Core
Jini

2nd Edition

W. KEITH EDWARDS

Prentice Hall PTR, Upper Saddle River, NJ 07458
www.phptr.com

Editorial/Production Supervision: *Kathleen M. Caren*
Acquisitions Editor: *Tim Moore*
Editorial Assistant: *Allyson Kloss*
Development Editor: *Russ Hall*
Marketing Manager: *Bryan Gambrel*
Manufacturing Manager: *Maura Goldstaub*
Cover Design: *Anthony Gemmallaro*
Cover Design Direction: *Jerry Votta*
Art Director: *Gail Cocker-Bogusz*
Technical Editors: *Peter van der Linden and Brian Murphy*

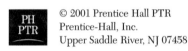

© 2001 Prentice Hall PTR
Prentice-Hall, Inc.
Upper Saddle River, NJ 07458

Printed in the United States of America

10 9 8 7 6 5 4 3 2 1

ISBN 0-13-089408-7

Prentice-Hall International (UK) Limited, London
Prentice-Hall of Australia Pty. Limited, Sydney
Prentice-Hall Canada Inc., Toronto
Prentice-Hall Hispanoamericana, S.A., Mexico
Prentice-Hall of India Private Limited, New Delhi
Prentice-Hall of Japan, Inc., Tokyo
Prenticd-Hall (Singapore) Pte. Ltd., Singapore
Editora Prentice-Hall do Brasil, Ltda., Rio de Janeiro

This book is gratefully dedicated to
Mark Weiser, who started me down this path
in the first place.

Contents

Contents

CHAPTER 10   Using the ServiceDiscovery Manager   354

CHAPTER 18 Distributed Applications 802

Foreword

Twenty years ago, I was a student at U.C. Berkeley, working on what would become a popular version of the UNIX operating system. At the time, computers were mostly used by professionals, and had software that was relevant to this use. In the last twenty years, we have seen the emergence of the personal computer, with much wider use, but the complexity of the systems today has exceeded the professional systems of twenty years ago, creating untold frustration. A better way of constructing new systems is needed, to reduce this frustration and better match the computing devices to human uses.

Almost a decade ago, I came across a book by Jacques Attali called *Lignes d'Horizon*. A colleague, John Gage, and I were traveling a lot together, and John was translating this book from French to English for his personal use. In this book we found great speculations about the computing world of the future, the idea of "nomadic computing," and we saw a linkage between these concepts and our desire for simpler, more reliable, and more human-centered computing. This set us off toward the design of a new computing substrate for the imagined future world of nomadic devices and pervasive embedded computing.

Hence Jini. Jini leverages the Java programming language to provide a simple substrate for distributed computing. Distributed computing is different, mostly because partial failures occur. If we don't handle failure, distributed systems paradoxically become less reliable as they get larger, rather than more reliable as the existence of redundant parts would suggest. Jini provides the tools for dealing with this and for dealing with the limited bandwidth and latency inherent in distributed computation.

The computing world of the future is a connected world, where "The Network is the Computer®." Java brings reliable object-oriented programming to the network. Its rapid rise reflects the power of objects to structure software, and the additional reliability and productivity that result from its modern design. Jini extends Java's benefits to distributed applications, which are structured as a set of communicating Java applications, without requiring complicated underlying operating systems to be understood to grasp the meaning of a distributed program.

Because Jini is simple, we can teach it and the principles of distributed programming to Java programmers in just a few days. By learning about the Jini philosophy, the uses of remote objects, leasing, distributed events, and transactions, you will be learning about both the essential elements of Jini and some basic principles of distributed programming. Core Jini will aid the student, the professional programmer writing a production application, and those curious about this new approach and new basic platform for distributed computing.

Bill Joy
Aspen, Colorado
June 1999

Foreword

I joined the Jini™ technology development team in 1997. At the time, I was designing and implementing middleware for a large distributed system at another company. The project was exciting and the work environment was one of the best I had ever experienced. When I was contacted about the possibility of joining the Jini development team, the Jini project was in its infancy and its future was still in doubt. Although the project's status might have made some people question the prudence of joining a project with such an uncertain future, five minutes into the description of the Jini vision, I knew this was where I wanted to be. I remember thinking to myself (with apologies to Jon Landau and Bruce Springsteen), "I've seen the future of software, and its name is Jini". The concepts being described to me, even at that early stage (and even though they were being presented by a manager!), were so elegant and so compelling that I knew this was an opportunity to be a part of something that could change the world.

By now, much of the early history of the Jini technology has been documented and, at least anecdotally, is well known. Most people who have followed the evolution of this technology know that Bill Joy provided the inspiration and initial direction, and that Jim Waldo — as lead architect — is the creator; without whom this truly revolutionary technology would not exist.

Most people also know that the work on which the Jini technology is based began within Sun Microsystems Laboratories at Sun's east coast facility just outside Boston. While with "the labs" Jim Waldo ran the Large Scale Distribution research project and, along with Ann Wollrath, Peter Jones and Ken Arnold, investigated and developed some of the key Jini concepts. The concepts developed in those early days, concepts such as leasing, distributed events and light-weight transactions, addressed issues in the field of distributed computing in a way that was contrary to the standard approach of attempting to hide distinctions between local and remote systems (sadly for some, this is still the standard approach).

The team of Waldo, Wollrath, Jones and Arnold made up the kernel of the

Jini engineering team. The team eventually moved from the labs into the Java-Soft product group where they began to investigate how a language-centric approach could be applied to the distributed computing concepts developed in the labs. As a result of this collaboration, Ann Wollrath created Java^{TM} RMI which has become one of the most interesting and useful components in the Java language; and Ken Arnold created the JavaSpaces^{TM} technology as well as began work on what would become the Jini lightweight transaction model.

What people probably don't know about the early history of the Jini technology is that when Bill Joy asked the team to expand their prior work to design a new platform for distributed computing, the team was moved out of JavaSoft in order to provide insulation from the kind of large company politics that can kill a new and radical idea. As a matter of fact, the Jini project actually began life in Sun Microsystems' Human Resources division! It was at about this time that Bob Scheifler (of X Consortium fame), Bryan O'Sullivan and Mark Hodapp joined the Jini team as architects and manager respectively. These individuals provided the missing pieces necessary for the project to continue to grow and thrive. The team eventually grew to include about fifteen development engineers. To this day, the development team here on the east coast remains small, focused and highly productive. The Jini team is made up of some of the finest people and brightest minds I have ever had the pleasure of knowing and working with.

After the initial release of the Jini technology, the team saw the need for utilities that could help developers be more efficient and productive when building their Jini applications. To address this need, John McClain, Bob Resendes, Gary Holness and Zane Pan were asked to design and implement a set of *helper* utilities and services. These individuals — managed by Jim Hurley and provided with superb technical leadership from both Jim Waldo and Bob Scheifler — produced the specifications and sample implementations for a set of Java classes and Jini services that encapsulate many of the desirable behaviors Jini applications should demonstrate when applying the various elements of the Jini technology programming model. Making up the bulk of the Jini 1.1 release, these new utilities and services can help many developers perform important duties such as discovery, join management, lease renewal, and event processing. (By the way, the names of the Jini 1.1 engineers should be familiar to anyone who subscribes to the JINI-USERS mail list. Those individuals are the "unsung heroes" who — along with Bob Scheifler — are responsible for much of the code making up the Jini releases. You'll not find a finer group of engineers.)

The next release of the Jini technology is a testament not only to the ability of the project engineers and managers, but also to the vision of Sun Microsystems as a company. Jini is revolutionary in all its aspects, not just its technical design. For example, although the Jini business model is the model from which the Sun Community Source License (SCSL — pronounced "scuzzle") originated, it began life steeped in controversy because it represented a significant move away from the safe confines of the status quo. The Jini project characterized the SCSL as a "call to arms" within the developer community, allowing *anyone* to participate in the growth and evolution of the Jini technology. Radical ideas such as those embodied in Jini would cause most companies to cancel the project. But Sun Microsystems has consistently demonstrated an ability to think and act in radically different ways. Just as the now legendary story tells how the Java language (known as Oak at the time) was one demo away from cancellation, the Jini project similarly rose from the ashes of pending cancellation. The project was allowed to survive because the culture established within Sun by its CEO, Scott McNealy, allows — even encourages — such radical thinking.

I had the pleasure of working with the author on the first edition of Core Jini. For those of you unfamiliar with the author's background, Keith Edwards is a highly respected researcher at Xerox's Palo Alto Research Center (PARC). His credentials in the field of distributed computing are distinguished and above reproach. Additionally, Keith is one of those rare individuals who not only has great skill and understanding in numerous technical disciplines, but also has the ability to communicate that knowledge to others. Because of Keith, Core Jini is truly something special.

Keith honored me once again by allowing me to participate in this next edition of Core Jini. In this edition, Keith has revised many of the original chapters as well as added new chapters covering all of the material included in the latest release of the Jini technology. The text covers everything you need to know to build clients and services that run in a Jini environment and which must behave as good "Jini citizens". The explanations are thorough and easy to follow, and are supplemented with example code that accurately demonstrates all of the important concepts. With respect to the new material, complete coverage is given to the helper utilities and services contained in the Jini technology 1.1 release. Of particular value will be the sections on the new ServiceDiscoveryManager helper utility and the new helper services. Keith also presents a number of examples which should help in understanding these new utilities and services.

Keith Edwards is one of the few authors to grasp the complete power and beauty of Jini, looking past the media hype and marketing demos to recognize the fact that Jini technology is not just for devices; a fact that many of the early adopters have come to discover for themselves. Keith not only understands the role that Jini technology can play both in the world of devices and the world of software services, but he presents the technology in a way that is easily accessible to both. With such a clear and complete picture, developers of device based systems or software service based systems can apply Jini technology as the infrastructure to create robust, reliable, and highly scalable distributed systems.

In addition to understanding the role Jini technology can play in the world of devices and software services, Keith Edwards also demonstrates a clear understanding of the concepts behind the Jini technology. He has thoroughly analyzed the Jini specifications and presents the designs reflected in those specifications in a way that will be accessible to the beginner as well as the hardened veteran. Keith presents an accurate description of the Jini philosophy on distributed computing, emphasizing the differences between local and remote systems; a description that remains true to the intent of the Jini architects. Keith's explanations of key concepts such as discovery, lookup, leasing, distributed events and transactions are excellent, and even the experienced reader will benefit from them.

It is worth noting that in addition to the fact that Core Jini will be an invaluable resource as a whole, the book is organized in such a way that the first four chapters should be required reading for three very different types of individual: Java programmers who are attempting to build their very first distributed system, experienced developers of distributed systems and, surprisingly, project managers faced with infrastructure decisions. For those new to distributed computing, the first four chapters contain a thorough and comprehensive introduction to distributed computing in general, and Jini technology in particular. For the more experienced in the field there is a detailed explanation of how distributed computing differs from almost all other computing environments, and how even the most experienced developer in the field must begin to view the world of distributed systems in a way that is probably very different from their current view. Finally, managers attempting to determine if Jini technology is the appropriate model on which to base their project will find the content of those chapters indispensable.

Thus, if you're planning on building a distributed system — whether that system consists of devices or software services, and whether that system is to be based on Jini technology or not — if you don't have a copy of Core Jini on your desk, you're doing yourself and your project a great disservice. Core Jini will help you gain not only a thorough understanding of this new and exciting technology called the Jini technology, but will also teach you the intricacies of distributed computing in general. Jump in and have fun as Keith introduces you to a radically new way to build distributed systems.

Brian Murphy
Sun Microsystems
Burlington, Massachusetts
April 2000

Introduction

This book provides a comprehensive guide to Jini, the new distributed systems technology from Sun Microsystems. Jini has the potential to revolutionize the way we build software. In a sense, Jini signals a change from a world in which devices are *networked* (meaning that computers simply have the ability to talk to one another) into one in which devices join together to form a true *distributed system*—a collection of networked components working together.

The distinction between networked systems and true distributed systems is an important one. Simple networked systems have simple communication patterns (usually peer-to-peer or client/server), and tend to be static, long-lived entities. Distributed systems, on the other hand, are composed of numerous constituent pieces. Any of these pieces can come or go without bringing down the whole system, and the system can respond to changes in its environment and its constituency in reliable and predictable ways. In a nutshell, Jini moves us from a world in which the "system" is the individual networked device, to one in which the "system" is the collection of all these devices working together.

This book serves two purposes. First, it provides a broad introduction to the core technologies of Jini. This introduction will be useful to Java developers who need to understand Jini, and to other technically-savvy readers who need to understand how Jini fits into the world, and why it is significant. Second, the book provides a deep understanding of how to build working software that leverages Jini. This second focus is intended for a range of developers, including those who are building Jini-enabled software for small devices such as Personal Digital Assistants (PDAs), to those building LAN-based (local area network) networked systems for the small-office/home-office (SOHO) or remote-office/home-office (ROHO), all the way up to those building enterprisewide network services and possibly software for the Internet itself.

These two goals of the book are largely represented by the book's two parts. Part I introduces Jini history, looks at Jini's place in the world—in particular, how Jini is different from what came before it—and provides some details on getting started with the technology and deploying it in actual use. Part II provides an in-depth look at the core Jini concepts, such as leasing, lookup, discovery, and transactions, as well as some extensive examples that illustrate particular aspects of Jini. Finally, the remainder of the book provides appendices and reference materials.

The philosophy taken by this book is that developers learn by reading code. You will no doubt notice if you page through this book, especially the chapters in Part II, that there are a great many code examples here. Some of these are "stand-alone" Jini programs—they typically introduce some concept in the smallest number of lines possible, in the interest of clarity. Others are utility programs that cover "holes" in the Jini APIs (Application Programming Interfaces). These programs will find their way into the toolchests of programmers working with Jini.

Throughout this book, though, I have provided a number of longer examples that share a common theme: Taken together, these examples can be used as applications in "live" Jini networks, and can interoperate with each other. This approach is very much in keeping with the Jini design philosophy itself—large numbers of cooperating applications working together to provide some service—and happens to be a good way to illustrate the ideas in Jini by using discrete chunks of code rather than monolithic, multithousand-line applications. Each of these examples illustrates one or more key points of the Jini architecture. They can be extended by you, and applied to any number of domains, from small, intelligent devices all the way up to enterprise software systems.

One thing this book does not provide is an introduction to Java itself. Jini is a layer atop Java—much like the Java Foundation Classes (JFC) or Java Database Connectivity (JDBC). Like these other layers, Jini introduces some new concepts and extends the Java programming model; but at its core, Jini remains pure Java. This book assumes that you are familiar with Java programming and, with one exception, does not cover the facilities available in the core Java class libraries or the language.

The one exception is the Java Remote Method Invocation system (RMI). RMI is used extensively in Jini. In fact, Jini leverages new features in RMI that only appeared in Java 2 (also popularly known as the JDK1.2 and later versions), such as the RMI activation framework. Thus, there is an RMI primer in Appendix A of this book that serves as an introduction to this technology for those who may be unfamiliar with it.

A Roadmap

Part I of this book, "Foundations," provides some necessary background reading on Jini. This information will be useful for savvy readers who just need to understand Jini, what it does, and how it works. But it's also required reading for developers who want to build actual, running Jini programs—the chapters in this part highlight the philosophical differences between Jini and "classical" networked and distributed systems technologies. If you have a good understanding of this material, you're ready to build software that's consistent with the Jini aesthetic.

Chapter 1, "A New Computing Paradigm," looks at the history and motivation of Jini. You'll see how Jini is really the fulfillment of the original Java promise: of collections of software and hardware, working together simply and without administration. This chapter also covers the process of getting and installing the Jini software.

Chapter 2, "Distributed Systems," provides a glimpse at the basics of distributed systems, and how Jini differs from traditional distributed systems software. Even if you're a handy network programmer, you may want to take a look at this chapter. Jini is fairly unique in the distributed systems world, and it's interesting to see the roots of Jini and understand what problems it's good at solving.

Chapter 3, "The Jini Model," introduces the basic concepts in Jini. Fortunately there are only a handful of these. Understanding these concepts and how they connect to each other will make later reading much easier and help you to understand how all the big pieces of the Jini design fit together.

Chapter 4, "Deployment Scenarios," covers some strategies for deploying Jini services. These are development targets, if you will—ways that you as a developer can deploy Jini code that you write. Jini is perhaps unique in all the Java libraries provided by Sun in that it is specifically designed to support devices which may *not* have Java Virtual Machines (JVMs) embedded in them. Jini can be used to connect devices with only limited computational ability, just as it can be used to connect large servers and other machines running full-fledged JVMs. This chapter will help you understand the options available to you if you're designing for Jini.

These first four chapters comprise Part I of this book—they provide a broad introduction to the Jini technology and how it fits into the world. Part II, "Building with Jini," is a very in-depth look at particular aspects of Jini. It is designed for the professional Java developer who is writing new Jini services or building Jini-enabled devices. Some of the chapters in this part are *In Depth* chapters that dive deeply into a particular aspect of the Jini technology. Others are structured around large examples that show Jini being applied to real problems.

Chapter 5, "Getting Started with Jini," begins with a series of programs designed to introduce you to the core Jini concepts. This series is a set of "Hello, World"-style programs that are evolved to illustrate ideas such as lookup, discovery, leasing, and remote events. This chapter is your first introduction to building Jini software from scratch, and covers almost all the basic Jini ideas, as well as provides an example of using Java's RMI framework.

Chapter 6, "In Depth: Discovery," is an in-depth chapter looking at Jini's discovery protocols. These are the means by which Jini services notify the world of their existence, and Jini client applications learn about the clusters or "communities" of services that are available to them. We'll look under the hood at these protocols—understanding what's really going on there is key to using them effectively. By the end of this chapter, you should understand these protocols well enough to be able to implement them "by hand" if you need to.

Chapter 7, "Attributes, Templates, and Service Matching," talks about the Jini notion of *attributes,* which are objects that can be associated with services to provide descriptive information about them. This chapter talks about how to use attributes, how the Jini attribute model meshes nicely with Java-Beans, and the rules for how clients search for services that they need to use.

Chapter 8, "The Service Join Protocol," moves on to the next major phase in a Jini application's life cycle, the use of the Jini lookup service by other services. Any Jini service will need to use the lookup service to join a community and make itself available to other members of that community. In this chapter, you'll learn about some of the responsibilities services have to be well-behaved, how they're assigned IDs that are unique over space and time, and some introductory details about how services are administered.

Chapter 9, "Using Low-Level Lookup Service Interfaces," continues the discussion of using lookup services started in Chapter 8. In this chapter, you'll learn how clients interact with Jini lookup services to find and use services. You'll also see how to write clients that can administer lookup services, and federate them into larger structures.

Chapter 10, "Using the Service Discovery Manager," discusses some new APIs introduced with Jini 1.1. If you've been programming with Jini 1.0, you'll want to pay special attention to this chapter; the `ServiceDiscoveryManager` provides a useful high-level interface to working with lookup services.

At this point, you should understand the basics of what you need to know to build a very functional and useful Jini client application that can participate in the discovery and lookup process, and allow you to find and browse any Jini service on the network. Chapter 11, "A Jini Lookup Service Browser," introduces a long application that exercises the ideas in the previous chapters. This application is a browser that can find lookup services and the services registered there, and allow you to view and control the attributes of those registered services. The code in this chapter builds up a toolkit of useful components for displaying and using service information, which you can reuse in your own applications.

Chapter 12, "In Depth: Leasing," gives in-depth coverage of the notion of leasing, which is how Jini manages resources held by remote systems. Leasing is also the key to Jini's ability to "self-heal" a large distributed system. In this chapter, we'll talk about the benefits of leasing, and cover some common idioms that arise again and again when programming with leases.

While Chapter 12's focus is on the ideas behind leasing, and in particular how clients can use leasing, Chapter 13, "Exporting Leased Resources," talks about how Jini services can implement leasing. This is the other half of the leasing equation that is started in Chapter 12. With these two chapters, you can "close the loop," exporting a leased resource to a client, which then uses the lease consumer APIs to control it.

While the chapters on discovery, lookup, and leasing provide the *basics* of what you have to do to write a functional Jini service, Chapter 14, "The Well-Behaved Service," provides a summary of the extra steps you can take to provide a *useful* and *useable* service. This chapter talks about service administration, the join protocol—which governs how services interact with their communities—and how to provide user interfaces for services.

After this coverage of what it takes to be a "good" service, you're ready to build a complete, sophisticated Jini application. Chapter 15, "A Complete Example: The Print Service," presents a long example of a service that allows clients to connect to it to print documents. This program supports administration, persistence, and self-description through attributes, and can serve as the basis for many of the services you will write. And, of course, you'll be able to use this service in conjunction with the other examples in this book.

Next, Chapter 16, "In Depth: Remote Events," provides a look at how Jini supports asynchronous notifications between programs. Jini extends the local Java event model with events that can be sent between objects in different JVMs. This remote event model has different semantics than the usual JavaBeans event model—this chapter looks at why this is, and explores some common idioms for using remote events. The remote event model lends itself to the creation of event "adaptors" that can plug into the event pipeline to provide such services as forwarding or storage of events. One of the examples here looks at an "event mailbox" adaptor that can be a useful service in many Jini communities.

While the preceding chapters cover topics that are considered core and fundamental to Jini, the next three chapters are a bit different. These last chapters cover topics that are actually implemented as services *atop* the core Jini infrastructure.

Chapter 17, "JavaSpaces," provides an introduction to Sun's JavaSpaces service. This service provides an extremely useful object storage engine. Many applications that use Jini will need a way to store persistent data, and share it for use by other applications. JavaSpaces provides an easy object-based way for them to do this. And JavaSpaces can even serve as the basis for new styles of distributed computation. This chapter looks at the JavaSpaces programming model and philosophy.

Chapter 18, "Distributed Transactions," covers transactions, which are one of the most technical concepts in Jini. Transactions are a way for cooperating processes to ensure the integrity of their data. Essentially, transactions are a way to make sure that either an entire set of operations happen completely, or that none of them happen at all. Those of you familiar with database programming are no doubt familiar with transactions and their power in preventing partial failures. The Jini model, while based on the familiar two-phase commit protocol used in database systems, is actually somewhat different. This chapter explores those differences, and shows how to build programs that can use transactions to safely group their operations.

Chapter 19, "Helper Services," covers some new services introduced in Jini 1.1 to aid in Jini development. Much like the Transaction Manager service, these are "utility" services that are meant to be used by other clients and services to simplify development. This chapter talks about the `EventMailbox` service, the `LookupDiscoveryService`, and the `LeaseRenewalService`. These are important new additions to Jini that should be in any programmer's toolbox.

Finally, the two appendices in this book provide some useful reference and background material. Appendix A is a primer on the RMI technology, in particular, the features that have been added as of the Java 2 release. The RMI activation framework, which provides a way for objects to be automatically reconstituted from persistent storage when needed, will be used heavily by many Jini applications, and is important to understand. In general, a good grounding in the ideas of RMI is necessary for getting the most from Jini.

Appendix B provides a reference to the various system properties that can be useful when developing with Jini. You can use these properties to control and tune the behavior of Jini, as well as some basic Java features, in your applications.

Conventions Used in This Book

This book follows a number of conventions to help you get the most out of it. Throughout the text, you'll see a number of callouts that designate particular items of interest. These callouts, called Core Note, Core Alert, and Core Tip, provide useful information that is important enough that it should not be lost in the text. Core Alerts are used for potential pitfalls in developing Jini applications. Examples might include portions of the Jini API that are unimplemented or perhaps behave differently than the specs indicate. Core Tips are pointers to common and useful ways to accomplish particular tasks. Examples might include common idioms or patterns that can make your life as a developer easier. Core Notes are extra information that might help you make sense of some aspect of Jini, or just provide fodder for Silicon Valley cocktail party conversations.

Getting Sample Code from the Internet

All the code samples in this book have been collected together, and are available electronically from my Web site. To download the code, point your Web browser to http://www.kedwards.com/jini/dl/corejini-2e.zip. Save the file to your computer's hard disk, and extract the contents. (You may also want to see the section "Further Information" below for details on other useful information at this Web site.) If you're on Windows, use your favorite unzipping utility, such as WinZip. On Solaris and other UNIX platforms, use a command like unzip corejini-2e.zip.

The unzip process will create a directory called corejini under whatever directory you ran the unzipper. For consistency with the rest of this book, I'd recommend unzipping the contents into C:\files\corejini (on Windows) and /files/corejini (on Solaris).

Under the corejini directory, you'll find separate subdirectories for each of the chapters in this book that contain code samples.

Feedback

No book is perfect, especially one that covers a topic as new and as rich as Jini. Even though this book has been thoroughly reviewed a number of times, I have no doubt that errors do remain, or that improvements can be made. If you find a "bug," either in the text or in one of the example programs, or if you think of anything that might make this book more useful to you or other readers, please drop me a note:

```
kedwards@parc.xerox.com
```

Further Information

Many of the chapters in this book have a "Further Reading" section at the end of them, with pointers to books, papers, and resources on the Internet that may extend your Jini knowledge.

However, for resources to extend this book itself, you should check out the *Core Jini* Web page, where I'll post news on updates, fixes, revisions, and so forth.

```
http://www.kedwards.com/jini
```

A Note on Versions

The 1.1 version of Jini is used throughout this book and in the examples. If you are using an earlier release, I strongly recommend upgrading to this new version. It fixes a number of bugs, and adds some important new features to the Jini class libraries.

For the most part, code written to version 1.0 (the first Jini release from January 1999) or 1.0.1 (a bug fix release from November 1999) will continue to run when used with Jini 1.1, although compilation is likely to produce a number of deprecation warnings. In particular, many of the classes and interfaces that were part of the com.sun.jini package hierarchy have been moved into the net.jini hierarchy. While the "original" versions of these classes and interfaces remain in com.sun.jini for compatibilitiy reasons, they have been deprecated and will be removed in a future release. You should replace them with the new versions, which in some cases have slightly different APIs.

Table I-1 lists deprecated classes and their replacements.

In addition to the classes and interfaces that got "promoted" in 1.1, a number of brand new classes and interfaces have been added to the net.jini packages. If you've been programming with Jini 1.0, you may want to keep an eye out for these additions to the Jini toolchest. Table I-2 lists the most important of these.

Table I-1 Deprecated 1.0 Classes and Their Replacements

`com.sun.jini.discovery.` `LookupLocatorDiscovery`	`net.jini.discovery.LookupLocatorDiscovery`
`com.sun.jini.lease.` `LeaseRenewalManager`	`net.jini.lease.LeaseRenewalManager`
`com.sun.jini.lease.` `LeaseListener`	`net.jini.lease.LeaseListener`
`com.sun.jini.lease.` `LeaseRenewalEvent`	`net.jini.lease.LeaseRenewalEvent`
`com.sun.jini.lookup.` `JoinManager`	`net.jini.lookup.JoinManager`
`com.sun.jini.lookup.` `ServiceIDListener`	`net.jini.lookup.ServiceIDListener`

Table I-2 New Classes and Interfaces in Jini 1.1

`net.jini.discovery.` `DiscoveryManagement`	An interface for classes used to control the discovery process, including adding and removing `DiscoveryListeners`, discarding registrars, and so forth.
`net.jini.discovery.` `DiscoveryGroupManagement`	An interface for classes that implement "group-oriented" discovery (such as via the multicast protocols).
`net.jini.discovery.` `DiscoveryLocatorManagement`	An interface for classes that implement "direct" discovery via a Jini-format URL (such as via the unicast protocol).
`net.jini.discovery.` `LookupDiscoveryManager`	This class unifies the "traditional" Jini multicast and unicast flavors of discovery into one utility. It should quickly become the most common class for automating the discovery process.

Table I-2 New Classes and Interfaces in Jini 1.1(continued)

`net.jini.lookup.` `ServiceDiscoveryManager`	This important class, which is an analog to `JoinManager`, can be used by clients (or services acting as clients) to handle the tasks of contacting lookup services and building lists of all available Jini services.
`net.jini.lookup.` `LookupCache`	This interface, which supports `ServiceDiscoverManager`, is implemented by classes that maintain a continually-updated set of all known services that match some criteria.
`net.jini.lookup.` `ServiceDiscoveryListener`	This interface, which supports `ServiceDiscoveryManager`, is used by clients that wish to be asynchronously notified of changes in the sets of available services.
`net.jini.lookup.` `ServiceItemFilter`	This interface is used to supply client-side filtering predicates that can restrict the set of services made available via `ServiceDiscoveryManager`.
`net.jini.lookup.` `ServiceDiscoveryEvent`	This event class represents a change in the set of services available through `ClientEventManager`.

Finally, in addition to the new and moved classes in Jini 1.1, there are a number of new services that come with the release. Whereas Jini 1.0 supplied a lookup service, transaction manager, and JavaSpaces storage service, Jini 1.1 adds three new "infrastructure" services that can be used by other Jini clients and services on the network (Table I-3).

As you can see, there are significant improvements in Jini 1.1, and plenty of reasons to upgrade!

Table I-3 New Services Included with Jini 1.1

`LookupDiscoveryService`	The `LookupDiscoveryService` is used by clients and services that wish to delegate the discovery process to an external entity. This can be useful, for example, when a service is inactive for periods of time. By delegating its discovery activities to the `LookupDiscoveryService`, the service can be awakened whenever new lookup services appear on the network; this allows it to remain inactive until it needs to join a community. Sun provides a sample implementation of this service called "`fiddler`."
`LeaseRenewalService`	This service can be used by clients and services that wish to delegate their lease renewals to an external entity. This can be useful when a service intends to be inactive for long periods of time. Sun provides a sample implementation of a lease renewal service called "`norm`."
`EventMailbox`	The `EventMailbox` service can be used to store events intended for clients and services that may be unavailable for periods of time. These entities can later reconnect to the network and fetch their events from the mailbox. Sun provides a sample implementation of an event mailbox called "`mercury`."

Acknowledgments

I n the fall of 1998, I received an e-mail from Mark Weiser, the Chief Technologist of Xerox PARC, asking me whether I'd be willing to evaluate a new technology called Jini. Mark had been involved for years in a vision of the future called "ubiquitous computing," in which our workspaces are filled with a variety of devices that are not only aware of us, but can work together with us to support us in our jobs. Much of the ubiquitous computing vision is predicated on the belief that technology should be a calming influence in our lives, rather than the often headache-inducing nightmare that it currently is.

When Mark asked me to see if Jini might be a viable substrate on top of which to base some of the grander ideas of ubiquitous computing (not to mention possible Xerox products), I had no idea that his simple e-mail would lead me down the path I've taken for the last few months.

Jini is an important technology. Jini is important because it has the potential to fundamentally change not only the way we build software, but the way we interact with the technology that is increasingly a part of our lives.

As I learned more about Jini, I became convinced that—even though it is a young technology—it could bring about a shift in what we expect from the technology in our lives. The ideas in Jini are simple. Perhaps deceptively so, because even simple ideas can be difficult to adopt, when they're so radically different than what's gone before. My goal in writing this book was to help, perhaps just a little bit, to change what we have come to expect from our computers. My method has been to focus on these simple ideas in Jini, and dig below the surface to see what the implications of these ideas really are.

Any book—even one with only one author's name on the cover—is always a collaborative effort to some degree. I believe this book has been more collaborative than most.

First, a sincere thanks to Mark Weiser for pointing me toward Jini in the first place, for encouraging me, and for setting *my* expectations about what a technology should be. Mark is, in many ways, the reason I came to Xerox PARC; I'm even more indebted to him after this project. Sadly, Mark passed away before this book could be published; the fact that this book is dedicated to him is appropriate, but doesn't begin to reflect his contributions to PARC and the world.

PARC's management team has been wonderfully supportive of this project, not only in terms of personal encouragement, but also by giving me the time to work on it. Richard Bruce, who is the manager of the Computer Science Lab, deserves thanks for allowing me to get so wrapped up in the writing. And a special thanks to Karin Petersen, my direct manager, for her constant support not only in terms of motivation, but also by giving me the freedom and flexibility to work on the book.

In hindsight, a word of thanks is due to Beth Mynatt, who through her encouragement managed to give me a solid shove off the face of this cliff, while somehow remaining safely on the edge herself. The edge of a precipice is a prime spot for spectators, and Beth has certainly gotten to observe my plummet for the last few months. Her turn will come...

My editors at Prentice Hall, Tim Moore and Ralph Moore (no relation, as Tim always tells me...I'm never sure if Ralph should be offended or relieved!), made this a smooth and *almost* enjoyable process! Russ Hall, my editor for the second edition, has likewise been a pleasure to work with.

I've had the extreme and unwarranted good fortune to have a truly stellar group of technical reviewers on this project. Peter van der Linden, whom many of you will know from his books such as *Deep C Secrets* and *Just Java*, provided excellent comments, especially on the book's examples. Marty Hall, author of *Core Web Programming*, provided great feedback throughout the early chapters, and also provided kind words in his first reviews that kept me from giving up hope. And a very special thanks to Brian Murphy. Brian is a member of the Jini team, and provided substantial comments on every single chapter in the book. Without his insight and feedback, this book would be far less useful, less accurate, and less clear than it is. Any readers who wish to thank Brian personally should certainly do so; take my word for it—he's saved you hours of aggravation.

A number of "unofficial" technical reviewers have also contributed to the book, especially in its early stages. Anind Dey provided great comments on the first few chapters. Beki Grinter, a dyed-in-the-wool Bell-head, provided excellent and insightful feedback on the telephone example in the first chapter. Beki, if I'd had the room, I would have expanded it into a full chapter, I promise.

My family, and especially my mother, will no doubt be single-handedly responsible for at least half of the sales of this book. I fully expect them to be handed out to old schoolmates, acquaintances from church, and casual passers-by on the streets. Go mom!

Finally, a special word of thanks and appreciation to Beki, who has certainly been the light at the end of this long tunnel. Thanks for supporting me, encouraging me, and not killing me during my mental and physical absences during the past few months.

And now, if you'll excuse me, I'm going to dig out from under the papers, books, and code littering my house, and resume my life where I left off.

Keith Edwards
San Francisco, California
November, 2000

FOUNDATIONS

A New Computing Paradigm

Topics in This Chapter

- The history of Jini
- Sun's licensing model for Jini
- Getting and installing the software
- Running Jini services from the command line

Chapter 1

T he computer on your desk is a remarkable device. It provides computational power, storage, and speed that would have been unthinkable only a few years ago. The fact that this statement is now such a cliché is only a testament to the incredible changes that have occurred in our industry.

Yet despite such advances, the basic structure of our computers remains much the same as it was in the 1950s: We have central processing units, memory, and disks. And, despite the fact that we now use computers with power that would have been unimaginable 40 years ago to play games and balance our checkbooks, we fundamentally interact with these machines in the same ways that our predecessors did: We install software on them, run applications, and manage the (always scarce) disk resources of our systems. A mainframe systems administrator from 1950 would understand these tasks immediately. In fact, in some sense, we've *all* become systems administrators—now each of us has to manage our own machines, doing tasks that would be familiar to systems administrators of an earlier era. The increase in speed and decrease in size has not brought about a qualitative change in how we manage, install, and use these machines.

The situation in desktop computers stands in stark contrast to the situation in telephony. The telephone network has grown exponentially since its humble beginnings, both in terms of raw capacity and the number of phones connected to the network. One can pick up a standard telephone virtually anywhere in the world and, nearly instantly, create a pipeline suitable for voice or data transfer to anyplace else in the world. And while this system's complexity has grown exponentially, it is largely hidden from its users. My perception of the phone system doesn't grow more complex as users in China come on line. The interface for connecting to any other place in the world stays largely the same, even as more of the world becomes accessible. And installation and maintenance of the small part of the global phone network that's housed in my residence couldn't be simpler— I simply plug in new devices and they become reachable from anywhere in the world. My own minute chunk of the phone network is owned by me and, if such a term even makes sense here, *administered* by me as well. And yet everything still "just works."

If we expect our computers to be useful—or even useable—as the number of interconnected devices on the network explodes, we have to reach this level of reliability, ease of deployment, and ease of administration. The most administration we have to do with the telephone system is the occasional replacement of a handset; why then should we take as a given that our current computers and computer networks require so much hand-holding to work properly?

Jini History

In some ways, the vision of Jini is the vision of Java—Jini is really the fulfillment of the original Java idea of groups of consumer-oriented electronic devices interchanging data and bits of code. Java started out as a language called Oak, designed as a portable way to write programs for embedded processors, at Sun Microsystems Labs in 1990. As the project matured, the language found its way into new types of devices. One of the first experiments resulted in Oak running on a handheld computer called the Star-7. In this guise, the language was used to build interfaces for digital TV and entertainment applications. In fact, the creator of Oak, James Gosling, decided to write the new language only after the team had tried to work with C++ and found it too complicated and "programmer-unfriendly."

In its second incarnation, Oak found its way onto the Web. In 1994, two engineers at Sun, Patrick Naughton and Jonathan Payne, wrote a Web browser completely in Oak. This browser, called WebRunner, later became the basis for the HotJava browser, and became famous for its ability to download executable programs, called applets, from Web servers and execute them securely within the browser. The language—rechristened Java for its launch in April 1995—was released with the browser and made Internet history.

Many of the goals of the original consumer electronics vision of Java—the ability to move code from device to device regardless of CPU type, security, compactness, and so on—made the language a natural for its new home on the Web.

The Jini Vision

Although Java got its start in consumer electronics, it is most commonly thought of as a tool for building applets. The original vision never died within Sun, however. A group of engineers realized that the original idea was still compelling. And although Java makes this idea *possible*—what with its ability to send portable code from machine to machine and execute it securely—there are other problems that must be solved to make the vision of constellations of easily administered and easily interconnected devices work in *practice*.

This vision requires mechanisms that we don't typically associate with desktop computers.

- The software infrastructure for these devices must be incredibly robust. Toasters and TV sets simply cannot fail with a message asking "Abort, Retry, Ignore?" The software must not only allow, but *encourage,* the development of reliable systems.

- The devices have to support true, effortless "plug and play." They should be the Internet equivalents of the telephone: You plug them in and they just work, without having to configure IP addresses, set up gateways and routers, install (and possibly remove) drivers, and so on. Upgrades of software are an important issue here—if an administrator has to be called in to upgrade the software for all the TVs in a large hotel, chances are the TVs simply won't get upgraded.

- Software systems for the Internet age must be evolvable. While creating software for stand-alone devices, such as the CPU in a microwave, is challenging enough, the potential problems are multiplied by the fact that networked devices must be able to communicate with any number of peer devices on the Internet. And, perhaps more problematic, the creator of the original device may not even know about the existence of new devices that will appear later. We'd like our software services and devices to be able to use each other without massive reconfiguration of the network.

- Devices like these will form spontaneous communities: Imagine a digital camera that's brought into proximity to a color printer. We'd like to be able to simply print the snapshots on the printer, without having to explicitly tell either device about the other. In many cases, the effort that would be required to tell the devices about one another would overwhelm any potential benefit to be gained from using them together—which is one reason we don't typically reconfigure our current networks at the drop of a hat. In this world, networking would become much more dynamic, and less the fixed, static organization that we have today.

The vision of legions of devices and software services working together, simply and reliably, had been espoused by a number of researchers and computer industry leaders before. Mark Weiser of Xerox PARC called this vision "ubiquitous computing," a term meant to connote the ready availability and useability of devices connected to the network. Bill Joy, one of the founders of Sun and the original creator of Berkeley UNIX, believed that the future would continue to hold traditional desktop computers, but also smart "appliances" in homes and vehicles.

With these visions in mind, a group at Sun set out to provide the infrastructure that would bring Java full circle—they intended to build the software layer that would sit atop Java to provide the benefits of reliability, maintainability, evolvability, and spontaneity that such a world would require. These developers set out to define a model that would be easy for programmers to understand, and yet would lend itself to this new way of building software—a way of building software that is probably foreign to many, even those used to writing network-aware code.

This project became known as Jini,[1] and many of the people who created and championed it are the same people who originally created and championed certain aspects of Java. Bill Joy would become one of the inspirations and chief supporters of the project, much as he was for the original Java work. Jim Waldo inspired much of the early work on Jini and would become the chief architect and designer of the system. Ann Wollrath invented Java's RMI facility, and continues her work in the context of Jini, where she has been one of the key designers of the system. And Ken Arnold would define Jini's transaction and storage models. One of the key Jini players who came from outside Sun is Bob Scheifler, who once led the X Consortium and has defined the Jini lookup and discovery protocols.

There are any number of exotic programming models that have attempted to solve the problems of distributed computing. The Jini designers could have selected one of these models—such as temporal logic, weakly-consistent databases, or agents—as the basis of a system to address the challenges that Jini addresses. But these systems typically require you to "start from scratch" when

---

1. The creators of the system explain that Jini was chosen because it is an energetic and easy-to-remember word that begins with "J" and has the same number of letters as "Java." Some of them will joke that Jini stands for "Jini Is Not Initials." The word is pronounced just like "genie."

learning them, because their programming models are so radical. Fortunately, the designers built their system on a set of core concepts that, at least individually, will be commonplace to Java developers: mobile code, strongly typed interfaces, and separation of interface and implementation. To this mix of old Java standbys they add some new concepts that are unique to Jini. These include a distributed storage model that can be used as a general-purpose facility for storing and retrieving objects. This storage model is based on the Linda system from David Gelernter at Yale. Jini also exposes a concept that has been used "under the covers" in RMI for years—the notion of "leasing" as a means to regulate access to resources on a network. Finally, Jini makes heavy use of periodic multicast to notify cooperating Jini applications and services of one another.

Again, the basic notions in Jini are familiar to any Java programmer. Jini adds a number of incremental changes to Java to extend it to this new world of lightweight distributed computing, but doesn't require developers to invest in learning entirely new programming paradigms from the ground up.

Not Just for Consumer Electronics

Interestingly, many of the attributes that are desirable in consumer devices turn out to be desirable in desktop and enterprise software as well. If you are a network or systems administrator, you're probably well aware of the problems of maintaining even stand-alone computers, much less a whole network of machines! PC networks have many of the same needs as consumer devices. We'd like them to be truly "plug and play" (not the weak sort of plug and play found on today's PCs, but real, reliable networking by just plugging into the wall). We'd like them to be evolvable in a consistent and reliable way—if I install an OS upgrade on one machine on the network, I'd like it (and the rest of the machines on the network) to keep working. These abilities are as important in home networks as they are in workgroup networks.

Enterprise systems have even more stringent requirements. Servers are meant to stay running for months or even years, so they need to be reliable. We'd like to be able to upgrade the software services on them without requiring a reboot or otherwise breaking the world. And we'd like to have much more flexibility in how we configure the services on the network—if my database server is underpowered, I'd like to be able to just move it to a new machine without having to touch every client to tell it where the database now lives.

This need for "administration-free" networking goes beyond simple convenience—it can actually allow us to do things that were so difficult as to be impractical before. For example, Jini enables a world in which you can visit a remote site—say, a customer's place of business—and be able to use all of the software services and devices on that remote network. Printers, fileservers, and scanners, as well as any number of purely software services, become accessible without any configuration, administration, or driver installation. Jini's administration-free properties lend themselves to the creation of spontaneous, ad hoc networks of computers, formed whenever and wherever needed.

Jini Becomes Public

The Jini project went on at Sun, hidden from public eyes, until *New York Times* technology reporter John Markoff broke the story in a front page article in 1998. Shortly thereafter, Jini—although still officially unannounced—appeared on the cover of *Wired* magazine. The technology was finally introduced to the public on January 25, 1999, with a host of licensees already on board.

These partners are building Jini-enabled services and devices, including disk drives, digital cameras, printers, and scanners. For its part, Sun is rapidly aligning behind Jini, in much the same way it aligned around Java back in 1995.

Licensees

At the time of this writing, Jini has already been licensed by nearly 40 companies that span a huge gamut from device vendors to enterprise software companies. These include disk drive manufacturers such as Quantum and Seagate, cellular phone manufacturers Nokia and Ericsson, printer vendors including Xerox, Canon, Epson, and Hewlett-Packard, camera manufacturer Kodak, networking vendors Cisco and 3Com, software producers BEA Systems, Novell, and Inprise, and a huge number of consumer electronics companies including Sony, Sharp, Philips, and Toshiba. Jini has also been licensed for use by companies as diverse as AOL and Kinko's.

Community Source Licensing

Sun provides access to Jini source code under what is called the Sun Community Source License (SCSL, often pronounced "scuzzle"). This license is designed to provide virtually free and easy access to all the Jini source code by developers, while allowing Sun to ensure that Jini products remain compatible with one another, and that the Jini source doesn't "splinter" into incompatible versions.

The community licensing model has many similarities to the "Open Source" movement. The Open Source movement espouses freely-available source code, available to anyone who needs it. This approach to software development has many benefits—look at the rapid development of large software systems such as Linux, for example. But it can have drawbacks. Most importantly, most Open Source arrangements either have minimal controls over the definition of the software (meaning that anyone can introduce an incompatible change), or they require anyone using the software to submit modifications they make back to an organizing body. The first drawback means that the original developer of the technology may be unable to prevent it from splintering into a morass of incompatible versions. The second drawback means that many companies who might otherwise be eager to develop for the technology may be reluctant to be required to turn over their intellectual property to a third party.

The community license model allows very open access to source code, while promoting compatibility among the developer community. And yet it does not require companies or developers to hand their developments back to Sun. How does it work? The SCSL defines two levels of usage of the source code; your responsibility to ensure compatibility increases as you move to the "higher" license level.

At the first level, you can obtain the source code for *Research Use*. This allows you complete access to the source for personal, research, and educational uses, or to evaluate the source for possible deployment. You can also distribute examples to other research use licensees. The license itself is just a "click through" page on the Sun download site; in fact, the Jini downloads that you get from Sun all include source code. At this level, there are practically no responsibilities imposed on you; primarily, Sun asks only that you notify it if you find bugs in Jini. You are free to learn about the technology, modify the source, create new implementations of the Jini components, and try it out in your applications. You can even create "clones" of the code, as long as you include the proper notices in the source.

When you get to the point of deploying your Jini project, whether internally or as a commercial product, then you move up to the *Commercial Use* license. This license grants you the right to distribute modified versions of Jini, as long as they conform to certain compatibility requirements. You should note that you can move to this level of access and responsibility without any extra legal overhead— there is nothing to sign, and you do not need to notify Sun of your new use of the technology. The only added responsibilities are that your modified code conform to the Jini naming conventions, that you openly publish the specifications to any extensions you may develop, and that your new implementation pass the Jini Platform Compatibility Kit. These requirements are intended to ensure that you will have complete interoperability and compatibility with any Jini services and applications that may be used with your code.

If you are a SCSL license, your Jini-based product can carry the "Jini compatible" logo if it passes the tests in the Jini Compatibility Kit and you sign and return to Sun a copy of the Jini Logo License agreement. There is *no* fee to use this logo (under the terms of the earlier Jini license, used in versions prior to 1.1, Sun charged a minimal fee for use of the logo—this charge has been done away with for version 1.1).

These guidelines allow you to have unfettered access to the source code for learning, experimenting, and teaching. As your code becomes more and more public, though, the community source license requires that your responsibilities to maintain compatibility increase as well. There are no requirements for you to hand over any of your code to other developers or to Sun. If you wish, however, you can choose to donate any code you write back to the community, in which case, Sun or other developers can redistribute it.

What does this mean for you? If you're developing a service for Jini that only depends on the Jini run-time framework and the Jini binaries as posted on the Sun Web site, you can distribute your program without having any source license at all, although you cannot redistribute the Jini binaries themselves (Sun requires a commercial license to redistribute their binaries). The SCSL model deals with access, modifications, and redistribution of the Jini *source* code, not the binaries. Only if you plan to use the source in your applications or make modifications to it will you need to follow the guidelines in the SCSL.

Sun intends the community licensing approach to afford the best of both worlds—easy and relatively unfettered access to source code, while still ensuring some degree of compatibility and co-evolution of the code. The SCSL process is still evolving, and Sun is actively soliciting feedback on their licensing strategies. The license has grown considerably simpler and less restrictive, just since the Jini 1.0 days.

Since this is my interpretation of the license, and I'm not a lawyer (thankfully!) you should read up on the full details of Jini's community licensing model at Sun's Web site. If you have any questions about the SCSL, you should consult the FAQs and other information at this page.

```
http://www.sun.com/jini/licensing/
```

Getting and Installing Jini

Obviously before you can start programming with Jini, you need to get the software set up! Chances are, if you're a Java developer, you've already got Java 2 installed on your system. If you don't have this version (or a later Java 2 point release), you're going to need it, because Jini requires some features that are only in Java 2.

Here's the checklist for getting Jini up and running:

1. Install Java 2, if you don't have it already.
   - Download the Java 2 software from Sun
   - Unpack the distribution
   - Examine the distribution

2. Install the Jini release.
   - Download Jini from Sun
   - Unpack the distribution
   - Examine the distribution

3. Set up your environment.
   - Make sure the Java binaries are in your PATH

4. Start the Jini run-time services, using either the GUI or the command line.
   - Configure and start the HTTP server
   - Configure and start the RMI activation daemon
   - Configure and start the Jini Lookup Service

5. Run the sample programs to make sure you've got everything correctly configured.

The remainder of this chapter details the steps required to download and install the Java 2 JDK (Java Development Kit) and Jini. The instructions for setting up Java 2 are particular to the Windows and Solaris implementations of the JDK that are available from Sun; if you run on a different platform—or simply use a different JDK implementation on one of these two platforms—then you should check with your operating system vendor for instructions on how to download and install Java 2.

Since the sample implementation of Jini that comes from Sun is itself implemented *completely* in Java, there is one version of the code for all platforms. The installation instructions given here for Jini should be useful for all machines and operating systems.

Core Note: Jini sample implementations and specifications

Jini, much like Java, is defined as a set of core specifications that detail how the software must work. And just as any operating system vendor or group of developers can create an alternate implementation of Java that conforms to these specifications, there

can be multiple implementations of Jini as well.

But just as Sun provides "sample" implementations of the Java technology for Windows and Solaris, it also provides a sample implementation of the Jini specifications. Sun's implementation is pure Java, and so should run on any platform with a fully conformant Java 2 implementation. This Jini sample implementation has been tested on the reference implementations of Java for Windows and Solaris; the Jini development team actively encourages developers to test Jini on other JDK implementations.

The installation and set-up instructions here detail the procedures for the sample implementations of both Java and Jini.

Installing Java 2

First, let's look at downloading and installing Java 2.

Downloading the JDK from Sun

The most current Java 2 JDK releases are always available from:

```
http://java.sun.com/jdk/
```

Click on the appropriate link for your operating system (currently either Windows or Solaris) and save the resulting file to your hard disk. There is also a documentation bundle separately available from the download site. You may wish to copy this bundle—which is available either as a ZIP file or as a compressed "tar" file—to your local system, if you don't otherwise have access to the Java 2 documentation.

Unpacking the Distribution

Next you need to unpack and actually install the JDK. In all of the examples in this book, I will use Java 2 version 1.3 (also called just JDK1.3). The examples should work fine with the earlier 1.2 release also though.

For Windows: If you're on the Windows platform, you've just downloaded a self-installing EXE file. You can just double-click on the file to install it. The installation script will copy two separate sets of files to your hard disk: the first is the JDK proper, which contains the compiler, debugger, and associated tools. The second is the Java Runtime Environment, which contains the Java Virtual Machine (JVM) and the class libraries for the language. In almost every case, simply installing these files to the default location suggested by the installer is fine.

For Solaris: Solaris users wind up with a self-installing shell script. You can run this script by invoking `sh` (the UNIX command shell interpreter) on the file you downloaded. For example, if you named the file `Solaris-install.bin`, you would type:

```
sh Solaris-install.bin
```

You'll be asked to accept the license agreement and provide a directory to unpack into.

Examining the Distribution

Once you've downloaded and installed the JDK, you should probably familiarize yourself with where all the important pieces live. Table 1–1 presents a list of the most important components of the JDK; I'll assume that you unpacked the contents into a directory called `jdk1.3`. It's important to understand where the essential components live, so that you can make sure your environment is properly configured for running Java.

Table 1–1 Layout for the JDK 1.3 Release	
`jdk1.3`	This is the root of the JDK installation.
`jdk1.3/bin`	Contains the Java executables, including `java`, which is the JVM; `javac`, the Java compiler; `rmic`, the RMI compiler; `rmid`, the RMI "activation daemon;" and `rmiregistry`, the RMI name server.
`jdk1.3/demo`	Various demonstration applets and programs.
`jdk1.3/doc`	Documentation for the Java platform, in HTML format. Note that this directory will *only* be available if you downloaded and unpacked the separate documentation bundle.
`jdk1.3/jre`	This directory contains the "Java Runtime Environment." This is the minimal set of tools and libraries required to run—but not develop—Java programs.
`jdk1.3/jre/ext`	This directory is for extensions to the Java platform. You can place JAR files here, as well as supporting native code, and the JVM will make it available to all Java applications in the VM.
`jdk1.3/lib`	This directory contains the JAR files for the Java class libraries, as well as supporting libraries that are not part of the Java API and are not directly callable by Java programs.

Installing Jini

Next, let's look at installing the Jini sample implementation on your system.

Downloading Jini from Sun

As of the writing of this book, the Jini code is available from the Java Developer's Connection Web site. This site requires a free registration before you can access the code there. (In general, if you're a Java developer, you should probably register at this site—it's the source of early access Java releases from Sun, bug listings, and many helpful articles on Java development.)

The version of Jini that this book is written against is called the "Jini System Software 1.1" release, or just "Jini 1.1." You may want to read the section, "A Note on Versions" at the end of the Introduction for a quick overview of what Jini versions are available and what has changed with each version. Before downloading from the Java Developer's Connection site, you should also check Sun's home page for Jini software to see if newer releases have become available since the writing of this book. The Jini home page is at:

```
http://www.javasoft.com/products/jini/
```

To download the software from the Developer's Connection, register with the site (if you haven't already), and then go to:

```
http://developer.javasoft.com/developer/products/jini/
index.html
```

This page has information on the latest versions of Jini, as well as information on how to submit bugs or requests for improvements. The "Product Offerings" link is where the actual downloadable Jini code comes from. There are a number of separate Jini-related downloads available, including:

- Jini Starter Kit. This download has the fundamental pieces of the Jini infrastructure, including the interfaces and library code that allow Java programs to interact with the key Jini services, as well as the Jini specifications for those services. This package includes not only public interfaces to the Jini software, but also implementations of several key Jini services, including—as of release 1.1—the JavaSpaces "storage service," which I'll discuss in Chapter 16. The Starter Kit also includes source code for the basic Jini classes.

- Jini Technology Compatibility Kit. This download contains code that can be used to test the compatibility of Jini services and applications. If you create custom services, or reimplement any of the core Jini interfaces, you should download the compatibility kit to test that your code will work properly when deployed against the Jini reference implementation.

At this point, you only need to download the Jini Starter Kit. In general, the compatibility kit is most useful for developers writing commercial Jini services or creating custom reimplementations of the core Jini functionality.

Unpacking the Distribution

Once you've downloaded the Jini Starter Kit ZIP file, which is called `jini1_1.zip`, you're set to unpack and install it. If you have decided to download the compatibility kit at this time, you should first install the basic Jini Starter Kit, and then install the other package "on top" of it. Again, however, you only need the Starter Kit, so here I'll only talk about installation of this package.

For Windows: You can use your favorite ZIP extraction utility, such as WinZip. If you want the Jini code to live under the `c:\` directory on your PC, you can extract to `c:` and the unzip utility will create a directory called `jini1_1` to hold the extracted software. Open the Starter Kit ZIP file and extract the contents to your desired directory.

For example:

```
cd c:\
unzip -d jini1_1.zip
```

For Solaris: Copy the ZIP files for the Starter Kit to the directory you want to contain the software, for example, `/files`, then unzip the file.

```
mkdir /files
cd /files
unzip jini1_1.zip
```

(Note that the `-d` option is not needed on Solaris.)

This process will create a directory called `jini1_1` under the directory in which you ran `unzip`.

Examining the Distribution

You'll use the code here pretty extensively during the course of this book, so you should make sure you understand what you've just unpacked and where everything lives. Table 1–2 shows the most important contents of the `jini1_1` directory.

Table 1–2 Layout of the Jini 1.1 Release	
`jini1_1`	This is the root of the Jini installation.
`jini1_1/index.html`	The `index.html` file is the root of all the documentation that ships with the Jini release.
`jini1_1/doc`	This directory contains documentation for the Jini release, including JavaDocs for the APIs, specifications, a glossary, and hints on running the Jini examples.
`jini1_1/doc/api`	This directory contains the API documentation for the system.
`jini1_1/doc/specs`	All the Jini specifications, which describe the Jini distributed computing model and all the core Jini services, live here.
`jini1_1/example`	The 1.1 release of Jini ships with a number of example programs. These include a ray tracing example and a distributed book bidding application. While the actual code for these examples lives in the `lib` directory, along with the rest of the Jini implementation, this directory contains security "policy" files that support these applications.
`jini1_1/lib`	This directory contains the JAR files that constitute the Jini implementation and interfaces. The `jini-core.jar`, `jini-ext.jar`, and `sun-util.jar` files contain the basic Jini interfaces that application writers will use. Other JAR files include the examples, the implementations of the core services, and some utility classes.
`jini1_1/source`	This directory contains the source code for the Jini distribution, under Sun's community source license.

Once you've downloaded and unpacked the files, you should read the `index.html` file to make sure that the installation and configuration instructions have not changed—the information below describes how to install and configure Jini for the release that was current at the time this book was written.

Set Up Your Environment

In this book, I'll follow a number of conventions when describing how to compile and run the example programs. One of those conventions is that I never set the CLASSPATH environment variable. Instead, I explicitly pass the JAR files and directories that a program may need on its command line via the `-cp` option. I'll go into more detail in Chapter 5 on the reasons for this, as well as other aspects of what I call "developing for deployment"—these are some simple rules to follow that can help identify configuration problems early.

The good news at this point though is that there's very little configuration you need to do to set up your environment to use Jini. In fact, at this point I'd recommend that you *unset* your CLASSPATH and just follow the instructions below to make sure your PATH is set correctly.

Setting Your PATH

To run any Java programs, you need to make sure that the `bin` directory from the Java 2 release is in your PATH. Setting your PATH correctly will ensure that all of the java binaries—including the compiler and RMI stubs generator— are accessible; these binaries will "automatically" augment your CLASSPATH to find the basic Java libraries when they are run, so you don't need to set any special CLASSPATH to use them.

For Windows: Type the following:

```
set PATH=c:\jdk1.3\bin;%PATH%
```

In this and later examples, you can change your Windows environment permanently by updating the Environment control pane under the System Control Panel.

For Solaris: The particular syntax varies depending on the shell that you use. If you use the common C-Shell, use the following command line and then type `rehash` to cause your change to the PATH variable to be reevaluated:

```
setenv PATH=/usr/java1.3/bin:${PATH}
```

You can make this change permanent by editing your `.cshrc` file.

Core Note: The JAR files in the Jini distribution

If you're curious, you've probably already poked around in the Jini distribution by now. The most important files here are the JAR files in the jini1_1/lib *directory, in particular the files* jini-core.jar *(which contains the core interfaces and classes that make up Jini),* jini-ext.jar *("extra" software, which will certainly prove useful to you, but aren't "annointed" as part of the central, core software package), and* sun-util.jar *(which contains some useful Sun-provided classes that are subject to change in future releases).*

You'll no doubt notice that there are a number of other JAR files in the lib *directory as well; many of these end in "-dl". These JAR files contain code that is meant to be downloaded to clients as they run.*

So, for example, you'll see reggie.jar *(which contains Sun's implementation of the Jini lookup service) as well as* reggie-dl.jar *(which contains only the code that clients need to use the lookup service).*

When you begin to create your own Jini applications, you may wish to make a similar separation, with the implementation of your application in one JAR file and the parts that will need to be downloaded to clients in another.

Start the Jini Run-Time Services

You've probably skimmed through the preceding sections with no problems whatsoever. Now, though, you're going to need to slow down a bit and take the time to start up the services that Jini needs at run time. The bad news is that figuring out the parameters and configurations needed to run these services can be a bit of work. The good news is that you rarely—if ever—have to restart them once they're going.

Jini depends on quite a bit of network infrastructure at run time. In a deployment setting, you would probably run most of these services on a compute server, or perhaps several compute servers for redundancy. To use Jini effectively, you will need one instance of most of these services running somewhere on your LAN; other services are more effectively deployed on all (or at least several) hosts. If you're doing your own development and experimentation with Jini, you can just run these services on your desktop computer, if you like.

The Jini distribution comes with the basic services needed to support Jini, as well as a few other "optional" services. The list below enumerates the various services that are *required* to run Jini applications on your network. In addition to these, there are a few other services—including the Jini "transaction manager" and the JavaSpaces "storage service," among others—that come with the distribution and that you should be aware of, but aren't required for most Jini work. So I won't talk about these until later in this book. But for development, you should go ahead and start all of the required services as described below. You can leave them running indefinitely, and pretty much forget that they're there.

The services that Jini requires are as follows:

- A simple Web server. Jini requires this facility because when downloaded code is needed through RMI, the actual transmission of the code happens via the HTTP protocol. Jini comes with a very simple HTTP server that's sufficient to supply code to applications that need it. A common configuration is to run an HTTP server on each host that needs to provide downloadable code to other applications.

- The RMI *activation daemon*. Despite its frightening name, the activation daemon is a very simple-to-use and useful piece of Java infrastructure. This process allows objects that may be invoked only rarely to essentially "go to sleep" and be automatically awakened when they are needed. This situation commonly arises in remote systems programming, where you may have a long-lived server object that is only rarely used. The RMI activation daemon manages the transition between active and inactive states for these objects, and is used extensively by the other core Jini run-time services. At a minimum, you will need to run the activation daemon on each host that runs a lookup service, described below.

- A lookup service. As you shall see, the lookup service is really the core of Jini. A lookup service keeps track of the currently active Jini services that are available on a LAN. Sun provides its own implementation of a lookup service that's custom-built for Jini. When you read the Jini documentation, you may notice that the RMI registry server that comes with the JDK can be used as a lookup service. While this option *can* be used, it is not recommended—the lookup service that comes with Jini is much more full-featured. I won't examine how to use the RMI registry as a lookup service in this book, because there is no good reason

to use it. The lookup service relies on activation to recover its
state after crashes or restarts. So you must run the activation
daemon on each machine that runs a lookup service.

This may seem like a lot of work, but these processes can be spread across the
machines in your network, and are largely self-maintaining: Once you start them,
they need virtually no caretaking. In the course of my Jini development, I leave
these processes running for weeks or even months. Many times I'm surprised to
see one still running on a server that I'd completely forgotten about.

There are two ways to start these services. If you want to get up and running
quickly, you can use a graphical user interface (GUI) that comes with the Jini distribution. This interface is only capable of starting Jini services on the *local*
machine, which is definitely not appropriate for debugging Jini applications that
will be run in multimachine environments! Still, the GUI can help you get started
more quickly than you could otherwise. I'll discuss this method first.

Most serious developers, though, will want to get "under the hood" to understand how to run the individual services "by hand" and pass any necessary arguments to them. So we'll also look at how to do this.

The next section discusses running the required Jini services via the GUI; the
following section gives more in-depth guidelines for running these services from
a command line on either Windows or Solaris.

Starting Required Services via the GUI

Jini ships with an easy-to-use GUI for starting the required Jini services. When
you use this interface, you start these services on the local machine—typically
the same machine on which you will be doing development. The GUI doesn't
hide all the details of these services—it just makes the most common configurations easy.

If you wonder about the various options for these services, read the next section on how to start these services from the command line. In general, having an
understanding of the options for these services will be useful as you get more
skilled in using Jini—so understanding how to start these services from the command line is important.

Core Note: A new service launcher has been added in Jini 1.1

*If you've been using Jini since the 1.0 days, you're probably
familiar with the use (and limitations) of the old StartService GUI
application that came with 1.0. One of the most severe problems with
this application was that the default parameters for starting different*

services was hard coded into the application—meaning that you would have to edit and recompile it if you wanted to change the defaults.

In 1.1, Sun has added a new, and greatly improved, service launcher in the package com.sun.jini.example.launcher.StartService. This new launcher lets you load pre-defined service configurations from property files, make changes, and then save these configurations. This new tool isn't just a Jini service launcher—it can be used to start any Java program you desire.

Although Jini 1.1 also ships with the old service launcher (in com.sun.jini.example.service.StartService), Sun's intent is to have the new launcher become the "standard" GUI for launching the Jini services. The old launcher will probably disappear in the next release.

Running the GUI

Once you've got your PATH set up, you can easily launch the configuration application. To do this, just run the following:

On Windows:

```
java -cp C:\jini1_1\lib\jini-ext.jar;
        C:\jini1_1\lib\jini-examples.jar
     com.sun.jini.example.launcher.StartService
```

On Solaris:

```
java -cp /files/jini1_1/lib/jini-ext.jar:
        /files/jini1_1/lib/jini-examples.jar
     com.sun.jini.example.launcher.StartService
```

Note that although I've broken the commands into separate lines for clarity, you should type all of the command on a single line Be sure, of course, to also use the correct directories for your Jini instalation, if you've installed Jini into someplace other than I have.

The `-cp` option sets the CLASSPATH for the JVM to include the `jini-examples` and `jini-ext` JAR files; the last argument is the fully qualified name of the `StartService` GUI.

Once this program launches, you'll see a window with two tabbed panes, as shown in Figure 1-1. The first is labeled *Template* and the second is labeled *Run*.

The *Template* tab is where you would create launching instructions for new services that you want to use the GUI to start. The *Run* tab will contain buttons to start and stop any service that has a template defined for it.

Figure 1–1   *The StartService launcher*

To begin, go to the *File* menu and select *Open Property File*. Jini 1.1 comes with property files that contain pre-defined templates for launching services on both Windows and Unix. The Windows property file can be found as

```
C:\jini1_1\example\launcher\jini11_win32.properties
```

The Unix property file lives in:

```
/files/jini1_1/example/launcher/jini11_unix.properties
```

Navigate down the directories and load the appropriate property file for your platform. After loading the property file, the GUI will display a separate tabbed pane for each service defined in the property file, and the *Run* tab will change to display start and stop buttons for each of the defined services. Figure 1-2 shows how the GUI should look after you've loaded the property file.

```
StartService                                          _□×
File
┌─────────┬──────┬───────────────┬──────────────┐
│ Mercury │ Norm │ TransientSpace│ FrontEndSpace │
├─────────┴──────┴───────────────┴──────────────┤
│  Transient_Fiddler    Activatable_Fiddler    Mahalo_TxnManager │
├────────┬─────┬──────┬──────────┬────────┬─────────────┤
│Template│ Run │ RMID │ WebServer│ Reggie │ LookupBrowser│
└────────┴─────┴──────┴──────────┴────────┴─────────────┘
              User Defined Labels       User Defined Values
   Service Name: [_____]      [_____]
       Entry1 : [_____]      [_____]
       Entry2 : [_____]      [_____]
       Entry3 : [_____]      [_____]
       Entry4 : [_____]      [_____]
       Entry5 : [_____]      [_____]
       Entry6 : [_____]      [_____]
       Entry7 : [_____]      [_____]
       Entry8 : [_____]      [_____]
       Entry9 : [_____]      [_____]
      Entry10 : [_____]      [_____]

                  [  Create  ]  [  Clear  ]
```

Figure 1–2   *The StartService GUI after loading a property file*

Flip through the panes and take a look at the configuration options for these various services. If you've installed Jini 1.1 in the "standard" locations, the defaults should work fine for you as-is. If not, you may need to tweak path names in a few places.

For most of the examples in this book, you will need to run only a subset of the services listed here. The most important of these is the Jini lookup service. Additionally, and as I mentioned before, you'll need a couple of "supporting" services that the lookup service needs to work properly. In particular, the *RMI activation daemon* (rmid) is needed, because the lookup service is implemented using the RMI activation framework. The activation daemon must run on the same machine as the lookup service, and must be started *before* the lookup service. Additionally, an HTTP server that provides access to the core Jini JAR files is also needed, somewhere on the network.

Take a look at the *RMID* tab to get the configuration panel for the activation daemon. You can see this panel in Figure 1-3. As you can see, there's not a lot to be configured! The *RMID Command* field specifies the command to run, and the *Options* field sets the security "exec policy" for the activation daemon (I'll describe this in more detail a bit later in the chapter). The only thing you may want to add is to give `rmid` a fixed log directory. By default, `rmid` creates a new log directory below whatever directory is current. It uses this log information to restart any activatable services the next time it is run. To be sure that you're getting the same log directory each time, you may want to explicitly set it in the *Options* field of the *RMID* configuration panel. You would do this by entering `-log directory` in the panel, where `directory` is replaced by a fully-qualified path to some existing directory.

Figure 1–3   *The RMID configuration panel*

Go to the *WebServer* configuration panel next, as shown in Figure 1-4. The *Java Options* and *JAR File* text areas are simply used to specify which JAR file contains the code for the web server. Make sure the path to the JAR file points to the `tools.jar` file that comes with Jini. The *Port* and *Document Area* tabs allow you to change the default port on which the web server runs, and the directory from which it will serve documents. You should probably leave these alone, with the exception of changing the web server port to 8080 (which I've done here with consistency with the rest of the book, and the other installation instructions that come with Jini). Of course, if you've installed Jini in some unusual location, you'll need to make the appropriate changes. Finally, the *Log Downloads* option passes the -verbose flag to the web server. This willl cause it to log all attempts to download files to standard output. I recommend leaving this option set to -verbose as it can be a great debugging aid.

StartService	_ □ ✕

File

Mercury	Norm	TransientSpace	FrontEndSpace

Transient_Fiddler	Activatable_Fiddler	Mahalo_TxnManager

Template	Run	RMID	WebServer	Reggie	LookupBrowser

Java Command :	java
Java Options :	-jar
Executable Jar File :	C:\files\jini1_1\lib\tools.jar
Port :	-port 8080
Document Area :	-dir C:\files\jini1_1\lib
Log Downloads :	-verbose

Figure 1–4   *The WebServer configuration panel*

Core Note: A word on port numbers

You may have wondered why I recommend changing the port number for the web server to 8080 in the instructions above. In all Jini releases prior to 1.1, port 8080 was the "recommended" port to use. Of course, you can use any port you wish for your webserver, as long as you're consistent. But all of the Jini documentation and installation instructions always used 8080 in the descriptions.

> *With 1.1, a few inconsistencies crept into the setup instructions. The StartService GUI uses 8081 while the instructions for running the services "by hand" still use 8080.*
>
> *In the interests of consistency in this book, I'm recommending that you use port 8080 if possible (that is, unless you've already got something else running at that port). This ensures that—whether you use the GUI or start things by hand—you'll be using the same configuration, and the rest of the instructions in the book will "just work."*
>
> *Be sure to note that there are a few other places in the GUI you'll have to make this change.*

Next, check out the *Reggie* configuration panel, as shown in Figure 1-5. This panel lets you configure the Jini lookup service. The *Security Policy File* option sets up a security policy file for the lookup service. The notion of security policies was introduced in Java 2 as a way to provide fine-grained control over the rights of Java code running in a JVM. If you're interested in the details of why this is needed for particular services, see the longer descriptions in the section on starting services from the command line. For now, however, all you have to do is edit the path here to point to the location of the policy file that ship with Jini.

![StartService window]

| StartService | | | | | | _ □ × |

File

Mercury	Norm	TransientSpace	FrontEndSpace
Transient_Fiddler		Activatable_Fiddler		Mahalo_TxnManager
Template	Run	RMID	WebServer	Reggie	LookupBrowser

Java Command :	java
Java Options :	-jar
Setup JVM Options :	
Executable Jar File :	C:\files\jini1_1\lib\reggie.jar
Codebase :	http://hostname:8080/reggie-dl.jar
Security Policy File :	C:\files\jini1_1\policy\policy.all
Log Directory :	C:\tmp\reggie_log
Groups :	public
Server JVM :	
Server JVM Arguments :	

Figure 1–5   *The Reggie configuration panel*

The *Executable JAR File* option should indicate the path to the `reggie.jar` file in the Jini distribution. The *Log Directory* specifies a path to a directory in which the lookup service will checkpoint its state. The lookup service can recover from crashes by using the information here. The lookup service will create the child-most directory (called `reggie_log` by default), so it shouldn't already exist. All the directories leading up to it *should* exist, however.

The *Groups* field lets you specify which *communities* this particular lookup service will support. You'll learn more about what this means in future chapters but for now, just leave it set to `public`.

The one option here that you will have to tweak is the *Codebase* field. This field specifies a URL from which *clients* of the lookup service can download the code needed to interact with the lookup service. You must provide a URL here that corresponds to the HTTP server you configured in the last step. In particular, you need to replace the string `HOSTNAME` with the name of your computer, and set the port number to 8080 as described in the Core Note previously.

You will not need to use the panels for the other services now. These are used to control the Jini transaction manager and JavaSpaces services, as well as a handful of Jini utility services; you'll see how to start these later in the book.

Finally, after all this, you're set to run! Click on the *Run* tab, which brings up the window shown in Figure 1-6. You can now click on *Start RMID*, *Start Web-Server*, and *Start Reggie* in that order (make sure that you start the reggie lookup service last, as it depends on the web server and activation daemon to be running).

StartService	
File	

Mercury	Norm	TransientSpace	FrontEndSpace			
Transient_Fiddler		Activatable_Fiddler		Mahalo_TxnManager		
Template	Run	RMID	WebServer	Reggie	LookupBrowser	

Start RMID	Stop RMID
Start WebServer	Stop WebServer
Start Reggie	Stop Reggie
Start LookupBrowser	Stop LookupBrowser
Start Transient_Fiddler	Stop Transient_Fiddler
Start Activatable_Fiddler	Stop Activatable_Fiddler
Start Mahalo_TxnManager	Stop Mahalo_TxnManager
Start Mercury	Stop Mercury
Start Norm	Stop Norm
Start TransientSpace	Stop TransientSpace
Start FrontEndSpace	Stop FrontEndSpace

Figure 1–6   *The Run panel*

Core Tip: Understanding the lifecycle of the lookup service

Chances are, you've never used an activatable program like the Jini lookup service before. What happens when you "start" an activatable service like reggie is that the launching program doesn't actually start the lookup service at all. Instead, it's merely a setup program that "registers" it with the activation framework, so that reggie can be started on demand.

The activation daemon, in turn, records information provided by the setup program so that it can start reggie in the future as needed. This is the information that's squirreled away in the activation daemon's log directory.

*Why do you need to care about this? Most importantly, this means that you generally need to only run the lookup service once, **ever**. "Running" the lookup service actually just does this registration process, which is typically a one time affair. After this, if your machine ever crashes or reboots, simply restarting* rmid *will cause the lookup service to be launched...as long as* rmid *can access its log files of course. Re-running the setup program just registers multiple copies of the lookup service on the same machine, which is probably not what you want.*

The later section on running the services by hand has more details on reggie lifecycle and interactions with activation.

At this point, you're set to start running some Jini examples. As mentioned earlier, getting the various services set up can be a pain, largely because of all the options that are needed, and uncommon JVM parameters (such as security policies) that have to be used. But once you've set up these services, you can likely leave them running for long stretches of time.

If you do want more details on the service launcher, read the file `NewStart-Service.txt` in the directory `jini1_1/doc/example` that comes with the distribution.

For those with a serious interest in how the Jini services work, I'll now present the details of starting these services from the command line, along with some helpful scripts for getting things going. If you're going to be starting these services automatically when servers boot, you need to understand how to launch them manually. The next section also looks behind the curtains at some of the options that I glossed over in the GUI walk-through.

Starting Required Services via the Command Line

If you have already started the required services from the GUI, you can skip over this section if you like. The purpose of spelling out how to run these by hand is to give you a bit more information about what the options for the various services are, and what common configurations of the Jini services are useful. And knowing how to start these services by hand is essential if you need to configure your machine to start Jini services at boot time.

This is the nitty-gritty on how to run these components. I'll walk through the steps required to start these services. In general, you should start them in the order listed. For each of these services, I'll provide short scripts for both Windows and UNIX that will save you time.

Start the Web Server

As mentioned, to support the downloading of code, you need to have an HTTP server that can provide the code needed by applications running somewhere on your network. The requirements of this server are minimal—it only really needs to support the "get" operation, so any old Web server that you're already running is probably sufficient.

Jini comes with a utilitarian Web server in its `tools.jar` package, though, so I'll show you how to get it running.

In the most basic case, all you have to do is type the following to run the HTTP server:

On Windows:

```
java -jar C:\jini1_1\lib\tools.jar
        -port 8080 -dir C:\jini1_1\lib
        -verbose
```

On UNIX:

```
java -jar /files/jini1_1/lib/tools.jar
        -port 8080 -dir /files/jini1_1/lib
        -verbose
```

Obviously, substitute whatever directory in which you have installed the Jini release. Here you see an example of an executable JAR file that has a default program that will be run when it is launched by the JVM.

There are a number of options you can pass to this server to customize its behavior. By default, the HTTP server runs on port 8080. If you already have a Web server running there, you may wish to launch the Jini HTTP server on a different port by passing the `-port <portnum>` option, as shown here. You can also set the root directory that will be served by passing `-dir <directory>` to the server; here I've shown the HTTP root directory to be set to the Jini `lib` directory, so that all of the core Jini code can be exported. Finally, the `-verbose` option is useful for debugging—it will cause the HTTP server to display each request made to it as well as where the request came from. You may wish to check the documentation that comes with the Jini release for more options, or in case you have specific configuration needs.

In general, any code that may need to be downloaded across the network has to be accessible from an HTTP server. This server doesn't have to be a full-blown, general-purpose Web server; it can be as simple as the HTTP service that comes with Jini. You can collect up all the downloadable code together and have one Web server serve it, or you can have a number of small servers running on your network. For development purposes, since Jini applications are generally deployed into multimachine environments, you will probably want to start multiple HTTP servers, one for each service.

How do you know whether or not code will need to be downloadable? This question will become clear as we delve into the Jini architecture. For now, you can assume that any core Jini component—such as the lookup service, the transaction manager, or JavaSpaces—may need to download code into other processes, and therefore their code should be accessible to at least one HTTP server running somewhere on your network.

Start the RMI Activation Daemon

Starting the RMI activation daemon couldn't be easier. The executable for this process lives in `jdk1.3/bin/rmid`. If you've added this directory to your path, the most expedient way to star the activation daemon is by typing:

```
rmid -J-Dsun.rmi.activation.execPolicy=none
```

The arguments on the command line cause the JDK 1.3 version of `rmid` to emulate the JDK 1.2 version security-wise. Essentially, it allows any program running on the machine full access to the facilities of `rmid`. With the tightening of security in the 1.3 platform, `rmid` no longer allows such access by default.

The security controls I've used here are acceptible on your own workstation or a "trusted" machine that you control access to, but is to general for a public server. For more details, read the manual pages for `rmid`, and see the information at:

```
http://developer.java.sun.com/developer/products/jini/
execpolicy.html
```

An instance of the activation daemon must run on each host where activatable objects reside. This includes the Jini lookup service, the transaction manager, and JavaSpaces. And, of course, if you create any activatable objects yourself, you will need to run an instance of the activation daemon on the machines that host those objects.

The only other option you may consider passing to `rmid` is an explicit path to a log directory, by using the `-log <directory>` argument. The activation daemon needs access to a directory in which to write information about the services that are registered with it. By default, it will simply create a directory called `log` underneath the current directory. So if you're not careful about where you start `rmid`, you may wind up with log directories scattered all over the system. You can use the `-log` argument to explicitly name a log directory that you can use each time you start `rmid`.

Start the Lookup Service

The Sun implementation of the lookup service is called "`reggie`," and it lives in the `reggie.jar` file that comes with the distribution. Starting this service is a little more complicated than starting the others. For one thing, there are more arguments that you need to pass to the program to tell it how to behave.

The basic form of running the lookup service is as follows:

```
java -jar <reggie jar file>
      <lookup client codebase>
      <lookup policy file>
      <log directory>
      <lookup groups>
```

This is quite an eyeful, so I'll walk through these options in a bit more detail. The first option here is an argument to the JVM itself, rather than to the Java program it will be running (`reggie`). The `-jar` option specifies that the `main()` routine for the program is contained in the specified JAR file; here, you should pass in the JAR file for the reggie service, `reggie.jar`, which lives in the `lib` directory of the Jini distribution.

Next are the arguments that are passed to the `reggie` program itself, rather than to the JVM that runs `reggie`. The next part of the command line is the *codebase* that specifies where code that will be downloaded to clients lives. The argument that you pass here should be a URL that points to the `reggie-dl.jar` file, which contains code used to access `reggie` that needs to be downloaded to callers. If you know *for certain* that all of your Jini services and applications will always run on the same machine, you can simply use a `file:` URL that points to the directory containing this JAR. As is more likely, though, you'll be running code all over your network. In this case, you should pass a URL for the machine running your Web server that will be used to serve up code, for example, `http://hostname/reggie-dl.jar` (replace "`hostname`" with the name of the machine that the Web server is running on, of course). You should make sure that the Web server can access the `reggie-dl.jar` file under its root directory.

Core Note: A word about codebase

There's a certain art to figuring out how to set the codebase property which, unfortunately, eludes many newcomers to RMI and Jini. The codebase property is used as a way for the server—a program which supplies callable code to a client—to inform the client of where the code can be retrieved from.

When you set the codebase property on a program, you're explicitly telling the server that, when it serializes an object for transmission to a client, it should "annotate" the serialized object with the codebase URL that says where to fetch the code for that object.

Serialization only transmits the member data within an object, not the code itself. Using codebase is a way for a server to tell a client how to download the code as well.

In general, an HTTP server will be running on each server machine that will export code. This HTTP server may be a separate process, such as you see here, or may be an extremely lightweight entity that lives within the server application itself.

There are two common mistakes to watch out for when using codebase. The first is that you should take great care when using file: *URLs.* File: *URLs specify that the code for a service is accessible through the filesystem. This will work great as long as both the client and the server share the same filesystem. But if one of these components is moved to a different host, your once-working code will now break, since the common filesystem is no longer accessible.*

*A second precaution is to never use "*localhost*" in a codebase URL. The hostname "*localhost*" is a shortcut for referring to the host that is evaluating the hostname. If you specify* localhost *in a codebase, this means that clients will attempt to load code from their own machines, rather than the server's machine. This is certainly not what you want, and the source of potentially hard-to-track bugs!*

You should always use the name or the IP address of the host on which the HTTP service will run—which is usually the same host that the Jini service itself will run on. We'll discuss codebase a bit more in the appendix on RMI.

Next you see a security policy file. Reggie, like many Jini services, registers itself with the RMI activation daemon. The activation daemon can start reggie "on demand," and can even restart it if the service crashes. The security policy file you specify here is passed as an argument to the RMI activation subsystem so that, whenever it activates a `reggie` process, it will begin running with the correct security permissions. Whenever you see a security policy file being passed on the command line like this (as opposed to being set via a property to the JVM), it is typically being used to set security for future activations of the service via the activation daemon.

The next option is a directory into which `reggie` will write its logs. You can pass any directory that is accessible on the filesystem where `reggie` is running; make sure you use an absolute pathname here. You should create any leading directories up to the actual log directory itself—although `reggie` will create its own log directory, it won't create any missing directories earlier in the path. You'll see many of the Jini services using log directories. These are used so that the services can checkpoint their state periodically, and recover after a crash. If you're planning on leaving the services up for long periods, you'll want to use a log directory that's on a stable, persistent filesystem.

Finally, you pass a list of *groups* for which the lookup server will provide service. Groups are further discussed a bit later, but essentially they are names that can be used to group clusters of Jini services together. `Reggie` understands two "special" group names that have particular meanings. Passing "`public`" here indicates to use an unnamed public group in which, by convention, services should register by default; passing "`none`" means to use no group at all (which is not of much value to us). For now, just use "`public`" as the group.

Here's a complete command line for starting `reggie`. Be sure, of course, to replace "`hostname`" and "`port`" with the name and port number you used to start the HTTP server in the earlier step.

On Windows:

```
java -jar c:\jini1_1\lib\reggie.jar
        http://hostname:port/reggie-dl.jar
        c:\jini1_1\example\lookup\policy.all
        c:\temp\reggie_log
        public
```

On UNIX:

```
java -jar /files/jini1_1/lib/reggie.jar
        http://hostname:port/reggie-dl.jar
        /files/jini1_1/example/lookup/policy.all
        /var/tmp/reggie_log
        public
```

When you run the lookup service, you'll notice that the command line returns to you after a few seconds (or perhaps longer if you're running on a slow machine or if there is a configuration problem). This is because the program that you've run has actually just registered `reggie` with the RMI activation daemon, so that it'll be started by the activation daemon the first time it is needed; the above command doesn't actually launch `reggie` itself. So the fact that the command returns after registration with the activation daemon is perfectly normal behavior.

You should be sure you understand the implications of the fact that `reggie` uses the activation daemon. First off, it means that this should be the *only* time you ever have to start `reggie` on the machine on which you just started it. The activation daemon will handle restarting it in the future, as long as (1) the activation daemon is running, and (2) the activation daemon has access to the log files it uses to save information about activatable programs. When you run `rmid`, it'll create a directory called `log` under the directory that was current when you ran it. Later— say, when the machine reboots—you should be able to start `rmid` in this same directory. It will find its log files and thus be able to restart any activatable programs that it knew about during its last run, including `reggie`.

For its part, `reggie` should be able to find the log directory *it* was using to store persistent information when it restarts. So you should make sure that the `reggie_log` directory provided on the command line above is in a location that will be stable and accessible across reboots, if you want service registrations to be persistent across reboots.

`Reggie` is a complicated program, and its interactions with the activation daemon make it even more complicated for the people unfamiliar with this facility. If you're having problems with `reggie`, you may want to take a look at the documentation and manual pages that come with the Jini distribution, or at `http://www.kedwards.com/jini/reggie.html`, which has a more thorough overview of the `reggie` lifecycle and details on how to configure the program.

Listings 1–1 and 1–2 offer scripts for Windows and UNIX that you can use to start the lookup service; these scripts are available from the FTP site as mentioned in the introduction.

Listing 1–1 `lookup.bat` Script for Windows

```
REM Set this to wherever Jini is installed
set JINI_HOME=C:\jini1_1
REM Set this to the host where the Web server runs
set HOSTNAME=hostname

REM Everything below should work with few changes
set POLICY=%JINI_HOME%\example\lookup\policy.all
set JARFILE=%JINI_HOME%\lib\reggie.jar
set CODEBASE=http://%HOSTNAME%:8080/reggie-dl.jar
set LOG_DIR=C:\temp\reggie_log
set GROUP=public

java -jar %JARFILE% %CODEBASE% %POLICY% %LOG_DIR% %GROUP%
```

Listing 1–2 `lookup.sh` Script for UNIX

```
#!/bin/sh

# Set this to wherever Jini is installed
JINI_HOME=/files/jini1_1

# Set this to wherever the Web server is running
HOSTNAME=hostname

# Everything below should work with few changes
POLICY=$JINI_HOME/example/lookup/policy.all
JARFILE=$JINI_HOME/lib/reggie.jar
CODEBASE=http://$HOSTNAME:8080/reggie-dl.jar
LOG_DIR=/var/tmp/reggie_log
GROUP=public

java -jar $JARFILE $CODEBASE $POLICY $LOG_DIR $GROUP
```

Running the Sample Program

At this point, you should have all of the required Jini services running on your machine, and you're ready to make sure everything works. We'll fire off a simple example—a browser application—that comes with the Jini distribution. To try out the browser, use the following command line:

On Windows:

```
java -cp c:\jini1_1\lib\jini-examples.jar
     -Djava.security.policy=
          c:\jini1_1\example\browser\policy
     -Djava.rmi.server.codebase=
          http://hostname:8080/jini-examples-dl.jar
     com.sun.jini.example.browser.Browser
```

On UNIX:

```
java -cp /files/jini1_1/lib/jini-examples.jar
     -Djava.security.policy=
          /files/jini1_1/example/browser/policy
     -Djava.rmi.server.codebase=
          http://hostname:8080/jini-examples-dl.jar
     com.sun.jini.example.browser.Browser
```

Be sure, of course, to substitute the paths you used to install the Jini JAR files, and to use the correct URL for your Web server, if you changed any of the default configurations.

You'll note that the browser requires its own codebase property—this is because the various Jini run-time services will actually download code that allows them to communicate with the browser as it runs. This code happens to be in the `jini-examples.jar` file, which is in the same directory as all of the rest of the Jini JAR files. So if you've already got an HTTP server that is exporting this directory, you can refer to this HTTP server in your codebase. Otherwise you'll have to start a new one that exports the browser's downloadable code.

At this point, you should see the browser application shown in Figure 1-7 running on your screen. This application lets you look at the Jini services running on your network, control them, and change the attributes associated with each of them. The display should indicate that one or more "registrars" (lookup services) are available. If you do not see this, then the most likely problem is that you've misconfigured your codebase for the lookup service.

You can leave this application running to monitor the status of any Jini lookup services running. For now, most of the controls in this application may not make much sense to you—we'll soon learn about Jini services and attributes, though. For now, if you see at least one Jini lookup service running—the one you just started—then things are set up properly.

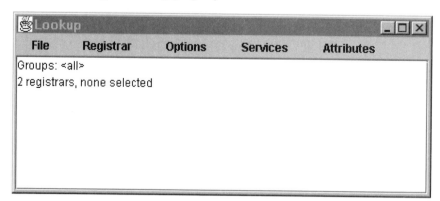

Figure 1–7   *Example Jini browser*

Further Reading and Resources

If you want to read more about the early history of the Java project (as well as see a photo of the Star-7 device), you can check out James Gosling's home page, which has an excellent introduction to the history of the project:

```
http://java.sun.com/people/jag/green/index.html
```

If you're curious about the integration of nondesktop computers into our daily lives, and how computers can be made to "disappear" into the fabric of our surroundings, you may want to check out Mark Weiser's vision of ubiquitous computing:

```
http://ubiq.com/hypertext/weiser/UbiHome.html
```

The *New York Times* article that broke the scoop on Jini still makes for some interesting reading:

```
http://www.nytimes.com/library/tech/98/07/biztech/articles/
15sun.html
```

The *Wired* interview with Bill Joy talks about Jini and the future visions of computing that inspired the Jini project:

```
http://www.wired.com/news/technology/story/13744.html
```

I've tried to keep track of some of the most common problems (and their solutions!) that arise when developing with Jini. These are collected on a troubleshooting page that I keep at my web site. If you have trouble getting services to run, you might visit the page to see if you recognize the problem you're having.

```
http://www.kedwards.com/jini
```

An excellent resource for Jini developers is the JINI-USERS mailing list. To subscribe, send mail to `listserv@java.sun.com`; the body of your message should contain the line `subscribe jini-users`. To unsubscribe, send a message to the same address, with the body containing `signoff jini-users`.

The RMI-USERS mailing list is also a great resource for getting help with RMI-related questions. To sign up, send a note to `listserv@java.sun.com` containing `subscribe rmi-users`. To sign off, send a note to the same address containing `signoff rmi-users`.

Finally, Sun has a Web site for the use of the larger Jini community. This Web site is a good place to check for code donated by community members, news, and upcoming Jini events. Registration is required, but grants you access to code from other community members, and gives you a space in which to upload your own code.

```
http://www.jini.org
```

DISTRIBUTED SYSTEMS

Topics in This Chapter

- The problems with distributed systems
- Why "classical" approaches aren't sufficient
- The Java model of distributed computing
- What dynamically downloadable code means for system designers

Chapter 2

We've all seen the error messages: *NFS server not responding; unable to locate the server; please check the server name and try again; no route to host; host unreachable.* As fallible as our desktop computers seem to be, somehow adding a network to the mix seems to make things break even faster than before.

There are a number of pretty apparent reasons for this fragility. Obviously, new ways for things to break exist in a networked system. The failure of a key router is a type of problem that can bring down a networked application, but simply has no effect on a truly *local* system—meaning an isolated, stand-alone application running on a single machine and in a single address space.

But there are deeper reasons for why distributed and networked systems are harder to build than stand-alone systems. In fact, these reasons point out *why* you cannot simply paper over the network, making remote resources look exactly like local ones, with exactly the same programming models, and expect your code to work.

This chapter provides some background reading on the philosophy of Jini; it looks at networked and distributed systems, and draws a distinction between the two. Most software these days, particularly with the advent of the Web, is networked. Jini, however, represents a more complex beast: a true dynamic distributed system. We'll look at the differences between these two types of software, and look at why there are some tough issues that an infrastructure for distributed systems programming needs to solve. Jini builds on Java to provide some particularly nice solutions to the problems of distribution; we'll look at what makes this Java-based approach different from what has come before.

What's So Hard about the Network?

To understand why building robust software for the network is difficult, it's useful to look at what approaches have been taken to solve the problems of network programming, and where those approaches break down.

Classical Networked Systems

A lot of the history of networked systems programming is about making the network appear to go away. If you look at the "classical" work in infrastructure for networked systems, you see a couple of common themes. First, they provide a way to move the data to the computation. Second, they provide a way to specify what to do to that data, out of a constrained set of possible options.

Finding a way to move the data to the computation is necessary because you cannot assume that the code needed for a particular operation will be available everywhere on the network. The fact that code has to be *compiled* and *installed* for a particular machine makes it difficult to have the code running everywhere. Thus, it's far easier to move the data to the code. But moving the data is no easy trick itself, because the machines on the network have different notions of byte order, floating-point format, word length, and so on. Data description tools such as XDR (External Data Representation, a Sun protocol from the mid-1980s used to package data for portability) make the network "disappear" by hiding the differences in machine-data formats so that any type of CPU can make sense of data it receives. These tools work by standardizing on a particular, portable wire format, which is independent of any machine-specific byte ordering, word length, etc. These tools let data flow around the network, so that it can make its way to wherever it may be needed.

The task of specifying what is to be done to this data once it has been shipped has typically been done via a remote procedure call (RPC) or remote object system. Remote procedure call systems attempt to make the call of a function on a different machine look (to the programmer) like the call of a local function in the same address space. Remote object systems such as CORBA and DCOM raise the level of programming from function calls to method invocations on objects, but essentially still try to mimic the semantics of local invocation. They are not *qualitatively* different from the RPC technology of the past 20 years.

There's one particularly good reason for these attempts to hide the network: Programmers are brought up to understand basic, local programming techniques practically from the time they are weaned. They *know* how to build reliable stand-alone programs. Adding specialized programming models to the mix just increases the time needed to learn the new models, and brings with it headaches, slipped deadlines, and hair loss.

All of these systems, therefore, try to make the network *transparent;* that is, they make the network simply "go away" from the perspective of the programmer.

The Network Is Not Transparent

Unfortunately, this simplification often turns out to be an oversimplification. These systems bring with them the implicit assumption that introducing a network wire between two software components will not affect the correctness of the program, only its performance. In fact, in traditional distributed object systems, hiding the location of a particular object is often seen as desirable—much as hiding the implementation of a function behind its interface is a desirable aspect of object-oriented programming. The behavior of a component in the face of network failures or poor performance is seen as another aspect of its implementation, not of its interface, or its contract with the rest of the system.

As it turns out, the hardest parts of building reliable distributed systems are not the parts that these systems address: packing data into portable forms, causing the invocation of a remote procedure somewhere on the network, and so forth. Instead, the hardest parts of building reliable distributed systems have to do with precisely those things about the network that *cannot* be ignored by the programmer—the fact that the time required to access a remote resource may be orders of magnitude longer than accessing the same resource locally; the fact that networks fail in ways that stand-alone systems do not; and the fact that networked systems are susceptible to partial failures of computations that can leave the system in an inconsistent state.

Computer scientist Peter Deutsch recognized these problems years ago, and called them "The Seven Fallacies of Distributed Computing." I won't go into all seven here, but see the sidebar for the list. Even with the support of all of these classical approaches, building reliable, scalable, robust distributed systems is still difficult—which is why we're all so familiar with the error messages at the start of this chapter. The problems come because the classical systems fool the unwary into believing that they can ignore the unhideable issues that lurk in distributed systems programming. I'll talk about some of these next.

The Seven Fallacies of Distributed Computing

Computer scientist Peter Deutsch has written about what he calls "The Seven Fallacies of Distributed Computing." Here are the fallacies, along with an introduction by him.

"Essentially everyone, when they first build a distributed application, makes the following seven assumptions. All prove to be false in the long run, and all can cause *big* trouble and *painful* learning experiences."

- The network is reliable
- Latency is zero
- Bandwidth is infinite
- The network is secure
- Topology doesn't change
- There is one administrator
- Transport cost is zero

Much of the work in Jini is designed to explicitly acknowledge these fallacies, rather than pretend they don't exist.

Performance and Latency

Clearly, accessing some resource—a file or an object—over a network is slower than accessing it locally. We all know this, and we know that the differences in access times, often several orders of magnitude, are enough to make the difference a *qualitative* one, rather than just a quantitative one.

But you may be saying to yourself, "What's the big deal? Accessing cache memory is orders of magnitude faster than accessing main memory, and accessing main memory is orders of magnitude faster than accessing the disk. Isn't this just yet another tier of performance?" The reason this is an issue in networked systems is that the differences in performance often make it impossible to distinguish a *failed* component from a *slow* component. Even though main memory is faster than a disk, both have performance characteristics that tend to stay within fairly fixed bounds. But as anyone who has used a Web browser can tell you, network performance can vary wildly, even within a short span of time. Access times in local systems simply cannot affect the program in quite the same way as remote access times.

And yet, systems such as RPC and CORBA do not even address these performance issues. By this, I don't mean that they should somehow work some magic to make the network hundreds of times faster so that the differences in latency go away. Obviously they cannot do this. But RPC and CORBA don't even consider performance and latency as part of their programming models— they simply ignore the issues entirely, treating them as "hidden" implementation details that the programmer must implicitly be aware of and deal with.

The fact that it is *possible* to ignore these differences when developing (because remote accesses are made to resemble, as closely as possible, local ones) means that designs can arise that not only have extremely poor performance, but also may be unable to handle the variations in performance that can happen in distributed systems. If the interfaces between objects in a system are designed before the "implementation detail" of location or "remoteness" is considered, very likely the system will have communication patterns that make it unacceptably slow, or not very robust.

Rather than ignoring the "remoteness" of components until late in a design, we must consider these architectural details at the same time that the interfaces for communicating between objects are designed.

New Failure Modes

Networked systems can fail in ways in which stand-alone systems cannot: Routers can fail, users can—intentionally or unintentionally—yank an Ethernet cable out of the wall, key machines with name servers and database servers can crash. A piece of code written to work in a stand-alone environment will be unprepared to deal with the new failure modes that can result if that same code is run in a networked environment.

Consider a simple example: a function to read a file from disk. This code fragment may be used over and over again in a large application, say a spreadsheet, and may be perfectly written for its original intended setting. It may catch and intelligently handle all sorts of errors, from the filesystem filling up to permission violations.

Now imagine this same application running in a situation where the file is on a disk attached to a network file server somewhere. This same code, which could handle all types of local failures in an intelligent way, must now deal with network failures as well. The fileserver machine may crash, or it may become unreachable. The application may, if it is lucky, fail in a "normal" way that mimics what would happen if one of the local error situations were to arise—it may treat a "server down" condition as a permissions violation, for example. But it may also crash in unexpected ways. Certainly, the code won't be able to respond intelligently to network errors, by retrying if the server is unreachable, or asking the user for a secondary fileserver if the primary one crashes.

You may be saying to yourself, again, "So what? I can just check to see whether a failure occurred after performing any operation that involves the network. The situation is the same in local programming—after writing to the disk, you check to make sure that the data was actually written." The reason this doesn't work is the fact that, very often in distributed settings, it may be difficult or impossible to even determine *if* an error occurred. In a local system, you can attempt to write some data to the disk and then check to see that the data was actually written. But in a distributed setting, there is often *no* centralized entity—like an operating system—which can be used to determine success or failure. Even "reliable" protocols like TCP/IP don't solve this problem—no matter how reliable TCP/IP is, it cannot distinguish between an application that has crashed and an application that is simply slow to respond; and there is no centralized entity that can detect the difference.

If our systems don't expose the types of failures that can occur in networked situations as part of the contract of dealing with resources—that is, in their interfaces—then these "hide the network" programming paradigms permit programmers to ignore them. By declaring the potential for remoteness in the interfaces to these objects, we can require programmers—via the compiler—to address these issues.

Concurrency and Consistency

Both of these differences between local and remote computing—performance and latency differences, and differences in failure modes—are significant, but they aren't nearly as devastating as the problems of concurrency and consistency that arise in distributed computing. When software components fail in a local setting—an application crashes, say—the failure is typically an all-or-nothing affair. If an entire machine goes down, all work on that machine is going to stop, regardless of what else is happening around the network. And if one of a set of components involved in some cooperative operation fails—say one of two applications involved in a cut-and-paste operation—a central component such as the operating system can detect this and signal the other involved parties.

Such a situation is not the case in distributed computing, however. In distributed computing, individual components can fail in ways that leave other components running and—as is often the case—unaware of their failure. This situation, called *partial failure*, is particularly insidious, and is the source of most of the evils that turn up in distributed computing. *Total failures*, which tend to crop up in local-only applications, are actually *easier* to deal with because at least the system winds up in a known state.

For example, think about a shared whiteboard application that allows a set of participants around the network to mark up and share a common drawing space. When one user makes a mark, the update must be sent to the other participants in the session. This update can be sent via repeated unicast—sending the same message repeatedly to each participant—or via multicast—sending once to a special network address that multiple parties can listen on. In either case, it is possible that one recipient's computer may crash or may become unreachable during the update process.

What happens now? If the sender cannot detect the failure (perhaps because the write routine was originally borrowed from some stand-alone application, or because the operating system simply cannot determine if a message has been delivered or not), it will have no way of knowing that one participant is out of sync with the rest. If the network is restored a moment later, the missed recipient will continue running, none the wiser that it has missed an update.

You may be thinking, well, obviously the thing to do is ensure that the sender is made aware when a message is not received by the recipient. Even if the operating system does not provide such notifications, application programmers can code them in by stamping messages with serial numbers and having recipients explicitly acknowledge receipt of updates. (The actual protocol that would be used is more complicated than this, because the sender of a receipt may not know that its receipt has been delivered correctly.) Even in this case, though, what's the original sender to do if it detects that an update has not been delivered to a recipient? One heavy-handed solution would be to assume that the recipient has crashed and will never come back up, and drop that participant from the session. A kinder, gentler solution would be to have the sender save the update, in the hopes that the recipient comes back on line at some point in the future and the message can be resent. But how long should the sender hold on to that update, and all future updates that happen before the recipient returns? We probably don't want the sender to queue *all* messages in the hopes that some recipient will eventually return, as this causes the sender to consume excess resources because of problems that aren't local to it, and over which it has no control.

This relatively trivial case—a shared whiteboard application—shows the problems that arise when the intricacies of distributed development are hidden below a veneer of library code. As detrimental as the problems of performance and failure modes are, the problems of partial failure, and maintaining consistency among participants, are the real show-stoppers for distributed computing. The classical solutions that try to paper over the differences between local and remote computing simply have nothing to say about these issues. And, in fact, one could argue that they *cannot* say anything about them: How to handle partial failures and consistency violations is an issue that each application writer must decide for him- or herself—it cannot be pushed into the operating system or toolkit and solved in a general way for all applications. Applications have different requirements, and will implement code to handle partial failures in different ways. An application that positively must have complete consistency may simply shut down if it detects some partial failure from which it cannot guarantee recovery. Another application may be willing to tolerate inconsistencies among participants, perhaps for some short period of time. The point of all of this is that our systems must rely on application code to deal with the handling of partial failures—programmers must acknowledge and deal with the possibility of these sorts of failures in their systems.

In all these cases, the developers of the distributed system have to consciously acknowledge the differences between networked and local programming, and decide what solution or set of trade-offs makes best sense for their applications. This is why building reliable distributed software remains so hard, even after 30 years of research into distributed computing—all of the work into making data portable and being able to move it to where computation occurs is necessary. It just isn't the hard part of the problem.

New Paradigms in Distributed Computing

Although not a panacea, Java makes some strong progress on the issues that make distributed systems programming hard. First off, Java provides a solution to many of the problems classical systems have focused on. Other problems that classical systems have addressed are simply not present in the Java world. The reason for this is that Java has the advantage of being a language-oriented system: The entire platform—from the run-time JVM, to the class libraries, to the bytecode verifier, to the security architecture—assume the existence of objects expressed using Java bytecodes. This assumption can greatly simplify many of the aspects of building distributed systems. In contrast to systems like CORBA and DCOM, where distribution is a bolted-on accessory to one or more languages, Java's approach to distributed computing assumes the existence of a *particular* language everywhere, with a favored data format and a favored code format.

For example, moving data around is no longer hard. The size and format of primitive types such as integers, floating-point numbers, strings, arrays, and even objects are defined by the Java specifications. No complex machinations are needed to handle conversions between the native data formats on one machine and the native formats on another. This is in stark contrast to C, where the language itself says little about the size or format of primitive types, and we have to rely on external, outside-the-language tools for describing portable data.

Even better, in addition to defining the primitive types, Java defines the format of complete *objects*, including such details as subclassing, method protection attributes, and type signatures. Assuming this lingua franca of data obviates the need for schemes such as XDR to homogenize data into portable forms.

Also, one of the key assumptions of pre-Java distributed computing—that data needs to move to the code, because the inverse is impractical—is done away with. Using Java, it's as easy for code to move from machine to machine, even machines with different operating systems or CPUs, as it is to move data. The Java bytecode format is the universal interchange format for executable code. Further, Java's security mechanisms ensure that code, once moved into your system, can execute with a degree of safety not found in other approaches. Although your operating system may support dynamic linking of, say, C code through shared object files or dynamic link libraries, Java's facilities for safe dynamic loading go far beyond what is possible in other environments.

For example, Java allows fine-grained access control to machine resources based on security policies. Code can be digitally signed, giving cryptographically secure guarantees about the authorship of classes. And, perhaps more importantly, Java's strong type safety, combined with the ability of the bytecode verifier to assure that malformed code will never be run, means that remotely loaded code can execute with a reduced chance of bringing down the entire process. For example, in C, it is possible—even easy—for a dynamically loaded piece of code to follow a null pointer, provide an out-of-bounds array index, or corrupt the heap, bringing down an otherwise long-running server. In Java, it is impossible to obtain a reference to unused data, and it is impossible to forge a new reference to an object you have not been explicitly given access to. Furthermore, in C, a function may return arbitrary (and possibly unexpected) values from a function to indicate errors. In Java, exceptional conditions must be declared as part of the signature of a method, *forcing* those who call the code to deal with them. These safety attributes of Java limit the ability of dynamically loaded code to corrupt the system.

The ability to move code from machine to machine is a dramatic change. Now, servers can be dynamically updated and maintained from authorized clients. Agent code can traverse the network, gaining performance by moving close to needed data. Systems built around rigidly defined, static interfaces can be dynamically evolved by supplying them with new implementations of those interfaces as needed.

So Java provides some novel solutions to many of the problems that classical systems have focused on, and makes some of the problems that those systems have addressed simply vanish. But what about the truly hard problems of distributed computing that I opened this chapter with? What does Java do to promote the distinction and fundamental differences between local and remote objects?

To understand how Java begins to address some of these harder problems, we first have to look at Java's model for strongly typed distributed computing. As you'll see, while Java doesn't provide magical solutions to the problems discussed earlier, its model of distributed computing explicitly acknowledges the differences in local and remote computation, and provides a toolset that allows programmers to deal with them.

The Need for Strong Typing

The previous section talked a lot about Java's ability to send code to running processes on demand. But is this really what we want? Is a world where executable code flies around really maintainable and understandable? As a language-based approach, Java is able to take the benefits that strong typing, true object orientation, and polymorphism bring to local computing and extend these benefits out to the Internet.

In Remote Method Invocation (RMI), the Java language's type definition facility is used to describe the interfaces for remote communication. This may seem like a subtle point, but it's actually very important—local types that you create when you declare a Java class or interface, as well as the types that are found in the Java libraries, are defined using the exact same mechanisms as the types used for remote communication. This means that a protocol for communicating with some remote server *is* a Java interface, which can be implemented by a class. Here's an example of an interface definition that would be found in a program using Java RMI:

```
public interface RemoteServer extends Remote {
     public int getLength(String s) throws RemoteException;
}
```

Now this example is actually defining a remote "protocol" between two remote processes—it defines the terms of interaction between two processes, including what is sent, what you can do, and what you might get back. This protocol will, of course, be implemented atop some lower-level protocol such as TCP/IP at run time—RMI will handle all the "convenience" tasks of setting up and tearing down sockets, and so forth—but the definition here provides the specification for how two processes will communicate at the *application* level. In a nutshell, the example says that a client can send a single message that transmits a string to a remote server, and the server returns an integer as a reply to this message. But—and this is perhaps the key idea with RMI—this example also defines a first-class interface in the Java language that can be implemented by classes, composed with other interfaces via multiple interface inheritance, passed as parameters, returned from methods, and introspected at run time.

You may be asking, "What's the big deal?" Other systems, such as CORBA's Interface Definition Language (IDL), for example, expose the remote protocol used for communication with services as a type in the native language. The difference is that in RMI, it is this type that completely defines the protocol. It represents "the truth" about the definition of the protocol, and can be manipulated freely in the Java language to extend and change the protocol. Systems like IDL, on the other hand, use some external expression of the protocol (typically a protocol definition written in a language-neutral format) to describe "the truth" about that protocol. The manifestation of the protocol as a Java type is done after the fact, and the Java (or other language) type is only a reflection of the protocol definition; it is not the protocol definition itself. Manipulating the Java type that results from an IDL specification, through subclassing, composition, or reflection, will do nothing to change the protocol used for communication, and it's likely to break your code.

Again, this may sound like a subtle, somewhat academic, distinction. But its importance is hard to overstate. By making protocol definitions first-class interfaces in a modern object-oriented language, we bring all of the power of object orientation that works so nicely in a single address space out to the world of distributed computation.

Polymorphism works in this world. For example, I can now define remote interfaces that are subinterfaces of other remote interfaces. The usual rules apply here—I can pass the more general interface around, cast it to the more specific interface if I need to, and reflect or use `instanceof` at run time to see what type of entity I am talking to. Just as interfaces allow multiple implementations, I can have any number of Java classes that implement a particular remote interface, and the compiler ensures that I live up to my obligations by implementing the methods I need to, with the correct signature. I can even write classes that implement multiple remote interfaces, just as I can write classes that implement multiple local interfaces.

Practical Remote Polymorphism

Even more radical than supporting polymorphism in remote interfaces, RMI supports full-fledged polymorphism in the types of objects passed as parameters or returned as results to or from remote methods. Consider this code example:

```
public interface MatrixSolver extends Remote {
    public Matrix crossProduct(Matrix m1, Matrix m2)
                                   throws RemoteException;
}
```

This code defines a remote interface for doing matrix math (presumably the remote object that implements this interface is running on some high-end processor that can do matrix math so quickly that the time required to send the parameters and receive the results is low relative to the time savings). This interface takes two instances of type `Matrix`, computes the cross product of them, and returns the result, also as a `Matrix`.

Clearly the designer of this remote interface expects callers to send and receive `Matrix` objects, and to understand the semantics of this class. Suppose, however, that I am a signal processing engineer, and I have developed my own special class for dealing with matrices that contain very few data elements. My implementation, called `SparseMatrix`, is far more space-efficient than the standard `Matrix` class that I subclass, so I use it everywhere in my program. I'd like to be able to take advantage of the matrix math remote object written by another group and running on a fast compute server, but the remote object that implements the math functions only understands the basic `Matrix` class, and has never heard of my `SparseMatrix`.

Clearly, in the local-only case, the polymorphism of the Java type system would give me what I want: I pass in `SparseMatrices` to code that expects plain `Matrices`, but the `crossProduct()` function works fine because it is written to use only the `Matrix` "part" of my class. A cleverly written `crossProduct()` function will even call `clone()` on one of its input parameters to create a new object of the same type as the input to stuff its result into, so that the return will be of the same type as one of the inputs.

But what happens in the remote case? If you're using RMI, the same thing as the local case! Even if the remote matrix math server object has never heard of `SparseMatrix`, even if the code for that class doesn't exist on its machine, RMI can package up instances of `SparseMatrix` and ship the data in these instances along. More importantly, RMI will even transmit the *code* for this class, if it is needed. It will ensure that `SparseMatrix` is an actual subclass of

`Matrix`, and implement all of its required methods so that it can be used safely and reliably wherever a `Matrix` is used.

Here you've seen a very pragmatic example. Dynamic, mobile code need not only be used for avant garde applications like active agents. It can play a very useful role in extending the benefits of object-oriented programming to the networked world.

Remoteness Is Part of the Interface, Not the Implementation

You'll also note from the short code examples in the preceding section one of the other benefits RMI brings to the table. The "remoteness" of an object—its ability to be used from another address space—is a part of the object's interface. This is another subtle change with big ramifications. It forces the developer to "design in" remoteness from the beginning, rather than adding it on as an afterthought. This choice by the RMI designers means that programmers must think up-front about the communication patterns they will support in their applications. The remoteness of a method is something that must be declared; it is not hidden as part of the implementation of the object. And, just like everything else in the Java type system, the remoteness of an object can be strongly typed at compile time and introspected at run time.

RMI requires that all interfaces that define a remote communications protocol extend the interface `java.rmi.Remote`. This interface is common to all "remotable" objects, so it is easy to test at run time or compile time whether something is remote or not. These objects have different semantics than simple local objects—their notions of equality are different, for example. Equality is based on whether two objects that implement `Remote` *refer* to the same remote object that lives on some server somewhere, not whether they *are* the same object. That is, if you have a reference to a remote object, what you actually refer to is a local proxy for the remote object, called a "stub." When you compare two such references, you do not want to know if they refer to the same local stub—you care about whether those stubs reference the same remote object on a different machine some place. So the notion of equality of references is extended to work in the remote case.

Perhaps more importantly, every remotely callable method on a remote object is declared to raise the exception `java.rmi.RemoteException`. This exception, along with its subclasses, defines the failure modes that can happen in a networked setting. By explicitly declaring these failures in the method signatures, RMI forces those who would use remote objects to provide exception-handling code to deal with these extra failure cases. And because Java declares exceptions as part of the signature of a method, any code that calls remote code will have to either handle the error conditions that remote exceptions represent, or propagate them up to code that can handle them—the compiler will not allow the programmer to ignore these conditions.

While the RMI facility is certainly not a panacea, and it won't make problems with distributed systems go away, or make distributed systems as easy to build as local ones, it is a step in the right direction. RMI uses the Java type system, but makes a clear semantic distinction between local and remote objects. It forces developers to handle the failure modes that can occur in a distributed setting, and requires them to decide about distribution "up front" rather than hiding it as an implementation detail. By leveraging the power of the Java language, RMI takes advantage of strong typing, extending it to the network domain. RMI makes the problems of data portability simply go away. And, by supporting secure and safe mobile code, RMI allows the benefits of object-oriented programming to now work across the network boundary, supporting flexible and evolvable remote code. It provides a powerful bag of tools for addressing the problems that developers face in building distributed applications.

Of course, Java is famous for mobile code, and not just in the context of RMI. The sidebar below contrasts the use of mobile code in RMI with other uses in Java.

Mobile Code in Other Contexts

You've seen several examples of the usefulness of mobile code in the preceding sections. How do these examples compare with mobile code in other settings... say, in applets? Let's summarize some of the contexts in which mobile code is used, and see what mobile code buys us in each circumstance.

- Applets. In Java's best-known role, applets provide a way for small applications to be installed automatically wherever they are needed, and removed when their users are through with them. In this context, mobile code is used as a way to remove the hassles of installing traditional applications on a system. With applets, installation of an application is as easy as browsing a Web page.

(continued)

- Agents. In the agent paradigm, small, autonomous bits of code travel the Internet, searching out desired data. For example, a "travel agent" might scour the Net looking for the best deals on a flight to Atlanta. In this context, mobile code is used for two things: performance and autonomy. Agents may provide a performance gain because code moves "nearer" the data (in the network sense). Autonomy is essential for agents because the user who started the agent may log off or shut down his or her machine. Once the agent has left the originator's computer, it can continue to run even if the originator disconnects.

- RMI. Java RMI is really an infrastructure for building many types of distributed systems, rather than a single distributed system itself. Thus, RMI can be used for automatic application installation (much as applets are), or to build agent-based systems. In its most basic uses, however, mobile code in RMI is primarily useful for extending the benefits of object orientation to networked systems, and for supporting evolvability by allowing new implementations of remote objects, and new implementations of parameter and return types.

- Jini. Although I haven't yet talked about Jini proper, Jini leverages RMI's semantics and uses mobile code as a way to achieve maintenance, evolvability, and ease of administration for networked devices and services. By using the RMI "way of doing things," Jini takes full advantage of the Java language; all of the benefits of mobile code are available to programs using Jini. (Note that I said that Jini uses RMI semantics, not the RMI implementation. Although Sun's current implementations use RMI extensively, other implementations could use whatever communications mechanisms they want, as long as they adhere to these semantics.)

Java is the first widely available and commercially viable system to support such a rich range of uses for mobile code.

All of the features of mobile code, mobile data, and strong typing (necessary for robustness) signal the possibility for a shift toward true dynamic distributed systems in which the "system" is composed of a number of components, all working together to achieve some result. This is in contrast to standard networked systems, where the "systems" are the individual components, which happen to connect to each other in fairly static patterns.

Let's look a bit more closely at some of the attributes of dynamic distributed systems.

- Dynamic distributed systems can potentially be called on to scale to very large numbers of machines.
- To scale, their code must be present on large numbers of machines. To be present on large numbers of machines, the code must be ubiquitously available. To be ubiquitously available, the code must be easy to install or—even better—automatically self-installing.
- Once deployed, dynamic distributed systems may need to stay running for long periods of time, even months or years. Thus, they must be robust and reliable, and be able to "self-heal" when errors occur.
- Any system that is in place for long periods of time will doubtless have to evolve to account for new network topologies, the presence of new devices, and the refinement of both interfaces and implementations. Thus, dynamic distributed systems must be easily adaptable and evolvable.

All of these attributes point to a class of software in which the system is composed of multiple discrete units that, when in the presence of others, offer a sort of emergent behavior—all of the components work together to create a symbiotic, self-healing system that is greater than the sum of its individual components.

In the next chapter, we will take our first look at Jini, a software system explicitly designed to support the creation of true dynamic distributed systems.

Further Reading

Much of the inspiration for this chapter came from two sources. The first was a lecture that Peter Deutsch gave to me after a presentation I made at Sun Labs, where I claimed "network transparency" as a benefit of a system I was working on. Peter—in his inimitable way—quickly convinced me that what I had claimed as a feature was really a devastating bug.

The second inspiration for this chapter came from an excellent report written by Jim Waldo, Geoff Wyant, Ann Wollrath, and Sam Kendall, also of Sun Labs. If some of these names sound familiar, it's because these folks are some of the brains behind the development of RMI and Jini. This report predates Jini by a few years, but it's just as true today as it was when it was written; reading it will give you some sense of where the Jini designers considered the big problems of distributed computing to be.

```
http://www.sunlabs.com/technical-reports/1994/
abstract-29.html
```

The Jini Model

Topics in This Chapter

- The goals of Jini
- What Jini is; what Jini isn't
- Basic concepts: discovery, lookup, leasing, remote events, transactions
- Downloadable proxies as the key to service delivery

Chapter

Now that you've seen the benefits Java can bring to distributed computing, it's time to see what Jini brings to Java. The Jini vision is simply this: You can walk up with any Jini-enabled device—be it a digital camera, a new printer, a PDA, or a cell phone—plug it into a TCP/IP network, and automatically see and use the variety of other Jini-enabled devices in your vicinity. Any resource available on the network is available to your Jini-enabled device, as if it were directly attached to it, or the device had been explicitly programmed to use it. And adding a new device to this "network community" is as simple as plugging it in.

Likewise, new software services can be added or moved without extensive configuration, and without having to tweak the clients of those services.

In this chapter, you'll learn about what Jini is: both in terms of the "center of gravity" of its design—what aspects the Jini developers considered crucial to focus on—and in terms of the new concepts Jini introduces.

Jini Design Center

In this section, I'll talk about Jini's "design center." This is the set of areas that the Jini designers felt were the most important to focus on.

Simplicity

Bill Joy, one of the inspirations and champions of Jini, once stated, "Large successful systems start out as small successful systems." This philosophy is very much a part of the Jini motivation. Essentially, if you already know Java, you almost know Jini. Jini is built using the fundamental Java concepts—especially as they relate to the distributed computing issues discussed in the last chapter—and adds only a thin veneer to allow services on the network to work with each other more easily.

This is important: Jini is, at its heart, about how services connect to one another—not about what those services are or what they do or how they work. In fact, Jini services can even be written in a language other than Java; the only requirement is that there exists, somewhere on the network, a bit of code that *is* written in Java that can participate in the mechanisms Jini uses to find other Jini devices and services.

I've been using the terms "devices" and "services" pretty interchangeably so far. But from the Jini perspective, everything—even a device such as a scanner or printer or telephone—is really a service. To use an object-oriented metaphor, everything in the world, even hardware devices, can be understood in terms of the interfaces they present to the world. These interfaces are the services they offer, so Jini uses the term "service" explicitly to refer to some entity on the network that can be used by other Jini participants. The services these entities offer may be implemented (here's the OO terminology again) by some hardware device or combination of devices, or some pure software component or combination of components.

Reliability

I've said that Jini provides the infrastructure that allows these services to find and use one another on a network. But what does this really mean? Is Jini simply a name server like the Internet's Domain Name Service (DNS) or the Lightweight Directory Access Protocol (LDAP) within an organization? As it turns out, Jini does have similarities to a name server; it even provides a service for finding other services in a community (though this service is actually much richer than a traditional name service, as you will see). But there are two essential differences between what Jini does and what simple name servers do:

- Jini supports serendipitous interactions among services and users of those services. That is, services can appear and disappear on a network in a very lightweight way. Interested parties can be automatically notified when the set of available services changes. Jini allows services to come and go without requiring any static configuration or administration. In this way, Jini supports what might be called "spontaneous networking"—services close to one another form a community automatically, with no need for explicit user involvement. This means that you don't have to edit configuration files, shut down or restart name servers, configure gateways, or anything else to use a Jini service—you literally just plug it in and Jini does the rest. Furthermore, every device or service that connects to a Jini community carries with it all the code necessary for it to be used by any other participant in the community.

- Communities of Jini services are largely self-healing. This is a key property built into Jini from the ground up: Jini doesn't make the assumption that networks are perfect, or that software never fails. Given time, the system will repair damage to itself. Jini also supports redundant infrastructure in a very natural way, to reduce the possibility that services will be unavailable if key machines crash.

Taken together, these properties make Jini virtually unique among commercial-grade distributed systems infrastructures. These properties ensure that a Jini community will be virtually administration-free. Spontaneous networking means that the configuration of the network can be changed without involving systems administrators. And the ability for a service to carry with it the code needed to use it means that there is no need for driver or software installation to use a service (other than installing the core Jini software itself, of course). Furthermore, the self-healing nature of Jini also reduces administrative load, and user headaches. A cooperating group of Jini services will be resilient to changes in network topology, service loss, and network partitions in a clean way. Jini services are able to cope with network failures. Perhaps they will not be able to fully do their jobs (even the telephone network may report errors to the user at times), but at least they will work predictably in the face of failures, and will recover by themselves over time.

Scalability

I've said that groups of Jini services join together in cooperating sets. In Jini, these groups of services are called *communities*; all services in a community are aware of each other and able to use each other.[1]

So Jini services band together to form communities. But how large are these communities? What did the Jini designers envision as the "target" size for a community? This is an important question. If Jini's design favors very large groups—say, a group composed of every Jini-enabled device in the continental United States—it will have very different performance and interaction characteristics than a design that favors very small groups. The key issue here is *scalability*—how Jini is designed to accommodate varying numbers of services, from the very large to the very small.

Jini addresses scalability through *federation.* Federation is the ability for Jini communities to be linked together, or federated, into larger groups. Ideally, the size for a single Jini community is about the size of a workgroup—that is, the number of printers, PDAs, cell phones, scanners, and other devices and network services needed by a group of 10 to 100 people. The reason for this workgroup focus is that, most often, people tend to collaborate with those they work closely with. Jini makes it easy to bring together this group of people into a community, and makes their resources shareable.

Even if you're part of a workgroup community, you may occasionally need access to resources "further" away (in the network sense)—for example, that fast, new color laser printer up in marketing. Jini supports access to services in other communities via federating them together into larger units. Specifically, the Jini lookup service—the entity responsible for keeping track of all the services in a community—is *itself* a Jini service. The lookup service for a given community can register itself in other communities, essentially offering itself up as a resource for users and services there. (As you'll see later, Jini actually bootstraps itself: Many of the core Jini features are themselves Jini services that can be shared and used by other services using the normal Jini mechanisms.)

The topology of these communities is very lightweight. When you install the Jini software, the system will, by itself, create communities that form along network boundaries. So, for example, if your engineering and marketing departments are on different networks, each will form a unique Jini community. If you want to federate these communities, it's trivial to do a tiny bit of administration to ensure that the lookup services for each community are known to the other.

---

1. If you peruse some older Jini technical documentation, you may see the word *djinn* used to refer to a community of Java services. Rather than using an obscure word (the original Arabic word from which "genie" is derived), I'll stick to the more meaningful "community." Often you may see the word "federation" used to describe a Jini community, and some wags, particularly those with a bent toward Star Trek, may refer to a Jini community as a "collective," reminiscent of the Borg.

Core Note: Jini and administration

Jini is designed to work well in an administration-free setting. But of course you can apply a bit of hand-holding to tailor the system for your particular circumstances.

Federating communities along organizational boundaries is a prime example of this sort of hand-holding: Jini knows enough by itself to form communities along network lines, but has no idea what your company's organizational structure is. So you have to tell Jini that information yourself.

Device Agnosticism

This was alluded to in the previous section, but is important enough that it deserves restating: Jini is agnostic with regard to devices. What does this mean? Essentially it means that Jini is designed to support a wide variety of entities that can participate in a Jini community. These "entities" may be devices or software or some combination of both; in fact, it's generally impossible for the user of one of these things to know which it is. This is one of the key contributions of Jini. To use something you don't have to know—and indeed, don't even care—whether that something is hardware or software. You only have to understand the interface it presents.

If an actual hardware device is connected to the network, Jini is flexible about how much computational power it needs to have. Jini can work with full-blown desktop or server computers, capable of running multiple JVMs and connecting with each other at gigabit speeds. It can also work with such devices as PDAs and cell phones that may have only limited Java capabilities—say, a Java 2 Micro Edition (J2ME) implementation with a limited set of class libraries.

In fact, Jini is actually able to accommodate devices that are so simple they may have no computation on them at all. As you'll see in the next chapter, Jini can accommodate devices with the computational intelligence of—literally—a light switch. The only requirement is that some other, perhaps shared, computational resource that can participate in the Jini community-building protocols on behalf of that device must exist.

Furthermore, and this may be somewhat surprising, Jini doesn't even require that the device or service be written in or understand Java! Again, all that is required is that some Java-speaking device be willing to act as a proxy on behalf of the Java-challenged device or service. You'll see how this works in the next chapter.

What Jini Is Not

Now that I've talked a bit about what Jini is, I should say a few words about what Jini is not.

Jini Is Not a Name Server

As mentioned previously, Jini is not just a name server. Some of what Jini does—like keeping track of the services known within a community—looks like a name server, and even uses the Jini lookup facilities, which provide functionality similar to (but not quite the same as) a name server. But Jini is much more. It is a paradigm for building distributed systems that support spontaneous appearance and disappearance in a community, and the ability to self-heal when things go wrong.

Jini Is Not JavaBeans

JavaBeans provides a way for software components—called beans—to find each other, use services provided by other beans, introspect each other, and so forth. But JavaBeans has a very different design center from Jini. Beans is largely intended for use within a single address space. The mechanisms used for communication between beans are based on direct method invocation, not remote protocols. The beans model, flexible as it is, is also far less dynamic than Jini. When a new bean appears on your system, the current beans in your application don't suddenly know about it and start using it. You—the designer of the system—have to explicitly link the bean into your application and "wire it up" to the other beans. JavaBeans is intended largely for design-time, and to a lesser degree for run-time use in a single address space. Jini is all about run-time use across address spaces. (This isn't to say that Jini and JavaBeans are incompatible systems, however. Jini can leverage JavaBeans in some nice ways. Later, you'll see how to use the JavaBeans event model from Jini, and how to attach beans to Jini services.)

Jini Is Not Enterprise JavaBeans

Likewise, Jini is not Enterprise JavaBeans (EJB). EJB has, on the surface, some characteristics of Jini. It provides the notion of services on the network. Enterprise beans can, and usually do, live in different address spaces. But again, the design center of EJB is quite different than that of Jini. EJB is designed to hook together legacy enterprise systems, covered by Java wrappers, to form the back-end business logic of enterprise applications. It is designed to support easy construction of this logic, and leverages the transaction, messaging, and database services already on the enterprise network. As such, EJB is largely used to configure relatively static pathways between enterprise software components. As long as the logic of the system doesn't change, there's probably little need to reorganize the connections between the beans. Again, defining how these connections will take place happens mostly at design time. In contrast, Jini is about dynamic, run-time discovery of services and run-time connectivity between them. (This is not to say that Jini and EJB can't interact. For example, an enterprise JavaBean could be "Jini-ized" so that it could discover and join a Jini community of services.)

Jini Is Not RMI

Jini is not the same thing as Java RMI. While Jini *uses* the RMI semantics extensively, particularly its rules for mobile code, Jini is a set of services and conventions built atop these semantics. As such, services that speak Jini can enjoy the full benefits of Jini's spontaneous networking and self-healing abilities. While it would be possible (although a lot of work) to build these abilities into a generic RMI application, they are not a part of RMI itself, and generic RMI applications do not see these advantages.

Jini Is Not a Distributed Operating System

Finally, Jini is not a distributed operating system. In some ways, it is much larger than a distributed operating system because pieces of it must run atop some platform that provides a JVM at a minimum; in other ways, it is much smaller than a distributed operating system—the facilities offered and the concepts used by Jini are very limited. Jini only has the notion of services, and the facilities for finding those services. True distributed operating systems provide all the services of traditional operating systems (file access, CPU scheduling, user logins), but do this over a connected group of machines. Jini allows much simpler devices to participate in Jini communities than would devices that rely on running a copy of a full-blown distributed operating system.

What Jini Is

So far in this chapter I've spent some time talking about the design center in Jini, as well as what Jini is not. Now it's time to say exactly what Jini is. I've said that conceptual simplicity was one of the key design goals of Jini, and now you'll get to see what that means in practice.

Broadly speaking, there are three main concepts that form the foundation for Jini. These work in concert to provide the ability for Jini services to spontaneously interconnect with each other, without cumbersome administration. The short sections below introduce these concepts briefly; I'll talk about them in more detail later in the chapter.

Services Carry the Code Needed to Use Them

Applications use services through objects called *proxies*, which provide all of the code needed to connect to a particular service. You can think of proxies as being similar to device drivers in that they allow an application program to interact with a service while shielding it from the details of that service.

But unlike device drivers, which are typically installed by some systems administrator and have to be in place before the device can be used, Jini proxies are carried by the services themselves, and are dynamically downloaded by clients when they wish to use a service. In essence, Jini services can "teach" clients how to use them by extending the capabilities of clients on-the-fly, using all the benefits of mobile code discussed in the last chapter. Applications don't have to know the implementation details of these proxies, and they don't have to be "compiled in"—or even known—when the applications are written.

These proxy objects typically communicate over the network with the back-end portion of the service using whatever protocols the back end was written to understand. Importantly, though, clients are shielded from having to know or care *how* a proxy does its communication with the back end.

A "Meta Service" Provides Access to All Other Services

The ability to dynamically download proxy code isn't enough, though. Simple dynamic downloading says nothing about how you know *what* services are available to you in the first place. Jini provides an interesting solution to this "service discovery" problem. It uses a special service that keeps track of all the other services in the community. This service, called the *lookup service*, is essentially a meta-service that provides access to all other services.

When a service wishes to make itself available, it "publishes" its proxy by storing it in a lookup service. Clients can then connect to the lookup service and ask it what services are available. The lookup service is the indispensible bit of infrastructure in a Jini community. It keeps track of the proxies of the services in the community, makes them available (and searchable) by clients, and can inform interested parties when new services appear or when services leave the community.

And yet, while the lookup service plays a very special role in Jini communities, it is still just a service, with all the characteristics of any other Jini service (including the ability to be deployed redundantly, the fact that lookup services are largely administration free, and so on).

A Bootstrapping Process is Used to Find Proxies for the Lookup Service

As I mentioned, the essential tasks of service discovery are performed by a Jini service, the lookup service. This begs the question: If applications use services by downloading their proxies from the lookup service, and yet the lookup service is *itself* a service, how do applications get the proxies for the lookup service? This is the bootstrapping problem—lookup services are the things that make other services available, but there has to be a way for lookup services themselves to be made available to applications.

You could imagine a couple of solutions to this problem, including providing some fixed "root" lookup service that provides proxies for all other lookup services in the known universe. But this solution isn't in keeping with the Jini spirit, since it depends on a centralized node (and a single point of failure). Another solution might be to simply pre-compile the proxy code that's used for talking to lookup services into every application. But this approach would negate the chief advantage of using downloadable proxies: that applications don't have to know ahead of time how a particular service is implemented. Ideally you'd like to have potentially many different implementations of the lookup service tuned for different environments, and thus each with their own proxy implementations for talking to the service's back end.

Jini's solution is simple and yet powerful. Jini uses a process called *discovery* by which lookup services, and the applications that wish to use them, periodically send out messages on the network. The end result of these messages is that an application will automatically find any lookup service in its vicinity, and will have an IP address and port number from which to download the proxy from the lookup service directly. This "out of band" protocol for discovering lookup services is how Jini services "self assemble" into communities. (There are other discovery protocols that allow other types of assembly; I'll talk about these later in this chapter.)

Fleshing Out The Key Ideas

Lookup and discovery are the key notions that Jini uses to allow an important Java feature—mobile code—to be used to allow applications to find and use services they may never have heard of before. Together, these technologies form the core infrastructure of Jini. If you only understand one key fact about how Jini works, this is the one to remember.

But while these features form the key to Jini, they're really only the most basic substrate on top of which other Jini concepts are layered. For example, the high-level descriptions above say nothing about the *particulars* of how these features are used. For example, they don't say anything about how lookup services come and go, or how clients actually use a lookup service to find services. In this section, I'll talk in more detail about the details of dynamic proxies, discovery, and lookup.

And, of course, these features aren't all there is to Jini. Layered atop these essential mechanisms are several other important concepts that affect the way you build Jini applications in practice. These include aspects of the Jini programming model such as remote events and transactions, as well as Jini's strategy for self-healing, called leasing. In the rest of this section, I'll flesh out the most fundamental concepts in Jini. In the next section, I'll talk about other important "supporting technologies" that you also need to understand to use Jini effectively.

Downloadable Proxies

Much of the power of Jini comes from its ability to effectively leverage a feature central to Java—the ability to download Java bytecodes from the network and execute them securely. In Jini, services are always accessed via an object provided by the service itself, called a proxy. This proxy is downloaded to the client—code and all—at the time the client wishes to use the service. The client then makes calls on it, just as it would any other object, to control and use the service.

This idea of downloadable service proxies is the key idea that gives Jini its ability to use services and devices without doing any explicit driver or software installation. Services publish the code that can be used to access them. A printer, for instance, publishes a proxy that understands how to control that particular printer.

A scanner publishes a proxy that knows how to talk to that particular scanner. An application that uses these services downloads their proxies and uses them without needing any understanding of how the proxies are implemented or how (or even whether) they talk to any back-end device or process.

In some ways, Jini proxies are analogous to Java applets: applets provide a zero-administration way to acquire and use an application; Jini proxies provide a zero-administration way to acquire and use the "glue logic" for communicating with any arbitrary service. But whereas applets are typically designed for "human consumption"—meaning that they usually appear in a Web page when a user asks for them, and come with a graphical interface—Jini proxies are designed to be found, downloaded, and used programmatically. They are essentially secure, network-aware, on-demand device drivers.

The particulars of how a proxy interacts with its service are completely up to the creator of the service/proxy pair. There are a number of common scenarios, though.

- The proxy can sometimes actually perform the service itself. In this case, the object that is sent to clients implements all of the service's functionality itself (and therefore, calling it a "proxy" is really unfair). This strategy is used when the service is implemented purely in software, and there are no external resources that need to be used. An example might be a language translation service that is completely implemented as in Java code and has no need to talk to any external processes to do its job.

- The proxy can be an RMI stub for talking to some remote service. If you've already got an RMI-based service running on the network, the stub for the service is fine for use as a Jini proxy. This is a particularly easy and minimal way to bring an RMI-based service into the Jini world. In this case, the proxy is a minimal, automatically-generated bit of code that has only the "intelligence" necessary to speak RMI.

- The proxy can be a "smart" proxy that can use any private protocol necessary to communicate with the service. Using a "smart" proxy (as opposed to an automatically generated RMI stub) allows more processing to be embedded in the client. For example, a smart proxy may cache data in the client. It may be able to "fail over" to multiple back-end services. And it fully hides the details of the communications protocol from the client. Smart proxies can be used to provide a Jini interface to legacy (non-Java) services that speak sockets or CORBA or some other protocol, and they can provide access to hardware devices that have their own communications protocols.

Proxies are the key to Jini's ability for clients to use services they may never have heard of before, and without any administration or driver installation. Even better, the client has no idea how the proxy is implemented. All the user of a printer service has to know is that the proxy implements the `Printer` interface—not the particulars of how it will talk to any specific printer.

Using Lookup Services

As mentioned earlier in the quick run-through of the main ideas in Jini, services store their proxies with lookup services, where clients can then find them.

You can think of Jini lookup services as being like name servers, since they keep track of all of the services that have joined a Jini community. But unlike a traditional name server, which provides a mapping from strings to stored objects, Jini lookup services support a much richer set of semantics. For one thing, the lookup service understands the Java type system. So you can search for proxies that implement particular Java interfaces, and the lookup service will return to you proxies that implement that interface. You can even search by looking for superclasses and superinterfaces of proxies.

How the internals of the lookup service are actually implemented is hidden from you. It may be built using a simple hashtable that gets saved to disk periodically, or it may be a high-powered directory service with lightning-fast lookups and logged writes to persistent storage. All you as the user of a lookup service knows is that the proxy for the lookup service implements the `ServiceRegistrar` interface, which is common to all lookup service implementations. You do not know the details of how it communicates with the lookup service itself—it may be using Java RMI, vanilla sockets, or smoke signals for all you know. This permits multiple, wildly varying implementations of the lookup service, with all of the details hidden behind the object you get that implements the lookup interfaces.

Publishing a Service

The most important thing a Jini service has to do is publish its proxy with the lookup service so that clients may use it. Abstractly, you can think of the lookup service as storing a set of "service items," each of which contains the proxy for a service, a unique ID for the service, and a set of descriptive "attributes" associated with the service. In Figure 3–1, you see a lookup service that's holding three service items.

Figure 3–1   *Lookup services maintain lists of service items*

If you are publishing a service (say, a printer) that you wish to make available to anyone who wants to use it, you *join* all the lookup services you find from the discovery process. The ServiceRegistrar interface has a method called reg-ister() that lets you join a lookup service. Figure 3–2 shows a service joining a community by registering its proxy with a lookup service.

Core Tip: Join every lookup service for your community

Note that any given community (that is, each unique group name on a given network) may have any number of lookup services supporting it. For fault-tolerance purposes, many redundant lookup services may be active.

Typically, a service that needs to join a community will join all the lookup services that support that community, so that if one lookup service fails, others can stand in for it. Unless you have some special need, or need to explicitly limit the scope of visibility of your service, you should usually join all of the lookup services that you discover.

A New Service

The service publishes ServiceItems with each Lookup Service it finds

Figure 3–2   *A service joins a Jini community*

You invoke the `register()` method by passing in a service item object as an argument. You fill in the attributes with objects that may describe your service. There are some standardized attributes provided by Jini for this purpose—service name, service location, comments, and so on. If your company sells a number of Jini services, you may even have your own standardized set of attributes that reveal extra information about the services.

Jini calls the process of publishing a proxy the *join protocol*. This isn't a protocol in the network sense, but rather a series of steps that services should take to ensure that they're well-behaved with respect to the other services in a community. Chapter 8 goes into quite a bit of detail on the join protocol and other aspects of how services interact with lookup services to publish their proxies.

Finding a Service

Once a service has joined a community by publishing its proxy, clients can use the service. Typically, clients will search the lookup services they have found for services that implement particular interfaces that they know how to use.

The lookup service provides a number of ways to search—you can search based on the type of the proxy, you can search for the service's unique ID if you happen to know it, or you can search based on the descriptive attributes associated with the service's proxy.

This process of finding the services you want to use is the core functionality of the lookup service and so, not surprisingly, the `ServiceRegistrar` interface defines a method called `lookup()` that does exactly this. By using this method, clients can retrieve the proxies needed to use the services they desire.

Chapters 9 and 10 go into detail on how clients interact with lookup services, but Figure 3–3 illustrates the high-level view of the process. Here you see a client application downloading the proxy for a particular service from a lookup service. Once the proxy has been downloaded, the client uses it as a "front end" to communicate directly with the service's "back end," which is typically a long-lived process or a hardware device connected to the network.

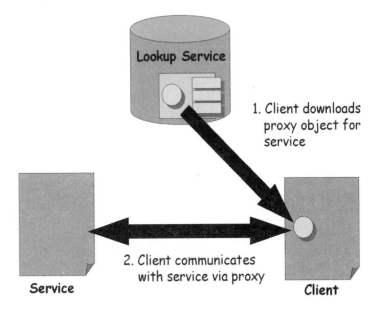

Lookup Service

1. Client downloads proxy object for service

2. Client communicates with service via proxy

Service

Client

Figure 3–3   *Using a Jini service*

Say you are writing the software for a digital camera and you want to be able to print from the camera directly to a printer when you detect that one is nearby. In this case, the most likely scenario is that the camera does a search of all the lookup services in its community, looking for proxies that implement the `Printer` interface. The lookup services may return one or more proxies that implement this interface, and the camera may choose to present them, possibly annotated with name, location, or comment information from their attributes, to the user on the LCD display of the camera. When the user prints a picture to a particular printer, the `Printer` methods on the front-end proxy object are invoked, and output is sent to the printer.

Common Interfaces, Divergent Implementations

You may be asking yourself, "How did the camera know to look for service items for the `Printer` interface?" Clearly, applications need to have at least *some* understanding of the semantics of the interfaces they are calling. You, as the writer of the digital camera software, may not know *how* the `Printer` interface works, but you have at least a basic idea of *what* it does—it causes things to be sent to the printer. If you were to encounter an interface with some unintelligible name, say the `Fleezle` interface, you would have no idea what it did, or what to pass as arguments to its methods, or what to do with its return values. In such a case, it's impossible to really use this unknown interface programmatically, without some end-user involvement to tell you what to do. For this reason, most Jini services will be written to implement well-known interfaces, and to expect the other services in a community to implement well-known interfaces. This is the only way they can know *how* to programmatically interact with services they encounter.

Sun, along with its partners and the wider Jini community of users, is working to define a set of common interfaces for printers, scanners, cellular telephones, storage services, and other common network devices and services. Development of these is ongoing at the time of this writing. If at all possible, writers of new services should use standardized interfaces wherever appropriate to ensure that Jini services can take advantage of each other.

It is, of course, possible to use unknown interfaces if the user can tell you what to do with them. For this reason, it's a good idea to create user interfaces (in addition to programmatic interfaces) to your services. Such interfaces can be displayed to a user and may allow them to interact "manually" with a service, even if a client doesn't know how to use it programmatically. Thus, a user might recognize the `Fleezle` service from its user interface, and control it directly from the camera, even if the camera's software could not.

Discovery

Before a Jini-aware application—either a service or client—can take advantage of Jini services, it must first find one or more Jini communities. The way it does this is by finding the lookup services that keep track of the shared resources of that community—this process of finding the available lookup services is called *discovery.*

There is not necessarily a one-to-one mapping of communities to lookup services. Each lookup service on a network may provide service for one or more communities, and each community may have one or more lookup services that support it, depending on how the lookup services were started.

The Discovery Protocols

There is not just a single discovery protocol—Jini supports several useful protocols in different situations.

- The Multicast Request Protocol is used when an application or service first becomes active, and needs to find the "nearby" lookup services that may be active.
- The Multicast Announcement Protocol is used by lookup services to announce their presence. When a new lookup service that is part of an existing community starts up, any interested parties will be informed via the Multicast Announcement Protocol.
- The Unicast Discovery Protocol is used when an application or service already knows the particular lookup service it wishes to talk to. The Unicast Discovery Protocol is used to talk directly to a lookup service, which may not be a part of the local network, when the name of the lookup service is known. Lookup services are named using a URL syntax with `jini` as the protocol specifier (`jini://turbodog.parc.xerox.com` specifies the lookup service running on the host `turbodog.parc.xerox.com` on the default port, for example). Unicast lookup is used when there is a need to create static connections between services and lookup services, such as when explicitly federating lookup services together.

The end result of the discovery process is that proxies for the discovered lookup services are returned to the application doing the discovery. As mentioned earlier, these proxies will all implement the `ServiceRegistrar` interface, and allow services to publish proxies, and clients to find them.

Supporting Multiple Communities

In Jini, communities can have names. In the Jini APIs, these names are called "groups," and during the discovery process, a service or application can specify the groups it wishes to find. The discovery protocols will return all of the lookup services it can find that are members of those groups. Lookup services can be members of multiple groups. (And, even though other types of services can register with any number of lookup services which have membership in any number of groups, you typically don't think of those services as being members of those groups. The Jini team thinks of "group membership" as being a trait of lookup services only, whereas other services simply join lookup services that are members of those groups.)

You can, in most cases, think of "groups" and "communities" as being the same things—groups are simply the names used to specify and represent communities. The most important difference to note between communities and groups is that because of network separation, different communities may have the same group name—the "public" group at Xerox PARC does not refer to the same "public" group at Javasoft, for example. Even though the names are the same, these names can refer to different actual communities depending on where they are. Put a different way, group names are not globally unique, nor are they necessarily globally accessible. But, for most purposes, you can think of groups and communities as being interchangeable.

How does a service know which community to join? In most cases, services will simply look for the "default" group, which is named by the empty string and—by convention—is treated as a "public" community, and then use the multicast protocols to connect to any and all lookup services they can find. The multicast protocols are designed to ensure that the discovery process will only reach lookup services running on the local network, to keep from blasting the entire Internet with discovery protocol packets.

In some cases, a service may need to join a non-default community. For example, a product development lab may test out new services in an "experimental" community that happens to exist on the same subnet as the "production" community, which might be the default. These two communities can share resources (if services join both communities), and even share lookup services (if the lookup services are members of both communities). To join the non-default experimental community, services would use the group name "experimental" to find the lookup services that are members of that community.

In other cases, a service may need to join a non-local community that is "out of range" of multicast discovery. Such services can be explicitly configured with a set of lookup services that they will connect to via unicast discovery. Since unicast discovery doesn't have the same range restrictions as multicast discovery, services can use this feature to join communities no matter where they are. The ability to use the unicast discovery protocol allows Jini to be flexible in creating its community structure.

While Chapter 6 goes into quite a bit of detail on the various discovery protocols, using them in practice is thankfully easy. Most applications will use a set of convenient utility classes that come with Jini and will never have to worry about interacting with discovery directly.

Supporting Technology

While the use of discovery and lookup to deliver service proxies is the central notion in Jini, this isn't enough in itself to really support rich, robust, distributed systems. So on top of this basic substrate, Jini layers some more technologies that are used to provide features like reliability and the ability to detect changes in services.

In this last section of the chapter, I'll talk about these supporting technologies and introduce several new concepts. You'll need to understand the ideas here—and the programming libraries that support them—to build real Jini software.

There are three particularly important ideas that are layered atop the basic Jini facilities:

- Jini's approach to self-healing is through a technique called *leasing*. Essentially, Jini never grants access to resources in perpetuity, but requires that resource holders continually "renew" their leases on resources.
- Jini provides a flexible *remote event* system to allow distributed applications to communicate with one another.
- Jini supports a lightweight model for *distributed transactions* to ensure that computations can reach a "safe" state.

The rest of this chapter provides an overview of these three important concepts in the Jini programming model.

Leasing

All the talk in this chapter about discovery and lookup covers the aspects of Jini that allow communities of applications to form spontaneously and exchange code. But I haven't said anything yet about how to ensure that these communities are stable, self-healing, and resilient in the face of (inevitable) network failures, machine crashes, and software errors.

Consider an example: Suppose our digital camera service joins a community by registering itself with a lookup service; presumably this happens whenever the camera is attached to a computer that is itself on the network. The camera publishes the fact that it is available for use, and all is well. That is, all is well until the user unceremoniously yanks the camera out of its cradle without turning it off first. What happens here? To the other members of the community, this may look like a classic partial failure situation—they may not be able to tell if the remote host to which the camera is connected has gone down, if it's simply slow to answer, if it's not answering network traffic because of a change in its configuration, if the camera's software has crashed, or even if the camera has been smashed with a hammer. But, regardless of how it was disconnected, the fact is that it has not had a chance to unregister itself before disconnecting because of its abrupt "termination."

The result of the user disconnecting the camera without shutting down properly—a completely understandable and common occurrence—is that, without some special facilities, a "stale" registration will linger in the lookup service for the community. Services that wish to use the camera will see it registered but will not be able to use it. But even more severe are the problems that the lookup service itself faces—if service registrations are never properly cleaned up, it will accrete registrations and slowly bog down under the weight of stale data.

This accumulation of state is a serious problem in long-lived distributed systems. You simply cannot ensure that services will never crash or become disconnected before they've had a chance to deregister themselves.

In the case I've described, the camera holds a *resource* in the lookup service—it is asking the lookup service to use some of its (possibly scant or expensive) storage and computation to maintain the camera's registration. If the Jini infrastructure used a traditional approach to *resource reservation*, the registration would simply stay active until it was canceled, or until some human administrator went through the logs and cleaned out the stale services.

Obviously, this solution violates everything that you want from Jini. First, it doesn't ensure that the system self-heals: Partial failures aren't recognized and cleaned up, and services that hold resources on behalf of others may grow without bound. Second, and perhaps even worse, it requires explicit human intervention to administer the system.

Time-Based Resource Reservation

To get around these problems, Jini uses a technique called *leasing*. Leasing is based on the idea that, rather than granting access to a resource for an unlimited amount of time, the resource is "loaned" to some consumer for a fixed period of time. Jini leases require demonstrable proof-of-interest on the part of the resource consumer to continue to hold onto the resource.

Jini leases work much like leases in "real life." Jini leases may be denied by the grantor of the lease. They can be renewed by the holder. Leases will expire at a predetermined date unless they are renewed. They can be canceled early (and, unlike in real life, Jini imposes no penalty on early lease cancellation). Finally, leases can be negotiated, but, as in real life, the grantor has the final word on the terms of the lease that is offered.

Leases provide a consistent means to free unused or unneeded resources throughout Jini: If a service goes away, either intentionally or unintentionally, without cleaning up after itself, its leases will eventually expire and the service will be forgotten. Leasing is used extensively by the lookup service and in other aspects of Jini, so it's important to understand how leases work.

One of the great aspects of leases is that they make it very hard to screw up the entire system: The system acts conservatively, so if you forget to do lease management, or a programming bug causes you to never renew your leases, your unreliable code simply drops out of the community without causing widespread damage to others. From the perspective of a community, buggy programs that forget to renew their leases look exactly the same as network errors and machine crashes—all the community sees is that the service's lease has expired and that it is no longer available.

The second great aspect of leasing is that it makes the persistent storage used by the members of a Jini community virtually maintenance-free. A systems administrator will never have to crawl through logs, trying to determine which services are active, which are inactive, and which have left stale data scattered throughout the system. Given a bit of time, the community will identify unused resources and free them, like antibodies attacking a virus. Certainly it would be a great day if we could erase all traces of unwanted applications, unused drivers, and obsolete OS upgrades from our PCs so easily.

Leasing is a rich topic in Jini, and there are many aspects of leases that don't warrant discussion in this (already long) chapter. I'll discuss leasing in detail in Chapters 12 and 13, though.

Remote Events

Jini services, like many software components in a system, whether distributed or local, occasionally need to be notified when some interesting change happens in the world. For example, in the local programming model, a software component may need to be notified when the user clicks a mouse, or when the user closes a window.

These are examples of *asynchronous notifications*. They are messages sent directly to a software component, and they are handled outside the normal flow of control of the component. That is, rather than continually polling to see whether some interesting change has occurred, a method on the component will be "automatically" called when the change occurs. The asynchronous nature of these notifications can often simplify programming, since you don't have to insert code to periodically check the state of some external entity.

Jini, like most of Java, uses *events* to do asynchronous notifications. An event is an object that contains information about some external state change that a software component may be interested in. For example, in AWT, a `MouseEvent` is sent whenever the mouse changes state—whenever it moves, or a mouse button is pressed or released. Events are injected into the system by an *event generator* that is watching for state changes. In AWT, there is a thread called the `AWTEventGenerator` that performs this service. In Java, once an event is introduced into the system, it is "sent" to the interested parties that want to hear about it. In this regard, Jini's event model works exactly the same as the standard event model used by JavaBeans and the Java Foundation Classes—all of these models support events and asynchronously call methods on listeners when events arrive.

How Jini Uses Events

There are many cases when a Jini application may need to receive a notification of a change in the state of the world. Earlier, I gave the example of a digital camera that wants to be able to use any printers available in its Jini community. I said that this camera would contact all of the lookup services it could find, and then search for services that implement the `Printer` interface. This example makes a grievous assumption that I completely glossed over: It assumes that the printers will be connected to the network and available for use *before* the camera. What if the inverse is true? In this case, there are no printers available when the camera first connects, although printers may come on line later. Certainly, you'd still like to be able to print, regardless of the order in which you plug in your devices.

The answer is that the camera needs to be notified when any services that it might be able to use appear in a community. It's easy to imagine the user interface to such a camera. The "Print" button on the LCD is grayed out. You plug a printer into the network, and suddenly the Print button comes alive! The camera has just received a notification that a printer is now active on the network.

This is only one example of how events are used in Jini. Obviously, the lookup service will generate events to interested parties when services appear, disappear, or change. But other Jini entities may generate or consume events as well. The `Printer` service may let other services listen for events that denote special printer conditions, such as `OutOfPaper` or `PrinterJammed`. Thus, events don't just have to go between the existing Jini infrastructure and services; they can fly among services themselves.

Remote vs. Local Events

But the Jini event model has some differences vs. the "normal" Java event model. Why this distinction? Aren't the Java event models good enough? As it turns out, the Java models are fine for what they were designed for: delivering asynchronous notifications within a single Java VM. The distributed computing world is a very different place, though, and calls for a slightly different event model to fully accommodate the kinds of programs that will run there.

There are a number of very important differences between events that are intended to be delivered locally and events that are intended for distributed delivery.

- In the local case, it's much easier to cause events to be delivered in the order in which they were generated. This is because local event delivery schemes can use a centralized queue that acts as a "choke point," forcing the events into a serial order. Distributed systems, because they lack this centralized event manager, and because of the issues of transporting the events over the network, cannot make this guarantee without serious performance penalties. (Java's AWT event dispatch mechanisms actually do *not* provide this guarantee of deterministic ordering for local events—but in general, local event delivery schemes can implement such an ordering relatively easily.)
- In the local case, an event that is sent will always be delivered, barring catastrophic failure (such as a crash of the entire application). Stand-alone systems are not susceptible to the kinds of partial failures that distributed systems are. Partial failures in a distributed system, whether a machine crash or a network partition, can cause events to go undelivered.
- The cost of sending a local event is typically small compared to the work that may be done to handle the event. Typically, "sending" an event is simply a method call to tell the interested party that the event has arrived. The computation that the recipient does as a result will likely dwarf the time required to send the event. In the remote case, the situation is reversed.

Delivery of the event may require orders of magnitude more time than the local case, and dominate the time spent in handling the event. The performance differences mean that distributed systems are likely to be architected to generate as few events as possible.

- Finally, in the local case, if a component has asked to be a recipient of events, the sender knows that it can safely deliver the event to that recipient. The remote case is far more complicated. The remote recipient of an event may be temporarily disconnected from the network, in which case the sender should probably keep trying to send. The recipient may have crashed, in which case the sender may wish to discard the event. Or, the recipient may be "inactive" for a period of time and not able to process the event. With this range of possibilities it's often impossible for a sender to know what the right response is.

As you can see, there are many more *policy* decisions to be made in the remote case—many more "knobs" that are available for turning. Does the order of delivery of events matter? Should events be delivered at all costs? If the recipient cannot be contacted, should the event be dropped? Stored until asked for? Resent?

There are no single answers to these questions. Each application must make its own decisions about what makes sense for it. An on-line banking application will almost certainly require very conservative answers to these questions—events should arrive, in order, and at all costs. If a recipient is down, the events should be logged until they can be resent. Other applications may have far less stringent requirements. An on-line game may be able to tolerate a few missed or badly sequenced events and still be fine.

Jini takes an interesting approach to solving this dilemma of how to express so many application constraints: It supports none of them directly, but provides generic mechanisms by which applications can extend the event processing behavior of the system. I'll talk about this ability in detail in Chapter 16, but the basic idea is that you can write new services that can receive and process *any* type of event from *any* Jini service, even if the new service doesn't understand the particular events types it's dealing with. These new services can implement particular policies that may be needed by applications.

The good news for application writers, though, is that for the most part, programming with Jini events looks very much like programming with "normal" events. Most of the time, you only need to understand the remote programming model insofar as you need to understand remote exception types and RMI. Only if you're planning on using (or writing) a new service to process events do you typically have to understand all the ins and outs of the Jini remote event model.

Distributed Transactions

The last major concept in the Jini programming model is *distributed transactions*. Unfortunately, this concept is one of the most difficult to master in Jini, but luckily many applications will never have to use transactions.

I've talked a lot about the need for reliability and robustness in distributed systems, and the evils that partial failures can cause. Recall that partial failures are when one stage of a computation fails, or when one component that's needed in a computation fails. If *every* stage that participated in a computation failed, then recovery would be easy—you would know that none of them had successfully completed, and you could simply retry the entire computation later. And, obviously, if every stage succeeded, then you would have no need to recover at all.

But the worst scenario, from the programmer's perspective, is when only a subset of the work that has to be done completes. Let's look at a classic example from database programming that exists in the local case. Bank databases need to be reliable, because millions or billions of dollars are moved through the databases each day. Many of the monetary exchanges are in the form of transfers between two accounts: The money is extracted from one account and added to another. Think about how you would program this transfer. Likely, you would write a bit of code to decrement the total in account A, and then write a bit of code to increment the total in account B by the same amount.

This is all simple and obvious, until you think about ways the transfer can fail. What if you crash just after you've decremented the total in account A? Account A may be out millions of dollars, but the money hasn't gone to B! It's simply lost in the ether, the victim of an accounting error caused by a program that wasn't resilient to partial failures.

Distributed systems compound the problems of partial failures: Each stage of your computation may involve contacting components that live somewhere on the network. These components may crash, or the network may become unstable, at some point midway through the computation. What do you do now? You need to either keep trying to contact the unreachable components (and you'd better succeed before you, yourself, crash), or you need to contact the successful components and tell them to undo whatever changes they've made. And, of course, there's always the chance that only a subset of the undo orders would succeed.

Ensuring Data Integrity

This is where transactions come to the rescue. Transactions are a way to group a series of related operations so that there can be only two possible outcomes: Either all of the operations succeed, or all of the operations fail. In either case, the system moves to a known state in which it is relatively easy to do the right thing—either move on if the transaction succeeds, or try again later if the transaction failed.

Transactions provide what are often called the "ACID" properties to data manipulations, so called because of the initials of the four individual properties.

- Atomicity. Either all of the operations grouped under a transaction succeed, or they all fail: They execute as if they were a single atomic operation.
- Consistency. After the transaction completes, the system should be in a consistent, understandable state. The notion of "consistency" is something that may only be discernible by the human users of the system—therefore, transactions are merely a way to help ensure consistency, not guarantees of consistency itself.
- Isolation. Transactions don't affect one another until they complete. That is, the effects of a transaction that is in the middle of executing will appear "invisible" to other computations outside of that transaction. This property ensures that computations won't be based on bogus data that may change if a transaction fails.
- Durability. Once a transaction completes successfully—meaning that all of its changes have been made permanent—then these changes must not be lost due to any subsequent failure or crash. The results of the transaction must be at least as persistent as the entities that use them.

Transactions work by coordinating all of the cooperating parties through a centralized entity. Essentially, this pushes the burden of getting all the parties to agree or all disagree, and tracking their states, into a piece of software called a *transaction manager*. Because the transaction manager is centralized with respect to the participants, it can have a "privileged" viewpoint, from which it watches all of the participants.

In the local cases, such as the bank database of our example, this centralized transaction manager is typically the database itself. Commercial databases have extensive facilities to ensure that sets of operations in a transaction either all complete or fail together. The database keeps logging information so that it can know whether a transaction has completed or failed if it crashes in the middle of executing a transaction.

Distributed databases—or any system that involves components running on multiple machines—are a little more complicated, though. In the local case, the crash of the database means that all of the operations in the transaction that were in progress also stopped at that point. The database can keep logs that are accurate, because all of the operations in a transaction happen locally to the database (they happen "within" the database itself).

In distributed databases, however, operations may be executed on remote machines that the database has no direct control over; the database may not be able to determine if an operation running on a remote machine has successfully completed or failed. All this may sound complicated but, as I said at the start of this section, the good news is that most Jini programmers are completely shielded from this complexity. I'll talk more about the nitty-gritty details of how transactions work under the covers in Chapter 18 but, for now, let's look at the programmer's view of how transactions work.

Transactions in Jini

Using transactions in practice is pretty easy, for three reasons. First, chances are you won't have to do a lot with transactions. Of the current Jini services, only the JavaSpaces storage service actively makes much use of transactions. So, if you never have to see a transaction, dealing with them is quite easy!

Second, even when you do have to deal with transactions, you really don't have to understand any of the mechanics of how the underlying distributed transaction protocols actually work to use them effectively as a *client*. (If you are *providing* an operation that can work in a transaction, then you have to do more work, though.)

Finally, when you do need to use transactions, the end-programmer transaction APIs are quite simple: You just create a transaction, pass it to all the operations you want to be grouped, and then tell it to try to execute all the operations atomically, which will either succeed or fail.

Programmatically, the first step in using transactions is to use the Jini `TransactionFactory` object to create a `Transaction` object to "hold" the grouped operations. Every service that knows how to participate in transactions will accept a `Transaction` parameter to its "transactable" methods. This is how you group an operation into a transaction: You simply pass in the `Transaction` object to one or more transactable methods to cause them to be grouped.

Once you've collected together the operations, you call `commmit()` on the `Transaction` object to call the Jini transaction system to attempt to execute all of these operations. The `commit()` call will either succeed, or an exception will be raised if one of the participants couldn't complete the operation. If this is the case, Jini will ensure that all of the other participants undo their operations.

In most cases, this simple explanation represents all you have to know about transactions. There are more complicated cases in the programming model (such as nested transactions), but these are rarely used. And, of course, if you wish to build a "transactable" service (meaning one that can participate in, rather than just originate, transactions), then you have to understand the transaction model deeply. But for most cases, using transactions is reasonably simple.

Because transactions are likely to be one of the aspects of Jini that you use the least, I'll save the in-depth discussion of them until near the end of this book.

What's Next?

I've introduced the most fundamental concepts in Jini—the notion that services carry the code needed to use them, the lookup process to finding and using that code, and discovery as a means to "jumpstart" a Jini community. I've also talked about three essential concepts in the Jini programming model that are built atop these basic ideas—leasing as a way to support self-healing, remote events for notifications, and distributed transactions for "safe" computing. I've talked about how all of these work conceptually, but haven't provided many details yet on how to actually program using these ideas.

In the chapters in Part II, I'll talk about each of these notions in greater detail. You'll see how to program against the Jini discovery and lookup APIs, see how to write downloadable proxy code for your services, and write services that make effective use of leasing, transactions, and remote events. You'll also learn how to use the various utility services that come with Jini.

Before Part II, however, there is one more chapter that provides a bit of introductory material before you jump into building real Jini services. If you're eager to get going, you may want to skip ahead. But if you do, I'd recommend revisiting Chapter 4, which has details on some common strategies for actually building and deploying "real world" Jini services later.

On to Chapter 4!

Deployment Scenarios

Chapter 4

This chapter completes a high-level look at the Jini technologies by examining the common ways that Jini can be deployed and used by devices and services. The Jini model is designed to accommodate a range of situations—from full-blown, general-purpose computers running JVMs, down to devices such as light switches that may have only a single bit of I/O and no computational power whatsoever.

What Does It Mean to Be a Jini Service?

Now that you know what Jini is, it's time to look at what it means to "speak" Jini—what are the minimum requirements for a device or piece of software that wishes to interact with the Jini infrastructure?

As it turns out, the minimum requirements are quite small. To make a piece of software or a device accessible through Jini, it, or another piece of software on its behalf, must do the following:

- Be able to connect to a TCP/IP network. This means that the device or service—or a piece of software on its behalf—should have an IP address and a complete TCP stack with the ability to send and receive multicast messages.

- Participate in the discovery process to find at least one lookup service. Most services should be capable of using both multicast and unicast discovery.
- Register with the lookup service by providing it with a proxy object that clients can download to use the service. This proxy object may call back to a back-end process or device, or may implement the service entirely by itself.
- Ensure that its leases for its lookup registrations are renewed for as long as the service is available.
- Maintain a bit of persistent storage to record certain configuration information, such as a service ID.

That's it! Any service you deploy must be capable of fulfilling all of these duties to work with Jini. These tasks can be implemented by your service itself, or by another piece of software on its behalf.

The requirements above represent the *minimum* that is required to participate in Jini. Of course, services can do a bit more work to be better behaved. For example, they can manage the set of lookup services that are discovered and discarded over the lifetime of the service, they can provide mechanisms for administration, support human interaction through user interfaces, and they can manage their event registrations and leases. But the proxy publishing mechanism is the star of Jini; everything else is just supporting cast.

You've no doubt noticed that I repeatedly said that another piece of software could enroll a device or service in a Jini community on its behalf. This use of third parties is the key to using Jini to control such devices as light switches and thermostats that may not have embedded JVMs in them, as well as legacy software services.

Let's look at what the consumer of a Jini service needs to be able to do.

- The consumer of a service (which need not be a service itself, although it might be) needs to be able to use the discovery process to find one or more lookup services. Nearly all consumers will use the multicast discovery process, and may be configurable to look for *specific* lookup services via the unicast discovery protocol.
- The consumer must be able to retrieve and use the proxy object for the service.
- (Optional, but highly recommended): If the desired service isn't found, the consumer may wish to solicit notifications from the lookup services it knows about, so the consumer will be informed if the desired service later becomes registered.

Again, this is pretty easy stuff. After the service proxy is found, it is down-loaded automatically to the client, which then uses it just as it would a class that was found at compile time. And even though I've belabored the fact that Jini services can include devices that don't run Java and aren't implemented in Java (through the use of some surrogate that *is* written in Java), you should note that Jini clients do have to be written in Java. This is because they must be able to deserialize and run the Java classes that constitute the service's proxy.

Minimal Jini services and consumers of services don't have to understand remote events, or transactions, and only need some minimal (and easily automat-able) support from leasing. But they do have to be able to use the discovery protocols and interact with lookup services.

How to Use Jini for Your Devices and Services

I'll now walk through some common scenarios for making your devices and networked services participate in Jini. As I've mentioned, Jini is designed to support a wide variety of hardware platforms, and can bring together hardware ranging from the very cheap (under a dollar) to the very expensive (million-dollar servers).

Understanding the options available to you when you decide to Jini-enable your product is crucial, because each of the options has different benefits and costs associated with it. In general, there are three common options for deploy-ment. In many cases, the particular option will be dictated for you by the type of device or service you are producing. The options are:

- Use Jini on a general-purpose computer. By "general-purpose" I mean that the machine has its own network connection, enough computational power to run a full-fledged JVM, and tends to stay up and connected to the network for long periods of time.
- Use Jini on a device with its own embedded JVM. These devices differ from general-purpose computers in that they have much less computational power (and, typically, a much lower cost), are only sporadically connected to the network, and tend to have much lower bandwidth to the network. More importantly from the standpoint of a Jini developer, these devices may only be able to run a subset of Java, such as Java 2 Micro Edition.
- Use Jini to control a device with no JVM. In this situation, a shared Jini-enabled computer is used to control a set of devices

that have very limited—and sometimes no—computing power, but do have a small amount of I/O capability. This scenario is ideal for things like switches around the home. Each switch may have a single bit I/O "port" (actually, a wire coming out of it) connected to a centralized Jini-enabled computer that handles communication with the switches, and exposes them as Jini services. Note that the centralized computer here need not be very powerful. It may look like a wall-mounted thermostat, or a stereo component, or a small "dongle" connected to another device.

I'll talk about each of these scenarios, and examine their relative strengths and weaknesses.

Jini on General-Purpose Computers

While much of the media focus surrounding Jini hypes its ability to link together small devices, Jini is perfectly at home running on a general-purpose computer as well. There are any number of services that can run on such machines, and Jini makes sense for exposing all of these to other members of a Jini community. For example, every desktop PC has a disk drive in it. There's no reason that this storage space couldn't be exposed to such devices as digital cameras (for picture storage), cellular telephones (for keeping backups of the on-board phone book), the answering machine (for providing long-term message storage), or even the VCR (to allow video to be digitized directly to the hard disk). This storage service would run directly on the PC, and would make the PC's hard drive accessible to any and all services that participate in Jini.

A little further up the scale, Jini can be run on large servers to provide a way to conveniently and robustly manage corporate data services. Jini in the enterprise can make corporate networks extremely reliable and resilient to network failures. It can also cut down on administration time. Consider a Jini document managment application. Such a system could be decomposed into a number of services, each of which could be available on multiple machines. Because the component services may be available redundantly, it is extremely reliable—a desirable attribute in a corporate data network. The services could provide user interfaces that could be used on any Jini-enabled device with a display. They could also easily interconnect with other services—perhaps text summarization tools, or email or pager gateways, or new search engines.

General-purpose machines such as these make the ideal hosts for Jini services that need to stay connected to the network for long periods of time (these include the "native" Jini services, such as lookup). There is a cost efficiency here, because multiple services can be run on a single computer. And they also provide convenient development platforms, because the services can be developed on the same machines on which they will be deployed.

Furthermore, the advantage of having a full-blown JVM cannot be overstated. Services that run on this platform have available to them all the standard Java class libraries. They would be able to take advantage of RMI to communicate with their proxies running on client machines. Additionally, RMI could be used to *upload* new code to the server, enabling on-the-fly maintenance and upgrades of the services running there. Such services could also connect to corporate databases using Java Database Connectivity (JDBC) software. And, a complete JVM with the entire Java class libraries ensures that virtually all downloadable code will run—which may not be the case when running on a machnie with only a subset of the Java class libraries available.

Figure 4–1 shows an example of a Jini service running on a general-purpose computer with a full array of class libraries, and using the network to communicate with its service proxy embedded in a client.

The downside of this strategy, obviously, is that it requires a general-purpose computer, which may be overkill in some cases. But in many situations, general-purpose machines will be on hand anyway, and using Jini on them does not significantly increase their load. In the context where general-purpose desktop or server machines are already available, running Jini services on these machines makes perfect sense.

Figure 4–1   *Using Jini on a general-purpose computer*

Jini on Java-Enabled Devices

As more and more devices in the world become Java-enabled, the option of deploying Jini on small devices with their own embedded JVMs becomes more common. More and more, devices such as cell phones, PDAs, printers, scanners, and cameras are coming with their own JVMs. In many ways, there is not much to distinguish running on a Java-enabled device from running on a general-purpose computer—in both cases, the devices are network-connectable and capable of executing the Java programs already contained on them, and, usually, downloading and running Java bytecodes from the network.

There are a few significant differences between running Jini on small devices and on general-purpose computers, however.

- Small devices may only run a subset of the entire Java platform.

- Small devices may only be intermittently connected to the network.
- Small devices typically have much less computational power and network bandwidth than their general-purpose cousins.

Of these, only the first is a real issue. Although you wouldn't want to run the Jini lookup service itself on a device that is off the network more than it is on, or that has extremely limited computing power, you're not likely to want to have the sole lookup service on your network running on a toaster or microwave oven anyway.

Core Alert: Jini and Java subsets

> *The issue of coping with different versions of Java is a significant problem for small devices. Such devices, because they are generally inexpensive, may have only a small subset of the full Java platform available to them, and may have very limited—if any—ability to display graphical interfaces.*
>
> *Think about how Jini works and you'll see why this is a problem. At the heart of Jini is the ability for a service to essentially send part of itself, its service proxy, to a client. When the service proxy is written, the developer makes an implicit assumption about what class libraries will be available on the client platform—if the service proxy uses JDBC, for example, he or she assumes that JDBC will be available wherever the proxy is run. This may not be the case if the more limited Java environments are being used as consumers of Jini services.*
>
> *These issues are particularly problematic for clients, which may not know ahead of time what services they will need to talk to, and thus what the requirements of those service's proxies may be.*

Limited Java Environments

The Core Alert above mostly deals with platform issues for Jini clients. Services are typically in better shape, platform-wise, since a service writer will know what class libraries he or she needs to implement the service. So the service's requirements are largely known ahead of time. But recall that even services are themselves clients of the lookup service—the lookup service downloads its own service proxy into the service providers. So at a minimum, a service would have to be able to download and run the lookup service's service proxy.

There is another option, however. A device could run a *custom* subset of the JVM that works with Jini even without the option of downloading code. Such a device would "hard code" the discovery protocols, and would carry with it the code for talking to particular implementations of the Jini lookup service. Such a device would be very restricted—it would not work outside its expected setting. If the implementation of the lookup service changed (perhaps because a vendor begins selling a newer, faster service that uses a different protocol for talking to lookup users), the device would not work.

One implementation strategy for such devices is that they could carry their own *custom* implementation of the lookup service that only holds the proxy for the device itself. This would limit the required interaction of the device with the rest of the Jini community—it would only have to serve up a proxy for its custom lookup service that clients can use to retrieve the device's proxy.

The benefit here is that the footprint of the JVM and class libraries required for such a device is *greatly* reduced. Because no code could be downloaded, there would be no need for the bytecode verifier or security manager. And the class libraries installed on the device could be pared down to the bare minimum required to participate in discovery and lookup.

Such a device would only be able to publish Jini services; it would not be able to consume Jini services, because using a service requires the ability to download its proxy. While these trade-offs are severe, they may be worthwhile in some extreme circumstances.

Versioning

All of these issues arise from the problem of ensuring that the version of Java on the host platform is compatible with the version of Java expected by a service proxy. The solution is to agree on a set of conventions, such as allowing service proxies to be stored with attributes that indicate the minimum level of Java functionality they require. Such an attribute would have information about needed class libraries, JVM versions, and so forth. Before attempting to use a service proxy, a consumer could check its attributes to make sure it was runnable.

At the time of this writing, the Jini community has not standardized on a set of such attributes. There are some steps you can take to create services that can run on as wide a set of host platforms as possible, though. Most importantly, you can limit the dependencies your proxy object has on the host platform. Usually this means excising dependencies on libraries that may not be present everywhere. If your service can be partitioned into chunks of functionality—some of which only depend on core libraries, and others that depend on less common libraries—then the extra functionality can often be attached to the service as attributes, or even broken out into separate services. By keeping questionable code out of the proxy, you ensure that clients can always download and use the proxy objects.

Jini Using Device Surrogates

This third approach is the one that will likely be taken by devices that tend to be attached to a host computer (including printers, scanners, and other devices), as well as extremely lightweight and cheap devices such as switches around the house.

In this approach, a machine capable of running a JVM is physically attached to one or more devices. This machine acts as a Jini *surrogate* on behalf of these devices—it participates in the lookup and discovery protocols, handles their service proxies, and manages their leases for them. In this case, the connection between the machine running the JVM and the device is typically not a network cable—more likely it's an RS-232, USB, Firewire, or perhaps even an X10 "home automation" connection.[1]

The machine running the JVM may actually *be* a general-purpose computer, say a spare PC in someone's basement, or it could be specialized for use as a Jini control box. Imagine a Jini controller that plugs into your stereo equipment, making your CD and DVD players, tuner, VCR, and television all accessible to your home Jini community. An even smaller device could resemble a wall-mounted thermostat, and would provide Jini services on behalf of your home alarm system, light switches, door locks, and so on. Whatever the shape of the controller, once the devices have been connected to it, they are fully available in the home Jini community.

A likely short-term scenario is a proxy application that runs on PCs. This application starts when the machine boots, and examines the Windows plug-and-play database to see if new hardware is added. If a recognized device, such as a printer or scanner, is added, the proxy application would publish services for

---

1. Current and older desktop computers are likely to connect with a standard serial RS-232 connection. Newer machines may use the faster Universal Serial Bus (USB) serial port. Firewire is a high-speed serial connection used in many high-end consumer electronics devices, and X10 is a set of technologies designed for building home automation and control systems. Sun's alliance with the HAVi group means that Firewire may serve a common role in connecting Jini stereos, VCRs, and DVD players—see the note at the end of this chapter.

these new devices, making them available on the network. Figure 4–2 shows an example of devices sharing a JVM that serves as a Jini proxy for them.

Figure 4–2 *A printer is made accessible through a surrogate*

There are obvious benefits to this approach. First, it enables "legacy" hardware to participate in Jini. There are huge numbers of printers, scanners, and other devices in the world that do not (yet) run Java; by installing a bit of software on a host computer, these devices are brought into the Jini world.

Second, the surrogate approach allows very cheap devices to be brought into a Jini community. If we all had to use light switches with embedded JVMs and eight megabytes of memory, chances are that not many of us would be buying them. If, on the other hand, large numbers of cheap devices could share a single Jini host, and could be indistinguishable from devices that run full JVMs, then we may begin to see more and more inexpensive Jini devices in the home.

There is currently an effort underway at the Jini Community website to create, in a systematic way, a set of standard APIs for creating surrogates. The Surrogate Architecture is still being defined at the time of this writing, but is making great progress. For more information, visit the Surrogate Project web pages at the Jini Community site:

```
http://developer.jini.org/exchange/projects/surrogate/
```

Requirements for Jini Lookup Services

The preceding sections talked about what platform requirements exist for running Jini services and consumers of Jini services. But for communities to form, lookup services must also be present on the network.

Jini defines interfaces to its services, not implementations. So a particular implementation of a lookup service may have more or less stringent requirements than an alternative implementation. For example, one lookup service may be built atop a full-blown commercial database, requiring JDBC support, while another may use an in-memory hashtable. But while it's impossible to make generalizations about what particular implementations a lookup service may require, you can talk about the absolute *minimum* functionality they will need.

Sun's current reference implementation of the lookup service is really at home on a general-purpose computer, running real, live Java. It makes use of RMI and activation, and its proxies generally require a full-fledged JVM environment. But a more minimal lookup service can actually be run on a far less-capable platform.

When Does Jini Make Sense?

Now that you've seen some common scenarios for enabling your device or service to participate in Jini, you can look at situations where using Jini may be appropriate from a technological or market perspective. These really boil down to a few common cases.

- If there exists, or you expect there to exist, Jini services that your device or software could use, then Jini may be a way to add value to your product. If you sell scanners, for example, and you see small Jini software services appearing that can provide image-to-e-mail or image-to-fax gateways, your scanner can easily use these to add value to itself. By making your scanner a consumer of Jini services, you enable it to appear as if it can directly scan to an e-mail message or a fax. You take instant advantage of all the developers in the world building these services. Essentially, you make these developers *your* developers.

- If your device can add value to other Jini services that exist, or you expect to exist, then Jini may open your product to new markets. For example, if you are in the market of selling printers, and you see Jini-enabled digital cameras coming to market, you have an opportunity to pitch your wares as an easy printing solution for those who have bought these devices.

- If your device already has an embedded JVM, or is usually deployed attached to a general-purpose computer, then adding Jini is likely a no brainer. Once you've got Java on or near your machine—or especially if your software is already written in Java—the work required to support Jini is minimal, and the potential gain is huge.

- If your non-Java software is running on a computer that can run a JVM—and practically all can, these days—then you can easily create a Jini wrapper for your service that makes it available in the Jini world. This is one of the great benefits of Jini—that it's easy to write a small bit of glue logic that makes an entire chunk of software, even one not written in Java, accessible to any other Jini device or service.

- If you have a software service that can be easily decomposed into constituent pieces, then it may make sense to represent each of those pieces as a Jini service. For example, an enterprise-scale document management system may have components that act as document storage repositories, document service engines, query engines, and so forth. By creating separate Jini services for each, you gain a number of benefits. First, you can easily move components to different machines as needed, without any need for reconfiguration or administration. Second, you gain built-in redundancy. Need a spare backup instance of one of these services? Just run another copy! Finally, by opening your architecture, you enable easy extensibility down the road.

- If you are creating a device that will typically be connected to other devices, then Jini may be a useful enabling technology for controlling these connections. For example, the components in a rack of stereo equipment are usually interconnected in a jumble of wires. Wouldn't it be nice if my preamp knew what devices were on the rack with it, what their levels and inputs were, and configured its controls accordingly?

- Finally, if your device can benefit from programmability, Jini may be a nice solution. Because Jini enables code downloading, your programmable devices can be upgraded on-the-fly. Even better, they can automatically control other devices in their Jini communities—imagine a central MIDI control panel that adds a new user interface for controlling a drum machine as soon as the drum machine is plugged in.

As Java appears on more and more devices and computers, and as more and more of our devices and software systems connect to each other, Jini becomes a logical solution for managing this interconnectivity. And—perhaps the point that will most encourage its adoption—if you've already got Java on your device or on your general-purpose computer system, adding Jini is trivial.

When Is Jini Not Appropriate?

Because Jini was explicitly designed to cover such a wide range of possible deployment scenarios—all the way from servers down to light switches—there are few hardware situations where Jini is not appropriate. There are a few factors that might argue against the cost of adding Jini to a device, however.

- First, if your device is *truly* isolated—meaning there isn't even a wire going to it—or is so fundamentally uninteresting that no one would want to use it over a network, then Jini is probably not for you. But fewer and fewer devices these days are truly isolated. And what would you be doing trying to sell such a boring device anyway?
- If your device is unlikely to be near any devices with a JVM, and needs to be so cheap that it cannot have a JVM embedded on it, then Jini is not a viable solution. Java has to exist *somewhere* in the loop for devices to participate in Jini.

Further Reading

If you're a fan of high-end audio and video equipment for the home, you might want to check out the *Home Audio/Video Interoperability* (HAVi) Web site. This group is a consortium of big A/V vendors who are promoting a set of very interesting standards. HAVi devices connect to one another via Firewire—an extremely high-speed serial connection, also known as IEEE1394 by those with a fondness for standards committees, and as i.LINK by Sony—and can transmit not only control information but also digital audio and video content from device to device.

Sun and the HAVi vendors have recently (at the time of this book's writing) agreed to integrate Jini with the HAVi technology. So we may soon be seeing "plug-and-play" stereo gear that both uses and provides Jini services.

```
http://www.havi.org
```

What's Next?

This chapter completes our broad look at the Jini technologies. In the next part, you'll start to build real Jini services, and look at the core Jini technology in depth.

Part 2

BUILDING
WITH JINI

Getting Started with Jini

Topics in This Chapter

- Guidelines for building, testing, and deploying Jini services
- Exploring lookup and discovery with the "Hello, World" service
- Using remote events to detect changes in a community
- Implementing leasing to enhance reliability and self-healing
- Using RMI to build service back ends

Chapter 5

In this chapter, you'll start building some actual Jini services, and the client applications to use them. The first pair of programs you'll look at are a "Hello, World" service and client. These are the minimal Jini programs—they use discovery and find a lookup service; the service publishes a service proxy, and the client fetches and uses it. The proxy for this service is pretty trivial—it returns the string "Hello, World" when asked. In this case, the proxy *is* the service, as it is capable of performing this task completely on its own. But it demonstrates how to begin working with Jini.

After this initial program, I'll begin iterating to show more and more Jini features. First, I'll expand the client to use events, so that it can be notified when services register with lookup services after it does.

The next iteration adds more sensible leasing. The first "Hello, World" service never renews the leases it holds on its registrations with lookup services. So I'll extend it to continually renew the leases it holds, so that the service's proxy will not "disappear" from the Jini community. Similarly, the client application needs to renew the leases it holds on its event registrations; in this iteration I'll extend it to manage its event registration leases so that it can be informed of changes in the state of its community.

Finally, I'll build a more complicated version of the "Hello, World" service that uses a proxy that communicates back to a remote server process. In this case, the proxy uses RMI to communicate back to the server to get the message to display. While the example is simple, it shows the way most Jini services will be architected—with a "thin" proxy communicating back to a "fat" server, which bears the burden of implementing the service.

This chapter starts to turn some of the abstract notions you learned about Jini in Chapter 3 into actual code. I'll do this progressively, improving the examples with each iteration, so that you can focus in on each feature as I present it.

If the examples in this chapter seem complex to you, don't worry! All of the examples here use very low-level Jini APIs. My philosophy about learning a new system is that it's important to understand the basics first, before learning about the higher level APIs that may be available to you. In these examples, you'll be learning the foundations of the Jini programming model. Most applications will rarely use these low-level APIs, but will instead use "helper" or utility classes. But by starting from the basics, you'll be in a better position to understand how these utility classes do their jobs.

Running the Jini Services

Before you can start writing your program, you need to make sure that the required Jini services are up and running. Check Chapter 1 for details on getting your environment set up to run Jini. For the examples in this chapter, you will not need to run a JavaSpaces storage service or a transaction manager. All of the iterations of "Hello, World" require only that a lookup service, an RMI activation daemon, and an HTTP daemon be running somewhere on the network. The RMI activation daemon (rmid) will need to run on the same host as the lookup service, since Sun's implementation of the lookup service uses activation.

Here's the checklist for getting set up, in case you've forgotten what you did in Chapter 1:

- Run the RMI activation daemon. You should run this on the same machine that you'll be running the lookup service on, and the activation daemon should be started *before* the lookup service.
- Run a Jini HTTP server which will supply downloadable code for the Jini lookup service; this server can be run on the same machine as the lookup service. You can set its "root" directory to point to the "lib" directory from the Jini distribution—this will ensure that your code will be able to download the classes in the reggie-dl.jar file, which contains the code needed to use the lookup service. Also, all of the example programs you'll write need to be able to supply code to Jini services and to each other.

So you'll also need to run an HTTP service to supply the code from these examples. I'll talk more about how to do this once I get into the example code itself.

- Run the Jini lookup service. You should run this service on a machine on the same network subnet on which you intend to run the sample programs—this is because Jini's multicast discovery protocols are, by default, only configured to find lookup services running "nearby" the object doing discovery.[1]

This configuration of services is sufficient to run all of the examples in this chapter, and most other Jini services as well. Throughout the book I will, however, follow some additional steps to make life easier when testing and deploying Jini services. I'll talk about these conventions in the next section.

Note that the examples in this chapter consist of both a Jini service—the entity that publishes a proxy—as well as a Jini client—essentially just an application that finds and uses a proxy. In many cases, services will use other services, so a Jini program is often both a service and a client. In the interest of simplicity, though, the client programs here are simple "stand-alone" applications.

While you can run all of these programs, lookup services, HTTP servers, activation daemons, clients, and servers on the same machine, I strongly advise you to read the next section. If you develop Jini applications in the same way that you probably develop "stand-alone" Java applications—by doing everything on one machine with the same CLASSPATH—you're likely to run into trouble when you deploy these programs on multiple machines. The next section offers some strategies for tuning your environment that can minimize these problems.

Developing with Deployment in Mind

Clearly, in the "real world," virtually all Jini services and clients will be run in multimachine environments. This means that services may be scattered across any number of machines on a network. The downloadable code for these services may be served by any number of HTTP servers, and clients may be connecting to these services from any machine.

But often—whether through convenience or necessity—you need to develop and test your code on only one machine. It's quite easy to run into problems in

---

1. In Chapter 6, which looks in depth at the discovery process, you'll find out exactly what Jini means by "nearness" in the network sense. But for now, you can be assured that any two machines on the same subnet are near enough to one another to share the same community.

such cases, simply because by running everything on one machine you're not exercising parts of your code that may cause things to break when the components of your distributed system run on different hosts.

Look a bit more closely at what this means. For most Jini development, you will have three Jini-aware applications running: a lookup service, the service you're testing, and a client that uses that service (these applications are in addition to whatever other programs are needed, such as HTTP servers and RMI activation daemons). If all of these programs run on the same machine, and share the same resources (the same CLASSPATH, the same HTTP server, and so on), then potential problems with dynamic class loading or with security may be masked. Developing and testing in such an environment can allow problems to lurk unnoticed in your code.

This is the great danger to only testing "locally." The apparent early convenience of taking the easy way out can result in greater headaches down the road. So even though a multimachine environment may require more "up-front" work, such as starting more HTTP servers, setting security policies, and so on, you'll be rewarded for this effort by easier debugging and deployment later. For this reason, it's a good idea to get in the habit of thinking about multimachine environments, and even "simulating" such environments when you develop and test.

Fortunately this "simulation" is fairly easy to do. There are some simple tips you can follow when you run and test your code to ensure that it will work in such a multimachine environment, even if you're developing on only one computer. These tips address most of the common problems in a multimachine setting.

Here are the tips you should follow when developing:

- Run a separate HTTP server for each program that provides downloadable code to other programs.
- Watch out for codebase problems.
- Always set a security manager.
- Pay attention to security policies.
- Take care with CLASSPATH.
- Consider bundling downloadable code into a JAR file.

Take a look at each of these in turn.

Run Multiple HTTP Servers

It's a good idea to run a separate HTTP server for each and every program that needs to provide downloadable code to other programs. This strategy allows you to clearly separate the downloadable code for each program from that of every other program. An alternative, like running one HTTP server with a root directory that points to the top of your Java development tree, will almost certainly be more convenient—because all of the classes you write will be accessible anywhere—but will keep you from identifying dependencies in your downloadable code that might keep your applications and services from working if they need to be moved to different machines.

If you can clearly separate all the downloadable code for a given program on one HTTP server, and then run that program with a codebase property that instructs clients of the program to fetch code only from that HTTP server, then you can tell when you don't have all the necessary code together in one place—the clients will complain that they cannot load certain needed classes.

Watch Out for Codebase Problems

Recall that the codebase property is set on a *server* (a program that exports downloadable code) to tell its *clients* (consumers of that code) where to load the required classes from. Appendix A has more details on codebase.

There are a few good general tips you should follow when setting the codebase property, though. First, never use `file:` URLs. If a server passes a `file:` URL to a client, the client will try to download any needed code from its own local filesystem. If you're developing and testing both your client and your server on the same machine, this may work—since the class files will live in the same place for both client and server. But if you ever run the client and server on separate machines that do not share a filesystem, your code will suddenly break.

Likewise, never use "`localhost`" in a codebase as a hostname. "`Localhost`" is used to refer to the current host, so if a server sets the codebase to a URL containing `localhost`, the client will evaluate this codebase and attempt to load the code from *its* system, rather than the server's. Again, this situation *may* deceptively work if you're testing the client and the server on the same machine, as you're likely to do. But if you use actual hostnames in codebase URLs, and run separate HTTP servers for each, as noted above, then you can identify potential problems in code loading early.

Always Set a Security Manager

Any Java program that will *use* downloadable code should set a security manager by calling `System.setSecurityManager()`. The security manager ensures that any classes that are loaded remotely—through a codebase that is provided via RMI—do not perform any operations they are not allowed to perform.

If you do not set a security manager, then no classes will be loaded other than those found in the application's CLASSPATH. So, if you only test locally, and do not set a security manager, your code may still work because the classes that would otherwise have to be downloaded may be found in your CLASSPATH. But your application will definitely fail in a multimachine setting.

Pay Attention to Security Policies

When you run a program with a security manager, the Java 2 security machinery will—by default—use a standard security policy. This standard policy is, unfortunately, often too restrictive to allow Jini applications to run. So in almost all cases, you will need to specify a new policy file that allows your program to run.

In these examples, I've used a very promiscuous security policy—it allows the example applications free and unfettered access to any resources. While this policy is fine for testing "known" code—meaning code that you have written—it's definitely not suitable for a production environment.

Take Care with CLASSPATH

As you've probably noticed, most of these development tips have to do with preventing unwanted sharing of resources—primarily, the sharing of code through unanticipated and nonrobust means, such as `file:` URLs or shared HTTP servers. One other way that code can be shared between two applications—and this is the way that most of us are familiar with—is by running the applications on the same machine and with the same CLASSPATH. If both a client and a server are sharing class files off the disk, then it's virtually impossible to tell what specific classes these programs will need to access remotely. So to prevent unanticipated sharing of class files, you may consider running *without* any CLASSPATH at all. Instead, try passing the `-cp` option to the `java` bytecode interpreter. This option lets you specify a series of directories and JAR files to load class files from. Even if you're developing your client and server on the same machine, you can keep the class files for each in separate directories, unset your CLASSPATH, and use a different `-cp` argument to the `java` interpreter for each to ensure that no unwanted crosstalk exists between your applications.

Furthermore, it's a good habit to provide *only* those classes the application needs to do its job, rather than all class files "just to be sure." You can start off with the three Jini JAR files in the `-cp` argument (`jini-core.jar`, `jini-ext.jar`, and `sun-util.jar`), and then copy in your own specific application class files as needed. The compiler is a great help in identifying which class files you need to install, as it will complain if it cannot find needed classes.

Under no circumstances should you put the -dl JAR files (`reggie-dl.jar` and so on) from the Jini distribution into your directory of classes—these are meant to be dynamically downloaded from the core Jini services. If you put these in with your application classes, you'll simply be ensuring that you're using the versions of these files that you got with Jini, and not the version that the lookup service *expects* and *tells* you to use.

Consider Bundling Downloadable Code into a JAR File

Perhaps the best way to make sure that you've isolated any unwanted dependencies from your code, and that you're providing exactly and only the code that other programs will need to download, is to create a JAR file that contains the classes that clients will have to download to use your program. This is the strategy taken by the core Jini services—the lookup service, for example, has the classes it needs for its implementation in `reggie.jar`, and the classes that will be downloaded to clients in `reggie-dl.jar`. The HTTP server that exports the lookup service's downloadable code has its root directory set to a directory containing `reggie-dl.jar`. The codebase property for the lookup service provides a URL naming the HTTP server that specifies where clients should download the classes in `reggie-dl.jar`.

You should consider breaking your classes into chunks for the implementation and the downloadable components. Creating separate JAR files for each is also handy when you need to move your service, or change where clients download your service's code.

Summary

These tips are designed to simulate the isolation that would exist between two Jini programs run on different machines—they share no common filesystem and no CLASSPATH. Security must be considered, since programs must go off-machine to access resources. And, in a real deployment setting, you cannot guarantee the existence of one global HTTP server for the network that contains all downloadable class files; instead, you must plan on separating class files for each service, and accessing them through individual HTTP servers.

Setting up your development environment in this way is a bit of trouble; but it can pay off in a big way as you begin to develop more complex services and applications.

Now that you've seen some strategies for developing Jini software, it's time to get into writing some actual code!

A First Jini Program: "Hello, World"

It's time to look at the minimal Jini programs. I'll show a simple service, and a client application to use that service, and step through how each of them works. The first thing any Jini service should have is an interface that defines what the service will do, such as in Listing 5–1. The service proxy object will implement this interface, and the client will use it whenever it searches the lookup services. In all of these examples, I'll include a package name that reflects where the code lives in the FTP'able bundle you can get from the FTP server as explained in this book's introduction. This will help to keep the code from different chapters partitioned.

Listing 5–1 `HelloWorldServiceInterface.java`

```
// This is the interface that the service's proxy
// implements

package corejini.chapter5;

public interface HelloWorldServiceInterface {
    public String getMessage();
}
```

This interface defines one simple method: When a caller asks for a message, a string is returned. The proxy object for the service will implement this interface.

Now look at the service. In this simple case, the "service" is really just the proxy object—which is perfectly capable of returning a string on its own without talking to any device or back-end process.

Even though the proxy implements the service itself, you will still need a program that handles finding a lookup service, publishing the proxy, and, in later examples, handling the leasing for the proxy to make sure that lookup services don't throw it away. This is called the "wrapper" process—it has a `main()` that takes care of the interactions with Jini needed to publish the proxy.

There are a few things to note about this example, as well as a few conventions that I'll be following in the code examples in the rest of this book. First, most of the Jini code lives in the `net.jini` package. This naming scheme follows the convention of using inverted domain names as package names—Bill Joy's Aspen SmallWorks, one of Sun's research labs, registered the domain "`jini.net`" in early 1997.

Second, Jini partitions its package namespace to reflect what is a core part of the system and what is built on top of the core. So the `net.jini.core.*` packages contains core, standard interfaces that constitute the heart of the system. These packages live in the `jini-core.jar` file. The `net.jini.*` packages contain libraries built using the core packages; this code lives in `jini-ext.jar`. Finally, Sun provides a set of "helper" classes in the `com.sun.jini.*` packages. These are considered "nonstandard" and subject to change. These classes reside in the `sun-util.jar` file. (If you unpack these JAR files, however, you will note that a few `com.sun.jini` classes *do* live in the `jini-core.jar` and `jini-ext.jar` files, as implementations of core interfaces...so the separation is not quite as clean as I've described here.)

In the code listings, I'll follow the convention of explicitly importing all of the Jini classes, so that you can tell which classes live in which packages.

The code in Listing 5–2 shows, in less than 100 lines of code, how to participate in a Jini community.

Listing 5–2 `HelloWorldService.java`

```
// This is the first iteration of a "Hello, World"
// service--it publishes a proxy that returns
// a string when asked by clients.

package corejini.chapter5;

import net.jini.discovery.DiscoveryListener;
import net.jini.discovery.DiscoveryEvent;
import net.jini.discovery.LookupDiscovery;
import net.jini.core.lookup.ServiceItem;
import net.jini.core.lookup.ServiceRegistrar;
import net.jini.core.lookup.ServiceRegistration;
import java.util.HashMap;
import java.io.IOException;
import java.io.Serializable;
import java.rmi.RemoteException;
import java.rmi.RMISecurityManager;

// This is the proxy object that will be downloaded
// by clients.  It's serializable and implements
// our well-known HelloWorldServiceInterface.
class HelloWorldServiceProxy implements Serializable,
    HelloWorldServiceInterface {
    public HelloWorldServiceProxy() {
    }
    public String getMessage() {
        return "Hello, world!";
    }
}
```

Listing 5–2 `HelloWorldService.java` (continued)

```java
// HelloWorldService is the "wrapper" class that
// handles publishing the service item.
public class HelloWorldService implements Runnable {
    // 10 minute leases
    protected final int LEASE_TIME = 10 * 60 * 1000;
    protected HashMap registrations = new HashMap();
    protected ServiceItem item;
    protected LookupDiscovery disco;

    // Inner class to listen for discovery events
    class Listener implements DiscoveryListener {
        // Called when we find a new lookup service.
        public void discovered(DiscoveryEvent ev) {
            System.out.println("discovered a lookup " +
                               "service!");
            ServiceRegistrar[] newregs = ev.getRegistrars();
            for (int i=0 ; i<newregs.length ; i++) {
                if (!registrations.containsKey(newregs[i])){
                    registerWithLookup(newregs[i]);
                }
            }
        }

        // Called ONLY when we explicitly discard a
        // lookup service, not "automatically" when a
        // lookup service goes down.  Once discovered,
        // there is NO ongoing communication with a
        // lookup service.
        public void discarded(DiscoveryEvent ev) {
            ServiceRegistrar[] deadregs =
                ev.getRegistrars();
            for (int i=0 ; i<deadregs.length ; i++) {
                registrations.remove(deadregs[i]);
            }
        }
    }
```

Listing 5–2 `HelloWorldService.java` (continued)

```
public HelloWorldService() throws IOException {
item = new ServiceItem(null, createProxy(), null);

// Set a security manager.
if (System.getSecurityManager() == null) {
    System.setSecurityManager(
            new RMISecurityManager());
}

// Search for the "public" group, which by
// convention is named by the empty string.
disco = new LookupDiscovery(new String[] { "" });

// Install a listener.
disco.addDiscoveryListener(new Listener());
}

protected HelloWorldServiceInterface createProxy() {
    return new HelloWorldServiceProxy();
}

// This work involves remote calls, and may take a
// while to complete.  Thus, since it's called from
// discovered(), it will prevent us from responding
// in a timely fashion to new discovery events.  An
// improvement would be to spin off a separate short-
// lived thread to do the work.
synchronized void registerWithLookup(ServiceRegistrar
                                      registrar) {
    ServiceRegistration registration = null;

    try {
        registration = registrar.register(item,
                                    LEASE_TIME);
    } catch (RemoteException ex) {
        System.out.println("Couldn't register: " +
                            ex.getMessage());
        return;
    }
```

Listing 5–2 `HelloWorldService.java` (continued)

```
    // If this is our first registration, use the
    // service ID returned to us.  Ideally, we should
    // save this ID so that it can be used after
    // restarts of the service.
    if (item.serviceID == null) {
        item.serviceID = registration.getServiceID();
        System.out.println("Set serviceID to " +
                            item.serviceID);
    }


    registrations.put(registrar, registration);
}

// This thread does nothing but sleep, but it
// makes sure the VM doesn't exit.
public void run() {
    while (true) {
        try {
            Thread.sleep(1000000);
        } catch (InterruptedException ex) {
        }
    }
}

// Create a new HelloWorldService and start
// its thread.
public static void main(String args[]) {
    try {
        HelloWorldService hws =
            new HelloWorldService();
        new Thread(hws).start();
    } catch (IOException ex) {
        System.out.println("Couldn't create service: " +
                            ex.getMessage());
    }
}
}
```

Writing the Service Proxy

Following the imports, you'll see the class definition for the service proxy, which here is called `HelloWorldServiceProxy`. There are a handful of points to make about this class.

- You'll notice it implements the `java.io.Serializable` interface. This is a *requirement* for a service proxy, because an instance of the class will have to be "pickled" and sent to each lookup service you contact, and then on to each client from there. Being serializable means that the proxy can be saved to a byte stream, sent down a socket to a remote system, and reconstituted at the other end.

- The service proxy also implements an interface, `HelloWorldServiceInterface`, that is known to the client. This is because, in the example, the client program will search the lookup services for service proxies that implement this interface. In general, you should try to use well-known interfaces wherever possible to make it easy for clients to know what your service does. In other words, the client must know what to ask for.

- The service proxy has a public, no-argument constructor. This is a requirement for any `Serializable` class that extends a non-`Serializable` class. While this isn't the case here, I try to get in the habit of creating no-argument constructors for my `Serializable` classes just in case I later change the class that they extend.

- In this example, the proxy is declared as a "top-level" but nonpublic class in the same file as the "wrapper" application that publishes it. The arrangement used here is fine—remember that the client will not need compile-time access to the proxy, so having it hidden here is not a problem.[2] The client gains access to this proxy at run time via serialization and code downloading. You can even declare a proxy as a nested inner class with one caveat—inner classes have a "hidden" reference to the instance of the class that created them. When an object is serialized, all of the nontransient, nonstatic references within it are serialized as well, which would cause the *wrapper* class to be bundled up with the

_____

2. Although the client *will* need compile-time access to the *interface* that the proxy implements. Otherwise, it would not know how to use the proxy programmatically.

proxy. This is almost certainly never what you want. If you declare your proxy as an inner class, be sure to declare it as a *static* inner class to avoid this problem. The keyword *static* on an inner class means that the class is nested simply for structural convenience—not for any run-time association between the nested and outer classes.[3] Static inner classes don't have the "hidden" reference to their enclosing classes, so your wrapper classes won't be serialized.

Core Alert: Forgetting serialization

If, as will sometimes happen, you do not make your service proxy `Serializable`, *the compiler cannot detect this error. Instead, you will get a run-time error when you attempt to register this proxy with a lookup service. The exact exception that will be raised is* `java.io.NotSerializableException`.

The `ServiceItem` *class, which is the class containing the service proxy that is passed to the registration process, is defined to hold an instance of type Object as the service's proxy. So you can pass any type of object here—although you should be aware that you will not get any compile-time warning if the object is not serializable.*

The "Wrapper" Application

Now it's time to walk through the application that will find lookup services and publish the proxy. This program isn't involved in helping the proxy perform its service; it only helps it manage its Jini responsibilities. In the example, the class that does this is called `HelloWorldService`. This class contains the `main()` function that begins the discovery process.

There is another inner class here that is used to interact with the Jini discovery system. The class, called `Listener`, implements the `DiscoveryListener` interface. By breaking the discovery-oriented code out into a separate inner class (as opposed to making the `HelloWorldService` wrapper class itself do discovery), you can keep a nice separation between the work required to participate in discovery and the work required by your particular service. I'll come back to the `Listener` class and describe how it works in just a bit.

---

3. Strictly speaking, "static" makes the class a "nested top-level class," not an inner class. But most people call it an inner class anyway.

After the declaration of the inner class for discovery, you get into the meat of this program. The constructor for `HelloWorldService` does four things. First, it creates an instance of `ServiceItem`. Instances of this class are what get passed to the lookup services during the registration process.

You'll notice three arguments to this constructor. The first is the *service ID* for the service. The service ID is a globally unique identifier for your service—even if you register the service on different lookup services, at different times, the service ID should be the same each time. This requirement that services remember their service IDs entails some bookkeeping on their part. This service isn't particularly well-behaved, as it requests a new service ID each time it is run.

To make the job of constructing an initial service ID easier, Jini uses a convention where, if you pass `null` as a service ID the first time you register it, the lookup service will assign a globally-unique service ID to it. Subsequent registrations should use this ID. You'll soon see how to do this for the simple service shown here. Chapter 8, which discusses lookup in depth, has more details on service IDs, their lifetimes, and how they are generated; you'll also see some convenient ways to manage this bookkeeping.

The second argument is an instance of the service proxy. This object will be serialized and, whenever a lookup service is discovered, sent to that lookup service to await a client who wants it. Here I've placed the construction of the proxy object in its own method, `createProxy()`, for clarity and for the ability of future subclasses to override this method.

The final argument, also `null` here, can contain a list of attributes you wish to associate with the service proxy. Interested clients can search these attributes. So, for example, if you are registering a printer, you might attach attributes that indicate the location and model of the printer. Clients could then retrieve this information for display to a user, or use it programmatically to find a particular printer. This argument is typed as an array of objects implementing the `Entry` interface. You'll see some examples of using attributes in future examples, but for now, this program will not attach any attributes to the service proxy.

Once the program has created the `ServiceItem` that it will register in the lookup services it discovers, it sets a security manager, if one is not yet set. Recall that any Java program that will download code—meaning load it from some location other than from a local directory specified by the CLASSPATH—must have a security manager to prevent that code from performing unauthorized operations. Since the service will need to download the proxy object for any lookup services it finds, it *must* set the security manager here.

After setting the security manager, the program creates an instance of `LookupDiscovery`. This class provides the mechanisms for using the multicast flavors of the Jini discovery protocol. Using it is amazingly simple. If you want to be told whenever a lookup service that is a member of the public group is found, you pass in an array of group names including only the empty string. (Recall that a "group" is simply a name that can be given to a Jini community. By convention, the group named by the empty string is taken to be a "public" community that services will join by default. Most of the time, using the approach taken here of passing the empty string is the appropriate one. If, on the other hand, you are running an experimental service, you might pass the string "experimental" here to look for that community. You would also have to run a lookup service that is configured to support that group name somewhere on your network.)

The `LookupDiscovery` object can call out to a `DiscoveryListener` whenever a new lookup service is found. The nested listener class implements this interface, so the constructor for `HelloWorldService` adds a new instance of `Listener` as the listener for discovery. After this, the discovery subsystem will call out to the `Listener` instance on the `DiscoveryListener` methods whenever a lookup service is found.

Core Note: The discovery API has an asynchronous look-and-feel

Clearly, if I want to write a Jini service that can be asynchronously notified whenever a new lookup service appears, I have to implement some listener interface so that the Jini libraries can call me back whenever a lookup service is started.

But why use an "asynchronous" interface—one in which notification is done outside the main flow of control—if I only want to connect to lookup services that are already running? Can I not get a "synchronous" API that blocks until it can return the lookup services to me?

The Jini APIs use this asynchronous style exclusively for discovery. The reason is that, in almost every case, a Jini service needs to be able to handle lookup services that start after it does. So ,using an asynchronous API everywhere has a number of advantages. First, it encourages "proper" behavior because services will have to be written to understand notifications of lookup services anyway. Second, it means that there is only a single way to get information about lookup services, so service code is simplified (as opposed to having both a blocking and a nonblocking API).

Finally, even if you know for a fact that lookup services are already running somewhere on your subnet, you don't know how long it will take them to respond to you. So, because you wouldn't know how long to block waiting for a response from a lookup service anyway, the asynchronous API is appropriate here too.

In general, the issues of designing good APIs that encourage the building of correct applications, and that make things that should be easy actually easy, are important to the Jini design. I'll highlight API design issues as they come up in later chapters.

Using Discovery and Lookup

Let's now look at how to build the code to support discovery. Recall that the code shown here uses an inner class called Listener to perform discovery. This class implements the DiscoveryListener interface, which has two methods: discovered() and discarded(). The former will be called whenever a lookup service is found that matches the group being looked for. The latter is called to indicate that a previously discovered lookup service should no longer be considered valid. Usually this happens because a lookup service has ceased to respond, and so you call the discard() method on LookupDiscovery to tell it that you are dropping the lookup service from the set you have found. The discarded() method may also be called if you change the groups you are searching for. This change would cause any lookup services you found previously that do not service your new groups to be discarded. Each of these methods will be passed a DiscoveryEvent object that describes the lookup services that have been discovered or discarded.

Core Tip: Understand when to discard lookup services

The discarded() *method on* DiscoveryListener *will be called in two circumstances. First, when the set of groups you're looking for changes, and* LookupDiscovery *needs to inform you that the lookup services you hold references to are no longer members of that set of groups. And second, when you explicitly discard a lookup service from the set of groups you are managing. The latter case is by far the more common.*

Why would you ever explicitly discard a lookup service? If you are performing an operation on a lookup service and get a RemoteException, *chances are the lookup service has gone down or is otherwise not accessible. When this happens, you should call the* discard() *method on* LookupDiscovery *to tell that class to drop the lookup service from the set of services it has found. Once this happens,* LookupDiscovery *will call out to your implementation of* discarded() *so that you can clean up your state.*

By discarding a failed lookup service, you're in a position to rediscover it once it returns to the network.

Misunderstanding how the `discarded()` *method is called is a common problem for beginning Jini programers—they mistakenly believe that when a lookup service crashes, some special post-mortem communication happens that causes the* `discarded()` *method to be called. This is not the case—once a lookup service has been found, there is no ongoing communication with it other than whatever methods you may call on it. So, you're responsible for dropping lookup services that begin to report errors.*

Look at the example's implementation of `discovered()`. The program keeps a hashmap that records all of the lookup services that have been found. Whenever the discovery protocol finds new lookup services, the program fetches them out of the `DiscoveryEvent` that it has been handed, and iterates through them to make sure it doesn't already have them in its hashmap. If the lookup service is indeed a new one, the program stores it in the hashmap and registers with the lookup service by calling `registerWithLookup()`.

Core Note: Redundant lookup services

In this example, I've done a bit of work to track the lookup services that have already been seen to ensure that I don't register with them twice. This isn't strictly necessary. A second registration at the same lookup service would simply overwrite the first one.

But tracking the registrations will turn out to be useful for managing leases anyway (something I'll get to later in this chapter), so keeping the hashtable is something that would have to be done in a program with proper leasing behavior. Plus, making sure that the program doesn't somehow do redundant registrations cuts down a bit on network traffic.

The process of registration with a lookup service is easy: You simply get the `ServiceRegistrar` instance that corresponds to the lookup service you've discovered, and call the `register()` method on it. As you can see, this call takes two arguments. The first is the service item, created earlier, and the second is the requested duration of the lease. This is the amount of time the wrapper asks the lookup service to hold the proxy without hearing from it again. In this case, the program asks for a 10-minute lease. Recall that the lookup service, as the grantor of the lease, may deny the request, or may grant a shorter lease. The status of the lease is returned in the `ServiceRegistration` object that results from this call. This result value allows a number of useful operations to be performed on it: You can get the ID of the newly registered service—this is how a program can get the service ID assigned to it the first time it runs. The returned `Service-Registration` also allows you to get the `Lease` object associated with the registration, and change the attribute set associated with the service item.

Core Tip: Do registration in a separate thread

In the example shown here, the work done by `registerWithLookup()` *happens in the same thread as discovery—that is, registration happens in response to a* `DiscoveryEvent`, *and occupies that thread until registration completes.*

In most cases, this work should be done in a separate thread of control, because the registration process involves a remote call which may take a relatively long amount of time to return: for example, the lookup service may crash, which means that a time out would occur before the call would return.

No other lookup services can be discovered while this registration process is in progress. So that lookup services can be discovered in a timely fashion, a better approach is to use a separate, short-lived thread to handle the registration tasks. The approach shown here should only be used when you really do want to block discovery until registration completes, but the code here is appropriate for illustrating the basics of how to do discovery and registration.

After registering the service proxy, the wrapper checks to see if this is the first time it has been registered. If this is the first time, it writes the service ID that's been returned into the service item, so that future registrations will use this same ID. It also stashes the registration result into a hashmap so that it can retrieve it in the future, if needed.

The code here follows that maxim that services should register themselves with any and all lookup services that they encounter for their specified groups. This way, if multiple lookup services are running on a network, you get built-in redundancy.

Note that this example shows the bare minimum necessary to register a service. There are a number of obvious and fairly important improvements you could, and will, make in the next iterations. Most crucial is leasing. As currently written, this program will register a service that will go away after 10 minutes, or whatever time the lookup service grants us as a registration duration. Secondly, there is very little error checking going on here. For example, what if the `register()` method fails? Remember that registration is defined so that if you re-register a service, it simply overwrites all previous registrations. Therefore, it's safe to simply retry a registration if it fails. This code gives up after the first attempt. I'll solve many of these problems in later iterations, but for now, it's important to get the basic concepts.

Last Details

The rest of the code is pretty much boilerplate. The service's class implements `Runnable`. This is to ensure that the little application won't simply stop when `main()` finishes. Without at least one active (non-daemon) thread in the application, it would simply terminate when `main()` "ran off the end" of available statements, which is likely before any lookup services are able to report their existence to us. So the service implements `Runnable` and causes a simple thread that sleeps forever to be started. If you happen to be doing any AWT or Swing work in your application, you won't need to start your own thread, as the Java windowing system starts its own threads as soon as you create any windows. But because the program here is not doing graphics, it'll have to start its own thread. Note that the back-end program will run forever, or until you kill it, as I've made no provision for breaking out of this thread.

The `main()` routine simply creates a `HelloWorldService` instance and starts the background thread to keep the application alive.

Now look at a simple client application (Listing 5–3) that can use this service.

Listing 5–3 `HelloWorldClient.java`

```java
// A simple client to exercise the HelloWorldService

package corejini.chapter5;

import net.jini.discovery.DiscoveryListener;
import net.jini.discovery.DiscoveryEvent;
import net.jini.discovery.LookupDiscovery;
import net.jini.core.lookup.ServiceRegistrar;
import net.jini.core.lookup.ServiceTemplate;
import java.io.IOException;
import java.rmi.RemoteException;
import java.rmi.RMISecurityManager;

public class HelloWorldClient implements Runnable {
    protected ServiceTemplate template;
    protected LookupDiscovery disco;

    // An inner class to implement DiscoveryListener
    class Listener implements DiscoveryListener {
        public void discovered(DiscoveryEvent ev) {
            ServiceRegistrar[] newregs = ev.getRegistrars();
            for (int i=0 ; i<newregs.length ; i++) {
                lookForService(newregs[i]);
            }
        }
        public void discarded(DiscoveryEvent ev) {
        }
    }

    public HelloWorldClient() throws IOException {
        Class[] types = {HelloWorldServiceInterface.class};

        template = new ServiceTemplate(null, types, null);

        // Set a security manager.
        if (System.getSecurityManager() == null) {
            System.setSecurityManager(
                    new RMISecurityManager());
        }

        // Only search the public group.
        disco = new LookupDiscovery(new String[] { "" });
```

Listing 5–3 `HelloWorldClient.java` (continued)

```java
        // Install a listener.
        disco.addDiscoveryListener(new Listener());
    }


    // Once we've found a new lookup service, search
    // for proxies that implement
    // HelloWorldServiceInterface.
    protected Object lookForService(ServiceRegistrar
                                    lusvc) {
        Object o = null;

        try {
            o = lusvc.lookup(template);
        } catch (RemoteException ex) {
            System.err.println("Error doing lookup: " +
                                ex.getMessage());
            return null;
        }

        if (o == null) {
            System.err.println("No matching service.");
            return null;
        }

        System.out.println("Got a matching service.");
        System.out.println("It's message is: " +
                        ((HelloWorldServiceInterface)
                            o).getMessage());
        return o;
    }

    // This thread does nothing--it simply keeps the
    // VM from exiting while we do discovery.
    public void run() {
        while (true) {
            try {
                Thread.sleep(1000000);
            } catch (InterruptedException ex) {
            }
        }
    }
```

Listing 5–3 `HelloWorldClient.java` (continued)

```java
    // Create a HelloWorldClient and start its thread.
    public static void main(String args[]) {
        try {
            HelloWorldClient hwc = new HelloWorldClient();
            new Thread(hwc).start();
        } catch (IOException ex) {
            System.out.println("Couldn't create client: " +
                               ex.getMessage());
        }
    }
}
```

This client program has some similarities with the server. It has an inner class that implements `DiscoveryListener`, as it has to participate in the discovery protocols. It spawns off a background thread so that its main program won't simply exit before any lookup services are found. And it installs a security manager since it will need to download and use the service proxy from the `HelloWorld-Service`.

But, instead of registering a service, this client program will *search* for a service proxy that implements `HelloWorldServiceInterface`. Whenever `discovered()` is called, the program is informed of one or more lookup services. For each of these, it'll look for the desired service. It does this by using a `ServiceTemplate` object, which is a way to describe the services being looked for.

Using Service Templates to Search for a Service

Each `ServiceTemplate` has three fields in it that control how search works. Here's part of the definition of a `ServiceTemplate`:

```java
public class ServiceTemplate {
    public ServiceID serviceID;
    public Class[] serviceType;
    public Entry[] attributeSetTemplates;
    // ... other details elided ...
}
```

The `ServiceTemplate` code acts like a query specification. When you pass a `ServiceTemplate` to a lookup service, the service searches all of its registered services for a match. A template matches a service if:

- The service ID in the template matches the ID of a registered service, or the template's service ID field is null; *and*
- The registered service is an instance or a subtype of *every* type in the template's `serviceType` field, or the template's type field is null; *and*
- The service's list of attributes contains at least one attribute that matches every entry in the template, or the template's attribute field is null. (Exactly what it means to "match" an attribute will be discussed in Chapter 7.)

By using a `ServiceTemplate`, you can search for services that match a known class or interface, or that have a desired set of attributes, or that have a specific service ID (if you happen to know it). Since Java type relationships are considered by the matching process, you can search for services that are subtypes of known types. For example, if class B extends class A, and if A is in the template, then a search will return all objects of type A or type B registered in the lookup service. Leaving one of the fields in a template set to null essentially makes it a wild-card value. A template with all fields set to null will match all services.

Core Tip: Finding the proxy for the lookup service

The proxy for a lookup service itself is stored along with the other registered services. So when you match all services, the call to `lookup()` *will return a reference to the lookup service itself, in addition to whatever other services are registered. Many users expect* `lookup()` *to return all services except the lookup service.*

Of course, you can always do a search for proxies that implement `ServiceRegistrar` *to return only proxies for lookup services.*

In this example, the program creates a template that searches based on the type of the service. In this case, it creates a template that's initialized by an array of `Classes` containing only the class of the desired interface, `HelloWorldServiceInterface`. Leaving the service ID and attributes fields blank means that the search will match any service that implements `HelloWorldServiceInterface`, no matter what its service ID is, or what attributes may be associated with it.

Looking Up a Service

The actual search is invoked by calling `lookup()` on the `ServiceRegistrar` object that represents a lookup service. This method contacts the lookup service and performs the search. If a match is found, the lookup service transmits the matching service's proxy back to the client, deserialized and ready to use, or `null` if there was no match.

Note that it's possible that a given Jini community may contain any number of services that implement a desired interface or, more generally, match any given query used to search. The form of the `lookup()` call used here only returns a single match—typically the first service found that matches the query. There is another form of the `lookup()` method that takes an extra parameter specifying the maximum number of matches to be returned.

In general, though, returning the first match from a specified query is good enough for most applications. If I create a query that only specifies the interface I'm searching for, I'm implicitly telling the lookup service that the interface is the only thing that matters to me. In such a case, one `HelloWorldServiceInterface` is as good as any other. Likewise, if I issue a query that specifies "any unjammed color printer on the third floor," then any single match satisfying that query is probably good enough.

If you need a very specific service, particularly if you need to find one that cannot be easily specified by using the matching facilities available in `Service-Templates`, then you can write a more general query to fetch a set of matching services, and then refine these (perhaps by presenting them to a user) to isolate a single service that you'll use. And clients like browsers will typically want to fetch all of the services they can find.

For this application, getting a single match is fine. Once you get a match, you can just cast it to its known type and use it! And while this particular service proxy is trivially simple, the fact that its implementation details are completely hidden means that a client can interact with arbitrarily complex services while knowing only their interfaces.

Compiling and Running the Examples

Once you've got the code typed in or downloaded, you can compile and then run the programs. For the examples in this chapter, I'll be following the somewhat tedious set of tips that I discussed earlier that are designed to "simulate" clients and services running on different hosts. I'd strongly recommend that you follow these steps, although if you want to jump in quickly, you can leave all the classes in your development directory and share a CLASSPATH. But if you do this, please come back to this example and walk through the procedure before you go on! The sidebar below presents a summary of the conventions and file locations that I'll be using in the rest of the book.

Conventions I'll Be Using

All the code examples in this book follow the set of guidelines presented earlier that are meant to mirror the effects of running clients and services on separate machines. Some of these guidelines may seem like a lot of extra work to you—after all, you want to jump in and get coding!

But most of the problems that starting Jini programmers face have to do with security and code loading: problems that are often hidden if you do not follow these guidelines.

In all the instructions for building and testing the code samples in this book, I've followed a set of conventions for where to put the code and how to run the services.

Most examples consist of a Jini service as well as a client that exercises that service. To ensure that the service and the client aren't inadvertently sharing class files, I will place the class files for each in a separate directory.

Likewise, in many of the examples, both the service and the client may need to export some downloadable code to another entity in the Jini community—services, for example, need to be able to export their proxy objects to Jini lookup services and to the clients that will use them. Clients often need to export downloadable code for their remote event listeners. In all these examples, I will also create and use a separate directory for the downloadable code that each entity exports; so the portions of the client that are meant to be downloadable are in a directory separate from the rest of the client's code, as are the portions of the service that are meant to be downloaded.

To simulate the effects of each of these bundles of downloadable code being on separate machines, I also will run separate HTTP servers to export the code in the service's export directory and the client's export directory; each will have its "root" directory set to point to one of the directories containing downloadable code. These HTTP servers can be run on the same physical machine, as long as they use different port numbers. In this book, I'll run the HTTP servers for services and clients on different ports: port 8085 for the services and port 8086 for the clients. The codebase properties for the client and the server will refer to the particular instance of the HTTP server that is exporting their code.

(continued)

The table below summarizes the conventions that I'll be using for directories, on both Windows and UNIX.

Class File Directory Conventions

Directory Contents	*Windows Location*	*UNIX Location*
Class files needed for the implementation of the service	`C:\service`	`/files/service`
Class files that the service makes available for download to other entities	`C:\service-dl`	`/files/service-dl`
Class files needed for the implementation of the client	`C:\client`	`/files/client`
Class files that the client makes available for download to other entities	`C:\client-dl`	`/files/client-dl`

When compiling a client, I'll set the CLASSPATH for the compiler to point to not only the three Jini JAR files, but also the client implementation directory, as specified above. This is necessary so that the compiler can find and use class files already generated for use by the client. Likewise, when compiling services, I'll set the CLASSPATH to the three Jini JAR files and the service's implementation code directory.

One advantage of this arrangement—in addition to maintaining separation between class files used by the client and the service—is that it's easy to create JAR files from these separate directories. Once your code has been partitioned like this, you can take the class files in each directory and create implementation and download JAR files for both the client and the service, much as the Jini reference implementation does (such as `reggie.jar` and `reggie-dl.jar`).

Refer back to the section, "Developing with Deployment in Mind," earlier in this chapter, for the rationale of these conventions.

Make sure you're ready to build and run the examples. First, unset your CLASSPATH to ensure that no extraneous class files leak across this boundary into either the client or the service; you'll be specifying the paths to find classes on the command line. Second, make sure that the source code for these examples is together in a well-known place. I suggest `C:\files\corejini` on Windows and `/files/corejini` on UNIX.

Compiling

Next, compile the programs. You want to keep the class files for the client and the service separated since, in general, clients and services share no code at compile time and will have no special knowledge of one another, other than some shared interfaces that the service's proxy may implement. You also need to separate code used in the implementation of a program from code meant to be downloaded *to* another program. In this case, the only application-specific downloadable code is the proxy object. Both the client and service will, of course, need to be able to download the lookup service's proxy, but you should have already configured an HTTP server that exports the `reggie-dl.jar` file somewhere on your network when you started the lookup service.

To keep the code separate, you can tell the `javac` compiler to output class files into separate directories. In fact, the best thing to do is create a directory called `client` for the client-side implementation, `service` for the service-side implementation, and `service-dl` for the downloadable code that the server exports (this is the downloadable code that the client will use; note the conventions being used for directory names here). You can create these directories under `C:\` on Windows and under `/files` on UNIX, and then pass the `-d` flag to the compiler to tell it where to output the class files it creates.

On Windows: First, create the directories you will need, and go to the directory that contains the sources you will compile.

```
mkdir c:\client
mkdir c:\service
mkdir c:\service-dl
cd c:\files\corejini\chapter5
```

Next, compile the source files needed for the service. The service relies on both `HelloWorldService.java` and `HelloWorldServiceInterface.java`. The `-d` option says to drop the resulting class files into `C:\service`.

```
javac -classpath C:\files;
                 C:\jini1_1\lib\jini-core.jar;
                 C:\jini1_1\lib\jini-ext.jar;
                 C:\jini1_1\lib\sun-util.jar;
                 C:\service
  -d C:\service
  C:\files\corejini\chapter5\HelloWorldServiceInterface.java
  C:\files\corejini\chapter5\HelloWorldService.java
```

Now, compile the source files needed for the client. The client also relies on
`HelloWorldServiceInterface.java`, as well as `HelloWorldCli-`
`ent.java`. Put these files in `C:\client`.

```
javac -classpath C:\files;
                  C:\jini1_1\lib\jini-core.jar;
                  C:\jini1_1\lib\jini-ext.jar;
                  C:\jini1_1\lib\sun-util.jar;
                  C:\client
  -d C:\client
  C:\files\corejini\chapter5\HelloWorldServiceInterface.java
  C:\files\corejini\chapter5\HelloWorldClient.java
```

Note that even though you already compiled the interface source file when you
built the service, you need to make sure that the resulting class file is present in
both the client and the server directories, since it's required by both. So the step
above compiles it into the client's directory as well.

Finally, in this example, the only newly-written code that will be downloaded
is the proxy's class file. This file should have been created when you compiled
the service, since the proxy is a nested class within the service. You can just copy
this file from the `C:\service` directory to the `C:\service-dl` directory. You
must follow the usual Java package name-to-directory conventions by placing the
class in a subdirectory called `corejini\chapter5`.

```
mkdir C:/service-dl/corejini/chapter 5
cd C:\service\corejini\chapter5
copy HelloWorldServiceProxy.class
     C:\service-dl\corejini\chapter5
```

On UNIX: First, create the directories you will need, and go to the directory
that contains the sources you will compile.

```
mkdir /files/client
mkdir /files/service
mkdir /files/service-dl
cd /files/corejini/chapter5
```

Next, compile the source files needed for the service. The service relies on both
`HelloWorldService.java` and `HelloWorldServiceInterface.java`. The
`-d` option says to drop the resulting class files into `/files/service`.

```
javac -classpath /files:
                  /files/jini1_1/lib/jini-core.jar:
```

```
                /files/jini1_1/lib/jini-ext.jar:
                /files/jini1_1/lib/sun-util.jar:
                /files/service
 -d /files/service
 /files/corejini/chapter5/HelloWorldServiceInterface.java
 /files/corejini/chapter5/HelloWorldService.java
```

Now, compile the source files needed for the client. The client also relies on
`HelloWorldServiceInterface.java`, as well as `HelloWorldCli-`
`ent.java`. Put these files in `/files/client`.

```
javac -classpath /files:
                /files/jini1_1/lib/jini-core.jar:
                /files/jini1_1/lib/jini-ext.jar:
                /files/jini1_1/lib/sun-util.jar:
 -d /files/client
 /files/corejini/chapter5/HelloWorldServiceInterface.java
 /files/corejini/chapter5/HelloWorldClient.java
```

Note that even though you already compiled the interface source file when you
built the service, you need to make sure that the resulting class file is present in
both the client and the server directories, since it's required by both. So the step
above compiles it into the client's directory as well.

   Finally, in this example, the only newly-written code that will be downloaded
is the proxy's class file. This file should have been created when you compiled
the service, since the proxy is a nested class within the service. You can just copy
this file from the `/files/service` directory to the `/files/service-dl` directory. You must follow the usual Java package name-to-directory conventions by
placing the class in a subdirectory called `corejini/chapter5`.

```
mkdir/files/service-dl/corejini/chapter 5
cd /files/service/corejini/chapter5
cp HelloWorldServiceProxy.class
   /files/service-dl/corejini/chapter5
```

Start an HTTP Server for the Service

Now that you've segregated the class files, you can start an HTTP server that
will export the downloadable class files that clients will need to use the service.
In this example, the service is the only entity that needs to export downloadable
code (in addition to the lookup service, that is, which should have its own
HTTP server already running), so you can run an HTTP server with a root
directory set to the location of the service's downloadable class files.

If you're developing everything on one machine, you're probably running the HTTP server that provides the class files for the core Jini services on your machine already. If this is the case, then you should pick a port number for the new HTTP server that's different than the one already running (which defaults to port 8080). Here, I'm starting the server on port 8085. In the rest of this book, I'll always run the HTTP server that exports code for services on this port.

On Windows: Launch the HTTP server that comes with Jini:

```
java -jar C:\jini1_1\lib\tools.jar
    -dir C:\service-dl -verbose -port 8085
```

On UNIX: Launch the HTTP server that comes with Jini:

```
java -jar /files/jini1_1/lib/tools.jar
    -dir /files/service-dl -verbose -port 8085
```

Set Up a Security Policy File

Since these example programs have a security manager set, they need to have a security policy provided for them at run time that tells the JVM what these programs are allowed to do. The policy file shown here in Listing 5–4 is very "promiscuous," in that it allows the programs to essentially do anything. This is fine in a testing environment, since you've written the code and know what it does. But you should not use this policy file in a production environment. Read the JavaSoft security tutorial, or *Just Java 1.2* by Peter van der Linden for more information on policy files.

Listing 5–4 A promiscuous policy file

```
grant {
    // Allow everyone access to everything
    permission java.security.AllPermission;
};
```

Drop this file into `C:\policy` on Windows, or `/files/policy` on UNIX. You'll need to pass the path to it on the command line when you run the programs.

Running

Now (finally!) you're ready to run the programs. One caveat with the version of the example programs shown in this section: You have to start the

`HelloWorldService` program *first*. This is because the client application only searches for services that are already in existence when it runs—there is no way for the client to be notified if the desired service comes along after the client has started. This is a problem that will be remedied in the next iteration of the example.

First, run the service. Make sure that you replace "`myhost`" in the codebase URL with the hostname on which the service's HTTP server is running.

On Windows:

```
java -cp C:\jini1_1\lib\jini-core.jar;
        C:\jini1_1\lib\jini-ext.jar;
        C:\jini1_1\lib\sun-util.jar;
        C:\service
    -Djava.rmi.server.codebase=http://myhost:8085/
    -Djava.security.policy=C:\policy
    corejini.chapter5.HelloWorldService
```

On UNIX:

```
java -cp /files/jini1_1/lib/jini-core.jar:
        /files/jini1_1/lib/jini-ext.jar:
        /files/jini1_1/lib/sun-util.jar:
        /files/service
    -Djava.rmi.server.codebase=http://myhost:8085/
    -Djava.security.policy=/files/policy
    corejini.chapter5.HelloWorldService
```

After you see the service report that it has "`discovered a lookup service`," run the client. Note that the client doesn't need to have a codebase property specified, as it is providing no downloadable code to other programs.

On Windows:

```
java -cp C:\jini1_1\lib\jini-core.jar;
        C:\jini1_1\lib\jini-ext.jar;
        C:\jini1_1\lib\sun-util.jar;
        C:\client
    -Djava.security.policy=C:\policy
    corejini.chapter5.HelloWorldClient
```

On UNIX:

```
java -cp /files/jini1_1/lib/jini-core.jar:
        /files/jini1_1/lib/jini-ext.jar:
```

```
    /files/jini1_1/lib/sun-util.jar:
    /files/client
-Djava.security.policy=/files/policy
corejini.chapter5.HelloWorldClient
```

The client will contact the lookup service, download the service proxy from it, as well as the code for the proxy from the HTTP server associated with the service, and execute it. You should see output like the following:

From the service:

```
discovered a lookup service!
Set serviceID to e91bb61d-b18e-447e-8935-adfd8bd741f5
```

From the client:

```
Got matching service.
Its message is: Hello, world!
```

Success! The client has contacted a Jini community, searched for a service that implements a particular Java interface, and downloaded code that implements that interface. All the setup here may seem at first like a lot of work with little payoff—certainly the "Hello, World" service isn't very compelling on its own. But you'll be able to extend this basic paradigm to richer and richer functionality. And—painful though it may be—following the tips to simulate a multimachine environment in which clients and services share no CLASSPATH will keep problems from cropping up later.

Now you're ready to move on and extend the client code by enabling event handling.

Extending "Hello, World" with Events

The previous example highlighted the basics of interacting with the discovery and lookup programming models. And, while unencumbered by some of the other Jini concepts, one would have to do a bit more to make these programs reliable and better behaved in a Jini community.

In this section, you will extend the client class with the ability to respond to remote events. By using remote events, you'll gain the ability to run the "Hello, World" service *after* the client has started. This is flexibility that's essential for a real-world application, and is missing from the prior iteration of the example.

My strategy for adding needed functionality while building on previous work is to subclass the earlier code. This makes it easy to see what has changed between iterations, and cuts down on the amount of redundant code that you as the reader have to parse.

For this example, most of the code—including `HelloWorldService` and `HelloWorldServiceInterface`—will stay exactly the same. You only need to extend the functionality of the `HelloWorldClient` code, as shown in Listing 5–5, to make it handle events properly.

Listing 5–5 `HelloWorldClientWithEvents.java`

```
// Extend the client so that it can receive events
// when new services appear.

package corejini.chapter5;

import net.jini.core.lookup.ServiceEvent;
import net.jini.core.lookup.ServiceItem;
import net.jini.core.lookup.ServiceRegistrar;
import net.jini.core.event.RemoteEvent;
import net.jini.core.event.RemoteEventListener;
import net.jini.core.event.UnknownEventException;
import java.io.IOException;
import java.rmi.RemoteException;
import java.rmi.server.UnicastRemoteObject;

public class HelloWorldClientWithEvents
        extends HelloWorldClient {
    // 10 minutes
    protected final int LEASE_TIME = 10 * 60 * 1000;

    // An inner class to listen for events.
    class MyEventListener
        extends UnicastRemoteObject
        implements RemoteEventListener {
        public MyEventListener() throws RemoteException {
        }
```

Listing 5–5 `HelloWorldClientWithEvents.java` (continued)

```java
    // Called when an event is received.
    public void notify(RemoteEvent ev)
        throws RemoteException, UnknownEventException {
        System.out.println("Got an event from: " +
                            ev.getSource());
        if (ev instanceof ServiceEvent) {
            ServiceEvent sev = (ServiceEvent) ev;
            ServiceItem item = sev.getServiceItem();
            HelloWorldServiceInterface hws =
                (HelloWorldServiceInterface)
                    item.service;

            System.out.println("Got a service.");
            System.out.println("It's message is: " +
                                hws.getMessage());
        } else {
            System.out.println("Not a service event, " +
                                "ignoring");
        }
    }
}

protected MyEventListener eventCatcher;

// Same as superclass, only create an event
// listener.
public HelloWorldClientWithEvents()
    throws RemoteException, IOException {
    eventCatcher = new MyEventListener();
}
```

Listing 5–5 `HelloWorldClientWithEvents.java` (continued)

```java
protected Object lookForService(ServiceRegistrar lu) {
    Object o = super.lookForService(lu);

    if (o != null) {
        return o;
    } else {
        try {
            registerForEvents(lu);
        } catch (RemoteException ex) {
            System.err.println("Can't solicit events: "
                               + ex.getMessage());
            // Discard it, so we can find it again
            disco.discard(lu);
        } finally {
            return null;
        }
    }
}


// Ask for events from the lookup service.
protected void registerForEvents(ServiceRegistrar lu)
    throws RemoteException {
    lu.notify(template,
            ServiceRegistrar.TRANSITION_NOMATCH_MATCH,
            eventCatcher, null, LEASE_TIME);
}

// Start the client.
public static void main(String args[]) {
    try {
        HelloWorldClientWithEvents hwc =
            new HelloWorldClientWithEvents();
        new Thread(hwc).start();
    } catch (IOException ex) {
        System.out.println("Couldn't create client: " +
                           ex.getMessage());
    }
}
}
```

This version of `HelloWorldClient` is a subclass of the original, and inherits all its functionality. The new code adds the ability to receive events from lookup services when a desired service is registered after the client has already done a `lookup()` operation. The changes needed to support this are quite small, and will be easily repeatable boilerplate for most applications.

Writing a Remote Event Listener

The most obvious feature of this revision of the client program is the inclusion of a nested class that will catch any events for the program. The Jini remote event model is based on RMI—that is, a remote process delivers an event to the receiver by calling the `notify()` method on the receiver. This is a "remote" method, since it is meant to be callable by a process in another JVM (and hence, the object defining it is a "remote object"). Here, I have created a new, nested class, called `MyEventListener`, whose sole purpose is to receive these events. In general, there's no reason that the class that registers the service cannot be the same class that receives the events. But, creating a separate class for listeners—whether local or remote—often results in a much cleaner design. In this case, the listener must extend the RMI class `UnicastRemoteObject`, so I have no choice but to create a separate nested class. Using separate nested classes for listeners is good practice in most cases.

If you are unfamiliar with RMI, now may be a good time to check out the RMI primer in Appendix A of this book. Basically, by making the listener class inherit from `UnicastRemoteObject`, I've said that its methods may be called from an object in a different JVM, either on the same host or on different hosts. In this case, the `notify()` method will be called by the lookup service to deliver an event whenever the desired service appears.

This event listener class needs to do several things.

- It must inherit from `UnicastRemoteObject` so that its methods can be called by objects in another JVM to deliver events.
- It must implement `RemoteEventListener`, which includes the `notify()` method. This method will be invoked whenever an event comes in.
- To work correctly with RMI, the class must declare that its constructor and any remotely callable methods may raise `RemoteException`. You'll notice that this is done in the example.

After defining a class to receive remote events, the client defines a constructor, which creates an instance of `MyEventListener` that will be used to receive events. Note that, as of now, the program has only declared and created one of these listeners—it hasn't actually "plugged it in" yet, because it hasn't yet found any lookup services from which it can receive events.

Soliciting Events via Notify()

The next change is in the `lookupService()` method. This implementation again calls its superclass—the behavior shown in the first `HelloWorldClient` is fine for the case when the service already exists when the client starts. But, if the superclass version of `lookupService()` doesn't find a service, it then solicits events from the discovered lookup service.

This is done by calling the `notify()` method on the lookup service. The `notify()` method is used to ask for event notifications from the lookup service. Thus, `notify()` is really a registration process, and its semantics involve the use of templates that play a role similar to the role they play in the `lookup()` method discussed earlier. You specify a template on which to search, and get informed of any matches. The difference is that `lookup()` finds matches that *already* exist in the lookup service; `notify()` finds matches *in the future*. Once you call `notify()`, you're asking the lookup service to hold on to your query, and inform you via an event whenever the service items in the lookup service change in a way that makes the query match.

There are a number of parameters to `notify()`.

- The first is the `ServiceTemplate`. This argument works just like it does in the `lookup()` method—you can specify explicit service IDs, service types, or attributes to match on. In this example, I use the same `ServiceTemplate` that I used for doing the original `lookup()`, because I'm searching for the same thing in both cases—a proxy that implements `HelloWorldService`.

- The second is the "transition" parameter. This value indicates when an event should be sent to you—when the lookup service changes so that a previously matching value no longer matches (indicated by the constant `TRANSITION_MATCH_NOMATCH`), when a matching value appears (indicated by `TRANSITION_NOMATCH_MATCH`), or simply when a matching value changes in some way (indicated by `TRANSITION_MATCH_MATCH`). By using this parameter, you can get notifications when services appear, disappear, or are modified. These values can be bitwise OR'ed together to solicit multiple types of matches. In the example, I care about when services start

up that didn't exist previously, so I use
`TRANSITION_NOMATCH_MATCH`.

- The third parameter indicates the object that should receive the events. This object must implement the `RemoteEventListener` interface. Here, I use the instance of the event listener that was created in the constructor.

- The fourth parameter, which is `null` here, is a `MarshalledObject` that will be returned to the caller when the event occurs. Any value that you pass here will be saved by the lookup service and returned to you in the `RemoteEvent` that you receive. By using this parameter, you can associate arbitrary, extra data with the events for which you register. You can use this data in a way that may be meaningful to your application, for example, to distinguish different contexts in which the events were solicited. The `MarshalledObject` class is new in Java 2; see the sidebar if you are unfamiliar with it.

- The final parameter is the requested duration of the lease. Event registrations, just like lookup service registrations, are leased to requestors. In the example, I have requested a 10-minute lease. Again, this example does not have adequate leasing behavior—it never renews its leases, so if you run the service after the client's event registration leases have expired, the client will receive no notifications. This defect will be remedied in the next iteration.

MarshalledObjects

The `MarshalledObject` class is a new addition to Java 2. It represents the serialized form of an object—essentially the raw bits that can be reconstituted into a "live" object upon demand, as well as an optional codebase URL that can be used to retrieve the bytecodes for the serialized object, if needed.

When you write out a `Serializable` object to an output stream, the Java serialization machinery is called to create a representation of the object that can be recreated as needed. A `MarshalledObject` is simply an object that represents the actual bytes that result from the serialization process. The `MarshalledObject` class itself can be thought of as the container for the bytes that result from serialization; the class only supports a few methods—basically just the ability to reconstitute the object, and the ability to compare two `MarshalledObjects` without having to reconstitute them into "live" objects again. Whenenever a `MarshalledObject` is converted into a "real" object, the bytecodes, which are needed to perform the conversion, will be downloaded from the codebase URL specified in the `MarshalledObject` if they aren't available locally.

While the Jini APIs could have used a `Serializable` parameter here, using a `MarshalledObject` can be more efficient—the object has already been serialized at this point, and can be shipped around, and compared without the overhead of reconstituting it into a "live" object each time it is needed. And if the client code wishes to use the same data in each event registration, it can "preserialize" the data into a `MarshalledObject` and use it over and over again.

Once the client has called `notify()`, the lookup service will send it an event whenever there is a match for the combination of template plus transition that was specified. In this example, since `TRANSITION_NOMATCH_MATCH` has been specified, the client will get an event whenever a service that matches the template is added to the lookup service. Whenever such a match occurs, the `notify()` method on the `MyEventListener` class will be invoked. The class implements this method by simply casting the found service to `HelloWorldServiceInterface` and printing out the message returned from the proxy.

The actual event that gets delivered when a match occurs is a subclass of `RemoteEvent` called `ServiceEvent`. So the implementation of `notify()` casts the event to a `ServiceEvent`, which contains detailed and specific information about the match. The event is set so that its source is the lookup service that matched the query. The `ServiceEvent` also has a `getServiceItem()` method that returns the service item that caused the event (or null if the event was sent because of a service item disappearing), a `getServiceID()` method that returns the ID of the service that caused the event, and a `getTransition()` method that returns the type of transition that caused the event to be sent. Here, the program gets the service item from the event so that it can fetch and use the proxy.

With the addition of this bit of code, I've made this little distributed system much more robust. Now, the client and service can be started in any order.

Compiling and Running the Code

Because the new code uses RMI to provide remote objects, there's one extra step in the compilation process: You need to run the RMI stub generator, called `rmic`, on the class files for the remote code to create "stub" classes for it. These stub classes are used internally by RMI to manage the over-the-wire communication with remote objects, and are downloaded to callers who need to invoke remote methods. Essentially, the stubs provide a bit of code that lives in the caller and takes care of the mechanics of performing the remote method invocation on the remote object. Also, I've added another entity to the system that must export downloadable code—since the client needs to pass the stubs for its listener class to the lookup service, it must export the necessary code so that the lookup service can access it.

Compiling

First, compile the classes. Again, I'll follow the rather intricate steps from before to ensure that unnecessary code sharing is prevented.

On Windows: Compile the client source file, and put the resulting code into `C:\client`.

```
javac -classpath C:\files;
                  C:\jini1_1\lib\jini-core.jar;
                  C:\jini1_1\lib\jini-ext.jar;
                  C:\jini1_1\lib\sun-util.jar;
                  C:\client
       -d C:\client
    C:\files\corejini\chapter5\HelloWorldClientWithEvents.java
```

On UNIX: Compile the client source file, and put the resulting code into `/files/client`.

```
javac -classpath /files:
                 /files/jini1_1/lib/jini-core.jar:
                 /files/jini1_1/lib/jini-ext.jar:
                 /files/jini1_1/lib/sun-util.jar:
                 /files/client
     -d /files/client
  /files/corejini/chapter5/HelloWorldClientWithEvents.java
```

Generating the RMI Stubs

Generating the RMI stubs is an easy task—one call to the `rmic` stubs compiler will do the trick, producing the code that will allow the lookup service to call the `notify()` method in the client remotely. You do, however, now need to create a new directory for this downloadable code that the *client* will provide. Although you created a directory for downloadable code from the *service* in the last example, here you need to export code from the client so that the lookup service can call the client. The stubs code necessary to call the `notify()` method remotely needs to be downloadable to callers, so it'll have to go in this download directory.

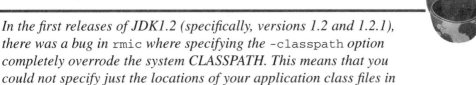

Core Alert: Bug in rmic in JDK1.2 and JDK1.2.1

In the first releases of JDK1.2 (specifically, versions 1.2 and 1.2.1), there was a bug in `rmic` *where specifying the* -classpath *option completely overrode the system CLASSPATH. This means that you could not specify just the locations of your application class files in the* -classpath *argument, or* rmic *would complain that it could not find various core Java classes (such as* java.lang.Object*).*

If you're using one of these earlier versions, you'll need to work around the bug by explicitly passing the JDK's rt.jar *file (found in the Java distribution in the* jre/lib *directory) to the* -classpath *option.*

Actually, a better solution if you're still using one of these earlier releases, is to consider upgrading to JDK 1.2.2 or 1.3 or later, which do not have the bug.

On Windows: Generate the RMI stubs. Remember that if you're using JDK 1.2 or 1.2.1, you'll have to pass `rt.jar` on the CLASSPATH also.

```
rmic -classpath C:\jini1_1\lib\jini-core.jar;
               C:\jini1_1\lib\jini-ext.jar;
               C:\jini1_1\lib\sun-util.jar;
               C:\client
    -d C:\client
corejini.chapter5.HelloWorldClientWithEvents.MyEventListener
```

On UNIX: Generate the RMI stubs. Remember that if you're using JDK 1.2 or 1.2.1, you'll have to pass `rt.jar` on the CLASSPATH also.

```
rmic -classpath /files/jini1_1/lib/jini-core.jar:
               /files/jini1_1/lib/jini-ext.jar:
               /files/jini1_1/lib/sun-util.jar:
               /files/client
    -d /files/client
corejini.chapter5.HelloWorldClientWithEvents.MyEventListener
```

Once you've run `rmic`, you can look in the `client` directory to see the generated stub file in the `corejini/chapter5` directory.

```
HelloWorldClientWithEvents$MyEventListener_Stub.class
```

This class file must be located in a directory that is accessible directly by the client, and it must also be in the `client-dl` directory so that it can be downloaded by the services that the client solicits events from. So, copy the class file into the `client-dl` directory so that it can be exported to a lookup service.

On Windows:

```
mkdir C:\client-dl
mkdir C:\client-dl\corejini
mkdir C:\client-dl\corejini\chapter5
cd C:\client\corejini\chapter5
copy HelloWorldClientWithEvents$MyEventListener_Stub.class
     C:\client-dl\corejini\chapter5
```

On UNIX:

```
mkdir /files/client-dl
mkdir /files/client-dl/corejini
mkdir /files/client-dl/corejini/chapter5
cd /files/client/corejini/chapter5
cp HelloWorldClientWithEvents\$MyEventListener_Stubb.class
     /files/client-dl/corejini/chapter5
```

Start an HTTP Server to Export the Client's Downloadable Code

You'll now need to start an HTTP server that can serve up the RMI stub files that the client needs to export. When you run the client, you'll set a codebase property that tells any interested parties where to find this code relative to the HTTP server. Since the client will be sending stubs to the Jini lookup service so that the lookup service can call the client's methods remotely, you'll actually be downloading a bit of custom behavior into a core Jini service. Nifty!

Once again, you may need to use a different port number, if you've got multiple HTTP services running on one machine. In this book, I'll use port 8086 for the HTTP server that exports client code.

On Windows: Launch the HTTP server that comes with Jini:

```
java -jar C:\jini1_1\lib\tools.jar
    -dir C:\client-dl -verbose -port 8086
```

On UNIX: Launch the HTTP server that comes with Jini:

```
java -jar /files/jini1_1/lib/tools.jar
    -dir /files/client-dl -verbose -port 8086
```

Running

Now you can run the example programs. Running the examples works just like before, except that you can now run the client and the service in either order. You can use the exact same service you created earlier with this new client.

But since you want to see the event behavior in action, run the client first. Make sure that you replace "myhost" in the codebase URL with the hostname on which the client's HTTP server is running; this is the HTTP server you just started. Also note that, unlike the previous version of the client, here you have to set a codebase, since you need to tell the lookup service where to download code from.

On Windows:

```
java -cp C:\jini1_1\lib\jini-core.jar;
        C:\jini1_1\lib\jini-ext.jar;
        C:\jini1_1\lib\sun-util.jar;
        C:\client
    -Djava.rmi.server.codebase=http://myhost:8086/
    -Djava.security.policy=C:\policy
    corejini.chapter5.HelloWorldClientWithEvents
```

On UNIX:

```
java -cp /files/jini1_1/lib/jini-core.jar:
        /files/jini1_1/lib/jini-ext.jar:
        /files/jini1_1/lib/sun-util.jar:
        /files/client
    -Djava.rmi.server.codebase=http://myhost:8086/
    -Djava.security.policy=/files/policy
    corejini.chapter5.HelloWorldClientWithEvents
```

Finally, you can run the service, just as you did before.

On Windows:

```
java -cp C:\jini1_1\lib\jini-core.jar;
        C:\jini1_1\lib\jini-ext.jar;
        C:\jini1_1\lib\sun-util.jar;
        C:\service
    -Djava.rmi.server.codebase=http://myhost:8085/
    -Djava.security.policy=C:\policy
    corejini.chapter5.HelloWorldService
```

On UNIX:

```
java -cp /files/jini1_1/lib/jini-core.jar:
        /files/jini1_1/lib/jini-ext.jar:
        /files/jini1_1/lib/sun-util.jar:
        /files/service
    -Djava.rmi.server.codebase=http://myhost:8085/
    -Djava.security.policy=/files/policy
    corejini.chapter5.HelloWorldService
```

If there are instances of the service running when the client starts, it will act exactly as it did before. Otherwise, it will simply wait for a `HelloWorldService` to appear, and display nothing.

From the client:

```
No matching service.
```

From the service:

```
discovered a lookup service!
Set serviceID to e91bb61d-b18e-447e-8935-adfd8bd741f5
```

From the client:

```
Got an event from: com.sun.jini.reggie.Registrar-
Proxy@9b559fd1
Got a matching service.
Its message is: Hello, world!
```

You should see the client detect the start of the new service and display the output from the proxy.

In this example, the client and the service can be started in any order. There's only one more necessary extension: The code must ensure that its leases, on both lookup and event registrations, are properly renewed. I'll solve this in the next iteration.

"Hello, World" with Leasing

The final major flaw in the example program is that it never renews—or even checks—the leases returned to it for lookup service registrations or event solicitations. To address this problem, the service should be extended so that it tracks the leases that are returned from each lookup service it registers itself with, and renews these before they expire, for as long as it wishes to make the service available. On the client side, the client should similarly renew its leases on its event solicitations from the lookup services for as long as it wishes to be informed about new services appearing. Finally, both applications should be "well-behaved" by canceling any leases they hold when they shut down. While this isn't a strict requirement—because the whole idea of leases is that they provide a way for the system to clean up after applications that do not or cannot clean up after themselves—it does allow the lease grantors to free up resources as soon as possible. I don't do this in these examples—because they never shut down—but canceling your leases just before you terminate is an easy task in most applications.

Doing lease management "by hand" in Jini can be a cumbersome aspect of developing clients and services. I've done it here to show the fundamentals of how leasing works, but fortunately there are some very nice helper utilities that take away most of the burden of leasing.

A Simple Approach

I will discuss strategies for effective leasing, including the use of external "leasing services," in Chapter 12. For now, though, I will add leasing directly to the "Hello, World" service and client applications. Once again, I'll subclass the code already written to add the new functionality.

Leasing is similar in both the client and service cases: The program needs to keep track of the leases that have been returned to it—for event registrations in the client, and for lookup service registrations in the service—and then renew them before they expire. In the earlier applications, you saw that the program started a thread that essentially did nothing. This thread was only used to keep the process alive so that the application could receive discovery or event notifications, even after `main()` had "run off the end" and completed.

In the next examples, I put this thread to good use. To use leasing properly, this thread will sit in the background, waking up when needed to renew leases. As you shall see, the structures of both the lease-augmented client and service are similar. First, take a look at a version of the "Hello, World" service, extended to do better leasing, as shown in Listing 5–6.

Listing 5–6 `HelloWorldServiceWithLeases.java`

```
// Extend HelloWorldService to renew its service
// registration leases.

package corejini.chapter5;

import net.jini.core.lookup.ServiceRegistrar;
import net.jini.core.lookup.ServiceRegistration;
import net.jini.core.lease.Lease;
import net.jini.core.lease.UnknownLeaseException;
import java.util.ArrayList;
import java.util.Iterator;
import java.io.IOException;
import java.rmi.RemoteException;

public class HelloWorldServiceWithLeases
    extends HelloWorldService {
    protected Thread leaseThread = null;

    public HelloWorldServiceWithLeases()
        throws IOException {
    }
```

```java
// Not only register, but also cause the lease
// thread to wake up.
protected void registerWithLookup(ServiceRegistrar
                                  lusvc) {
    super.registerWithLookup(lusvc);
    leaseThread.interrupt();
}
// run now maintains our leases
public void run() {
    while (true) {
        try {
            long sleepTime = computeSleepTime();
            Thread.sleep(sleepTime);
            renewLeases();
        } catch (InterruptedException ex) {
        }
    }
}

// Figure out how long to sleep.
protected synchronized long computeSleepTime() {
    long soonestExpiration = Long.MAX_VALUE;
    Iterator iter = registrations.keySet().iterator();
    while (iter.hasNext()) {
        Lease l = ((ServiceRegistration)
                   iter.next()).getLease();
        if (l.getExpiration() - (20 * 1000) <
            soonestExpiration) {
            soonestExpiration = l.getExpiration() -
                                (20 * 1000);
        }
    }

    long now = System.currentTimeMillis();

    if (now >= soonestExpiration) {
        return 0;
    } else {
        return soonestExpiration - now;
    }
}
```

Listing 5–6 `HelloWorldServiceWithLeases.java` (continued)

```java
    // Do the work of lease renewal.
    protected synchronized void renewLeases() {
        long now = System.currentTimeMillis();
        ArrayList deadLeases = new ArrayList();

        Iterator keys = registrations.keySet().iterator();
        while (keys.hasNext()) {
            ServiceRegistrar lu =
                (ServiceRegistrar) keys.next();
            ServiceRegistration r =
                (ServiceRegistration) registrations.get(lu);
            Lease l = r.getLease();
            if (now <= l.getExpiration() &&
                now >= l.getExpiration() - (20 * 1000)) {
                try {
                    System.out.println("Renewing lease.");
                    l.renew(LEASE_TIME);
                } catch (Exception ex) {
                    System.err.println("Couldn't renew: " +
                                        ex.getMessage());
                    deadLeases.add(lu);
                }
            }
        }

        // clean up after any leases that died
        for (int i=0, size=deadLeases.size(); i<size; i++){
            registrations.remove(deadLeases.get(i));
        }
    }

    // Create the service and start the leasing
    // thread.
    public static void main(String args[]) {
        try {
            HelloWorldServiceWithLeases hws =
                new HelloWorldServiceWithLeases();
            hws.leaseThread = new Thread(hws);
            hws.leaseThread.start();
        } catch (IOException ex) {
            System.out.println("Couldn't create service: " +
                                ex.getMessage());
        }
    }
}
```

While the code for the leasing-enabled version of the service has grown a bit, most of the changes are fairly easy to understand. I'll start by looking at the heart of the changes, in the `run()` method.

Prior to this example, the service process created a new thread that essentially did nothing but sleep. While it accomplished no useful work, this thread was actually required to keep the JVM from exiting, because without a live, non-daemon thread, the JVM will exit as soon as `main()` returns. In all of the examples, `main()` simply creates an object representing the service, starts a new thread of control, and then returns (by simply "running off the end" of the available statements).

Here, however, I actually have a need for a thread to do some work. In the new service, `run()` handles lease management. The new implementation of `run()`, which overrides the one from the original `HelloWorldService`, basically loops forever. For each iteration, it determines how long it should sleep until it needs to do some leasing work, sleeps for that amount of time, and then wakes up to renew any leases that are coming due.

Look at how this works in more detail. Ignoring the code that handles `InterruptedException` for the moment, you see that for each iteration in `run()`, the program first computes the time it should sleep, via `computeSleepTime()`. This method iterates through all of the leases for service registrations that have been received from lookup services and finds the one that expires the soonest. Once it has determined which lease is coming due first, it computes how long it has to sleep in order to wake up just before the lease expires. To do this, it stores in the variable `now` the current time (in milliseconds) and compares it to the needed wake-up time. If the method has already missed the next wake-up time, it returns 0, indicating that the thread should not sleep at all, but rather should go ahead and try to renew the expiring lease if it can (chances are it may be too late if this happens, though). Otherwise, the method returns the number of milliseconds the thread should sleep.

You'll note that this code, rather than using the "raw" expiration time for leases, "fudges" the amount a bit. Here, it adjusts the expiration time by 20 seconds. This is meant to give time to do any processing needed to send the renewal message, allow transit time over the network to the lease grantor, and provide a bit more time just to be safe.

After figuring the amount of time the thread should sleep, `run()` sleeps for that amount, and then calls `renewLeases()` to do the actual lease renewal.

The `renewLeases()` method again iterates through all the leases. Whenever it finds a lease that expires at any point between now and now plus the 20-second fudge factor, it tries to renew the lease for the 10-minute lease time used in all these examples. If the lease renewal fails for any reason (such as the lease grantor is unwilling to renew it, or the network is down), `renewLeases()` adds it to a list of "dead leases" until it finishes all the renewal attempts. Once it's done with renewals, it then walks through the dead leases and removes them from the list of registrations.

Core Note: Handling "dead" leases

This example takes the simple and expedient approach of simply disposing of troublesome leases. An actual service, however, would probably be coded to be a little more persistent than this.

For example, a service may continue to retry the renewal for some period of time. If the registration is with a lookup service that is especially important—perhaps because a human user has told the service to register itself there, for instance—then it may periodically try to re-register itself there.

This example shows lease management in its most basic form—simply waking up periodically to renew leases before they expire. You've seen how `run()` works by computing a sleep time, sleeping, and then renewing all the leases that are about to expire.

But what happens to this code when a new lease is added after the thread starts? Remember that discovery is an asynchronous process. New lookup registrations may happen at any arbitrary point in the future, not just when you start to run the lease thread. If a new lease is added while the thread is blocked in `sleep()`, it may need to wake up sooner than it otherwise would. Perhaps the new lease will expire before the thread is due to wake. To deal with this case robustly, the code should wake the sleeping thread and recompute the sleep interval whenever a new lease is added.

The key to handling this case is already in the code you see here. As you may have guessed, the `try-catch` block to handle the `InterruptedException` in `run()` has something to do with it.

Whenever a new registration is done in the `registerWithLookup()` method, the code not only calls the superclass version of this method to cause the registration to happen and be recorded, it also interrupts the thread that's doing lease management. The `run()` method, because it catches and handles `Interrupte-dException`, will simply restart another iteration of its internal loop when it is interrupted. This causes the sleep time to be recomputed, which will correctly account for any change in the set of managed leases. Notice how the `main()` routine stores the `Thread` object for the lease management thread in the `Hel-`

loWorldServiceWithLeases instance so that this interrupt process can happen.

Next, let's move on to the client example. Whereas the service used leases to handle its registrations with lookup services, the client uses leases to handle its registrations for events. As you shall see in Listing 5–7, while the basic implementation details are just a bit different, the "big picture" of leasing is exactly the same in the client as it is in the service.

Listing 5–7 HelloWorldClientWithLeases.java

```java
// Extend the client to renew its event registration
// leases.

package corejini.chapter5;

import net.jini.core.lookup.ServiceRegistrar;
import net.jini.core.event.RemoteEvent;
import net.jini.core.event.RemoteEventListener;
import net.jini.core.event.EventRegistration;
import net.jini.core.lease.Lease;
import net.jini.core.lease.UnknownLeaseException;
import java.util.ArrayList;
import java.io.IOException;
import java.rmi.RemoteException;

public class HelloWorldClientWithLeases
    extends HelloWorldClientWithEvents {
    protected ArrayList eventRegs = new ArrayList();
    protected Thread leaseThread = null;

    public HelloWorldClientWithLeases()
        throws RemoteException, IOException {
    }
```

Listing 5–7 `HelloWorldClientWithLeases.java` (continued)

```java
// When we register for events, add the event's
// registration to the set of managed
// registrations.
protected void registerForEvents(ServiceRegistrar lu)
    throws RemoteException {
    EventRegistration evreg;

    evreg = lu.notify(template,
            ServiceRegistrar.TRANSITION_NOMATCH_MATCH,
            eventCatcher, null, LEASE_TIME);

    eventRegs.add(evreg);
    leaseThread.interrupt();
}

// Run maintains our leases.
public void run() {
    while (true) {
        try {
            long sleepTime = computeSleepTime();
            Thread.sleep(sleepTime);
            renewLeases();
        } catch (InterruptedException ex) {
        }
    }
}

// Figure out how long to sleep.
protected synchronized long computeSleepTime() {
    long soonestExpiration = Long.MAX_VALUE;
    for (int i=0, size=eventRegs.size(); i<size; i++) {
        Lease l = ((EventRegistration)
                    eventRegs.get(i)).getLease();
        if (l.getExpiration() - (20 * 1000) <
            soonestExpiration) {
            soonestExpiration = l.getExpiration() -
                                (20 * 1000);
        }
    }
```

Listing 5–7 `HelloWorldClientWithLeases.java` (continued)

```java
        long now = System.currentTimeMillis();

        if (now >= soonestExpiration) {
            return 0;
        } else {
            return soonestExpiration - now;
        }
    }


    // Do the lease renewal work.
    protected synchronized void renewLeases() {
        long now = System.currentTimeMillis();
        ArrayList deadLeases = new ArrayList();

        for (int i=0 , size=eventRegs.size(); i<size; i++) {
            Lease l = ((EventRegistration)
                        eventRegs.get(i)).getLease();
            if (now <= l.getExpiration() &&
                now >= l.getExpiration() - (20 * 1000)) {
                try {
                    System.out.println("Renewing lease.");
                    l.renew(LEASE_TIME);
                } catch (Exception ex) {
                    System.err.println("Couldn't renew: " +
                                        ex.getMessage());
                    deadLeases.add(eventRegs.get(i));
                }
            }
        }

        // Clean up after any leases that died.
        for (int i=0, size=deadLeases.size(); i<size; i++) {
            eventRegs.remove(deadLeases.get(i));
        }
    }
```

Listing 5–7 `HelloWorldClientWithLeases.java` (continued)

```
// Start the service.
public static void main(String args[]) {
    try {
        HelloWorldClientWithLeases hwc =
            new HelloWorldClientWithLeases();
        hwc.leaseThread = new Thread(hwc);
        hwc.leaseThread.start();
    } catch (IOException ex) {
        System.out.println("Couldn't create client: " +
                            ex.getMessage());
    }
}
```

The extensions to the client code to do leasing are much the same as the extensions required in the service code. Here again you see an extended `run()` method, which allows a thread to do lease management duties. You also see the use of interrupts to cause the leasing thread to recompute the required sleep time after a change in the set of managed leases.

In fact, the only real difference here is that the client and the service use different data structures in which to store their registrations, because they're storing different types of registrations—`ServiceRegistrations` in one case and `EventRegistrations` in the other. So the code to iterate over them is a bit different. The fact that two applications serving two very different roles—client and service—in a Jini community have nearly identical lease management code is a big hint that lease management can be largely automated with some helper classes. You'll see how to do this in Chapter 12.

For now, though, you've seen the basics of how to manage leases in both clients and services, and extended the simple "Hello, World" examples through several iterations to the point that they can become full-fledged participants in a Jini community.

Compiling and Running the Code

You've already set yourself up with HTTP servers for the downloadable code from the services (their proxies), the downloadable code from the clients (the stubs for their event listeners), and the core services (the lookup service). To run the leasing examples, all you have to do is compile the client and the service into their appropriate directories. This extension of the "Hello, World" examples adds no *new* downloadable code, so you don't have to copy any class files into the download directories that are served by the HTTP servers.

Compiling

Compile the client and the service just as in the previous examples. Here again, I'm sending the class files that result from the compilation into separate directories, to ensure that the class paths of the two programs are isolated, just as they would be when the programs are running on two different machines on the network.

On Windows: Compile the client source file, and put the resulting code into C:\client.

```
javac -classpath C:\files;
                 C:\jini1_1\lib\jini-core.jar;
                 C:\jini1_1\lib\jini-ext.jar;
                 C:\jini1_1\lib\sun-util.jar;
                 C:\client
      -d C:\client
  C:\files\corejini\chapter5\HelloWorldClientWithLeases.java
```

And then compile the service source file, putting the resulting class files into C:\service.

```
javac -classpath C:\files;
                 C:\jini1_1\lib\jini-core.jar;
                 C:\jini1_1\lib\jini-ext.jar;
                 C:\jini1_1\lib\sun-util.jar;
                 C:\service
      -d C:\service
  C:\files\corejini\chapter5\HelloWorldServiceWithLeases.jav
a
```

On UNIX: Compile the client source file, and put the resulting code into /files/client.

```
javac -classpath /files:
                 /files/jini1_1/lib/jini-core.jar:
                 /files/jini1_1/lib/jini-ext.jar:
                 /files/jini1_1/lib/sun-util.jar:
                 /files/client
      -d /files/client
```

```
/files/corejini/chapter5/HelloWorldClientWithLeases.java
```

And then compile the service source file, putting the resulting class files into
`/files/service`.

```
javac -classpath /files:
                 /files/jini1_1/lib/jini-core.jar:
                 /files/jini1_1/lib/jini-ext.jar:
                 /files/jini1_1/lib/sun-util.jar:
                 /files/service
    -d /files/service
    /files/corejini/chapter5/HelloWorldServiceWithLeases.java
```

Running

Now you're set to run the extended example programs. Since the client in this
case extends the earlier version that uses events, you can run these programs in
either order. And, unlike previous versions, these programs will continually
renew their leases so you don't have to run them within a few minutes of one
another!

On Windows: Run the service and the client in either order. Here I'm starting
the service first.

```
java -cp C:\jini1_1\lib\jini-core.jar;
         C:\jini1_1\lib\jini-ext.jar;
         C:\jini1_1\lib\sun-util.jar;
         C:\service
    -Djava.rmi.server.codebase=http://myhost:8085/
    -Djava.security.policy=C:\policy
    corejini.chapter5.HelloWorldServiceWithLeases
```

```
java -cp C:\jini1_1\lib\jini-core.jar;
         C:\jini1_1\lib\jini-ext.jar;
         C:\jini1_1\lib\sun-util.jar;
         C:\client
    -Djava.rmi.server.codebase=http://myhost:8086/
    -Djava.security.policy=C:\policy
    corejini.chapter5.HelloWorldClientWithLeases
```

On UNIX: Run the service and the client in either order. Here I'm starting the
service first.

```
java -cp /files/jini1_1/lib/jini-core.jar:
         /files/jini1_1/lib/jini-ext.jar:
```

```
      /files/jini1_1/lib/sun-util.jar:
      /files/service
-Djava.rmi.server.codebase=http://myhost:8085/
-Djava.security.policy=/files/policy
corejini.chapter5.HelloWorldServiceWithLeases

java -cp /files/jini1_1/lib/jini-core.jar:
      /files/jini1_1/lib/jini-ext.jar:
      /files/jini1_1/lib/sun-util.jar:
      /files/client
-Djava.rmi.server.codebase=http://myhost:8086/
-Djava.security.policy=/files/policy
corejini.chapter5.HelloWorldClientWithLeases
```

The output of running this client and service pair is much the same as in the first example: The client will contact the lookup service, download the service proxy (including getting the code for the proxy from the HTTP server associated with the service), and run it. But in this case, both the client and the service will periodically renew their leases. You should see output like the following:

From the service:

```
discovered a lookup service!
Set serviceID to e91bb61d-b18e-447e-8935-adfd8bd741f5
Renewing lease.
Renewing lease.
Renewing lease.
```

From the client:

```
Got matching service.
Its message is: Hello, world!
Renewing lease.
Renewing lease.
Renewing lease.
```

These programs will continue to renew their leases indefinitely, until you kill them.

The last example of the chapter doesn't focus on any new Jini concepts per se. Instead it shows an alternative architecture for the "Hello, World" service that more closely mirrors the way a "real" Jini service will be built: It consists of a separate "back-end" portion of the service that the proxy communicates with. In this last example, you'll learn how to use RMI to create proxies that can communicate with off-machine resources.

Using a Proxy that Communicates with a Back-End Process

In this last example of the chapter, I'll focus on a new architecture for this little "Hello, World" example, one that is closer to what you're likely to see in "real world" Jini services. In this version of the service, the proxy that clients download will communicate to a "back-end" server process to get the messages it will return.

While this example—like the other versions of the "Hello, World" service—is a bit contrived because the actual role the service performs is so simple, it does represent a very realistic strategy for building Jini services. Very often a long-lived server process will run on a machine someplace, and the proxies it publishes allow clients to connect to it over the network. And, of course, since the proxy is defined by the service writer and downloaded dynamically by clients, the clients do not need to know how—or even whether—the proxy communicates over a network or not.

An architecture like this one can arise when there is some remote physical resource (like a printer) that the proxy must communicate with, or when the computation that the service must do is hefty enough that it makes little sense for the proxy to do it itself, or if there is a need to coordinate multiple clients through some central server.

In this example, the proxy will communicate with the back-end server via RMI, although this is not a requirement. You could just as easily define a proxy that communicates using raw TCP/IP sockets or CORBA or whatever. But RMI is an easy solution for a pure-Java system and, since RMI and RMI concepts are used throughout Sun's sample implementation of Jini, I've chosen to use it in this example to illustrate some basics of how it works. If you're just getting started with RMI, you might want to read Appendix A, which gives a more detailed introduction to the technology.

One nice thing about this last version of the service is that, even though the architecture here is quite different than previous versions, very little code has to change. The `HelloWorldInterface` used as the interface for previous proxies is used here too. So the same clients that happily used the old, purely local proxy will now find and use the new networked proxy. The service wrapper will, of course, have to define and publish this new proxy that has the smarts to connect up over the network. And, in addition to its Jini responsibilities, it'll have to set up an RMI remote object—meaning an object that can have its methods invoked remotely—that the proxy will communicate with.

I should note, just in case you're wondering, that this version of the example doesn't really show off any new Jini techniques per se. But it does show some important ancilliary techniques that will be handy for any Jini programmer.

Defining the Remote Protocol

The first thing to do is to define the protocol that the proxy will use to communicate back to the server (Listing 5-8). RMI defines communication protocols via Java interfaces that extend the `java.rmi.Remote` interface. (Again, see Appendix A if you want some background reading on RMI. If you feel comfortable with this short example, though, read on!)

Listing 5-8 BackendProtocol.java

```
// Define a communication protocol that
// allows the proxy to talk to the back-
// end service.

package corejini.chapter5;

import java.rmi.Remote;
import java.rmi.RemoteException;

public interface BackendProtocol extends Remote {
    public String fetchString() throws RemoteException;
}
```

This is a simple interface with only one method, called `fetchString()`. This method will be invoked by the proxy on the remote object in the server to return a new string to display. Note that the method is declared to raise `RemoteException`; this exception will be raised if there is some network communication failure at any point when the proxy tries to invoke the method.

Defining a New Network-Aware Proxy

The next step is to create a new proxy that, rather than simply returning a string, will communicate with a remote object that implements the `Backend-`

`Interface` to get the string to return. This new proxy is called, unimaginatively, `HelloWorldServiceProxy2` (Listing 5-9)

Listing 5–9 HelloWorldServiceProxy2.java

```
// A "smarter" proxy for the "Hello, World" service.
// This one knows how to talk to a remote object
// that implements the BackendProtocol interface.

package corejini.chapter5;

import java.io.Serializable;
import java.rmi.Remote;
import java.rmi.RemoteException;

public class HelloWorldServiceProxy2
    implements HelloWorldServiceInterface,
            Serializable {
    protected BackendProtocol backend;

    public HelloWorldServiceProxy2() {
    }

    public HelloWorldServiceProxy2(BackendProtocol
                                    backend){
        this.backend = backend;
    }

    // Note getMessage() now calls backend.fetchString()
    public String getMessage() {
        try {
            return backend.fetchString();
        } catch (RemoteException ex) {
            return "Couldn't contact backend: " +
                    ex.getMessage();
        }
    }
}
```

The first thing to note here is that the new proxy isn't much more complicated than the original one! Once again, the proxy implements the same `HelloWorldServiceInterface` as well as `Serializable`. There's a no-argument constructor here, since I'm again following my habit of creating such constructors for all `Serializable` classes.

The second constructor takes a parameter of type `BackendProtocol`. As you'll see when I discuss the service back end itself, this constructor will be used to intialize the proxy with a reference to the service's remote object before it is registered with lookup services. By initializing the proxy with a reference to an object implementing `BackendProtocol`, it can be serialized and stored in a lookup service, and then be ready to use once it is downloaded by a client.

The "smarts" of the proxy are in its new implementation of the `getMessage()` method. Unlike the first version, which simply returned a string, this version invokes the `fetchString()` method on the remote object to get a string to return.

Because the proxy is now communicating with a remote object, network failures can occur. Therefore, the `getMessage()` method has to catch any `RemoteExceptions` that may be raised during the course of getting the string. If an exception occurs, there is no way of returning the "correct" string to the caller, so the code returns the text of the exception.

Core Tip: Plan on remoteness early

There's an interesting and subtle design error that this code raises. The old version of the proxy didn't declare any exceptions as being raised from its `getMessage()` method—and, in fact, the interface that it implements says that it cannot raise any exceptions in this method.

So in the example here, you're forced into a bad situation—the only way to report the error to the client is to return it through the "normal" channels used for data: as the return value of the function. In a "real-life" service, you would not want to expect your clients to be able to distinguish strings that represent real data from strings that represent exceptional conditions.

Likewise, you could raise a nondeclared run-time exception here. But this would almost certainly cause any clients to exit immediately, as few run-time exceptions are caught by programmers.

The situation here points to an important design goal for defining the interfaces for your services: Decide early whether any potential implementation of your service may involve remoteness. Even though your particular implementation may not require remote communication now, some future implementation may need it. And, because Java requires the possibility of `RemoteExceptions` to be

*declared in the interface, it is extremely hard to evolve a system
toward remoteness if the design didn't account for it up front.*

Defining the New Service Wrapper

The only thing left to do at this point is define a new service wrapper (Listing
5-10). This new wrapper extends the last one, HelloWorldServiceWithLe-
ases, and so it gets proper leasing behavior for free.

The only extra work that this new wrapper has to do is define and create a new
remote object that implements BackendProtocol to respond to fetch-
String() requests from the service's proxies, and then to create and publish the
new network-aware proxy, instead of the old "network-dumb" one.

Listing 5-10 HelloWorldServiceBackend.java

```java
// A version of HelloWorldService that creates a "back-end"
// remote object for the proxy to communicate with.

package corejini.chapter5;

import net.jini.core.lookup.ServiceItem;
import java.io.IOException;
import java.io.Serializable;
import java.rmi.Remote;
import java.rmi.RemoteException;
import java.rmi.server.UnicastRemoteObject;


// HelloWorldServiceBackend is the "wrapper" application
// that creates a remote object and publishes a proxy that
// can refer to it.
```

Listing 5-10 HelloWorldServiceBackend.java

```java
public class HelloWorldServiceBackend
    extends HelloWorldServiceWithLeases {

    // Backend is the RMI server object that receives
    // remote method invocations from the proxy.  It simply
    // cycles through a set of strings each time it is
    // called.

    static class Backend extends UnicastRemoteObject
        implements BackendProtocol {
        protected int nextMessage = 0;
        protected String[] messages = { "Hello, World",
                                        "Goodbye Cruel World",
                                        "What's Up, Doc?" };

        // Nothing for the constructor to do but let the
        // superclass constructor run.
        Backend() throws RemoteException {
        }

        public String fetchString() throws RemoteException{
            System.out.println("Back-end: fetching string");
            String str =  messages[nextMessage];
            nextMessage = (nextMessage + 1) %
                            messages.length;
            return str;
        }
    }

    // Constructor doesn't have to do anything
    // except let the superclass constructor run.
    public HelloWorldServiceBackend() throws IOException {
    }
```

```
Listing 5-10 HelloWorldServiceBackend.java

    // Since we're using a different proxy, we have to
    // reimplement createProxy().  This new version creates
    // a remote server object that will receive method
    // invocations from the proxy, and creates a
    // HelloWorldServiceProxy2 object that refers to it.
    protected HelloWorldServiceInterface createProxy() {
        try {
            BackendProtocol backend = new Backend();
            return new HelloWorldServiceProxy2(backend);
        } catch (RemoteException ex) {
            System.err.println("Error creating backend: " +
                                ex.getMessage());
            ex.printStackTrace();
            System.exit(1);
            return null;          // NOT REACHED
        }
    }


    // Main creates the wrapper and starts the lease
    // thread.
    public static void main(String args[]) {
        try {
            HelloWorldServiceBackend hws =
                new HelloWorldServiceBackend();
            hws.leaseThread = new Thread(hws);
            hws.leaseThread.start();
        } catch (IOException ex) {
            System.out.println("Couldn't create service: " +
                                ex.getMessage());
        }
    }
}
```

The first important bit of this code defines the remote object that proxies will call out to to get their strings. The class `Backend` extends `java.rmi.UnicastRemoteObject`. This is the most common superclass for objects that can have their methods called remotely. The constructor for `Backend` is declared to raise `java.rmi.RemoteException` since the constructor for `UnicastRemoteObject` may raise this exception.

The implementation of `fetchString()` cycles through a set of three possible strings it may return. Here is an example—albeit a simple one—of how a back-end service can be used to coordinate multiple clients. The server will cycle through these strings, returning a different one to each request in turn, no matter how many clients are connected to it. This same sort of strategy could be used to coordinate a locked resource among several clients, for example.

The other important method here is `createProxy()`. Recall back from the very first version of the "Hello, World" service that the code that published the proxy called `createProxy()` to get the object to publish. This design was intentional, to allow subclasses an easy way to use new proxies.

The prior implementation of `createProxy()` returned an instance of the first `HelloWorldProxy`. This new version first creates the remote object—an instance of `Backend`—that answers calls from the proxy. It then creates and returns an instance of the *new* proxy, `HelloWorldProxy2`, initializing it with a reference to the newly-created remote object.

The code in the service's superclass will register this object with a lookup service, causing it to be serialized and stored there until a client needs it. The reference to the remote object will arrive intact when the client gets it, allowing the proxy to do its job by calling on the remote object it was initialized with when it was created in the back end.

Compiling and Running the Example

Getting this example up and running is basically the same as that for any of the previous examples.

Compiling

Compile the Java source files, putting the resulting code into the service's implementation code directory. All the class files resulting from the compilation will be used by the service, and should go in the service's implementation directory. Additionally, the new proxy defined by this service, as well as the classes it needs, must reside in the service's directory of exportable, downloadable code so that it can be fetched by lookup services and clients. So, after compilation, copy the class file for the proxy and the classes it references out to the export directory.

On Windows:

```
javac -classpath C:\files;
              C:\jini1_1\lib\jini-core.jar;
              C:\jini1_1\lib\jini-ext.jar;
              C:\jini1_1\lib\sun-util.jar;
              C:\service
```

```
    -d C:\service
  C:\files\corejini\chapter5\HelloWorldServiceBackend.java
  C:\files\corejini\chapter5\BackendProtocol.java
  C:\files\corejini\chapter5\HelloWorldServiceProxy2.java

cd C:\service\corejini\chapter5
copy HelloWorldServiceProxy2.class
C:\service-dl\corejini\chapter5
copy BackendProtocol.class C:\service-dl\corejini\chapter5
```

On UNIX:

```
javac -classpath /files:
                /files/jini1_1/lib/jini-core.jar:
                /files/jini1_1/lib/jini-ext.jar:
                /files/jini1_1/lib/sun-util.jar:
                /files/service
  -d /files/service
  /files/corejini/chapter5/HelloWorldServiceBackend.java
  /files/corejini/chapter5/BackendProtocol.java
  /files/corejini/chapter5/HelloWorldServiceProxy2.java

cd /files/service/corejini/chapter5
cp HelloWorldServiceProxy2.class
  /files/service-dl/corejini/chapter5
cp BackendProtocol.class /files/service-dl/corejini/chapter5
```

Generating the RMI Stubs

The service uses a nested class, `Backend`, that implements the remote protocol that the proxy will talk to. Since the methods on this nested class will be callable remotely, you need to invoke the RMI stubs compiler (`rmic`) on it to generate the class file for the stubs that callers will use to talk to the back-end object. The generated stubs file will need to be accessible to the service (which means that it should live in the `service` directory), and must be downloadable as well (which means that it should be copied into the `service-dl` directory).

Remember the **Core Alert** from the previous event example: If you're running JDK 1.2 or 1.2.1, there is a bug in `rmic` that requires you to pass the core Java libraries in `rt.jar` via the `-classpath` argument.

On Windows:

```
rmic -classpath C:\jini1_1\lib\jini-core.jar;
                C:\jini1_1\lib\jini-ext.jar;
                C:\jini1_1\lib\sun-util.jar;
```

```
            C:\service
      -d C:\service
corejini.chapter5.HelloWorldServiceBackend.Backend


cd C:\service\corejini\chapter5
copy HelloWorldServiceBackend$Backend_Stub.class
      C:\service-dl\corejini\chapter5
```

On UNIX:

```
rmic -classpath /files/jini1_1/lib/jini-core.jar:
                /files/jini1_1/lib/jini-ext.jar:
                /files/jini1_1/lib/sun-util.jar:
                /files/service
      -d /files/service
corejini.chapter5.HelloWorldServiceBackend.Backend


cd /files/service/corejini/chapter5
cp HelloWorldServiceBackend\$Backend_Stub.class
      /files/service-dl/corejini/chapter5
```

After running `rmic` and copying the file, you should see that the stub file is located in `service-dl` under the `corejini/chapter5` subdirectory.

```
HelloWorldServiceBackend$Backend_Stub.class
```

Now that the service's code is in the implementation directory, and the necessary class files are in the export directory, you're ready to run!

Running

You can start the service just as before. For the client, you can "reuse" any of the clients you've used before—since the new service simply provides a reimplementation of *exactly* the same interface as before, the clients are none the wiser. This is the power of Jini: You can swap particular implementations of a service in and out at run time, and clients will simply use whichever one they find that meets their requirements.

Next it's time to run the service and the client. Here I'm reusing the leasing client from the previous example.

On Windows:

```
java -cp C:\jini1_1\lib\jini-core.jar;
        C:\jini1_1\lib\jini-ext.jar;
        C:\jini1_1\lib\sun-util.jar;
        C:\service
    -Djava.rmi.server.codebase=http://myhost:8085/
    -Djava.security.policy=C:\policy
    corejini.chapter5.HelloWorldServiceBackend

java -cp C:\jini1_1\lib\jini-core.jar;
        C:\jini1_1\lib\jini-ext.jar;
        C:\jini1_1\lib\sun-util.jar;
        C:\client
    -Djava.rmi.server.codebase=http://myhost:8086/
    -Djava.security.policy=C:\policy
    corejini.chapter5.HelloWorldClientWithLeases
```

On UNIX:

```
java -cp /files/jini1_1/lib/jini-core.jar:
        /files/jini1_1/lib/jini-ext.jar:
        /files/jini1_1/lib/sun-util.jar:
        /files/service
    -Djava.rmi.server.codebase=http://myhost:8085/
    -Djava.security.policy=/files/policy
    corejini.chapter5.HelloWorldServiceBackend

java -cp /files/jini1_1/lib/jini-core.jar:
        /files/jini1_1/lib/jini-ext.jar:
        /files/jini1_1/lib/sun-util.jar:
        /files/client
    -Djava.rmi.server.codebase=http://myhost:8086/
    -Djava.security.policy=/files/policy
    corejini.chapter5.HelloWorldClientWithLeases
```

Since the service's proxy is communicating with a back-end process, you'll actually get different results each time you run the client! Even if you start multiple clients at the same time, each will download a separate copy of the proxy for the service. Each of these proxy objects will come with the RMI code needed to communicate with the back-end process, which actually determines which string to return.

Here's a sample run:

From the service: This output is the same as before.

```
discovered a lookup service!
Set serviceID to e91bb61d-b18e-447e-8935-adfd8bd741f5
```

From the client: Run the service four times in a row and see what happens.

```
Got matching service.
Its message is: Hello, world!

Got a matching service.
Its message is: Goodbye, Cruel World

Got a matching service.
Its message is: What's Up, Doc?

Got matching service.
Its message is: Hello, world!
```

Here you can see the back-end portion of the service cycling through the strings it provides. Even if the proxies are running in clients on different machines, they will all communicate with the single back-end process to get the string to display. This is a classic—albeit simple—example of using a back-end process as a "choke point" to synchronize multiple clients.

One Final Iteration

One more advanced feature of RMI that can often be useful for building Jini services is the RMI *activation framework*. This is a facility that can be used to start services on demand as they are needed. The discussion of how to use the activation framework is beyond the scope of this chapter, but see Appendix A for one final iteration of the trusty "Hello, World" service that uses activation.

What's Next?

You've seen how to create simple Jini clients and services that do all of the basics—lookup and discovery, leasing and event registration, and even remote method invocations. The goal of this chapter was to get your hands dirty by working with the various Jini facilities at a very low level. But while you've seen all of the basics here, this isn't the end-all and be-all of building with Jini. These services don't do a very good job of remembering their service IDs, and they have no way for users or administrators to interact with them. For example, I cannot tell the `HelloWorldService` that I'd like it to register itself with a lookup service that's not on the local network.

In future chapters, you'll see convenience APIs that make many of the chores done "by hand" in this chapter easier. These same APIs make services better behaved by taking over many of the details that were ignored here. By now, though, you should have a good grounding in what's going on "behind the scenes" whenever a Jini service or client runs.

Next, in Chapter 6, you'll learn about one of the most important topics in Jini: the discovery process.

In Depth: Discovery

Topics in This Chapter

- Multicast and unicast discovery protocols
- How IP multicast works
- Using the discovery programming interfaces
- Discovery packet formats

Chapter

6

In this chapter, you'll look in depth at the protocols and APIs used to locate lookup services. The discovery protocols are at the core of Jini, and are the mechanisms by which Jini services and applications bootstrap themselves into Jini communities when they start up. Discovery also provides a means for services that may have been separated from the network to reestablish their participation when they are once again able to communicate.

This chapter covers discovery in brutal detail. If you're only interested in building applications and services, then you probably only care about the "higher level" details of discovery—how discovery works and what APIs are available to control it. This chapter covers these aspects of discovery up front. The first two sections provide an overview of the goals and methods of discovery, while the third section discusses how to use discovery in applications via the various class libraries that Jini provides.

Some of you will want to get under the hood and get your hands dirty, though. This may be because you are interested in how discovery works, or even because you want to build your own lookup service that implements discovery. So later in this chapter you'll see what the APIs are actually *doing* when you're finding lookup services, and how the various discovery protocols are structured. You'll even learn about the raw, on-the-wire formats of the discovery protocols, which you'll need if you're implementing discovery from scratch.

Much of the material in this chapter is equally applicable whether you're building clients or services: The discovery protocols are used by both. There are a number of places, however, where services interact with discovery in particular ways unique to them. I'll highlight those points throughout the text via **Core Notes**.

What's Discovery?

You saw a quick overview of discovery in Chapter 3. Basically, discovery is the process by which Jini applications find the lookup services that serve their communities. A Jini community is a group of services that are available—both to each other and to consuming applications—on the network. All of the members of a community are available and visible to all other members of that community, and to any application that "looks" at that community.

The end result of the discovery process is that an interested party learns about a set of lookup services, and acquires service proxies for them so that it can interact with them using whatever protocols they speak. Recall that lookup services are accessed through their proxies, just like any other Jini service. But whereas "normal" proxies are retrieved by talking to a lookup service, proxies for the lookup service itself are retrieved via discovery—it's how Jini bootstraps itself. And, of course, like any other service proxy, the actual protocol that the proxy uses to speak to the lookup service is hidden from the proxy's user.

The discovery process is designed so that, by default and without any special knowledge of what communities may exist, a service that starts up will find and register itself with the "nearby" lookup services. The discovery protocol's notion of "nearness" is based on network topology—services that are on the same or a closely connected network will, by default, share the same lookup services. What nearness means for a particular network will largely depend on how that network was configured by its administrator. I'll talk more about network nearness a bit later in this chapter.

The use of network nearness doesn't, however, preclude other forms of nearness, possibly with their own future discovery protocols to support them. For example, a device with an infrared transceiver may join communities based on physical proximity. Such a device could use a special discovery protocol to find and join communities within IR range. These IR-located communities may or may not be the same, or overlap with, the network-based communities.

Groups Partition the Community Namespace

Typically, one or more lookup services will exist on a subnet. Each of these lookup services will serve a set of "groups," which are essentially names for their communities. Groups might be created for organizational entities within a company ("Engineering" or "Marketing"), or for physical distinctions that might not be reflected in the network topology ("first floor" or "commons area"), or for deployment distinctions ("production" versus "experimental"). Figure 6–1 shows how a group of lookup services may support a number of groups, and how those groups may be "overlapped" across lookup services. Here you see three groups, called "Engineering," "Marketing," and "Accounting." The Engineering and Marketing groups share a lookup service that is a member of both of these groups. Marketing and Accounting also have their own individual lookup services that are members of only those groups. You can see here that a given group may be supported by multiple lookup services (as in the case of Marketing), and that a lookup service can support multiple groups (as in the one supporting both Engineering and Marketing).

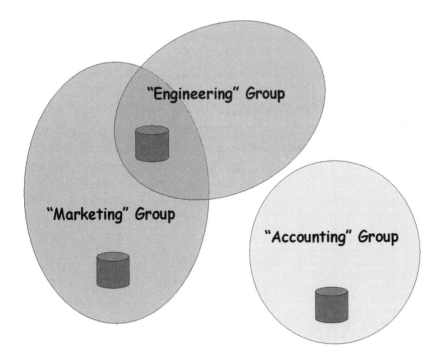

Figure 6–1   *Multiple lookup services supporting multiple groups*

When a service starts, it may be configured to search out and join certain groups that it finds on its subnet—such a service would either have some persistent state that recorded the groups it should join, or might have a user interface by which an actual human tells it which groups it should become a part of.

In most cases, however, services and applications will always join the *default* group. This is the public group, named by the empty string, that will contain most of the services in a Jini community.

Types of Discovery

Broadly, there are two basic forms of discovery. One form is used to support "serendipitous" interaction between services and lookup services. Serendipitous interaction means that the lookup services and Jini services find each other without any previous configuration or advance knowledge of one another, and without being explicitly told to search for one another.

This form of discovery is used when a service starts and needs to find all the lookup services that may be running in its vicinity. It's also used when a lookup service starts and needs to announce its presence to any Jini services that may be running, in case they wish to register with it. These two sorts of discovery—discovery that originates from the joining service, vs. discovery that originates from the lookup service—actually use different but similar protocols. You'll learn about these protocols in this chapter.

The second form of discovery is used to "hard wire" a Jini service to a lookup service. Unlike the serendipitous forms of discovery, where services find any and all lookup services in their vicinity, this "direct" form of discovery allows services to contact particular lookup services that they may know about ahead of time. This form of discovery uses its own protocol that is distinct from the serendipitous forms of discovery, and has a URL-based naming scheme for specifying lookup services.

Together, these three protocols—two serendipitous and one direct—form the core of discovery.

An Overview of Discovery

It's time to look at how discovery works in practice. Each of the three discovery protocols is designed to be used in different scenarios, so I'll talk about each in turn. But first, you should understand an important technology that is the basis for the serendipitous discovery protocols: IP multicast. The next section provides a background introduction to this technology.

An IP Multicast Primer

Both of the serendipitous discovery protocols use the IP (Internet Protocol) multicast facility. Multicast is a way to send one message that may be received by any number of parties. It is not broadcast, because it does not go to every party on the network; it only goes to those who are explicitly listening for it. And it is not unicast, which would entail sending a separate message to each intended recipient, and would require that the sender know the IP addresses of each recipient ahead of time. Multicast makes efficient use of network resources, because a message sent to multiple receivers is transmitted as a single message wherever possible. (Of course, if the parties are on two completely different networks, at some point the multicast routers will have to copy the message to reach the recipients on the second network.)

The form of multicast used by Jini is based on the UDP/IP protocol. UDP provides a connectionless, unreliable transport. This means that UDP provides no guarantees that a packet sent will actually arrive, and it provides no guarantees about the order in which a series of packets will arrive. These properties are the same as in normal, unicast UDP. (I should note, though, that UDP is pretty reliable in practice.)

In UDP multicast, a range of special IP addresses are used as *multicast groups*. Interested parties can effectively "join" a group by listening for messages sent to that IP address. Any message sent to the address will be received by all parties listening to it.

Each message sent via multicast has a *scope* associated with it, which is used to limit the "distance" the message will travel. The benefit of scoping is that an IP address used as a multicast group for one set of hosts may be invisible to another set of hosts using the same IP address, if the hosts are far enough away and their messages are scoped so that they do not reach each other. In this way, scoping effectively limits the visibility of multicast groups, and allows the addresses used for multicast to be reused many times across the Internet. Parties don't have to agree on which multicast addresses will be "owned" by which organizations. (This situation is in contrast to the domain naming system used to associate host names with IP addresses. Because these addresses are visible globally across the network, they must be registered and owned by a centralized facility.)

Scoping also allows efficiency in routing. If a sender sends a message to a multicast address, it may not know ahead of time if anyone has joined that group (that is, is listening on that address). If the routers had to send the message into every nook and cranny of the Internet, looking for interested recipients, the Internet would be swamped in short order. Instead, a sender can set the scope of its messages, which would cause the routing infrastructure of the Internet to only let the message go so far in its search for recipients.

In UDP multicast, the scope of a message is set by specifying the value of the IP "Time-to-Live" (TTL) parameter. The TTL of a message specifies how many "hops" it will take. When the message is routed through the network, every router that it crosses increments its hop count. Once the hop count exceeds the TTL parameter, the message is dropped. Setting the TTL limits the range of multicast messages. A TTL of 1 will cause the message to only reach machines on the same network segment; longer TTLs can cause a message to span the entire Internet. TTLs effectively let you set a "radius" within which any interested parties will hear your message.

Network administrators can also control message scope. Routers are configured with settings that cause them to drop packets beyond a certain configured radius, to prevent packet storms that can be caused by abusive senders. So the *particular* notion of what constitutes the "nearness" of some host on the network depends largely on the configuration of the network.

Service-Initiated Discovery

When a new service starts and wishes to join the community in its vicinity, it uses the *multicast request protocol*. This protocol is used to find all of the nearby lookup services that may be running. As its name implies, this protocol uses IP multicast to find lookup services. The service sends a multicast message to a well-known multicast address; this address is agreed upon ahead of time by all the Jini lookup services and all other services, and the message is scoped so that it will only travel a set distance. This is how a Jini service finds the lookup services nearby—the scoping limits the discovery request so that it only reaches lookup services that might be listening on a multicast address and are running on the same subnet as the service.

Once a lookup service receives a multicast discovery request, it replies by connecting directly to the requesting service and sending a unicast (point-to-point) message. This message contains the proxy object that the service can use to contact the lookup service. Depending on network latencies and the speeds of the machines running the lookup services, these answer messages may "trickle in" over a short period of time.

Lookup Service-Initiated Discovery

Lookup services periodically announce their existence using the *multicast announcement protocol*. This protocol works much the same as the multicast request protocol, only it is initiated by the lookup services themselves.

In multicast announcement, interested parties on the network listen on a well-known multicast address for announcements about the existence of lookup services. Periodically, all lookup services send a multicast message to this address; the message is scoped so that it only reaches interested parties on the local area network.

Once an interested party has received an announcement of the existence of a lookup service, it can then ask the lookup service for its service proxy. It contacts the lookup service using a direct unicast connection, and the lookup service replies with the proxy object that the client can use to communicate with it.

You may be wondering why the lookup service doesn't just multicast out its proxy object when it announces its presence. This would allow any interested recipients to immediately get the proxy, without requiring them to do a separate round-trip message to fetch it. There are two reasons Jini does not take this approach. The first is that, because most announcements are likely to go unused except when a lookup service is just starting or reconnecting to the network, keeping the message size as small as possible can greatly cut down on network traffic. But a second, even more severe, reason is that multicast messages *must* be kept to a reasonable size. The multicast protocol itself dictates a maximum packet size, which is fairly small. Because serialized proxy objects can be arbitrarily large, there is no way to guarantee that they'll fit within the bounds of a multicast message. You'll see later in this chapter why multicast imposes this size restriction.

"Direct" Discovery

In addition to listening on a multicast address for multicast discovery requests from services, each lookup service also listens on a normal, unicast address. Any service can connect directly to this address to access the lookup service, using the *unicast discovery protocol*. In this sense, the protocol isn't so much a "discovery" protocol as a way to contact an already known lookup service in order to download its service proxy. The client sends a message to the lookup service, which replies with its service proxy.

Unicast discovery is based on a URL naming scheme, where lookup services are named using URLs of the form `jini://turbodog.parc.xerox.com:4160/foobar`. The protocol name, `jini`, specifies that the URL represents a

Jini lookup service. The next component is the hostname, in this case, tur-bodog.parc.xerox.com. The next part, containing the colon and the number, is optional—if present, it represents the port number on which the lookup service is listening. Port number 4160 is the default port for Jini lookup.[1] The last part, /foobar in this case, while a legal component of a URL, is generally not used in Jini and should not be a part of a Jini URL specification. Jini lookup services are typically not searchable by name, so the part of the URL trailing the host and port specification is superfluous.

Core Note: The service "join" protocol adds more requirements

This chapter just addresses the core mechanisms of discovery; most of these mechanisms are equally valid whether your code is providing a service or simply consuming services that it finds on the network.

There are, however, a few guidelines and conventions that service builders must follow. These guidelines dictate what "well-behaved" services will do, and result in a bit of extra work for services. While much of this extra work happens after discovery—registering with the lookup service, maintaining leases, and so on—some of the tasks affects how the service interacts with discovery.

Collectively these guidelines are called the service "join" protocol, because they control how services join communities.

These guidelines dictate how services should try to reconnect to lookup services that have disappeared from the network, what services should do if they are specifically configured with unicast URLs to connect to, and so on.

All the details of being a "well-behaved" service are grouped together in Chapter 14. I'll wait until that chapter to cover the join protocol, because join involves details of lookup services and persistence that I haven't covered yet. There, you'll see the particular conventions that govern how services use discovery; in this chapter, you'll look only at the mechanisms that control what discovery does.

---

1. The decimal number 4160 is the same in value as the subtraction of the two numbers, expressed in hexadecimal, as 0xCAFE - 0xBABE. The hexadecimal number 0xCAFEBABE also happens to be the "magic number" that identifies Java class files.

Using Discovery in Applications

As you saw in Chapter 5, the basic discovery APIs are quite simple. The discovery API is based on the listener paradigm, common throughout Java. Parties that are interested in being informed of the discovery of new lookup services implement this listener interface, and will receive events detailing the state of lookup services. There are also a number of common interfaces—and classes that implement those interfaces—for controlling the discovery process.

I'll start by walking through the listener interfaces.

DiscoveryListeners Are Informed of Discoveries

The basic interface for Jini-aware applications that need to work with discovery is called `DiscoveryListener`. This is a very simple Java interface with only two methods.

```
package net.jini.discovery;

import java.util.EventListener;

public interface DiscoveryListener extends EventListener {
        public void discovered(DiscoveryEvent ev);
        public void discarded(DiscoveryEvent ev);
}
```

Any object that needs to find lookup services via the high-level discovery APIs that Jini provides must implement this interface. The first method, `discovered()`, will be called whenever a new lookup service is found via the discovery protocols. The Jini class libraries that implement the discovery protocols will invoke the method "automatically" when necessary.

The second method, `discarded()`, is a bit more interesting. This method will be called when a previously found lookup service is no longer relevant. This may happen, for example, when the set of groups you are interested in changes. Any previously found lookup services that do not support one of the new groups will be discarded.

But most often, this method is called whenever problems develop when communicating with a lookup service. If you've implemented a program that communicates with a lookup service, and you begin getting `RemoteExceptions` whenever you try to talk with that lookup service, then chances are that it's crashed or is unreachable. In such a case, you can actually tell the discovery machinery to "undiscover" an already discovered lookup service (this is done through a method called `discard()` on classes that implement the `Discovery-Management` interface that you'll see in a bit). When this happens, the Jini class libraries will call out to the `discarded()` method so that your `DiscoveryListener` can clean up any state to reflect the fact that a lookup service has been discarded.

Many beginning Jini programmers believe that `discarded()` is somehow called automatically whenever a lookup service crashes. This isn't the case. Once a lookup service has been found, there is no ongoing communication with it—especially no post mortem communication. Your code is responsible for discarding lookup services that you detect are misbehaving; the `discarded()` method here will be called by the Jini discovery machinery in response to that.

DiscoveryChangeListeners Are Informed of Changes in Group Membership of Lookup Services

In some cases, you may wish to determine when there is a change in the set of groups to which a previously-discovered lookup services belongs. If you wish to be informed of such changes, you may use the `DiscoveryChangeListener` interface. This interface is a subinterface of `DiscoveryListener`, so you can use it everywhere you use a `DiscoveryListener`. The new interface adds a single method, `changed()`, which is called whenever the set of groups of which a lookup service is a member changes:

```
package net.jini.discovery;

public interface DiscoveryChangeListener
          extends DiscoveryListener {
     public void changed(DiscoveryEvent ev);
}
```

If you provide a class that implements `DiscoveryChangeListener` you must, of course, provide implementations of not only `changed()` but also `discovered()` and `discarded()` (because `DiscoveryChangeListener` extends the `DiscoveryListener` base interface). The `changed()` method will be invoked by the discovery subsystem whenever it detects that the group membership for a lookup service has changed.

Be sure to note one caveat about using `DiscoveryChangeListeners`—you will only receive change notifications for lookup services which were discovered using the group (multicast) forms of discovery. A lookup service discovered solely through direct locator-based discovery will produce no change events.

In general, few applications explicitly care about being informed of group membership changes in lookup services. Most applications will simply provide an implementation of `DiscoveryListener` and use it to be notified when any lookup service that's a member of any of the groups they are discovering is found.

DiscoveryEvents Encapsulate Discovery Information

You'll notice that `discovered()`, `discarded()`, and `changed()` all take an instance of `DiscoveryEvent`. Look at the relevant parts of that class now:

```
package net.jini.discovery;

import java.util.EventObject;
import java.util.Map;

public class DiscoveryEvent extends EventObject {
      // ... some methods elided ...
      public ServiceRegistrar[] getRegistrars();
      public Map getGroups();
}
```

Some of the methods in this class, like the constructor, are not shown here because they will not be used by Jini applications directly (only the internals of the Jini libraries will create new `DiscoveryEvents`, for example). For receivers of these events, the most important method of interest is `getRegistrars()`. This method returns an array of `ServiceRegistrar` instances. Each of these is a service proxy for a lookup service somewhere on the network. The underlying Jini libraries may batch together multiple `ServiceRegistrars` into one event, which is why an array of `ServiceRegistrars` is returned here.

Receivers of `DiscoveryEvents` can determine the current groups that a given lookup service supports by calling the `getGroups()` method. This method returns a `Map` containing the associations between every registrar referenced by the event to the registrar's current member group set. Each key in the map will be a `ServiceRegistrar`; each value in the map will be a `String` array containing the names of the groups in which that registrar is a member.

The `DiscoveryEvent` class extends the `EventObject` class, and therefore inherits a number of methods from it. The only one of importance is `get-Source()`, which returns the instance of the class that generated this event. In most cases, this will be a class that implements the discovery protocols (and thus

caused the event to be generated), such as `LookupDiscoveryManager`, which
you'll learn about next.

Using LookupDiscoveryManager to Control Discovery

By far, the most convenient way to control the discovery process in Jini is via
the `LookupDiscoveryManager` class. This class, which was introduced in Jini
1.1, provides a complete suite of functionality for controlling both multicast
and unicast forms of discovery, and for doing general "housekeeping" on the
discovery process.

There are a few other discovery classes that may be used in some specialized
circumstances, which I'll discuss a bit later. But, `LookupDiscoveryManager` is
certainly the most important. Jini also provides a general framework of interfaces
that "factor" the various aspects of discovery nicely. These interfaces allow you
to very easily plug in new discovery implementations—perhaps with different
performance characteristics, or even that work over different, non-IP transports—
and have these implementations be available to the rest of Jini.

As you shall see, `LookupDiscoveryManager` implements three of these
"general" discovery interfaces, called `DiscoveryManagement` (which defines
bookkeeping and listener control), `DiscoveryGroupManagement` (which
defines APIs for controlling multicast discovery), and `DiscoveryLocatorMan-
agement` (which defines APIs for controlling unicast discovery). I'll talk more
about these interfaces later in the chapter. But for now, look at `LookupDiscov-
eryManager`.

```
package net.jini.discovery;

public class LookupDiscoveryManager
                implements DiscoveryManagement,
                            DiscoveryGroupManagement,
                            DiscoveryLocatorManagement {
    //
    // constructor
    //
    public LookupDiscoveryManager(
                        String[] groups,
                        LookupLocator[] locs,
                        DiscoveryListener listener)
                throws IOException;

    //
```

```
// bookkeeping and listener control
//
public void addDiscoveryListener(
                          DiscoveryListener listener);
public void removeDiscoveryListener(
                          DiscoveryListener listener);

public ServiceRegistrar[] getRegistrars();
public void discard(ServiceRegistrar proxy);
public void terminate();

//
// multicast discovery controls
//
public String[] getGroups();
public void addGroups(String[] groups)
    throws IOException;
public void setGroups(String[] groups)
    throws IOException;

public void removeGroups(String[] groups);

//
// unicast discovery controls
//
public LookupLocator[] getLocators();
public void addLocators(LookupLocator[] locs);
public void setLocators(LookupLocator[] locs);
public void removeLocators(LookupLocator[] locs);
}
```

This is a fairly hefty class with a lot of functionality, so you should take time to understand it well.

Start with the constructor. The constructor for the class provides a handy way to initiate both multicast and unicast discovery, and to install a single listener. The first argument to the constructor is a string array that is used to specify the groups you wish to discover using the multicast protocols. Most applications will search for the public group, and will thus pass in a string array of a single element containing the empty string (expressed in Java by writing `new String[]{""}`).

The second argument is an array of `LookupLocators`. The `LookupLocator` class is simply a way to represent a Jini-formatted URL that names a lookup service. I'll discuss this class in a bit, but for now you can just think of it as a URL that names a lookup service you wish to discover via unicast discovery. If you want to have your program explicitly connect to one or more named lookup services, you can pass locators here that represent those lookup services. Most applications, though, will simply pass null here.

The final argument to the constructor is a reference to an object that implements the `DiscoveryListener` interface you saw before. Typically this will be an object you define in your program that will take some action when new lookup services are found.

Once a properly configured `LookupDiscoveryManager` has been created (where "properly configured" means that a `DiscoveryListener` has been specified, and at least one group or locator has been provided), your listener will be called whenever lookup services are found. The `DiscoveryEvents` passed to this listener will contain the proxies for these lookup services.

Core Note: Dealing with catastrophic failure

The volume of network traffic required for one service to participate in discovery is relatively small. But imagine a situation where a whole network of machines is coming back up after a power failure or other catastrophic failure that causes an entire network of machines to crash. Hundreds, perhaps thousands, of services would begin at about the same time and begin pummeling their lookup services with multicast requests. In addition to swamping the network with multicast traffic, they will also swamp the lookup services and the machines hosting them.

This situation is called a packet storm, and it is a very real consequence of having network services that need to interact with each other upon start up. A packet storm can easily bring an entire network to its knees and even cause machines running some less-than-robust operating systems to simply crash. Clearly, this is a situation you want to avoid.

Therefore, a well-behaved Jini service should wait for some random period of time before initiating a multicast request. This delay will help to reduce the odds that enough services will start at once to create packet storms and flood the network. This safeguard can help a Jini network restart itself safely after a catastrophic failure. While a service can wait for a random time within any range it desires, a range of 0 to 15 seconds is probably fine.

If you're using the standard Jini classes for discovery— `LookupDiscoveryManager` *and the others—you don't have to worry about this requirement, since those classes handle such duties for you.*

The rest of the class provides three main types of functionality: some bookkeeping methods for controlling listeners and a few other discovery chores, methods to control multicast discovery, and methods to control unicast discovery.

The bookkeeping methods allow you to add and remove listeners via the `add-DiscoveryListener()` and `removeDiscoveryListener()` methods. The `LookupDiscoveryManagement` class remembers all of the lookup services it has found to date and, when a new listener is added, will report all the previously found lookup services to it. By batching up previous discoveries and sending them to listeners who may be added later on, the `LookupDiscoveryManagement` class avoids race conditions where discovery is started and a lookup service is found before any listeners have been registered.

Be sure to note that you can, of course, pass an implementation of `DiscoveryChangeListener` to the add and remove methods, because `DiscoveryChangeListeners` *are* `DiscoveryListeners`. Doing so would allow you to receive notification whenever the set of groups of which a lookup service is a member changes.

Since the `LookupDiscoveryManagement` class batches discoveries, you can use the add and remove methods to effectively "turn off" discovery events for your application, should you ever have a need to do so. The `LookupDiscoveryManager` will continue collecting details about lookup services it finds, and these will be delivered to you if you reinstall a listener—you don't have to worry about "missing" any discovery events.

What happens when a previously discovered lookup service crashes, becomes unreachable, or ceases to be a member of one of the groups that you are interested in? In each of these cases, the offending lookup service should be "undiscovered." That is, it should be dropped out of the set of discovered lookup services (because it is either dead or no longer relevant), and any registered `DiscoveryListeners` should be called so that they can do any housekeeping that may be necessary.

This is where the `discard()` method comes in. Calling `discard()` essentially causes the `LookupDiscoveryManager` instance to "forget" about a previously seen lookup service. If the lookup service appears again later, or once again joins a group in which you're interested, it will then be eligible for rediscovery.

Who calls `discard`? This is actually an interesting question! The `LookupDiscoveryManager` class can itself discard lookup services in some circumstances. For instance, if a lookup service ceases to be a member of any of the groups in which you are interested, the `LookupDiscoveryManager` can detect this by looking at the multicast traffic from the lookup service. In this case it will automatically discard the lookup service, which will cause the `discarded()` method to be invoked on any `DiscoveryListeners` you have registered. In some circumstances, the `LookupDiscoveryManager` may also be able to detect that a lookup service discovered through group discovery is unreachable and may be discarded.

But in general, *you* are responsible for calling `discard()`! Typically you will do this if the proxy for the lookup service begins raising `RemoteExceptions`—these mean that the proxy is unable to communicate with the backend part of the lookup service, and it has probably either crashed or become unreachable. The discovery utilities may have no idea that the lookup service has crashed, because there is no ongoing communication with a lookup service once it has been discovered. In this case, *it is your responsibility* to invoke `discard()`. This drops the registrar from the `LookupDiscoveryManager`'s list of discovered lookup services, which makes it elegible for re-discovery in the future, if it comes back.

Be sure to note the difference between the `discard()` method on `Lookup-DiscoveryManager` and the `discarded()` method on `DiscoveryListener`. Your code is responsible for calling `discard()` and, because of that call, `LookupDiscoveryManager` calls the `discarded()` method on the listener. You don't call `discarded()` to drop a lookup service; that method is invoked "automatically" for you when a lookup service is dropped via `discard()`.

Calling `terminate()` ends the discovery process. When this method is called, no more `DiscoveryEvents` will be sent to any already registered listeners, although new listeners added after the call to `terminate()` will be notified of all of the lookup services found prior to the call to `terminate()`. Calling `terminate()` stops the process of discovery irreversibly for the particular instance of `LookupDiscoveryManager` that you call it on—you can never restart discovery again without creating a new `LookupDiscoveryManager`. Trying to change the state of the instance via `setGroups()`, `addGroups()`, or `removeGroups()` after termination will cause an `IllegalStateException` to be raised.

The second big block of functionality in this class has to do with control of multicast discovery, particularly controlling the set of groups for which the class will search. The `setGroups()` method explicitly sets the groups for discovery, overwriting any existing groups. By convention, a null array of groups indicates that all groups should be searched for. An empty array indicates that no groups should be searched for. Two special constants, `ALL_GROUPS` and `NO_GROUPS`, are used to indicate these cases, and are provided in the `DiscoveryGroupManagement` interface that this class implements. These special values work in all of the group control methods, and also in the constructor. If the set of groups grows, then the `LookupDiscoveryManager` instance will initiate a new round of multicast requests to find lookup services supporting the new groups.

Addition and deletion of individual groups can be done via `addGroups()` and `removeGroups()`. If groups are dropped from the active search set, either through `setGroups()` or `removeGroups()`, then this may cause already found lookup services to become "uninteresting"—if a lookup service is no longer a member of any of the groups being searched for, then it will be discarded from the set of active lookup services. When this happens, all listeners will have their `discarded()` methods invoked.

Because both `setGroups()` and `addGroups()` may cause the multicast request protocol to begin again, these methods may raise `IOException` if they encounter problems starting the protocol.

The final set of methods here control unicast discovery. These methods are very much analogous to the methods that control multicast discovery. But whereas the multicast methods control the set of *groups* being searched for, these methods control the set of *names* of lookup services being searched for. The `LookupDiscoveryManager` class can use the unicast protocols to attempt to fetch proxies for a whole set of explicitly named lookup services. Recall that lookup services are named via Jini-formatted URLs, which are represented in the APIs by instances of the `LookupLocator` class. (I'll provide details of this class a little later in this chapter.)

The methods here do exactly what you would expect. Calling `getLocators()` returns all of the locators currently being searched for, including ones corresponding to lookup services that have already been found. The `setLocators()`, `addLocators()`, and `removeLocators()` methods control the set of lookup services being searched for.

An Example

I'll walk through a short example of how to use discovery in applications via the `LookupDiscoveryManager` class. This program starts up and participates in both the multicast and the unicast discovery protocols until you press the Enter key to stop it. It will print out details about each lookup service that it can find on your local network.

Obviously, to get the most out of this application, you need to be running a lookup service somewhere on your network! If you haven't followed the instructions in Chapter 1 for installing and running the core Jini services, now would be a good time to do that. Without a lookup service on your network, the program in Listing 6–1 will simply sit around doing nothing.

Before I get into the meat of the program, though, I first need to define a `DiscoveryListener` that will receive notifications of discovery events. This listener, called `PrintingListener`, can be used in this and other programs to print out details about the lookup services you find.

Listing 6–1 `PrintingListener.java`

```
// This is a simple DiscoveryListener that will
// print when it receives discovery events.

package corejini.chapter6;

import net.jini.discovery.DiscoveryManagement;
import net.jini.discovery.DiscoveryListener;
import net.jini.discovery.DiscoveryEvent;
import net.jini.discovery.DiscoveryGroupManagement;
import net.jini.core.lookup.ServiceRegistrar;
import java.rmi.RemoteException;

public class PrintingListener
    implements DiscoveryListener {
    protected DiscoveryManagement dm;
```

Listing 6–1 `PrintingListener.java` (continued)

```java
// The PrintingListener keeps a handle to a
// DiscoveryManagement instance.  It will use this to
// discard lookup services that raise exceptions,
// allowing them to be discovered again.
public PrintingListener(DiscoveryManagement dm) {
    this.dm = dm;
}

// Print out some simple debugging information
public void discovered(DiscoveryEvent ev) {
    ServiceRegistrar[] regs = ev.getRegistrars();

    for (int i=0 ; i<regs.length ; i++) {
        try {
            System.out.println("Discovered: ");
            System.out.println("\tURL:     " +
                                    getURL(regs[i]));
            System.out.println("\tID:      " +
                                    regs[i].getServiceID());
            System.out.println("\tGroups: " +
                                    getGroups(regs[i]));
        } catch (RemoteException ex) {
            // Discard lookup services that raise remote
            // exceptions
            System.err.println("Error: " + ex);
            dm.discard(regs[i]);
        }
    }
}
```

Listing 6–1 `PrintingListener.java` (continued)

```java
// Print out details of discarded lookup services.
public void discarded(DiscoveryEvent ev) {
    ServiceRegistrar[] regs = ev.getRegistrars();

    for (int i=0 ; i<regs.length ; i++) {
        System.out.println("Discarded: " + regs[i]);
    }
}

// A helper method to get the URL for a
// lookup service.
static String getURL(ServiceRegistrar reg)
    throws RemoteException {
    return reg.getLocator().toString();
}

// A helper method to get the groups that a
// lookup service is a member of.
static String getGroups(ServiceRegistrar reg)
    throws RemoteException {
    String[] groups = reg.getGroups();

    if (groups == DiscoveryGroupManagement.ALL_GROUPS){
        return "<all groups>";
    }

    if (groups == DiscoveryGroupManagement.NO_GROUPS) {
        return "<none>";
    }
```

Listing 6–1 `PrintingListener.java` (continued)

```
        StringBuffer buf = new StringBuffer();
        for (int i=0 ; i<groups.length ; i++) {
            if (groups[i] == null) {
                // This should never happen. The Discovery
                // libraries should exclude all nulls.
                buf.append("NULL ");
            } else if (groups[i].equals("")) {
                buf.append("PUBLIC ");
            } else {
                buf.append(groups[i]);
            }
        }

        return buf.toString();
    }
}
```

The `PrintingListener` class implements `DiscoveryListener`, so it can be installed as a listener in an instance of `LookupDiscoveryManager` (or in any of the other discovery classes, which you'll see later in this chapter).

The constructor for the listener takes as an argument a class implementing `DiscoveryManagement`. This is an interface that defines a set of methods for the "bookkeeping" functions needed to control discovery. In fact, these methods are exactly the same as the bookkeeping methods you've already seen on `LookupDiscoveryManager`, since this class implements the `DiscoveryManagement` interface. I'll explain these "generic" discovery interfaces a little later in the chapter. For now, though, all you have to know is that `LookupDiscoveryManager` implements this interface, so it can be passed here. But by defining the argument as the generic interface I need, rather than a specific class, I leave the possibility that other discovery implementations can be used with this `PrintingListener`.

Why is a `DiscoveryManagement` object passed to the constructor? It's so that if the `PrintingListener` runs into trouble any time it uses a lookup service's proxy object, it can tell the `DiscoveryManagement` class to discard the proxy.

You can see this behavior in the implementation of `discovered()`. The listener cycles through all of the proxies contained in the `DiscoveryEvent` it receives, and prints details about each of them (the name, the proxy, and which groups it supports). If any of this causes the proxy to raise a `RemoteException`, the listener assumes that the lookup service has died or is otherwise inaccessible. By calling `discard()`, it causes the `LookupDiscoveryManager` (or whatever other class is managing the discovery process) to drop the errant lookup service so that it can be found again when it reconnects to the network.

The `discarded()` method simply prints out the URL of the lookup service that was dropped. This method will be called for every lookup service that you `discard()` as above.

The rest of this class simply defines a couple of helper methods to print out the URL for the service, and the set of groups that the service is a member of. I've defined these methods to be static, since I'll be using them as "helpers" in later examples in this chapter.

The `getURL()` class shows something I haven't covered before: how to get the URL for a lookup service. The code here calls `getLocator()` on a `ServiceRegistrar`, which returns a `LookupLocator`. The `LookupLocator` class is a representation for the URL name of a lookup service, and has a few other convenient methods as well. You'll see the ins and outs of this class a bit later in this chapter.

Next, it's time to start looking at the heart of the discovery example, which can be seen in Listing 6-2.

Listing 6–2 `DiscoveryExample.java`

```java
// Exercise the DiscoveryListener class through
// LookupDiscoveryManager.

package corejini.chapter6;

import net.jini.core.discovery.LookupLocator;
import net.jini.discovery.DiscoveryListener;
import net.jini.discovery.DiscoveryEvent;
import net.jini.discovery.DiscoveryGroupManagement;
import net.jini.discovery.LookupDiscoveryManager;
import net.jini.core.lookup.ServiceRegistrar;
import java.util.ArrayList;
import java.rmi.RemoteException;
import java.rmi.RMISecurityManager;
import java.net.MalformedURLException;
import java.io.IOException;
```

Listing 6–2 `DiscoveryExample.java` (continued)

```java
public class DiscoveryExample {
    protected LookupDiscoveryManager discoveryMgr = null;
    protected DiscoveryListener myListener;
    protected String[] groups;
    protected LookupLocator[] locs;

    public DiscoveryExample(ArrayList groups,
                            ArrayList locs) {
    // To mirror the DiscoveryGroupManagement constants,
    // an empty groups array indicates NO_GROUPS, while a
    // null groups array indicates ALL_GROUPS.
    if (groups == null) {
        System.out.println("searching for all groups");
        this.groups =
        DiscoveryGroupManagement.ALL_GROUPS;
    } else if (groups.size() == 0) {
        System.out.println("searching for no groups");
        this.groups =
        DiscoveryGroupManagement.NO_GROUPS;
        } else {
            this.groups = (String[])
                groups.toArray(new String[0]);
        }
        this.locs = (LookupLocator[])
            locs.toArray(new LookupLocator[0]);
    }

    synchronized void startDiscovery() throws IOException {
        if (discoveryMgr == null) {
            discoveryMgr =
                new LookupDiscoveryManager(groups,
                                           locs, null);
        myListener = new PrintingListener(discoveryMgr);
            discoveryMgr.addDiscoveryListener(myListener);
        }
    }

    synchronized void stopDiscovery() throws IOException {
        if (discoveryMgr != null) {
            discoveryMgr.terminate();
        }
    }
```

Listing 6–2 `DiscoveryExample.java` (continued)

```java
public static void main(String[] args) {
    ArrayList groups = new ArrayList();
    ArrayList locs = new ArrayList();
    boolean doingGroups = false;
    int index = 0;

    if (System.getSecurityManager() == null) {
        System.setSecurityManager(
            new RMISecurityManager());
    }

    try {
        for (int i=0 ; i<args.length ; i++) {
            if (args[i].equals("-groups")) {
                doingGroups = true;
            } else {
                if (doingGroups) {
                    if (args[i].equals("public")) {
                        groups.add("");
                    } else if (args[i].equals("none")) {
                        // make it an empty arraylist
                        groups.clear();
                        break;
                    } else if (args[i].equals("all")) {
                        // make it a null array list.
                        groups = null;
                        break;
                    } else {
                        groups.add(args[i]);
                    }
                } else {
                    locs.add(new LookupLocator(args[i]));
                }
            }
        }
    }

    DiscoveryExample ex =
        new DiscoveryExample(groups, locs);
    ex.startDiscovery();
```

Listing 6–2 `DiscoveryExample.java` (continued)

```
                    System.out.println("Hit return to terminate " +
                        "discovery.");

                    while (((char) System.in.read()) != '\n')
                        /* loop */ ;

                    System.out.println("Terminating discovery.");
                    ex.stopDiscovery();
                } catch (MalformedURLException ex) {
                    System.err.println("Bad URL: " +
                                            ex.getMessage());
                } catch (IOException ex) {
                    System.err.println("Problems with discovery: " +
                                            ex.getMessage());
                }
            }
        }
```

When you run this program, you can specify on the command line what groups you're interested in discovering, as well as the names of any lookup services you wish to find. The `main()` for this program does some argument processing—you can first specify the Jini-format URLs for any lookup services on the command line. To specify groups, you use the token `-groups`, followed by the names of any groups. The special value "`public`" can be used to search for the public group (you have to use a keyword for the public group because it is named by the empty string). Similarly, "`all`" and "`none`" can be used to search for all groups, and no groups, respectively.

The `main()` then passes the arrays of desired groups and locators into the `DiscoveryExample` class, starts the discovery process by calling `startDiscovery()`, and waits until a return is typed at the keyboard. The discovery process will run in the background continuously until you press a key, at which point `main()` calls `stopDiscovery()`. This particular program halts the discovery process by calling `terminate()`, which is irreversible. If you want to build a version of this program that temporarily keeps any discovery events from being sent to you, you could simply remove any listeners from the object doing discovery.

In the `startDiscovery()` method, you see how a new `LookupDiscovery-Manager` is created and set up. The code passes it the arrays of groups and locators, and then installs a new `PrintingListener` to receive discovery events.

While in this example I've used a separate top-level class to receive discovery events, using an inner class is common practice as well.

Security and LookupDiscovery

Jini provides a way, using the Java 2 security mechanisms, for you to limit what lookup services a service or application can discover. This can be very useful, for example, if you download new Jini services from the Internet. If you don't trust the source of the service, and cannot guarantee that it won't try to do something malicious, you can restrict it to only lookup services that are members of certain groups. An "unsafe" group might exist just for experimenting with untrusted services, for example.

When a service or other application creates a `LookupDiscoveryManager` object, or tries to change the set of groups for which the `LookupDiscoveryManager` object is searching, the code checks to see whether the creator has permission to try to discover each of the desired groups. `LookupDiscoveryManager` will raise a `java.lang.SecurityException` if the proper privileges aren't in place.

But permissions need to be set even for *trusted* programs because, by default, applications are allowed to discover *no* groups. So you *must* pass in *some* form of policy file, to allow even lookup services themselves to be able to perform discovery. These same mechanisms can be used to selectively restrict the groups that applications can discover and ultimately join.

So to allow a service access to certain groups, you can create a policy file and pass the file to the JVM via the `java.security.policy` property. The policy file would be used to restrict and allow accesses made by the *discovering* application, whether it's a service or a client or a lookup service itself (since lookup services use the normal discovery process to find other lookup services).

Jini introduces its own permissions class just for granting access to groups. This class is called `net.jini.discovery.DiscoveryPermission`, and can be used in a policy file just like any other permission. The permission takes an argument that indicates the group to which access should be allowed, and supports the use of "*" as a wildcard character. Here are some examples. This permission entry in a policy file allows discovery of all groups on the network.

```
permission net.jini.discovery.DiscoveryPermission "*"
```

This entry allows applications to discover and join one specific group, the "unsafe" group.

```
permission net.jini.discovery.DiscoveryPermission
          "unsafe"
```

And finally, this entry grants applications the right to discover and then join the default, public group:

```
permission net.jini.discovery.DiscoveryPermission ""
```

You should note that when you set a security policy for a JVM, that policy restricts *all* the code that runs in the JVM by default, not just downloaded code. You can, however, use the features of Java 2 security to create policy files that selectively grant code certain permissions based on where it came from. So, for instance, you could create policy files that grant more permissions to locally loaded classes than downloaded ones, or to classes "digitally signed" by a known person.

Compiling and Running the Program

Build the program and try it out. Compilation is pretty easy—the class exports no downloadable code (it isn't a Jini service), and has no remote methods. So, you won't have to worry about using the RMI stubs compiler or copying downloadable code to a Web server's root directory. But I will follow the standard guidelines here of specifying the CLASSPATH on the command line, both when compiling and running.

On Windows:

```
javac -classpath C:\files;
                  C:\jini1_1\lib\jini-core.jar;
                  C:\jini1_1\lib\jini-ext.jar;
                  C:\jini1_1\lib\sun-util.jar;
                  C:\client
  -d C:\client
  C:\files\corejini\chapter6\DiscoveryExample.java
```

On UNIX:

```
javac -classpath /files:
                  /files/jini1_1/lib/jini-core.jar:
                  /files/jini1_1/lib/jini-ext.jar:
                  /files/jini1_1/lib/sun-util.jar:
                  /files/client
  -d /files/client
  /files/corejini/chapter6/DiscoveryExample.java
```

Now you're set to run the program. Since this program will *use* downloaded code, and since it must perform discovery to find lookup services, you must pass it a policy file. The "promiscuous" policy file that you used in Chapter 5 will work just fine. Make sure you specify which groups and/or locators you're looking for. Here I'm searching for the public group. If you specify a locator URL, make sure it comes before the `-groups` flag, and make sure it's a valid Jini URL; otherwise, you'll get an exception.

On Windows:

```
java -cp C:\jini1_1\lib\jini-core.jar;
       C:\jini1_1\lib\jini-ext.jar;
       C:\jini1_1\lib\sun-util.jar;
       C:\client
     -Djava.security.policy=C:\policy
     corejini.chapter6.DiscoveryExample -groups public
```

On UNIX:

```
java -cp /files/jini1_1/lib/jini-core.jar:
       /files/jini1_1/lib/jini-ext.jar:
       /files/jini1_1/lib/sun-util.jar:
       /files/client
     -Djava.security.policy=/files/policy
     corejini.chapter6.DiscoveryExample -groups public
```

When the program starts, it will wait for discovery events until you press the Enter key. Every time a new lookup service is discovered, some information about it will be printed to standard out.

Hit return to terminate discovery.

Discovered:

      URL: jini://grouper.parc.xerox.com/

      ID: 90afbd9d-3103-48f9-b3de-b7db0b37095b

      Groups: PUBLIC

Discovered:

      URL: jini://turbodog.parc.xerox.com/

      ID: c498f93c-9c3c-4c71-94b4-92bc63d863e3

      Groups: PUBLIC

Discovered:

      URL: jini://rubberducky.parc.xerox.com:40437/

      ID: 8311f536-7f1c-4c69-bfef-f009542f9f8c

      Groups: PUBLIC

Terminating discovery.

This program shows the basics of using `LookupDiscoveryManager` to interact with the discovery protocols and find the lookup services that are members of a Jini community.

Common Interfaces for Controlling Discovery

As I mentioned briefly, Jini provides a set of "generic" interfaces that define methods for controlling the various aspects of discovery. The `LookupDiscoveryManager` class, as a general tool for doing both unicast and multicast discovery, implements *all* of these interfaces.

So why does Jini have these interfaces? Why not just use `LookupDiscoveryManager` everywhere and be done with it? The answer is that—while `LookupDiscoveryManager` is a powerful class, useful in many situations—it may not serve all discovery needs. Some applications may only need to do either unicast or multicast discovery, but not both. Others may want to restrict the "bookkeeping" that can be done (by preventing the removal of listeners, for example). And most likely, some services and infrastructure may need to work over non-TCP/IP networks (such as infrared connections, FireWire, or other transports).

If Jini mandated the use of `LookupDiscoveryManager` everywhere, you'd be out of luck. This class, powerful as it is, provides a discovery implementation only for TCP/IP networks, using the default discovery semantics defined by Jini's creators.

Fortunately, you can define your own *custom* discovery implementations. What's more, the Jini APIs are defined so that the generic discovery *interfaces* are specified as parameters to methods, not any particular implementation of those interfaces. So you can easily create your own discovery implementation, perhaps with different performance characteristics, or designed to operate over different networks, and "plug it in" to the rest of the Jini machinery. This extensibility is an essential trait in a system designed to span such a range of hardware and software.

Most applications will simply use `LookupDiscoveryManager`. But even the writers of such applications should understand these "generic" discovery interfaces, because they're referenced in the Jini APIs to keep from being implementation-dependent. Having a good grounding in these interfaces will help you understand which particular aspects of discovery are needed by different applications.

All of the methods in `LookupDiscoveryManager`, with the exception of the constructor, come from these three interfaces. The `DiscoveryManagement` interface defines the methods for listener control (`addListener()` and removeListener()), as well as the other bookkeeping methods (getRegistrars(), discard(), and terminate()).

The DiscoveryGroupManagement interface defines the methods used to control group-based discovery. While LookupDiscoveryManager (and hence most current Jini programs) will use multicast IP to implement these APIs, other implementations could exist. The methods in this interface define the common group constants (ALL_GROUPS and NO_GROUPS), as well as the methods to change and retrieve the set of managed groups (getGroups(), addGroups(), setGroups(), and removeGroups()).

Finally, the DiscoveryLocatorManagement interface defines the methods used to control "direct" location-based discovery using LookupLocator URLs to specify the locations of lookup services (getLocators(), addLocators(), setLocators(), and removeLocators()).

It's highly likely that in the near future, Sun or other third parties will produce novel new discovery implementations that implement these same interfaces.

Other Discovery Classes

For most applications, the LookupDiscoveryManager class, along with DiscoveryListener and DiscoveryEvent, are the only classes that will be used. There are, however, a handful of other classes that may come in handy in certain circumstances.

These include the net.jini.discovery.LookupDiscovery class, which implements *only* the multicast discovery protocols, and the net.jini.discovery.LookupLocatorDiscovery class, which implements *only* the unicast protocols. These classes provide implementations of DiscoveryGroupManagement and DiscoveryLocatorManagement, respectively.

These classes provide subsets of the functionality of LookupDiscoveryManager, so I won't discuss them in depth here. You should be aware that they exist, however, and can be used if your application needs only multicast or unicast discovery behavior. See the Jini documentation and API reference for more details on these classes.

One other discovery-related class that made its appearance in the discussion of the LookupDiscoveryManager class is LookupLocator. As I said at the time, LookupLocator is primarily used as a way to represent the "location" of a lookup service, encoded as a URL.

LookupLocator does provide a few other useful functions, however. Most importantly, LookupLocator can be used to drive the entire unicast discovery protocol to fetch lookup proxies. The section below provides more details on this class, and an example of its use.

Using LookupLocator to Control UnicastDiscovery

You've seen how to use the `LookupDiscoveryManager` class to control unicast and multicast forms of discovery. `LookupDiscoveryManager` uses an asynchronous programming model, where proxies—whether fetched via unicast or multicast discovery—are returned via a callback to a listener.

The `LookupLocator` class, which you've already seen used in the `LookupDiscoveryManager` class and the `DiscoveryLocatorManagement` interface, can provide a *synchronous* way to fetch the proxy for a lookup service, given its location. In unicast discovery, you already *know* where the lookup service resides; all you need is to get the proxy for it. In this case, either the process succeeds or it fails; there is no trickle in of answers as when the multicast protocol is used. This functionality might be useful to you if you don't want or need a full-blown `LookupDiscoveryManager` or `LookupLocatorDiscovery` in your program, or if you want a synchronous programming model for some reason. This role of `LookupLocator` is in addition to its role as "handle" or name for a lookup service.

```
package net.jini.discovery;

public class LookupLocator implements Serializable {
    public LookupLocator(String host, int port);
    public LookupLocator(String url)
                throws MalformedURLException;
    public String getHost();
    public int getPort();
    public ServiceRegistrar getRegistrar()
          throws IOException, ClassNotFoundException;
    public ServiceRegistrar getRegistrar(int timeout)
          throws IOException, ClassNotFoundException;
}
```

Each `LookupLocator` instance represents the location of a single lookup service—running on some host and listening on some port on that host—somewhere on the network. The lookup service need not be nearby on the local network as in the case of multicast discovery, since the unicast protocol underlying this class can go directly to any lookup service anywhere on the network, regardless of distance.

You construct a new `LookupLocator` by providing it with the location of the lookup service you want to talk to. The *location* of a lookup service comprises two parts: the address of the host on which the service is running, and the IP port number on which the service is listening for incoming requests. The address of the host may take the form of a fully qualified domain name or an IP address (e.g., 13.2.116.134).

In the first version of the constructor, you pass these two parameters in separately. In the second, you pass a specially formatted Jini URL that contains the name of the lookup service. This URL has the form `jini://hostname:port/data` or `jini://hostname/data`. The `port` is optional, and defaults to the standard Jini lookup service port number (4160). The `data` part, while valid in the URL syntax, is meaningless to Jini and should be omitted (in the current implementation, this part of the URL is simply ignored). The constructor that takes a string representation of the URL may raise a `MalformedURLException` if the string isn't a properly formatted Jini URL.

The methods `getHost()` and `getPort()` simply return the values for the host and port extracted from the parameters to the constructor. They do not contact the remote lookup service, and do no validation on the values that were passed to the constructor.

Invoking either of the `getRegistrar()` methods actually initiates the unicast discovery protocol. Each of these methods returns the service proxy for the lookup service specified in the constructor, or raises an exception if it fails. There are two ways that the methods may fail. If they run into trouble with the discovery protocol itself, they raise an `IOException`. If the service proxy that is received from the lookup service cannot be reconstituted, they raise a `ClassNotFoundException`.

The first version of the `getRegistrar()` method blocks for a predetermined amount of time, currently one minute in the default implementation.[2] The second version takes a parameter that specifies a timeout, expressed in milliseconds. If either form of the method waits for the duration of its timeout period without hearing from the lookup service, it raises `java.io.InterruptedIOException` (which is a subclass of the basic `java.io.IOException`).

An Example

Next, look at an example (Listing 6–3) of how to use the `LookupLocator` class. This program is similar to the one you saw in the section on `LookupDiscoveryManager`—it contacts a lookup service and then prints out details about

---

2. The timeout value can be set via the `net.jini.discovery.timeout` property. See Appendix B for a complete list of the Jini and RMI properties that are relevant.

it. The difference here is that you provide a URL that names the desired lookup service on the command line. The program uses unicast discovery to go directly to the lookup service and fetch its service proxy and other information about it.

Listing 6–3 `LocatorExample.java`

```java
// Exercise the LookupLocator class

package corejini.chapter6;

import net.jini.core.discovery.LookupLocator;
import net.jini.core.lookup.ServiceRegistrar;
import java.io.IOException;
import java.net.MalformedURLException;
import java.rmi.RemoteException;

public class LocatorExample {
    public LocatorExample() {
    }
```

Listing 6–3 `LocatorExample.java` (continued)

```java
    public ServiceRegistrar getRegistrar(String url)
        throws MalformedURLException, IOException,
                ClassNotFoundException {
        LookupLocator loc = new LookupLocator(url);
        System.out.println("Host: " + loc.getHost());
        System.out.println("Port: " + loc.getPort());
        return loc.getRegistrar();
    }

    public static void main(String[] args) {
        if (args.length != 1) {
            System.out.println(
                    "Usage: LocatorExample <url>");
            System.exit(1);
        }

        LocatorExample loc = new LocatorExample();
        ServiceRegistrar reg;

        try {
            reg = loc.getRegistrar(args[0]);

            System.out.println("Got registrar: ");
            System.out.println("\tURL:     " +
                        PrintingListener.getURL(reg));
            System.out.println("\tID:      " +
                        reg.getServiceID());
            System.out.println("\tGroups: " +
                        PrintingListener.getGroups(reg));
        } catch (MalformedURLException ex) {
            System.err.println("Not a valid jini URL.");
            System.exit(1);
        } catch (Exception ex) {
            System.err.println("Error getting proxy: " +
                            ex.getMessage());
            System.exit(1);
        }
    }
}
```

This example is quite straightforward, because there's not all that much you can *do* with a `LookupLocator`. Here you see that `main()` extracts a string from the

command line and passes it to the `LocatorExample` instance by calling `getReg-`
`istrar()` to attempt to fetch the actual service proxy. The `getRegistrar()`
method creates a `LookupLocator`, dumps out some details about it (which it can
do without going over the wire—the host and port are simply extracted from the
URL), and then tries to get and return its service proxy. The code shown here
reuses the methods from the `PrintingListener` of the earlier example to display the group and URL information about the lookup service.

Compiling and Running the Program

Run this program and see what it does. The compilation instructions are basically the same as for the last example.

On Windows:

```
javac -classpath C:\files;
                  C:\jini1_1\lib\jini-core.jar;
                  C:\jini1_1\lib\jini-ext.jar;
                  C:\jini1_1\lib\sun-util.jar;
                  C:\client
        -d C:\client
  C:\files\corejini\chapter6\LocatorExample.java
```

On UNIX:

```
javac -classpath    /files:
                  /files/jini1_1/lib/jini-core.jar:
                  /files/jini1_1/lib/jini-ext.jar:
                  /files/jini1_1/lib/sun-util.jar:
                  /files/client
  -d /files/client
  /files/corejini/chapter6/LocatorExample.java
```

Now you're set to run the program. You'll have to pass a valid Jini URL on the
command line. You can use one of the URLs that was returned from the `Dis-`
`coveryExample` program earlier.

On Windows:

```
java -cp C:\jini1_1\lib\jini-core.jar;
         C:\jini1_1\lib\jini-ext.jar;
         C:\jini1_1\lib\sun-util.jar;
         C:\client
       -Djava.security.policy=C:\policy
       corejini.chapter6.LocatorExample
```

```
jini://turbodog.parc.xerox.com
```

On UNIX:

```
java -cp /files/jini1_1/lib/jini-core.jar:
        /files/jini1_1/lib/jini-ext.jar:
        /files/jini1_1/lib/sun-util.jar:
        /files/client
      -Djava.security.policy=/files/policy
      corejini.chapter6.LocatorExample
      jini://turbodog.parc.xerox.com
```

The program will perform unicast discovery on the URL you provide to it. Once the service registrar proxy has been downloaded, the program will use it to print out some information about the just-discovered lookup service.

> *Host: turbodog.parc.xerox.com*
>
> *Port: 4160*
>
> *Got registrar:*
>
> > *URL: jini://turbodog.parc.xerox.com/*
> >
> > *ID: c498f93c-9c3c-4c71-94b4-92bc63d863e3*
> >
> > *Groups: PUBLIC*

This program illustrates how to use the `LookupLocator` class to discover a lookup service given its URL-formatted name, and retrieve its service proxy.

Under the Hood: The Discovery Protocols

If you're just writing Jini services and need to have a grasp of the basics of how discovery works, the previous sections should be enough for you. With the overview of discovery and the details about how to actually program against the Jini APIs, you should be all set to tackle most discovery tasks.

But some of you may need more details, either to solve discovery problems, or perhaps because you are building your own custom lookup services that need to correctly interact with services using the discovery protocols. In this section, I'll take an in-depth look at the nitty-gritty details of the three discovery protocols and how they're implemented.

The Multicast Request Protocol

The multicast request protocol is a service-initiated protocol that is used when a service needs to discover all the lookup services that may already exist on a local network. The protocol is implemented using a low-level multicast facility, so it does not require full-fledged Java RMI or CORBA or any other more heavyweight protocol. If, as is usually the case, the multicast request protocol is being run in a standard TCP/IP setting, then multicast UDP datagrams are used as the basis for the protocol. This section describes the implementation of the protocol on top of multicast UDP.

Communication Flow

The initiating service—called the discoverer here, for clarity—sets itself up to both send multicast request messages and receive unicast replies. This is done by creating a couple of sockets, one for outgoing multicast UDP messages and one for incoming TCP messages. Likewise, a lookup service that participates in the multicast request protocol will set up a socket for receiving multicast UDP messages (it *joins* the multicast group represented by the address, in multicast parlance), as well as a socket for sending outgoing TCP messages. These sockets are the twins of those on the service side, as Figure 6–2 shows.

The discoverer then sends the multicast request message, which contains the set of groups in which the discoverer is interested. This message must fit in a single packet, so that it can be contained in a single UDP multicast datagram message. This requirement is because UDP provides no guarantees that a message spanning multiple packets will arrive in order or without packet loss; by making the messages simple, Jini guards against partial message loss.

Further, the message contains only simple data types—no objects—because the discovery protocols are designed to be easy to implement by very lightweight entities. Since these entities may not even have a JVM available to them, the discovery request cannot take advantage of Java serialization or other features.

Packet Format

Figure 6–3 shows the format of the packet.

Wherever a data type such as `int` or `string` is used in the protocol, you can assume that the message was written using the same semantics that you would get if you called `DataOutputStream.writeInt()` or `writeUTF()`. That is, integers are written as four-byte (32-bit) values, with the most-significant byte first (that is, in standard network byte order). Strings are written in UTF-8 character encoding; the first two bytes of a string representation will be the length,

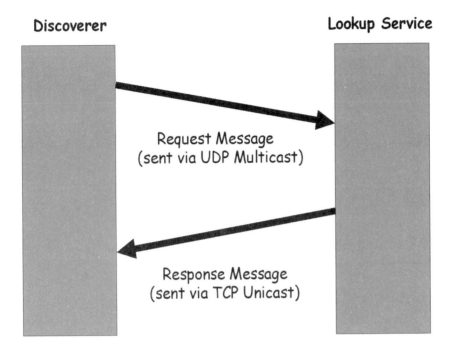

Discoverer

Lookup Service

Request Message
(sent via UDP Multicast)

Response Message
(sent via TCP Unicast)

Figure 6–2   The multicast request protocol

most-significant byte first, and the remaining bytes will contain a representation of the characters in the string. UTF-8 uses one, two, or three bytes to encode each character, depending on its value. Check out the documentation for the `DataOutputStream` class for details on how specific types are written.

The header portion contains the following items:

- The `Protocol Version` is an integer that denotes the version of the discovery protocol being used; explicitly providing the version number allows implementors of future discovery protocols to know when they are speaking with a party that implements an earlier version of the protocol. In the current version of Jini, the version should be set to 1.

- The `Port` field is an integer that should contain the TCP port number that the discoverer is listening on for unicast replies from the lookup service. The lookup service will reply to the port number contained here when it sends its unicast response.

Header

Proto Version <int>	Port <int>

Heard From

Heard Len <int>	Heard 1 <svc id>	Heard 2 <svc id>	...

Groups

Group Len <int>	Group 1 <string>	Group 2 <string>	...

Figure 6–3   *The multicast request packet*

After this short, fixed-length header, come two variable-length chunks of data. The first, called Heard From, contains a list of lookup services from which the discoverer has already heard. If a lookup service receives the multicast request, but is in the "heard from already" set, it should not reply. This allows some optimization of the protocol. This first variable-length block of data consists of the Heard Length field and the Heard field.

- The Heard Length field is an integer containing the number of heard-from lookup service identifiers that follow. The length may be zero if no lookup services have yet been heard from.
- Each Heard item is a representation of a Jini service ID. Each ID is a 128-bit value that will uniquely identify a lookup service (see Chapter 8 for more details on service IDs). Each item is written as a 16-byte chunk, with the most-significant byte first.

The second block of variable-length data, called Groups, contains the set of groups the discoverer is interested in. All lookup services that are members of one of the specified groups should answer the request. This second block of data is described by the `Group Length` field and the `Group` field.

- The `Group Length` field is an integer containing the number of groups that follow. If the length is zero, then the discoverer is indicating that all groups are being searched for.
- Each `Group` denotes the name of a group that is being searched for. Each item here is a string encoded in UTF-8 format. The number of groups should, of course, match the number indicated in the length field.

Jini requires that any message sent via multicast be, at most, 512 bytes long (see the section "Other Internal Discovery Issues," later in this chapter, for details on why this is so). Since there are two components of the request that are variable length, either or both may cause the size of the packet to exceed the size limit of 512 bytes. The Jini discovery specifications dictate that if the `Groups` component causes the packet to exceed 512 bytes, then a discoverer should perform multiple requests. Each request should have a subset of the total group list such that there is no overlap between the groups specified in each request.

If the `Heard From` component causes the packet to exceed 512 bytes, then the set of lookup service IDs from which the discoverer has already heard must be left incomplete. Remember that this is only an optimization, so excluding lookup services from the list, while unfortunate, will not "break" anything. How a discoverer chooses to exclude lookup service IDs from this list is up to it—however, simply truncating the request to 512 bytes is not an option. No matter what solution you take, the packet must be correctly formatted, with a `Heard Length` that correctly denotes the number of service IDs, and no partially sent service IDs.

Once a lookup service receives the multicast message, it can reply to the discoverer. To do this, it must figure out where to send the reply. It builds the Internet address to send its response to by using the port number from the request, and getting the host address by determining the source of the incoming request, using the `getAddress()` call on `java.net.DatagramPacket`.

The message it sends is essentially the same as the response used in the unicast discovery protocol, which I will discuss later. This response transmits a serialized service proxy for the lookup service back to the discoverer, at which point it can reconstitute the object and use the lookup service.

Using the Multicast Request Protocol

Once the discoverer has set itself up for sending requests and receiving responses, it periodically sends multicast request messages. These messages are sent to a well-known address that Jini lookup services listen on (the IP address is 224.0.1.85 and the port number is 4160). While the interval between requests is up to the service, five seconds is a good number to use. As responses come in, the discoverer adds the service IDs of the discovered lookup services to the set of lookup services it has heard from. After some period of time, the discoverer ceases using multicast request, presuming that it has found all active lookup services already running. While the length of time that a service will use multicast request is up to it, seven rounds of messages is recommended by the Jini specifications. After this point, it can stop sending messages and shut down the socket it has been using for receiving requests. Most discoverers at this point will switch over to listening for multicast announcement messages to detect lookup services that start in the future or that reconnect to the network.

As mentioned earlier in the chapter, services should wait for some random period of time before initiating multicast request. This random wait helps to reduce "packet storms" that may flood a network after a power outage or other large failure.

Remember that the details here of using the multicast request protocol are primarily for developers who need to implement the protocol "by hand" for some reason. The Jini class libraries providing the nice set of APIs discussed in this chapter make the job of discovery easier.

The Multicast Announcement Protocol

The multicast announcement protocol is used by lookup services to announce their presence to any interested parties that may be listening and "in range" of the multicast scope of the lookup service. Unlike multicast request, which typically only is used during the start-up phase of a service or when the set of groups it wishes to be a member of changes, multicast announcement is used for the duration of the life of a lookup service. It will periodically announce its existence to any parties that may care to listen.

Communication Flow

The announcement protocol is a bit simpler than the request protocol. The lookup service creates a multicast UDP socket on which to send messages, and a unicast TCP socket on which it will receive messages from interested parties. Services and other applications that wish to receive announcements of new lookup services, again called discoverers here, create a socket to listen for the multicast UDP announcements.

When discoverers receive an announcement from a lookup service they have not heard from, they can contact it by creating a TCP socket and sending a message to the TCP socket the lookup service is listening on for requests. This second half of the protocol is essentially the same as the unicast discovery protocol, which will be discussed shortly. The first half is literally only used to announce the presence of lookup services, so that discoverers can then use the unicast discovery protocol to find out more information about them. The communications flow is shown in Figure 6–4.

Discoverer   **Lookup Service**

Announcement Message
(sent via UDP Multicast)

Request Message
(sent via TCP Unicast)

Response Message
(sent via TCP Unicast)

Figure 6–4   *The multicast announcement protocol*

Packet Format

Figure 6–5 shows the format of the outgoing announcement message that lookup services will send. This packet has essentially the same requirements as the multicast request that discoverers send in the multicast request protocol: it must be no longer than 512 bytes, and should be as simple as possible to encode and decode (thus, it cannot require Java serialization, since the lookup service may not be implemented using Java).

Header

Proto Version <int>	Host <string>	Port <int>	My ID <svc id>

Groups

Group Len <int>	Group 1 <string>	Group 2 <string>	...

Figure 6–5   *The multicast announcement format*

Just as in the request protocol, all data elements are written as if encoded via a `java.io.DataOutputStream`. So, integers are written in standard network byte order (most-significant byte first), and strings are encoded as UTF-8, with the character data preceded by two bytes containing the length. The header of the message contains the following items:

- The `Protocol Version` is an integer, indicating the version of the protocol to accommodate possible future revisions. In the current Jini implementations, this value should always be set to 1.

- The `Host` field is a string containing the name of the host on which the lookup service is running. A discoverer can use this hostname to connect to the lookup service using the unicast discovery protocol.

- The `Port` field contains the port number on which the lookup service is listening for incoming unicast discovery requests. This value is also needed for the discoverer to initiate the second half of the discovery protocol.

- The `Service ID` field represents the globally unique identifier for the lookup service generating the announcement. It represents a `net.jini.lookup.ServiceID` object, a 128-bit value that discoverers can use to determine whether they have heard from this lookup service already. It is encoded as a 16-byte chunk, written with the most-significant byte first.

After this fixed-length header, a variable-length component called `Groups` indicates the names of the groups of which the lookup service is a member.

- The `Group Length` field is an integer that indicates the number of group names to follow.

- Each `Group` item is a string, encoded as UTF-8, that represents one of the groups of which the lookup service is a member. The number of groups should, of course, match the length specified.

Since the variable-length portion of the message may cause the packet to exceed 512 bytes, the lookup service must generate multiple announcements if it supports too many groups to fit into a single message. These messages will each contain a subset of the groups that the service supports, organized in such a way that there is no overlap between messages.

Using the Multicast Announcement Protocol

When a lookup service starts, it creates a UDP multicast socket on which to send its announcement messages. This socket is bound to the well-known address on which discoverers will listen for announcements (the IP address is 224.0.1.84 and the port number is 4160). It also creates a TCP socket to listen for incoming unicast messages from discoverers that have heard the announcements and wish to fetch the lookup service's proxy object using unicast discovery. The lookup service then periodically sends announcement messages. The time between sends is up to the lookup service, but the Jini specifications recommend 120 seconds between announcements.

A discoverer that wishes to receive announcements creates a multicast UDP socket and "joins" this socket to the well-known multicast address on which lookup services will announce themselves. When the discoverer receives an announcement on this socket, it looks at the service ID and list of groups contained in the message. If the service ID is one that the service has already seen, or if the group list doesn't contain any groups the discoverer is interested in, it can ignore the message. Otherwise, it adds the service ID to the list of IDs it has heard from and may initiate unicast discovery to fetch the lookup service's proxy object.

Core Note: Knowing when groups change

The actual implementation of the protocol may be a bit trickier than this, because the set of groups of which a lookup service is a member may change. There is no indication in the multicast announcement protocol when a lookup service suddenly joins, and therefore begins to support, new groups.

Therefore, an interested party should also track the set of groups joined by each of the lookup services it has seen. Then, if a lookup service was ignored because it previously belonged to no interesting groups, the discoverer can see whether an interesting group has been added and continue on to unicast discovery. By tracking group membership, a discoverer can also invoke discard() *if it notices that a previously discovered lookup service no longer belongs to any of the desired groups.*

The LookupDiscoveryManager *class does this for you, which is yet another reason to use these convenience APIs if at all possible.*

Like in multicast discovery, the standard Jini APIs provide an easy way to use multicast announcement—especially since the fact that there is a distinction between multicast request and multicast announcement is hidden from the programmer behind a listener-style interface.

Core Note: Automatic switching between multicast discovery modes

The current implementation of the multicast protocols provided by Jini will start off in the mode of sending multicast requests, and then switch into a mode where they merely wait for multicast announcements from lookup services. Services and applications that implement their own discovery code can choose whether or not to switch modes, and can provide their own policies about when and whether to do so. The current Jini discovery specs recommend that a discovering entity make seven attempts at the multicast request protocol, with five seconds between each attempt. After this, the discovering entity should only listen for announcement messages.

If the set of groups that the discoverer is interested in changes, it may begin multicast request again.

The LookupDiscoveryManager *class handles all of this for you, so you don't have to worry about it if you're using the Jini class libraries for discovery.*

The Unicast Discovery Protocol

Both of the multicast protocols are used in situations where lookup services and other Jini services that are located on a local area network need to find each other. These protocols, since they both involve some element of periodicity—that is, the discovery process continues at intervals for a period of time—also help Jini communities repair themselves after network, machine, and software crashes.

But sometimes, services need to search or join groups associated with lookup services that may not be nearby in the network sense. In these cases, a service needs to be able to retrieve a proxy for a lookup service that may be running on the other end of the building or the other side of the planet. The unicast discovery protocol is used in these situations. And, as you've seen, unicast discovery is also used during the course of the two multicast protocols: when multicast request runs, the service proxy is delivered using the lookup service-to-discoverer half of the unicast discovery protocol. And in multicast announcement, once a discoverer has been made aware of a lookup service, it requests its service proxy using unicast discovery.

In both of these contexts, the multicast protocols are essentially used as a way to "jump start" the unicast discovery process. Unlike multicast, where lookup services and discoverers find each other merely via the fact that multicast will reach all hosts within range, unicast requires *explicit* information about the location of the lookup service. This information includes the name of the host that the lookup service is running on, and the port that the lookup service is listening on for incoming requests. Essentially, in the two serendipitous protocols, multicast is used as a convenient way to provide this information about the location of the lookup service so that unicast can proceed from there.

In this section, you'll learn about the basic unicast discovery protocol, which may be used as part of multicast request, multicast announcement, or as a "stand-alone" protocol for connecting to lookup services whose locations are already known.

Communication Flow

The unicast discovery protocol is very simple. It involves a simple request to the lookup service and a response back to the discoverer. The response always contains the service proxy for the lookup service.

The initial request can come from a number of sources. If unicast discovery is being used as a "stand-alone" protocol, then a discoverer will, through some means, have obtained the location (hostname and port number) of the lookup service, possibly through direct user configuration. It will then make a connection to the lookup service, which will respond with the proxy. Figure 6–6 shows the communication flow for stand-alone discovery.

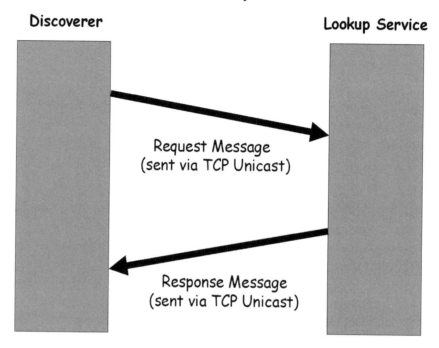

Figure 6–6   *The unicast discovery protocol*

If unicast discovery is being used as a part of the multicast request protocol, the multicast request message serves as the initial request for unicast discovery. It contains all the information needed for the lookup service to respond with its service proxy. In Figure 6–2, which shows the complete multicast request protocol, the final message in the protocol is a unicast discovery response.

If unicast discovery is being used as a part of multicast announcement, then the protocol works just like in the stand-alone case. Announcement distributes the location of the lookup service, and discoverers are then free to use full unicast discovery to get the service proxy. In Figure 6–4, which shows the complete multicast announcement protocol, the second half of the exchange is unicast discovery.

In all these cases, the lookup service can determine the host of the discoverer (which it needs in order to send back its service proxy) by getting the source of the incoming request. The lookup service still needs to know the port number at which the discoverer is listening for its response, though. When unicast discovery is being used as a "stand-alone" protocol, or as part of multicast announcement, the lookup service always connects to the default port (4160) on the discoverer's host. When unicast discovery is being used as part of multicast request, the port number is included as part of the original multicast request message.

Packet Format

Next, take a look at the request that a discoverer uses to initiate unicast discovery. This message is used in stand-alone unicast discovery, or in the second half of the multicast announcement protocol. As mentioned, in multicast request, there is no need for a discoverer to send a separate unicast discovery request, as the multicast request message serves this purpose without requiring that the discoverer already know the location of the lookup service.

The unicast discovery request message is very simple—it contains only one field. Figure 6–7 shows the format of the packet.

- The `Protocol Version` field, an integer, indicates which version of the protocol is being used. This field allows for possible future expansion of the protocol. In all current Jini implementations, this field should be set to 1.

Header

Figure 6–7   *The unicast discovery request format*

Like all Jini discovery messages, the field here is encoded using normal network byte order.

The response is only slightly more complicated. This is the response message that is the end result of *all* the discovery protocols—it delivers a lookup service's proxy, as well as a list of the groups that it supports. Figure 6–8 shows the format of the packet. Here are the fields of the response:

- The message begins with the `Service Proxy` for the lookup service. This is a representation of a `java.rmi.MarshalledObject` for the proxy, written out using Java object serialization.
- The `Group Length` field is an integer containing the number of group names that follow.

Each `Group` item that follows is a UTF-8 encoded string representing the name of a group of which the lookup service is a member. Obviously, the number of group names here should match the length sent.

Service Proxy

Proxy <object>

Groups

Group Len <int>	Group 1 <string>	Group 2 <string>	...

Figure 6–8   *The unicast discovery response format*

Using Unicast Discovery

As I mentioned, unicast discovery is used as a part of the other discovery protocols. A discoverer can initiate unicast discovery using a number of means: multicast request, multicast announcement, or "directly." Initiating direct discovery means that the discoverer has, somehow, learned the location of a lookup service and has sent a unicast discovery request to it. Such a location could be provided by a user or as part of the discoverer's persistent configuration.

The lookup service replies with the response format just given. Once the discoverer receives this response, it can deserialize the `MarshalledObject` included in it, and then call the `get()` method that `MarshalledObject` supports to get the actual service proxy. This proxy implements the `net.jini.core.lookup.ServiceRegistrar` interface and can be used to communicate with the lookup service.

An Example

Let's look at one last example program in this chapter. This is the "lowest level" example here, because it shows how to build the "consumer" side of one of the discovery protocols by hand. The code here implements the requestor half of unicast discovery. As you'll note, it includes *none* of the Jini discovery packages, as it completely implements the protocol itself.

While the example here (Listing 6–4) is of the unicast protocol, which is the simplest of all the discovery protocols, the basic layout of the code here will be the same for any of the protocols.

Listing 6–4 `Unicast.java`

```
// Implement the unicast protocol "by hand"

package corejini.chapter6;

// look ma, no discovery packages.
import net.jini.core.lookup.ServiceRegistrar;
import java.net.Socket;
import java.rmi.MarshalledObject;
import java.io.DataOutputStream;
import java.io.ObjectInputStream;
import java.io.IOException;

public class Unicast {
    public static final int protoVersion = 1;

    public Unicast() {
    }

    public ServiceRegistrar getRegistrar(String host,
                                         int port)
    throws IOException, ClassNotFoundException {
        Socket sock = new Socket(host, port);

        // send the request
        DataOutputStream out =
            new DataOutputStream(sock.getOutputStream());
        out.writeInt(protoVersion);
        out.flush();
```

Listing 6-4 Unicast.java (continued)

```java
// Receive the reply
ObjectInputStream in =
    new ObjectInputStream(sock.getInputStream());
MarshalledObject mobj =
    (MarshalledObject) in.readObject();

System.out.println("Received serialized proxy " +
                   "from registrar.");

int groupLen = in.readInt();
String[] groups = new String[groupLen];

System.out.println("Registrar supports " +
                   groupLen + " groups.");
for (int i=0 ; i<groupLen ; i++) {
    groups[i] = in.readUTF();
    System.out.println("Group " + i + ": " +
                       groups[i]);
}

// Convert the marshalled object into a "live"
// registrar
ServiceRegistrar reg =
    (ServiceRegistrar) mobj.get();

return reg;
}
```

Listing 6–4 `Unicast.java` (continued)

```java
public static void main(String[] args) {
    String host = null;
    int port = 4160;

    if (args.length >= 1) {
        host = args[0];
    }
    if (args.length == 2) {
        try {
            port = Integer.parseInt(args[1]);
        } catch (NumberFormatException ex) {
            System.err.println("Bogus port: " +
                                ex.getMessage());
            System.exit(1);
        }
    }
    if (args.length == 0 || args.length > 2) {
        System.err.println(
                "Usage: Unicast <host> [<port>]");
        System.exit(1);
    }

    Unicast unicast = new Unicast();
    ServiceRegistrar reg;

    try {
        reg = unicast.getRegistrar(host, port);

        System.out.println("Got registrar: ");
        System.out.println("\tURL:      " +
                    PrintingListener.getURL(reg));
        System.out.println("\tID:       " +
                    reg.getServiceID());
        System.out.println("\tGroups: " +
                    PrintingListener.getGroups(reg));
    } catch (Exception ex) {
        System.err.println("Error getting proxy: " +
                            ex.getMessage());
        ex.printStackTrace();
    }
}
}
```

From the user's standpoint, this program works almost the same as the `Loca-torExample` did. Both do essentially the same thing—download the service proxy for a lookup service—only they do it in different ways. Here the program handles the protocol itself, directly, rather than relying on `LookupLocator` to do it. From the user's perspective, the only difference is that a hostname and port number for a lookup service get passed on the command line, rather than a URL (this is just to save the tedium of dissecting the URL in this short example). If no port number is provided, the code will default to 4160, the standard Jini discovery port.

The `Unicast` class does the work. When `getRegistrar()` is called with a host and port number, it creates a socket bound to the address of the lookup service. It then wraps the socket's `OutputStream` in a `DataOutputStream` and writes the protocol version number to the lookup service. The version number is the only outgoing component of the unicast request.

Next, `getRegistrar()` needs to assemble the reply from the lookup service. It gets the socket's input stream and wraps it in an `ObjectInputStream`, because it'll be reading a serialized object from this stream—the actual raw service proxy of the lookup service just found. The code here fetches the proxy, which is stored as a `MarshalledObject` on the stream, and then gets the number of supported groups, and the groups themselves. Once it's got all of the contents of the reply, the code reconstitutes the `MarshalledObject` back into a "live" `ServiceRegistrar` and returns it.

Compiling and Running the Program

Compile this last example of the chapter and give it a run. The compilation instructions are basically the same as for the last example.

On Windows:

```
javac -classpath C:\files;
                 C:\jini1_1\lib\jini-core.jar;
                 C:\jini1_1\lib\jini-ext.jar;
                 C:\jini1_1\lib\sun-util.jar;
                 C:\client
  -d C:\client
  C:\files\corejini\chapter6\Unicast.java
```

On UNIX:

```
javac -classpath  /files:
                 /files/jini1_1/lib/jini-core.jar:
                 /files/jini1_1/lib/jini-ext.jar:
```

```
                       /files/jini1_1/lib/sun-util.jar:
                       /files/client
   -d /files/client
   /files/corejini/chapter6/Unicast.java
```

Now you're set to run the program. Remember that instead of a URL, this program takes a hostname and, optionally, a port number on the command line.

On Windows:

```
java -cp C:\jini1_1\lib\jini-core.jar;
        C:\jini1_1\lib\jini-ext.jar;
        C:\jini1_1\lib\sun-util.jar;
        C:\client
        -Djava.security.policy=C:\policy
        corejini.chapter6.Unicast
        turbodog.parc.xerox.com
```

On UNIX:

```
java -cp /files/jini1_1/lib/jini-core.jar:
        /files/jini1_1/lib/jini-ext.jar:
        /files/jini1_1/lib/sun-util.jar:
        /files/client
        -Djava.security.policy=/files/policy
        corejini.chapter6.Unicast
        turbodog.parc.xerox.com
```

The program will perform unicast discovery on the URL corresponding to the hostname and port you provide to it. Once the service registrar proxy has been downloaded, the program will use it to print out some information about the just-discovered lookup service.

Registrar supports 1 groups.

Group 0:

Got registrar:

    URL: jini://turbodog.parc.xerox.com/

    ID: c498f93c-9c3c-4c71-94b4-92bc63d863e3

    Groups: PUBLIC

This program essentially does the same thing as the `LookupExample` earlier—it uses unicast discovery to find a lookup service and download its service proxy. But in this case, the program implements the entire client side of the unicast protocol "by hand."

Other Internal Discovery Issues

In this section, I'll discuss some other issues that may concern implementors of new lookup services that will use discovery, and network administrators who plan to deploy Jini lookup services. You'll also learn about the rationale for one of the restrictions imposed on the multicast discovery protocols—namely, that protocol messages must fit in one packet.

Multicast Restrictions and Guidelines

As mentioned, the multicast discovery protocols require that all multicast data fit in packets with a maximum length of 512 bytes. The reason for this is that multicast is based on UDP, which makes no guarantees that a series of packets will arrive in the correct order, or even arrive at all. Rather than layering a more heavyweight control protocol atop UDP multicast to ensure that multipacket chunks of data arrive intact, Jini simply requires that each message fit in a single packet, and that each packet be understandable by a receiver without any other context.

The 512-byte requirement comes from the fact that this is the smallest size that IP mandates to be supported by all implementations. So, no matter what actual transport it is running over, IP guarantees that packets of this size or less will arrive intact if they arrive at all.

When multicast protocols are in use, senders should take care to ensure that they limit the scope of their transmissions to keep from flooding a large portion of the network. While the scope of messages is not mandated by the Jini specifications, a TTL value of 15 is recommended for the UDP multicast environment.

While the "under-the-hood" details in this chapter cover the implementation of the discovery protocols atop TCP and UDP multicast, it is possible to implement a protocol for communication between a discoverer and a lookup service over other protocols, even reliable ones. Jini takes the approach that the protocol used for communication *may* run over an unreliable, connectionless transport that makes no guarantee about the order of delivery of packets. By imposing such "lowest common denominator" demands on the network, the Jini concepts should map well to other transports.

Multicast Routing Infrastructure

While most modern IP routers support multicast, there are still some older machines on the Internet that do not. If a router connecting two network segments does not support multicast, then multicast traffic originating on one segment will not be forwarded on to the second segment (although it would still appear on the first and be available to hosts there).

If your network is in such a situation, there are a number of options available to you. The first is simply to run a Jini lookup service on each network segment. This means that only services on the same segment will be able to find each other, unless you explicitly federate your lookup services by providing each lookup service with the name of its peer and having them use unicast discovery to join each other.

A second alternative is to "bridge" between the two segments in such a way that multicast traffic passes between them, even though the routers do not support it. In IP multicast, this technique is called *multicast tunneling*, and is fairly easy to set up. You could even write a simple tunnel yourself: You just create a program that joins a multicast group and forwards all messages it receives on to an IP address for a host on another network segment. The program also reads from a standard socket and relays messages received there on to the multicast socket. By running two of these on machines on different segments, you can relay multicast traffic on distinct segments using unicast IP.

Security

Be forewarned—in the current Jini implementation and specifications, there is no authentication performed on either the discovery requests or responses. This means that it is impossible to know whether the entity contacting you is a "legitimate" lookup service or other service, or what actual human user "owns" those processes.

Sun promises to extend Jini with better distributed security based on the RMI security model being proposed for a future version of Java.

Host and Network Requirements

Let's look at the minimal software support required to run each side of discovery—the requirements for lookup services and the requirements for parties finding lookup services.

In order to run the portions of the discovery protocols required by a lookup service, your machine must have a network stack that can support both multicast UDP and unicast TCP protocols. Implicit in this requirement is that the machine has an IP address. Other than these two requirements, the Jini discovery protocols impose no other burdens on the machine that will host a lookup service. There is not even a requirement for a JVM on this machine—the portion of the discovery protocols that run in the lookup service could easily be implemented in C or any other language. Of course, a particular implementation of a lookup service that uses these protocols may impose its own requirements on the host platform, over and above these.

Parties that are searching for a lookup service have slightly expanded requirements of their host platforms. First, like lookup services, they must have a properly configured network stack capable of UDP multicast and TCP unicast messages. They must also, however, have a JVM available to them. The JVM is needed by these parties because any lookup services that are found will transmit to them a serialized Java object that will be used to communicate with the lookup service. These applications will need a JVM in order to reconstitute and run the proxy objects returned from discovery.

Interfaces for Discovery Implementors

This chapter has gone into some fairly nitty-gritty details about the discovery protocols and how messages are encoded. Most developers who need this information will be building their own lookup services, possibly with different performance and administration characteristics, or that use different network transports. Others may use this information to create alternative APIs to the discovery process, perhaps because the default APIs discussed in this chapter are not flexible enough.

If you find that you need to implement the discovery protocols yourself, you should know that Jini provides a set of APIs that encapsulate the encoding for the messages in the discovery protocols. Writing code that does the actual encoding and decoding of the data in the messages is one of the most potentially error-prone tasks that a discovery implementor could face. To ensure that the on-the-wire format of the discovery messages is the same, the net.jini.discovery package provides classes to do this for you.

While the description of these classes is outside the scope of this book—because they will be used by very few people—you should know that the classes exist, and where to find them. Table 6–1 gives a list of these classes.

Table 6–1 Classes for Discovery Implementors

Class Name	*Description*
OutgoingMulticastRequest	Marshals a multicast discovery request into an array of instances of class `java.net.DatagramPacket`.
IncomingMulticastRequest	Unmarshals a single `DatagramPacket` into a class with methods to access the relevant message fields.
OutgoingMulticastAnnouncement	Marshals a multicast announcement message into an array of `Datagram-Packets`.
IncomingMulticastAnnouncement	Unmarshals a single `DatagramPacket` into a class with methods to access the relevant message fields.
OutgoingUnicastRequest	Marshals a unicast discovery request onto an `OutputStream`.
IncomingUnicastRequest	Unmarshals a unicast request from an `InputStream`.
OutgoingUnicastResponse	Marshals a unicast discovery response onto an `OutputStream`.
IncomingUnicastResponse	Unmarshals a unicast discovery request from an `InputStream` into a class with methods to obtain the service proxy and supported groups.
Constants	Provides a number of useful static constants and methods for accessing common discovery constants, such as addresses and port numbers.

Summary

This chapter has shown how the Jini discovery protocols allow services to come together to form communities. The discovery protocols can support "serendipitous" connectivity—so that spontaneous communities can form based simply on the "nearness" of services to one another—and can also support "direct" connectivity, in which explicit associations are created between services and communities.

A thorough understanding of the protocols underlying discovery is essential if you ever need to debug problems with discovery, or are just curious about how Jini's much-lauded spontaneous networking actually works. But for most developers, the handy `LookupDiscoveryManager` class will be just about all they ever need to use discovery.

What's Next?

Now that you know how to find the lookup services in a Jini community, it's time to move on. The next chapter talks about how to *describe* the services that you find using Jini's notion of *attributes*. The techniques you'll see there will allow you to attach arbitrary Java objects to services, and retrieve and use them later.

Attributes, Templates, and Service Matching

Topics in This Chapter

- Search using attributes
- The Jini standard attributes
- Writing new attributes
- Attributes and JavaBeans
- Using `ServiceTemplates` to combine search criteria
- Service matching rules

Chapter 7

A s you saw in the example programs in Chapter 5, services create and publish records called `ServiceItems` that contain information about themselves. These `ServiceItems` contain the proxy for the service, the service's unique ID, and also any attributes that may describe the service. While you've already seen the basics of how `ServiceItems` get published, and how clients use them, you'll learn much more about these topics in the next few chapters. Chapter 8 covers how services join communities; Chapter 9 shows the low-level interfaces available for interacting with lookup services; and Chapter 10 covers some useful higher level interfaces for clients.

Before delving into how services and clients use lookup, though, I need to spend some time talking about attributes and templates, which are the subjects of this chapter. Jini attributes provide a rich and very flexible way for services to "annotate" their proxies with information describing the service.

Jini provides a set of "standard" attributes—essentially well-formatted information that both clients and services understand and can use to communicate with one another. But service developers can also write their own custom attributes. You'll learn how to do this, and also explore the integration of attributes with the JavaBeans framework.

When clients search for services, they do so by creating templates that describe the services that they're looking for. This template will be *matched* against the `ServiceItems` stored in a lookup service. Templates provide a way for you to search for a service given its unique ID, the interfaces its proxy implements, or the attributes attached to it.

In this chapter, I'll start off by showing how attributes work—what they are, how they're matched, and how you can create new ones. After this, I'll move on to talk about templates and template matching. As you'll see, Jini attributes have a set of rules that determine whether one attribute matches another one. You should understand these rules before you move on to look at template matching. Template matching provides a way to match against *multiple* attributes, as well as other search criteria. The attribute matching rules are a building block for full service template matching.

Understanding how to use attributes and how searching works in Jini is important for creating well-behaved services, and will be essential for your exploration of how to effectively use lookup services in the next few chapters.

Attributes Basics

In the examples in Chapter 5, you saw how to register services using the `ServiceRegistrar` object returned from the discovery process, and how clients can search for services using this same object. When the "Hello, World" services published their proxy objects, they created a `ServiceItem` containing a service ID, the proxy, and a set of attributes. Likewise, when the clients from that chapter connected to a lookup service, they searched by providing template objects that could contain an ID, the class of a proxy, and some attributes.

None of the examples so far, though, have actually *used* any attributes. All of the examples in Chapter 5 simply passed in a null array of `Entry` objects for the attributes.

It's time now to look at what attributes are, how to use them, and what you can do with them. This chapter lays the groundwork for a more in-depth look at how services and clients use lookup in the next few chapters. Much of the work that Jini programs need to do involves using the lookup service and managing attributes. Understanding attributes gives you not only a great tool for describing your services to clients (and end-users), but also gives you powerful ways to search for particular services that you need to use.

What Are Attributes?

Attributes are Java objects that are attached to service proxies. Services attach these attributes when they publish their proxies, and clients can search for proxies by looking for certain attribute patterns, and can download the attributes of a service to examine them closely.

Attributes are used to associate extra descriptive information with a service that might otherwise be unavailable. So, for example, a printer service might have a location attribute that specifies where the printer is, as well as a status attribute that indicates whether the printer is out of paper. These two attributes—location and status—would be Java objects that you created and attached to your service proxy.

Every Java object that you wish to use as an attribute must implement the `net.jini.core.entry.Entry` interface. This interface is a subinterface of `java.io.Serializable`, but adds no new methods itself. Much like `Serializable`, it's merely a "marker" or "tag" interface that you use to indicate that you're allowing a certain class to be used in a certain way.

Search Using Attributes

As I said in the introduction to this chapter, clients search for services by constructing `ServiceTemplates` that describe the matching criteria for the services they are looking for. These `ServiceTemplates` can be used to find services based on their unique IDs, their types, or the attributes attached to them. In this section, I'll talk about the basic rules for how individual attributes are matched. It's essential that you understand the basics of what it means for one attribute to match another one, before moving on to the slightly more complicated topic of how `ServiceTemplates` can be used to match whole *sets* of attributes. That discussion will come in the second half of this chapter; right now, I'll just focus on matching individual attributes.

Jini's attribute mechanisms are designed to make searching for particular attributes simple, quick, and effective. Think about what it might mean to "search" for an arbitrary Java object, however. What would you specify as the search criterion? You could imagine searching based on the class of the object, which would certainly be useful. By using this form of searching, you could find every attribute that is of a certain type. If you were writing a client application that presented a list of all the printers in a building, you might search for all service proxies of type `Printer` that have an attribute of type `Location` on them.

While useful, this form of search is not sufficient for many applications, though. Suppose you want to find only printers on the third floor. If you can search only on the type of the attribute, you'd have to find all printers that have a `Location`, and then manually check each of these to see if the printer is on the third floor. So, a more powerful form of searching would let you match attributes based on their *contents*, not just on their *types*.

Content-based searching allows you to ask the lookup service for those proxies whose attributes contain data that match some pattern you supply. And, importantly, you don't have to provide the *exact* value of the attribute object to match it. If the attribute contains a number of fields, you can specify which you are interested in matching and which you don't care about.

Think about a `Location` attribute. In an office setting, such an attribute might include several fields, including building, floor, and office number. Jini's attribute searching mechanisms allow you to formulate a query that will match any printer in a specified building, any printer on the third floor of *any* building, or any combination of matches on these fields.

The facilities in Jini support both of these search styles. You can use a type-based search to find all proxies that have attributes of a certain type. And you can use a content-based search to find proxies whose attributes match some value.

An attribute search uses the notion of *attribute templates* that are checked for *matches* against the set of attributes on a service. It works like this: When you perform a search, you give it a template. A template is itself just an attribute—no more and no less. The template is compared to all of the stored attributes to see if any match. For the template to match an attribute, the attribute must be of the same class, or a subclass, of the template. Further, the data fields in the template that are non-null must match *exactly* the corresponding data fields in the attribute. If a template has a null data field, it is considered to be a "wildcard" that matches any value in the attribute.

When I say that a data field must exactly match the value in the template, I mean that two data fields, when serialized, produce the same bytes. In the lookup service, the fields of templates and attributes are stored in their already serialized forms as `MarshalledObjects`. Comparison of two fields calls the `equals()` method on `MarshalledObject`, which reports true if the fields serialize to the same sequence of bytes (ignoring the codebase that may be attached to the object by RMI). Note that the `equals()` method on the `Object` class, as well as any `equals()` method that may exist on the attribute class, is never called. So you cannot override this method to change matching behavior.

The template matching scheme is convenient because it allows a program to search based on any part of an attribute that it considers salient—a program need not match the *entire* attribute completely to have a match; it can use wildcards for fields that it doesn't care about, and specify those that it does care about.

Because templates can potentially match attributes that are of the same class or a subclass of the attribute, templates can be used to find extensions of types known to the searching program.

The template matching mechanisms used by Jini are simple, intuitive, and easy for the system to implement. They allow wildcard searches without necessitating any changes to the objects that you're searching for, or complicated edifices of pattern-matching code. But you should be aware of one minor limitation of the way Jini templates work—because a null field is "reserved" to indicate a wildcard value, there is no way for you to explicitly search for attributes whose fields are set to null. To find an attribute that has a null field, you must use a template with a wildcard that will match *any* value in that field. You will then need to retrieve all matching attributes, and skim out only the ones that have the null fields you are looking for.

The Special Semantics of Attributes

While you can think of attributes as simply arbitrary serializable Java objects—because that's what they are—Jini doesn't use all the "objectness" of these objects in performing its searches. To Jini, a searchable attribute is simply a collection of its data fields. All of the methods of the object are ignored for purposes of searching, as are various "special" data fields: static, transient, non-public, or final fields. Likewise, all fields that are primitive types (such as ints and booleans) are ignored; only references to other objects within an attribute are considered for searching.

In fact, the best way to think of Entries is not as single Java objects—they should be thought of as *collections* of Java objects, because what really matters from the search standpoint are the individual fields in an Entry. Each member in an Entry is a separate item in the collection, independent from all others for the purposes of a search. Figure 7–1 illustrates this notion.

Paring down the searchable parts of objects to this bare minimum means that Jini can implement attribute searching very simply, and without requiring the writers of attributes to implement any special code. One could imagine an alternative where every attribute had to have a searchMe() method that participated in the search process; Jini uses nothing so complicated, and thus allows more types of objects to be used as attributes.

Entry objects are Serializable, so they can be transmitted to lookup services when a service registers itself, and so they can be downloaded to clients when proxies are retrieved. Like all Serializable objects, Entry objects must have a no-argument constructor if they extend a non-Serializable class.

But Entry objects have a few more special semantics than regular objects, even regular Serializable objects. First, all the fields of a given entry are serialized *separately* and *independently* from one another. This means that if a given entry has two fields that refer to the same object, two copies of that object will be

A "Service Version" Entry

For Content-Search, an Entry is the Collection of its Members

Figure 7–1   *Entries are collections of objects*

serialized. This is different than the standard serialization behavior, where normally any object written to a serialization stream twice will result in only one copy of the object being stored. When an Entry is reconstituted, each of its fields will point to a separate copy of the object.

Why is this so? Why do Jini attributes diverge from the normal semantics of serialization? If all references in an entry were "chunked" together into one serialized stream, searching for particular references would involve either deserializing the entire Entry (an expensive operation), or "understanding" the serialized format well enough to crawl through it, looking for particular references. Because the ability to search on individual fields in an object is essential, serializing members separately means that search code can provide this behavior while executing quickly, with no understanding of the particular serialized format of an attribute. This is why it's useful to think of attributes as being collections of their members, rather than indivisible objects.

Figure 7–2 shows how this works. On the left is an Entry object before it has been serialized. Note that two of its member references point to the same object. On the right, you see this same object after it has gone through the process of serialization and reconstitution. Note that the references that originally pointed at the same object now point to two separate objects. Each of these is a copy of the original, created because the original was serialized separately for each of the two references to it.

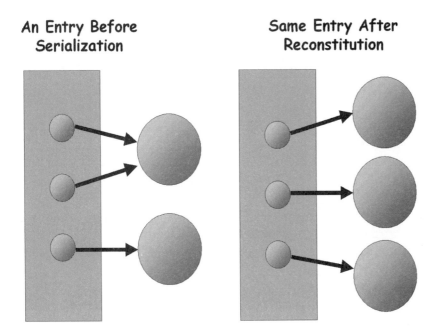

An Entry Before Serialization

Same Entry After Reconstitution

Figure 7–2 *An entry before and after serialization*

The peculiar semantics of `Entry` objects have implications for you as a writer of services and clients. Even though only the public, nonstatic, nonfinal, nontransient object references "matter" from the standpoint of searching, you can still include whatever code, data, and methods in your attributes that you want—the code, etc. just won't be considered in the search process. These attributes can be transmitted to clients who can use them just as they would any other object returned through RMI or dynamically loaded via a class loader. You simply have to realize that all of the data members in your object will be reconstituted separately when the attribute is reconstituted at the client. This is the real reason that Jini has the `Entry` "tagging" interface that adds no methods—it is to ensure that you have considered the implications of using your code as an attribute when you write it.

If, for some reason, your attribute cannot be properly deserialized (probably because it contains a reference to a nonserializable object), any client that tries to retrieve your attribute will get a `net.jini.core.entry.UnuseableEntryException` when it tries to fetch it. You'll learn about this exception, and about how clients search for and fetch attributes, a bit later in this chapter. For now, however, let's continue our look at how attributes are used.

Who Changes Attributes?

I've talked about the fact that attributes are used to describe services. Occasionally, the description of a service may need to change—if a printer is moved, the location attribute on it must be updated; if it runs out of paper, its status attribute should reflect this fact.

Who is actually responsible for changing these attributes that describe services? Clearly, the service itself can take charge of some of these. If a printer can tell that it's out of paper, there's no reason it shouldn't advertise this fact via an attribute; requiring a human to notice that the printer is out of paper and attaching a status attribute to it is just extra work that we shouldn't need to do. So some attributes represent information that the service and the service alone should have control over.

Other attributes reflect information that a particular service may have no inkling of, however. If you pack up and move a printer to a new office, the printer will have no idea where it is. Some human, likely the printer's owner, will have to explicitly set the location attribute of the printer, if he or she wants to advertise its location to the rest of the world. In cases like this, there is no way the service can know the correct value of an attribute ahead of time, and an actual human *must* set the value, if it is to be set.

There are actually a wealth of human-attachable attributes that one might want to add: attributes to comment on a particular service, to leave helpful hints about its use, or to leave the e-mail address of the resident expert on using the service. So in general, Jini services should provide a way for users to create and add new attributes; some of these may be from the "standard" set of attributes, and others may be "home-grown" attributes that have meaning only to a particular individual or organization.

Jini provides a convention that attribute writers can use to describe which type of attribute they are creating. If an attribute is meant to be changed *only* by a service, it should implement the `net.jini.lookup.entry.ServiceControlled` interface. This interface, much like `Entry`, is merely a "tagging" interface that says that the attribute should not be changed by anyone or anything other than the service that added it. This interface has no methods; it's merely a way for Jini to tell what kind of access control to grant to the particular attribute that implements it.

An attribute that does not implement `ServiceControlled` is effectively saying that it is freely writable, and can be used by humans, other services, or applications to squirrel away information that may be useful in the future.

Services that wish to change the set of attributes associated with themselves can use the various interfaces available to services, described in the next chapter. But how do users and client programs change the attributes on a service? The answer is that services should *allow* them to add attributes to their proxies. Most services in Jini should provide an "administration" interface that allows client programs—as well as users, through those client programs—to change the set of attributes on a service. These same administration interfaces can often be used to start or stop a service, change the set of groups it joins, and change the set of explicit lookup services it registers itself with.

Chapter 14 has all the details on service administration. For the discussion of attributes here, though, all you need to know is that certain attributes are controllable by either users or the services that published them, while others "belong" solely to the service. This latter type of attribute should implement the `Service-Controlled` interface.

The Standard Attributes

The Jini class libraries provide a number of "standard" attribute types that should be used to provide information about services. By agreeing on a set of these types, services can publish information about themselves in a well-understood format, and clients can have an idea of what they should be searching for.

The Jini standard attributes are defined in the `net.jini.lookup.entry` package. Hopefully, as the industry gains more experience with Jini, more and more attributes will become standardized, and applications can be written to expect these types. Sun believes that the Jini community process will lead to the creation and adoption of new attribute types.

Table 7–1 provides a list of the basic standard attribute types.

Table 7–1 Standard Jini Attributes

Attribute	*Purpose*
`Address`	Provides information on the geographical location of a service, such as country, city, and street address. This attribute type is distinct from `Location`, which describes a location within an organization. This attribute is not `ServiceControlled`.
`Comment`	Used to provide a free-form string comment on a service. This attribute is not `ServiceControlled`.
`Location`	Provides information on the location of a service within an organization—building, floor, and room number. This attribute is not `ServiceControlled`.
`Name`	Used to designate a human-readable name for the service that will be seen by its users. The name of a service should be something that users will naturally understand, like "Fred's VCR." This attribute is not `ServiceControlled`.
`ServiceInfo`	Used to provide generic information about a service's manufacturer, model name, serial number, and so on. This attribute has a name field, which should provide the "generic" name of the product, rather than the specific name of an instance of the product (so, "Fleebtix VideoStar 1500" rather than "Fred's VCR," for example). This attribute is `ServiceControlled`.
`ServiceType`	Used to associate human-readable information that can describe a service. The `ServiceType` attribute includes a localized name for the service, a short description for it, and an icon to use for it. This attribute is `ServiceControlled`.
`Status`	Used to provide information on the current operating state of a service. The `Status` class is meant to be used as a superclass for service-specific types of status. The class, along with its supporting `StatusType` class, supports the designation of multiple error levels, from NORMAL up through ERROR. Users can search for particular error levels without having to understand the specifics of the `Status` subclasses used by individual services.

Writing New Attributes

The Jini standard attributes provide tools to associate information with services in ways that will be understood by nearly every Jini-aware application that will be written. Because these attributes are standardized and included with Jini itself, information such as comments, locations, and manufacturer details will be encoded using these types, and applications will be written to look for and use them.

But sometimes you may need to create your own attributes. Sometimes the standard types are insufficient for the information you'd like to reveal about your service, and sometimes your organization may have decided on its own set of conventions for the kinds of information to associate with services. In these situations, you should create your own attribute types to store information about your service. Creating new attribute classes is easy—nearly as easy as just writing a Java object—and gives you complete freedom in how to represent the information that you will attach to your service.

You should, however, try to use the standard attributes wherever possible. Jini services can have any number of attributes attached to them, and can even have multiple attributes of the same type attached to them (a computer may have multiple `Name` attributes, for example). Because so many applications will expect the standard attributes, you should use them in addition to whatever extra information you provide.

I've already covered most of the details of writing new attribute classes: For the most part, you simply have to create a class that implements the `Entry` interface. Because this interface requires no methods, "implementing" it is trivial. `Entry` is a subinterface of `Serializable`, so you do have to take the normal steps that you would take to write a `Serializable` class—have a default, no-argument constructor if it extends a non-serializable class, ensure that anything you *don't* want to be serialized is flagged with the `transient` keyword or is static, and make sure that all the data that you reference is itself `Serializable`. This last requirement—making sure that all objects you reference are `Serializable`—is easily forgotten and can lead to great pain and misery when debugging.

Also, remember to take into consideration the special semantics of `Entry` objects with regard to searching and serialization. Searches involve only the public, nontransient, nonstatic, nonfinal object reference fields in an attribute. So, if you want clients to be able to search your attributes based on some data they contain, make sure that the data is stored as an object, and that the reference to it is public, nonstatic, nonfinal, and nontransient.

With regard to serialization, recall that all object reference fields in an attribute are serialized independently from one another, and will be reconstituted independently from one another when a client downloads your attribute. You must take special care to ensure that your object has no cross-field dependencies that will cause strange or broken behavior after reconstitution.

If you are writing a simple attribute that doesn't need to inherit from some pre-existing class, you can use the Jini `AbstractEntry` as your attribute's superclass. This class, which lives in `net.jini.entry`, provides some handy methods that override some of the methods in the `Object` class: `AbstractEntry` provides new implementations of `equals()`, `hashCode()`, and `toString()` that are useful in the context of `Entry` objects. For example, `toString()` returns a string containing each field's name and value. And `equals()` performs the `Entry` comparison test—it sees if the relevant (nonstatic, public, etc.) fields in two `Entry` objects match.

You don't have to use the `AbstractEntry` class, but if you're not already subclassing an existing class, you may find it useful. All of the Jini standard attributes use `AbstractEntry` as their superclass.

Finally, you should plan on human readability of your new attribute type. At a minimum, you should provide a sensible implementation of the `toString()` method, so that users who view your attribute will be able to read it. If you are implementing complex attribute types, you should also consider providing ways to integrate your attribute with the JavaBeans framework, as described in the next section.

An Example: A Capacity Attribute

Take a look at an example of a new attribute. Many services and devices have some innate capacity associated with them. For example, a storage service may have a maximum number of bytes that it can store; a digital camera can only store so many pictures before it exceeds its limits.

You can define a *capacity* attribute that captures this sort of information. A "generic" capacity attribute could be reused by many services, because it is not dependent on the "units" of storage (megabytes, or photos, or documents).

You can see how such an attribute might be implemented in Listing 7–1.

Listing 7–1 `Capacity.java`

```
package corejini.chapter7;

import net.jini.entry.AbstractEntry;
import net.jini.lookup.entry.ServiceControlled;

public class Capacity extends AbstractEntry
        implements ServiceControlled {
    public Integer maxCapacity;
    public Integer inUse;
    public Integer freeSpace;

    public Capacity() {
        maxCapacity = new Integer(0);
        inUse = new Integer(0);
        freeSpace = new Integer(0);
    }

    public Capacity(int max, int used) {
        maxCapacity = new Integer(max);
        inUse = new Integer(used);
        freeSpace = new Integer(max - used);
    }
}
```

This new `Capacity` attribute starts off by extending the `AbstractEntry` class. By extending this class, it inherits useful implementations of `toString()` and other methods. The new class also implements `ServiceControlled` because the amount of free space in a service is intrinsic to that service and should not be altered directly by a user or a client (of course, the free space available in a service can and will change through administration of the service. But the attribute itself should never be changed or overwritten by anyone other than the service itself).

Although this class is straightforward, there is one interesting design point to make. Here, the three aspects of capacity—the maximum amount of storage, the amount of storage currently in use, and the amount of storage currently available—are stored as separate `Integer`s. At first glance this may appear wasteful. Certainly, given any two of these you could compute the other one.

The reason for "breaking out" these details as separate objects is to facilitate a search for them. Some searches may be interested in all storage services that have a maximum total capacity of a certain size; other searches may be looking for storage services with a given amount of free capacity, and yet others may be looking for heavily used storage services that are holding some given number of items. By using individual members for each of these, they can be searched individually. You could imagine other computed values that might be of interest and could be stored as separate members in this attribute. A "percent full" member might be of interest to some applications, for instance.

Unfortunately, there is no way to construct an attribute search to perform comparisons of data members in an attribute. So there is no way, using the `lookup()` method, to directly ask for all services with a maximum capacity *over* a given amount. A client that needs to do this sort of query would retrieve everything with a capacity and then look for those with particular values. Chapter 10 presents some high-level client-side APIs that make this job a bit easier, though.

Next, I'll build on this simple `Capacity` attribute to explore the relationship of attributes and JavaBeans.

Attributes and Beans

As I've said many times in this chapter, attributes are simply Java objects, albeit with some special serialization behavior to make searching more effective. As full-blown Java objects, you can set member fields in attributes and call methods on those attributes, if they have them.

But, just as "normal" Java objects can sometimes be difficult to work with—because they may not follow certain design patterns that indicate how to use them—attributes can also be somewhat opaque. In the Java world, special objects that follow certain design patterns are called *beans*. A bean is simply a Java object, just like any other, but it follows a set of conventions about how it will work and what its methods will be named.

For example, all beans have a no-argument constructor. Most beans are `Serializable`. If a bean has data in it that is accessible from outside the bean, it must have "get" and "set" methods that allow access to the data; these methods must follow JavaBeans-prescribed naming conventions.

All of these requirements are so that programs—particularly development tools—can *introspect* these objects and, if not understand *what* they do, at least get a sense of *how* they might do it. That is, they can figure out what methods are available to change the bean's state, and get some idea of how those methods work together. The JavaBeans `Introspector` class has the intelligence to look at a class that follows the bean conventions, and report on how to interact with the bean.

Beans also follow conventions that allow them to provide extra information describing their use. Any bean class will typically also come with a corresponding `BeanInfo` class that provides details on the fields and methods of the bean, as well as extra useful information such as icons that can be used to represent the bean on a palette of tools.

If an attribute followed the bean conventions or, alternatively, there were a way to associate a bean with an attribute at run time, then you could leverage all the power of the JavaBeans framework when working with attributes.

Using Entry Beans to Map Entries to Beans

Fortunately, Jini provides just such a facility. Jini uses the notion of *entry beans*, which are beans that correspond to particular `Entry` classes (recall that `Entry` is simply the interface that all attributes will implement). An entry bean for a given entry will provide "get" and "set" methods for every data member that the `Entry` contains. Entry beans "wrap" normal `Entry` objects, and allow them to participate in the JavaBeans framework. In Jini, all beans that represent entries implement the `EntryBean` interface.

Next I'll show how you create and use entry beans. If you have an entry— whether as a service or as a client—and you want to create an associated bean for it so that you can use the bean programmatically or introspect on it, you go through the `net.jini.lookup.entry.EntryBeans` class. This class provides some static utility methods for finding and instantiating entry beans for a given `Entry`. Take a look at the methods it provides:

```
package net.jini.lookup.entry;

public class EntryBeans {
        public static EntryBean createBean(Entry ent)
                    throws ClassNotFoundException,
                            IOException;
        public static Class getBeanClass(Class c)
                    throws ClassNotFoundException;
}
```

The `createBean()` method instantiates an `EntryBean` given a particular `Entry` instance. The method will search for an `EntryBean` class that corresponds to the specified `Entry`, instantiate it, connect it to the `Entry` instance you passed in, and return it.

The `getBeanClass()` method simply tries to load the class of the `EntryBean` that corresponds to the `Entry` class you pass in (if you pass the class of something that's not an `Entry`, you'll get a `ClassCastException` run-time error). Once you've got the class, you can instantiate it yourself.

How Are Entry Beans Found?

The scheme that the `EntryBeans` utility class uses to find beans is simple, and is very similar to the method used by the "regular" JavaBeans bean-loading facilities. For an `Entry` with a given class name, say `Foo`, the `EntryBeans` class tries to find a class called `FooBean`. It tries to find this class by calling first the class loader that originally loaded the `Entry`, and then by calling its own default class loader.

The fact that the `EntryBeans` class first tries the class loader that was responsible for loading the `Entry` means that you can engineer some elegant code with beans. For example, if the original `Entry` was loaded remotely, say via RMI, then the code that implements the entry's bean can be stored on the same HTTP server and will be transmitted to the caller when it is needed. Once a bean is loaded, you can use the same class loader to fetch any extra information, such as `BeanInfo` classes, that may exist to describe how to use the bean.

If you create your own attribute classes, you should definitely consider creating corresponding `EntryBeans` and storing the code for them on the same server that manages the code for your `Entry` classes.

The Entry Bean Class

The Jini `net.jini.lookup.entry` package contains an interface that should be implemented by all entry beans. This interface is called, logically enough, `EntryBean`. If you create a new attribute type and want to make a new bean to go along with it, there are a few standard steps that you must take.

1. Create your bean class by implementing `EntryBean`.
2. Name your bean class by taking the name of your `Entry`'s class and appending "`Bean`" to it. So, for example, if your `Entry` is of class `Fleezle`, your bean should be of class `FleezleBean`. The bean should be in the same package as your `Entry` class.
3. Make sure your bean has a public, no-argument constructor and implements `Serializable` (so that it can be transmitted to clients as needed).
4. For every significant data member in the `Entry`, provide "get" and "set" methods in your bean. So, for example, if your `Entry` has a reference to an object called `foo`, you should provide meth-

ods called `getFoo()` and `setFoo()`, following the standard Java capitalization conventions.

The `EntryBean` interface is quite simple. It requires that you implement only two methods. Take a look at that interface:

```
package net.jini.lookup.entry;

public interface EntryBean {
        public void makeLink(Entry e);
        public Entry followLink();
}
```

The first method, `makeLink()`, is used to "wire up" the bean to an existing `Entry`. By calling this method, you create the association between a particular bean and a particular attribute. Your implementation of this method will typically be quite simple: You stash the reference to the `Entry` in your bean, and then all of your "get" and "set" methods simply access the data members in that `Entry`. If, for some reason, a caller passes in an `Entry` which is of the wrong type for your bean, you should raise a `ClassCastException`.

The next method, `followLink()`, simply provides a way to access the original `Entry`, given the bean.

While the requirements of implementing the `EntryBean` interface are practically trivial, you should make sure that you do, in fact, implement this interface. The `EntryBeans` utility class will complain loudly (through the use of `ClassCastExceptions`) if your bean doesn't implement this interface, even if it is named correctly.

If the `Entry` class that you're wrapping is particularly complex, you may want to consider making your bean a `java.awt.Component`, a `javax.swing.JComponent`, or some other "active" entity so that it can be displayed and edited properly. Ensuring that actual human users can understand, use, and edit your attributes is an important requirement, and providing a user interface for your attributes via a bean is an easy way to do this.

The Standard Entry Beans

Just as Jini provides a standard set of attributes, it also provides a standard set of beans that can wrap those attributes. In fact, for each of the standard `Entry` types, the `net.jini.lookup.entry` package contains a corresponding `EntryBean`.

In their current implementation, these bean classes only wrap their corresponding Entry classes; they do not provide any extra BeanInfo descriptions or icons or anything fancy like that. Future Jini releases should provide a richer set of Entry classes, along with more complex beans to support them.

An Example: A Capacity Bean

Look at a minimalist bean for the Capacity attribute in Listing 7–2. This bean is simply a wrapper for a Capacity instance.

Listing 7–2 CapacityBean.java

```
package corejini.chapter7;

import net.jini.core.entry.Entry;
import net.jini.lookup.entry.EntryBean;
import java.io.Serializable;

public class CapacityBean
            implements EntryBean, Serializable {
    protected Capacity assoc = null;

    public CapacityBean() {
    }
```

Listing 7–2 `CapacityBean.java` (continued)

```java
public Entry followLink() {
    return assoc;
}
public void makeLink(Entry e) {
    if (e != null && !(e instanceof Capacity)) {
        throw new ClassCastException(
            "Expected corejini.chapter7.Capacity");
    }
    assoc = (Capacity) e;
}
public Integer getMaxCapacity() {
    return assoc.maxCapacity;
}
public void setMaxCapacity(Integer maxCapacity) {
    assoc.maxCapacity = maxCapacity;
}
public Integer getInUse() {
    return assoc.inUse;
}
public void setInUse(Integer inUse) {
    assoc.inUse = inUse;
}
public Integer getFreeSpace() {
    return assoc.freeSpace;
}
public void setFreeSpace(Integer freeSpace) {
    assoc.freeSpace = freeSpace;
}
}
```

Here you see the basics of creating a bean for an attribute. The `CapacityBean` class implements `EntryBean` and is `Serializable` because, obviously, it will be downloaded to clients as needed. The class implements the simple `makeLink()` and `followLink()` methods by using an internal reference to a `Capacity` entry; note that `makeLink()` raises a `ClassCastException` if a caller tries to create a link to an `Entry` that's not a `Capacity`.

By following the bean naming conventions, you can allow the data in a `Capacity` object to be introspected and used programmatically—all of the members of the attribute are mapped into "get" and "set" functions that access the wrapped `Capacity`.

Once you've created a bean class for your attribute, you can go further and create extra information that can describe how to use the bean. For example, you can create `BeanInfo` and `BeanDescriptor` classes that provide guidelines on how the bean should be used. If you define any exotic types in your attribute, you can provide bean `PropertyEditors` that allow users to display and edit these types, or `Customizers` that allow users to interact with the entire bean as a whole.

Listing 7–3 shows an example of a `BeanInfo` class for the above bean. It's pretty simple: Because `Capacity` defines no unusual types, there is no need for specialized `PropertyEditors` or `Customizers`. The only "extra" information provided here is a `BeanDescriptor` that has an extended description of the `CapacityBean`.

Listing 7–3 `CapacityBeanBeanInfo.java`

```java
package corejini.chapter7;

import java.beans.BeanInfo;
import java.awt.Image;
import java.beans.BeanDescriptor;
import java.beans.MethodDescriptor;
import java.beans.EventSetDescriptor;
import java.beans.PropertyDescriptor;

public class CapacityBeanBeanInfo implements BeanInfo {
    protected BeanDescriptor beanDesc = null;

    public CapacityBeanBeanInfo() {
    }

    public BeanInfo[] getAdditionalBeanInfo() {
       return null;
    }
    public BeanDescriptor getBeanDescriptor() {
       if (beanDesc == null) {
          beanDesc = new BeanDescriptor(
                  corejini.chapter7.CapacityBean.class,
                  null);
          beanDesc.setShortDescription(
              "This Jini attribute shows the capacity "
              + "of a storage service.");
          }
       return beanDesc;
    }
    public EventSetDescriptor[] getEventSetDescriptors()
{
       return null;
    }
```

Listing 7–3 `CapacityBeanBeanInfo.java` (continued)

```
    public int getDefaultEventIndex() {
        return -1;
    }

    public PropertyDescriptor[] getPropertyDescriptors() {
        return null;
    }
    public int getDefaultPropertyIndex() {
        return -1;
    }

    public Image getIcon(int param1) {
        return null;
    }
    public MethodDescriptor[] getMethodDescriptors() {
        return null;
    }
}
```

For most of the `BeanInfo` methods, the class returns null, indicating that it is providing no special information over what can be determined by the JavaBeans `Introspector` class. If you wanted, you could return extra information here, describing which parts of the `CapacityBean` are considered to be for "expert" use only, and provide icons for your bean.

Here, I've implemented the `getBeanDescriptor()` method to return a new `BeanDescriptor` with a short description of the `CapacityBean`. This is meant to be a human-readable message that can be presented to users.

The JavaBeans loading facilities dictate how `BeanInfo` objects must be named. A `BeanInfo` class for a given bean is named by taking the name of the original bean and appending "`BeanInfo`" to it. So here, I've given the class the rather awkward name of `CapacityBeanBeanInfo` so that it can be found at run time.

A Second Bean Example: Using GUI Beans

The `CapacityBean` is certainly a JavaBean—it follows all of the patterns and naming conventions of the beans framework—but it doesn't provide much other value. The information contained in a `Capacity` object is amenable to a graphical presentation, so you could create a new `CapacityBean` class that is a graphical component.

This new bean would still follow all of the bean conventions, and would implement all of the methods shown above. But it would also be a full-fledged component that clients could drop into GUI applications as needed.

You can see such a bean in Listing 7–4.

> **Listing 7–4 Another Version of** `CapacityBean.java`

```
package corejini.chapter7;

import net.jini.core.entry.Entry;
import net.jini.lookup.entry.EntryBean;
import java.io.Serializable;
import javax.swing.JLabel;
import javax.swing.JPanel;
import javax.swing.JProgressBar;
import javax.swing.BoxLayout;

public class CapacityBean extends JPanel
            implements EntryBean, Serializable {
    protected Capacity assoc = null;

    public CapacityBean() {
        super(true);
        setBackground(java.awt.Color.white);
        setLayout(new BoxLayout(this, BoxLayout.Y_AXIS));
        add(new JLabel("Not initialized"));
    }

    public Entry followLink() {
        return assoc;
    }
    public void makeLink(Entry e) {
        if (e != null && !(e instanceof Capacity)) {
            throw new ClassCastException(
                "Expected corejini.chapter7.Capacity");
        }

        assoc = (Capacity) e;

        init();
    }
```

> **Listing 7–4** Another Version of `CapacityBean.java` (continued)

```
protected void init() {
    // Clear out anything lingering from a
    // previous init()
    removeAll();

    JLabel label = new JLabel("Max = " +
                        getMaxCapacity() +
                        ", used = " + getInUse() +
                        ", free = " +
                        getFreeSpace());
    JProgressBar slider = new JProgressBar(0,
                        getMaxCapacity().intValue());
    slider.setValue(getInUse().intValue());

    add(slider);
    add(label);
}

public Integer getMaxCapacity() {
    return assoc.maxCapacity;
}
public void setMaxCapacity(Integer maxCapacity) {
    assoc.maxCapacity = maxCapacity;
}
public Integer getInUse() {
    return assoc.inUse;
}
public void setInUse(Integer inUse) {
    assoc.inUse = inUse;
}
public Integer getFreeSpace() {
    return assoc.freeSpace;
}
public void setFreeSpace(Integer freeSpace) {
    assoc.freeSpace = freeSpace;
}
}
```

This class is a reimplementation of the first `CapacityBean`. The most notable difference is that the new implementation is a subclass of `JPanel`. This means that it inherits full functionality as a Swing component—it can be nested within other components and used just as you would any other widget in the Swing package.

I'll walk through how this code works. First, notice that the class implements all of the "standard" "get" and "set" methods that are required if the code is to be a bean for the `Capacity` class. But here, whenever `makeLink()` is called, `CapacityBean` initializes two subcomponents that provide a graphical view of the capacity of a service. The code creates a `JLabel` and a `JProgressBar` that provide a view of current capacity.

To use GUI beans such as this, clients must do the following:

- For a given attribute, fetch its bean.
- Introspect the bean, to see if it is a subclass of `Component`.
- If the bean is a component, it can be displayed on the screen; otherwise, the client should create a default label or other display by calling the `toString()` method on the original attribute.

If you write your clients to test whether beans it retrieves are `Components`, you can greatly enhance the appearance and usefulness of your code.

Core Note: User interfaces for Jini services

Actually, as you'll see in Chapter 14, there are a number of options available to you when you want to associate a user interface with a Jini service or attribute. Each of these approaches has different trade-offs. Check out Chapter 14 for a discussion of some strategies for building user interfaces for Jini; there is no single strategy that is best for all applications.

Matching using ServiceTemplates

So far in this chapter I've focused mainly on attributes—what they are, how they differ from "normal" serializable Java objects, how to create them, and how they're matched. As I said in the introduction, the primary use of attributes is to *describe* services so that clients can find them easily. You've seen the rules for how individual attributes match one another, and how to create templates to match attributes. Now it's time to look at the `ServiceTemplate` class. This is the class that clients use to construct their search criteria, which may include an attribute search as described earlier.

The Jini service template matching system is extremely flexible and yet simple to use. When searching, you can find services based on the set of attributes associated with them (using the type- and content-based attribute matching rules I've already described); you can search for one *explicit* service by looking it up via its service ID; and you can search for services that implement particular interfaces that your client knows how to use.

The way you describe what you'd like to search for is by using the `ServiceTemplate` class. Each `ServiceTemplate` has fields for specifying service IDs, service types, and desired attributes. Any or all of these can be null to specify a "wildcard" value which will match any service. Here are the relevant parts of the `ServiceTemplate` definition.

```
package net.jini.core.lookup;

public class ServiceTemplate
            implements Serializable {
        public ServiceTemplate(ServiceID serviceID,
                                Class[] serviceTypes,
                                Entry[] attrSetTmpls);
        public ServiceID serviceID;
        public Class[] serviceTypes;
        public Entry[] attrSetTemplates;
}
```

When you create a `ServiceTemplate`, you simply "fill in" the fields that you care about with appropriate values. If you know the ID of the service you're searching for, you can fill it in and leave the other fields null. Likewise, if you know the class of the service you're searching for, or any of its attributes, you can fill these in and leave other fields empty.

When a lookup service looks for matches against a given `ServiceTemplate`, it compares the template to all of the `ServiceItems` it stores. The rules that determine whether a `ServiceTemplate` matches a `ServiceItem` are analogous to the rules that determine whether an attribute template matches an attribute. In short, a given `ServiceItem` stored in a lookup service matches a `ServiceTemplate` if:

- The service ID in the template matches the ID of a registered service, or if the template's `serviceID` field is null; *and*
- The registered service is an instance of *every* type in the template's `serviceTypes` field, or the template's `serviceTypes` field is null; *and*
- Every entry in the template's set of attributes must be matched (according to the rules defined for matching individual attributes)

by at least one entry in the set of attributes associated with the service.

To boil these rules down, a template matches a service item if every field in the template matches the corresponding field in the service item. Fields that are null in the template always count as matches. And the individual elements in the attributes field are matched using the standard attribute matching rules that I covered in the first half of this chapter.

The array fields, `serviceTypes` and `attributeSetTemplates`, allow you to specify multiple "tests" that a service item must pass. If you provide multiple classes in `serviceTests`, for example, you're saying that for any service to match, its proxy must implement *every* one of the types (classes or interfaces) that you specify. Passing multiple attributes means that every attribute in the template must find a match in the attributes stored on the service.

An Example of Matching Multiple Attributes

Since the rules for matching against multiple attributes are commonly misunderstood, it may be helpful to walk through a set of short examples that show how the rules are applied in practice.

For these examples (Tables 7-2 through 7-4), assume that if two items from different columns have the same letter, then those items match by the normal attribute matching rules (that is, their fields match). The "A-super" and "A-super-super" notation means that an entry contains a superclass or super-superclass of A.

Suppose you have the situations shown below:

Table 7–2 Scenario 1

Service Template	*Service's Attributes*
A	*A*
A-super	*B*
A-super-super	*C*
	D

In this first scenario, the template would match the service because every entry in the template finds a corresponding match in the service's attributes. Even though the service has *extra* attributes, this does not prevent the template from matching.

Table 7–3 Scenario 2

Service Template	Service's Attributes
A	A
B-super	B
C	C
D-super-super	D
	E
	F
	G

In this second scenario, the template would also match the service. Be sure to note here that the template does not directly contain the attributes *B* or *D*. Instead it contains superclasses (or super-superclasses) for these attributes. Jini's matching rules allow superclasses to match more specific types. And again, the presence of extra attributes on the service does not affect matching.

Table 7–4 Scenario 3

Service Template	*Service's Attributes*
A	A
B	B
C	C
D	E
	F
	G

Finally, in this third scenario, the template does *not* match the service item. This is because the template contains the attribute *D*, which does not match any attribute on the service.

As you can see, the rules for matching entire templates are an extension of the rules for matching individual attributes. I've devoted an entire chapter to the topic of attributes, templates, and matching rules because these concepts are commonly misunderstood—particularly the rules for matching multiple attributes.

The next chapter begins an in-depth look at the actual programmatic APIs available for controlling and using lookup services. You'll begin to learn about how to use the `ServiceRegistrar` interfaces directly. Chapter 9, in particular, presents a number of examples that show how to use these matching rules in practice to find services.

Further Reading

If you're new to the world of JavaBeans, a great way to get your feet wet is to check out *How to be a Good Bean*, a short tutorial on what a class needs to do to play well with other JavaBeans. This is a short but informative paper from Javasoft, written by Eduardo Pelegri-Llopart and Larry Cable.

```
http://java.sun.com/beans/docs/goodbean.pdf
```

The on-line tutorial from Javasoft is a more comprehensive introduction to the world of JavaBeans.

```
http://java.sun.com/docs/books/tutorial/javabeans/
```

The Service
Join Protocol

Topics in This Chapter

- Overview of lookup
- Using the `JoinManager` class
- The join protocol
- Service responsibilities

Chapter

8

In Chapter 6, you saw how to find lookup services for Jini communities via the process of discovery. Now you'll learn about what you can actually *do* with those lookup services once you've found them. The collection of lookup services that support a Jini federation is the heart of that community—the lookup services have shared responsibility for keeping an accurate picture of the services available to the community.

Jini lookup services provide a rich but simple set of APIs for service producers and consumers, both of which use the lookup facilities. Services use lookup to store their proxies, and to describe these proxies by attaching attributes to them. Consumers of services use lookup to search for services, and to be notified when new services become available.

In this chapter you'll see how services join their communities via the facilities provided by lookup services. You'll be exploiting a set of much higher level APIs than those used in the "Hello World" examples in Chapter 5. In the two chapters following this one, you'll learn about the client side of the equation—how clients use lookup to search for services, solicit events, and federate Jini communities.

Overview of Lookup

You saw a basic overview of what Jini lookup services do and how to use them in Chapters 3 and 5. Basically you can think of a lookup service as a big networked storage engine. Each lookup service stores a set of `ServiceItems` that describe the particular services that the lookup service knows about. When a new service starts, it tells lookup services about itself by *registering* `ServiceItems` with them. When a new client starts up and wants to use a service, it contacts any lookup services it finds and *searches* for the desired service.

Both clients and services find lookup services by using the discovery mechanisms outlined in Chapter 6. The discovery process returns the lookup service's proxy, which implements the `ServiceRegistrar` interface. `ServiceRegistrar` is the interface that *all* Jini lookup services must implement, and so it forms the most basic API for dealing with lookup services. Most programs, however, will rarely use the `ServiceRegistrar` proxies directly. Instead, they will go through intermediate class libraries that make the job of dealing with lookup services easier. I'll discuss the class libraries useful for building services in this chapter (the libraries for clients will have to wait until the next chapter).

Remember that Jini lookup services are full-fledged Jini services, and support all the abilities and properties of other Jini services. They are accessed through their proxies, have unique service IDs, manage leases, publish attributes that describe their proxies, and can be administered using the same mechanisms as other services. The only difference between a lookup service's proxy and any other service proxy is that lookup proxies can be found by discovery; this is how Jini applications bootstrap themselves into a community.

As you shall see, the fact that lookup services are Jini services means that you can configure groups of lookup services in very powerful ways: Any given lookup service can, in addition to whatever other service proxies it holds, keep a reference to its *own* proxy, as well as proxies for other lookup services.

Why would a lookup service want to hold on to proxies for itself and other lookup services? There are three reasons. First, proxies that are stored in a lookup service can have attributes associated with them. So a lookup service can "annotate" itself by attaching attributes to its service proxy. Clients can, when they connect to a lookup service, search for that lookup service's `ServiceItem`, and view any attributes attached to it. Storing the proxy in the lookup service means that these same descriptional capabilities are available to lookup services.

Second, allowing access to the lookup service's service proxy through the lookup service itself provides a very uniform and elegant way to access resources on a Jini network. A lookup service holds proxies for *all* the services it knows about, including itself. So, an application that iterates over all the service proxies held by a lookup service will actually get every proxy available to it, including that of the lookup service.

Finally, by making lookup services themselves Jini services, Jini supports the ability to *federate* lookup services together. You can make one Jini community reachable through another one by having the first community's lookup service register itself with the second community. By connecting communities, you can create arbitrary structures of Jini communities—groups of lookup services can be organized into a hierarchy, for example, or all the communities in your organization can also connect to a larger "clearinghouse" lookup service that only maintains pointers to other lookup services. You'll see an example in the next chapter of federating lookup services together.

Publishing a Service Proxy: The Join Protocol

From the earlier examples, you've seen that publishing a proxy for a service is a pretty easy task—even when you're managing your interactions with a lookup service "by hand," as in the examples in Chapter 5. The most basic steps that a service needs to do are:

- Create a `ServiceItem` that holds both the proxy object for the service and any attributes that describe it.

- Publish the service by calling `register()` on any `ServiceRegistrars` found through the discovery process.

- Maintain the leases on service registrations returned from the lookup services.

These are the most *basic* steps that need to happen when a service makes itself available. But, as alluded to in Chapter 5, there are many other things that well-behaved services should do in order to play nicely with other members of a Jini community.

Some of these were discussed in the chapter on discovery—services should switch from multicast request to waiting for multicast announcement after a period of time, services should wait some random amount of time before attempting discovery, and so forth.

But other requirements concern how services interact with lookup services. These requirements are collectively called the *join protocol*, because they regulate how services join communities. The basics of join are exactly the same as those just described, and exactly what you saw in Chapter 5: Services simply publish proxies and remember their IDs. But, well-behaved services need to do this in a constrained way, in particular:

- Services should use unique service IDs, even across restarts of the service and across whatever lookup services they are registered with. The first time—meaning the *very first time ever*—that a service is run, it needs to ask for a service ID from the first lookup service it contacts.

- Services should keep a list of *specific* lookup services that they are expected to join. This list may be configured by a human user or administrator. The list should be "remembered" to persistent storage when the service shuts down so that it can recover it later.

- When a service starts, it should register itself with all of the specific lookup services named in this list. The service uses unicast discovery to turn these lookup service URLs into `ServiceRegistrars` for the lookup services.

- Services renew their leases on registrations. If, at any point, communication with a lookup service fails, what steps the service takes depend on how the lookup service was discovered. If the lookup service was discovered through multicast discovery, the service should instruct the group discovery mechanisms to explicitly "forget" about it by calling `discard()` on the `LookupDiscoveryManager` (or other) object that is managing the discovery process. If the lookup service later recovers, it will announce its presence via multicast announcement and will be rediscovered. If the lookup service was discovered through unicast discovery—that is, it was one of the explicit lookup services to which the service connected—then the service should try periodically to reconnect. It will typically do this by instructing the object used to manage locator discovery (typically either `LookupDiscoveryManager` or `LookupLocatorDiscovery`) to discard the locator and periodically try to reconnect. The join protocol dictates this requirement because explicit lookup services were likely configured by humans, and should be remembered at all costs; also, since these lookup services are likely to be on a different network, they will not be rediscovered automatically via the serendipitous forms of discovery.

- If a service changes the set of attributes that it keeps—or is *asked* by a user or administrator to change the set of attributes—then it makes this change at *every* lookup service it is registered with. This stipulation is because a user or administrator ideally wants to be able to simply change *one* instance of an attribute and have it propagated to whatever lookup services are necessary.

- If a service changes the set of groups it is a member of—or is *asked* by a user to change the set of groups—then it must drop its registration at any discovered lookup services that are not members of the new groups. If groups are added, the service should begin discovery again to find lookup services that are members of these groups.

As you can see, while services at a *minimum* need only call `register()` to publish their proxies, there is quite a bit more work that needs to happen for services to interact cleanly with their communities. All the requirements of the join protocol are designed to make services easy to administer and maintain.

Clearly, there is a lot of bookkeeping that needs to happen for services to use the join protocol. Services need to *persistently*—meaning even across restarts of the service—remember a number of details, including their service IDs, the set of groups they are members of, the set of explicit lookup services they are to connect to, and any attributes attached to them.

The "Hello, World" service examples in Chapter 5 showed only the bare minimum of how to register with a lookup service in the interest of clarity. Now it's time to see how to "really" do it.

The JoinManager Class

Clearly, if you were a masochist, you could implement all of the requirements of the join protocol yourself, using the simple `ServiceRegistrar` interface described earlier. This interface is, in fact, the "base" level interface that describes all that you can guarantee a lookup service knows how to do. But fortunately, Jini provides some convenient classes to help you manage the process. The most important of these is called `JoinManager`, and lives in the `net.jini.lookup` package.

The `JoinManager` class provides all of the functionality necessary to implement the join protocol, with the exception of persistent storage. Here are the relevant parts of the API for the `JoinManager` class:

```
package net.jini.lookup.JoinManager;

public class JoinManager {
        public JoinManager(Object proxy, Entry[] attrs,
                        ServiceIDListener callback,
                        DiscoveryManagement discMgr,
```

```
                           LeaseRenewalManager leaseMgr)
            throws IOException;
    public JoinManager(Object proxy, Entry[] attrs,
                       ServiceID serviceID,
                       DiscoveryManagement discMgr,
                       LeaseRenewalManager leaseMgr)
        throws IOException;

    //
    // Access to the various managers...
    //
    public DiscoveryManagement getDiscoveryManager();
    public LeaseRenewalManager
                  getLeaseRenewalManager();

    //
    // Attribute controls
    //
    public void addAttributes(Entry[] attrs);
    public void addAttributes(Entry[] attrs,
                              boolean checkSC);
    public Entry[] getAttributes();
    public void modifyAttributes(Entry[]
                                  attrTemplates,
                                  Entry[] attrs);
    public void modifyAttributes(Entry[]
                                  attrTemplates,
                                  Entry[] attrs,
                                  boolean checkSC);
    public void setAttributes(Entry[] attrs);

    //
    // Miscellaneous controls
    //
    public ServiceRegistrar[] getJoinSet();
    public void terminate();
}
```

From just perusing this API, you can see that using `JoinManager` will make the job of participating in the join protocol much easier. The `JoinManager` takes care of participating in discovery, propagating attributes, handling group membership changes, and additions and deletions of explicit lookup service names. You can control all of these easily, just by using the methods that control the state of the various parameters.

Let's walk through the API. The first thing you see are the constructors. The `JoinManager` class provides two constructors, which are used at different times during a service's life cycle. The first constructor is used when a service *first* starts, before it has a service ID. The first two parameters to this contstructor represent the proxy for the service and the attributes to be attached to it.

After this, however, are a few extra parameters you haven't seen before. The first is the `ServiceIDListener`. This is an object that will receive notification when the service ID has been set; likely, this object will try to save the service ID to persistent storage so that it can be reused if the service ever shuts down or restarts. The listener doesn't, however, have to do anything special to tell the `JoinManager` about the service ID. The `JoinManager` automatically notices that an ID has been assigned to the service and will use it in any future registrations until it shuts down or the service goes away (recall that the `JoinManager` doesn't handle the persistent state itself—so it's up to the user of `JoinManager` to take care of remembering things like service IDs across runs). If you leave off the `ServiceIDListener` by just passing in null, the `JoinManager` will continue to work, but you will not be called when the ID is first set.

Here's the definition of `ServiceIDListener`. It has only one method, which passes the newly-set ID for the service.

```
package net.jini.lookup.ServiceIDListener;

public interface ServiceIDListener {
    public void serviceIDNotify(ServiceID serviceID);
}
```

The next parameter in the constructor is defined to accept any object that implements the `DiscoveryManagement` interface. Recall from Chapter 6 that `DiscoveryManagement` is an interface that defines methods for administering the discovery process. The handy `LookupDiscoveryManager` class implements this interface, and will be used by most applications. But because `JoinManager`'s constructor is defined to take the interface type, you can easily pass in whatever implementation you want and the `JoinManager` will happily use it.

To make the job of using `JoinManager` even easier, you can simply pass null here, and the constructor will create a "default" `LookupDiscoveryManager` to use to participate in the discovery process. This default instance will attempt to join only the public community. Many applications will simply pass null here, unless they need to use a different `DiscoveryManagement` implementation, or—more likely—need to preconfigure their discovery behavior before the join process begins.

The last parameter is a thing called a `LeaseRenewalManager`. This is simply an object that takes care of managing and renewing leases for you, much like the "helper" code you saw in Chapter 5. The `LeaseRenewalManager` lives in the `net.jini.lease` package. Basically, a `LeaseRenewalManager` will automatically try to renew any leases that it manages, and can call out to a listener if a renewal ever fails. You'll see a few examples of how it works in this chapter, and explore it more fully in Chapter 12 (you'll also, in that chapter, see how to go about building custom lease renewal services). The `LeaseRenewalManager` passed to the constructor will be used to renew the leases on the service's proxies.

If you don't need any specialized lease renewal behavior, and don't care to be informed whenever leases cannot be renewed, you can just pass in null here. The `JoinManager` will create a "default" `LeaseRenewalManager` to handle leasing for you. This is the approach that most applications will take.

The second constructor is used when a service is being rerun, perhaps after being shut down for maintenance or being moved to a new machine. The difference between this constructor and the previous one is that, rather than taking a `ServiceIDListener` to be called when the service's ID is set, this constructor takes the ID of the service as an explicit argument. When the `JoinManager` starts its work, it will use this ID at every lookup service it registers with.

The `getLeaseRenewalManager()` and `getDiscoveryManager()` methods return the `LeaseRenewalManager` and `DiscoveryManagement` instances, respectively, that the `JoinManager` is using to do its work. These may be the instances that were explicitly passed in to the constructor, or the instances that were implicitly created by the `JoinManager` if null was passed for the corresponding arguments to the constructor.

Most of the rest of the methods have to do with setting and changing the set of attributes associated with a service's registrations. All of these methods are a great time saver, because they allow you to perform operations across *all* of a service's registrations with one method call. Calling, for example, `setAttributes()` doesn't just change the set of attributes cached locally in the `JoinManager`. It actually goes out and updates all of the service's current registrations to have the new attributes. Likewise, any future registrations will acquire the new attributes. You'll see how to use these methods a bit later in the examples.

The `getJoinSet()` method returns the proxies for all of the lookup services with which the `JoinManager` has successfully registered. If the `JoinManager` hasn't yet managed to register with any lookup services, this method will return an empty array.

Finally, the `terminate()` method is used to stop the discovery process, cancel the leases held on any registrations, and generally shut down the join process. This is how you shut down a service. If you passed a `DiscoveryManagement` instance to the constructor of the `JoinManager`, it will still be "intact" after this call. Otherwise, it will be shut down via its `terminate()` call, which is irreversible. If you passed in your own reference to a `LeaseRenewalManager`, or otherwise held on to a reference to this object after termination, your reference will still be valid. That is, you can still reuse this `LeaseRenewalManager` for other work. The leases for registrations created by the `JoinManager` will be cancelled, though, resulting in the service's proxy disappearing from its communities.

Managing Service IDs

I've talked both in this chapter and in Chapter 5 about the need to keep service IDs unique, and for services to use the same service ID across runs and on every lookup service they register with. Why is this?

To answer this question, you need to understand how Jini applications use service IDs. If you are a client application that wishes to use, say, a printer service, you start out by contacting all of the lookup services you can find. A well-written printer service will have registered itself with all the lookup services for the groups it wishes to join. If this printer service used a different ID each time it registered, the client would have no way of knowing that the registrations at each lookup service represented the *same* printer. It might display to its users a list of dozens of printers, each of which was actually the same device. By requiring services to use the same ID at each lookup service, you can *know* that two `ServiceItems` with the same IDs actually represent the same device or service.

So this is why services use the same IDs at each lookup service they find. But why is it so important for services to remember their IDs across crashes, and use the same ID after they've been restarted, or even if they're disconnected, moved to a different computer, and reattached?

The answer is that you, as the service writer, cannot ensure that a given client will not hold on to your service ID indefinitely. Say that your service controls a printer. Another service, say a digital camera, might be a *consumer* of your service—when a printer is available, the "Print" button on the camera's display highlights to mean that printing is possible. If there are several printers on the network, the user of the camera may have configured the camera to print to *your* printer, and so the camera has recorded the service ID of your print service as the "preferred" printer.

Now suppose the printer is disconnected momentarily from the network—either because the computer it attaches to crashes, or maybe because someone needs to rework its cabling to add a scanner or other device. If the printer were to come back up with a new ID, the camera would have no way to find the printer's proxy using the information it retains—the old ID of the service. In this case, the user's configuration of the camera would be lost, and he or she would have to reset the default printer for the camera. This is the sort of unhappy and frustrating chore that gives computers a bad name, and is exactly the thing that Jini is designed to prevent.

The solution is for the printer to remember its ID and reuse it when it reconnects to the network. Because the writer of the printer service can't guarantee that no client will be holding on to its ID, it should make every effort to reuse the ID that it was originally granted.

The underlying key to all of this is a simple concept: Service IDs uniquely represent services. That is, a service ID will globally and for all time refer to *exactly* one printer, or camera, or software service, even if that printer, camera, or software moves to a different machine or disappears off the network for long periods of time. You can think of the service ID as the "serial number" of a service. Even two cameras from the same manufacturer, identical in every other regard, still have different serial numbers to identify them as different cameras. Like serial numbers, each *instance* of a Jini service has a unique identifier—even if I have one class that implements a printer service, each instance of that class would represent a different physical printer and thus would have its own ID. And also like many serial numbers, Jini service IDs are quite large so that they can uniquely distinguish all the potential Jini-enabled devices that may come along—Jini service IDs are 128 bits long, which is more than enough to last virtually *forever.* (Even if the world's population reaches 100 billion, and each of these people have, say, a million Jini-enabled VCRs, cameras, and DVD players to their name—a situation that would make Sun quite happy indeed— assigning unique IDs to these devices would only take around 64 bits of the service ID address space.)

But unlike a serial number, which is typically burned into a device or piece of software when it leaves the factory, Jini assigns service IDs to services when they first run. This practice is in keeping with Jini's philosophy of decentralized control—there is no need for any central, global registry to keep track of all service IDs and dole them out to applicants. There is likewise no bureaucratic paperwork to go through to get a unique service ID assigned to your service. All you have to do is use the proper constructors of `JoinManager` to ensure that a service ID that is globally unique and yours for all time is assigned to you the first time you run. The `JoinManager` gets the service ID from the first Jini lookup service that happens to respond to it.

Core Note: How are service IDs generated?

The fact that programs that need an ID that is theirs forever, across all space and time, can simply have one handed to them is great. But how does this actually work? What's the magic that allows any Jini lookup service to create one of these almighty IDs? The truth is that there's no magic. In fact, the size of the bit space makes it rather improbable that any two 128-bit random numbers ever generated would be the same, as long as they start from different seed values. Jini uses a somewhat more sophisticated technique than just cranking out random 128-bit numbers, though. I won't go into the details here; see the "Further Reading" section at the end of this chapter if you really care. But basically, the service ID is created by stuffing together 60 bits of system clock, expressed in 100 nanosecond chunks since the year 1582, a bunch of random "noise" thrown in for good measure, and, on some implementations, a unique host address for the lookup service (usually its Ethernet address, if it has one). This scheme guarantees unique numbers until the year 3400 A.D., at which point the clock rolls over. Even then, however, the host identifiers and random number components will likely provide uniqueness, although it can no longer be guaranteed. (And, by that time, the smart money says that any Jini printers bought in the late 20th or early 21st century will be out of warranty, so you should probably consider upgrading anyway.)

Core Note: What if I want to create my own service ID?

While the ability to simply ask the lookup service for a service ID is certainly useful, you may be wondering whether Jini allows you to create your own service ID internally. The answer is yes; this is certainly something the Jini creators expect to happen.

While using the first constructor of the `JoinManager` *(on the "first ever" join) to acquire a service ID is the most common usage pattern to assign a service ID, it is not a requirement. Any service is free to create its own service ID—it simply needs to follow the format and rules for service ID generation that are defined in the lookup service specification. In the future, services that assign their own service IDs will probably be quite common. For example, the designers of Jini expected the possibility that hardware services would have their IDs burned into ROM or PROM when the hardware was manufactured.*

This then begs the question: If this is accepted behavior, why doesn't Jini then provide a `uuidgen()` *method that creates a universally unique ID and can be called directly by clients? The answer is that the best way to create a unique ID is by using the hardware network address (the MAC address) information, which is not accessible through Java.*

So, if you do choose to have your service assign its own ID, you simply have to make sure that it (1) generates the ID using the format and rules specified in the lookup service specification, to ensure that the ID is unique across space and time, (2) uses only the second constructor of the JoinManager, *supplying your self-assigned ID, and (3) uses the same service ID each time it registers with a lookup service.*

Using the JoinManager in Applications

It's time to look at how to use the JoinManager to implement services. In this example, you'll see the use of a new kind of service wrapper. Recall that a service wrapper is a program that publishes a service proxy and takes care of the chores of renewing leases for it. In many services, the wrapper process will also serve as the "back-end" portion of the service (if there is one).

In the examples in Chapter 5, the "Hello, World" services all used a process that continually ran to manage their simple service proxies. In all of these cases, the wrapper simply handled lease management (although the last example of Chapter 5 did use a back-end object that the proxy communicated with to accomplish its service).

Here you'll see an example of a service wrapper that uses the JoinManager APIs. You'll also see how to use persistence to store some of the state that services need to keep between runs—the service ID, attribute sets, groups, and explicit lookup URLs. In the "Hello, World" examples, every time the service ran, it "forgot" all of its old state—it would try to acquire a brand new service ID for each run, and it did nothing to store the state of any attributes or other data.

The example here (Listing 8–1) will "checkpoint" its state to persistent storage whenever it first receives a service ID from a lookup service. When subsequently run, it will recover this state from persistent storage, and use it to reset all its internal data, including its service ID. In this simple example, there is no way for users to *change* the set of groups, attributes, or lookup URLs that the wrapper uses. You can easily extend this program to provide a way to programmatically change these parameters; the wrapper can then checkpoint these whenever they are updated.

Take a look at the wrapper code:

Listing 8–1 `ServiceWrapper.java`

```java
// A basic wrapper that uses JoinManager

package corejini.chapter8;

import net.jini.core.lookup.ServiceID;
import net.jini.core.discovery.LookupLocator;
import net.jini.core.entry.Entry;
import net.jini.lookup.JoinManager;
import net.jini.lookup.ServiceIDListener;
import net.jini.discovery.LookupDiscoveryManager;
import java.io.File;
import java.io.Serializable;
import java.io.IOException;
import java.io.ObjectInputStream;
import java.io.FileInputStream;
import java.io.ObjectOutputStream;
import java.io.FileOutputStream;
import java.rmi.RMISecurityManager;

class MyProxy implements Serializable,
    corejini.chapter5.HelloWorldServiceInterface {

    public MyProxy() { }
    public String getMessage() {
        return "Bonjour, my little turnip...";
    }
}
```

Listing 8–1 `ServiceWrapper.java` (continued)

```java
public class ServiceWrapper implements Runnable {
    protected JoinManager join = null;
    protected File serFile = null;
    protected Object proxy = new MyProxy();

    // Note static!
    static class PersistentData implements Serializable {
        ServiceID serviceID;
        Entry[] attrs;
        String[] groups;
        LookupLocator[] locators;

        public PersistentData() {
        }
    }

    // An inner class to catch ID changes
    class IDListener implements ServiceIDListener {
        public void serviceIDNotify(ServiceID serviceID) {
            System.out.println("Got service ID " +
                                    serviceID);
            PersistentData state = new PersistentData();
            state.serviceID = serviceID;
            state.attrs = join.getAttributes();
            LookupDiscoveryManager luMgr =
                (LookupDiscoveryManager)
                    join.getDiscoveryManager();
            state.groups = luMgr.getGroups();
            state.locators = luMgr.getLocators();

            try {
                writeState(state);
            } catch (IOException ex) {
              System.err.println("Couldn't write to file:"
                                    + ex.getMessage());
                ex.printStackTrace();
                join.terminate();
                System.exit(1);
            }
        }
    }
```

Listing 8–1 `ServiceWrapper.java` (continued)

```java
public ServiceWrapper(File serFile,
                        boolean firsttime)
        throws IOException, ClassNotFoundException {
    this.serFile = serFile;

    if (System.getSecurityManager() == null) {
        System.setSecurityManager(
            new RMISecurityManager());
    }

    if (firsttime)
        register();
    else
        reregister();
}

public void run() {
    while (true) {
        try {
            Thread.sleep(Long.MAX_VALUE);
        } catch (InterruptedException ex) {
        }
    }
}

protected void register() throws IOException {
    if (join != null) {
        throw new IllegalStateException(
            "Wrapper already started.");
    }


    System.out.println("Starting...");
    LookupDiscoveryManager luMgr =
        new LookupDiscoveryManager(new String[]{ "" },
                                    null,
                                    null);
    join = new JoinManager(proxy, null,
                new IDListener(), luMgr, null);
}
```

Listing 8–1 `ServiceWrapper.java` (continued)

```java
protected void reregister()
    throws IOException, ClassNotFoundException {
    if (join != null) {
        throw new IllegalStateException(
            "Wrapper already started.");
    }

    PersistentData state = readState();

    System.out.println("Restarting:  old id is " +
            state.serviceID);

    LookupDiscoveryManager luMgr =
        new LookupDiscoveryManager(state.groups,
                                   state.locators,
                                   null);
    join = new JoinManager(proxy, state.attrs,
                    state.serviceID, luMgr, null);
}

protected void writeState(PersistentData state)
        throws IOException {
    ObjectOutputStream out =
        new ObjectOutputStream(
            new FileOutputStream(serFile));

    out.writeObject(state);
    out.flush();
    out.close();
}

protected PersistentData readState()
    throws IOException, ClassNotFoundException {
    ObjectInputStream in =
        new ObjectInputStream(
    new FileInputStream(serFile));

    PersistentData state = (PersistentData)
                            in.readObject();
    in.close();
    return state;
}
```

Listing 8–1 `ServiceWrapper.java` (continued)

```java
static void usage() {
    System.err.println("Usage: ServiceWrapper " +
            "[-f] serialization_file");
    System.exit(1);
}

public static void main(String[] args) {
    boolean firsttime = false;
    String serFileName = null;
    File serFile = null;

    if (args.length < 1 || args.length > 2) {
        usage();
    }

    if (args.length == 2) {
        if (args[0].equals("-f")) {
            firsttime = true;
            serFileName = args[1];
        } else {
            usage();
        }
    } else {
        serFileName = args[0];
    }

    serFile = new File(serFileName);

    try {
        ServiceWrapper wrapper =
    new ServiceWrapper(serFile, firsttime);
        new Thread(wrapper).start();
    } catch (Exception ex) {
        ex.printStackTrace();
    }
}
}
```

This is a fairly involved example that shows how a service might make its state persistent between runs. Here, because the point is to show how to use JoinManager and how to make the data that JoinManager needs be persistent, rather

294

than to show off any particularly fancy service, I've reused the "Hello, World" interface from earlier examples.

The first thing to notice is that the code required to deal with the mechanics of discovery and lookup is actually significantly *shorter* than the prior examples. And, not only is the code shorter, it is actually better behaved as well: This version has proper leasing behavior and fully participates in the join protocol.

Let's look at how the wrapper works. When you run the `main()` provided here, you need to specify a file in which to store the persistent state between runs. Also, if this is the first time that the service is being brought up, you specify `-f` on the command line, to indicate that this is the service's "first time." I'm using these special command-line arguments for flags and to specify the storage location so that I can simplify the concepts being illustrated. Your services will most probably automatically detect whether they are being run for the first time by looking to see if a service ID has already been written to persistent storage. And, rather than specifying the location of that storage on the command line, they will support selectively changing the storage location through the service administration interfaces you'll see in Chapter 14.

The code for `main()` checks the command-line arguments and instantiates the wrapper, which calls `register()` if this is the first time it's been run, or `reregister()` otherwise. The `register()` call simply instantiates a `JoinManager` to handle the wrapper's participation in the join protocol. It then passes the proxy object and a null list of attributes. It registers an instance of a nested listener class as the `ServiceIDListener` for the protocol (the code must be informed when it gets a `ServiceID` for the first time, so that it can checkpoint it), and passes a `LookupDiscoveryManager`—initialized to join the public group—and a null for the lease manager, which causes the `JoinManager` to implicitly create a `LeaseRenewalManager` internally.

The first time a `ServiceID` is assigned, `serviceIDNotify()` will be called by virtue of the fact that the wrapper has registered a `ServiceIDListener` with the `JoinManager`. This is where the service checkpoints its state out to stable storage. In this particular case, the `ServiceID` is the *only* thing that can change. It's easy to imagine an extension of this code that allows users to set attributes, groups, and lookup URLs, however, and the wrapper could just as easily checkpoint these when they change.

When the wrapper checkpoints its state, it saves everything as an instance of `PersistentData`, a class defined here to collect together all the parameters in the `JoinManager` and `LookupDiscoveryManager` that may change. Note here that `PersistentData` is a *static* nested class. If this class weren't declared static, it would have an implicit reference to the `ServiceWrapper` that created it, causing the entire wrapper to be saved to the disk along with it! This clearly isn't what you want; declaring the class static means that it's nested purely for purposes of scoping, not because of any run-time association between the nesting and the inner class.

Data is written to stable storage by extracting the state to save out of the `Join-Manager`, putting it in a `PersistentData` object, and then calling `write State()`. The `writeState()` call simply creates an `ObjectOutputStream` for the file being saved to, and writes the object.

If the service is terminated—or crashes—and is run again later, you can leave off the `-f` flag and the `reregister()` method will be invoked. This method loads in the persistent state by calling `readState()`, which works just the same as `writeState()` but in reverse. It wraps an `ObjectInputStream` around the data file and loads in the `PersistentData` object that was written earlier. A new `JoinManager` is created from this data—note how `reregister()` passes in the service ID and other data that were retrieved from stable storage so that it registers itself in the same state it had the last time it was run.

Core Note: The service writer's toolkit

This simple service wrapper for the "Hello, World" example shows the beginnings of a toolkit of sorts for service writers. In later chapters, I'll expand on this code and turn it into a full-fledged toolkit that supports persistence, administration, event handling, and leasing.

Chapter 14 lays the groundwork for some service administration components; Chapter 15 has a reworking of this code into a more modular basis for creating robust services; and Chapter 16 extends the toolkit to support services that need to generate events.

You can also download a more full-featured version of the toolkit from http://www.kedwards.com/jini/swt.html.

Compiling and Running the Example

This example program is a service, so it both needs to consume downloadable code (the lookup service's proxy) and export downloadable code (its service proxy). So, following the normal conventions, you'll need to compile the service and then copy any class files that are meant to be downloadable out to the `ser-vice-dl` directory. This is the directory that's exported by the HTTP server that's handling the downloadable code from services. You'll also need to provide the name of a file for persistent storage, and the `-f` flag the first time you run.

On Windows:

```
javac -classpath C:\files;
                 C:\jini1_1\lib\jini-core.jar;
                 C:\jini1_1\lib\jini-ext.jar;
                 C:\jini1_1\lib\sun-util.jar;
                 C:\service
      -d  C:\service
      C:\files\corejini\chapter8\ServiceWrapper.java

mkdir C:\service_dl\corejini\chapter8
cd C:\service\corejini\chapter8
copy MyProxy.class
                 C:\service-dl\corejini\chapter8

java -cp C:\jini1_1\lib\jini-core.jar;
         C:\jini1_1\lib\jini-ext.jar;
         C:\jini1_1\lib\sun-util.jar;
         C:\service
     -Djava.security.policy=C:\files\policy
     -Djava.rmi.server.codebase=http://myhost:8085/
corejini.chapter8.ServiceWrapper -f C:\temp\foo
```

On UNIX:

```
javac -classpath /files:
                 /files/jini1_1/lib/jini-core.jar:
                 /files/jini1_1/lib/jini-ext.jar:
                 /files/jini1_1/lib/sun-util.jar:
                 /files/service
      -d  /files/service
      /files/corejini/chapter8/ServiceWrapper.java

mkdir C:\service_dl\corejini\chapter8
cd /files/service/corejini/chapter8
copy MyProxy.class
                 /files/service-dl/corejini/chapter8

java -cp /files/jini1_1/lib/jini-core.jar:
         /files/jini1_1/lib/jini-ext.jar:
         /files/jini1_1/lib/sun-util.jar:
         /files/service
     -Djava.security.policy=/files/policy
     -Djava.rmi.server.codebase=http://myhost:8085/
corejini.chapter8.ServiceWrapper -f /tmp/foo
```

Using Attributes through the JoinManager

Next I'll show how to add and change attributes on your service through the JoinManager interface. The JoinManager supports a handful of calls to control attributes on a service: addAttributes() allows new attributes to be added to the existing set of attributes; removeAttributes() discards a set of attributes for the service; setAttributes() overwrites the current attributes with new ones; getAttributes() fetches the current set of attributes for the service; and modifyAttributes() changes sets of attributes according to pattern-matching rules similar to those used for search.

All of these calls share one thing in common—any change they make to the set of attributes is used for all future registrations, and is also propagated to all current registrations. These methods provide an extremely convenient way to change whole batches of attributes across all the lookup services that a particular service is registered with.

Most of these methods are self-explanatory, but a few deserve some extra attention. The first thing to note is the modifyAttributes() method. This is a fairly complex—but very useful—method that can be used to change a whole series of attributes in one shot.

The modifyAttributes() call takes two parameters, each an array of Entries. The call modifies the current set of attributes based on these parameters. The first parameter, called the *attribute templates*, is used to specify which attributes to change. The second parameter, called the *attributes set*, specifies what to do to attributes that match the templates.

Here's how it works. Both of the arrays of Entries must be the same length; if they are not, an IllegalArgumentException is thrown. Next, the method iterates through the arrays, looking pair-wise at Entries from both the attribute template and attribute set arrays (so, after the third iteration, the method will look at attrTemplate[3] and attrSet[3]).

For each attribute template, the method finds all attributes attached to the service that match the template—this means that the system finds all attributes that have the same class as the template's class, and any non-null fields in the template that exactly match the corresponding field in the attribute being tested for a match.

Once all the matches for the template have been found, the method looks at the corresponding element in the attribute set array (that is, the element that has the same index as the template it just tested). The value of the Entry in the attribute set array determines what will happen to the matches. If the attribute set Entry is null, then all matched attributes are deleted. Otherwise, every non-null field in the Entry is copied into the corresponding field of every matched attribute.

Using `modifyAttributes()` lets you make wholesale changes to entire sets of attributes—removing groups of attributes that match a template, and making prescribed changes to groups of attributes—all in one operation.

Restricting Changes to ServiceControlled Attributes

As you have no doubt noticed, the `JoinManager` class provides two versions of each of the `addAttributes()` and `modifyAttributes()` methods. The first version of each of these methods, the ones without the boolean `checkSC` parameter, are meant to be used by the service itself to add and change any of its attributes. These calls simply perform the requested change when they are invoked.

There are second versions of each of these methods, however, that take a boolean called `checkSC`. The `checkSC` parameter says whether to check if the attributes being added or changed implement the `ServiceControlled` interface. If any added or changed attribute *does* implement this interface, and `checkSC` is true, then a `SecurityException` will be raised. This version of the call is meant to be used when an attribute addition or change may originate with an external client application or end-user.

Recall the details of service administration from the last chapter: Services should provide some means for users and programs to change their attributes. Typically, this will be done through an object that implements one or more service administration APIs. Service consumers will typically ask the service proxy for its administration object, and any method calls on this administration object will—in a service-specific way—make their way back to the service's back end for processing.

This is where the `checkSC` versions of these methods come in. A client may interact with a service's proxy to cause new attributes to be added. The proxy bundles this request up however it sees fit—using RMI or sockets or whatever—and transmits it back to the "back-end" process or device that handles the service proxy's registration. This back-end process will most likely be a wrapper like the one you've just seen; and this wrapper, if it is implemented in Java, will almost certainly be built using the `JoinManager` class. So, when these client-originated requests for attribute changes come in, the back-end process can simply pass them through the `checkSC` versions of the `addAttributes()` and `modifyAttributes()` methods of the `JoinManager`. If the client is attempting to add or change an attribute that should be under the sole control of the service, a `SecurityException` will be raised and the back-end process can abort the change.

Figure 8–1 shows the basic idea—a client asks for an administration object by calling getAdmin(). Once it has this delegate object, which it can use to administer a service, it can call methods defined on it to interact with the service. In this illustration, calling addAttributes() on the administration object will cause a message to be sent to the wrapper for the service, which will then invoke the "safe" version of addAttributes() defined by the JoinManager. If the client attempts to change any ServiceControlled attributes, the call will fail with a SecurityException. The exact way in which an administration object calls back to the wrapper is dependent on the way in which the service author chose to build administration.

Client Application

Service Proxy

getAdmin()

Service Wrapper

Join Mgr

Admin Object

addAttribute()

Figure 8–1   *Attributes are added through administration delegates*

Further Reading

If you're interested in the nitty-gritty details about how Jini lookup services generate their globally-unique service IDs, you should check out this draft document from the IETF (Internet Engineering Task Force, the body that decides on all Internet standards) that describes the process. The draft is written by Paul Leach and Rich Salz, and is available at:

```
http://www.kedwards.com/jini/draft-leach-uuids-guids-01.txt
```

Summary

This chapter has presented an overview of how to use Jini lookup services—from the perspective of services. You've looked at the Jini join protocol and seen how to use the `JoinManager` to publish your proxies, change attributes, and so on. You've also seen how to create a simple service wrapper that can support the persistence requirements of the join protocol. Together with the discovery protocols that allow you to find lookup services in the first place, these operations form the core of Jini. They allow you to create applications that bind together to form communities of services with minimal advance knowledge of each other.

What's Next?

In the next chapter, you'll learn about how clients use lookup services. You'll see how to search for services, and solicit events so you can stay informed of changes in your community. Much like the `JoinManager` shields services from having to interact with "raw" `ServiceRegistrar` proxies, you'll see what useful libraries are available to help clients interact with lookup services. Finally, you'll learn about how to administer lookup services to interconnect Jini communities into rich federations.

Using Low-Level Lookup Service Interfaces

Topics in This Chapter

- Searching for services
- Soliciting events from lookup services
- Administering and configuring lookup services

Chapter 9

In the previous chapter, you learned how services can use the Jini lookup service to publish proxies and describe those proxies using attributes. In that chapter, you saw that even though the "raw" `ServiceRegistrar` interface—which forms the base level API to the lookup service—is available for use, most services will take advantage of the more convenient `JoinManager` class. This class handles most of the responsibilities imposed on services by Jini's join protocol.

In this chapter, you'll learn about the low-level lookup service interfaces, with a special focus on how clients use lookup services. At a very basic level, clients typically need two things from a lookup service: they need to be able to search for service proxies, and they need to be able to ask for events to tell them when the set of available services has changed. And, while clients *can* make use of the low-level `ServiceRegistrar` interface to accomplish these tasks, they—like services—will usually interact with a set of higher level class libraries that makes their lives easier. I'll save the discussion of these high-level APIs for building clients until the next chapter.

This chapter covers two major topics. First, I'll talk about how clients interact with the low-level `ServiceRegistrar` interface. You'll see how to search for proxies and how to solicit events from lookup services using these interfaces. Second, I'll talk about how clients can manage *topologies* of Jini communities. You'll learn how to administer lookup services and interconnect them into new structures.

How Clients Use Lookup

In the "Hello, World" examples of Chapter 5, you saw the basics of how clients use lookup services. For the most part, client interactions with a lookup service involve either searching for services, or soliciting events to be informed of changes in the state of available services. All of the "Hello, World" examples used the `ServiceRegistrar` interface directly, using the `lookup()` method to search and the `register()` method to solicit events.

Using the raw `lookup()` interface, there are a few ways clients can search—all of which use the rules you saw in Chapter 7. You'll see some examples in this chapter of how to construct templates to search for services.

Depending on the particular search API used, the lookup service will either return to the client a single service proxy object, or a set of `ServiceItems`, each of which contains a proxy as well as any attributes associated with the proxy. Once a client has a proxy in its hands, it can invoke methods on the proxy to interact with the service.

In addition to searching, clients can also ask a lookup service to send it notifications when new services appear, existing services change, or previously registered services go away. The mechanisms for asking for events are very similar to the mechanisms used to search. In fact, the actual calls are almost identical. You can think of lookup services as providing two kinds of search—one for services that were registered in the past, and one for services that will be registered in the future. The tools used for describing what you're interested in are virtually the same in either case.

Clients begin their search for services in the same way that services begin their lives: They use discovery to find lookup services. Services can use the `Lookup-DiscoveryManager` class (or another discovery class), either directly or via the `JoinManager`. Clients also use these same classes for discovery and, like services, can optionally "hide" the discovery process behind the `ServiceDiscoveryManager` utility class, which I'll discuss in the next chapter.

While there is no equivalent of the join protocol for clients, clients do typically have to do a fair amount of bookkeeping to interact with services. You saw a bit of this in Chapter 5: Clients will typically keep lists of all of the lookup services they've found; they will keep a table of the services maintained by those lookup services, perhaps keyed by service ID; and, they will solicit events from all discovered lookup services so that they can keep apprised of changes in the state of available services (and they will, of course, renew their leases on these event registrations). All of these tasks are automated by the `ServiceDiscoveryManager`, which makes the job of writing robust clients significantly easier. This useful class is the subject of the next chapter.

In the next section, you'll learn about how clients interact directly with the raw `ServiceRegistrar` interface to do searching and event solicitation.

Using the ServiceRegistrar Interface

In this section, you'll see the ins and outs of using the `ServiceRegistrar` interface directly. While most clients won't do the work you'll see here—they'll use the more convenient `ServiceDiscoveryManager`—it's important to have a good understanding of what's going on under the covers so that you'll know what the `ServiceDiscoveryManager` is doing. And, in any event, the semantics of searching and event registration are the same regardless of whether you're doing these tasks through `ServiceRegistrar` or through `ServiceDiscoveryManager`. I'll start with the searching APIs.

Searching for Services

You saw an overview of the basic rules for searching in Chapter 7. In that chapter, you saw that searching was based on a simple idea: You submit a *template* that describes the service you are searching for to the lookup service. The lookup service then returns the matches for your template. In this chapter, I'll talk about the actual `ServiceRegistrar` APIs that use these rules to match and return services; I'll also walk through some search examples.

The Search APIs

The `ServiceRegistrar` interface supports two variants of a method called `lookup()` for performing searches. One variant is intended for clients that can completely specify the service they need by using the template mechanism. The other is appropriate either if a client cannot fully specify the service it is looking for using a template, or for "browser"-style applications that may need to find all available services. Here are the two versions of the `lookup()` method:

```
Object lookup(ServiceTemplate tmpl)
                throws RemoteException;
ServiceMatches lookup(ServiceTemplate tmpl, int maxMatches)
                throws RemoteException;
```

All the classes and interfaces used here are part of the net.jini.core
.lookup package, since they are the foundation for interaction with lookup services.

In both versions of the lookup() method, the client provides a template that
describes the services for which it is searching. This template is represented as a
class, called ServiceTemplate. In the first version of lookup(), the client provides only the template; the lookup service will do the search and return the
proxy—if a matching one exists—or null if no services are found that match the
template. Be sure to test the reference you get back to see if it is null—assuming
that the template will always match and return a non-null value is a common programming error in Jini.

Core Tip: Codebase errors can also cause null proxies

*While you'll get a null if your search template doesn't match any
services, another likely cause of null proxies is a configuration error.
If the matching service's codebase is misconfigured—meaning that
the code needed to implement the proxy can't be found at the URL
indicated by the codebase property—then the proxy won't be
properly deserialized and a null will be returned.*

*Unfortunately, the Jini APIs tend to be silent in the face of such
errors. You should be on the lookout for this symptom and know its
cause. Be aware that this sort of misconfiguration can also cause
null proxies in the second form of the lookup call as well.*

*You may want to pay a visit to Appendix B, which lists some
properties you can set to cause the Jini libraries and services to
print extra debugging information. In particular, you can set the two
properties:*

```
com.sun.jini.reggie.proxy.debug=true
net.jini.discovery.debug=true
```

*The first causes the lookup service proxy to display information
about any problems it encounters when it attempts to download
service proxies and their associated attributes. The second prints
information about problems during the discovery process.*

If one or more services match, however, then *one* will be selected by the
lookup service as the matching service. The proxy object of this service will be
returned to the caller.

This version of the lookup() method is quite simple to use, because it trades ease of use for some loss of power. Even though multiple services may match the template you specify, only one will be returned; you have no control over *which* matched service will be returned.

In practice, this limitation will not be a problem for the clients that use this version of the call. Many times, clients will be capable of *fully* specifying the service that they want using the template mechanisms, in which case there will be only one service that matches. This situation might be the case for a Jini "universal remote control" that needs to talk to *exactly* one particular DVD player in your house, and knows this device by its service ID or by enough descriptive information that it can uniquely identify it. Either the desired DVD player is there, or it isn't, and no fancier search techniques are needed to determine whether it's there.

In other situations, if the desired service can be specified *well enough* by the template, the client may not *care* which of a number of possible choices it gets back. If a client needs a TIFF to JPEG image format conversion service, it can simply formulate a query that asks for any such converter. If multiple TIFF to JPEG services are running on a network, the client doesn't particularly care which one is returned—any of the alternatives will do, as long as it meets the needs that the client has specified.

You should be aware that this version of lookup() returns *only* the service proxy object for the matched service. There is no way to get the service ID of the matched service, or any of its attributes. This method is the "quick and dirty" version of search, where clients know exactly what they want, and intend to use the service proxy returned with a minimum of fuss.

The second version of lookup() is more flexible, but not quite as easy to use as the first. In this version, the client again passes in a ServiceTemplate that describes the services it wishes to find. But it also passes in an integer, describing the maximum number of matches it wishes to have returned to it. The lookup() method, rather than simply returning a single service proxy, returns an object called ServiceMatches that contains an array of complete ServiceItems (containing proxy, service ID, and attributes) that matched the query. If you need to find *all* the matching services known to a lookup service, you can pass in Integer.MAX_VALUE as the number of items to find. This is the largest number that can fit in 32 bits, which should far outstrip the number of individual services registered with any one lookup service.

The ServiceMatches class is simply a container for an array of ServiceItems. Here are the relevant parts of that class:

```
package net.jini.core.lookup;

public class ServiceMatches
            implements Serializable {
        public ServiceMatches(ServiceItem[] items,
                                int totalMatches);
        public ServiceItem[] items;
        public int totalMatches;
}
```

The items array is public, so once you get back a ServiceMatches object from the ServiceRegistrar, you can just grab this array to see all the return results. The ServiceItem class contains public members for the service proxy, the service ID, and any attributes that are associated with the service. You already saw in the earlier examples how services create ServiceItems when they join a Jini community; the ServiceItems returned from lookup() are simply copies of the same ServiceItems published by services. Here are the relevant portions of that class:

```
package net.jini.core.lookup;

public class ServiceItem implements Serializable{
        public ServiceItem(ServiceID serviceID,
                                Object service,
                                Entry[] attributeSets);
        public ServiceID serviceID;
        public Object service;
        public Entry[] attributeSets;
}
```

The service field here is the proxy object for the service. This is the same object that would be returned from the simpler version of lookup() you saw before.

Once a client retrieves this array of ServiceItems, it can iterate over them to look for exactly the services it needs or, in the case of browser-style applications, simply display them all to the user.

An Example: Searching for Service Information

Listing 9-1 shows an example of searching. In it, you see how a client searches using the ServiceRegistrar to look for all services that have a specific type of attribute. In this case, the code is looking for all services that have a ServiceInfo attribute, with any values in that attribute. Such a function might be used by a Jini browser, for example, to show to users all of the services that have human-readable information attached to them.

This example also shows how client code can distinguish among multiple ServiceItems that they may receive from a collection of registrars by looking at their ServiceIDs. Since any given service uses its unique ID everywhere it registers itself, clients can eliminate duplicates by examining the IDs of newly found services with those of services they've already seen (this is one of the tasks that the ServiceDiscoveryManager handles itself, as you'll see later in the next chapter).

Listing 9–1 ServiceInfoSearcher.java

```java
// Find and print services that have ServiceInfo
// attributes.

package corejini.chapter9;

import net.jini.discovery.LookupDiscoveryManager;
import net.jini.discovery.DiscoveryManagement;
import net.jini.discovery.DiscoveryEvent;
import net.jini.discovery.DiscoveryListener;
import net.jini.core.lookup.ServiceMatches;
import net.jini.core.lookup.ServiceItem;
import net.jini.core.lookup.ServiceTemplate;
import net.jini.core.lookup.ServiceRegistrar;
import net.jini.lookup.entry.ServiceInfo;
import net.jini.core.entry.Entry;
import java.util.HashMap;
import java.rmi.RemoteException;
import java.rmi.RMISecurityManager;
import java.io.IOException;
```

Listing 9–1 `ServiceInfoSearcher.java` (continued)

```java
public class ServiceInfoSearcher implements Runnable {
    protected HashMap registrars = new HashMap();
    protected HashMap services = new HashMap();
    protected ServiceTemplate tmpl;

    class Discoverer implements DiscoveryListener {
        public void discovered(DiscoveryEvent ev) {
            ServiceRegistrar[] newregs = ev.getRegistrars();
            for (int i=0 ; i<newregs.length ; i++) {
                addRegistrar(newregs[i]);
            }
        }
        public void discarded(DiscoveryEvent ev) {
            ServiceRegistrar[] newregs = ev.getRegistrars();
            for (int i=0 ; i<newregs.length ; i++) {
                removeRegistrar(newregs[i]);
            }
        }
    }

    public ServiceInfoSearcher() throws IOException {
        if (System.getSecurityManager() == null) {
            System.setSecurityManager(
                new RMISecurityManager());
        }

        // build our template
        Entry[] attrTemplates = new Entry[1];
        attrTemplates[0] =
            new ServiceInfo(null, null, null,
                            null, null, null);
        tmpl = new ServiceTemplate(null,
                                   null,
                                   attrTemplates);

        // set up for discovery
        LookupDiscoveryManager disco =
            new LookupDiscoveryManager(
                    LookupDiscoveryManager.ALL_GROUPS,
                    null, new Discoverer());
    }
```

Listing 9–1 `ServiceInfoSearcher.java` (continued)

```java
    protected synchronized void addRegistrar(
                                ServiceRegistrar reg) {
        if (registrars.containsKey(reg.getServiceID()))
            return;

        registrars.put(reg.getServiceID(), reg);
        findServices(reg);
    }
    protected synchronized void removeRegistrar(
                                ServiceRegistrar reg) {
        if (!registrars.containsKey(reg.getServiceID()))
            return;

        registrars.remove(reg.getServiceID());
    }

    void findServices(ServiceRegistrar reg) {
        try {
            ServiceMatches matches =
                reg.lookup(tmpl, Integer.MAX_VALUE);

            for (int i=0 ; i<matches.totalMatches ; i++) {
                if (services.containsKey(
                            matches.items[i].serviceID))
                    continue;


                addService(matches.items[i]);
            }
        } catch (RemoteException ex) {
            System.err.println("Couldn't search: " +
                            ex.getMessage());
        }
    }

    protected void addService(ServiceItem item) {
        services.put(item.serviceID, item);
        System.out.println("New service found: " +
                        item.serviceID);
        printServiceInfo(item);
    }
```

Listing 9–1 `ServiceInfoSearcher.java` (continued)

```java
public static void printServiceInfo(serviceItem item) {
    for (int i=0 ; i<item.attributeSets.length ; i++) {
        if (item.attributeSets[i] instanceof
                                    ServiceInfo) {
            ServiceInfo info =
                (ServiceInfo) item.attributeSets[i];
            System.out.println("  Name = " +
                            info.name);
            System.out.println("  Manufacturer = " +
                            info.manufacturer);
            System.out.println("  Vendor = " +
                            info.vendor);
            System.out.println("  Version = " +
                            info.version);
            System.out.println("  Model = " +
                            info.model);
            System.out.println("  Serial Number = " +
                            info.serialNumber);

            System.out.println("  Proxy is " +
                            item.service);
        }
    }
}

public void run() {
    while (true) {
        try {
            Thread.sleep(Long.MAX_VALUE);
        } catch (InterruptedException ex) {
        }
    }
}
```

Listing 9–1 `ServiceInfoSearcher.java` (continued)

```
    public static void main(String args[]) {
        try {
            ServiceInfoSearcher searcher =
                new ServiceInfoSearcher();
            new Thread(searcher).start();
        } catch (Exception ex) {
            System.err.println("Error starting searcher: " +
                                ex.getMessage());
            ex.printStackTrace();
        }
    }
}
```

The search program participates in discovery to find all lookup services on its local network. The program does some bookkeeping as results come in—it records all the registrars it finds by putting them in a hash map keyed by the ID of the service. As it finds lookup services, it executes a query by calling `lookup()` on the `ServiceRegistrars` for each of the discovered lookup services.

The `ServiceTemplate` is created by initializing the service ID to null (since the program isn't looking for specific IDs) and by setting the `types` array to null also (since it's not looking for specific types of services). The code *does* however pass in a template for the attribute it's looking for: The program creates an empty `ServiceInfo` entry, which is one of the standard Jini attribute types, and makes sure that all its fields are set to null. This will cause it to match *any* `ServiceInfo` attribute, regardless of content.

Whenever services are returned from the search, the code scans a list of all services found so far, looking for each returned service's ID. If a newly found service is just a duplicate of one that has already been seen, it is ignored. Otherwise, the code adds it to the hash map of all known services on the network, and prints the details it can learn about it from its `ServiceInfo`. This keeps duplicate registrations from showing up as separate services.

Compiling and Running the Example

This example is one of the more simple to compile and run. This code is only a consumer of downloadable code (the proxies for the lookup services it finds), and it exports no downloadable code of its own. I'll compile the program into the `client` directory since it doesn't export a service.

On Windows:
```
javac -classpath C:\files:
                 C:\jini1_1\lib\jini-core.jar;
                 C:\jini1_1\lib\jini-ext.jar;
                 C:\jini1_1\lib\sun-util.jar;
                 C:\client
    -d C:\client
        C:\files\corejini\chapter9\ServiceInfoSearcher.java

java -cp C:\jini1_1\lib\jini-core.jar;
         C:\jini1_1\lib\jini-ext.jar;
         C:\jini1_1\lib\sun-util.jar;
         C:\client
    -Djava.security.policy=C:\files\policy
corejini.chapter9.ServiceInfoSearcher
```

On UNIX:
```
javac -classpath /files:
                 /files/jini1_1/lib/jini-core.jar:
                 /files/jini1_1/lib/jini-ext.jar:
                 /files/jini1_1/lib/sun-util.jar:
                 /files/client
    -d /files/client
        /files/corejini/chapter9/ServiceInfoSearcher.java

java -cp /files/jini1_1/lib/jini-core.jar:
         /files/jini1_1/lib/jini-ext.jar:
         /files/jini1_1/lib/sun-util.jar:
         /files/client
    -Djava.security.policy=/files/policy
corejini.chapter9.ServiceInfoSearcher
```

Soliciting Events from a Lookup Service

Searching is a tool that you can use to see what services are *already* registered at a particular lookup service. But you can also ask a lookup service to tell you when *new* services arrive by requesting that it send you events. Such events allow clients to be notified of changes in the state of a lookup service without having to contact the lookup service to poll it for changes. Events are a far more efficient way for clients to become aware of changes in lookup service state, since messages are sent *only* when a change actually occurs.

The process of asking a lookup service to send you an event is called *soliciting* the event. The Jini facilities for event solicitation are very rich—not only can you become informed when new services appear, you can also be informed when existing services go away, or when the set of attributes on a service changes in an "interesting" way. And you don't simply ask the lookup service to send you an event when *anything* happens to it—you can specifically describe which changes you wish to be informed of.

Specifying When Events Should Be Sent

The facilities for describing when lookup services should send events are very similar to the facilities for describing search queries. In both cases, you use a `ServiceTemplate` that describes the types of services you consider interesting. In searching, any services matching that template will be returned to you; event solicitation allows you to have somewhat richer control over how the template is used to determine when to send events.

When you ask for events to be sent to you, you provide a special flag that determines how the template is used. This flag can have any or all of three possible values, indicating that an event should be sent when:

- A service suddenly matches the provided template.
- A service which *used* to match the template no longer does.
- A service which matches the template changes in some way, while still matching the template.

The first case is used when you are looking for particular types of services, or services with particular attributes associated with them, and want to be informed when one of these registers itself. For example, if you're an application that needs a storage service, you may ask for events to tell you when any new storage services appear in a community. If you're a printer administration client, you may ask that an event be sent to you when any printer service suddenly has an "out of paper" status attribute attached to it.

The second case is used to detect when services are unregistered with a lookup service (possibly because the service crashes and its leases expire), or when an attribute on a service goes away. For example, a browser application may clean up its display, removing icons for services that are no longer registered with a lookup service. A printer administration application might remove a printer from its trouble logs once it determines that an error condition has been corrected.

Finally, the third case is used simply to keep clients' views of the state of the community up-to-date. By using this flag value, you can determine when the set of attributes on a service changes in some way, even if that change does not cause it to no longer match the template. For example, if a user adds a comment to a service, you could detect the change with this flag value, and update any display you were presenting to a user.

Using Notify() to Ask for Events

In this section, I'll only look at the basics of how to use events to retrieve information from lookup services. I won't go into a full-blown design discussion of how events in Jini work, or some of the interesting ways you can alter the Jini event behavior—these topics will have to wait until Chapter 16, in which you'll get to take an in-depth look at events.

But even the basics presented here allow you to do enough to deal with nearly all the requirements that clients have when using events. Clients ask for events by calling the `notify()` method on a `ServiceRegistrar`. Here is the definition of that method, along with the definition of the "transition" flags that govern when events are sent.

```
int TRANSITION_MATCH_NOMATCH = 1 << 0;
int TRANSITION_NOMATCH_MATCH = 1 << 1;
int TRANSITION_MATCH_MATCH = 1 << 2;

EventRegistration notify(ServiceTemplate tmpl,
                         int transitions,
                         RemoteEventListener l,
                         MarshalledObject data,
                         long leaseDuration)
                                  throws RemoteException;
```

The arguments here are mostly self-explanatory. You pass in a `ServiceTemplate` that describes a pattern to match, and a `transitions` flag to indicate how the template should be used. The valid values of `transitions` are specified by the integer flags shown here. `TRANSITION_MATCH_NOMATCH` indicates that an event should be sent when the template ceases to match a given service; `TRANSITION_NOMATCH_MATCH` indicates that an event should be sent when the template begins to match a service; and `TRANSITION_MATCH_MATCH` means that an event should be delivered when a previously matched service changes in some way, yet still matches the template. The flag values shown here can be bitwise OR'ed together so that you can specify that any or all of these transitions should result in events.

Next, you specify a `RemoteEventListener`. This is an object that the lookup service will call when an event is generated; this should be an object in your client that implements the `RemoteEventListener` interface and is equipped to deal with messages from the lookup service. `RemoteEventListener` is an RMI remote interface, so the object that implements this interface must fit into the RMI framework—by extending `UnicastRemoteObject`, and so on. (You'll see an example of how to do this in this chapter; see Appendix A if you need some background information on how RMI works.)

The third parameter to `notify()` is a `MarshalledObject` that specifies an arbitrary, preserialized Java object that you wish to be returned to you when an event is sent. You can use this parameter to store any information that you may need to process the event once it arrives; by having necessary information returned in the event itself, you can often simplify your bookkeeping.

Finally, the last parameter is a requested duration for the lease on your event solicitation. Remember that event solicitations, just like lookup service registrations, are leased in Jini. You have to request that the lookup service send you events in the future, and you must renew the lease that's returned to you if you want to continue receiving events.

The `notify()` method returns an `EventRegistration` to you. This is a simple container class that contains the source of the event (which, when registering with lookup services, will be the `ServiceRegistrar` that will send events to you), the lease for the event registration, and a few other pieces of data that I'll talk more about later. When you receive an `EventRegistration`, you should hold on to the lease that comes with it so that you can renew it when you need to.

Receiving Events

When you request that events be delivered to you, you provide an object that implements the `RemoteEventListener` interface to receive the events. The `RemoteEventListener` interface is extremely simple—it only has one method. Here's the interface:

```
package net.jini.core.event;

public interface RemoteEventListener
            implements java.rmi.Remote,
                        java.util.EventListener {
        public void notify(RemoteEvent ev)
            throws java.rmi.RemoteException,
                UnknownEventException;
}
```

Whenever the lookup service changes state in such a way that an event should be sent to you, the lookup service will construct an event, and deliver it by calling the `notify()` method on the `RemoteEventListener` you specified when you originally solicited the event.

The `notify()` method is declared to take a `RemoteEvent` parameter. The lookup service actually delivers to you a *subclass* of `RemoteEvent` that provides extra information about the change that took place in the lookup service. This subclass is called `ServiceEvent`.

```
package net.jini.core.lookup;

public class ServiceEvent extends RemoteEvent {
        // ... some details elided ...
        public ServiceID getServiceID();
        public ServiceItem getServiceItem();
        public int getTransition();
}
```

When your listener receives the event, it can cast it to `ServiceEvent` and then access details about the change that occurred in the lookup service. The `get-ServiceID()` method returns the ID of the service that caused the event to be triggered. The `getServiceItem()` method returns the complete service item that caused the event to be sent. This item is the *new* state of the service item, if it changed, or null if the service was deleted. Finally, `getTransition()` returns a flag value indicating what type of transition occurred—a service matched, a previously matched service disappeared, or a matching service changed in some way.

An Example: Using Events to Find Services

Next take a look at an extension of the previous attribute-based search example. This new example (Listing 9–2) subclasses the previous `ServiceInfo-Searcher` to display information for when services with `ServiceInfo` attributes start up, go away, or have their attributes changed.

Listing 9–2 `ServiceInfoWatcher.java`

```java
// like lookup searcher, only uses events

package corejini.chapter9;

import net.jini.core.lookup.ServiceRegistrar;
import net.jini.core.lookup.ServiceEvent;
import net.jini.core.lookup.ServiceItem;
import net.jini.core.lookup.ServiceID;
import net.jini.core.event.RemoteEvent;
import net.jini.core.event.EventRegistration;
import net.jini.core.event.RemoteEventListener;
import net.jini.core.lease.Lease;
import net.jini.lease.LeaseRenewalManager;
import java.rmi.RemoteException;
import java.rmi.server.UnicastRemoteObject;
import java.util.HashMap;
import java.io.IOException;
```

Listing 9–2 `ServiceInfoWatcher.java` (continued)

```java
public class ServiceInfoWatcher
        extends ServiceInfoSearcher {
    protected Listener listener;
    protected LeaseRenewalManager mgr;
    protected HashMap leases = new HashMap();
    protected int transitions =
    ServiceRegistrar.TRANSITION_MATCH_NOMATCH |
        ServiceRegistrar.TRANSITION_NOMATCH_MATCH |
        ServiceRegistrar.TRANSITION_MATCH_MATCH;

    class Listener extends UnicastRemoteObject
        implements RemoteEventListener {

        public Listener() throws RemoteException {
        }

        public void notify(RemoteEvent ev)
            throws RemoteException {
            if (!(ev instanceof ServiceEvent)) {
                System.err.println("Unexpected event: " +
                                ev.getClass().getName());
                return;
            }

            ServiceEvent serviceEvent = (ServiceEvent) ev;
```

Listing 9–2 `ServiceInfoWatcher.java` (continued)

```java
        switch (serviceEvent.getTransition()) {
        case ServiceRegistrar.TRANSITION_NOMATCH_MATCH:
            addService(
                serviceEvent.getServiceItem());
            break;
        case ServiceRegistrar.TRANSITION_MATCH_NOMATCH:
            removeService(
                serviceEvent.getServiceID());
            break;
        case ServiceRegistrar.TRANSITION_MATCH_MATCH:
            serviceChanged(
                serviceEvent.getServiceItem());
            break;
        }
    }
}

public ServiceInfoWatcher()
        throws IOException, RemoteException {
    mgr = new LeaseRenewalManager();
    listener = new Listener();
}

protected void removeService(ServiceID serviceID) {
    services.remove(serviceID);
    System.out.println("Service no longer available: "
                        + serviceID);
}

protected void serviceChanged(ServiceItem item) {
    services.put(item.serviceID, item);
    System.out.println("Service updated: " +
                        item.serviceID);
    printServiceInfo(item);
}
```

Listing 9–2 `ServiceInfoWatcher.java` (continued)

```java
// Overrride addRegistrar and removeRegistrar to
// have them ask for/terminate event solicitations
// whenever we find a lookup service.
protected void addRegistrar(ServiceRegistrar reg) {
    try {
        super.addRegistrar(reg);

        EventRegistration er = reg.notify(tmpl,
                        transitions,
                        listener,
                         null,
                        10 * 60 * 1000);
        // do something with lease
        leases.put(reg.getServiceID(), er.getLease());
        mgr.renewUntil(er.getLease(), Lease.ANY, null);
    } catch (RemoteException ex) {
        System.err.println("Can't solicit event: " +
                        ex.getMessage());
    }
}
protected void removeRegistrar(ServiceRegistrar reg) {
    try {
        super.removeRegistrar(reg);

        // Terminate leases on this dude.
        Lease lease = (Lease)
            leases.get(reg.getServiceID());

        if (lease == null)
            return;

        leases.remove(reg.getServiceID());
        // May raise unknown lease exception or
        // remote exception. Should be ok to ignore
        // here...
        mgr.cancel(lease);
    } catch (Exception ex) {
    }
}
```

Listing 9–2 `ServiceInfoWatcher.java` (continued)

```
public static void main(String[] args) {
    try {
        ServiceInfoWatcher watcher =
                            new ServiceInfoWatcher();
        new Thread(watcher).start();
    } catch (Exception ex) {
        System.err.println("Error starting watcher: " +
                            ex.getMessage());
    }
}
}
```

This code is a subclass of `ServiceInfoSearcher`, so it reuses all of the existing behavior for searching for services registered at lookup services. Unlike the search example, here you have to use RMI to receive remote events; this adds a bit of complexity that wasn't in the search version of the program.

Before I get to how RMI works in this case, take a look at the `addRegistrar()` and `removeRegistrar()` methods. These override the previous implementations from the search example so that the new program can solicit events whenever it finds a new lookup service. Look at `addRegistrar()` first. The code calls the superclass version of `addRegistrar()`, so that it still gets all of the default searching behavior. But, it also solicits events from the newly found registrar. Here, I've used the same template used for searching—which finds any service that has a `ServiceInfo` attribute on it. The code specifies that it's interested in any type of transition of those services, passes in a listener object for remote events (more on this in a bit), and requests an initial lease time of 10 minutes.

The call to `notify()` returns an `EventRegistration` that contains the lease for the registration. Here again, the code has to do a bit of extra bookkeeping. The code will need to be able to cancel its event leases whenever a lookup service goes away. So it stores the lease in a hash map, keyed by the lookup service's ID. That way, if the program ever detects that a lookup service is being dropped, it can find its lease and cancel it. Here you also see that the code is asking a `Lease-RenewalManager` to take care of its leases. You'll learn about lease managers in Chapter 12, which covers leasing in depth. For now, you can just rest easy knowing that the lease renewals will be taken care of until the `ServiceInfoWatcher` program shuts down or until you tell the lease renewal manager to cease renewing this lease.

The reimplementation of removeRegistrar() also calls out to the superclass version of removeRegistrar(), so that it can update its bookkeeping of active lookup services. But here, the code also finds the event registration it had on the newly irrelevant lookup service and asks the lease renewal manager to cancel the lease on that event registration. The lease is also removed from the bookkeeping hash table.

You should note that the cancel() method on the lease renewal manager may raise exceptions if it runs into trouble canceling the lease (it may raise either an UnknownLeaseException or a RemoteException). Since the reason for calling cancel() in the first place is to tell the manager to stop trying to renew leases with a lookup service that seems to be failing, ignoring the exceptions in this *particular* case is okay.

All of this work is to properly solicit events and manage event leases. Let's now look at how the actual delivery of an event works.

ServiceInfoWatcher defines a class called Listener that will receive remote events from lookup services. Note the format of this class, because the basics will be common to all receivers of remote events: It's a java.rmi.server.UnicastRemoteObject, because its notify() method needs to be callable from the lookup service running in a separate address space. It implements RemoteEventListener, because this is the way Jini knows to deliver remote events.

Whenever an event is delivered to this class, the notify() method will be invoked to deliver a RemoteEvent. As I mentioned before, the lookup service will actually send a subclass of RemoteEvent called ServiceEvent, which contains details of the service that has changed.

When the ServiceEvent comes in, this implementation of notify() looks at the transition in the event that specifies what type of change occurred. If a new service has appeared, it calls the addService() method that was defined in the ServiceInfoSearcher superclass. If the transition indicates that a service has been removed or changed in some way, notify() calls removeService() or serviceChanged(), respectively. These simply update the bookkeeping required to track the known services and print out details of the affected service.

Compiling and Running

This program not only uses proxy objects downloaded from the lookup services it finds, but it also needs to export the stubs for its RemoteEventListener implementation to those lookup services. So in addition to compiling, you'll have to use rmic to generate RMI stubs, and be sure to set a codebase so that lookup services can find the implementation of the stubs.

You should consider leaving this program running; it'll allow you to see how services come and go in your Jini community as you run other examples from this book.

On Windows:

```
javac -classpath C:\files;
                 C:\jini1_1\lib\jini-core.jar;
                 C:\jini1_1\lib\jini-ext.jar;
                 C:\jini1_1\lib\sun-util.jar;
                 C:\client
    -d C:\client
        C:\files\corejini\chapter9\ServiceInfoWatcher.java

rmic -classpath C:\files;
                 C:\jini1_1\lib\jini-core.jar;
                 C:\jini1_1\lib\jini-ext.jar;
                 C:\jini1_1\lib\sun-util.jar;
                 C:\client
    -d C:\client
        corejini.chapter9.ServiceInfoWatcher.Listener

mkdir C:\client_dl\corejini\chapter9
cd C:\client\corejini\chapter9
copy ServiceInfoWatcher$Listener_Stub.class
    C:\client-dl\corejini\chapter9

java -cp C:\jini1_1\lib\jini-core.jar;
        C:\jini1_1\lib\jini-ext.jar;
        C:\jini1_1\lib\sun-util.jar;
        C:\client
    -Djava.security.policy=C:\files\policy
    -Djava.rmi.server.codebase=http://myhost:8086/
corejini.chapter9.ServiceInfoWatcher
```

On UNIX:

```
javac -classpath /files:
                 /files/jini1_1/lib/jini-core.jar:
                 /files/jini1_1/lib/jini-ext.jar:
                 /files/jini1_1/lib/sun-util.jar:
                 /files/client
    -d /files/client
        /files/corejini/chapter9/ServiceInfoWatcher.java

rmic -classpath /files:
                 /files/jini1_1/lib/jini-core.jar:
                 /files/jini1_1/lib/jini-ext.jar:
```

```
            /files/jini1_1/lib/sun-util.jar:
            /files/client
    -d /files/client
       corejini.chapter9.ServiceInfoWatcher.Listener

mkdir C:/client_dl/corejini/chapter9
cd /files/client
cp ServiceInfoWatcher\$Listener_Stub.class
   /files/client-dl/corejini/chapter9

java -cp /files/jini1_1/lib/jini-core.jar:
         /files/jini1_1/lib/jini-ext.jar:
         /files/jini1_1/lib/sun-util.jar:
         /files/client
    -Djava.security.policy=/files/policy
    -Djava.rmi.server.codebase=http://myhost:8086/
corejini.chapter9.ServiceInfoWatcher
```

Other Client Issues

Search and event solicitation are the two most important items in your bag of tricks as the developer of a Jini client. Using these simple APIs, you can select the services you need to do your job.

There are, however, a few more details that you might need to be aware of. These include a few additional ServiceRegistrar APIs, as well as some programming techniques you can use to build more effective clients.

You Cannot Change a Service's Attributes Without Going through the Service

First, you should be aware that there is no API on the ServiceRegistrar class to change the attributes associated with a service. This means that clients have no *direct* way to update, modify, or remove any attributes attached to the services they find.

While search and notification may return to you a list of ServiceItems, which contain attributes for the services you've found, these are merely *copies* of the attributes that reside in the lookup service. In almost every case, any changes you make to these attributes will have no effect on the attributes stored in a lookup service. (One exception is if the attributes are themselves remote objects. In this case, calling methods on these objects to change them will change some centralized object, and the change you make will be visible everywhere.)

This restriction is by design—clients cannot just rampage over the set of attributes associated with a service without telling that service. If Jini allowed this sort of operation, it would have to provide security primitives that would allow services to dictate exactly what changes could be made to which attributes. Also, if a client could change a service's attributes directly, the service may have no way of detecting this change, and would be unable to propagate the change out to the other lookup services it is registered with—a requirement of the join protocol.

So then, how do client applications change service attributes, say, to add a comment or to update a location? The answer is that the client *must* go through an API provided by the service to do this. By going through the service, Jini allows the service a chance to veto any proposed change that it does not approve of. And this approach also gives the service a chance to "notice" the change, so that it can write the attribute to persistent storage and propagate it out to any other lookup services it may be registered with.

Jini provides conventions that services can use to allow clients to change their attributes. These conventions are made manifest through the *service administration* APIs—these are a set of interfaces that services may implement which allow clients to change their attributes, set the groups to discover and join, and so on. I'll talk more about service administration, and how to make your services administrable, in Chapter 14. For now, however, just remember that you shouldn't make the mistake of trying to change an attribute that you get back from search or from an event and expect it to affect any attributes stored in a lookup service.

Downloaded Service Proxies Are Not Leased

A second point to make is that once you've downloaded a service proxy to your client, it's yours until you decide you no longer need it. A client's copy of a service proxy is not leased *to it* (even though the proxy may be leased to the lookup service). So it will not be automatically cleaned up if the service crashes.

Why is this? In a nutshell, leasing is intended as a way for "the system"—meaning the collection of all of these autonomous services—to ensure that it returns to a safe state, without requiring the participation of any one member. Even if a service goes berserk, leasing ensures that the system as a whole will clean up after it, even if the individual services that make up the greater system are poorly written or ill-behaved.

Leasing is not intended as a way to yank a proxy out of the hands of a client. In fact, you could argue that such an operation would be "un-Jini-like" since, in large part, the behavior of a client in the face of failure should *not* be determined by the rest of the system; it should be the responsibility of the application writer to deal with failures in a way that makes sense for his or her application.

To sum it up, leasing is a tool to protect the *system* as a whole, not to ensure that any one *application* works without fail. And, since leasing provides a "semantically neutral" solution—if a lease expires the resource is dropped, no matter what else happens—this approach may not be best for particular clients.

There are implications in this for you as the writer of client code. Most importantly, the client must make sure that it has some way to detect if a service crashes while the client is using it. Typically, this means that you must write your code to catch any exceptions raised by the proxy, and consider certain errors (such as RemoteException) as indications that the service has crashed. What you choose to actually *do* in such circumstances is up to you. You may periodically retry the service, you may dispose of its proxy, or you may terminate the client program with extreme prejudice. The correct behavior is for you to decide, not Jini.

In addition to this requirement of catching and properly dealing with exceptions, clients may also wish to solicit events from the lookup service that the proxy came from. These events can tell the client if the service has failed to renew its lease and has disappeared from the community. Doing this is simple— once you download a proxy, you create a template that has the ID of the service, and tell the lookup service to send you an event if the service ever disappears.

This approach is not an *alternative* to catching and dealing with exceptions raised by the service's proxy—because, depending on the duration of the registration's lease, the service may crash some time before you ever get an event telling you that the service is no longer available. But it can provide you with extra information about what's going on in your Jini community.

Service IDs Are Unique Across Lookup Services

Finally, the fact that service IDs are unique across all space and time is of great importance to client writers. Once you've found a service, you know that any time you encounter that service's ID, it represents the same service. So, if your client application contacts multiple lookup services (as it is almost certain to do), you can "prune" the lists of services you find at each one to eliminate multiple registrations of individual services.

Likewise, since service IDs are the same across time, if you ever find an ID for a service you wish to use, you can safely store that ID away and know that it will *always* refer to that service. Of course, there is no guarantee that the service will be up and reachable when you want to use it, but know you can always *try* to find and use the service given its ID.

"Browser-Oriented" Lookup APIs

In addition to the basic APIs that clients use for searching for services and soliciting notifications, lookup services support a handful of methods designed to simplify the creation of browsers.

These methods allow you to contact a lookup service and download all the classes that any registered service proxies implement, or the classes of attributes on the services, or the values of particular fields in the attributes of registered services. These APIs are typically not used by most clients—most commonly, they're used by browsers that may need to quickly determine what services are registered, or get a "slice" of the values of some attributes, without having to download the attributes themselves. The method definitions from the `Service-Registrar` API are:

```
public Class[] getEntryClasses(ServiceTemplate tmpl)
                throws RemoteException;
public Object[] getFieldValues(ServiceTemplate tmpl,
                                int setIndex,
                                String field)
            throws NoSuchFieldException,
                RemoteException;
public Class[] getServiceTypes(ServiceTemplate tmpl),
                                String prefix)
            throws RemoteException;
```

The `getEntryClasses()` method finds all service items whose types match the `ServiceTypes` field of the specified template. It then finds every entry on those service items that either is a subclass of at least one entry class mentioned in the template, or that doesn't match *any* of the templates. The classes of these entries are then returned. This method can be used by a browser (or other client) to assess whether certain entry classes are in use, and then to prepare itself for dealing with these classes. The sample lookup service browser that comes from Sun uses this method, for instance, to build the menu of entry classes.

The `getFieldValues()` method is used to "slice" out certain field values from an attribute on a set of services. This might be used, for instance, to select only the `name` field of the `ServiceInfo` attributes on a set of services. The specified template is used to match a set of services known to the lookup service. Out of these matches, the method then finds the attributes on these services that match the `setIndex`-*th* attribute in the template, and returns an array of the values of the field specified by the `field` parameter.

This is a fairly confusing method, so I'll walk through an example. Suppose you want to display the `name` field from all `ServiceInfo` attributes of some particular set of services. You'd first create a template that specifies the services for which you're interested in getting this value. This template will be used to find a set of services in the lookup service, using the normal matching rules. Now, you need to select out the `name` field of any `ServiceInfo` attributes on these services. Presumably, the template you used to search contains a `ServiceInfo` attribute somewhere in the template's array of attributes (since you are, after all, wanting to display the names of services). If this attribute appears at slot 2 in the array, you would pass a value of `setIndex` equal to 2 to tell `getFieldValues()` that the `ServiceInfo` attribute is the *particular* one you want to fetch values from. Finally, you pass the string "name" for the value of the `field` parameter to select out the `name` field. If you specify a field that doesn't exist, you'll get a `java.lang.NoSuchFieldException`.

This method, while perhaps a bit confusing, can be very handy for selecting out particular bits of data to display about services, without requiring you to download and reconstitute large numbers of services. A classic example is a browser that wants to produce lists of available services—shown by their names or icons—without having to download the services' proxies and all of their attributes.

Finally, the `getServiceTypes()` method is roughly analogous to `getEntryTypes()`. But whereas `getEntryTypes()` fetches information about the classes of attributes, `getServiceTypes()` fetches information about the classes of service proxies.

The method follows what is standard operating procedure for these methods by using the template to match a set of service items. Then, the method finds all of the most specific types that the service item is an instance of that are *not* specified by the template and whose fully qualified class names begin with the specified prefix. What this method allows you to do, in effect, is say, "I know there are some printers out there that I'd like to use, but I don't know the *particular* models that are on this network. I'd like to find out what my options are." Or, alternatively, "I do know that Xerox sells a wide array of printers whose proxies live in the package *com.xerox.docuprint*. I'd like to see if anything in this package is available."

To accomplish the first sort of query, you would build a template that specifies the common `Printer` interface to find all printer services. The method would then return the *most specific* classes of all proxies that are `Printers`, allowing you to determine what sorts of printers are available on the network before downloading them all. Likewise, the second sort of operation could be done by specifying the string "`com.xerox.docuprint`" in the query to find any and all proxy classes that live under this package, again, without having to download the services or their attributes.

These browser-oriented APIs really constitute a third way of extracting information about available services from a lookup service. And like the first two—polling using `lookup()` and soliciting events via `register()`—these methods all use `ServiceTemplates` to identify services. The primary difference is that these browser-oriented APIs, rather than returning entire `ServiceItems` or proxies, with all of their downloading overhead, return only the information you ask for. So you incur no huge downloads of things you don't want or need.

So, to answer the common question of "Why would I ever want to use these methods when I can just call `lookup()` or `register()`?" these methods are used when you need to know *something* about some set of registered services, but may not *necessarily* need to *use* those services. These methods allow you to write clients that get the needed information in a very lightweight way.

Federating and Administering Lookup Services

I've alluded a few times in this book to the ability of services to be controlled through a set of administrative interfaces. I'll talk about how to build administrable services in quite a bit of detail in Chapter 14, and look closely at all of the various administrative interfaces that are available for controlling services.

Lookup services, you will remember, are themselves Jini services. And, as Jini services, they provide a set of administrative interfaces that can be used to control them. Through these interfaces, you—or your programs—can tune various parameters to control a lookup service. For example, you can change the set of groups of which a lookup service is a member, and you can cause it to register itself with specific lookup URLs that represent other lookup services. You can change the attributes that the lookup service attaches to its service proxy. You can also change the logging directory that a lookup service uses for checkpointing its data, and even shut down a lookup service.

In this section, I'll focus just on the interfaces that govern how lookup services may be administered. I'll save the more general discussion of service administration until Chapter 14.

A Quick Overview of Service Administration

Services use a "delegation" model of administration. This means that you can ask a service for an object that can be used to administer it. Once you have this administration object, you can test it to see if it implements certain standard interfaces for controlling the service.

Jini services that are administrable will have service proxies that implement the `net.jini.admin.Administrable` interface. This interface has only one method on it:

```
package net.jini.admin;

public interface Administrable {
        public Object getAdmin()
                throws java.rmi.RemoteException;
}
```

If you want to administer a service, you test its proxy to see if it implements `Administrable` and, if it does, call the `getAdmin()` method on it to fetch an object that can be used to administer the service. The `getAdmin()` method is declared to raise a `RemoteException`. This is because certain services may implement `getAdmin()` by contacting a back-end process to retrieve an administrative object. Declaring this exception in the interface gives service writers freedom in how they choose to fetch and return administration objects to callers.

Once you've gotten an administrative object, you can test whether it implements various well-known interfaces that can be used to control a service. Most services will provide a single administrative object that implements a handful of different administrative interfaces.

Jini defines one core administrative interface that is used to control a service's participation in the join protocol. This interface, called `net.jini.admin.Join-Admin`, can be used to set the groups that a service tries to join, the lookup URLs it contacts when it starts, and the attributes it attaches to its proxies.

Other, specialized services may implement their own administrative interfaces on top of the core ones. In fact, Jini defines one such interface that the administrative objects of all lookup services should implement.

Lookup Administrative Interfaces

The interface `net.jini.lookup.DiscoveryAdmin` is used to control a lookup service. Through its methods, you can read or change the set of groups of which a lookup service is a member, and read or change the port that the lookup service uses for unicast discovery.

Be sure to note the distinction between `JoinAdmin` and `DiscoveryAdmin`. The former controls which lookup services a Jini service joins, while the second controls which groups a lookup service supports for discovery. While a lookup service may implement `JoinAdmin` to allow it to become a member of multiple groups, it may answer discovery requests for a potentially different set of groups.

```
package net.jini.lookup;

import java.rmi.RemoteException;
import java.io.IOException;

public interface DiscoveryAdmin {
        public void addMemberGroups(String[] groups)
                    throws RemoteException;
        public String[] getMemberGroups()
                    throws RemoteException;
        public int getUnicastPort()
                    throws RemoteException;
        public void removeMemberGroups(String[] groups)
                    throws RemoteException;
        public void setMemberGroups(String[] groups)
                    throws RemoteException;
        public void setUnicastPort(int port)
                    throws RemoteException, IOException;
}
```

The methods on this interface should be mostly self-explanatory. The `addMemberGroups()`, `setMemberGroups()`, and `removeMemberGroups()` methods change the set of groups that the lookup service *supports*. This is not necessarily the set of groups that the lookup service registers its own proxy with, although these are likely to be the same; instead, it is the set of groups for which this lookup service will answer a discovery request.

Calling `setUnicastPort()` changes the port number on which the lookup service listens for unicast discovery requests. If you set the port to zero, the lookup service will try to establish itself on the default port, and then choose an arbitrary port if it cannot acquire the default one.

In addition to the `DiscoveryAdmin` interface, which all administrable lookup services are required to implement, most lookup services will also implement a handful of other administrative interfaces. Many of these are "suggested" administrative interfaces that live in `com.sun.jini.admin`; these interfaces can be used to shut down a service, or to change where the service keeps its persistent storage.

A particular lookup service also may implement any number of interfaces specific to it. So, for example, a lookup service based on an SQL database implementation may provide an administrative interface for tuning the database, setting database permissions, and so forth.

Administering the Reggie Lookup Service Implementation

Sun provides a default lookup service implementation that ships with Jini. This service, called `reggie`, is administrable through all the standard interfaces. Calling `getAdmin()` on its service proxy returns an object that implements not only `net.jini.admin.JoinAdmin` and `net.jini.lookup.DiscoveryAdmin`, but also two "optional" administrative interfaces from `com.sun.jini.admin`: `DestroyAdmin` and `StorageLocationAdmin`, which are used to shut down services and change a service's persistent storage location.

Additionally, `reggie`'s administrative object also implements the `com.sun.jini.reggie.RegistrarAdmin` object. This object allows clients to control `reggie`-specific parameters, such as how the internal algorithm used by `reggie` to grant lease times is used, and how the logging file is used.

I won't go into all of the details of how to administer `reggie` here. For most uses, the standard lookup service administrative interfaces are sufficient for anything a client application or an administrator will need to do. If you're seeing poor lease performance on your network, or need to manage the growth of `reggie`'s log files, then you can use the `reggie`-specific administrative interfaces to do this. See the documentation on the `com.sun.jini.reggie.RegistrarAdmin` class that comes with Jini for more details.

Federating Lookup Services

By default, the multicast forms of discovery will only find lookup services that are "nearby," in a network sense. As discussed in the chapter on discovery, this is because of the way that multicast works, and Jini's desire to support work-group-sized communities easily and with no administration. "Nearness" depends on the number of "hops" a packet requires to travel to a destination, which in turn depends on the local network configuration.

Often, you may need to take the ad hoc collection of communities that Jini lookup services will naturally create, and shape it into a form that represents boundaries other than simple network dividing lines. For example, you might wish to create a hierarchy of Jini communities that mirrors an organizational structure in your company. Or, if you're in a large building, you may want to connect a group of Jini communities together in a way that mirrors the physical layout of your work space.

Both of these cases are examples of how you may need to *federate* Jini communities together into new topologies that do not necessarily reflect simple network boundaries. In Jini, complex organizational structures like this are created by explicitly connecting the lookup services for various communities to one another.

Let's look at an example. Suppose I want to create an enterprisewide collection of Jini communities that will allow me access to any resource, anywhere on my company's network, anywhere in the world.

One solution I could take to this problem is to create *one* Jini community, and configure each and every service with a set of URLs that points to the lookup services supporting this community. In this case, my entire enterprise is one huge Jini community.

This approach may not be the best one, however. I'm putting a huge load on each of the lookup services in this case—every one of them needs to be able to hold the entire set of services that are available. If you work for a large company, you'd better be running these lookup services on some pretty high-powered machines! Even worse, having a centralized set of lookup services means that most services will live far away (networkologically speaking) from the lookup services back at company HQ (headquarters). If a branch office's connection to HQ is severed, all work stops. Even though my computer may be sitting right next to a printer at the branch office, I cannot use it because I cannot contact the central lookup services back at HQ. This setup also increases your administrative workload—every service that anyone in the company brings up must be explicitly configured with the "magic" URLs for the HQ lookup services.

A far better approach is to create clusters of interlinked communities that reflect natural working patterns. In this approach, every branch office might have its own Jini community that supports only the services available locally; since these services only talk to local lookup services, they require no extra administration. Another lookup service might represent the Sales division of my company. This service would support a "community of communities," linking all of the branch offices together. All of the lookup services for each of the branch offices would register themselves in this "metacommunity," and the lookup services for the larger Sales division metacommunity would register themselves in the branch office lookup services. I could continue up the organizational hierarchy, finally creating a "root" community that contains proxies for the lookup services supporting Sales, Engineering, Accounting, and so on.

In this scenario, I have created a hierarchy of Jini lookup services. At each level, the lookup services register both with those "above" them and those "below" them in the hierarchy. When you browse your local community's lookup service, you not only see all the services in your neighborhood, but you see the lookup services for higher level organizational units. You can "open" these (by searching them) to find other offices that are peers of yours, and to find further parent communities.

This hierarchical arrangement has great benefits. Not only does it provide a structure that mirrors that of the organization—providing clear administrative boundaries—it also means that the services of a local community will *always* be available, even if a network connection to HQ goes down. Each community can function autonomously, even if it is isolated from the others. And, since you only have to set explicit lookup URLs in the federated lookup services, not every service anywhere on the network, this approach keeps the amount of explicit administration work low.

Other topologies are possible. You might create a "star" arrangement, where each local community connects to a centralized community whose job it is to maintain references to all other communities. Or, you might have a completely ad hoc organization, where you have Jini "islands" connected to one another as users need to access resources in other communities. Figure 9–1 shows a few of these.

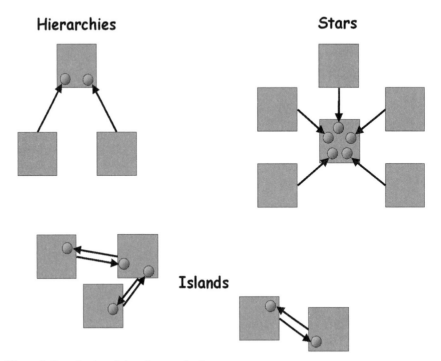

Figure 9–1   *Lookup federation topologies*

This freedom to federate lookup services together is one of the great strengths of Jini. It allows administrators and users to create connections between clusters

of Jini services as needed; every organization or individual is free to create whatever structures it needs across its communities.

Take a look at an example (Listing 9-3) of how to federate two lookup services
together. This program would be used by an administrator to create a two-way
connection between two lookup services: You provide it with URLs that name
two separate lookup services, and the tool creates the link between them. Each
lookup service registers itself with the other one.

Listing 9–3 `Federate.java`

```
// Cause two lookup services to register with each
// other.

package corejini.chapter9;

import net.jini.core.discovery.LookupLocator;
import net.jini.core.lookup.ServiceRegistrar;
import net.jini.admin.Administrable;
import net.jini.admin.JoinAdmin;
import java.net.MalformedURLException;
import java.io.IOException;
import java.rmi.RMISecurityManager;

public class Federate {
    public Federate() {
        if (System.getSecurityManager() == null) {
            System.setSecurityManager(
                new RMISecurityManager());
        }
    }
```

> ### Listing 9–3 `Federate.java` (continued)

```java
public boolean federate(String url1, String url2)
    throws MalformedURLException, IOException,
        ClassNotFoundException {
    // Get service registrars for both servers
    LookupLocator loc1 = new LookupLocator(url1);
    LookupLocator loc2 = new LookupLocator(url2);

    ServiceRegistrar reg1 = loc1.getRegistrar();
    ServiceRegistrar reg2 = loc2.getRegistrar();

    Object admin1 = null, admin2 = null;

    if (reg1 instanceof Administrable) {
        admin1 = ((Administrable) reg1).getAdmin();
    } else {
        System.err.println("Registrar " + reg1 +
                " is not administrable");
        return false;
    }

    if (reg2 instanceof Administrable) {
        admin2 = ((Administrable) reg2).getAdmin();
    } else {
        System.err.println("Registrar " + reg2 +
                " is not administrable");
        return false;
    }

    if (!(admin1 instanceof JoinAdmin)) {
        System.err.println("Registrar " + reg1 +
                            " doesn't support " +
                "join administration");
        return false;
    }
    if (!(admin2 instanceof JoinAdmin)) {
        System.err.println("Registrar " + reg2 +
                            " doesn't support " +
                "join administration");
        return false;
    }

    JoinAdmin jadmin1 = (JoinAdmin) admin1;
    JoinAdmin jadmin2 = (JoinAdmin) admin2;
```

Listing 9–3 `Federate.java` (continued)

```java
        // Now, actually do the federation
        LookupLocator[] locs = new LookupLocator[1];

        locs[0] = loc1;
        jadmin2.addLookupLocators(locs);

        locs[0] = loc2;
        jadmin1.addLookupLocators(locs);

        return true;
    }

    public static void main(String[] args) {
        if (args.length != 2) {
            System.err.println("Usage: Federate " +
                            "<url1> <url2>");
            System.exit(1);
        }

        String url1 = args[0], url2 = args[1];

        Federate fed = new Federate();

        try {
            if (fed.federate(url1, url2)) {
                System.out.println(
                        "Lookup services federated!");
            } else {
                System.err.println(
                        "Couldn't federate.");
            }
        } catch (Exception ex) {
            System.err.println("Error federating: " +
                            ex.getMessage());
        }
    }
}
```

This is a rather straightforward program that illustrates a powerful concept. The program takes URLs for two Jini lookup services. The two lookup services represented by these URLs will be registered with each other as services. Any program contacting either one of these lookup services will find the proxy for the other, and can then "jump" to that lookup service simply by downloading and using its proxy. Since I'm explicitly providing URLs here, there is no requirement that the federated lookup services exist on the same network; they can exist on opposite sides of the world from each other. (Indeed, the connection of lookup services in different network "regions" is the entire point of federation. Lookup services that are near one another already will likely find each other through multicast discovery.)

This is a minimalist example; you can probably imagine improvements on it. For one thing, rather than connecting individual lookup services, you will more likely want to connect entire communities. This would entail finding all the lookup services that support a given group, and connecting them to all the lookup services that support a second group. Once you contact any lookup service in the first group, you should be able to find the other lookup services supporting that group, since they will most likely be registered with the lookup service you just found.

One other point to make about this example is that all I'm doing here is causing two lookup services to publish their service proxies in one another. Any client that stumbles across the proxy as it scans a lookup service would have to be written to realize that what it has in its hands is, in fact, a federated lookup service that it may want to contact to search for other services. This is behavior that most clients will want to support—since, presumably, the whole point of a user federating two lookup services is to allow clients to make use of services on either one.

But it's easy to imagine—and even easy to build—a more complicated sort of federating tool. You'll see such a tool as the last example in this chapter.

Compiling and Running

This code exports no remote objects, so you don't have to use rmic here. Make sure when you run that you pass in the Jini URLs for two lookup services on the command line.

On Windows:

```
javac -classpath C:\files;
                C:\jini1_1\lib\jini-core.jar;
                C:\jini1_1\lib\jini-ext.jar;
                C:\jini1_1\lib\sun-util.jar;
                C:\client
    -d C:\client
        C:\files\corejini\chapter9\Federate.java
```

```
java -cp C:\jini1_1\lib\jini-core.jar;
        C:\jini1_1\lib\jini-ext.jar;
        C:\jini1_1\lib\sun-util.jar;
        C:\client
    -Djava.security.policy=C:\files\policy
        corejini.chapter9.Federate
                jini://turbodog.parc.xerox.com
    jini://foundation.parc.xerox.com
```

On UNIX:
```
javac -classpath /files:
                /files/jini1_1/lib/jini-core.jar:
                /files/jini1_1/lib/jini-ext.jar:
                /files/jini1_1/lib/sun-util.jar:
                /files/client
    -d /files/client
        /files/corejini/chapter9/Federate.java

java -cp /files/jini1_1/lib/jini-core.jar:
        /files/jini1_1/lib/jini-ext.jar:
        /files/jini1_1/lib/sun-util.jar:
        /files/client
    -Djava.security.policy=/files/policy
        corejini.chapter9.Federate
                jini://turbodog.parc.xerox.com
    jini://foundation.parc.xerox.com
```

Example: A Lookup Service Tunnel

The last example showed how to federate lookup services by cross-publishing their proxies with each other. I mentioned that clients that come across a lookup service proxy would have to be written to realize that the proxy represents a registrar, and to search it and present the services that exist there.

In this example, you'll see a type of federation that doesn't require *any* special client-side smarts. This example is a *lookup service tunnel*. This program connects two lookup services in a much deeper way than simply asking them to publish their proxies with each other. The tunnel makes the individual services registered with one lookup service *directly* available on another.

The tunnel actively finds all of the services that are known to one lookup service, called the *from* service. It then contacts a second lookup service, called the *to* service. Any services found in the *from* service are registered in the *to* service. The tunnel solicits events from the *from* service so that it can ensure that its picture of the services available there is up-to-date and reflected in the services it makes available on the *to* lookup service.

Essentially the tunnel is a service that acts as a wrapper for other services. It finds their proxies on a given lookup service (one might say it *absconds* with the proxies for these services), and then republishes them on a different lookup service. It also takes over responsibility for managing the leases on the republished proxies for these services, and ensures that the attributes on them accurately mirror the attributes on the originals.

With a lookup service tunnel, clients don't need *any* special smarts to use services that used to reside on a distant lookup service—because the tunnel makes all of those services locally available.

Take a look at the program, as shown in Listing 9-4.

Listing 9–4 `TunnelService.java`

```java
// Create a tunnel between two lookup services

package corejini.chapter9;

import net.jini.core.lookup.ServiceEvent;
import net.jini.core.lookup.ServiceRegistrar;
import net.jini.core.lookup.ServiceTemplate;
import net.jini.core.lookup.ServiceItem;
import net.jini.core.lookup.ServiceMatches;
import net.jini.core.event.RemoteEventListener;
import net.jini.core.event.RemoteEvent;
import net.jini.core.event.EventRegistration;
import net.jini.core.discovery.LookupLocator;
import net.jini.core.entry.Entry;
import net.jini.core.lease.Lease;
import net.jini.lookup.entry.Name;
import net.jini.lookup.entry.ServiceInfo;
import net.jini.lookup.JoinManager;
import net.jini.lookup.ServiceIDListener;
import net.jini.lease.LeaseRenewalManager;
import net.jini.discovery.LookupDiscoveryManager;
import net.jini.discovery.DiscoveryGroupManagement;
import java.io.Serializable;
import java.io.IOException;
import java.util.HashMap;
import java.rmi.server.UnicastRemoteObject;
import java.rmi.RemoteException;
import java.rmi.RMISecurityManager;

class TunnelServiceProxy implements Serializable {
    // Currently this is an "empty" proxy.
}
```

Listing 9–4 `TunnelService.java` (continued)

```java
public class TunnelService {
    protected JoinManager join;
    protected ServiceTemplate tmpl =
        new ServiceTemplate(null, null, null);
    protected LeaseRenewalManager leaseMgr =
        new LeaseRenewalManager();
    protected HashMap leases = new HashMap();
    protected HashMap joinManagers = new HashMap();
    protected LookupLocator toLoc;
    protected ServiceRegistrar fromReg;
    protected int transitions =
        ServiceRegistrar.TRANSITION_MATCH_NOMATCH |
        ServiceRegistrar.TRANSITION_NOMATCH_MATCH |
        ServiceRegistrar.TRANSITION_MATCH_MATCH;
    protected Listener listener;

    // Listen for changes in the source lookup service
    class Listener extends UnicastRemoteObject
        implements RemoteEventListener {
        public Listener() throws RemoteException {
        }

        public void notify(RemoteEvent ev)
            throws RemoteException {
            if (!(ev instanceof ServiceEvent)) {
                return;
            }

            ServiceEvent sev = (ServiceEvent) ev;
            ServiceItem[] items = new ServiceItem[1];
            items[0] = sev.getServiceItem();
```

Listing 9–4 `TunnelService.java` (continued)

```java
        switch (sev.getTransition()) {
        case ServiceRegistrar.TRANSITION_MATCH_NOMATCH:
            withdrawServices(items);
            break;
        case ServiceRegistrar.TRANSITION_NOMATCH_MATCH:
        case ServiceRegistrar.TRANSITION_MATCH_MATCH:
            // New service has shown up, or an old one
            // has changed--push it to the dest.  If
            // it's a change, we'll overwrite
            pushServices(items);
            break;
        }
    }
}

public TunnelService() throws RemoteException {
    listener = new Listener();

    if (System.getSecurityManager() == null) {
        System.setSecurityManager(
                new RMISecurityManager());
    }
}

public void createTunnel(String from,
            String to) throws Exception {
    LookupLocator fromLoc = new LookupLocator(from);
    toLoc = new LookupLocator(to);
    fromReg = fromLoc.getRegistrar();

    publishProxies(fromLoc, toLoc);
    solicitEvents();
    ServiceItem[] fromServices = getServices();
    pushServices(fromServices);
}
```

Listing 9–4 `TunnelService.java` (continued)

```java
protected ServiceItem[] getServices()
    throws RemoteException {
    ServiceMatches matches = fromReg.lookup(tmpl,
                                Integer.MAX_VALUE);
    return matches.items;
}

protected void publishProxies(LookupLocator from,
                LookupLocator to)
    throws IOException {
    Name name = new Name("Tunnel service");
    ServiceInfo info = new ServiceInfo(
                        "Tunnel service",
                        "Prentice-Hall",
                        "Your local bookseller",
                        "v1.0",
                        null, null);
    Entry[] entries = new Entry[2];
    entries[0] = name;
    entries[1] = info;

    LookupLocator[] locators = new LookupLocator[2];
    locators[0] = from;
    locators[1] = to;

    String[] groups =
        DiscoveryGroupManagement.NO_GROUPS;

    LookupDiscoveryManager luMgr =
        new LookupDiscoveryManager(groups,
                                locators,
                                null);
    join = new JoinManager(new TunnelServiceProxy(),
                        entries,
                        (ServiceIDListener) null,
                        luMgr, leaseMgr);

    System.out.println("Join manager started...");
}
```

Listing 9–4 `TunnelService.java` (continued)

```
protected void solicitEvents() throws IOException,
        ClassNotFoundException {
    EventRegistration er = fromReg.notify(tmpl,
                                    transitions,
                                    listener,
                                    null,
                                    10 * 60 * 1000);

    leases.put(fromReg.getServiceID(), er.getLease());
    leaseMgr.renewUntil(er.getLease(), Lease.ANY,
                    null);
}

protected void pushServices(ServiceItem[] items) {
    for (int i=0 ; i<items.length ; i++) {
        try {
            LookupLocator[] toArray =
            new LookupLocator[] { toLoc };
            System.out.println("Pushing service to " +
                        toLoc + ": " +
                            items[i].service);
            LookupDiscoveryManager luMgr =
                new LookupDiscoveryManager(
                    DiscoveryGroupManagement.NO_GROUPS,
                    toArray, null);
            JoinManager j =
                new JoinManager(items[i].service,
                            items[i].attributeSets,
                            items[i].serviceID,
                            luMgr,
                            leaseMgr);
            joinManagers.put(items[i].serviceID, j);
        } catch (Exception ex) {
            System.err.println("Couldn't tunnel svc: " +
                        ex.getMessage());
        }
    }
}
```

Listing 9–4 `TunnelService.java` (continued)

```java
protected void withdrawServices(ServiceItem[] items) {
    for (int i=0 ; i<items.length ; i++) {
        try {
            System.out.println("Withdrawing service " +
                                items[i].service);
            JoinManager j = (JoinManager)
                joinManagers.get(items[i].serviceID);
            j.terminate();
            joinManagers.remove(items[i].serviceID);
        } catch (Exception ex) {
            System.err.println("Couldn't withdraw svc: "
                                + ex.getMessage());
        }
    }
}

public static void main(String[] args) {
    if (args.length != 2) {
        System.err.println("Usage: TunnelService " +
                            "<from_url> <to_url>");
        System.exit(1);
    }

    String from = args[0], to = args[1];

    try {
        TunnelService tunnel = new TunnelService();
        tunnel.createTunnel(from, to);
    } catch (Exception ex) {
        System.err.println("Error creating tunnel: " +
                            ex.getMessage());
        System.exit(1);
    }
}
}
```

The tunnel service program is the most complex example you've seen so far. This program is both a service, and a fairly complex client application. The heart of the program is the `createTunnel()` method. This method creates `LookupLocator` instances from the string URLs it is passed. It then publishes proxies for its service on both the *to* and the *from* lookup services—in the code shown here, this is a "no op" proxy; it is simply published to give a representation of the tunnel service on both of the lookup services. You can easily extend this proxy to implement administrative interfaces that could be used to control the behavior of the tunnel, and save selected parameters to persistent storage.

After registering its proxies, the tunnel solicits events from the *from* lookup service. This step is necessary so that the tunnel will be made aware when the state of the set of services registered there changes—it must update the proxies it will create on the *to* lookup service to reflect changes in the original service.

Once it has solicited events, the tunnel retrieves all of the services currently registered at the *from* lookup service and "pushes" them out to the *to* lookup service.

In this one example, you see illustrated many of the concepts discussed in this chapter. TunnelService needs to be able to search for services in the *from* registrar, and publish new service proxies on the *to* registrar. It must also be a recipient of remote events—when new services appear, they are pushed to the destination registrar; when services disappear, they are removed; and, when they change, their ServiceItems are written to the destination, overwriting whatever attributes were there before.

As new services are pushed, the code in pushServices() is run to create the proxying behavior. Every new service has its own JoinManager that is responsible for its registration. The JoinManager essentially creates a new service, copying the original service's ID, attributes, and proxy. The LookupDiscoveryManager's parameters are set so that it will only connect to the destination lookup service—it will never try to perform multicast discovery, because DiscoveryGroupManagement.NO_GROUPS is passed as the set of groups it should connect to.

This code also maintains its own LeaseRenewalManager, which manages the leases for not only the TunnelService's proxy object, but also the leases for event registrations, and all the registration leases for the proxy objects that it tunnels through to the *to* lookup service.

When services disappear from the original lookup service, they are removed from the destination service. This is done by terminating the join protocol—the service's ID is mapped to the JoinManager that was created for it. When the JoinManager is retrieved, the terminate() method is called, and the bookkeeping entry for the service is removed from the hash map that maps from services to their JoinManagers.

Compiling and Running

This is the most complicated example of the chapter to compile and run. First, the program—like any Jini program—needs to be able to use downloaded lookup service proxies, so you must take the usual care to run it with a security policy file. Second, the code exports two downloadable classes: the RMI stub for its event listener, and the proxy for the tunneling service. So, you need to run the rmic stubs compiler and make sure you copy the proxy class file out to the service-dl directory, as well as set a codebase property to tell other programs where to find the implementations for these classes.

On Windows:

```
javac -classpath C:\files;
                 C:\jini1_1\lib\jini-core.jar;
                 C:\jini1_1\lib\jini-ext.jar;
                 C:\jini1_1\lib\sun-util.jar;
                 C:\service
     -d C:\service
         C:\files\corejini\chapter9\TunnelService.java

rmic -classpath C:\files;
                 C:\jini1_1\lib\jini-core.jar;
                 C:\jini1_1\lib\jini-ext.jar;
                 C:\jini1_1\lib\sun-util.jar;
                 C:\service
     -d C:\service
         corejini.chapter9.TunnelService.Listener

mkdir C:\service_dl\corejini\chapter9
cd C:\service\corejini\chapter9
copy TunnelServiceProxy.class
         C:\service-dl\corejini\chapter9
copy TunnelService$Listener_Stub.class
         C:\service-dl\corejini\chapter9

java -cp C:\jini1_1\lib\jini-core.jar;
         C:\jini1_1\lib\jini-ext.jar;
         C:\jini1_1\lib\sun-util.jar;
         C:\service;
         C:\service-dl
     -Djava.security.policy=C:\files\policy
     -Djava.rmi.server.codebase=http://myhost:8085/
     corejini.chapter9.TunnelService
     jini://turbodog.parc.xerox.com
     jini://foundation.parc.xerox.com
```

On UNIX:

```
javac -classpath/files:
              /files/jini1_1/lib/jini-core.jar:
              /files/jini1_1/lib/jini-ext.jar:
              /files/jini1_1/lib/sun-util.jar:
              /files/service
      -d /files/service
              /files/corejini/chapter9/TunnelService.java

rmic -classpath /files:
              /files/jini1_1/lib/jini-core.jar:
              /files/jini1_1/lib/jini-ext.jar:
              /files/jini1_1/lib/sun-util.jar:
              /files/service
-d /files/service
              corejini.chapter9.TunnelService.Listener


mkdir/files/service_dl/corejini\chapter9
cd /files/service/corejini/chapter9
cp TunnelServiceProxy.class
        /files/service-dl/corejini/chapter9
cp TunnelService\$Listener_Stub.class
        /files/service-dl/corejini/chapter9

java -cp /files/jini1_1/lib/jini-core.jar:
        /files/jini1_1/lib/jini-ext.jar:
        /files/jini1_1/lib/sun-util.jar:
        /files/service
    -Djava.security.policy=/files/policy
    -Djava.rmi.server.codebase=http://myhost:8085/
        corejini.chapter9.TunnelService
        jini://turbodog.parc.xerox.com
        jini://foundation.parc.xerox.com
```

Summary

This rather long chapter has shown the low-level details of how clients interact with lookup services. You've seen how to use the `ServiceRegistrar` interface to perform lookup and event solicitation. You've also started to look at service administration with some examples of how lookup services can be configured and controlled.

What's Next?

Just as Jini services have the high-level `JoinManager` class that shields them from the intricacies of the join protocol and using the `ServiceRegistrar` interfaces directly, clients can take advantage of the `ServiceDiscoveryManager`. In the next chapter, you'll learn about this useful class, which will almost certainly be the most common Jini class you use in your own applications.

Using the
ServiceDiscoveryManager

Topics in This Chapter

- Basics of the `ServiceDiscoveryManager`
- Common programming idioms
- Creating `LookupCaches`
- Soliciting events

Chapter 10

I n the previous chapter, you learned how to use the `ServiceRegistrar` interface. This interface, common to all lookup service implementations, is the "lowest common denominator" API for accessing lookup functionality. You can count on the basic interfaces for `lookup()` and `register()` being available on every lookup service you encounter.

Now, in this chapter, you'll learn about how to use the `ServiceDiscovery-Manager` class. This class is built using the "raw" `ServiceRegistrar` interface, and provides higher level functionality on top of it. In this chapter, you'll learn how to use the `ServiceDiscoveryManager` to maintain client-side caches of services, search for services, and receive event notifications when services appear, disappear, or are modified. While you can certainly do all of these functions directly using `ServiceRegistrar`, in most cases, the `ServiceDiscoveryManager` will provide a simpler programming model and more functionality.

I'll talk about the API provided by this important class, and cover the most common programming "idioms" that it supports. As you'll see, the `ServiceDiscoveryManager` is a complicated class that can support a number of styles of interaction. Beginners are often confused by the behavior of this class because they don't understand the different ways to use it, and how those programming styles interact. In this chapter, I'll cover each of these styles, and provide example programs that show you practical details about how to use them.

Higher Level APIs for Client Lookup

You've no doubt noticed that many of the clients you've seen so far exhibit many of the same behaviors—they discover lookup services, search for desired services, and solicit events to be informed of changes in the available services. In the examples in this book, I've typically done some bookkeeping to keep track of the lookup services and service proxies that I'm using. Certainly much of the `ServiceInfoWatcher` and `ServiceInfoSearcher` code from the last chapter is devoted to these sorts of chores.

There are a number of good reasons for this bookkeeping. First, by holding on to the proxies for lookup services, you don't have to reinitiate the costly discovery process if you need to do future queries or event solicitations. Second, by holding on to the services found at these lookup services, you can very quickly iterate over the available services, perhaps to present them to a user. Keeping information about the service IDs of lookup—and other—services allows you to recognize duplicate registrations, which is a useful thing to do.

Of course, not *all* clients will, or should, do this bookkeeping. Limited memory clients, for instance, may be willing to pay the time penalty required to query lookup services again and again, rather than keeping references to many service proxies around. But, many clients will follow the "cache and bookkeep" paradigm. (And, now is probably a good time to point out that many services will themselves be clients of other services. So, they are likely to follow many of these same patterns and have the same requirements for bookkeeping.) Sun realized this common behavior and created a class—called the `ServiceDiscoveryManager`—to support it in Jini 1.1.

The ServiceDiscoveryManager

The `ServiceDiscoveryManager` is an incredibly flexible class. It can serve as a "substitute" for using the raw `ServiceRegistrar` methods for doing lookup. It can also create a cache of services based on some search criteria. This cache can be polled by a client application that wishes to determine what services are available, and the cache can also deliver events to the client when a service is added, removed, or changed. One of its benefits is that it largely hides the entire notion of lookup services and the `ServiceRegistrar` API. You only deal with services—the `ServiceDiscoveryManager` takes care of finding lookup services, eliminating duplicate services, and so on. Most client applications written to Jini 1.1 or later will use the `ServiceDiscoveryManager` class as their sole interface for service location.

Here is the declaration of the class:

```
package net.jini.lookup;

public class ServiceDiscoveryManager {
    public ServiceDiscoveryManager(
                        DiscoveryManagement discoveryMgr,
                        LeaseRenewalManager leaseMgr)
        throws IOException;

    public LookupCache createLookupCache(
                        ServiceTemplate tmpl,
                        ServiceItemFilter filter,
                        ServiceDiscoveryListener listener)
        throws RemoteException;

    public ServiceItem lookup(ServiceTemplate tmpl,
                        ServiceItemFilter filter);
    public ServiceItem lookup(ServiceTemplate tmpl,
                        ServiceItemFilter filter,
                        long waitDur)
        throws InterruptedException, RemoteException;
    public ServiceItem[] lookup(ServiceTemplate tmpl,
                        int maxMatches,
                        ServiceItemFilter filter);
    public ServiceItem[] lookup(ServiceTemplate tmpl,
                        int minMatches,
                        int maxMatches,
                        ServiceItemFilter filter,
                        long waitDur)
        throws InterruptedException, RemoteException;

    public DiscoveryManagement getDiscoveryManager();
    public LeaseRenewalManager getLeaseRenewalManager();
    public void terminate();
}
```

I'll cover how the constructor for this class works before jumping in to the other methods on the class and how they're used.

The constructor for ServiceDiscoveryManager takes as arguments an object implementing the DiscoveryManagement interface, and a LeaseRenewalManager. The semantics are much the same as for the service-side Join-Manager: You can pass in any object that implements DiscoveryManagement (typically a LookupDiscoveryManager) to have control over the discovery process. You can also pass in your own `LeaseRenewalManager` if you wish to reuse an instance of this class that you may already have "sitting around" in your program. If you pass null for either of these parameters, a default implementation will be created (a `LookupDiscoveryManager` initialized to find lookup services in the public group, and a "fresh" `LeaseRenewalManager`).

Notice that the constructor is declared as raising `IOException`. This is because the constructor may have to initiate the multicast discovery protocols, which can cause this exception.

A Word on Usage Patterns

The `ServiceDiscoveryManager` is a commonly misunderstood class, not only because it provides a lot of functionality, but because it supports three broad patterns of usage. Before I continue with the description of the other methods in the class, I should say a few words about these patterns, how they work, and how they relate to one another.

In the first pattern, there is no need to create a `LookupCache` at all. In this style of use, you only need to create a `ServiceDiscoveryManager` and then invoke whichever version of `lookup()`—on the `ServiceDiscoveryManager` itself—that is applicable to the needs of your application.

In the other two usage patterns, after creating a `ServiceDiscoveryManager`, you use that object to create one or more `LookupCaches`. From that point on, you *typically* interact only with the `LookupCache`, not the `ServiceDiscovery-Manager` that you initially created. Of course, you are free to invoke methods on `ServiceDiscoveryManager` at any time, even if you've created a `Lookup-Cache`, although this style of programming isn't common in the two patterns that involve `LookupCaches`.

Once a `LookupCache` has been created, if you need to query for a particular service, you will typically invoke one of the versions of `lookup()` provided by the `LookupCache`, not the `ServiceDiscoveryManager`. This is the second usage pattern.

The third and final usage pattern involves the event mechanisms of the `Lookup-Cache`. That is, if you wish to be notified of the arrival, departure, or modification of services, you must register for events with the `LookupCache`, not with the `Ser-viceDiscoveryManger` or the underlying `ServiceRegistrar`.

These three patterns will become more clear as I walk through the rest of the methods on the class. But it's important to keep these in mind in the discussions below, so that you can see the "big picture."

Creating Lookup Caches

Perhaps the most important method on this class, because it's used in the two most common usage patterns, is `createLookupCache()`. Clients use this method to instruct the `ServiceDiscoveryManager` to create a cache of all of the available services that match some search criteria. The `ServiceDiscoveryManager` will discover lookup services and then search them to find the desired services. It will also solicit events from these lookup services to ensure that the cache is kept relatively up-to-date—as new matching services appear in the community, they will also appear in the cache.

The cache that is returned by this method is a local repository of all matching services, and is "back-filled" by the `ServiceDiscoveryManager` (meaning that the set of services it contains may change, even after you've acquired a reference to the cache). You should be sure that you understand this point: The proxies and attributes of any matching services will be stored locally by the cache. So, if your client is running in a memory-constrained environment, you should take great care when using caches.

Using methods that you'll see below, you can use the cache to return all matching services, and can ask the cache to inform you about changes in the status of matched services.

The `createLookupCache()` method takes three arguments. The first is an instance of `ServiceTemplate`, which works just as in the earlier examples of the previous chapter: The template is used to query lookup services to find desired services, using the normal template-matching semantics. The second argument is a `ServiceItemFilter`. This is a *client-side* filtering mechanism that lets you have fine-grained control over which services show up in the cache.

I talked in the last chapter about how `ServiceTemplates`, while powerful and simple-to-use, don't always give you all of the control over service matching that you may like. They don't, for instance, allow you to do any comparisons over numeric attributes other than simple equality. The `ServiceItemFilter` used here allows you greater control over matching. Any `ServiceItems` that match the template are returned to the client where they are evaluated by the filter. The filter has a method that can return true or false to indicate whether the service is considered a match or not.

Core Tip: Optimizing your searches

Be sure you understand the relationship between `ServiceTemplates` *and* `ServiceItemFilters`. `ServiceTemplates` *are sent "over the wire" to lookup services. The matching of services against* `ServiceTemplates` *happens inside the*

> *lookup service, using the fast (but relatively coarse) rules I outlined
> before. Any matched services are then returned to the client, where*
> ServiceItemFilters—*which execute completely in the client—
> have an opportunity to further prune the results.*
>
> *Usually, you will look for a design that partitions a search
> between these two classes in a way that minimizes the amount of
> data returned from the lookup service. Since sending a lot of data
> over a network is a relatively expensive operation, you should use*
> ServiceTemplates *that, as closely as possible, cull out only the
> services that you're interested in. Once this small set of possibly
> interesting services is returned, you can use* ServiceFilters *to
> refine the result set.*

The final argument to the constructor is an object that implements the `Ser-viceDiscoveryListener` interface. This argument allows you to supply a listener to the cache that will be called whenever the cache updates its state to reflect the addition, removal, or change of a service. The cache will deliver a `ServiceDiscoveryEvent` that encapsulates this information. Unlike `ServiceEvents`, which are sent from lookup services to reflect their changes in state, `ServiceDiscoveryEvents` are purely *local* events; that is, they originate in the cache in the client's VM, rather than some remote VM.

There are some other important differences between `ServiceDiscoveryEvents` and `ServiceEvents` in addition to just the local versus remote distinction. In particular, the cache will try to *coalesce* multiple remote `ServiceEvents` into a single `ServiceDiscoveryEvent`. I'll talk more about this in the section on `ServiceDiscoveryListeners` a bit later.

I'll continue walking through the rest of the methods in `ServiceDiscoveryManager`, and then talk about the supporting classes such as `LookupCache`, `ServiceDiscoveryEvent`, and so on.

New Versions of Lookup()

The `ServiceDiscoveryManager`, in addition to supporting the ability to create caches of services, also provides "wrapper" implementations of the lookup method that appears in the `ServiceRegistrar` interface. I call these implementations "wrappers" because they allow clients to essentially search a whole *set* of lookup services at once. That is, while the `ServiceRegistrar` version searches only one particular lookup service, these versions are "front ends" that provide a slightly richer API and can search all of the lookup services that have been discovered so far.

All versions of the `lookup()` method take a `ServiceTemplate` and a `ServiceItemFilter` as arguments; these parameters are used in exactly the same way as described above. The `ServiceDiscoveryManager` uses the template to get an initial set of matching services from the lookup services it has discovered, and then uses the filter to further cull this list.

The first two versions of `lookup()` return only a single `ServiceItem`. If the template and filter together match multiple services, an arbitrary one is selected and returned. If no matching services are available at the lookup services (that is, if the template query returns no matches), then the filter will not be run and a null will be returned to the caller.

The second two versions return an array of all matching service items. Note that these versions of `lookup()` take extra parameters describing how many matches should be returned. If no matches are found, then an empty array will be returned to callers.

One single-valued version of `lookup()` and one multi-valued version of `lookup()` are also defined to be *blocking*. This means that they will wait for some specified amount of time until the requested number of matches is found. The versions of `lookup()` that take a wait duration parameter have this behavior.

If the wait duration expires without the requested number of services being found (either one service for the single-valued version, or `minMatches` for the multi-valued version), then the blocking methods will return an empty result. Otherwise, they complete successfully and return the service items they have found.

Contrast this to the non-blocking versions (the versions *without* the wait duration parameter), which return a result immediately. Be aware that if these versions of `lookup()` report that no matching services have been found, it may be because there actually are no matching services in the community, or it may be because no lookup services have been discovered yet.

This is a common mistake when using this class! Callers create a `ServiceDiscoveryManager` and immediately use the non-blocking version of `lookup()`, which will often return null. The error isn't that the service isn't available—it's just that the lookup service holding it may not have been discovered yet.

Note that the blocking methods may raise `java.lang.InterruptedException`. This is because, sometimes, a caller may wish to interrupt a thread that is blocked executing one of these methods. If you interrupt a thread in this way (by calling `Thread.interrupt()`), then the method will raise an `InterruptedException`.

The blocking methods provide you with an easy-to-use way to allot a fixed period of time to try to find a service.

Miscellaneous Methods

After the lookup() methods, there are a handful of useful utility methods on ServiceDiscoveryManager. The getDiscoveryManager() and getLease-RenewalManager() methods return the DiscoveryManagement object and LeaseRenewalManager object in use, respectively. If you explicitly passed in instances in the constructor, these methods will return these same objects; otherwise, they will return the implicit objects created by the ServiceDiscoveryManager.

The terminate() method is used to shut down the ServiceDiscoveryManager. Specifically, this means that all DiscoveryListeners and RemoteEventListeners will be removed, and any leases on event registrations will be cancelled. All internal threads will also be stopped.

Much as in the case of JoinManager, calling terminate() is an irreversible operation. Calling any method on ServiceDiscoveryManager after calling terminate() will result in a RuntimeException.

Receiving Remote Events

You've no doubt noticed that some of the methods of this class raise RemoteExceptions while others do not. This is because the methods that raise RemoteExceptions (including createLookupCache() and the blocking versions of lookup()) register remote event listeners with lookup services so that they can be informed of changes in the set of available services.

This fact isn't a mere curiosity of the implementation, though—it puts requirements on you to ensure that your client program correctly exports the listener code that lookup services will use to call back to the ServiceDiscoveryManager.

Remember that remote events are delivered from one JVM to a listener in another. The actual mechanics of how this happens are that the listener is defined as an RMI remote object, typically extending java.rmi.Unicast-RemoteObject. The *stub* for this object is automatically downloaded into the caller—the program that will *generate* the remote event—so that it can know how to connect back to the receiving listener.

Just like any remote event listener, `ServiceDiscoveryManager` comes with a listener class that will receive events, and an `rmic`-generated stub class that is meant to be downloaded into callers. Even though the stub comes as a part of the standard Jini client libraries, *it is your responsibility* to provide the facilities for this stub to be downloaded by lookup services.

The common way to do this is to extract the stub class along with the classes it uses from the Jini JAR files and bundle them into a separate JAR file that will be served by the client's HTTP server. You can, of course, bundle these into the JAR file that contains any other client-exported code so that you have everything in one place. After doing this, you must set a codebase that tells the lookup service where the needed code can be found.

The stub class is called `net.jini.lookup.ServiceDiscoveryManager$LookupCacheImpl$LookupListener_Stub.class`, and it lives in `jini-ext.jar`. This class depends only on `net.jini.core.event.RemoteEventListener.class`, from `jini-core.jar`. While technically you don't need to export the class file for the `RemoteEventListener` interface—because any lookup service should already have it—it's a good idea to keep all necessary code together, just in case.

Remember that you *must* make some provision for exporting these class files, or the methods on `ServiceDiscoveryManager` that use events—which are the most powerful and useful methods—will not be useable by you!

In the interest of keeping the descriptions of how to run the example programs short, I will take the expedient approach of simply placing these class files in the client's downloadable code directory, where they will be served by the "normal" HTTP server that exports the rest of the client's code. I would recommend producing a single JAR file of all downloadable code exported by the client for a "production" system, though.

Supporting Classes

As you saw above, there are a number of supporting classes used alongside the `ServiceDiscoveryManager`.

LookupCache

For many clients, the most common idiom of using the ServiceDiscovery-
Manager will be to create one or more LookupCaches, each of which reflects a
different pool of services that the client is interested in. LookupCache is actually an interface, which allows future implementations of ServiceDiscoveryManager to provide different sorts of caches, perhaps with different
performance characteristics.

The cache provides a handful of methods that allows clients to retrieve services out of the cache, and ask the cache to notify them upon changes.

```
package net.jini.lookup;

public interface LookupCache {
    public ServiceItem lookup(ServiceItemFilter filter);
    public ServiceItem[] lookup(ServiceItemFilter filter,
                                int maxMatches);

    public void addListener(ServiceDiscoveryListener l);
    public void removeListener(ServiceDiscoveryListener l);

    public void discard(Object serviceReference);
    public void terminate();
}
```

The lookup() methods work similarly to the versions in ServiceDiscoveryManager that you saw before, with a couple of important differences. First,
these methods do not take the ServiceTemplate parameter. This is because
they do not actually cause any network traffic to go between the client and the
lookup service. Instead, the query is answered completely from the services that
happen to be contained in the cache at the time the call to lookup() is made.
Recall that the contents of the cache will eventually be all of the services that
match both the template and the filter specified when the cache was set up (I say
"eventually" because it may take some time for the cache to fill). The Service-
ItemFilter provided here allows you to further refine the services you select
from the cache.

A second difference is that both versions of lookup() here are non-blocking.
The first will return a matching ServiceItem if it exists in the cache, or null otherwise, but will return immediately. Likewise, the second will return a matching
array of ServiceItems, or an empty array if no matches exist, but will still
return immediately. Again, this behavior is because both of these methods

involve no remote calls—they go directly to the cache and try to satisfy the requests based on the information available locally.

While the `lookup()` calls allow you to "poll" the cache to find out if desired services are available, sometimes you may want the cache to asynchronously notify you when services are available. Thus, the `LookupCache` provides a way for you to install and remove listeners for service-related events. The `addListener()` and `removeListener()` methods let you install and uninstall `ServiceDiscoveryListeners` that will be called when services are added, removed, or changed. (See below for details on `ServiceDiscoveryListeners` and the `ServiceDiscoveryEvents` that they will receive.)

Finally, the last two methods are used for housekeeping in the cache. The `terminate()` method simply shuts down all of the activities of the `LookupCache`: It halts all threads and cancels any event registrations with lookup services. This method is irreversible, and is typically called when the client is no longer interested in the contents of the cache.

The `discard()` method is used to drop a service from the cache. The argument here should be the service's proxy object. Once a proxy has been dropped, all references to it in the cache are removed, and the cache's `ServiceDiscoveryListeners` will be notified. This operation is often done if a service seems to have failed or has become unreachable—you will usually detect this because the service's proxy will begin to raise `RemoteExceptions`. Discarding the service means that the service may be rediscovered later, if it recovers and registers itself with lookup services.

Core Note: Understanding the semantics of discard

As mentioned, calling `discard()` *causes a reference to a service to be dropped from the cache so that it can be rediscovered. Generally, the only time you will explicitly discard a service is when it seems to have failed—meaning that attempts to use its proxy result in* `RemoteException` *being thrown.*

If the service has genuinely crashed or been shut down then, over time, its registrations with lookup services will expire. When the service comes back online, it will reregister with these lookup services, the lookup cache will detect this fact, and the service will be rediscovered and added to the cache once again. Any listeners registered with the cache will be notified.

There is, however, an insidious condition which the `LookupCache` *must deal with. What happens if the service hasn't actually crashed, but merely become unreachable because of some network partition? In this case, your attempts to use it will certainly result in*

RemoteExceptions being raised. But it may be possible, depending on the partition, that the service is still in perfect communication with all of the lookup services with which it is registered!

In this case, the service will never "reappear" in the lookup service, since it will never have left it. Does this mean that the LookupCache will never rediscover the service, and that it is lost forever?

Fortunately, no. The algorithm that the LookupCache uses to determine when a service is to be rediscovered is a bit more complex than you might first think; it can be helpful to understand how this works in case you're debugging problems with service discovery.

When you first call discard() on a service, the LookupCache removes the reference to the service from the cache. But it also keeps a copy of this reference in a separate "limbo" storage area. It then waits for a some amount of time to pass; typically this will be some span that is longer than the typical lease duration with a lookup service. If, during this interval, the service disappears from the lookup services, then the cache assumes that the service has in fact crashed, and removes its reference from the limbo area. If the service returns later, it will then be rediscovered.

However, if this timeout elapses and the service is still registered with the lookup services, the cache assumes that the service has not actually crashed—since it is apparently renewing its leases with the lookup services. In this case, the service is then "rediscovered" by the cache, and its reference is moved from limbo back into the cache's regular storage space. Any listeners are informed of this fact. This mechanism provides a way for the cache to recover from network partitions and "rediscover" inaccessible services, even if those services have never left the community.

The timeout period can be controlled by the property com.sun.jini.sdm.discardWait, and is set to 10 minutes by default (which is twice the maximum lease granted by reggie).

ServiceItemFilter

The ServiceItemFilter interface provides a way to do client-side "filtering" of service query results. The basic idea is that you provide a class that implements the ServiceItemFilter interface to calls that create caches or do a lookup(). Any results returned by matching a ServiceTemplate are returned to your client, where your filter gets a chance to veto whether a service should be returned.

```
package net.jini.lookup;

public interface ServiceItemFilter {
    public boolean check(ServiceItem item);
}
```

The `check()` method will be called to evaluate whether a service is considered to match the filter. The filter should return true if the service matches, or false otherwise.

Filtering provides you with a way to do searches that are impossible using the standard `ServiceTemplate` semantics. For example, you can write filters that apply numerical comparison tests to attributes.

ServiceDiscoveryListener

The `ServiceDiscoveryListener` interface is used by clients that wish to be asynchronously notified of changes in the available services known to a `LookupCache`. You can install a `ServiceDiscoveryListener` when you first create a cache via a call to `createLookupCache()`, and you can also add listeners after the fact by calling `addListener()` directly on the `LookupCache`.

The interface itself is fairly simple:

```
package net.jini.lookup;

public interface ServiceDiscoveryListener {
    public void serviceAdded(ServiceDiscoveryEvent event);
    public void serviceChanged(ServiceDiscoveryEvent event);
    public void serviceRemoved(ServiceDiscoveryEvent event);
}
```

In many ways, the information available through this interface is analogous to the information available through the low-level `ServiceEvents` that are sent from lookup services. The primary differences are that the `ServiceDiscovery-Listener` methods are locally invoked from the cache (rather than remotely by the lookup service), and correspond to changes in the cache rather than just one particular lookup service. This means that the `LookupCache` will try to *coalesce* multiple `ServiceEvents` into single `ServiceDiscoveryEvents`.

Why is this? Think about how services are registered in Jini. Typically, a service will start up and join any and all lookup services that it finds that are "relevant" (meaning that they are members of a group, or named by a locator, that the service is searching for). So any given service will usually be registered with *many* lookup services. The `LookupCache` will register with *each* of these to receive notifications in changes in the set of services each provides.

But of course, when you're interested in a service, you typically just want to acquire *a* reference to it, not *all* references to it. So the `LookupCache`, even though it receives multiple `ServiceEvents` about a given service, will typically generate only a single corresponding event to its listeners.

This is done in the following way:

- The `serviceAdded()` method is called when a cache receives notification that a service has been registered *for the first time* in a community. This means that even if a service registers itself with multiple lookup services, the cache will notice these multiple registrations, determine that the multiple registrations are for the same service, and generate only one invocation of `service-Added()`.

- The `serviceRemoved()` method is called when a service disappears from *all* of the lookup services that it knows about. The method will not be called if a service is dropped merely from one of a set of lookup services with which it is registered.

- The `serviceChanged()` method is invoked once for each *distinct* change in attributes it detects. That is, the cache keeps one "canonical" set of attributes associated with each service in the cache. When the attributes change at one lookup service, the cache updates its record of the service's attributes and generates an event. Future notifications of updates do not generate events, if those updates produce attributes that are the same as those already known to the cache. Typically, when a service changes its attributes, it does so by updating each lookup service with which it is registered. The first such change will be detected by the cache and will result in an event. As the other lookup services are updated to the same attribute set, further events are not generated by the cache.

- Finally, the `serviceChanged()` method is invoked when a unique change occurs in the service's proxy object.

Be sure to note that the `serviceChanged()` method, in addition to being called when an attribute on a service changes, will also be called when the *proxy* for a service changes. This may happen if a service updates or revises its published proxy. But, two proxies *for the same service* that are registered at different lookup services may not be "equal" if you don't take special precautions. If you write your own services, you should be aware that proxies that have inconsistent equality comparisons with each other can cause the `LookupCache` to report that a proxy has changed.

Core Alert: Controlling proxy changes

As a service writer, you will often want to have control over whether the proxies for your service are considered equal to, or different from, each other. The best way to do this—and a good rule of thumb to follow in any case—is to override the `equals()` *and* `hashCode()` *methods on your service proxies.*

Think about what happens if your service registers itself at multiple lookup services. Each registration will result in a new copy of the proxy being stored at each of those lookup services. If your service doesn't override `equals()` *and* `hashCode()`, *you've effectively given up control over how the* `LookupCache` *will determine if these proxies are the same or not. And, without doing anything explicit, the default implementation of these methods is likely to report that each proxy is different from all others, resulting in many* `serviceChanged()` *invocations.*

(If your proxies are simply RMI stubs, then you'll get the correct behavior—since stubs override `equals()` *and* `hashCode()` *to be based on whether the remote objects referred to by the stubs are equal to each other. If, as is commonly the case, you're using smart proxies that contain a single remote reference to a back-end server, a common implementation for* `equals()` *is to simply invoke the* `equals()` *method on the remote reference.)*

The rule of thumb is to always provide "smart" implementations of these two methods on your service proxies. Remember that if two objects are equal to each other, they must return the same hash code.

ServiceDiscoveryEvent

The `ServiceDiscoveryEvent` encapsulates the information about service changes, additions, and removals that the `LookupCache` produces.

```
package net.jini.lookup;

public class ServiceDiscoveryEvent
    extends java.util.EventObject {
```

```
// ... constructor elided ...
public ServiceItem getPostEventServiceItem();
public ServiceItem getPreEventServiceItem();
}
```

The declaration here doesn't show the constructor for the class, since it's only of interest to the implementors of the `LookupCache` class. The two methods of interest here are `getPostEventServiceItem()`, which returns the `Service-Item` for the changed service *after* the change has taken place, and `getPreEventServiceItem()`, which returns the `ServiceItem` for the changed service *before* the change has taken place.

If the event is being sent because a service was removed, then `getPostEventServiceItem()` will return null. Likewise, if the event is sent because a service was added, `getPreEventServiceItem()` will return null. If the service merely changed (it wasn't added or removed), then neither will return null—the pre-event method returns the state before the change and the post-event method returns the state after the change.

Neither of these methods actually copy the cached `ServiceItem` before returning it, since this can be a potentially expensive operation. So you should take care to not modify the `ServiceItems` returned by these methods, or you will seriously corrupt your `LookupCache`.

The only other method of interest on this class is `getSource()`, which is inherited from `java.util.EventObject`. This method will return the `Lookup-Cache` that generated the event.

Core Tip: Troubleshooting multiple service events

One common problem symptom when you use the event facilities in the `ServiceDiscoveryManager` is that you may receive mulitple, repeated `ServiceDiscoveryEvents` for the same service. Often these will show the service constantly appearing and disappearing rapidly.

Such problems are typically the result of one of two errors. The first, and easiest to fix, is that you are not correctly exporting the remote event listener that the `ServiceDiscoveryManager` uses to receive events. Without this working, the `ServiceDiscoveryManager` will be unable to correctly determine when services come or go after initial discovery time See the section, Receiving Remote Events for details.

The second, and somewhat more insidious cause, results from services that do not properly override `equals()` and `hashCode()`

on their proxies. This means that each proxy registration is likely to look like a new and different proxy version to the ServiceDiscoveryManager, *resulting in unnecessary events. See the section on* ServiceDiscoveryListener *for details.*

If you're experience this symptom, check both of these potential causes.

A Basic Example

In this example, you'll see how to use the ServiceDiscoveryManager in its most straightforward settings. The example demonstrates how to use both the blocking and non-blocking forms of lookup, as well as the LookupCache. You should pay special attention to the output of this program! Misunderstanding how the ServiceDiscoveryManager reports its results is a common source of errors.

Look at the code in Listing 10-1:

Listing 10–1 ClientLookupExample.java

```
// Explore the ServiceDiscoveryManager

package corejini.chapter10;

import net.jini.core.lookup.ServiceItem;
import net.jini.core.lookup.ServiceTemplate;
import net.jini.lookup.ServiceDiscoveryManager;
import net.jini.lookup.LookupCache;
import net.jini.lookup.ServiceItemFilter;
import net.jini.lookup.ServiceDiscoveryListener;
import net.jini.discovery.LookupDiscoveryManager;
import net.jini.lease.LeaseRenewalManager;
import java.io.IOException;
import java.rmi.RemoteException;
import java.rmi.RMISecurityManager;
import corejini.chapter9.ServiceInfoSearcher;

public class ClientLookupExample  {
    protected LookupDiscoveryManager discoveryMgr;
    protected LeaseRenewalManager leaseMgr;
    protected ServiceDiscoveryManager lookupMgr;

    public ClientLookupExample() throws IOException {
        if (System.getSecurityManager() == null) {
            System.setSecurityManager(
                    new RMISecurityManager());
        }

        lookupMgr =
            new ServiceDiscoveryManager(null, null);
    }
```

Listing 10–1 ClientLookupExample.java (continued)

```java
// Subclasses may override...
public ServiceDiscoveryListener getListener() {
    return null;
}

// subclasses may override...
public ServiceItemFilter getFilter() {
    return null;
}

// Do a bit of work here...
public void runTests() {
    ServiceTemplate tmpl =
        new ServiceTemplate(null, null, null);
    ServiceItem service = null;

    service = lookupMgr.lookup(tmpl, null);

    if (service == null) {
        System.out.println("Non-blocking lookup " +
                           "found no services.");
    } else {
        System.out.print("Non-blocking lookup found: ");
        ServiceInfoSearcher.printServiceInfo(service);
    }

    try {
        service = lookupMgr.lookup(tmpl, null, 20000);
    } catch (RemoteException ex) {
        System.out.println("Error: " + ex);
    } catch (InterruptedException ex) {
    }

    if (service == null) {
        System.out.println("Blocking lookup found " +
                           "no services.");
    } else {
        System.out.print("Blocking lookup found: ");
        ServiceInfoSearcher.printServiceInfo(service);
    }

    LookupCache cache = null;
```

Listing 10–1 ClientLookupExample.java (continued)

```
    try {
        cache = lookupMgr.createLookupCache(tmpl,
                                    getFilter(),
                                    getListener());
    } catch (RemoteException ex) {
        System.out.println("Error: " + ex);
    }

    service = cache.lookup(null);

    if (service == null) {
        System.out.println("Cache lookup found " +
                        "no services.");
    } else {
        System.out.print("Cache lookup found: ");
        ServiceInfoSearcher.printServiceInfo(service);
    }

    System.out.println("Pausing...");
    try {
        Thread.sleep(5000);
    } catch (Exception ex) {
    }

    System.out.println("Trying again...");
    service = cache.lookup(null);
    if (service == null) {
        System.out.println("Cache lookup found " +
                        "no services.");
    } else {
        System.out.print("Cache lookup found: ");
        ServiceInfoSearcher.printServiceInfo(service);
    }

    System.out.println("Getting all cached services.");
    ServiceItem[] services = cache.lookup(null,
                                Integer.MAX_VALUE);
```

Listing 10–1 ClientLookupExample.java (continued)

```
        if (services == null || services.length == 0) {
            System.out.println("No services in cache");
        } else {
            for (int i=0 ; i<services.length ; i++) {
                System.out.print("[" + i + "] ");
                ServiceInfoSearcher.printServiceInfo(
                                            services[i]);
            }
        }

        cache.terminate();
    }

    public static void main(String[] args) {
        try {
            ClientLookupExample cle =
                new ClientLookupExample();
            cle.runTests();
        } catch (IOException ex) {
            System.err.println(ex.toString());
        }

        System.exit(0);
    }
}
```

The `main()` for this example creates an instance of `ClientLookupExample` and then calls `runTests()`, which exercises the `ServiceDiscoveryManager`. Note that the constructor for the example installs a security manager—which it must do in order to download code, just the same as all the rest of the examples in this book—and creates a new `ServiceDiscoveryManager`, passing in nulls as arguments. This causes the `ServiceDiscoveryManager` to create its own `LookupDiscoveryManager` and `LeaseRenewalManager`.

Most of the work here happens in `runTests()`. The code exercises the `ServiceDiscoveryManager` in several ways. First, it calls `lookup()` directly, using the non-blocking APIs. In this example, the program always uses a template that matches all services. After this, it tries the blocking version of `lookup()` with a wait duration of 20000 milliseconds (20 seconds). It then creates a `LookupCache`, and invokes `lookup()` on it to fetch a service. Note that the code calls `getFilter()` and `getListener()` to get a `ServiceItemFil-`

ter and a `ServiceDiscoveryListener` to use when creating the cache. In this example, these methods always return null; later examples will override these to test filtering and event processing. The code then sleeps for a few seconds, does another lookup, and—finally—prints out the entire contents of the cache. Any services that are found are printed by calling the `printServiceInfo()` method from the earlier `ServiceInfoSearcher` program.

While this example may seem to be going all over the map, invoking `lookup()` over and over again, first on the `ServiceDiscoveryManager` and then on the `LookupCache`, it's important to understand the different behaviors that these calls can produce. So, the next step is to move on and compile the example and see what it does.

Compiling and Running the Example

Compile this example using the standard operating procedure. Remember that the client will need to export downloadable code to services. For this to work, you must ensure that you're running an HTTP server to export the client's downloadable code. Refer back to the client examples in Chapter 5 if you haven't started this Web server.

On Windows:

```
javac -classpath C:\files;
              C:\jini1_1\lib\jini-core.jar;
              C:\jini1_1\lib\jini-ext.jar;
              C:\jini1_1\lib\sun-util.jar;
              C:\client
     -d C:\client
C:\files\corejini\chapter10\ClientLookupExample.java
```

The one extra step you must take is to ensure that the class files for the `ServiceDiscoveryManager`'s remote event listener are also exported correctly! Here, I'm taking the quick-and-dirty approach of extracting the needed files from the Jini JARs directly into the client's download directory. This makes them available from the same codebase, and uses the same HTTP server, as the rest of the client's code.

The syntax to extract a single file from a JAR is `jar xvf <jar_file> <file_to_extract>`. Make sure you're in the `client-dl` directory when you run the extraction commands.

```
cd C:\client-dl
jar xvf C:\jini1_1\lib\jini-ext.jar net\jini\lookup\Service-
DiscoveryManager$LookupCacheImpl$LookupListener_Stub.class
```

```
jar xvf C:\jini1_1\lib\jini-core.jar
   net\jini\core\event\RemoteEventListener.class
```

If you look at the contents of the client-dl directory, you should see that jar created a net directory, as well as subdirectories, to contain the class files.

```
java -cp C:\jini1_1\lib\jini-core.jar;
        C:\jini1_1\lib\jini-ext.jar;
        C:\jini1_1\lib\sun-util.jar;
        C:\client
    -Djava.security.policy=C:\files\policy
    -Djava.rmi.server.codebase=http://myhost:8086/
corejini.chapter10.ClientLookupExample
```

On UNIX:

```
javac -classpath /files:
                 /files/jini1_1/lib/jini-core.jar:
                 /files/jini1_1/lib/jini-ext.jar:
                 /files/jini1_1/lib/sun-util.jar:
                 /files/client
    -d /files/client
/files/corejini/chapter8/ClientLookupExample.java
  C:\files\corejini\chapter10\ClientLookupExample.java
```

The one extra step you must take is to ensure that the class files for the ServiceDiscoveryManager's remote event listener are also exported correctly! Here, I'm taking the quick-and-dirty approach of extracting the needed files from the Jini JARs directly into the client's download directory. This makes them available from the same codebase, and uses the same HTTP server, as the rest of the client's code.

The syntax to extract a single file from a JAR is jar xvf <jar_file> <file_to_extract>. Make sure you're in the client-dl directory when you run the extraction commands. On most UNIX shells, you will have to preface the dollar sign character by a backslash to "escape" it.

```
cd /files/client-dl
jar xvf /files/jini1_1/lib/jini-ext.jar net/jini/lookup/Ser-
viceDiscoveryManager\$LookupCache-
Impl\$LookupListener_Stub.class
jar xvf /files/jini1_1/lib/jini-core.jar
   net/jini/core/event/RemoteEventListener.class
```

If you look at the contents of the `client-dl` directory, you should see that `jar` created a `net` directory, as well as subdirectories, to contain the class files.

```
java -cp /files/jini1_1/lib/jini-core.jar:
        /files/jini1_1/lib/jini-ext.jar:
        /files/jini1_1/lib/sun-util.jar:
        /files/client
    -Djava.security.policy=/files/policy
    -Djava.rmi.server.codebase=http://myhost:8086/
corejini.chapter10.ClientLookupExample
```

The results that you see will actually vary depending on the performance of the machine you run the example on, and the performance of the machines running lookup services in your community. Here's a sample run, though:

Non-blocking lookup found no services.
Blocking lookup found: Name = Lookup
  Manufacturer = Sun Microsystems, Inc.
  Vendor = Sun Microsystems, Inc.
  Version = 1.1 alpha
  Model =
  Serial Number =
  Proxy is com.sun.jini.reggie.RegistrarProxy@af330156
Cache lookup found no services.
Pausing...
Trying again...
Cache lookup found: Name = Address Book Service
  Manufacturer = Xerox PARC
  Vendor = Xerox PARC
  Version = 1.0
  Model = null
  Serial Number = null
  Proxy is com.xerox.dispatch.addressbook.AddressBookServiceProxy@0
Getting all cached services...
[0] Name = Address Book Service
  Manufacturer = Xerox PARC
  Vendor = Xerox PARC
  Version = 1.0
  Model =
  Serial Number =
  Proxy is com.xerox.dispatch.addressbook.AddressBookServiceProxy@0
[1] Name = Lookup

Manufacturer = Sun Microsystems, Inc.
Vendor = Sun Microsystems, Inc.
Version = 1.0
Model =
Serial Number =
Proxy is com.sun.jini.reggie.RegistrarProxy@f16dfd46
[2] Name = Authentication Service
Manufacturer = Xerox PARC
Vendor = Xerox PARC
Version = 1.0
Model =
Serial Number =
Proxy is com.xerox.dispatch.authenticator.AuthenticatorProxy@0
[3] Name = Lookup
Manufacturer = Sun Microsystems, Inc.
Vendor = Sun Microsystems, Inc.
Version = 1.1 alpha
Model =
Serial Number =
Proxy is com.sun.jini.reggie.RegistrarProxy@af330156

Note that, here, the first call to `lookup()` returns null while the second finds a valid service! Remember that invoking `lookup()` on the `ServiceDiscovery-Manager` only searches for services on the lookup services that have been discovered so far. In this run, the first call to `lookup()` happens before any lookup services have been found, so it returns null. The second blocks for a few seconds, and then gives a chance for some lookup services to be discovered, so it returns a service. These two similar calls produce different results, and you should make sure you understand why.

After this, the program creates and exercises the `LookupCache`. The first operation is to call `lookup()` on this cache. In the example run you see here, notice that the cache returns no service. This is because calling `lookup()` on the cache only returns results that have already been stored in the cache. In this case, the cache has not yet been filled with any services and so nothing is returned. After sleeping for a bit, the next call to `lookup()` returns a service. Again, it's important to notice the differences here. Even though prior calls to `lookup()` on the `ServiceDiscoveryManager` itself may return results, here the call to `lookup()` on the cache returns nothing. A later call, made after a pause, returns a service because the cache has had a chance to fill.

Finally, the example dumps out all of the services in the cache; in this example, there are several—they've just taken a few moments to show up.

Be sure you understand the differences in behavior between the "raw" `ServiceRegistrar` version of `lookup()` and the versions here. The versions here have timing dependencies that do not exist in the `ServiceRegistrar` version—and these timing dependencies are a common source of confusion when using the `ServiceDiscoveryManager`. Even though you must understand these differences, most users will still prefer to use the `LookupCache`, since it provides so many benefits (the ability to search for services across many lookup services, the fact that it essentially "hides" the existence of lookup services at all, the ability to run client-side filtering predicates, and so on).

Using Filters

Listing 10-2 demonstrates how to use `ServiceItemFilters`. In this program, you'll see three filters, and learn how to combine them together to extract specific services in ways that are impossible using just `ServiceTemplates`.

The first filter shows how you can do substring matching of attributes. This filter allows you to find all services that contain a given string in the `vendor` field of their `ServiceInfo` attributes.

```
Listing 10-2 ServiceInfoVendorFilter.java
```

```java
// A filter that matches services whose ServiceInfo.vendor
// contains a given substring.

package corejini.chapter10;

import net.jini.core.lookup.ServiceItem;
import net.jini.lookup.ServiceItemFilter;
import net.jini.lookup.entry.ServiceInfo;
import net.jini.core.entry.Entry;

public class ServiceInfoVendorFilter
        implements ServiceItemFilter {
    protected String substring;

    public ServiceInfoVendorFilter(String substring) {
        this.substring = substring;
    }

    public boolean check(ServiceItem item) {
        Entry[] attrs = item.attributeSets;
        for (int i=0 ; i<attrs.length ; i++) {
            // If it's a ServiceInfo or subclass
            if (ServiceInfo.class.isAssignableFrom(
                                attrs[i].getClass())) {
                return ((ServiceInfo)
                attrs[i]).vendor.indexOf(substring) != -1;
            }
        }

        return false;
    }
}
```

The `ServiceInfoVendorFilter` is pretty simple. Instances of the class are constructed with a string to search for. The `check()` method iterates over the attribute set on the service item, looking for `ServiceInfo` attributes or its subclasses. When one is found, the method simply looks to see if the parameter occurs as a substring in the vendor string. If it does, the method returns true.

The second filter is a little more complicated. It lets you match services that have a certain version number in the `version` fields of their `ServiceInfo` attributes. Using this filter, you can find services that are exactly at a given version (say, version "1.0.1"), or services that are *greater* than a given version (version "1.2.7" is greater than version "1.2" or version "1.2.6").

Version numbering is a black art at best, and this particular filter (Listing 10-3) only makes a best effort attempt at comparing versions. But, it shows the power of being able to use arbitrary filters to prune the set of matched services.

Listing 10-3 ServiceInfoVersionFilter.java

```java
// A filter that matches services whose ServiceInfo.version
// matches a search parameter

package corejini.chapter10;

import net.jini.core.lookup.ServiceItem;
import net.jini.lookup.ServiceItemFilter;
import net.jini.lookup.entry.ServiceInfo;
import net.jini.core.entry.Entry;
import java.util.ArrayList;
import java.util.StringTokenizer;

public class ServiceInfoVersionFilter
        implements ServiceItemFilter {
    public static final int EQUAL = 1;
    public static final int EQUAL_OR_GREATER = 2;

    protected String test;
    protected String[] testTokens;
    protected int cond;

    public ServiceInfoVersionFilter(String test, int cond){
        this.test = test;
        this.cond = cond;
        testTokens = makeVersionTokens(test);
    }
```

Listing 10-3 ServiceInfoVersionFilter.java (continued)

```java
// Version numbering is an inexact science, but
// this covers many cases.
public boolean check(ServiceItem item) {
    Entry[] attrs = item.attributeSets;
    for (int i=0 ; i<attrs.length ; i++) {
        // If it's a ServiceInfo or subclass
        if (ServiceInfo.class.isAssignableFrom(
                attrs[i].getClass())) {
            String target = ((ServiceInfo)
                                attrs[i]).version;

            if (target.equals(test)) {
                return true;
            }

            switch (cond) {
            case EQUAL:
                return false;
            case EQUAL_OR_GREATER:
                String[] targetTokens =
                    makeVersionTokens(target);

                // Cycle through each.  If any element
                // in target is less than the
                // corresponding element in test,
                // report false.
                int min = Math.min(testTokens.length,
                                    targetTokens.length);
```

Listing 10-3 ServiceInfoVersionFilter.java(continued)

```
                    for (int j=0 ; j<min ; j++) {
                        try {
                            int testVal =
                            Integer.parseInt(testTokens[j]);
                            int targetVal =
                        Integer.parseInt(targetTokens[j]);

                            if (targetVal < testVal) {
                                return false;
                            }
                        } catch (NumberFormatException ex) {
                            System.err.println(
                                    "Unexpected format: " +
                                    testTokens[i] + ", " +
                                    targetTokens[i]);
                            ex.printStackTrace();
                        }
                    }

                return testTokens.length <=
                        targetTokens.length;
            }
        }
    }

        return false;
    }
```

Listing 10-3 ServiceInfoVersionFilter.java(continued)

```
        // Convert a string of the form 1.2.2.1 into a
        // string array.
        static String[] makeVersionTokens(String v) {
            String str = v;
            // Jettison everything after a space.
            if (str.indexOf(' ') != -1) {
                str = str.substring(0, str.indexOf(' '));
            }
            StringTokenizer t = new StringTokenizer(str, ".");
            ArrayList arr = new ArrayList();
            while (t.hasMoreTokens()) {
                arr.add(t.nextToken());
            }
            return (String[]) arr.toArray(new String[0]);
        }
    }
}
```

This filter is quite a bit more complicated than the previous one. Instances of the ServiceInfoVersionFilter are constructed with a string representing a version and a parameter indicating whether the filter should look for exact version matches, or versions that are equal to or greater than the specified version. The input version number is "tokenized" into an array of strings.

The check() method finds any ServiceInfo attribute that is on the service and checks its version against the original input version. If the two match exactly, then the predicate method returns true. The complicated case is when the filter is looking for versions that are greater than or equal to the input version. The code here tokenizes the service's version and walks down the two token arrays, pairwise matching version numbers. If any token in the input version is greater than the service's version, the method returns false. While this code isn't perfect, it is capable of comparing many styles of version numbers correctly.

The previous two filters give you a way to do very flexible matching over fields of the ServiceInfo attribute. But this begs a question: How can you use *two* filters at the same time? The ServiceDiscoveryManager APIs only allow you to pass in a single filter to any call to lookup() or createLookupCache().

The answer is to use a filter that can aggregate other filters, and this is exactly what the third filter example does. This filter lets you connect up other filters by logical operators (either AND or OR), and evaluates all of them in turn. The

AggregationFilter can be a useful way to chain together sets of filtering operations, as shown in Listing 10-4.

Listing 10-4 AggregationFilter.java

```java
// A filter that joins other filters together.

package corejini.chapter10;

import net.jini.core.lookup.ServiceItem;
import net.jini.lookup.ServiceItemFilter;
import java.util.ArrayList;
import java.util.Iterator;
```

Listing 10-4 AggregationFilter.java(continued)

```java
public class AggregationFilter
        implements ServiceItemFilter {
    private ArrayList list = new ArrayList();
    private int operator;

    public static final int AND = 1;// all must match
    public static final int OR = 2;// any must match

    public AggregationFilter(int operator) {
        if (operator == AND || operator == OR) {
            this.operator = operator;
        } else {
            throw new IllegalArgumentException(
                                "Bogus operator");
        }
    }

    public void add(ServiceItemFilter filter) {
        list.add(filter);
    }

    public boolean check(ServiceItem item) {
        if (list.size() == 0) {
            return true;
        }

        Iterator iter = list.iterator();

        while (iter.hasNext()) {
            ServiceItemFilter filter =
                (ServiceItemFilter) iter.next();

            boolean result = filter.check(item);


            if (result && operator == OR) {
                return true;
            }

            if (!result && operator == AND) {
                return false;
            }
        }
```

Listing 10-4 AggregationFilter.java (continued)

```
        // If we've made it to the end without shortcutting,
        // then we're in OR and have seen nothing but falses
        // (and should return false), or we're in AND and
        // we've seen nothing but trues (and should return
        // true).
        return (operator == AND);
    }
}
```

The `AggregationFilter` is created by specifying an operand that dicates whether the supplied filters are to be combined by a logical AND operation or a logical OR operation. Filters are added to the aggregation by the `add()` method. The implementation of `check()` simply iterates through the supplied filters, evaluating each in turn according to the specified combination rule.

Finally, the last bit of code is an example to show off how these filters work. Listing 10-5 is an extension of the original `ClientLookupExample`. The only major difference is that the `getFilter()` method has been overridden to use the `AggregationFilter` to connect together a `ServiceInfoVersionFilter` with a `ServiceInfoVendorFilter`.

Listing 10-5 ClientLookupWithFiltering.java

```java
// A version of ClientLookupExample to use filtering

package corejini.chapter10;

import net.jini.lookup.ServiceItemFilter;
import java.io.IOException;

public class ClientLookupWithFiltering
        extends ClientLookupExample {
    public ClientLookupWithFiltering() throws IOException {
    }

    public ServiceItemFilter getFilter() {
        AggregationFilter filt =
            new AggregationFilter(AggregationFilter.AND);

        filt.add(new ServiceInfoVendorFilter("Sun"));
        filt.add(new ServiceInfoVersionFilter("1.0",
            ServiceInfoVersionFilter.EQUAL_OR_GREATER));

        return filt;
    }

    public static void main(String[] args) {
        try {
            ClientLookupWithFiltering cle =
                new ClientLookupWithFiltering();
            cle.runTests();
        } catch (Exception ex) {
            System.err.println(ex.toString());
        }

        System.exit(0);
    }
}
```

This short snippet of code is simply an extension of the original `ServiceDiscoveryManager`. The only significant change is that this version overrides the `getFilter()` method, which is used when the example creates a lookup cache.

Here, `getFilter()` creates an `AggregationFilter` holding a `ServiceIn-foVendorFilter` and a `ServiceInfoVersionFilter`.

Compiling and Running the Example

Before running, make sure that the class files needed for the `ServiceDiscov-eryManager`'s remote event listener are still present in the `client-dl` direc-tory—you'll need them for this example too. If you've deleted them, follow the instructions from the earlier example to extract them again.

On Windows:

```
javac -classpath C:\files;
                  C:\jini1_1\lib\jini-core.jar;
                  C:\jini1_1\lib\jini-ext.jar;
                  C:\jini1_1\lib\sun-util.jar;
                  C:\client
    -d C:\client
  C:\files\corejini\chapter10\ClientLookupWithFiltering.java

java -cp C:\jini1_1\lib\jini-core.jar;
         C:\jini1_1\lib\jini-ext.jar;
         C:\jini1_1\lib\sun-util.jar;
         C:\client
    -Djava.security.policy=C:\files\policy
    -Djava.rmi.server.codebase=http://myhost:8086/
corejini.chapter10.ClientLookupWithFiltering
```

On UNIX:

```
javac -classpath /files:
                  /files/jini1_1/lib/jini-core.jar:
                  /files/jini1_1/lib/jini-ext.jar:
                  /files/jini1_1/lib/sun-util.jar:
                  /files/client
    -d /files/client
  /files/corejini/chapter10/ClientLookupWithFiltering.java

java -cp /files/jini1_1/lib/jini-core.jar:
         /files/jini1_1/lib/jini-ext.jar:
         /files/jini1_1/lib/sun-util.jar:
         /files/client
    -Djava.security.policy=/files/policy
    -Djava.rmi.server.codebase=http://myhost:8086/
corejini.chapter10.ClientLookupWithFiltering
```

This program runs the same sequence of tests that the previous example ran. But here you see that the searches involving the cache return only a select few services—those that contain the string "Sun" in the vendor identification, and those with a version greater than or equal to "1.0." (The first calls to lookup() do not use a filter, and thus here you see a "Xerox PARC" service being returned.)

Non-blocking lookup found no services.
Blocking lookup found: Name = Address Book Service
Manufacturer = Xerox PARC
Vendor = Xerox PARC
Version = 1.0
Model =
Serial Number =
Proxy is com.xerox.dispatch.addressbook.AddressBookServiceProxy@0
Cache lookup found no services.
Pausing...
Trying again...
Cache lookup found: Name = Lookup
Manufacturer = Sun Microsystems, Inc.
Vendor = Sun Microsystems, Inc.
Version = 1.0
Model =
Serial Number =
Proxy is com.sun.jini.reggie.RegistrarProxy@f16dfd46
Getting all cached services...
[0] Name = Lookup
Manufacturer = Sun Microsystems, Inc.
Vendor = Sun Microsystems, Inc.
Version = 1.1 alpha
Model =
Serial Number =
Proxy is com.sun.jini.reggie.RegistrarProxy@af330156
[1] Name = Lookup
Manufacturer = Sun Microsystems, Inc.
Vendor = Sun Microsystems, Inc.
Version = 1.0
Model =
Serial Number =
Proxy is com.sun.jini.reggie.RegistrarProxy@f16dfd46

Using Events

The final example of this chapter shows you how to use the event mechanisms provided by the `ServiceDiscoveryManager`. In both of the earlier examples, you saw how the `LookupCache` initially contained no information. The first call to `lookup()` on this cache returned no results; only after waiting for the cache to fill did `lookup()` return services to the caller.

For many clients, this will be perfectly acceptable behavior. Certain clients may be content to examine the contents of the cache only after it has had time to fill, perhaps after some predetermined blocking period has expired.

Other clients, though, may want fine-grained information about available services, *as they become available*. A Jini service browser, for instance, may want to display services to the user as they "trickle in." You probably wouldn't want to write a browser so that it had to wake up every few seconds and do a `lookup()` on the cache to try to figure out what's changed.

Such clients will want to use the event mechanisms provided by `Lookup-Cache` to get information about changes in the state of the cache, as described in the discussion of events earlier.

This example presents an extension of the earlier code, modified to install an event listener to detect changes in the cache. The code you'll see here creates an instance of a class called `DiffListener`, which is a `ServiceDiscoveryLis-tener` that prints out information about changes in the state of the cache. Once this listener is installed, you can see the services trickle in to the `LookupCache` between the time the example program first calls `lookup()` and after the wait.

Listing 10-6 shows the code for `DiffListener`.

Listing 10-6 DiffListener.java

```java
// A ServiceDiscoveryListener that shows what's changed

package corejini.chapter10;

import net.jini.core.lookup.ServiceItem;
import net.jini.lookup.ServiceDiscoveryListener;
import net.jini.lookup.ServiceDiscoveryEvent;
import net.jini.lookup.LookupCache;
import net.jini.core.entry.Entry;

public class DiffListener implements ServiceDiscoveryLis-
tener {
    public DiffListener() {
    }

    // The preEventServiceItem will be null, while the
    // postEventServiceItem will hold the newly-added
    // service item
    public void serviceAdded(ServiceDiscoveryEvent ev) {
        System.out.println("+++ SERVICE ADDED");
        ServiceItem item = ev.getPostEventServiceItem();
        printServiceItem(item);
    }

    // The preEventServiceItem holds the newly-removed
    // service, while the postEventServiceItem is null
    public void serviceRemoved(ServiceDiscoveryEvent ev) {
        System.out.println("+++ SERVICE REMOVED");
        ServiceItem item = ev.getPreEventServiceItem();
        System.out.println("Service's ID was " +
                           item.serviceID);
    }
```

Listing 10-6 DiffListener.java

```java
public void serviceChanged(ServiceDiscoveryEvent ev) {
        System.out.println("+++ SERVICE CHANGED");

        // Get both the pre and post service items.
        ServiceItem pre = ev.getPreEventServiceItem();
        ServiceItem post = ev.getPostEventServiceItem();

        // This shouldn't happen!
        if (pre == null && post == null) {
            System.out.println("Null service items!?");
            return;
        }

        // This block of code looks at the proxies to determine
        // if they've changed.  It also looks for some common
        // error cases...notably, if the proxy is null, chances
        // are you've got codebase problems.
        if (pre.service == null && post.service == null) {
            System.out.println(
                "The service's proxy is still null");
            System.out.println("Codebase problem?");
        } else if (pre.service == null && post.service != null) {
            System.out.println("The service's proxy is no " +
                            "longer null");
            System.out.println("Proxy now: " + post.service +
                            " (" +
                            post.service.getClass().getName()
                            + ")");
        } else if (pre.service != null && post.service == null) {
            System.out.println(
                "The service's proxy has become null");
            System.out.println("Check codebase");
        } else if (!pre.service.equals(post.service)) {
            System.out.println("The service's proxy has changed");
            System.out.println("Proxy was: " +  pre.service +
                            " (" +
                            pre.service.getClass().getName() +
                            ")");
            System.out.println("Proxy now: " + post.service +
                            " (" +
                            post.service.getClass().getName()
                            + ")");
        }
```

Listing 10-6 DiffListener.java

```java
            // The ID of a service should *never* change. If it
            // does change, chances are you've changed the ID
             // in a ServiceItem in the cache!  Remember that you
            // should never write to ServiceItems in the cache.
            if (!pre.serviceID.equals(post.serviceID)) {
                System.err.println("Uh oh, the ID has changed");
                System.err.println(
                    "Don't muck with the service items!");
                System.out.println("ID was: " + pre.serviceID);
                System.out.println("ID now: " + pre.serviceID);
            } else {
                System.out.println("ID: " + pre.serviceID);
            }
        }

        // Other changes can happen because of attribute
        // modifications.  This code doesn't detect those...
    }

    // A helper method to print out a service item
    public static void printServiceItem(ServiceItem item) {
        if (item == null) {
            System.out.println("Bogus: null service item");
            return;
        }

        if (item.service == null) {
            System.out.println("Bogus: service proxy is null");
            System.out.println("This service's codebase is " +
                                "probably misconfigured");
        } else {
            System.out.println("Proxy: " + item.service);
            System.out.println("Class: " +
                                item.service.getClass().getName());
        }

        System.out.println("ID:     " + item.serviceID);
```

Listing 10-6 DiffListener.java

```
        Entry[] attrs = item.attributeSets;

        if (attrs == null || attrs.length == 0) {
            System.out.println("Service has no attributes");
        } else {
            for (int i=0 ; i<attrs.length ; i++) {
                System.out.print("[" + i + "] ");
                if (attrs[i] == null) {
                    System.out.println("null entry (possible " +
                                        "codebase problem)");
                } else {
                    System.out.println(attrs[i]);
                }
            }
        }
    }
}
```

To meet the `ServiceDiscoveryListener` interface, `DiffListener` must implement three methods. The first, `serviceAdded()`, is called whenever a new service has appeared in the cache. The implementation here simply gets the `ServiceItem` for the new service and calls the static method `printService()` on it to display some details about the service.

The second method, `serviceRemoved()`, is called whenever a service has been dropped from the cache. Typically this will be because the service has disappeared from the lookup services for the community. Note that the code here fetches the `ServiceItem` for the service as it existed *before* the change, by using `getPreEventServiceItem()`. When a service is dropped from the cache, the `getPostEventServiceItem()` method will return null.

Finally, the last method this class must implement is `serviceChanged()`. The implementation of this method shown here does a bit of work to try to figure out what aspects of the service changed. The code also looks a bit for common error cases. The method first gets both the pre- and post-event `ServiceItem`s. It then examines the proxies for each service. A null proxy typically indicates that you've got either a problem with codebase (meaning that the code for the proxy can't be found), or you've got a problem with security (either no security manager, or an overly-restrictive security policy, which means that *no* non-local code will be loaded). The method will detect null proxies, and will note if a proxy becomes null, or ceases to be null. The code here will also compare the two proxies (using `equals()`) to see if the proxies report that they are different.

Next, the code compares the IDs for the two service items. This is a bit of sanity checking: recall that services should *always* use the same ID, everywhere. If you ever see different service IDs for the "same" service, then chances are you've modified one of the ServiceItems stored in the cache. Remember that any ServiceItems returned to you from the cache should be considered immutable; if you change them, you are likely to corrupt the cache.

Change events for services will often be sent because the set of attributes on a service changes. This code, unfortunately, doesn't detect such changes. You could easily modify it to walk over the two sets of attributes, seeing if attributes were added, removed, or modified.

Next, take a look at the final extension of the main example code in Listing 10-7:

Listing 10-7 ClientLookupWithEvents.java

```
// A version of ClientLookupExample that uses events

package corejini.chapter10;

import net.jini.core.lookup.ServiceTemplate;
import net.jini.core.lookup.ServiceItem;
import net.jini.lookup.ServiceDiscoveryListener;
import net.jini.lookup.LookupCache;
import java.io.IOException;

public class ClientLookupWithEvents extends ClientLookupEx-
ample {
    protected ServiceDiscoveryListener myListener;

    public ClientLookupWithEvents() throws IOException {
        System.out.println("Creating with events");
        myListener = new DiffListener();
    }

    public ServiceDiscoveryListener getListener() {
        return myListener;
    }

    public static void main(String[] args) {
        try {
            ClientLookupWithEvents cle =
                new ClientLookupWithEvents();

            cle.runTests();
        } catch (Exception ex) {
            System.err.println(ex.toString());
        }

        System.exit(0);
    }
}
```

This class is a very short extension of the first ClientLookupExample. The only substantial change here is that the getListener() method is overridden to return an instance of the DiffListener class.

If you look back to `ClientLookupExample`, you'll see that `getListener()` is called when the program first creates its `LookupCache`. The listener that is returned from this call is installed so that it will receive `ServiceDiscovery-Events` as the cache is updated.

Compiling and Running the Example

Once again, before running, make sure that the class files needed for the `ServiceDiscoveryManager`'s remote event listener are still present in the `client-dl` directory—you'll need them for this example too. If you've deleted them, follow the instructions from the earlier example to extract them again.

On Windows:

```
javac -classpath C:\files;
                C:\jini1_1\lib\jini-core.jar;
                C:\jini1_1\lib\jini-ext.jar;
                C:\jini1_1\lib\sun-util.jar;
                C:\client
    -d C:\client
  C:\files\corejini\chapter10\ClientLookupWithEvents.java

java -cp C:\jini1_1\lib\jini-core.jar;
        C:\jini1_1\lib\jini-ext.jar;
        C:\jini1_1\lib\sun-util.jar;
        C:\client
    -Djava.security.policy=C:\files\policy
    -Djava.rmi.server.codebase=http://myhost:8086/
corejini.chapter10.ClientLookupWithEvents
```

On UNIX:

```
javac -classpath /files:
                /files/jini1_1/lib/jini-core.jar:
                /files/jini1_1/lib/jini-ext.jar:
                /files/jini1_1/lib/sun-util.jar:
                /files/client
    -d /files/client
    /files/corejini/chapter10/ClientLookupWithEvents.java

java -cp /files/jini1_1/lib/jini-core.jar:
        /files/jini1_1/lib/jini-ext.jar:
        /files/jini1_1/lib/sun-util.jar:
        /files/client
    -Djava.security.policy=/files/policy
```

```
-Djava.rmi.server.codebase=http://myhost:8086/
    corejini.chapter10.ClientLookupWithEvents
```

This program runs exactly the same sequence of calls as the first example. Again, note that the non-blocking lookup finds no services and, more interestingly for the purposes of this example, the call to `lookup()` on the `Lookup-Cache` also reports that no services were found.

Non-blocking lookup found no services.
Blocking lookup found: Name = Lookup
  Manufacturer = Sun Microsystems, Inc.
  Vendor = Sun Microsystems, Inc.
  Version = 1.1 alpha
  Model =
  Serial Number =
  Proxy is com.sun.jini.reggie.RegistrarProxy@af330156
Cache lookup found no services.
Pausing...

After this sequence, however (which is the same as the previous run), you see a number of `ServiceDiscoveryEvents` being received by the `DiffListener`. These events show the changes to the cache as they happen.

+++ SERVICE ADDED
Proxy: com.xerox.dispatch.addressbook.AddressBookServiceProxy@0
Class: com.xerox.dispatch.addressbook.AddressBookServiceProxy
ID: dbc234f7-defb-4dc4-9a22-97361fd89172
[0] net.jini.lookup.entry.ServiceInfo(name=Address Book Service,manufac-turer=Xerox PARC,vendor=Xerox PARC,version=1.0,model=,serialNumber=)
+++ SERVICE ADDED
Proxy: com.sun.jini.reggie.RegistrarProxy@dd2c2c30
Class: com.sun.jini.reggie.RegistrarProxy
ID: aaf8f7d8-e76c-424a-8862-a37c18da37de
[0]   net.jini.lookup.entry.ServiceInfo(name=Lookup,manufacturer=Sun Microsystems, Inc.,vendor=Sun Microsystems, Inc.,version=1.0,model=,serial-Number=)
+++ SERVICE ADDED
Proxy: com.xerox.dispatch.authenticator.AuthenticatorProxy@0
Class: com.xerox.dispatch.authenticator.AuthenticatorProxy
ID: 3131ea32-e31d-4047-9e21-f1bf4eb95d60
[0] net.jini.lookup.entry.ServiceInfo(name=Address Book Service,manufac-turer=Xerox PARC,vendor=Xerox PARC,version=1.0,model=,serialNumber=)
+++ SERVICE ADDED

Proxy: com.sun.jini.reggie.RegistrarProxy@af330156
Class: com.sun.jini.reggie.RegistrarProxy
ID: 5b41c161-dab6-47a9-b22a-bbd29cee3c4c
[0]   net.jini.lookup.entry.ServiceInfo(name=Lookup,manufacturer=Sun Microsystems,   Inc.,vendor=Sun   Microsystems,   Inc.,version=1.1 alpha,model=,serialNumber=)

After a number of events have been received, the final call to `lookup()` shows the new state of the cache, which reflects the changes represented by the various `ServiceDiscoveryEvents`.

Trying again...
Cache lookup found: Name = Address Book Service
 Manufacturer = Xerox PARC
 Vendor = Xerox PARC
 Version = 1.0
 Model = null
 Serial Number = null
 Proxy is com.xerox.dispatch.addressbook.AddressBookServiceProxy@0
Getting all cached services...
[0] Name = Address Book Service
 Manufacturer = Xerox PARC
 Vendor = Xerox PARC
 Version = 1.0
 Model =
 Serial Number =
Proxy is com.xerox.dispatch.addressbook.AddressBookServiceProxy@0
[1] Name = Lookup
 Manufacturer = Sun Microsystems, Inc.
 Vendor = Sun Microsystems, Inc.
 Version = 1.0
 Model =
 Serial Number =
 Proxy is com.sun.jini.reggie.RegistrarProxy@f16dfd46
[2] Name = Authentication Service
 Manufacturer = Xerox PARC
 Vendor = Xerox PARC
 Version = 1.0
 Model =
 Serial Number =

Proxy is com.xerox.dispatch.authenticator.AuthenticatorProxy@0
[3]   Name = Lookup
Manufacturer = Sun Microsystems, Inc.
Vendor = Sun Microsystems, Inc.
Version = 1.1 alpha
Model =
Serial Number =
Proxy is com.sun.jini.reggie.RegistrarProxy@af330156

Summary

This chapter has shown the details of how clients interact with lookup services using the high-level—and very powerful—`ServiceDiscoveryManager`. This class provides a layer of "insulation" between your application code and the low-level `ServiceRegistrar` interface.

The interfaces you've seen here will, in all likelihood, be the most common APIs you use when building Jini applications.

What's Next?

In the next chapter, you'll put your newly-found knowledge of lookup services to good use by building a complete lookup service browser from the ground up.

A Jini Lookup Service Browser

Topics in This Chapter

- Implementing a lookup service browser
- Building interfaces for service administration
- GUI components for Jini services and attributes
- Using JavaBeans attributes in a browser

Chapter 11

This chapter builds on all the tricks of the trade that you've learned in the previous chapters. Here, the focus is on one large application: a full-blown Jini service browser. This browser allows you to view the lookup services on your network, find the services available at each, view the attributes associated with services, and administer services.

You'll see how to apply many of the concepts you learned earlier. For example, you'll see how to retrieve beans from attributes and display them to users; you'll also see how to wrap a service's administrative APIs in easy-to-use GUI components.

While much of the Jini code in this chapter is similar to what you've seen in the individual, smaller examples earlier, here I'll pull all the concepts into one large application. I'll also build a number of Swing GUI components that can be dropped into your custom applications to allow you to view attributes and administer services. In this chapter, I've broken many of the GUI classes out into separate chunks to not only enhance clarity, but also to facilitate reuse of the code in your own applications.

What Does a Browser Do?

There are many possible browsers that one could build for the Jini environment. In general, a browser is a tool that allows users to see a whole set of the services available on a Jini network. How these services are organized and presented is up to the *particular* browser; Jini doesn't dictate how this should be done and, in fact, there are a number of logical choices.

For example, a browser could be "attribute-oriented." Such a browser may search for specific attributes, such as GUI components, and only display those services that have rich representations. A "universal remote control" might be this sort of browser—it would display the "control panels" for each of the devices it manages in turn.

Other browsers might be "service-oriented." That is, they might show all the services available (removing duplicates, of course), and what the attributes of those services are, while hiding details about which lookup services the services came from (and perhaps even hiding the notion of lookup services at all). Such a browser might look like a conventional computer desktop, with icons representing all the available services. Clicking on an icon might open it up to display its user interface or information about the services. The `ServiceDiscoveryMan-ager` class is an excellent tool for building browsers such as this, since it largely hides lookup services from its callers.

Another type of browser—and this is the type you will see here—is "lookup-oriented." This means that, rather than hiding details about what lookup services are out there and which services are registered with particular lookup services, this information is presented to the user. I believe that such a tool is perhaps more useful for debugging a Jini community than as an actual end-user tool. End-users most likely do not *care* about where services are registered, and most likely they don't even want to know what a lookup service is. They're just interested in getting work done by interacting with the services made available through each of those lookup services.

But, as a Jini developer, you will certainly have a need to do occasional debugging of your Jini community—to see if your newly created service has registered itself on all the lookup services it can find, and to administer services and lookup services as needed. This example allows you to do that. And, perhaps more importantly, it illustrates a number of idioms for building browsers. At the end of this chapter, you'll have a set of building blocks that you can use in new applications (including new browsers), and can fine-tune as needed.

Using the Browser

This lookup-oriented browser uses a three-paned display to show lookup services, services registered at a particular lookup service, and the attributes attached to a particular service. This layout is reminiscent of the class browser for the Smalltalk language, which may be familiar to you. Figure 11–1 shows the basic display.

Browser		
Lookup Services	**Services**	**Attributes**
Jini://turbodog.parc.xerox.com/	My Service	ServiceInfo [net.jini.lookup.entry.ServiceIn
	RegistrarProxy	
		Max = 64, used = 10, free = 54
		Name [net.jini.lookup.entry.Name(name=N

Figure 11–1   *Lookup service browser*

The left panel displays all the lookup services found through multicast discovery. The center panel shows the services registered at the currently selected lookup service. And the right panel shows all the attributes for the currently selected service.

The browser application will also allow graphical administration of any lookup service or any service that supports the `Administrable` interface. See Figure 11–4 for an example of what this graphical administration interface looks like. The browser also has a tight integration with the JavaBeans framework. In the screenshot shown here, you see the `CapacityBean` developed earlier being used as an attribute; the browser will locate beans for attributes and display them inline if they are graphical components.

Building Administration Components

As mentioned in earlier chapters, most services—and certainly all well-behaved ones—support administration through delegation. What this means is that the proxy for a service may implement the `Administrable` interface, which allows a client to ask the proxy for an object that can be used to control the service.

The returned "administration object" is a delegate that can be used to control the service. How do clients know how to interact with this object? They test it to see whether it implements one or more well-known administrative interfaces. Services, depending on their type, may implement several different administrative interfaces for controlling the communities a service joins, for adding and removing attributes, for changing the location of its persistent storage, and so on. In addition to a handful of "standard" well-known administrative interfaces, services can implement any number of implementation-specific administrative interfaces that they like. Of course, only clients written to understand these special-purpose APIs will be able to call them programmatically.

Of course, you'd like to be able to make your services afford administration by actual human users—and not merely programmatically by client applications that understand a particular service's administrative interfaces. What would be ideal is the ability to take *any* administrative interface, even one you've never seen before, and create a GUI for it to display to a user.

There are a number of ways a service could provide its own GUI for administration. One possibility would be to have the administrative object itself be a full-blown GUI object; clients could test to see whether it subclasses the `Component` class and, if so, display it. This approach has a drawback though: On restricted platforms without the GUI class libraries available, a client would never be able to instantiate this administrative interface because its superclasses would be unavailable. This would prohibit *any* use of it on such platforms, even direct programmatic use through its APIs that never even use the object's "`Component`-ness."

An alternative would be to define a type of attribute, perhaps called `AdministrationGUI`, that contains the GUI for service administration. Once retrieved, a well-known method on the attribute could be called to "activate" it with a service's administration object. Unfortunately, Jini has not yet provided any such conventions for use.

A third option—and the one taken here—is to explicitly create a custom GUI for the administrative object in the client. In the browser example in this chapter, this creation happens by introspecting the administration object to see whether it implements any of a few well-known administrative interfaces. Each of these interfaces has a GUI associated with it that you'll see shortly. One could get even fancier—perhaps using the JavaBeans introspection facilities to create custom GUIs for a service's administration object *on-the-fly*. This approach would work much like the way JavaBeans property sheets are created for beans after they are loaded. The on-the-fly approach is beyond the scope of this chapter, though, so here I'll just build a custom set of administration GUIs "by hand."

The administrative interfaces this code supports are `DiscoveryAdmin`, `StorageLocationAdmin`, `DestroyAdmin`, and `JoinAdmin`. I will define a component called `AdminPanel` that takes as an argument to its constructor an administration object from a service's proxy. It will then create a tabbed panel with separate GUIs for each of the administrative interfaces that the object implements.

Each of the panes of the tabbed panel is a separate custom GUI that "understands" how to present the features of a particular administrative interface. I'll talk about the most simple of these first, and then move up to the more complex examples.

DestroyAdminPanel

The `DestroyAdmin` interface (Listing 11–1) has only one method, which allows a caller to shut down a service. So, as you might expect, the GUI to this interface is equally simple: a single button to invoke the shutdown operation! Like all the separate administrative GUIs you'll see here, the `DestroyAdmin-Panel` is a subclass of `JPanel`. As such, it inherits all the Swing component functionality and can be inserted into any other type of container component— so it can be displayed in lists, or inserted into frames, or placed in any other Swing container.

Listing 11–1 `DestroyAdminPanel.java`

```java
// A user interface for DestroyAdmin

package corejini.chapter11;

import com.sun.jini.admin.DestroyAdmin;
import javax.swing.JPanel;
import javax.swing.JOptionPane;
import javax.swing.JLabel;
import javax.swing.JButton;
import java.awt.event.ActionListener;
import java.awt.event.ActionEvent;
import java.awt.BorderLayout;
import java.rmi.RemoteException;
```

Listing 11–1 `DestroyAdminPanel.java` (continued)

```java
// Initialize with a ref to the admin object
public class DestroyAdminPanel extends JPanel {
    public DestroyAdminPanel(final DestroyAdmin admin) {
        super();

        setLayout(new BorderLayout());

        JLabel label;
        JButton button;

        add(new JLabel("CAUTION:"), BorderLayout.NORTH);
        add(new JLabel("Clicking will terminate " +
                    "the service!"),
            BorderLayout.CENTER);

        button = new JButton("Terminate");

        button.addActionListener(new ActionListener() {
            public void actionPerformed(ActionEvent ev) {
                try {
                    admin.destroy();
                } catch (RemoteException ex) {
                    JOptionPane.showMessageDialog(null,
                            "Couldn't destroy service:\n"+
                            ex.getMessage(), "Alert",
                            JOptionPane.ERROR_MESSAGE);
                }
            }
        });

        add(button, BorderLayout.SOUTH);
    }
}
```

The constructor for the panel simply creates the button and a couple of labels to warn the user that clicking will shut down the service. The heart of the code is in the `ActionListener` for the button: This code calls the `destroy()` method on the service's administration object. If an error occurs (perhaps because the service has crashed or is disconnected from the network), a `RemoteException` will be raised, which causes a warning dialog box to be displayed.

Figure 11–2   *The DestroyAdminPanel*

Figure 11–2 shows the `DestroyAdminPanel`, nested in an `AdminPanel` (which I will discuss shortly), along with the other administration interfaces.

StorageLocationAdminPanel

The second simplest standard administrative interface is called `Storage-LocationAdmin`. This interface (Listing 11–2) allows a caller to change the location of a service's persistent storage. It supports only two methods: one to get the current storage location, and one to set a new storage location.

Take a look at the code:

Listing 11–2 `StorageLocationAdminPanel.java`

```java
// A user interface for StorageLocationAdmin

package corejini.chapter11;

import com.sun.jini.admin.StorageLocationAdmin;
import javax.swing.JPanel;
import javax.swing.JTextField;
import javax.swing.JButton;
import javax.swing.JLabel;
import javax.swing.JOptionPane;
import java.awt.event.ActionListener;
import java.awt.event.ActionEvent;
import java.awt.BorderLayout;
import java.awt.GridLayout;
import java.rmi.RemoteException;

// Initialize with a ref to the admin object
public class StorageLocationAdminPanel extends JPanel {
    public StorageLocationAdminPanel(
                final StorageLocationAdmin admin) {
        setLayout(new BorderLayout());
        final JTextField loc = new JTextField();
        JButton button = new JButton("Set");
        JPanel panel = new JPanel();
        final JLabel currentLoc = new JLabel();
        panel.setLayout(new GridLayout(2, 2));
        panel.add(new JLabel(
                    "Current storage location: "));
        try {
           currentLoc.setText(admin.getStorageLocation());
           panel.add(currentLoc);
        } catch (RemoteException ex) {
           JOptionPane.showMessageDialog(null,
                        "Couldn't get location:\n" +
                            ex.getMessage(), "Alert",
                        JOptionPane.ERROR_MESSAGE);
        }
```

Listing 11–2 `StorageLocationAdminPanel.java` (continued)

```
    panel.add(new JLabel("New storage location: "));
    panel.add(loc);
    add(panel, BorderLayout.NORTH);

    button.addActionListener(new ActionListener() {
        public void actionPerformed(ActionEvent ev) {
            try {
                admin.setStorageLocation(loc.getText());
                currentLoc.setText(
                        admin.getStorageLocation());
            } catch (Exception ex) {
                JOptionPane.showMessageDialog(null,
                        "Couldn't set location:\n" +
                            ex.getMessage(),"Alert",
                        JOptionPane.ERROR_MESSAGE);
            }
        }
    });

    add(button, BorderLayout.SOUTH);
    }
}
```

This code is only slightly more complex than the `DestroyAdminPanel` you saw earlier. This example lays out a 2x2 grid. On the top row are two labels which provide the current storage location of the service; the bottom contains a text field and a button to cause any text in the field to be used as the new storage location.

Once again, the heart of this code is in the `ActionListener` attached to the button. This code fetches the text out of the text field and calls `setStorageLocation()` to attempt to change the service's location of its persistent storage. To see if the change took effect, the code then asks the service for its new storage location and displays that in the panel. This allows users to confirm what actually happened when they tried to change the storage location.

An attempt to change a service's storage location can fail for two reasons. First, the network connection to the service may be down, in which case, a `RemoteException` will be raised. Second, the user may specify a location that makes no sense for the particular service. Examples of this might include providing a

DOS-style pathname to a service running on UNIX. Jini makes no assumptions about how services will interpret the storage location passed to them; it's merely a string, which they are free to interpret or reject as they see fit. If a user passes in a bogus storage location, an IOException will be raised. Both of these conditions are trapped in this example, and a warning dialog is presented to the user.

Figure 11–3 shows the simple user interface for this administrative API.

Figure 11–3   *The StorageLocationAdminPanel*

Both of the next two administrative interfaces are significantly more complex than what you've seen so far. And, both of them happen to require a particular style of interaction—adding and removing items from a set. Before going on with the next two administrative GUIs, take a look at a "helper" class that will be used to manage sets of items.

A ListBox for Managing Sets

The JoinAdmin and DiscoveryAdmin APIs have methods for controlling sets of groups a service should join, sets of attributes that should be attached to it, and sets of lookup locator URLs that it should explicitly connect to. To facilitate controlling sets like these, I'll create a ListBox class (see Listing 11–3) that allows a user to view the items in a set, and add and remove items from it. The ListBox supports "plug-in" actions that can be used to map the GUI behavior of the ListBox onto whatever particular sort of set it is managing. I'll use this class extensively in the next two administration panel examples.

Listing 11–3 ListBox.java

```java
// A list component for this application.

package corejini.chapter11;

import javax.swing.JPanel;
import javax.swing.JList;
import javax.swing.JLabel;
import javax.swing.JTextField;
import javax.swing.JButton;
import javax.swing.JScrollPane;
import javax.swing.Action;
import javax.swing.event.ListSelectionEvent;
import javax.swing.event.ListSelectionListener;
import java.awt.BorderLayout;
import java.awt.GridLayout;
import java.awt.event.ActionEvent;

public class ListBox extends JPanel {
    protected Action addAction, removeAction, updateAction;
    protected JList list = new JList();
    protected JTextField field = new JTextField();
    protected JButton addButton = new JButton("Add");
    protected JButton removeButton = new JButton("Remove");
    protected Object lastSelected = null;

    public ListBox(String title, int rowCount) {
        this(null, null, null, title, rowCount);
    }
```

Listing 11–3 `ListBox.java` (continued)

```java
// Create a ListBox initialized with our actions
public ListBox(Action addAction, Action removeAction,
               Action updateAction, String title,
               int rowCount){
    super();
    this.addAction = addAction;
    this.removeAction = removeAction;

    setLayout(new BorderLayout());
    removeButton.setEnabled(false);
    list.setVisibleRowCount(rowCount);
    list.addListSelectionListener(
      new ListSelectionListener() {
        public void valueChanged(ListSelectionEvent ev){
            int idx = ev.getFirstIndex();

            if (idx == -1)
                lastSelected = null;
            else
                lastSelected =
                    ((JList)
          ev.getSource()).getModel().getElementAt(idx);

            if (ev.getValueIsAdjusting())
                return;

            if (((JList)
          ev.getSource()).getSelectedIndex() == -1)
                removeButton.setEnabled(false);
            else
                removeButton.setEnabled(true);
      }
    });
```

Listing 11–3 `ListBox.java` (continued)

```java
        setLayout(new BorderLayout());
        JPanel listPanel = new JPanel();
        listPanel.setLayout(new BorderLayout());
        JPanel gridPanel = new JPanel();
        gridPanel.setLayout(new GridLayout(2, 2));

        listPanel.add(new JLabel(title),
                    BorderLayout.NORTH);
        listPanel.add(new JScrollPane(list,
                JScrollPane.VERTICAL_SCROLLBAR_ALWAYS,
             JScrollPane.HORIZONTAL_SCROLLBAR_AS_NEEDED),
                    BorderLayout.CENTER);

        gridPanel.add(addButton);
        gridPanel.add(field);

        gridPanel.add(removeButton);
        add(listPanel, BorderLayout.CENTER);
        add(gridPanel, BorderLayout.SOUTH);

        if (addAction != null)
            addButton.addActionListener(addAction);

        if (removeAction != null)
            removeButton.addActionListener(removeAction);

        // also update after add/remove
        if (updateAction != null) {
            addButton.addActionListener(updateAction);
            removeButton.addActionListener(updateAction);

            updateAction.actionPerformed(
                        new ActionEvent(this, 0, null));
        }
    }
```

Listing 11–3 `ListBox.java` (continued)

```java
// Change the action set
public void setActions(Action add, Action remove,
                       Action update) {
    if (addAction != null)
        addButton.removeActionListener(addAction);

    if (removeAction != null)
        removeButton.removeActionListener(
                              removeAction);

    if (updateAction != null) {
        addButton.removeActionListener(updateAction);
        removeButton.removeActionListener(
                              updateAction);
    }

    addAction = add;
    removeAction = remove;
    updateAction = update;

    if (addAction != null)
        addButton.addActionListener(addAction);

    if (removeAction != null)
        removeButton.addActionListener(removeAction);

    if (updateAction != null) {
        addButton.addActionListener(updateAction);
        removeButton.addActionListener(updateAction);

        updateAction.actionPerformed(
                    new ActionEvent(this, 0, null));
    }
}

// Some "helper" list methods
public Object getSelectedValue() {
    return lastSelected;
}
```

Listing 11–3 `ListBox.java` (continued)

```
    public JList getList() {
        return list;
    }
    public JTextField getField() {
        return field;
    }
}
```

This component groups together four controls. There is a list widget within a scrolling pane, a text field, an associated Add button that attempts to add whatever text is entered in the text field, and a Remove button that attempts to remove whatever item in the list is selected.

To be useful for our different administration panels, this component needs to be able to interact with different sorts of lists—lists of attributes, lists of groups, and lists of lookup URLs. And, when the Add and Remove buttons are clicked, the component needs to call out to different code that invokes the appropriate administration methods for whatever type of list is being edited.

The `ListBox` supports editing different types of lists by abstracting out the application behavior that says what to actually *do* when the Add or Remove buttons are clicked, and by abstracting away the details about how the list gets populated. A caller will pass the `ListBox` three `Action` objects representing the code to invoke whenever the Add button is pressed, the Remove button is pressed, or when the list needs to be updated.

The `Action` class is an addition to the Java GUI programming model made by the Java Foundation Classes. It provides a way to represent a single callable operation as an object that implements the `ActionListener` interface. `Actions` can be installed in buttons, where they will be automatically invoked whenever the button is pressed, or they can be called "manually" by invoking the `actionPerformed()` method on them.

The `ListBox` class, in addition to creating its subcomponents, also handles making sure that the Remove button is properly enabled or disabled whenever an item is selected or unselected in the list. The `ListBox` also remembers what the last selected item in the list was, by watching for change events in the list.

Whenever the add or remove actions are performed by clicking the appropriate button, the `ListBox` will also manually invoke the update action to cause the contents of the list to be redisplayed. By providing an update action, which queries a service for the state of a particular administrable item, clients can cause the

ListBox to properly reflect the contents of service group, attribute, and locator lists.

The constructor for the ListBox also allows callers to pass in two parameters that control aspects of the appearance of the control: The rowCount integer specifies the desired minimum number of rows in the list, and the title string allows callers to provide a descriptive title over the ListBox.

Now that we've got a ListBox widget that can be reused in the examples, it's time to move on to the next administration panel.

DiscoveryAdminPanel

Jini lookup services will implement the DiscoveryAdmin interface. This interface controls the way the service supports Jini communities—it allows callers to change the set of groups in which a lookup service is a member, and also allows them to change the port number on which the lookup service listens for unicast discovery messages.

In this section, you'll see a reuseable GUI component for interacting with DiscoveryAdmin objects. This control provides a ListBox for viewing, adding, and removing groups from the lookup service's set of supported groups, and provides a text entry field and a button for changing the lookup service port as shown in Listing 11–4.

Listing 11–4 DiscoveryAdminPanel.java

```
// A user interface for DiscoveryAdmin

package corejini.chapter11;

import net.jini.lookup.DiscoveryAdmin;
import javax.swing.JPanel;
import javax.swing.JTextField;
import javax.swing.JLabel;
import javax.swing.JButton;
import javax.swing.AbstractAction;
import java.awt.event.ActionEvent;
import java.awt.BorderLayout;
import java.awt.GridLayout;
```

Listing 11–4 `DiscoveryAdminPanel.java` (continued)

```java
public class DiscoveryAdminPanel extends JPanel {
    protected ListBox listbox;
    protected JTextField portField = new JTextField();
    protected JLabel currentPort = new JLabel();
    protected DiscoveryAdmin admin;

    // An action for adding new groups
    class AddAction extends AbstractAction {
        public void actionPerformed(ActionEvent ev) {
            System.out.println("In add!");
            String[] newGroups = new String[1];

            newGroups[0] = listbox.getField().getText();
            if (newGroups[0].equals("<public>"))
                newGroups[0] = "";

            try {
                admin.addMemberGroups(newGroups);
            } catch (Exception ex) {
                System.err.println("Couldn't add group: " +
                                    ex.getMessage());
            }
        }
    }
}
```

Listing 11–4 `DiscoveryAdminPanel.java` (continued)

```java
// An action for removing groups
class RemoveAction extends AbstractAction {
    public void actionPerformed(ActionEvent ev) {
        Object sel = listbox.getSelectedValue();

        if (sel == null) {
            return;
        }

        try {
            String[] items = new String[1];
            sel = (sel.equals("<public>") ? "" : sel);
            items[0] = (String) sel;
            admin.removeMemberGroups(items);
        } catch (Exception ex) {
            System.err.println("Couldn't remove group:"
                                + ex.getMessage());
        }
    }
}

// An action for changing groups
class UpdateAction extends AbstractAction {
    public void actionPerformed(ActionEvent ev) {
        try {
            String[] members = admin.getMemberGroups();
            for (int i=0 ; i<members.length ; i++) {
                if (members[i].equals(""))
                    members[i] = "<public>";
            }
            listbox.getList().setListData(members);
        } catch (Exception ex) {
            System.err.println("Couldn't update: " +
                                ex.getMessage());
            listbox.getList().setListData(
                                new String[0]);
        }
    }
}
```

Listing 11–4 `DiscoveryAdminPanel.java` (continued)

```java
class SetPortAction extends AbstractAction {
    public void actionPerformed(ActionEvent ev) {
        try {
            admin.setUnicastPort(
                    Integer.parseInt(
                        portField.getText()));
            currentPort.setText(
                    Integer.toString(
                        admin.getUnicastPort()));
        } catch (Exception ex) {
          System.err.println("Couldn't change port:" +
                             ex.getMessage());
        }
    }
}

public DiscoveryAdminPanel(DiscoveryAdmin da) {
    super();

    admin = da;
    setLayout(new BorderLayout());

    // Create a ListBox and initialize it with our
    // actions
    listbox = new ListBox("Member Groups", 12);
    listbox.setActions(new AddAction(),
                        new RemoveAction(),
                        new UpdateAction());
    JPanel portPanel = new JPanel();
    portPanel.setLayout(new BorderLayout());
    JPanel gridPanel = new JPanel();
    gridPanel.setLayout(new GridLayout(2, 2));
    gridPanel.add(new JLabel("Current port: "));
    try {
        currentPort.setText(
                Integer.toString(
                    admin.getUnicastPort()));
    } catch (Exception ex) {
        System.err.println("Error setting port: " +
                           ex.getMessage());
    }
```

Listing 11–4 `DiscoveryAdminPanel.java` (continued)

```
        gridPanel.add(currentPort);
        gridPanel.add(new JLabel("New port: "));
        gridPanel.add(portField);
        portPanel.add(gridPanel, BorderLayout.CENTER);
        JButton button = new JButton("Set");
        button.addActionListener(new SetPortAction());
        portPanel.add(button, BorderLayout.SOUTH);

        add(listbox, BorderLayout.CENTER);
        add(portPanel, BorderLayout.SOUTH);
    }
}
```

This code is a heavy user of the `ListBox` control shown earlier; it creates three actions that understand how to interact with objects implementing the `DiscoveryAdmin` interface to present lists of lookup groups to a user.

The `AddAction` class retrieves the text out of the `ListBox`'s text field. The text is treated as the name of a group that the lookup service is being asked to support, and so it is passed to the `addMemberGroups()` call to tell the lookup service to begin supporting the named group. The code here allows the user to type "`<public>`" to indicate the default, unnamed public group; more on this a bit later. Note that this code doesn't have to handle updating the list itself—it only need concern itself with how to add an item to the list. The updating of the list is done by the `ListBox`, which automatically calls out to whatever update action has been installed in it after the add action is invoked.

The `RemoveAction` class fetches the selected item from the `ListBox` that, because of the data the actions install in the list, will be a string. The selected string is then passed to `removeMemberGroups()` to ask the lookup service to remove it from the set of groups it supports. Note here the special handling for the default, unnamed public group. Because the default group is unnamed (or, more precisely, it is named by the empty string), the actions use the convention of showing the string "`<public>`" in the list instead of an empty list item. So, if the selected item is called "`<public>`," the `RemoveAction` replaces it with the empty string so that it will properly name the default group. Like `AddAction`, this code doesn't have to update the list after removing an item, because the `ListBox` automatically invokes the update action after removal.

The `UpdateAction` simply asks the `DiscoveryAdmin` object for all the groups of which the lookup service is a member. These are displayed in the list;

note that the unnamed group is "translated" into the string "`<public>`" for display here. If an exceptional condition results from the operation, the list is cleared and an error is reported.

Finally, even though management of the unicast port number isn't done through the `ListBox` class, here I've defined a `SetPortAction` that will be bound to a button to change the port number. This code calls out to `DiscoveryAdmin` to set the port from whatever text is contained in the text entry field, and then sets the displayed port number to whatever the `DiscoveryAdmin` object reports as its true, current port number. Note that, unlike the remove and add actions, this code *must* update the display itself after it is executed—there is no `ListBox` class automatically performing updates for it after invocation.

Figure 11–4 shows this interface.

Figure 11–4 *The DiscoveryAdminPanel*

The rest of the code is in the constructor for `DiscoveryAdminPanel`, and is straightforward. The code creates the layout by constructing a `ListBox` and then the grid of controls for displaying and updating the port number. All the appropriate action classes are instantiated and installed in the `ListBox` so that it will automatically call out to methods to add, remove, and update list elements whenever the `Listbox`'s buttons are pressed.

JoinAdminPanel

The final administration GUI is the most visually complicated. The JoinAdminPanel (Listing 11–5) presents an interface for controlling services that support the JoinAdmin interface. This interface should be implemented by every
Jini service: it is used to control the groups that a service will try to join, the
attributes that should be installed on every one if its registrations, and the set of
explicit lookup locator URLs that it should try to connect to. Essentially, this
interface controls the aspects of a service's participation in the Jini join protocol.

All three of these controllable parameters—groups, attributes, and locators—
are sets from which items can be added and removed. So all three of these can
use the ListBox class to permit editing. The code will, of course, need different
action objects to support interacting with the various JoinAdmin APIs.

Listing 11–5 JoinAdminPanel.java

```
// A user interface for JoinAdmin

package corejini.chapter11;

import net.jini.admin.JoinAdmin;
import net.jini.core.discovery.LookupLocator;
import javax.swing.JPanel;
import javax.swing.BoxLayout;
import javax.swing.AbstractAction;
import java.awt.event.ActionEvent;
import java.awt.BorderLayout;
import java.rmi.RemoteException;

public class JoinAdminPanel extends JPanel {
    protected ListBox groupsList, locsList, attrsList;
    protected JoinAdmin admin;

    // An action for adding groups
    class AddAction extends AbstractAction {
        ListBox listbox;

        AddAction(ListBox lb) {
            listbox = lb;
        }
```

Listing 11–5 `JoinAdminPanel.java` (continued)

```java
public void actionPerformed(ActionEvent ev) {
    String newItem = listbox.getField().getText();

    try {
        if (listbox.equals(groupsList)) {
            String[] items = new String[1];
            items[0] = newItem;
            if (items[0].equals("<public>"))
                items[0] = "";

            admin.addLookupGroups(items);
        } else if (listbox.equals(locsList)) {
            LookupLocator[] items =
                new LookupLocator[1];
            items[0] = new LookupLocator(newItem);
            admin.addLookupLocators(items);
        } else if (listbox.equals(attrsList)) {
            // noop for now...
        }
    } catch (Exception ex) {
        System.err.println("Error adding item: " +
                            ex.getMessage());
    }
}
}
```

Listing 11–5 JoinAdminPanel.java (continued)

```java
// An action for removing groups
class RemoveAction extends AbstractAction {
    ListBox listbox;

    RemoveAction(ListBox lb) {
        listbox = lb;
    }
    public void actionPerformed(ActionEvent ev) {
        Object sel = listbox.getSelectedValue();

        if (sel == null)
            return;

        try {
            if (listbox.equals(groupsList)) {
                String[] items = new String[1];
                sel = (sel.equals("<public>") ? "" :
                        sel);
                items[0] = (String) sel;
                admin.removeLookupGroups(items);
            } else if (listbox.equals(locsList)) {
                LookupLocator[] items =
                    new LookupLocator[1];
                items[0] = (LookupLocator) sel;
                admin.removeLookupLocators(items);
            } else if (listbox.equals(attrsList)) {
                // noop for now...
            }
        } catch (Exception ex) {
            System.err.println("Error removing item: "
                            + ex.getMessage());
        }
    }
}
```

Listing 11-5 `JoinAdminPanel.java` (continued)

```java
// An action for updating groups
class UpdateAction extends AbstractAction {
    ListBox listbox;

    UpdateAction(ListBox lb) {
        listbox = lb;
    }
    public void actionPerformed(ActionEvent ev) {
        Object[] items = null;
        try {
            if (listbox.equals(groupsList)) {
                items = admin.getLookupGroups();
                for (int i=0 ; i<items.length ; i++) {
                    if (items[i].equals(""))
                        items[i] = "<public>";
                }
            } else if (listbox.equals(locsList)) {
                items = admin.getLookupLocators();
            } else if (listbox.equals(attrsList)) {
                items = admin.getLookupAttributes();
            }
            listbox.getList().setListData(items);
        } catch (Exception ex) {
            System.err.println("Error updating: " +
                                ex.getMessage());
            listbox.getList().setListData(
                                new String[0]);
        }
    }
}
```

Listing 11–5 `JoinAdminPanel.java` (continued)

```
public JoinAdminPanel(JoinAdmin ja) {
    super();

    admin = ja;

    groupsList = new ListBox("Lookup Groups", 4);
    groupsList.setActions(new AddAction(groupsList),
                          new RemoveAction(groupsList),
                          new UpdateAction(groupsList));

    attrsList = new ListBox("Lookup Attributes", 4);;
    attrsList.setActions(new AddAction(attrsList),
                         new RemoveAction(attrsList),
                         new UpdateAction(attrsList));
    locsList = new ListBox("Lookup Locators", 4);
    locsList.setActions(new AddAction(locsList),
                        new RemoveAction(locsList),
                        new UpdateAction(locsList));

    setLayout(new BorderLayout());

    JPanel panel = new JPanel();
    panel.setLayout(new BoxLayout(panel,
                                  BoxLayout.Y_AXIS));
    panel.add(groupsList);
    panel.add(attrsList);
    panel.add(locsList);

    add(panel, BorderLayout.CENTER);
    }
}
```

The constructor for this class simply creates the three `ListBoxes` and arranges them into a panel. Look at the three action classes used by this example, which are where the action is.

The `JoinAdminPanel` uses one add, one remove, and one update action class for all of the three types of lists that it manages (groups, attributes, and locators). The constructors for these actions are parameterized by the particular `ListBox` they are asked to manage. So, in the constructor, you see the creation of three separate instances of `AddAction`, one for each of the three `ListBoxes`. And, each of these takes the particular `ListBox` it is associated with as a parameter.

Whenever an action is invoked, it compares the `ListBox` it was passed as a parameter to the three `ListBoxes` it knows are used in this panel. By doing this, it can tell if it is meant to manage groups, attributes, or locators. This "trick" saves the trouble of creating three separate add action classes, three separate remove action classes, and three separate update action classes, one for each type of list.

Now look at how `AddAction` works. When it is invoked, it fetches any text from the text entry field of its `ListBox`. It then checks to see whether the `List-Box` it was parameterized by was the groups `ListBox`, the attributes `ListBox`, or the locators `ListBox`. Depending on which list it is managing, it invokes the appropriate method, with the appropriate arguments, on the `JoinAdmin` object. For example, if the `AddAction` is associated with the groups `ListBox`, it calls `addLookupGroups()` and passes the selected string as an argument. If it is associated with the locators `ListBox`, it converts the string to a `LookupLocator` and passes this to `addLookupLocator()`.

Note that this code currently ignores attributes—there is no way to add a new attribute to a service using this GUI as presented. The reason for this is that specifying attributes and filling out all of their member data is a fairly long process— a bit too long to present readily in book format. Properly adding an attribute would require that the GUI allow users to enter the name of an attribute class, load that class, and then introspect on it to determine what member data it supports. The GUI would then allow the users to "fill in" each of these attributes in the appropriate type, probably by using the JavaBeans `PropertyEditor` mechanisms.

One less powerful, but quite easy, alternative would be to simply take the strings that are typed and install them as `Comment` attributes on the current service. As mentioned, though, the code here does not support adding attributes to services.

The `RemoveAction` class is structured much the same as `AddAction`. Depending on the `ListBox` it was parameterized with, it will invoke either `removeLookupGroup()` or `removeLookupLocator()` on the `JoinAdmin` object with the appropriate parameters. Again, this code does not support removing attributes from services. Note here again how this action translates the string "`<public>`," meant for display in a list, into the empty string for manipulating the default group.

The `UpdateAction` class does this same translation, and invokes the appropriate methods on `JoinAdmin` for fetching groups, locators, and attributes (the code here does allow *viewing* all the attributes on a service in a list).

Figure 11–5 shows the JoinAdminPanel.

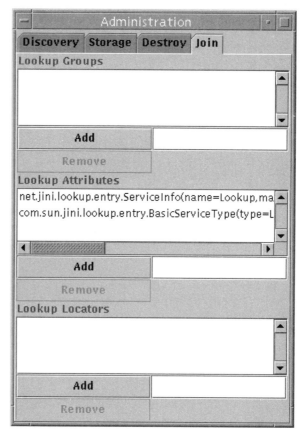

Figure 11–5 *The JoinAdminPanel*

AdminPanel

Now that all of these separate panels are finished, they can be grouped together to form an easy solution for administering all four of these common service behaviors.

The AdminPanel class simply provides a panel with a tabbed pane containing separate tabs for each of the four administrative interfaces that a service may implement. You can create one of these by simply passing in the administration object for a service to the AdminPanel constructor, as shown in Listing 11–6.

Listing 11–6 `AdminPanel.java`

```java
// This is the overall administration GUI.   You pass it
// an admin object, it introspects it to figure out which
// interface it implements, and puts up the tabbed panes.

package corejini.chapter11;

import net.jini.admin.JoinAdmin;
import net.jini.lookup.DiscoveryAdmin;
import com.sun.jini.admin.DestroyAdmin;
import com.sun.jini.admin.StorageLocationAdmin;
import javax.swing.JPanel;
import javax.swing.JTabbedPane;
import java.awt.BorderLayout;

public class AdminPanel extends JPanel {
    public AdminPanel(Object admin) {
        setLayout(new BorderLayout());
        JTabbedPane pane = new JTabbedPane();

        if (admin instanceof DiscoveryAdmin) {
            DiscoveryAdminPanel panel =
                new DiscoveryAdminPanel((DiscoveryAdmin)
                                            admin);
            pane.addTab("Discovery", panel);
        }
        if (admin instanceof StorageLocationAdmin) {
            StorageLocationAdminPanel panel =
                new StorageLocationAdminPanel(
                        (StorageLocationAdmin) admin);
            pane.addTab("Storage", panel);
        }
        if (admin instanceof DestroyAdmin) {
            DestroyAdminPanel panel =
                new DestroyAdminPanel((DestroyAdmin) admin);
            pane.addTab("Destroy", panel);
        }
        if (admin instanceof JoinAdmin) {
            JoinAdminPanel panel =
                new JoinAdminPanel((JoinAdmin) admin);
            pane.addTab("Join", panel);
        }

        add(pane, BorderLayout.CENTER);
    }
}
```

This code simply introspects on the administration object passed to it. For each known administrative API that it implements, the constructor creates a new tab in the tabbed pane with the appropriate administration GUI. This class is ready-to-use in your own applications.

JList Cell Renderers for Common Jini Types

You're now ready to move on from building the administrative GUI to creating other components needed for the browser. As you saw in the screenshot of the browser in Figure 11–1, the browser organizes a view of a Jini community as a set of individual lists, displaying lookup services, services contained within those lookup services, and attributes attached to services.

The Swing JList class provides some handy facilities for controlling how the items in a list will appear. The JList class can contain any type of object as an element in a list. By default, these objects are displayed in the list via JLabel instances: In most cases, the text of the label will be set by invoking toString() on the object. If the object contained in the list's model is an icon, then the label that displays that object will be set to display that icon instead of any text.

You can, however, override this default behavior by specifying a new List-CellRenderer for the JList. A ListCellRenderer examines each item in a list and returns an appropriate Component type to display it. Custom cell renderers can, for example, be used to display a list of java.awt.Color objects as color swatches, rather than simply the toString() representation of colors stuffed into a label. A cell renderer must simply override one method, called getListCellRendererComponent(), to return a custom component for an object stored in a list.

Because the browser organizes lookup services, other services, and attributes into JLists, you can take advantage of Swing's custom cell rendering behavior to generate appropriate Components for each of these Jini object types. The browser will use these renderers when it creates its display lists. The cell renderers presented here can be reused in your own code when you have a need to display Jini types in a Swing container.

LookupCellRenderer

First, look at a ListCellRenderer (Listing 11–7) that can help display objects of type ServiceRegistrar. These will be the proxy objects for the various lookup services that are discovered; by creating a custom cell renderer for these proxies, you can display them in a more sensible form than whatever the implementor happened to provide for the toString() return value.

Listing 11–7 LookupCellRenderer.java

```
// A ListCellRenderer for Lookup ServiceRegistrars --
// draws a ServiceRegistrar as its locator URL

package corejini.chapter11;

import java.awt.Component;
import javax.swing.JList;
import javax.swing.JLabel;
import javax.swing.DefaultListCellRenderer;
import java.rmi.RemoteException;
import net.jini.core.lookup.ServiceRegistrar;

public class LookupCellRenderer extends DefaultListCellRen-
derer {
    public Component getListCellRendererComponent(
                        JList list,
                        Object value,
                        int index,
                        boolean isSelected,
                        boolean cellHasFocus) {
        Component c =
            super.getListCellRendererComponent(list, value,
                                        index,
                                        isSelected,
                                        cellHasFocus);
```

Listing 11–7 `LookupCellRenderer.java` (continued)

```
            if (c instanceof JLabel) {
                JLabel l = (JLabel) c;
                if (value instanceof ServiceRegistrar) {
                    ServiceRegistrar reg =
                        (ServiceRegistrar) value;
                    try {
                        l.setText(reg.getLocator().toString());
                    } catch (RemoteException ex) {
                        System.err.println(
                            "Error getting locator: " +
                            ex.getMessage());
                        l.setText(reg.toString());
                    }
                }
            }
            return c;
        }
    }
```

Here you see a short cell renderer that creates a label containing the Service-
Registrar's locator URL. Recall that ServiceRegistrar is only an interface—the code has no idea what actual class it is, and so cannot predict what
APIs it may have available other than those defined in ServiceRegistrar, and
cannot know what its toString() method may return. A LookupLocator URL
is a common representation of *all* ServiceRegistrars, however, and so I'll use
that, rather than an arbitrary toString() result, as the value to display.

Note here how the code interacts with the superclass' implementation of
getListCellRenderer(). By subclassing DefaultListCellRenderer, the
code has access to all of that class' methods, including the default functionality
for creating a new JLabel from an object stored in a list. The behavior in the
default cell renderer is actually a bit more complicated than simply creating a
label and returning it. It considers whether the object in the list is selected, and
whether it has the focus, to properly assign colors and highlighting information
to it.

Because recreating all of that work in this class would be excessive, the code
reuses the label handed to it from the superclass, and changes the text of it to be
the URL for the ServiceRegistrar. This is a fairly simple example of a List-
CellRenderer; the next examples will be a bit more complex.

ServiceCellRenderer

The next type of Jini object the browser will need to display in lists is a service proxy. Service proxies, as you will recall, are even more free-form than lookup `ServiceRegistrars`. There are *no* standard interfaces that they typically implement, other than `Administrable`, which will not help you create an easily recognizable representation of a service.

You'd like to be able to display lists of service proxies in a way that helps users to quickly identify and use them. Again, if you have to rely on whatever `toString()` implementation the writer of the proxy may—or may not—have provided, you may be in trouble.

Instead, the alternative used here is to search the attributes associated with a service for helpful information on how to display it (see Listing 11–8).

Listing 11–8 `ServiceCellRenderer.java`

```java
// A ListCellRenderer for services -- draws a service
// as its name if it has one, or a cleaned-up
// representation of the proxy's class

package corejini.chapter11;

import java.awt.Component;
import javax.swing.JList;
import javax.swing.JLabel;
import javax.swing.DefaultListCellRenderer;
import net.jini.core.lookup.ServiceItem;
import net.jini.lookup.entry.Name;

class ServiceCellRenderer extends DefaultListCellRenderer {
    public Component getListCellRendererComponent(
                            JList list,
                            Object value,
                            int index,
                            boolean isSelected,
                            boolean cellHasFocus) {
        Component c =
            super.getListCellRendererComponent(list, value,
                                        index,
                                        isSelected,
                                        cellHasFocus);
```

Listing 11–8 `ServiceCellRenderer.java` (continued)

```
            if (c instanceof JLabel) {
                JLabel l = (JLabel) c;
                if (value instanceof ServiceItem) {
                    ServiceItem item = (ServiceItem) value;
                    String s = null;
                    // Use the Name attribute, if there is one.
                    for (int i=0 ;
                            i<item.attributeSets.length ; i++) {
                        if (item.attributeSets[i] instanceof
                                                        Name) {
                            s = ((Name)
                                    item.attributeSets[i]).name;
                            break;
                        }
                    }
                    if (s == null) {
                        s = Browser.declassify(
                            item.service.getClass().getName());
                    }
                    l.setText(s);
                }
            }
        return c;
    }
}
```

The basic structure of this `ListCellRenderer` is the same as the previous one—it calls out to its superclass to create a default label, and then changes it based on information it can determine about the object it is displaying.

In this case, I assume that the objects in the lists of services are `Service-Items`. When the cell renderer is asked to display a `ServiceItem`, it scans over the attributes associated with it. If a `Name` attribute is found (which will contain a human-readable name like "`Fred's VCR`" or "`OCR Service`"), it is used as the text of the label. If no `Name` is associated with the service's proxy, then the class name of the service is used; here, I call a method called `declassify()`, which is defined in the `Browser` class you'll see shortly, to strip off leading package names from a class. Displaying the name of the proxy's class isn't the best solution—because whatever the proxy's author named the class is really an implementation detail which may not be fit for human consumption—but it's all there is to go on.

You could easily change this example to search for a `ServiceType` attribute and fetch the `Icon` member out of it to display a graphical representation of the service; most of the services shipped by Sun as a part of Jini do not have such icons, though, so I haven't taken that approach here.

AttrCellRenderer

Now for the fun one: lists of attributes. You'll remember from Chapter 7 that attributes have a nice synergy with beans—the Jini APIs provide a way for developers to associate beans with attribute classes, and clients can take advantage of these beans for display or programmatic purposes.

The cell renderer for attributes (Listing 11–9) follows the same basic paradigm of the others—it asks its superclass for a default `Component` to be used to display an object. In this case, however, it also uses the beans facilities to see if it can recover a bean for the attribute. If the bean it gets back is itself a `Component`, then the code can display this instead of the boring old label it gets from the default renderer.

Listing 11–9 `AttrCellRenderer.java`

```
// A ListCellRenderer for attributes -- draws attributes
// as components if they are, or uses the name of the class
// along with its toString() representation

package corejini.chapter11;

import java.awt.Component;
import javax.swing.JList;
import javax.swing.DefaultListCellRenderer;
import net.jini.core.entry.Entry;

public class AttrCellRenderer extends DefaultListCellRenderer
{
    public Component getListCellRendererComponent(
                            JList list, Object value,
                            int index,
                            boolean isSelected,
                            boolean cellHasFocus) {
        Component c =
            super.getListCellRendererComponent(list, value,
                                        index,
                                        isSelected,
                                        cellHasFocus);
        return Browser.getComponentForEntry(
                            (Entry) value, c);
    }
}
```

The `getListCellRendererComponent()` method again calls the superclass to fetch a `JLabel`, which will be the default component to return. But, the code also calls `getComponentForEntry()` to see if a "better" one can be returned. This method takes the `Entry` for which the code is looking for a `Component`, as well as the default `Component`, which will be returned if an alternative cannot be found.

The `getComponentForEntry()` method—a static method defined in the `Browser` class that you'll see later—first calls out to the `EntryBeans` class to try to create a bean for the specified `Entry`. This will result in an attempt to locate and load a bean that corresponds to whatever `Entry` class was passed in. The code here ignores any exceptions that may result; if the bean is null then it will just use the default.

After trying to load the bean, the code checks to see if a bean was successfully loaded and, if so, whether the bean is a subclass of `Component`. If it is, then `setVisible()` is called on it to make it appear on the screen, and it is returned. If no bean was loaded, or if the loaded bean was not a `Component`, then the default component (most likely a `JLabel`) is returned. Here, I've tried to make sure that the display is somewhat sensible, by setting the label to the de-packaged class name and then appending the `toString()` representation of the attribute. (Here, you see yet another example of why providing intelligent implementations of `toString()` is so important for classes like this, which will be displayed to users.)

With the bag of tricks accumulated so far, you can create administrative GUIs for arbitrary services, and create nice-looking and intuitive lists of services, registrars, and attributes. Now, it's time to move on to the browser itself.

The Core Browser Framework

Now that you've got a set of building blocks to work from, you can begin looking at the core code of the browser application. The basic functionality of the browser is fairly simple; it needs to do the following things:

- Create the three-paned user interface you saw in Figure 11–1.
- Perform discovery, and be prepared to receive events from the lookup services that are discovered.
- Monitor for mouse clicks on the list panes; clicks and double-clicks will cause other panes to update, and may contact Jini lookup services to find available services, and solicit events from these services.

I've tried to create a "natural" set of bindings between mouse clicks and operations in this interface. Clicking on the various panels will produce the actions shown in Table 11–1.

Table 11–1 Operations in the Jini Browser	
Lookup Service Clicked	Clicking on a lookup service causes the service list to be updated with the set of services contained in that lookup service. The code will also solicit events from the lookup service so that new services will be found. Event registrations from any previously selected lookup service are canceled.
Lookup Service Double-Clicked	Double-clicking on a lookup service causes the administration panel for that service to appear, if the lookup service is administrable.
Service Clicked	Clicking on a service causes the attribute list to display the set of attributes associated with that service. Any beans that may exist for the attribute classes will be found and, if those beans are `Components`, will be displayed in the list.
Service Double-Clicked	Double-clicking on a service causes the administration panel for that service to appear, if the service is administrable.
Attribute Clicked	Clicking on an attribute has no effect in this example. One could extend this example to pop up a panel containing more information about the attribute—such as the short description that can be retrieved from the attribute's bean.
Attribute Double-Clicked	Double-clicking on an attribute has no effect in this example. One could extend this example to pop up a JavaBeans PropertyEditor to edit the attribute, and then set its value through the service's administrative APIs.

Storing Data in Lists

Now that you have some idea of the requirements for the browser, it's time to flesh out the individual components of the core program. From the screenshot you saw in Figure 11–1, you no doubt noticed that the browser is organized as three lists, each in separate panes. These lists are `JLists`, which are quite flexible in how the data contained in them is represented. If you peruse the documentation for this class, you'll notice that you can create new `JLists` by passing in arrays or `Vectors` of objects, or by passing in something called a `JListModel`. If you pass in a simple type—such as an array or `Vector`—the

JList class will create a default list model that it will use internally to represent the data stored in it. The *bad* thing about using this default model is that if you ever add, remove, or change anything in the array or Vector you passed to the list, the JList object will not notice this fact. The default list model expects the input data to be unchanging; if your data will ever change, you need to define a new list model that will "poke" the JList whenever it is updated.

Clearly, the data in the browser's lists may change. Services may appear and disappear from the services pane; lookup services may come and go. So, the code for the browser creates an extremely simple new list model called the ArrayListModel. This class implements the various ListModel interfaces, and wraps a simple ArrayList. Whenever items are added to or removed from this model, it calls out to any listeners that may be waiting for changes. The visible JList components in the application register themselves as listeners for changes in their respective models, so they will be updated as the set of managed list items changes.

Listing 11–10 shows the ArrayListModel class.

Listing 11–10 ArrayListModel.java

```java
// Wrap an array list so that we notify listeners
// when a change occurs.

package corejini.chapter11;

import java.util.ArrayList;
import javax.swing.AbstractListModel;

public class ArrayListModel extends AbstractListModel {
    ArrayList a = new ArrayList();

    public Object getElementAt(int index) {
        return a.get(index);
    }
    public int getSize() {
        return a.size();
    }
    boolean contains(Object o) {
        return a.contains(o);
    }
```

Listing 11–10 `ArrayListModel.java` (continued)

```
synchronized void addElement(Object o) {
    a.add(o);
    fireIntervalAdded(this, a.size(), a.size());
}
synchronized void removeElement(Object o) {
    int index = a.indexOf(o);
    if (index != -1) {
        a.remove(index);
        fireIntervalRemoved(this, index, index);
    }
}
synchronized void setData(ArrayList newArrayList) {
    int len = a.size();
    a = newArrayList;
    fireIntervalRemoved(this, 0, len);
    fireIntervalAdded(this, 0,  a.size());
}
}
```

This simple class extends `AbstractListModel`, so it inherits all the basic `ListModel` functionality. It also contains an enclosed `Vector`, and exposes some handy `Vector`-like methods on it (such as `addElement()`, `contains()`, and so on). Whenever these methods are called to update the contents of the contained `Vector`, any listeners for the model will be messaged.

This list model will serve as the basis for all three of the list panes in the browser example. Next, take a look at some classes that will be used to facilitate the browser's integration with Jini.

Using Discovery

As I mentioned at the start of this chapter, there are many possible ways to build a browser. The approach that this browser takes might be called "lookup-oriented." That is, it organizes services based on the lookup services that hold their proxies. Other arrangements are certainly possible, and even desirable in many circumstances. But because of this browser's requirements—to track individual lookup services, solicit events from the currently-viewed lookup service, and organize services based on the lookup service they came from—the code here does not use the `ServiceDiscoveryManager`. The `ServiceDiscoveryManager` effectively "hides" individual lookup services from callers. So while it's amenable to building other sorts of browsers, it's not really what this code needs. In this example, I'm using the low-level discovery classes and the `ServiceRegistrar` interface for event solicitation.

Since I'm using these lower level APIs, there are two special interfaces that code in the browser will need to implement to be "plugged in" to the Jini runtime system. First, it will have to leverage the `DiscoveryListener` interface to be informed about new lookup services. Second, it will have to use `RemoteEventListener` so that it can be informed of changes in the set of services known to particular lookup services.

There is no reason why you couldn't have one big `Browser` class that does all of this by implementing both interfaces. For clarity, though, here I've broken out the implementations of these two interfaces into separate classes (see Listings 11–11 and 11–12). These could easily be inner classes, which would allow them to have direct access to the members of the `Browser` class that created them; in the interests of clarity, I've tried to lessen the amount of cross-talk between the classes here and the larger `Browser` class by writing these as separate, non-nested classes. I'll talk about the one for discovery first.

Listing 11–11 `Discoverer.java`

```
// A class to manage discovery for us

package corejini.chapter11;

import net.jini.discovery.DiscoveryListener;
import net.jini.discovery.DiscoveryEvent;
import net.jini.core.lookup.ServiceRegistrar;

public class Discoverer implements DiscoveryListener {
    protected Browser browser;

    Discoverer(Browser browser) {
        this.browser = browser;
    }
    public void discovered(DiscoveryEvent ev) {
        ServiceRegistrar regs[] = ev.getRegistrars();
        System.out.println("discovered! " + regs.length);
        for (int i=0 ; i<regs.length ; i++) {
            if (!browser.getLookups().contains(regs[i])) {
                System.out.println("adding " + regs[i]);
                browser.getLookups().addElement(regs[i]);
            } else {
                System.out.println("already contains...");
            }
        }
    }
    public void discarded(DiscoveryEvent ev) {
        ServiceRegistrar regs[] = ev.getRegistrars();
        for (int i=0 ; i<regs.length ; i++) {
            browser.getLookups().removeElement(regs[i]);
        }
    }
}
```

This class is instantiated by passing it an instance of a `Browser`. Basically, all it does is wait around for new `DiscoveryEvents` to be passed to it via its `dis-covered()` and `discarded()` interfaces. When `discovered()` is called, each registrar is compared to the list of registrars already known to the browser; if the registrar is a new one, it is added to the browser's list of registrars. When a registrar is discarded, it is removed from the browser's list of registrars.

This code requires that the Browser implement a method called getLookups() that returns a list of lookup services known to it. As you'll see in the discussion of the Browser class, the object that is returned from this call is an instance of the ArrayListModel defined earlier. By using this list, the Discoverer can simply add and remove registrars, safe in the knowledge that the Browser's lists will be updated appropriately.

Receiving Service Events

The second class that is needed to play well with Jini is an implementation of RemoteEventListener. Whenever the user selects a new lookup service, the browser needs to search that lookup service to see which services are known to it. It *also* must solicit events from the lookup service so that it will be informed when new services appear, or old services disappear, so that it can update the lists that it presents to users; the Listener object will receive these events.

The RemoteEventListener interface is implemented by a separate object. Again, this interface could be implemented by the larger Browser itself, or by an inner class. But here, I've pulled it out as a separate, non-nested class.

Listing 11–12 `Listener.java`

```java
// A class to receive RemoteEvents

package corejini.chapter11;

import java.rmi.server.UnicastRemoteObject;
import java.rmi.RemoteException;
import net.jini.core.event.RemoteEvent;
import net.jini.core.event.RemoteEventListener;
import net.jini.core.lookup.ServiceEvent;
import net.jini.core.lookup.ServiceRegistrar;

public class Listener extends UnicastRemoteObject
    implements RemoteEventListener {
    Browser browser;

    Listener(Browser browser) throws RemoteException {
        super();
        this.browser = browser;
    }
    public void notify(RemoteEvent ev) {
        if (!(ev instanceof ServiceEvent))
            return;

        // We just update the whole set of services --
        // not efficient, but shorter than mucking our
        // way through the lists.
        browser.updateServices((ServiceRegistrar)
                                ev.getSource());
    }
}
```

The `Listener` class extends `java.rmi.server.UnicastRemoteObject`, so that its methods can be called by objects in other JVMs. The single essential method in this class is `notify()`, which will be passed a `RemoteEvent` as a parameter. The parameter is tested to see if it is a `ServiceEvent`—meaning that it came from a registrar containing news of service changes—and if it is not, the event is ignored. If it *is* a `ServiceEvent`, however, then the source of the event (which will be the `ServiceRegistrar` object representing the lookup service

that generated it) is passed to a method on the browser called updateSer-
vices().

Note that the ServiceEvent contains details about the changes in the state of
services at a particular registrar. So, the code here could use this information to
update the various lists in the browser directly—by seeing if a changed service
was the currently selected service and, if so, selectively updating its list of
attributes. By passing only the source of the event to updateServices(), the
code is losing much of this information; and in fact, updateServices() (as you
shall see) simply rebuilds the entire service list when a change is detected. While
this is a bit wasteful, the set of services and attributes available to a lookup service will likely not change very often. And avoiding a "widening" of the interfaces between Listener and Browser keeps the connections between these two
classes as simple as possible.

Handling List Events

Finally, before moving on to the large Browser class, take a look at one more
piece of infrastructure that the application will need. As you know if you've
done much Java GUI programming, events such as mouse clicks are handled by
listener classes that are set up to receive certain events. The most convenient
way to create a listener is to make a small inner class—perhaps even an *anony-
mous* inner class (meaning one that is defined "in line" and has no name)—that
implements whatever particular interfaces you need.

From the table of actions that you saw earlier, you know that the browser
needs some listener class to handle all of the various sorts of clicks and double-
clicks on its lists. Here is the listener (Listing 11–13) I've defined for the browser.
Once again, code like this is most often seen as an inner class, but here it's broken
out for better clarity.

Listing 11–13 `ListClickListener.java`

```java
// Better as an inner class, but I've broken it out
// for legibility.  This handles clicks on list items

package corejini.chapter11;

import java.awt.event.MouseAdapter;
import java.awt.event.MouseEvent;
import javax.swing.JList;

public class ListClickListener extends MouseAdapter {
    Browser browser;

    ListClickListener(Browser browser) {
        this.browser = browser;
    }
    public void mouseClicked(MouseEvent ev) {
        boolean doubleClick = ev.getClickCount() == 2;

        if (ev.getSource() instanceof JList) {
            JList list = (JList) ev.getSource();
            int index = list.locationToIndex(ev.getPoint());

            if (index == -1)
                return;

            if (list.getModel().equals(
                        browser.getLookups())) {
                if (doubleClick) {
                    browser.lookupDoubleClicked(index);
                } else {
                    browser.lookupClicked(index);
                }
            } else if (list.getModel().equals(
                        browser.getServices())) {
                if (doubleClick) {
                    browser.serviceDoubleClicked(index);
                } else {
                    browser.serviceClicked(index);
                }
            }
        }
    }
}
```

You'll note that this code really has nothing to do with Jini, but lots to do with Swing. The listener class extends `MouseAdapter`, which provides default implementations for all the various `MouseListener` methods. The only thing the code cares about is when the mouse is clicked, so the `ListClickListener` overrides `mouseClicked()`, which will receive a `MouseEvent` whenever a click occurs.

This method determines if the event represents a single-click or a double-click. Then, it checks the source of the event to ensure that it is, in fact, a `JList` object (if the source is some other class, then the `ListClickListener` was in all probability installed as a `MouseListener` for some other component on the screen by accident). The method then computes the newly selected index from the *X, Y* coordinates of the mouse click. Finally, it asks the source list for its model, and compares it to the `Browser`'s models for the lookup list and the service list. These models, stored by the `Browser`, are instances of the `ArrayListModel` defined earlier, and are accessed by calling `getLookups()` and `getServices()` on the `Browser` instance.

The Browser Class

Now that I've finally covered all the individual "support" classes the browser will be using, it's time to move on to the `Browser` class itself.

Listing 11–14 shows this rather involved class.

Listing 11–14 `Browser.java`

```
// Behavior:
//
// lookup single-click -- update services
// service single-click -- update attrs
// attr single-click -- noop
//
// lookup double-click -- bring up admin panel
// service double-click -- bring up admin panel
// attr double-click -- noop

package corejini.chapter11;
```

Listing 11–14 Browser.java (continued)

```java
import net.jini.admin.Administrable;
import net.jini.discovery.DiscoveryGroupManagement;
import net.jini.discovery.LookupDiscoveryManager;
import net.jini.core.lookup.ServiceRegistrar;
import net.jini.core.lookup.ServiceItem;
import net.jini.core.lookup.ServiceTemplate;
import net.jini.core.lookup.ServiceMatches;
import net.jini.core.event.EventRegistration;
import net.jini.lookup.entry.EntryBean;
import net.jini.lookup.entry.EntryBeans;
import net.jini.core.entry.Entry;
import net.jini.lease.LeaseRenewalManager;
import javax.swing.JLabel;
import javax.swing.JList;
import javax.swing.JPanel;
import javax.swing.JFrame;
import javax.swing.JOptionPane;
import javax.swing.JScrollPane;
import javax.swing.JDialog;
import java.awt.event.MouseListener;
import java.awt.event.WindowEvent;
import java.awt.event.WindowAdapter;
import java.awt.Component;
import java.awt.BorderLayout;
import java.awt.GridBagLayout;
import java.awt.GridBagConstraints;
import java.util.ArrayList;
import java.io.IOException;
import java.rmi.RemoteException;
import java.rmi.RMISecurityManager;
```

Listing 11–14 `Browser.java` (continued)

```java
// This is the overall browser application.  It's a panel,
// so it can be embedded in other JComponents
public class Browser extends JPanel {
    // Models for the three panes
    protected ArrayListModel lookups, services, attrs;
    protected ServiceRegistrar currentLookup = null;
    // Search for everything
    protected ServiceTemplate template =
        new ServiceTemplate(null, null, null);
    // Current event registration
    protected EventRegistration er = null;
    protected Listener eventListener;
    protected LeaseRenewalManager leaseMgr =
        new LeaseRenewalManager();
    protected LookupDiscoveryManager disco;

    public Browser() throws IOException, RemoteException {
        MouseListener listener =
            new ListClickListener(this);

        // Make an event listener
        eventListener = new Listener(this);

        // Create the list models
        lookups = new ArrayListModel();
        services = new ArrayListModel();
        attrs = new ArrayListModel();

        GridBagLayout layout = new GridBagLayout();
        GridBagConstraints c = new GridBagConstraints();

        setLayout(layout);

        c.fill = GridBagConstraints.BOTH;
        c.weightx = 1.0;
        c.gridx = GridBagConstraints.RELATIVE;
        c.gridy = 0;
```

Listing 11–14 `Browser.java` (continued)

```java
// Do labels across the top
JLabel label = new JLabel("Lookup Services");
layout.setConstraints(label, c);
add(label);

label = new JLabel("Services");
layout.setConstraints(label, c);
add(label);

label = new JLabel("Attributes");
layout.setConstraints(label, c);
add(label);

// Do scrolling lists across the bottom
c.gridy = 1;
c.weighty = 1.0;
JList list = new JList(lookups);
list.addMouseListener(listener);
list.setCellRenderer(new LookupCellRenderer());
JScrollPane scroller = new JScrollPane(list);
layout.setConstraints(scroller, c);
add(scroller);

list = new JList(services);
list.setCellRenderer(new ServiceCellRenderer());
list.addMouseListener(listener);
scroller = new JScrollPane(list);
layout.setConstraints(scroller, c);
add(scroller);

list = new JList(attrs);
list.setCellRenderer(new AttrCellRenderer());
list.addMouseListener(listener);
scroller = new JScrollPane(list);
layout.setConstraints(scroller, c);
add(scroller);

// Set up for discovery
disco = new LookupDiscoveryManager(
        DiscoveryGroupManagement.ALL_GROUPS,
        null,
new Discoverer(this));
}
```

Listing 11–14 `Browser.java` (continued)

```java
ArrayListModel getLookups() {
    return lookups;
}
ArrayListModel getServices() {
    return services;
}
ArrayListModel getAttrs() {
    return attrs;
}

// Find all services in "reg"
void updateServices(ServiceRegistrar reg) {
    ServiceMatches matches;

    try {
        matches = currentLookup.lookup(template,
                                    Integer.MAX_VALUE);
    } catch (RemoteException ex) {
        showDialog("Problem contacting registrar:\n" +
                ex.getMessage());
        disco.discard(reg);
        return;
    }

    ArrayList newServices =
        new ArrayList(matches.totalMatches);
    for (int i=0 ; i<matches.totalMatches ; i++) {
        newServices.add(matches.items[i]);
    }

    services.setData(newServices);
}

// Handle single-clicks on lookup services--update the
// list of services
protected void lookupClicked(int index) {
    unsolicitEvents();
    currentLookup = (ServiceRegistrar)
                        lookups.getElementAt(index);
    updateServices(currentLookup);
    solicitEvents();
}
```

Listing 11–14 `Browser.java` (continued)

```
// Handle double-clicks on lookup services--administer
// the lookup service
protected void lookupDoubleClicked(int index) {
    currentLookup = (ServiceRegistrar)
                      lookups.getElementAt(index);

    if (!(currentLookup instanceof Administrable)) {
        System.out.println(
            "Lookup service is not administrable");
        return;
    }

    Object o;

    try {
        o = ((Administrable) currentLookup).getAdmin();
    } catch (RemoteException ex) {
        showDialog("Problem contacting registrar:\n" +
                   ex.getMessage());
        disco.discard(currentLookup);
        return;
    }

    if (o != null) {
        System.err.println(
            "GOT AN ADMINABLE REGISTRAR!");
        AdminPanel panel = new AdminPanel(o);
        JFrame frame = new JFrame("Administration");
        frame.getContentPane().add(panel);
        frame.pack();
        frame.setVisible(true);
    }
}
```

Listing 11–14 `Browser.java` (continued)

```java
// Handle single-clicks on services--update the
// attr list
protected void serviceClicked(int index) {
    ServiceItem item = (ServiceItem)
                            services.getElementAt(index);
    ArrayList newEntries =
        new ArrayList(item.attributeSets.length);
    for (int i=0 ; i<item.attributeSets.length ; i++) {
        newEntries.add(item.attributeSets[i]);
    }

    attrs.setData(newEntries);
}

// Handle double-clicks on services--try to administer
// them
protected void serviceDoubleClicked(int index) {
    ServiceItem item = (ServiceItem)
                            services.getElementAt(index);

    if (!(item.service instanceof Administrable)) {
        System.out.println(
            "Service is not administrable");
        return;
    }

    Object o;

    try {
        o = ((Administrable) item.service).getAdmin();
    } catch (RemoteException ex) {
        showDialog("Problem contacting registrar:\n" +
                    ex.getMessage());
        return;
    }
```

Listing 11–14 `Browser.java` (continued)

```java
    if (o != null) {
        AdminPanel panel = new AdminPanel(o);
        JFrame frame = new JFrame("Administration");
        frame.getContentPane().add(panel);
        frame.pack();
        frame.setVisible(true);
    }

    System.out.println("Got admin object: " + o);
}

// Ask a lookup service for events
void solicitEvents() {
    System.out.println("Soliciting events");
    try {
        er = currentLookup.notify(template,
            ServiceRegistrar.TRANSITION_MATCH_NOMATCH

            ServiceRegistrar.TRANSITION_NOMATCH_MATCH

            ServiceRegistrar.TRANSITION_MATCH_MATCH,
            eventListener, null, 10 * 60 * 1000);

        leaseMgr.renewUntil(er.getLease(),
                            Long.MAX_VALUE, null);
    } catch (RemoteException ex) {
        er = null;
        disco.discard(currentLookup);
    }
}
```

Listing 11–14 `Browser.java` (continued)

```java
// Stop receiving events
void unsolicitEvents() {
    if (er == null)
        return;

    System.out.println("UN-Soliciting events");
    try {
        leaseMgr.cancel(er.getLease());
    } catch (Exception ex) {
    }
}

// Clean up a classname (strip off package part)
static String declassify(String name) {
    if (name == null) return null;

    int idx = name.lastIndexOf('.');

    if (idx == -1)
        return name;
    else
        return name.substring(idx+1);
}

void showDialog(String message) {
    JOptionPane pane = new JOptionPane(message,
                        JOptionPane.DEFAULT_OPTION,
                        JOptionPane.ERROR_MESSAGE,
                        null, null, null);
    JDialog dialog = new JDialog(
            JOptionPane.getFrameForComponent(this),
                "Alert!");
    dialog.getContentPane().setLayout(
                        new BorderLayout());
    dialog.getContentPane().add(pane,
                        BorderLayout.CENTER);
    dialog.pack();
    dialog.show();
}
```

Listing 11–14 `Browser.java` (continued)

```java
static Component getComponentForEntry(Entry e,
                    Component defaultComponent) {
    EntryBean bean = null;

    // If we're passed a null entry, return the
    // default component (if it's a label, make
    // it say "NULL")
    if (e == null) {
        if (defaultComponent instanceof JLabel) {
            ((JLabel)
                defaultComponent).setText("NULL");
        }
        return defaultComponent;
    }

    try {
        bean = EntryBeans.createBean(e);
    } catch (Exception ex) {
    }

    // Now beanInstance will be either null or
    // will ref a bean. If it's null or it's not
    // a component, we just tostring it.  If
    // it's a component, we return that.
    if (bean == null || !(bean instanceof Component)) {
        if (defaultComponent instanceof JLabel) {
            String cname =
                Browser.declassify(
                        e.getClass().getName());
            ((JLabel) defaultComponent).setText(
                    cname + " [" +
                    e.toString() + "]");
        }
        return defaultComponent;
    } else {
        ((Component) bean).setVisible(true);
        return (Component) bean;
    }
}
```

Listing 11–14 `Browser.java` (continued)

```
public static void main(String[] args) {
    try {
    if (System.getSecurityManager() == null) {
        System.setSecurityManager(
                new RMISecurityManager());
    }

    JFrame frame = new JFrame("Browser");
    frame.addWindowListener(new WindowAdapter() {
        public void windowClosing(WindowEvent ev) {
            System.exit(1);
        }
    });
    frame.getContentPane().add(new Browser());
    frame.pack();
    frame.setVisible(true);
    } catch (Exception ex) {
      System.err.println("Couldn't create browser:" +
                        ex.getMessage());
      ex.printStackTrace();
    }
  }
}
```

The `Browser` class is an extension of `JPanel` so that you can embed it in a `JFrame`, or any other Swing container that needs the ability to browse lookup services and other Jini services. The code here declares three separate `ArrayList-Models`—these are the models that represent the data stored in the three panes of the interface. It also declares a reference to the currently-selected lookup service, the `EventRegistration` object for event solicitations on that current lookup service, a template for searching for services, the event listener, and a `LeaseRe-newalManager` to handle event solicitations.

The constructor for the `Browser` class sets up the user interface and readies all the objects that it needs for Jini participation. All the required `ArrayListModels` are created, and `JLists` are built to view them; each `JList` has an instance of `ListClickListener` installed as its `MouseListener` so that the list data will be updated properly on single- and double-clicks. Each list is also passed the appropriate list cell renderer for it to draw its contents. And finally, the constructor initiates discovery by creating a `Discoverer` and using it as the `DiscoveryListener` on a `LookupDiscoveryManager` instance.

The `Browser` is responsive to several sorts of occurrences: user input on the lists, events from lookup services telling the `Browser` that the set of services has changed, and discovery events that tell the `Browser` that the set of lookup services has changed. All of these three types of input are handled by the objects created earlier, but all of these objects call back into the `Browser` to change its state.

When new discovery events are received, the `Discoverer` simply updates the list of available lookup services by changing the `ArrayListModel` that represents these services; changes to these models cause the display to automatically update. The other two input handlers have slightly more complex interactions with the `Browser`, though.

When new `ServiceEvents` are received by the `Listener` class that handles remote events from lookup services, the `updateServices()` method on `Browser` is called. This method simply executes a `lookup()` search on the changed lookup service, and rebuilds the data stored in the `ArrayListModel` representing the services pane. As discussed in the section on the implementation of the `Listener` class, this isn't the most efficient implementation, but it's easy to implement and show here, and the performance hit shouldn't be too bad for most applications. If you have services that continually update their attributes, say several times a minute—which is probably a bad idea anyway—you can change the code to dissect the `ServiceEvent` and only update those portions of the lists that have been affected.

Note that many of the methods here that contact the lookup service may run into problems if the lookup service is down. These methods (such as `solicitEvents()`) always catch any `RemoteExceptions` from the lookup service and call `discard()` on the `LookupDiscoveryManager` instance to drop the lookup services from use. The list pane will be updated (since calling `discard()` causes the `discarded()` method on `Discoverer` to be called), and—if the lookup service ever returns—it will be rediscovered.

The `ListClickListener` calls several methods on `Browser` that update its state in response to user input. These methods are the "meat" of the code shown here. I'll talk about each in turn.

The `lookupClicked()` method needs to update the services list display to reflect all of the services available on the newly selected lookup service. This method first "unsolicits" events from the currently selected lookup service, if any. This is necessary so that it will not continue to receive events from a lookup service that the user is not even looking at, and will also reduce the bandwidth requirements the code places on the network. Next, it records the currently selected lookup service, so that it will have it available when it does any event processing. The code then calls the same `updateServices()` method that is used during `ServiceEvent` handling. And finally, it solicits events from the lookup service, so that as services come and go, the display of available services will be changed.

Administration of lookup services is done via the `lookupDoubleClicked()` method. This method simply tests the selected item to see if it implements the `Administrable` interface and, if it does, creates a new `AdminPanel` and nests it in a frame to display it.

The `serviceClicked()` method needs to update the list of attributes to show the attributes for the currently-selected service. It fetches the `ServiceItem` that corresponds to the selected index, and retrieves the attributes out of it, setting the data in the `ArrayListModel` for the attribute list.

The implementation of `serviceDoubleClicked()` is similar to `lookupDoubleClicked()`—it fetches the selected item and tests to see whether it is `Administrable`. If it is, it creates a new frame containing the `AdminPanel` for the service and displays it.

Most of the rest of the methods on this class are "helpers" that are called from one of the input-handling routines. The `solicitEvents()` method is used to ask for events from a newly selected lookup service. It uses the stored value of `currentLookup` to ask for notifications, and saves the returned `Event-Registration` so that it will be available later when the program needs to cancel the event leases. It also passes the lease from this registration to the `LeaseRenewalManager` for automatic renewal.

When the user changes the currently-selected lookup service, the lease on the event registration of the previously-selected lookup service must be canceled before registering for events with the new lookup service. The `unsolicitEvents()` method takes care of this. It finds the current event registration and asks the `LeaseRenewalManager` to cancel the lease for it.

The other methods in this class are quite simple. The `declassify()` method is simply a helper to strip any leading package name off a class name, for a cleaner display. It is called from the various `ListCellRenderers` you saw before. And, `showDialog()` simply displays an error dialog when something goes wrong; it is invoked from several of the methods in `Browser`.

The `main()` shown here creates a new `JFrame`, and adds a new `Browser` instance to it. Once created, the `Browser` will handle all the Jini interactions and display updates on its own.

Building and Running the Browser

There are three steps to getting this new browser up and running. First, you must compile the source. Follow the guidelines used elsewhere in this book to ensure separation between the browser's class files and the class files of any services that may be on your machine. If you're using Sun's `javac`, you can just pass the "root" class (`Browser`) to the compiler and it will generate code for all reachable classes.

Next, you'll have to run `rmic` to generate the stubs for the event listener class. Make sure that these go in the `client-dl` directory, since they'll be downloaded to lookup services.

Finally, you're set to run the browser. Make sure you specify a codebase that refers to the HTTP server that is exporting the RMI stubs class file, and provide a security policy file.

On Windows:

```
javac -classpath C:\files;
                C:\jini1_1\lib\jini-core.jar;
                C:\jini1_1\lib\jini-ext.jar;
                C:\jini1_1\lib\sun-util.jar;
                C:\client
    -d C:\client
            C:\corejini\chapter11\Browser.java

rmic -classpath C:\files;
                C:\jini1_1\lib\jini-core.jar;
                C:\jini1_1\lib\jini-ext.jar;
                C:\jini1_1\lib\sun-util.jar;
                C:\client
    -d C:\client
        corejini.chapter11.Listener

mkdir C:\client_dl\corejini\chapter11
cd C:\client\corejini\chapter11
copy Listener_Stub.class C:\client-dl\corejini\chapter11

java -cp C:\jini1_1\lib\jini-core.jar;
        C:\jini1_1\lib\jini-ext.jar;
        C:\jini1_1\lib\sun-util.jar;
        C:\client
    -Djava.security.policy=C:\files\policy
    -Djava.rmi.server.codebase=http://myhost:8086/
corejini.chapter11.Browser
```

On UNIX:

```
javac -classpath /files:
                /files/jini1_1/lib/jini-core.jar:
                /files/jini1_1/lib/jini-ext.jar:
                /files/jini1_1/lib/sun-util.jar:
                /files/client
        -d /files/client
            /files/corejini/chapter11/Browser.java

rmic -classpath /files:
                /files/jini1_1/lib/jini-core.jar:
                /files/jini1_1/lib/jini-ext.jar:
                /files/jini1_1/lib/sun-util.jar:
                /files/client
    -d /files/client
        corejini.chapter11.Listener

mkdir C:\client_dl\corejini\chapter11
cd /files/client/corejini/chapter11
copy Listener_Stub.class /files/client-dl/corejini/chapter11

java -cp /files/jini1_1/lib/jini-core.jar:
        /files/jini1_1/lib/jini-ext.jar:
        /files/jini1_1/lib/sun-util.jar:
        /files/client
    -Djava.security.policy=/files/policy
    -Djava.rmi.server.codebase=http://myhost:8086/
        corejini.chapter11.Browser
```

What's Next?

This chapter has looked at the first fairly large Jini client of the book. And while most of the Jini-specific interactions shown here should be fairly familiar to you by now, you've seen how to create the "glue" between Jini and Swing applications. Many of the components here can be reused in applications you build in the future.

In the next chapter, I'll continue the in-depth look at Jini by focusing on one of its core concepts: leasing. You'll learn how to use leasing in your applications, and how to create services that export resources through leasing.

In Depth: Leasing

Chapter 12

I n this chapter, you'll look in depth at the leasing paradigm used throughout Jini. As you will see, leasing provides a solution to many of the problems inherent in distributed computing—it allows for a distributed system to clean up when parts of it fail, and prevents the accretion of persistent state in long-lived systems.

Leasing is not without its problems, though. In particular, managing leases can be one of the more difficult aspects of building with Jini. Fortunately, most of the lease management chores you will face are mechanical enough that they can be easily automated by class libraries or third-party services.

In this look at leasing, I'll reexamine the rationale for leases as opposed to other solutions for designing reliability into distributed systems. After this introduction, I'll walk through a close look at the programming interfaces for using, renewing, and canceling leases, and focus on some common idioms that programmers use to handle leases. These common idioms are implemented as a set of classes that application writers can use to make the job of managing leases easier.

Being a well-behaved consumer of leases is only half of the story, though. In the chapter after this one, you'll see how you can export resources you hold to other applications via leasing.

Reliability in Distributed Systems

I'll briefly reexamine the problems of designing reliability into a distributed system, and the approach that Jini takes.

Any system, distributed or not, will never be completely reliable: software can crash: machines and networks will fail. Sometimes failures seem as if they must be caused by the phase of the moon, or perhaps cosmic rays. But distributed systems—systems comprised of multiple, cooperating components distributed across a network—compound the problems of failure greatly. In a distributed system, the failure of any one component may *potentially* bring down the entire system. And not only do distributed systems suffer because they necessarily have more components that might fail, they also suffer simply because they can fail in ways that stand-alone systems cannot. A dead power supply in a key router is unlikely to bring down a purely stand-alone application; that same failure can cripple a distributed system, however.

The challenge here is not to design distributed systems so that none of their components can fail—this is clearly impossible. Nor is it to design distributed systems that appear to fail in the same ways that stand-alone systems can—work over the years has shown that this is impractical at best, and at worst hides important information that developers need to make informed decisions about how to handle failures. Instead, the challenge is to design distributed systems using concepts that promote reliability wherever possible, acknowledge the inevitability of failures, and provide a way for the system itself (and not developers) to clean up from failures. The reason that the system itself should be empowered to clean up from failures isn't that programmers are too dim to do it; it's that, often, the software component that would do the cleaning up is itself the one that has failed or become disconnected from the network. So, the need for "self-healing" distributed systems is critical.

The Need for Self-Healing

Self-healing also addresses one of Jini's primary concerns—that distributed systems should function for long periods of time without the intervention of a human administrator. If a human has to come in and clean up the mess (reconfigure the software, move machines, reinstall applications, juggle network topologies) every time a component crashes, the system will become simply unworkable as it grows to hundreds, thousands, or even millions of components.

What is inarguably the most successful distributed system in history—the Internet—has many of these self-healing properties. Routing tables are automatically distributed around the world as network configurations change. Domain name service entries are propagated to secondary servers and cached locally as they change. And packets that are unable to reach a destination through one route may be re-sent along a different one.

The Need for Evolvability

Many distributed systems do, however, share a reliability problem that stand-alone systems also have: They are often designed to run for long periods of time without interruption. While many stand-alone systems, such as Web servers and database servers, are designed to stay up for months or even years, distributed systems typically have even greater needs in this area.

There are a couple of reasons for this. The first is that distributed systems potentially reach many, many more people than any application running on a stand-alone machine. Thus, the costs of bringing the entire system down may be astronomically greater. Chances are that it would be impossible to even inform all of the users, distributed across a campus or across the planet, about the impending downtime.

A second reason that distributed systems must be designed to stay up for longer periods of time is simply that distributed systems are hard to control. Because a distributed system is spread across many machines on a network, there may be no centralized point of control for the entire system. Can you imagine what it would even mean to "shut down the Internet" over a weekend for maintenance? These systems, once they've started, rarely stop running.

Both of these facts point to one of the big problems of distributed systems—once started, these systems may be difficult or impossible to upgrade. Think about how tricky it is to introduce new versions of a software program on even a stand-alone computer—file formats change, other applications expect the old version to still exist, and so on. In a distributed system, the problem is exponentially compounded because it is impossible to upgrade all the components across the world at the *same time*—you cannot take the system down for maintenance, and even if you could, chances are you wouldn't be able to reach every machine to upgrade everything smoothly without failures. One must be able to evolve or upgrade the system *incrementally*—on a component-by-component basis—rather than upgrading the entire system as a whole. This problem of *software evolution* is a serious one in distributed systems and needs to be specifically addressed by any design for reliability we use in our systems.

Leasing as a Solution

The problems inherent in distributed computing point to the fact that programmers should design to accommodate these problems explicitly. That is, the concepts and idioms that are used to build systems should be created based on the understanding that distributed systems can fail, that they should heal themselves wherever possible, and that they may be long-lived beasts once they've been started.

Leasing in Jini is an attempt to address these issues. Jini uses this one central concept—that access to resources is leased to consumers, rather than granted to them in perpetuity—as a way to acknowledge that systems fail. The common idioms of using leases, and the code in the Jini class libraries that supports leasing, are designed to promote self-healing and provide a degree of maintainability in long-running distributed systems.

The Leasing Approach

Let's look at exactly what problems leasing addresses, and how leasing can provide some solutions—not to the problems of keeping components in a distributed system from failing, but to the problem of building software that reacts predictably and safely in the face of those failures.

The primary idea behind leasing is that a lease holder must establish a continued proof-of-interest in using some resource if it is to be allowed access to it. If the lease holder fails to demonstrate interest, then the lease expires and the resource is released.

There are a couple of key points to make here:

- The resource that a lease grants access to can be essentially anything—a bit of storage, some computation, or a promise for the lease grantor to act in the future on behalf of the requestor. The core Jini services use leases to grant access to event and lookup service registrations; your own services can use leases to grant access to any resources you export.
- The failure of a lease holder to demonstrate proof-of-interest may be because the holder is honestly no longer interested in using the resource. But it may also be because the lease holder has crashed or become disconnected from the network.

Leasing is a very simple idea conceptually. But the notion that resources are leased, rather than granted indefinitely, provides some real benefits to distributed systems.

Leasing provides a way to address two central problems in distributed computing. First, failures are guaranteed to be detected. If the system were to grant access to resources indefinitely, then the holder of a resource may crash, perhaps never to return, and the grantor of the resource would be unable to allow its use by other interested parties. By granting a lease, the system guarantees that failures will be detected without requiring any separate component other than the lease grantor to be involved in the process of determining that the failure exists. Leasing also puts a hard deadline on when failures will be detected—if a lease is granted for 10 minutes, then 10 minutes is the longest window during which an unnoticed failure may exist.

Second, leases provide a way for a distributed system to *automatically* clean up after failed components. This is especially important in long-lived software systems. If the system didn't discard irrelevant information, then it would accrete state for all the components that had been a part of the system but hadn't cleaned up after themselves. Clearly, a component that fails won't have the opportunity to free up its resources. Leasing guarantees that irrelevant data will simply be forgotten when leases expire.

The use of leases to detect failures and to clean up after them happens completely within the lease grantor. Because there is no need for the holder of the resource or any centralized authority to be involved, you can say the system is self-healing in the face of failures of resource holders. The leasing paradigm doesn't depend on the failed component being able to somehow communicate that it has failed.

The fact that a service that does not renew its lease is completely forgotten from the system provides a way to evolve components of a distributed software system in isolation. When a service is cleaned up after its leases expire, you know for a fact that its service proxy is no longer installed in any lookup service, it will never receive any events, and no other service will be able to find it. The entire service and every trace of it has been removed from the lookup services in the Jini community. Once the service is "off line," you are free to run a different version of the same service, perhaps using the same API but with a different implementation, and plug it into all the same communities of which the original service was a member.

Issues in Leasing

Simply saying that "resources are leased rather than granted indefinitely" gives a flavor of Jini leasing, but provides no specifics. The Jini designers had to make a number of other crucial design choices to ensure that leasing works to promote reliability in distributed systems.

Relative vs. Absolute Time

The first design choice, which may be unintuitive at first, is that Jini leases are specified using a desired lease *duration*, rather than an explicit lease expiration *time*. While absolute times are useful and natural for many applications, they are unworkable in a distributed system, particularly one where you may not have control over all the computers that are participating in the system.

Suppose leases were specified in terms of absolute time. You might ask a resource provider for a lease that lasts until, say, 10PM Tuesday night. You have no idea what kind of machine the resource provider is running on, how well-maintained it is, or even where it is. The clock on the machine may not have been set in years, or it may have missed the last switch to daylight savings time. The two machines involved in this operation—the machine that your service is running on and the machine that the resource provider is running on—may have completely different notions of what absolute time of day it is.

Now look at a lease specified in terms of relative time. In such a system, a resource consumer requests a lease for a duration, say one hour. Even though the systems may have completely different ideas about the time of day, their clocks are probably more or less capable of timing the passage of one hour accurately.

But, you may be asking, if the clock of one machine is wildly wrong in the first place, isn't that probably because the machine's clock is keeping inaccurate time? That is true. But the amount of clock skew that can accrue for the typical duration of a lease is far, far less than the total amount of error that the clock may have accumulated since it was last set. So, except in the case of disastrous clock failures of the sort that would likely keep the machine from functioning anyway, specifying leases in terms of duration is more accurate than specifying leases in terms of absolute times.

You may also be wondering about the time required to send the message to renew the lease. If I ask for a lease for one second, how can I guarantee that my message to renew the lease will arrive before the lease expires? The answer is that you should request leases large enough that the time required to send a renewal message will, in all probability, be in the noise. While you cannot guarantee that your renewal request will arrive in *any* fixed time (or even whether it will arrive at the destination at all), you can make some good guesses about the order of magnitude differences between network transmission time and lease duration. So most leases will be on the order of five or ten minutes and will completely dominate the time required to send a renewal message on any network.

Lease Negotiation

A second design choice, perhaps an obvious one, is that leases in Jini are negotiated. Without some form of negotiation, resource consumers could simply ask for an impossibly large lease duration, and you would be back with the problems that happen when access to resources is granted for a virtually infinite period of time.

So Jini works more like "real-life" leases: The grantor and the lease holder (the lessor) must agree on the terms of the lease. And, also like in the real world, the grantor has the final say on the lease that is offered.

Real-life leases may involve many rounds of negotiation. Fortunately, Jini uses a much simpler approach that is easy-to-use by programs. A lease requestor asks for a lease of a given duration, and the grantor replies with the *actual* duration, which may be the requested value, zero (thus denying the lease), or any value in between. At the point that the grantor returns the lease, the receiver effectively holds it; there is no need for it to acknowledge or accept the duration of the lease, and it cannot propose a new duration without going through the normal lease renewal process.

In practice, this approach works well. While it is not as flexible as an involved, multiround lease negotiation, it involves only one round-trip message between the requestor and the grantor, the request process can be done simply via one method invocation, and the process is good enough for nearly all applications.

Leasing Done by Third Parties

A third choice of the Jini designers was that leases could be acquired by third parties on behalf of the resource consumer. This is an interesting design decision—it says that while a resource may be held by the original resource consumer, the task of providing proof-of-interest can be delegated to an external entity. What happens is that the external third party goes through the mechanics of acquiring and renewing the lease, but the lease is actually in the "name" of the original resource consumer.

Clearly, this may make the life of the resource consumer easier: It can delegate all (or at least most) of the mechanics of leasing to someone else, and go about the job of using its resources. And, such a strategy may be a requirement in situations where services are running on computationally-impoverished devices that may not have the horsepower, connectivity, or bandwidth to handle all of the chores of lease management. Such devices can hand off the task of leasing to a third party to be done for them.

But, third-party leasing can bring problems with it. Most of these problems arise from the separation noted earlier: that the resource still resides in the consumer, but the task of providing proof-of-interest has been removed from the consumer. You'll learn about all the implications of third-party leasing, and strategies for services that are using third-party leasing, in this chapter.

Core Note: Leasing analogies

Actually, the third-party leasing situation is analogous to what can happen in "real-life" leases via power of attorney. When you delegate power of attorney to an individual, you give that person "signing authority" on your behalf to enter into contracts. Although the attorney is doing the signing, you are still the one bound to the contract.

There are few, if any, situations in Jini where an unscrupulous third party would take out a lease on your behalf and gain any benefit from it. So, third-party leasing is almost entirely used as a convenience by the lessor.

The Cost of Leasing

This ability to automatically detect failures and clean up after them is the benefit that leasing brings to a distributed system. But it also brings a bit of a burden to the users—both consumers and grantors—of leasing. In a system where access to resources is granted in perpetuity, the programming model for resource consumers is simple: They simply ask for the resource and, if they get it, continue to use it until they are finished. Well-behaved consumers will hopefully remember to free the resource when they shut down. Likewise, the job of the resource provider is also easy: It simply grants the resource when asked for it, and forgets about it until the consumer says otherwise.

This simplicity is where the problems come in. Because the provider forgets about the resource until the consumer says otherwise, it may not be able to detect when the consumer has failed. Likewise, for the consumer to notify the provider when it fails, the programmer must remember to put in the code for the notification, and the program must be able to call it—meaning that it has not crashed before it can free the resource.

So leasing presents some benefits, but at the cost of a more heavyweight programming model. Leasing requires that a consumer of a resource be actively engaged in showing the provider that it is interested in holding on to that resource. The resource provider must actively keep an eye on the resources it has granted so that it can free them when leases expire.

This chapter looks at leasing from the perspective of a lease consumer. In the next few sections, you'll see the programming interfaces available to resource consumers for managing and using leases. Virtually all of the Jini code you write will be a consumer of resources in some way, so these sections are crucial for writing reliable Jini code. The following chapter looks at how services that grant access to resources can use leasing to manage these resources.

Building Lease Consumers

In this section, you'll look at the programming interfaces that are used by lease consumers—that is, services and applications that hold leases on some resource provided by another service. Here you'll see the most basic leasing interfaces, which allow you to renew and cancel leases. These are the lowest level leasing APIs, which you've seen in the "Hello, World" examples. There are a number of higher level APIs built on top of these, which I'll talk about a bit later.

The process of how a lease is created—or *granted*—varies depending on how you gain access to the resource that the lease represents. For example, lookup service registrations are leased, so the process of registering a service causes a lease to be returned. Likewise, since event registrations are leased, asking for notifications returns a lease. In these situations, leases aren't ever created directly by the consumer of a lease—instead, they are created by the provider of the lease, and returned as a natural part of asking for access to a particular resource.

Both lookup and event registration mechanisms provide their own APIs that return leases, often bundled together with some other information about the registration. If you write a service that provides some resource to other services and wish to use leasing to control access to that resource, you can choose your own APIs for how the lease is returned to callers.

The Lease Interface

Here, assume that—through some means such as service or event registration—a lease has been returned to a consumer. Take a look at the basic `Lease` interface first.

```
package net.jini.lease;

import java.rmi.RemoteException;

public interface Lease {
```

```
long FOREVER = Long.MAX_VALUE;
long ANY = -1;

int DURATION = 1;
int ABSOLUTE = 2;

long getExpiration();
void cancel() throws UnknownLeaseException,
                            RemoteException;
void renew(long duration) throws LeaseDeniedException,
                            UnknownLeaseException,
                            RemoteException;
void setSerialFormat(int format);
int getSerialFormat();
LeaseMap createLeaseMap(long duration);
boolean canBatch(Lease lease);
}
```

The first thing to notice here is that `Lease` is an interface, not a class. In Jini, the `Lease` object that is returned to a caller is used to manage the lease. Invoking the remote methods on the `Lease` object causes messages to travel to the lease grantor (the service that controls the underlying resource) to update the grantor's notion of the lease's state. Some of the `Lease` methods are local accessors. The `getExpiration()` method, for instance, returns a value that is stored locally by the `Lease` object. It causes no communication between the lease grantor and the lease holder. The grantor's notion of the state of a lease is, ultimately, the "true" one, since the grantor is the entity that controls the underlying resource that the lease grants access to. The object returned to callers is merely a "proxy" that can be used to effect changes in the state of the grantor's internal lease representations. Figure 12–1 shows an illustration of this—the lease object held by a consumer is a proxy that's used to communicate with a lease grantor; the grantor maintains the actual resource and any information it uses to track the status of leases.

Lease grantors decide how they will communicate with the `Lease` proxy objects that they return to callers. This is why `Lease` is an interface and not a class—different lease grantors may use different mechanisms for communication between the `Lease` proxy objects handed out to callers and themselves. One implementation might use RMI, another might use raw TCP/IP sockets, and a third might use CORBA. But whatever type is actually returned to callers, it must implement the `Lease` interface defined here.

The interface defines a number of constants that can be useful when managing leases. The FOREVER token can be used to indicate that the requestor wishes a

Figure 12–1   *Leases are proxies for communication with grantors*

lease granted in perpetuity. Most lease grantors will be unwilling to grant such a lease, as it circumvents the nice "fail and forget" properties that Jini promotes. If a requestor does receive such a lease, however, it should be very conscientious about canceling the lease when it has finished with it.

The ANY token indicates that a requestor is asking for a lease of any duration. Usually this will result in the grantor's default lease duration being assigned.

I'll skip the next two constants, DURATION and ABSOLUTE, for now, and come back to them when I talk about serialized formats for leases.

Determining When a Lease Expires

The first method in the interface, getExpiration(), returns the expiration time of the lease. The return value is a long, representing the number of milliseconds since the start of "Java time" (January 1, 1970). You'll note that this value is an absolute one. Even though leases are requested in terms of relative time durations, the getExpiration() method returns expirations in terms of absolute time as a convenience to the programmer: You can very easily call

`System.currentTimeMillis()` to check the current clock against the expiration time of the lease.

The fact that the method expresses time in terms of absolute expirations, rather than durations, doesn't circumvent the desirable properties of using durations in leasing. Durations are still transmitted over the wire when requesting leases and doing lease management. But, leases will convert durations into absolute times for convenience. This is a local-only operation that is not affected by any differences in machine clocks.

Canceling a Lease

The `cancel()` method does just what its name suggests—it cancels the lease represented by the `Lease` object. A lease that is explicitly canceled has the same effect as a lease that expires through neglect: the resource that the lease grants access to is freed, and possibly made available for others to use. In general, you should not call `cancel()` on a lease that has already expired, as this simply makes extra work for the lease grantor, and increases network traffic.

You'll note that `cancel()` can raise two exceptions. The first, `Remote-Exception`, is raised if the `Lease` object has trouble communicating with the lease grantor. Remember that the `Lease` object is used for manipulating state in the lease grantor; so, methods like `cancel()` must cause some message to be sent to the grantor in order to cancel the lease. The second exception, `UnknownLeaseEx-ception`, means that the grantor does not know about the lease represented by the `Lease` object you hold. Most likely this will happen when a lease expires automatically, and yet you still hold the `Lease` object representing it and try to call `cancel()` on it. Lease grantors are free (and encouraged) to clean up all remnants of expired leases. If you hold on to a reference to the `Lease` object representing this lease longer than the grantor does, you can get this exception. Most often it indicates an error in your lease management logic.

Renewing a Lease

The `renew()` method is used to renew an already granted lease. The parameter to this method is the duration, in milliseconds, of the desired lease. If the grantor grants this renewal, the specified duration here will become the *new* lease duration—it is not added to whatever time is left on the old duration.

The `renew()` method returns no value to its caller. Instead, after the method contacts the lease grantor to request a new expiration time, the method will update the locally cached expiration field to reflect the new expiration time. This new value is available through the `getExpiration()` method of the `Lease` object as soon as `renew()` returns. If, for some reason, the grantor decides to deny the request entirely, then the `LeaseDeniedException` is raised. If this happens, the original lease duration remains intact and will expire at whatever point in the future it originally would have. Like `cancel()`, `renew()` may raise `RemoteException` if communication with the grantor fails, or `UnknownLease-Exception` if the grantor no longer knows about the lease represented by this `Lease` object.

Ensuring That Leases are Serialized Correctly

The next set of methods are used to control how a `Lease` object is serialized. Leases are commonly serialized for two reasons. The first is when a `Lease` is transmitted across machines. If a `Lease` is used as a parameter or a return value in an RMI call, it is serialized—written out as a sequence of bytes—sent over the wire, and then reconstituted into a complete `Lease` object at the other end.

The second case is when a service needs to record its persistent state. Services may "checkpoint" themselves from time to time, so that if they crash, they can recover the information that they once held. They may also become inactive for a period of time (typically using the Java RMI activation mechanisms), particularly if they only need to do work infrequently. In this case, a service may wish to write the `Lease` objects it holds to persistent storage as well as any other important state it needs to maintain.

Whenever a `Lease` is transmitted between two machines via serialization, you need to make sure that the lease expiration time is sent as a duration, rather than an absolute value. This is because you cannot guarantee that the clocks of the two machines are in sync, and is exactly the case that was discussed earlier in this chapter.

But what happens when you need to save a `Lease` to persistent storage for later retrieval on the *same* machine? If you write those `Leases` to disk in such a way that their expiration times are saved as durations, you are in trouble when you read them back. Suppose that you save your `Leases` to disk, go inactive for a period of time, and then wake up and recover the saved data. The expiration times for the `Leases` are now expressed as a duration relative to the last time the program ran. To make sense of these times, you'd also need to store the times at which the `Leases` were granted and do some math to figure out how to normalize the times. This is a lot of extra work, and introduces the potential for errors. The problem would be a lot simpler if, when storing `Leases` for later use on the same machine, you could just tell them to write themselves as absolute times.

This is where the `setSerialForm()` and `getSerialForm()` methods come in. These methods are used to ensure that `Lease` objects have the correct behavior whenever they are serialized, either for transmission to another machine or for persistence on the same machine.

The `Lease` interface provides two constants that can be used as arguments to `setSerialForm()` and are returned as results from `getSerialForm()`. The `DURATION` value is used to indicate that, when serialized, the `Lease` should be written in a form so that times are expressed as durations rather than absolute expirations. This value should be used whenever a `Lease` is to be sent to a different machine on the network, and is the default for all `Lease`s. The value of the constant `ABSOLUTE` is used to indicate that whenever a `Lease` object is serialized, its expiration time should be represented as an absolute time, not a duration. This value should be used whenever a `Lease` is serialized for writing to persistent storage for later retrieval on the same machine.

Batching Leases for Performance

In many cases, a resource consumer will have to manage many leases at the same time. For example, a service may have several lookup service registrations, may be registered to receive multiple event notifications, and may have leases on other types of resources owned by other entities.

The `Lease` APIs provide the foundation for *batching* lease operations together to make lease management more efficient, in terms of computation required to do lease management, network bandwidth required for doing lease updates, and programmer effort required to write lease management code.

In lease batching, a number of leases are grouped together using a data structure called a `LeaseMap`, and can all be renewed or canceled at the same time. This permits easier lease management and can drastically cut down on the network traffic required to do renewals or cancellations—if leases are managed individually, each will require a separate round-trip message to the lease grantor to renew or cancel it.

Not all leases held by a lease consumer can be batched, however. `LeaseMap`s are designed to group together only the `Lease` objects held by a consumer that *can* be batched together. Typically, this means that a `LeaseMap` can only contain `Lease`s that originated from the same lease grantor. `Lease`s that come from different grantors each need to talk to their particular grantor in order to do renewals or cancellations, and each of these `Lease` objects may use a different protocol to talk back to the grantor.

Because of these constraints, not all leases can be batched together into a `LeaseMap`. In fact, the decision about whether two `Lease` objects can be batched together depends on the particular implementation of the `Lease` that is in use; some `Lease`s may support batching in some circumstances, others may not.

The `Lease` interface has two methods to support lease batching: `create-LeaseMap()` and `canBatch()`. The `canBatch()` method is used to determine whether an object from a particular `Lease` implementation can be batched with another `Lease` object. The method returns a boolean indicating whether batching is possible; if batching is possible, then these two `Lease` objects can coexist in the same `LeaseMap` for efficiency.

Typically, a `Lease` implementation that supports batching will return `true` from `canBatch()` if the argument `Lease` uses the same implementation and communicates back to the same lease grantor. Smarter implementations could, in theory anyway, batch with `Leases` of other implementations.

The `createLeaseMap()` method creates a new `LeaseMap` object, initialized to contain the `Lease` instance on which the method was called. The argument to the method associates a duration in milliseconds with that particular `Lease` object. Each `Lease` added to the map will have its own duration associated with it; whenever the `Leases` in the `LeaseMap` are all renewed together, a renewal request will be made for each `Lease` using its associated duration.

The LeaseMap Interface

Now take a look at the API provided by the `LeaseMap` interface:

```
package net.jini.lease;

import java.rmi.RemoteException;

public interface LeaseMap extends java.util.Map {
    boolean canContainKey(Object key);
    void renewAll() throws LeaseMapException,
                            RemoteException;
    void cancelAll() throws LeaseMapException,
                            RemoteException;
}
```

`LeaseMap` extends the `java.util.Map` interface, part of the Java 2 collections library. A `Map` is much like a hash table, and provides a way to associate keys with values; any key can exist only once in the map. Since `LeaseMap` extends `Map`, all the usual `Map` methods for adding and removing key-value pairs from the object are available here. Check out the documentation for the Java 2 `Map` class for all the basic details of how this form of associative collection works.

The `LeaseMap` maintains an association between keys which are `Lease` objects and values which are objects of class `Long`. These `Longs` are the desired duration for the `Lease`. Whenever the `Leases` in the map are renewed, the map will attempt to renew each `Lease` for its associated duration.

The `LeaseMap` will ensure that any `Lease` you attempt to add to it is compatible with the other `Leases` already there. That is, it will verify that any `Lease` whose addition is requested can be batched with the `Leases` already in the map. If you try to add a `Lease` that cannot be batched with the other `Leases` in a `LeaseMap`, an `IllegalArgumentException` will be raised. So you should be prepared to catch this exception, or—even better—check that the `Lease` can be added before you try. The method `canContainKey()` is used to determine whether a candidate `Lease` would be compatible with the other `Leases` in a `LeaseMap`.

The usual `Map` methods for adding key-value pairs will also raise an `IllegalArgumentException` if you try to add in a key which is not a `Lease` or a value which is not a `Long`.

Once you've added your `Leases` to your `LeaseMap`, you can efficiently control all of them at once using the `renewAll()` and `cancelAll()` methods. Calling `renewAll()` will attempt to renew all the `Lease` objects in the `LeaseMap` for the duration associated with each. If all the renewals are done successfully, then nothing is returned and control flow continues as normal. If, however, any of the renewals fail, those objects will be dropped from the `LeaseMap`. This is so that a renewal failure will not cause repeated failures in the future when `renewAll()` is again called on the `LeaseMap`. In this case, a `LeaseMapException` will be raised. This exception contains all the `Leases` for which renewal failed. The program can then take steps to deal with the failure, most likely by letting the leases expire, or scheduling a retry for sometime in the future—which are the standard strategies to take when a single `Lease` renewal is denied.

The `cancelAll()` method works in much the same way as `renewAll()`: The method attempts to cancel all `Leases` in the `LeaseMap`. If the operation completes successfully, nothing is returned and the program continues as normal. If any of the cancellations fail, however, they are removed from the `LeaseMap` and a `LeaseMapException` is raised which contains the failed cancellations. In this case, a program may either let the `Lease` objects involved in the failed cancellation expire on their own, or may attempt to retry the cancellation at some point in the future.

Now look at a portion of the `LeaseMapException` class to see how to extract bad `Leases` from it:

```
package net.jini.lease;

import java.util.Map;
```

```
public class LeaseMapException extends LeaseException {
      public Map exceptionMap;

      // ... other methods and constructor elided ...
}
```

The `LeaseMapException` class has a public member, called `exceptionMap`, which is a `Map` containing all the `Leases` involved in a failed renewal or cancellation operation. Since this member is publicly accessible, you can just poke around in the contained `Map` to see where the problems are.

The keys in this `Map` are the `Lease` objects involved in failed operations. The values are the `Exceptions` that were raised when the renewal or cancellation was attempted. By using the `Exception` associated with each `Lease`, a program can make a determination about what caused the failure, how to proceed, and how to report the failure to a user.

Higher Level APIs for Lease Consumers

Chapter 5 presented a version of the "Hello, World" example that was enhanced to use leasing. Clearly, managing the leases used by that simple application was a big part of the programming there. In the case of that trivially simple service, leasing consumed a big fraction of the total number of code lines.

Fortunately, the work that programmers have to do to manage leases is pretty mechanical. A set of leases is acquired and remembered and, for most services, these leases will be held for as long as the service lasts. This is because the leases typically represent things like lookup service registrations, which most services want to maintain indefinitely. There's not a lot of fine-grained juggling of leases in most applications.

These characteristics of application behavior lend themselves well to library code that can handle the chores of lease management. In the last section, you learned about the "foundation" level APIs for leasing, because it's important to understand the groundwork on which higher level APIs are based. In the next few sections, you'll see some examples of common leasing idioms, and see how these can be expressed in helpful, higher level lease management tools that developers can use.

The first of these tools is provided by Jini itself, and you've already seen some examples of it in previous chapters. It's called the `LeaseRenewalManager`, and it can offload some of the leasing chores from applications. In this section, you'll explore the `LeaseRenewalManager`. A bit later, you'll see how to create and use completely external third-party services to handle leasing.

The `net.jini.lease` package defines a handful of classes that are ready-to-use for lease management. The most important of these is the `LeaseRenewalManager`. The `LeaseRenewalManager` is a class that can manage the renewals for whole sets of leases. The basic programming paradigm is that you create a `LeaseRenewalManager` and give it leases to manage. Whenever you pass it a lease, you also tell it how long the lease should be held. At any point in the future, you can tell the `LeaseRenewalManager` to extend the expiration time on the lease, remove the lease from the set of managed leases, or cancel the lease.

You may be asking yourself, "So what does this buy me? I've still got to figure out how long my leases should be for, and ask the `LeaseRenewalManager` to renew them for me. I'm doing the same work, only I'm talking to this new class, rather than a generic lease object." The big difference between using a `LeaseRenewalManager` and handling "raw" leases by yourself is that you typically ask the `LeaseRenewalManager` for lease expiration times that are *far* longer than a normal lease grantor would provide as a lease duration. The `LeaseRenewalManager` takes care of repeatedly contacting the grantor and renewing the leases, no matter what actual duration the grantor was willing to give for a single duration. So you can ask a `LeaseRenewalManager` for a lease of days, weeks, or even years. It will dutifully continue renewing the lease at whatever duration it can get until the time expires, or you tell the manager to drop the lease.

The fact that you can ask for long leases does not violate the self-healing properties of Jini, because the `LeaseRenewalManager` itself will deal with the shorter leases that services grant. And, if the JVM containing your service terminates, it will bring down the `LeaseRenewalManager` as well. So the failure behavior is the same whether or not you use this class—there's a "window" of error during which an unexpired lease may exist for a client that has gone away.

If a lease cannot be renewed by the `LeaseRenewalManager`, it will call out to a listener that can decide what to do—clean up any state that may be lingering around in the lease consumer, pop up a message to the user, and so on. Users of the `LeaseRenewalManager` can have listeners on a lease-by-lease basis—each lease can have its own listener, so you can use different listeners for, say, leases for event registrations and leases for service registrations. Lease listeners should implement the `LeaseListener` interface, which includes one method, called `notify()`, which receives a `LeaseRenewalEvent` whenever a lease expires.

You've seen the use of the `LeaseRenewalManager` a number of times in the preceding chapters, so here I'll focus on the APIs for the classes you need to use to work with the `LeaseRenewalManager`.

First, look at the `LeaseRenewalManager` itself:

```
package net.jini.lease;

import net.jini.core.lease.Lease;
import net.jini.core.lease.UnknownLeaseException;
import java.rmi.RemoteException;

public class LeaseRenewalManager {
    public LeaseRenewalManager();
    public LeaseRenewalManager(Lease lease,
                        long expiration,
                        LeaseListener listener);

    public void renewFor(Lease lease,
                        long desiredDuration,
                        LeaseListener listener);
    public void renewFor(Lease lease,
                        long desiredDuration,
                        long renewDuration,
                        LeaseListener listener);

    public void renewUntil(Lease lease,
                        long desiredExpiration,
                        LeaseListener listener);
    public void renewUntil(Lease lease,
                        long desiredExpiration,
                        long renewDuration,
                        LeaseListener listener);

    public long getExpiration(Lease lease)
                        throws UnknownLeaseException;
    public void setExpiration(Lease lease,
                            long desiredExpiration)
                        throws UnknownLeaseException;
    public void remove(Lease lease)
                        throws UnknownLeaseException;
    public void cancel(Lease lease)
                        throws UnknownLeaseException,
                            RemoteException;
    public void clear();
}
```

A new `LeaseRenewalManager` can be created "empty" (meaning that it manages no leases initially), or it can be created with a single initial lease to manage.

In the form of the constructor that takes a lease, you see that the call also takes an expiration time (expressed in milliseconds, as you might expect), as well as a `LeaseListener` that will be associated with this lease and will be notified if a request for renewal is ever denied. Using this second form of the constructor is equivalent to creating an empty `LeaseRenewalManager` and then calling `renewUntil()` to add a lease to it.

The `renewFor()` and `renewUntil()` methods are the ways to add new leases to the set of managed leases. These calls work exactly the same, except that `renewFor()` takes a long indicating a duration from the present time, and `renewUntil()` takes a long indicating an absolute expiration time. (Both of these calls still result in relative durations being sent to the lease grantor; the call that takes an absolute expiration time is simply for programmer convenience.)

Core Alert: There's a bug in renewFor() in Jini 1.0

If you're still using the initial release of Jini, version 1.0, you should be aware that this version contains a bug in the implementation of `renewFor()`. *The* `renewFor()` *method doesn't test for overflow, so if someone inputs the value* `Lease.FOREVER` *(or another large value), overflow will occur because* `renewFor()` *adds the duration input to the current time. This problem doesn't exist in* `renewUntil()`.

The bug was fixed in version 1.0.1 and later releases, which is yet another fine reason to upgrade if you're still using version 1.0.

When a lease is added to the managed set, it will be continuously renewed until the requested expiration time passes, the lease cannot be renewed by its grantor, or it is explicitly canceled or removed from the managed set. If you try to add an already managed lease, the lease will be removed and then added back to the set. This may be useful if you change some parameter of a lease, or renew it "manually" without going through the `LeaseRenewalManager`; adding the lease again gives the manager a chance to refresh its sense of when it should wake up to renew the lease. If you happen to pass in an expiration time that is sooner than the current expiration time, then the current expiration time is not changed.

Note that there are two versions each of `renewFor()` and `renewUntil()`. The versions with the `renewDuration` parameter allow you to specify the duration that will be requested from the original lease grantor, each time the `LeaseRenewalManager` contacts it to renew the lease. You can pass `Lease.ANY` to these methods to have the grantor use it's "default" renewal time. In the versions of these methods without the `renewDuration` parameter, `Lease.ANY` is the default requested renewal duration.

One very common idiom that is used by most clients and services is to continually renew a lease until the program using the resource goes away. For example, a Jini service browser will typically want to continue to receive events until the user shuts the program down. If you only use the LeaseRenewalManager to ask for very long leases, you haven't actually saved yourself much work: You still have to be prepared to wake up and ask the LeaseRenewalManager to extend the leases for you.

Fortunately, when you add a lease using renewUntil(), you can pass the special token Lease.ANY. As you remember from the discussion of the "raw" leasing APIs, the ANY flag indicates that the grantor is free to grant a lease for any duration that is most convenient for it. Essentially, this is the grantor's "preferred" lease duration. In the context of the LeaseRenewalManager, passing this flag as the expiration time for your lease means that the lease will be *continually* renewed in whatever chunks the grantor sees fit to use, until the owner cancels it or the LeaseRenewalManager goes away (including when the JVM containing it exits). This is the way most applications will use the LeaseRenewalManager—they will use the special Lease.ANY flag to renew leases continually until they shut down. Note that you *cannot* pass this flag to renewFor(), which renews a lease for a requested duration. Or, more precisely, you *could* use Lease.ANY here, but it will be interpreted purely as a duration, not as a special flag to be used to indicate continuous renewal forever.

Core Note: What happens if you pass Lease.ANY to renewFor()?

The value of the ANY flag is actually –1, and renewFor() *computes an absolute time for renewal by adding the duration flag to the current time, as mentioned in the Core Alert earlier. So the end result of passing* Lease.ANY *to* renewFor() *is that you wind up with a lease that is set to expire one millisecond before now—not very useful.*

Confusing the renewFor() *and* renewUntil() *methods is a common mistake; it would be good if* renewFor() *complained if a user passed in* Lease.ANY *as a duration, but it doesn't.*

I'll quickly walk through the rest of the methods on the LeaseRenewalManager, which are, for the most part, self-explanatory.

Calling getExpiration() returns the *desired* expiration time that was associated with the lease through the LeaseRenewalManager. Note that this isn't the time that the lease's currently granted duration runs out—the LeaseRenewalManager hides this from you. The return value is the time you've asked the LeaseRenewalManager to stop automatically renewing the leases.

The `setExpiration()` method allows you to change the desired expiration time for a lease. Calling this method is equivalent to calling `renewUntil()` on a new lease. So, you can pass `Lease.ANY` to go into the same renew-forever mode that you get when you pass this flag to `renewUntil()`.

Both of the expiration times in these methods are expressed in milliseconds, represented as a long. And both may raise `UnknownLeaseException` if the lease that you're changing isn't known to its grantor for some reason; this may occur if you hold on to a lease outside the lease manager after it's already been canceled or has expired.

The `cancel()` method cancels a lease, if it was in the set of managed leases known to the `LeaseRenewalManager`. The lease is also removed from the set of managed leases. Calling `remove()` simply removes the lease from the set of managed leases, perhaps because a caller wishes to control a particular lease "by hand." And finally, `clear()` removes all leases from the managed set; it does not cancel them, however.

Internally, the `LeaseRenewalManager` creates a new thread that will wake up periodically to renew leases. It also tries to batch leases together into `LeaseMaps` wherever possible.

Let's look now at the way that listeners are notified when leases expire. There are two ways in which a lease might expire—either because there is a failure with renewal, and the desired expiration time cannot be met, or when the lease expires at its normal expiration time (when it "dies a natural death," if you will). The Jini leasing utilities define two listener interfaces for receiving notifications of these types of expiry. Each lease in a `LeaseRenewalManager` can have its own listener associated with it, so you can determine on a lease-by-lease basis whether—and why—a lease has expired.

The first interface is the `LeaseListener` interface. Listeners that implement this interface will only be called when a lease expires "early" because of a renewal failure:

```
package net.jini.lease;

import java.util.EventListener;

public interface LeaseListener extends EventListener {
    public void notify(LeaseRenewalEvent ev);
}
```

A `LeaseListener` need only implement one method, `notify()`. This method will be called with a `LeaseRenewalEvent` as a parameter whenever a lease expires early or cannot be renewed. By the time this method is invoked, the

`LeaseRenewalManager` will have already removed the expired lease from its set of managed leases.

The second interface is called `DesiredExpirationListener`. This is a sub-interface of `LeaseListener`, and will be called whenever a lease expires "naturally," because it has reached it's desired expiration time:

```
package net.jini.lease;

public interface DesiredExpirationListener
        extends LeaseListener {
        void expirationReached(LeaseRenewalEvent ev);
}
```

Note that because `DesiredExpirationListener` is a subinterface of `LeaseListener`, your implementations of it will receive notifications when a lease expires naturally and, via the `notify()` method declared in `LeaseListener`, when a lease expires early. Like `notify()`, the `expirationReached()` method receives a `LeaseRenewalEvent` when natural expiration occurs. Also like `notify()`, when `expirationReached()` is called, the newly-expired lease will already have been removed from the set of leases managed by the `LeaseRenewalManager`.

These two listener interfaces allow you to be informed of any expiry in the leases managed by the `LeaseRenewalManager`, whether expected or unexpected.

Next, let's look at the `LeaseRenewalEvent` class, which defines the event type that will be received by both these listeners:

```
package net.jini.lease;

import java.util.EventObject;
import net.jini.core.lease.Lease;

public class LeaseRenewalEvent extends EventObject {
        // ... some details elided ...
        public Throwable getException();
        public long getExpiration();
        public Lease getLease();
}
```

Since `LeaseRenewalEvent` extends the standard Java `EventObject`, it inherits a `getSource()` method from there that will return the `LeaseRenewalManager` that resulted in this event being sent. The `getExpiration()` method returns the original desired expiration time that was requested of the

`LeaseRenewalManager` for the now-defunct lease; the `getLease()` method returns the lease itself. Finally, `getException()` returns an exception that explains why the lease renewal failed. If the lease was denied, this will be a `net.jini.core.lease.LeaseDeniedException`; if the lease expired unnaturally, the exception may be `net.jini.core.lease.UnknownLease-Exception`, `java.rmi.RemoteException`, or null. Note that if the lease expires naturally—meaning at its desired expiration time—then there is no exception, and the `getException()` method returns null.

Because the `LeaseRenewalManager` does such a fine job of handling leases, most lease users will never use the low-level APIs. But by seeing the example in Chapter 5 of how these low-level APIs work, you've got a solid understanding of how the `LeaseRenewalManager` works internally.

A Leasing Service

The `LeaseRenewalManager` is an example of how a generic class can satisfy leasing on behalf of an application—as a lease user, you can simply pass your leases to the manager and forget about them.

There are other ways you could imagine delegating lease behavior. Jini's leasing mechanisms are flexible enough that they can support *third-party leasing*, which means that a completely external entity, outside the lease owner's JVM, can take care of leasing for you. Essentially, you delegate the chore of lease management to a process running outside your address space.

This section presents an example of just such an entity, which here is implemented as a complete Jini service, called the `LeaseService`. The `LeaseService` registers itself in Jini communities and makes its facilities available to all parties on the network; the service can be shared by any number of other services and can perform the leasing operations for all of them. This strategy is useful for services that will be inactive for long periods of time (and therefore will be unable to do their own lease management without waking up continually), but still wish to hold on to leases. It may also be useful for small devices that have very limited computational ability or bandwidth, but tend to be always connected to the network.

While delegating lease renewals to an external process makes good sense in many settings, there are some downsides to the strategy as well. After I walk through the implementation of the lease renewal service, I'll discuss some of the pros and cons of using a facility like this.

Core Note: Jini 1.1 provides the "norm" leasing service

When I originally wrote the first edition of this book, there was no leasing service in Jini. One of the additions in Jini 1.1, however, was a full-fledged leasing service, provided by Sun, called "norm."

If you have need of a real leasing service, I encourage you to use the Sun-provided one, and not the version I'll present here. Norm has a much more industrial-strength implementation, and—because it ships as a standard part of Jini—will be common on many networks. Chapter 19 in this book covers norm, as well as two other important "infrastructure" services that appeared with Jini 1.1.

While I don't encourage you to use this leasing service in a production environment, I have kept this example for the second edition of Core Jini because I feel that the example illustrates a number of important issues in leasing and in building and using lease services. What you learn here should serve you well as you build other Jini services, and should help you know what to expect when you use norm.

An Overview of a Leasing Service

A leasing service is a complete, stand-alone Jini service that exposes callable methods to other Jini services and applications. In this case, the methods that are exposed help a program to delegate the management of its leases.

The `LeaseRenewalManager` has a well-crafted API that makes the task of delegating the management of leases within a JVM an easy task. So, for the example leasing service that you'll see here, I'll keep the same basic "look and feel" of the interfaces: Callers will be able to add new leases to the set of managed leases, using both relative durations and absolute expiration times; callers can cancel and remove leases from the set; and callers can receive notification via a listener mechanism when leases expire prematurely.

There are some niceties of the `LeaseRenewalManager` API that will take some work to preserve in this new, remote setting, however. In particular, even though the "wire" format of leases is always a duration, the `LeaseRenewal-Manager` allows lease times to be specified in either relative durations or absolute expiration times. This works great because the owner of the lease and the `Lease-RenewalManager` are running on the same machine—they will both see the system clock, and therefore, they can easily convert from absolute to relative times as needed by simply adding or subtracting the current time.

Such is not the case with a remote lease manager, though. If a client asks for an absolute expiration time, this needs to be converted into a relative duration for transmission to the remote manager. Once there, it can be converted into whatever the *manager's* sense of absolute time is. This is because you cannot guarantee that both the client and the lease service have the same sense of absolute time, so working with relative durations is the only way to approach an accurate lease time.

I'll also have to make a few other changes to the basic `LeaseRenewalManager` API. For example, all the methods that callers use to manage leases will now need to raise `RemoteException` since they involve going "over the wire" to a remote process. For the remote lease service to call back to clients to deliver lease expiration events when their leases expire prematurely, lease listeners will have to be remotely callable objects.

With these considerations in mind, it's time to begin to flesh out what a remote leasing service might look like. The client-side API should look as close to the `LeaseRenewalManager` as possible; this will be the API that's implemented by the service proxy object that clients use. It will be essentially identical to the methods available on `LeaseRenewalManager` except for the raising of `RemoteExceptions`. The proxy object will communicate with the back-end leasing service using a private protocol that handles the translation to and from relative and absolute times. And, clients that wish to receive events when their leases expire early will need to implement a special remote version of the `LeaseListener` interface.

Remote Leasing APIs

I'll start off by talking about the APIs for the service. You'll see both the client-side API (that is, the API supported by the service proxy object as shown in Listing 12–1), as well as the remote interface that's used for communication between the proxy and the back-end part of the service as shown in Listing 12–2.

Listing 12–1 `LeaseRenewalService.java`

```java
// Interface for the proxy -- clientside api.

package corejini.chapter12;

import net.jini.core.lease.Lease;
import net.jini.core.lease.UnknownLeaseException;
import net.jini.core.event.RemoteEventListener;
import java.rmi.RemoteException;

public interface LeaseRenewalService  {
    public void renewUntil(Lease lease, long expiration,
                           RemoteEventListener listener)
                   throws RemoteException;
    public void renewFor(Lease lease, long duration,
                         RemoteEventListener listener)
                   throws RemoteException;
    public void clear() throws RemoteException;
    public void remove(Lease lease) throws RemoteException,
                           UnknownLeaseException;
    public void cancel(Lease lease) throws RemoteException,
                           UnknownLeaseException;
    public long getExpiration(Lease lease)
                   throws RemoteException,
                           UnknownLeaseException;
    public void setExpiration(Lease lease, long expiration)
                   throws RemoteException,
                           UnknownLeaseException;
}
```

The `LeaseRenewalService` interface is the API that the service proxy will implement, and that clients will use to interact with the leasing service. This API is designed—intentionally—to reflect as closely as possible the interfaces of the `LeaseRenewalManager`. Since, unlike the `LeaseRenewalManager`, this interface provides access to remote leasing agents, all the methods are declared to raise `RemoteException` since they can fail in various network-oriented ways. Other than this, the API is largely the same as that of the local-only leasing manager; the only other significant difference is that I've omitted the versions of `renewFor()` and `renewUtil()` that take the `renewDuration` parameter, for brevity.

Take a look now at the interface that the proxy will use for communication with the back-end portion of the service. This interface defines the remote protocol that the back-end part of the service speaks.

Listing 12–2 `RemoteLeaseRenewer.java`

```java
// Defines the remote (RMI) protocol between the proxy and
// the back end.

package corejini.chapter12;

import net.jini.admin.Administrable;
import net.jini.core.lease.Lease;
import net.jini.core.lease.UnknownLeaseException;
import net.jini.core.event.RemoteEventListener;
import java.rmi.Remote;
import java.rmi.RemoteException;

public interface RemoteLeaseRenewer
        extends Remote, Administrable {
    public void renewAny(Lease lease,
                        RemoteEventListener listener)
        throws RemoteException;
    public void renewFor(Lease lease, long duration,
                        RemoteEventListener listener)
        throws RemoteException;
    public void clear() throws RemoteException;
    public void remove(Lease lease) throws RemoteException,
        UnknownLeaseException;
    public void cancel(Lease lease) throws RemoteException,
        UnknownLeaseException;
    public long getRemainingDuration(Lease lease)
        throws RemoteException, UnknownLeaseException;
    public void setRemainingDuration(Lease lease,
                                    long expiration)
        throws RemoteException, UnknownLeaseException;
}
```

You'll note that the protocol defined here is very *similar*, but not exactly the *same*, as the client interface. Instead of a `renewUntil()` interface, here you see a `renewAny()`. And, `getExpiration()` and `setExpiration()` are replaced by `getRemainingDuration()` and `setRemainingDuration()`.

The reason for these differences is that the remote protocol used for communication between the proxy and the service must *only* traffic in relative durations. You can expose the *appearance* of absolute time in the proxy but, whenever you send lease times out across the wire, you must convert them into relative times for the reasons mentioned before.

For most client-side uses of `renewUntil()`, you can simply convert the absolute time passed there into a duration and send that to the service using `renewFor()`. However, recall that one of the uses of `renewUntil()` is to support the perpetually renewing behavior that passing an expiration time of `Lease.ANY` indicates. Since this is a special-case behavior that `renewFor()` doesn't support, here I've added a special `renewAny()` that specifically turns on this behavior. Likewise, `getRemainingDuration()` and `setRemainingDuration()` do simple conversions to and from absolute and relative time.

This interface is defined as a remote interface—by virtue of the fact that it extends `Remote`—which means that the proxy object and the back-end service will communicate using RMI. The interface also extends `Administrable`, so it provides a way for proxies to call back to the service to fetch an administration object for them.

Listing 12–3 shows the implementation of the proxy object that will mediate between these two APIs. You can think of this proxy as essentially a converter box that maps from the client-side interface to the wire protocol used to communicate with the back-end service.

Listing 12–3 `LeaseServiceProxy.java`

```
// This intentionally has nearly the same api as
// LeaseRenewalManager only here we raise remote
// exceptions.
//
// The reason we don't use the rmi stub for the
// leasing svc directly is that the proxy here must
// translate between absolute and relative time.
//
// The back-end methods traffic *only* in relative time.
//
package corejini.chapter12;
```

Listing 12–3 `LeaseServiceProxy.java` (continued)

```java
import net.jini.core.lease.Lease;
import net.jini.core.lease.UnknownLeaseException;
import net.jini.core.event.RemoteEventListener;
import net.jini.admin.Administrable;
import java.io.Serializable;
import java.rmi.RemoteException;

public class LeaseServiceProxy
        implements LeaseRenewalService,
                    Serializable, Administrable {
    protected RemoteLeaseRenewer backend;

    public LeaseServiceProxy(RemoteLeaseRenewer backend) {
        this.backend = backend;
    }

    public void renewUntil(Lease lease, long expiration,
                            RemoteEventListener listener)
        throws RemoteException {
        // Translate between time formats.
        if (expiration == Lease.ANY) {
            backend.renewAny(lease, listener);
        } else {
            long duration =
                expiration - System.currentTimeMillis();
            backend.renewFor(lease, duration, listener);
        }
    }

    public void renewFor(Lease lease, long duration,
                            RemoteEventListener listener)
        throws RemoteException {
        backend.renewFor(lease, duration, listener);
    }

    public void clear() throws RemoteException {
        backend.clear();
    }
```

Listing 12–3 LeaseServiceProxy.java (continued)

```java
public void remove(Lease lease) throws RemoteException,
    UnknownLeaseException {
    backend.remove(lease);
}

public void cancel(Lease lease) throws RemoteException,
        UnknownLeaseException {
    backend.cancel(lease);
}

public long getExpiration(Lease lease)
    throws RemoteException,
            UnknownLeaseException {
    // Translate between time formats
    long dur = backend.getRemainingDuration(lease);
    return System.currentTimeMillis() + dur;
}

public void setExpiration(Lease lease, long expiration)
    throws RemoteException, UnknownLeaseException {
    // Translate between time formats
    backend.setRemainingDuration(lease,
            expiration - System.currentTimeMillis());
}

public Object getAdmin() throws RemoteException {
    return backend.getAdmin();
}
}
```

When the proxy is created, it is passed a reference to an object that implements the back-end protocol; it will use this object to make calls on the service. The rest of the code here is pretty simple; in fact, most of the mappings between the client-side APIs and the server-side APIs are simple "pass throughs," meaning that there is no special conversion to be done.

Only the methods noted earlier have anything special to do. The renewUntil() method checks its parameters to see if Lease.ANY was passed to it. If it was, then the code maps the method invocation into renewAny() on the server; otherwise, it calculates a duration by subtracting the current time from the requested expiration time, and calls renewFor() on the server. Likewise, getExpiration() and setExpiration() convert to and from the absolute expiration times that are used locally and the durations that must be sent over the wire; these methods call getRemainingDuration() and setRemainingDuration(), respectively.

Note that the proxy shown here implements Administrable by calling back to the remote leasing service. The remote service will return an object that can be used for administration.

Events and Listeners for Remote Leasing

The classes and interfaces used for delivering leasing events from the Lease-RenewalManager will not work in the remote case—LeaseListener is not a remote interface, so listeners cannot be called from JVMs on remote machines, and LeaseRenewalEvent provides a local LeaseRenewalManager as its source, which is not useful in the remote case.

So, the program here will need some new interfaces and classes for dealing with remote leasing services. And, just like the interfaces for LeaseRenewalService, I'll try to stay as close to the semantics of the existing classes as possible.

First, look at a remote version of LeaseRenewalEvent, as shown in Listing 12–4.

Listing 12–4 RemoteLeaseRenewalEvent.java

```
// A subclass of RemoteEvent for lease events.

package corejini.chapter12;

import net.jini.core.lease.Lease;
import net.jini.core.event.RemoteEvent;
```

> **Listing 12–4** `RemoteLeaseRenewalEvent.java` (continued)

```java
public class RemoteLeaseRenewalEvent extends RemoteEvent {
    protected Lease lease;
    protected long expiration;
    protected Throwable throwable;

    public RemoteLeaseRenewalEvent(long eventID,
                                   long seqNum,
                                   LeaseRenewalService renewer,
                                   Lease lease,
                                   long expiration,
                                   Throwable throwable) {
        super(renewer, eventID, seqNum, null);
        this.lease = lease;
        this.expiration = expiration;
        this.throwable = throwable;
    }
    public Lease getLease() {
        return lease;
    }
    public long getExpiration() {
        return expiration;
    }
    public Throwable getException() {
        return throwable;
    }
}
```

Here I've defined a new event class, which is a subclass of the Jini `RemoteEvent` class, as all good Jini remote events should be. Unfortunately, subclassing `LeaseRenewalEvent` is not really an option here—pragmatically, to initialize a `LeaseRenewalEvent` superclass, you'd have to pass in a `LeaseRenewalManager`, which you don't have in the remote case. Also, making `RemoteLeaseRenewalEvent` a subclass of `LeaseRenewalEvent` really says that the remote event is just a special case of the local event, which isn't exactly true—they're fundamentally different types of events that just happen to report similar occurrences.

All of the methods defined here return exactly the same values that they do in the local case, with one exception. The `getSource()` method, defined by the `EventObject` superclass of `RemoteEvent`, returns the `LeaseRenewalService` that caused the event to be fired, rather than the `LeaseRenewalManager` that's returned in the local case.

There are a few other details here that will be discussed more fully in Chapter 16 when I talk about remote events. For example, the constructor takes an "event ID" and a "sequence number," which are simply passed through to the superclass constructor. These values are used to allow clients to route and order events. For our purposes here, though, you can pretty much ignore them for the time being.

Since the `RemoteLeaseRenewalEvent` is a subclass of `RemoteEvent`, I can just use the regular Jini `RemoteEventListener` interface as the interface that receivers of these events will implement. So I don't need to create any new listener classes here. In other words, the Jini `RemoteEventListener` will become the remote analog of the local `LeaseListener` interface. Note that using `RemoteEventListener` implies that classes that implement it must be RMI server objects, which means that most likely, they will be subclasses of `java.rmi.server.UnicastRemoteObject`, so that they can receive the remote method invocation of `notify()`.

Leasing Service Implementation

Now that the interfaces and protocols used for communication have been defined, and the details of how events and listeners work have been decided, I'll focus on the construction of the actual leasing service (see Listing 12–5).

First and foremost, the code shown here *is* a Jini service. Much of the code is involved with creating a `JoinManager` to participate in discovery, and handling persistent state so that the service can recover itself after restarts or crashes.

Since the back-end service shown here needs to communicate via RMI with its proxies in various clients, it extends `UnicastRemoteObject` so that its implementations of the methods in `RemoteLeaseRenewer` can be called remotely.

The code in the service that actually implements lease management is fairly simple. All of the `RemoteLeaseRenewer` calls are implemented by calling out to our old friend, the local `LeaseRenewalManager`! The service essentially wraps up one of these and makes it available to any other services around the network via RMI.

Most of the rest of the code is concerned with two tasks. The first is mapping to and from local `LeaseListeners` (which are what the `LeaseRenewalManager` used by the implementation understands) and `RemoteEventListeners` (which are what clients provide to the service). The second is checkpointing lease information out to persistent storage whenever something changes (so that the code can recover the state of its leases after a crash), and recovering that checkpointed state after a restart.

Take a look at the code now:

Listing 12–5 `LeaseService.java`

```java
// A service back end to manage leases.

package corejini.chapter12;

import net.jini.core.lease.Lease;
import net.jini.core.lease.UnknownLeaseException;
import net.jini.core.event.RemoteEvent;
import net.jini.core.event.RemoteEventListener;
import net.jini.core.event.UnknownEventException;
import net.jini.core.discovery.LookupLocator;
import net.jini.core.lookup.ServiceID;
import net.jini.core.entry.Entry;
import net.jini.lookup.JoinManager;
import net.jini.lookup.ServiceIDListener;
import net.jini.discovery.LookupDiscoveryManager;
import net.jini.lease.LeaseRenewalManager;
import net.jini.lease.LeaseRenewalEvent;
import net.jini.lease.LeaseListener;
import java.rmi.RemoteException;
import java.rmi.RMISecurityManager;
import java.rmi.server.UnicastRemoteObject;
import java.util.HashMap;
import java.util.Iterator;
import java.io.File;
import java.io.Serializable;
import java.io.IOException;
import java.io.ObjectOutputStream;
import java.io.ObjectInputStream;
import java.io.FileOutputStream;
import java.io.FileInputStream;
```

Listing 12–5 `LeaseService.java` (continued)

```java
public class LeaseService  extends UnicastRemoteObject
    implements RemoteLeaseRenewer, ServiceIDListener {
    protected JoinManager joinMgr = null;
    protected LeaseRenewalManager leaseMgr =
        new LeaseRenewalManager();
    protected String storageLoc = null;
    protected LeaseRenewalService proxy;
    protected HashMap allLeases = new HashMap();
    protected File file = null;
    protected ServiceID serviceID = null;
    protected long eventID = 0;

    // Maps from local lease listeners to remote event
    // listeners
    class LeaseListenerConduit implements LeaseListener {
        RemoteEventListener remote;
        long eventID;
        long seqNum = 0;

        LeaseListenerConduit(RemoteEventListener remote,
                             long eventID) {
            this.remote = remote;
            this.eventID = eventID;
        }

        public void notify(LeaseRenewalEvent ev) {
            // Always remove the lease from
            // the set of leases
            allLeases.remove(ev.getLease());
            try {
                checkpoint();
            } catch (IOException ex) {
                System.err.println("Couldn't checkpoint " +
                                    storageLoc +
                                    ": " + ex.getMessage());
                System.err.println(
                    "Service not removed from storage.");
            }
```

Listing 12–5 `LeaseService.java` (continued)

```java
        try {
            if (remote != null) {
                remote.notify(remotify(ev, eventID,
                                       seqNum++));
            }
        } catch (RemoteException ex) {
            System.err.println(
                    "Couldn't notify remote listener: " +
                    ex.getMessage());
        } catch (UnknownEventException ex) {
            System.err.println("UnknownEvent: " +
                               ex.getMessage());
            remote = null;
        }
    }

    // Produce a RemoteLeaseRenewalEvent from a
    // local LeaseRenewalEvent.
    RemoteLeaseRenewalEvent remotify(
                            LeaseRenewalEvent ev,
                            long eventID,
                            long seqNum) {
        return new RemoteLeaseRenewalEvent(
                            eventID,
                            seqNum,
                            proxy,
                            ev.getLease(),
                            ev.getExpiration(),
                            ev.getException());
    }
}
```

Listing 12–5 `LeaseService.java` (continued)

```
// This is the state that we need to keep around to
// manage leases.
static class LeaseEntry implements Serializable {
    long expiration;
    RemoteEventListener listener;
    long id;    // ID to use when sending events

    LeaseEntry(long expiration,
               RemoteEventListener listener,
               long id) {
        this.expiration = expiration;
        this.listener = listener;
        this.id = id;
    }
}

// All of this service's persistent data...
static class LeaseServiceData implements Serializable {
    ServiceID id;
    Entry[] attrs;
    String[] groups;
    LookupLocator[] locs;
    HashMap leases;

    LeaseServiceData(ServiceID id,
                     Entry[] attrs, String[] groups,
                     LookupLocator[] locs,
                     HashMap leases) {
        this.id = id;
        this.attrs = attrs;
        this.groups = groups;
        this.locs = locs;
        this.leases = leases;
    }
}
```

Listing 12–5 `LeaseService.java` (continued)

```java
public LeaseService(String storageLoc)
    throws RemoteException, IOException,
    ClassNotFoundException {
    if (System.getSecurityManager() == null) {
        System.setSecurityManager(
                new RMISecurityManager());
    }

    this.storageLoc = storageLoc;

    proxy = new LeaseServiceProxy(this);

    file = new File(storageLoc);

    // If the file exists, treat this as a restart.
    // Otherwise, it's the first time the service has
    // been run.
    if (file.exists()) {
        restore();
    }

    // We'll use the "initial" form of the join manager
    // constructor if the file didn't exist or restore()
    // didn't work.
    if (joinMgr == null) {
        LookupDiscoveryManager luMgr =
          new LookupDiscoveryManager(new String[]{ "" },
                                     null,
                                     null);
        joinMgr = new JoinManager(proxy, null, this,
                                  luMgr, null);
    }
}
```

Listing 12–5 `LeaseService.java` (continued)

```java
protected void checkpoint() throws IOException {
    LeaseServiceData data;

    // Cycle through allLeases and chuck the ones that
    // have expired.
    Iterator keys = allLeases.keySet().iterator();
    while (keys.hasNext()) {
        Lease lease = (Lease) keys.next();
        LeaseEntry entry = (LeaseEntry)
                                allLeases.get(lease);
        if (entry.expiration >=
                System.currentTimeMillis())
            allLeases.remove(lease);
    }

    LookupDiscoveryManager luMgr =
        (LookupDiscoveryManager)
            joinMgr.getDiscoveryManager();
    data = new LeaseServiceData(serviceID,
                            joinMgr.getAttributes(),
                            luMgr.getGroups(),
                            luMgr.getLocators(),
                            allLeases);
    ObjectOutputStream out = new
        ObjectOutputStream(new FileOutputStream(file));

    out.writeObject(data);
    out.flush();
    out.close();
}
```

Listing 12–5 `LeaseService.java` (continued)

```java
protected void restore() throws IOException,
                                ClassNotFoundException {
    ObjectInputStream in = new
        ObjectInputStream(new FileInputStream(file));
    LeaseServiceData data = (LeaseServiceData)
                            in.readObject();

    if (data == null) {
        System.out.println(
            "No data in data file, although it exists.");
    } else {
        allLeases = data.leases;
        // fill the lease manager with the leases...
        Iterator iter = allLeases.keySet().iterator();
        while (iter.hasNext()) {
            Lease lease = (Lease) iter.next();
            LeaseEntry entry = (LeaseEntry)
                            allLeases.get(lease);

            if (entry.expiration >=
                    System.currentTimeMillis()) {
                allLeases.remove(lease);
                continue;
            }

            leaseMgr.renewUntil(lease, entry.expiration,
                LeaseListenerConduit(entry.listener,
                                    entry.id));

        }
        serviceID = data.id;
        LookupDiscoveryManager luMgr =
            new LookupDiscoveryManager(data.groups,
                                    data.locs,
                                    null);
        joinMgr = new JoinManager(proxy, data.attrs,
                                data.id, luMgr, null);
    }
}
```

Listing 12–5 `LeaseService.java` (continued)

```java
public void serviceIDNotify(ServiceID serviceID) {
    this.serviceID = serviceID;

    try {
        checkpoint();
    } catch (IOException ex) {
        System.err.println("Couldn't checkpoint to " +
                            storageLoc +
                            ": " + ex.getMessage());
        System.err.println("Service ID not saved.");
    }
}

// These are the methods of RemoteLeaseListener that
// our proxy will use to communicate with us.

public void renewAny(Lease lease,
                     RemoteEventListener listener)
    throws RemoteException {
    long id = eventID++;
    lease.setSerialFormat(Lease.ABSOLUTE);
    allLeases.put(lease,
                new LeaseEntry(Lease.ANY,
                                listener, id));

    try {
        checkpoint();
    } catch (IOException ex) {
        System.err.println("Couldn't checkpoint to " +
                            storageLoc +
                            ": " + ex.getMessage());
        System.err.println("New lease not saved.");
    }

    LeaseListenerConduit conduit =
        new LeaseListenerConduit(listener, id);

    leaseMgr.renewUntil(lease, Lease.ANY, conduit);
}
```

Listing 12–5 `LeaseService.java` (continued)

```
public void renewFor(Lease lease, long duration,
                     RemoteEventListener listener)
    throws RemoteException {
    long id = eventID++;
    lease.setSerialFormat(Lease.ABSOLUTE);
    allLeases.put(lease,
                  new LeaseEntry(duration +
                                 System.currentTimeMillis(),
                                 listener, id));

    try {
        checkpoint();
    } catch (IOException ex) {
        System.err.println("Couldn't checkpoint to " +
                           storageLoc +
                           ": " + ex.getMessage());
        System.err.println("New lease not saved.");
    }

    LeaseListenerConduit conduit =
        new LeaseListenerConduit(listener, id);

    leaseMgr.renewFor(lease, duration, conduit);
}

public void clear() throws RemoteException {
    allLeases.clear();

    try {
        checkpoint();
    } catch (IOException ex) {
        System.err.println("Couldn't checkpoint to " +
                           storageLoc +
                           ": " + ex.getMessage());
        System.err.println(
                    "Lease storage not cleared.");
    }

    leaseMgr.clear();
}
```

Listing 12–5 `LeaseService.java` (continued)

```java
public void remove(Lease lease) throws RemoteException,
    UnknownLeaseException {
    allLeases.remove(lease);

    try {
        checkpoint();
    } catch (IOException ex) {
        System.err.println("Couldn't checkpoint to " +
                            storageLoc +
                            ": " + ex.getMessage());
        System.err.println(
                "Lease not removed from storage.");
    }

    leaseMgr.remove(lease);
}
public void cancel(Lease lease) throws RemoteException,
    UnknownLeaseException {
    allLeases.remove(lease);

    try {
        checkpoint();
    } catch (IOException ex) {
        System.err.println("Couldn't checkpoint to " +
                            storageLoc +
                            ": " + ex.getMessage());
        System.err.println(
                "Lease not removed from storage.");
    }

    leaseMgr.cancel(lease);
}


// Note the absolute/relative time conversions.
public long getRemainingDuration(Lease lease)
    throws RemoteException,
            UnknownLeaseException {
    long expiration = leaseMgr.getExpiration(lease);
    return expiration - System.currentTimeMillis();
}
```

Listing 12–5 `LeaseService.java` (continued)

```java
public void setRemainingDuration(Lease lease,
                                 long duration)
    throws RemoteException, UnknownLeaseException {
    LeaseEntry entry = (LeaseEntry)
                        allLeases.get(lease);
    long expiration = System.currentTimeMillis() +
                      duration;

    if (entry != null) {
        entry.expiration = expiration;
        allLeases.put(lease, entry);
    }

    try {
        checkpoint();
    } catch (IOException ex) {
        System.err.println("Couldn't checkpoint to " +
                            storageLoc +
                            ": " + ex.getMessage());
        System.err.println(
            "Lease expiration not updated in storage.");
    }

    leaseMgr.setExpiration(lease, expiration);
}

// For now, don't return an administration object.
public Object getAdmin() {
    return null;
}
```

Listing 12–5 `LeaseService.java` (continued)

```java
public static void main(String[] args) {
    if (args.length != 1) {
        System.err.println(
                "Usage: LeaseService <storage_loc>");
        System.exit(1);
    }

    try {
        LeaseService src = new LeaseService(args[0]);
        while (true) {
            try {
                Thread.sleep(Long.MAX_VALUE);
            } catch (InterruptedException ex) {
            }
        }
    } catch (Exception ex) {
        System.out.println("trouble: " +
                            ex.getMessage());
        ex.printStackTrace();
    }
}
}
```

This is a rather involved piece of code, so I'll start from the top. The `Lease-Service` is an application—meaning it has a `main()` to start it—that extends `UnicastRemoteObject`, because some of its methods will be callable remotely; implements `RemoteLeaseRenewer`, because this is the way that its proxies will communicate with it; and implements `ServiceIDListener`, because it needs to know its ID so that it can save it to persistent storage.

I'll first discuss how the service starts up, how it checkpoints itself to persistent storage, and how it resumes after a restart. The `main()` here takes a single parameter on the command line—the location of the service's persistent storage. If the indicated file does not exist, then the service assumes that this is the first time it is being run, and will use the `JoinManager` to retrieve a fresh `ServiceID` for it. If the file *does* exist, then the service assumes that it is being restarted after a crash or other shutdown. The constructor for `LeaseService` calls `restore()` if the file exists. If the file doesn't exist, or if for some reason `restore()` doesn't create a `JoinManager`, the constructor creates a `JoinManager` using the "initial" form of the constructor and sets its instance up as the `ServiceIDListener` so that the `LeaseService` can be informed when an ID is assigned to it.

The constructor also creates the proxy for the service, which is just an instance of the `LeaseServiceProxy` class you saw earlier. This instance is initialized by passing it a handle to the `LeaseService`, which is the way the proxy will communicate back to the service.

In the case of the leasing service here, there will always be a back-end process, chugging away, to do the lease renewals. Using the RMI activation framework to have the back-end process sleep until it was needed wouldn't really buy you a lot here, at least not on a busy network. The service would spend most of its time working to renew leases; and when no leases needed renewing, the `LeaseRenewalManager` used internally would just go to sleep. You could write a version of this code that uses the activation framework, though. Such a version could deactivate itself if it had no leases to renew and after no clients had contacted it for some period of time. This strategy would allow the back-end service to consume *no* resources until a caller used its proxy. And—always one of the more compelling reasons to use activation—this would allow the service to automatically restart after a crash; you wouldn't have to monitor the process for crashes and manually restart it. Of course, if the service were allowed to be inactive, some other entity would then have to be active to renew the `LeaseService`'s registration leases.

The `restore()` method tries to reload all of the saved state of the service. It creates an `ObjectInputStream` from the storage file, and reads in an instance of `LeaseServiceData`, which is a class used here to group all of the persistent state together. This class contains the service's ID, and the set of groups, lookup locators, and attributes it is to use. In addition to all of this state used by the `JoinManager`, `LeaseServiceData` also keeps all the leases that were in use the last time the service was checkpointed, stored as a hash map. This hash map is keyed by the leases themselves, and maintains a `LeaseEntry` for each lease. The `LeaseEntry` class defined here is a way to keep track of all the state that the `LeaseRenewalManager` needs for each lease—its desired expiration time, and the listener that is associated with it. Whenever `restore()` is called, the code fetches all the saved leases and re-inserts them into the `LeaseRenewalManager` so that they will be managed again. As it processes each lease, it eliminates any stored leases that have already passed their expiration times.

Note that this operation doesn't guarantee that leases will be saved across crashes or restarts. If a lease has expired during the time the `LeaseRenewalService` was down, there will be no way to renew it. But clearly, a leasing service should be as conservative as possible, so the code here dutifully tries to save lease data and restore it when possible. If no leases expired during the time the service was down, it should be able to successfully recover and continue managing all the leases that were in effect before it crashed.

The `checkpoint()` method is the inverse of `restore()`: It writes all necessary data to persistent storage. This method will be called from each and every one of the other methods in `LeaseRenewalService` that cause the state of managed leases to change, or from any code that changes any state that might be needed by the join protocol.

Each time the set of managed leases is checkpointed, any already expired leases are eliminated from the set of `allLeases`. The code does this since there is no "automatic" way to determine when a managed lease has expired—listeners are only called when some "exceptional" condition occurs, such as when a lease expires before the desired period has elapsed. Rather than spinning off a thread to clean up the managed lease set, the program simply removes dead leases whenever it checkpoints or resumes.

Most of the work described above has little to do with leasing per se. It's more about the things that "good" services have to do to ensure that they can recover properly, rather than specifically about how to build a service that does leasing. In future chapters, I'll expand on the code here to create a generic service framework to handle persistence. But for now, I'll focus on the code that's specific to leasing.

Take a look at the `renewFor()` method, since it's typical of the other methods from the `RemoteLeaseRenewer` interface that this service implements. When `renewFor()` is invoked, it is passed a lease, a duration, and a `RemoteEventListener`. The first thing this method does is set the serialization format of the lease so that it will be stored as an absolute time whenever it is checkpointed to disk. Remember that whenever the code saves leases to disk, it *must* save them in absolute time format—otherwise, when it wakes up, it will have no idea how to convert the stored durations into new absolute times.

Next, the code stores the lease in the `allLeases` hash map, along with a new `LeaseEntry` for it that records the expiration time (computed by adding the duration to the current time—it must always save times as absolutes here), and the listener that was passed to it. Then, `checkpoint()` is called to write the change in the state of managed leases out to persistent storage. If the service crashes at this point, it can recover not only the lease itself, but the desired expiration time and the listener that the client wished to be used for it.

Finally, after all the checkpointing, the method actually calls to the local `LeaseRenewalManager` to have it manage the lease. The `renewFor()` implementation passes the lease and the given duration. But what about the listener? The client has sent the service a `RemoteEventListener` class—which it must do since the service needs to call it back remotely—but `LeaseRenewalManager` only understands the local `LeaseListener` class.

The answer to this conundrum is to create a custom class that maps between local and remote listeners, called the `LeaseListenerConduit`. This class is an implementation of the `LeaseListener` interface, so it can be used as a listener in the `LeaseRenewalManager`. It takes a `RemoteEventListener` as an argument and saves it, so that whenever its `notify()` method is called, it can forward the invocation to the `RemoteEventListener`. Whenever any new lease is passed to the `LeaseService`, it "wraps" the `RemoteEventListener` in a new `LeaseConduit` and passes the conduit to the `LeaseRenewalManager` as the listener for the lease.

Look at the `LeaseListenerConduit` a little more closely. The implementation of `notify()` actually has to do a few things. First, it needs to remove the lease from the set of all managed leases. Recall that the listener is called whenever a lease expires prematurely or cannot be renewed. If this happens, the code needs to remove it from the set of managed leases and checkpoint it to persistent storage.

The code also invokes the remote listener if it is not null. Clients can easily pass in a null `RemoteEventListener`; the various methods on `LeaseService` still create conduits, though, since they need to make sure that they have a conduit for every lease to remove failed leases from the managed set. The null check here is necessary so that the code doesn't try to call out to a nonexistent remote listener.

Note here that the invocation of `notify()` passes in an *event ID* and a *sequence number* when it creates the remote version of the event. As you'll see in Chapter 16, Jini remote events should have a unique ID and increasing sequence numbers stored in them. This service doesn't really *use* these numbers in any way, but they should be generated correctly in any case. The strategy taken here is to simply keep a counter for event IDs and assign each new lease registration a new ID. The ID number is stored in the `LeaseEntry` for the lease. Sequence numbers are stored in the conduit and incremented each time an event is generated. Again, if you're curious about how this works and what it does, you can jump ahead to Chapter 16 or—probably better—just ignore it for now.

Finally, the code traps any exceptions that may result from calling the remote listener. The `LeaseListener` API doesn't specify any exceptions that may be thrown from `notify()`. So, since the conduit must meet this interface, it cannot raise any exceptions it receives. `RemoteException` may be raised if there is trouble communicating with the receiver. If such an exception is caught, the service simply prints a message but does nothing else. Since it doesn't remove the listener, the service will try to re-send events in the future, if any arise. The `UnknownEventException` is an exception type that the Jini `RemoteEventListener` class may raise. You'll learn about the full meaning of this exception in

Chapter 16, but you can basically treat it as a request to not send future events to this recipient. The service "disables" the recipient by setting the listener to null, ensuring that it will receive no further events.

The implementation of `LeaseService` shown here implements the `getAdmin()` interface required by `RemoteLeaseRenewer`, but it returns null. So in practice, this service is not administrable. I will, however, come back to this service in Chapter 14, when I talk about building service administration objects and graphical interfaces. At that time, I'll re-implement this method to do "real" administration.

Compiling and Running the Example

On Windows: First, compile the main program file. The Java compiler should build all of the class files needed by `LeaseService`. You can compile all of the implementation code for the service into the `service` directory.

```
javac -classpath C:\files;
                 C:\jini1_1\lib\jini-core.jar;
                 C:\jini1_1\lib\jini-ext.jar;
                 C:\jini1_1\lib\sun-util.jar;
                 C:\service
       -d C:\service
       C:\corejini\chapter12\LeaseService.java
```

Next, you need to ensure that downloadable code is copied to a directory that is being exported by the service's HTTP server. Clients will download the service's proxy, so `LeaseServiceProxy.class` needs to be copied to the `service-dl` directory. Also, the implementation of the proxy depends on `RemoteLeaseRenewer` and `LeaseRenewalService`, so those class files are necessary as well. (If you ever have trouble figuring out what files are needed in the download directory, you can simply try running a client—it will tell you if needed classes cannot be found with a `ClassNotFoundException`.)

```
mkdir C:\service_dl\corejini\chapter12
cd C:\service\corejini\chapter12
copy LeaseServiceProxy.class
    C:\service-dl\corejini\chapter12
copy RemoteLeaseRenewer.class
    C:\service-dl\corejini\chapter12
copy LeaseRenewalService.class
    C:\service-dl\corejini\chapter12
```

The only bit of shared state that both a client of the service and the service itself have is the interface that the service's proxy implements: `Lease-RenewalService`. So here I've also copied that class file out to the `client` directory, where presumably clients would be able to link against it.

```
copy LeaseRenewalService.class C:\client\corejini\chapter12
```

The last step is to run the RMI stubs compiler on `LeaseService`. The stubs also need to be downloadable, so make sure you put them in the `service-dl` directory that's exported by the HTTP server.

```
rmic -classpath C:\service;
               C:\jini1_1\lib\jini-core.jar;
               C:\jini1_1\lib\jini-ext.jar;
               C:\jini1_1\lib\sun-util.jar;
       -d C:\service-dl
       corejini.chapter12.LeaseService
```

Finally, you're set to run! Make sure you pass in a security policy file, a correct codebase, and a file to use for persistent storage for the service.

```
java -cp C:\jini1_1\lib\jini-core.jar;
         C:\jini1_1\lib\jini-ext.jar;
         C:\jini1_1\lib\sun-util.jar;
         C:\service
             -Djava.rmi.server.codebase=http://myhost:8085/
             -Djava.security.policy=C:\policy
       corejini.chapter12.LeaseService C:\temp\leasedata
```

On UNIX: First, compile the main program file. The Java compiler should build all of the class files needed by `LeaseService`. You can compile all the implementation code for the service into the `service` directory.

```
javac -classpath /files:
                 /files/jini1_1/lib/jini-core.jar:
                 /files/jini1_1/lib/jini-ext.jar:
                 /files/jini1_1/lib/sun-util.jar:
                 /files/service
         -d /files/service
       /files/corejini/chapter12/LeaseService.java
```

Next, you need to ensure that downloadable code is copied to a directory that is being exported by the service's HTTP server. Clients will download the service's proxy, so `LeaseServiceProxy.class` needs to be copied to the `service-dl` directory. Also, the implementation of the proxy depends on `RemoteLeaseRenewer` and `LeaseRenewalService`, so those class files are necessary as well. (If you ever have trouble figuring out what files are needed in the download directory, you can simply try running a client—it will tell you if needed classes cannot be found with a `ClassNotFoundException`.)

```
mkdir C:/service_dl/corejini/chapter12
cd /files/service/corejini/chapter12
cp LeaseServiceProxy.class
    /files/service-dl/corejini/chapter12
cp RemoteLeaseRenewer.class
    /files/service-dl/corejini/chapter12
cp LeaseRenewalService.class
    /files/service-dl/corejini/chapter12
```

The only bit of shared state that both a client of the service and the service itself have is the interface that the service's proxy implements: `LeaseRenewalService`. So here I've also copied that class file out to the `client` directory, where presumably clients would be able to link against it.

```
copy LeaseRenewalService.class
    /files/client/corejini/chapter12
```

The last step is to run the RMI stubs compiler on `LeaseService`. The stubs also need to be downloadable, so make sure you put them in the `service-dl` directory that's exported by the HTTP server.

```
rmic -classpath /files/service:
              /files/jini1_1/lib/jini-core.jar:
              /files/jini1_1/lib/jini-ext.jar:
              /files/jini1_1/lib/sun-util.jar:
       -d /files/service-dl
corejini.chapter12.LeaseService
```

Finally, you're set to run! Make sure you pass in a security policy file, a correct codebase, and a file to use for persistent storage for the service.

```
java -cp /files/jini1_1/lib/jini-core.jar:
        /files/jini1_1/lib/jini-ext.jar:
        /files/jini1_1/lib/sun-util.jar:
        /files/service
```

```
-Djava.rmi.server.codebase=http://myhost:8085/
-Djava.security.policy=/files/policy
corejini.chapter12.LeaseService /tmp/leasedata
```

Leasing in Practice

In the very first "Hello, World" examples you looked at, you may have wondered about the wisdom of requiring a long-lived server process to sit around on a machine someplace, just to renew the leases for a trivially simple proxy object that never even needs to contact the server. So this raises the question—who *should* do the leasing for a particular service?

As it turns out, there are a number of leasing strategies you might use; which one you actually implement depends almost entirely on how your service is structured. In this section, you'll learn about some of the strategies and the pros and cons of each.

Who Handles Lease Renewals?

There are three common service architectures used in Jini: services may be implemented using back-end processes, services may be implemented through a combination of hardware and software, or services may be implemented completely in the service proxy object that is sent to clients. In this section, I'll talk about leasing strategies for each of these architectures.

Many Jini services are implemented as proxies that communicate with back-end software processes. If you build a new network software service, in most cases, the service will be implemented as a long-lived process that runs on a machine somewhere on the network; a custom proxy object will be used to communicate with this back end. In nearly all of these cases, it makes sense to have this back-end process handle the lease renewals for the proxy. This arrangement is an easy and natural fit for the Jini leasing model, and makes intuitive sense—the service is only "up" for as long as the back end is running; if the back end ever goes away, the leases for its proxy should expire on their own.

There are a couple of mitigating factors that may argue against using this strategy, however, even when a service has a long-lived process associated with it. First, the back end of a service may not be implemented in Java. This will usually be the case when you need to make some legacy software service accessible through Jini. In such situations, it will likely be impossible for a back end written in, say, C to fulfill all of the obligations of Jini lease management (it will not, for example, be able to deserialize and use `Lease` implementations received from lease grantors). With such an arrangement, a *separate* back-end "wrapper" process may be created in Java, solely to handle various Jini chores, and to publish the service proxy that will be used to communicate with the "native" back end. This wrapper can stay active, handling the leasing itself, or it can delegate leasing to an external lease service and exit.

A second mitigating factor is if the back-end process, while long-lived, is typically inactive for long periods of time. A service may be idle because it has to do work only infrequently—typically when required by its service proxy or some external scheduling constraints. A monthly disk backup service might fall into this class of application. Services like this can either wake up as needed to manage lease renewals, or they can delegate their lease management to an external lease service, like the one you've already seen in this chapter.

Waking up as needed to perform leasing makes sense, if the service can acquire very long leases, or if the service doesn't consume many system resources while it is in its "sleeping" state. Delegating leasing to an external service may be easier, though, and allows the back-end process to completely deactivate itself (possibly via the RMI activation mechanisms) when it is not in use. While the external leasing service would have to stay running the entire time, just as the back end would do if it were to manage leases itself, the external service has the advantage that it can be shared among *many* services.

If a service is implemented as a proxy object that communicates with a hardware device, then the approaches are much the same as in the software-only case. If the device has a JVM on it, it can easily do its own lease management during the time it is connected to the network. Much like a software service that consists of a back-end process and a proxy, this architecture is a natural fit for Jini: As long as the device is connected to the network, its proxies will be available since the device itself will manage its participation in a Jini community.

If the device does not have a JVM on it, then the most typical solution is to provide an external Java "surrogate" that does the leasing. This surrogate will typically run on a computer that the device is connected to (the host for a printer, for example). The surrogate may handle leasing itself, which means that it must stay active, or it can delegate lease management to an external service and then exit.

The final common type of service is where the service proxy *is* the service—it contains all the intelligence to implement all of its operations itself, without having to communicate with any external software process or hardware device. The first versions of the "Hello, World" service are examples of this type. Services like this must create some form of a wrapper process which will, at a minimum, do discovery to publish the proxy on lookup services. This wrapper can work just like the Chapter 5 examples—by staying active to manage leases—or it can use a leasing service and shut down after the proxy has been registered with a lookup service.

Table 12–1 summarizes the leasing strategies commonly taken by services. The first column, *Service Architecture*, denotes how the service is structured. All services have proxies; some may have active back-end services, or devices that can handle their leasing for them. Others must take alternative approaches.

I should also note that this table only shows leasing strategies for services, which have a variety of implementation characteristics and expected lifetimes. Clients—applications that are merely consumers of Jini services—may have entirely different behaviors. In most cases, a client exists solely to make use of a service to accomplish some task. The task has a natural lifetime and the client will typically be running until the task is complete. Once the task is finished, the client's job is done, and it will usually cease running at that point. Since most clients will use resources leased from Jini services, they will need to continually renew the leases held on those resources. In such cases, it makes sense for a client's process to manage the leases used by that client, rather than delegating to a third party.

Table 12–1 Leasing Strategies

Service Architecture	*Leasing Strategy*
Always-active back-end process written in Java	Back-end process handles lease renewal for the service proxy.
Always-active back-end process not written in Java	An external "wrapper" process manages Jini participation and lease renewal. This wrapper can do leasing itself internally, or can delegate it to an external leasing service.
Rarely-active back-end process	Either wake up the back-end process periodically to handle lease renewals, or defer to an external leasing delegate.
Device with embedded JVM	The device handles lease renewal for the service proxy.
Device without embedded JVM	Create an external surrogate for the device that runs on a nearby computer; this surrogate may defer to an external leasing service for lease renewal.
Proxy-only	Create an external wrapper for the proxy; this wrapper may stay running to do lease management, or may defer to an external leasing service for lease renewal.

The Perils of Leasing

Clearly, applications that have some device or process that is naturally associated with the service, and can handle leases for it, map most directly to the Jini model. And, while Jini is explicitly designed to accommodate the model where leases can be delegated to external services, this model has some weaknesses compared to allowing services to handle lease management themselves.

The external lease service is designed to automatically renew leases for a longer period of time than is typically granted in a single lease. This strategy, while it makes certain types of services possible (those that don't have any long-lived component, or have a back end that cannot for some reason do lease management), also weakens the durability of a Jini community because it separates the process performing the service from the process performing its leasing. This weakness happens in two ways.

First, using an external service to do leasing extends the "effective" duration of a lease, without requiring the extra proof-of-interest that such a duration would normally expect. That is, once a service asks a leasing service to renew its leases for the next month or year, the leasing service will handle this even if the original service dies. As long as the leasing service continues showing proof-of-interest by renewing the lease, most lease grantors will be more than happy to grant the renewal. Put succinctly, lease delegation grants the power of lease renewal without the natural lease expiration that would happen when a service goes away; the service process can crash without bringing down lease renewal with it.

Second, using an external service introduces another point of failure into the system: the leasing service itself. Since a resource consumer does not have to periodically check the leasing service, the leasing service can die without any of its services becoming aware of its death. Not only is the service unable to contact the leasing service to check or update the status of its leases, but the leases granted by the original grantor may silently expire without the service being any the wiser.

Obviously, using a third-party lease manager that runs in a separate JVM is a two-edged sword. There are situations in which such a strategy is very useful. For example, if a hardware device (like an air conditioner) that will almost certainly never move or crash is installed, a leasing service could perpetually renew its leases with little fear that the hardware will go away. Despite these benefits, however, leasing by an external process can seriously weaken the robustness and durability of a Jini community in which it is used, and you should think seriously about whether it makes sense for you to follow this strategy.

Delegation to an External JVM vs. Delegation to an Internal Class

Even though the basic code for `LeaseRenewalManager` and `LeaseService` look very similar, I need to reiterate the fundamental differences between them. While the `LeaseRenewalManager` class shown earlier in this chapter is a "third party" in the sense that it is a separate object meant to do lease negotiations, it is not a lease renewal *service*, and does not suffer from the same weaknesses of using an external process to do leasing. This is because the `LeaseRenewalManager` utility class is used *within* the back-end process that manages leases. When the back-end process fails, the lease renewal class also fails, and the system cleans up after itself in a normal way. By tying lease management to the service in this way, you gain the expected lease benefits of reliability and self-healing. It is only when lease management is done in a separate process, isolated from the service on whose behalf it is working, that you can potentially run into trouble.

Leasing vs. Garbage Collection

Those of you with experience with garbage collection (GC) may be thinking that leasing is essentially a duplication of what Java currently does with its garbage collector. In a sense, this is accurate: Both GC and leasing have to do with clearing out unused resources from a system. And, Java's RMI facility even comes with a distributed garbage collector that can free up a resource across a network when no *remote* reference to it exists.

So, what's the difference? The key difference is that GC is used to free resources when there is no active reference in a program that could be used to reach the resource. In leasing, there are typically *never* any references to the resource to begin with. For example, the proxy for a digital camera service may sit happily on its lookup service, never to be used by any other Jini participant. Just because this service hasn't yet been used doesn't mean that it should be unregistered and deleted—someone may come along later and want to use it. Leasing is the appropriate solution for resources that are stored for later use by some party; unlike GC, leasing works even if the party that originally stored the resource no longer has any use for it, or any outstanding references to it.

Just as an aside, RMI's distributed garbage collector has used leases internally since the beginning. In RMI, leases are used as a tool to implement the distributed GC algorithms robustly, and solve many of the same problems in RMI that they do in Jini. For example, one of the key differences between local and remote GC is that in the local case, all references to objects are known when the garbage collector begins to run. In the remote case, a program may have shipped off a reference to some internally held object to another machine. The distributed garbage collector must try to determine whether that other machine still holds a reference to the object in order to make a decision about whether it is collectible. Leasing is used as part of the distributed GC process to allow the collector to free resources referenced by clients that may have crashed. RMI hides leases by using them only internally; Jini exposes leases and makes them available as one of the core elements of its programming model.

Summary

This chapter has looked at the rationale behind leasing as a way to bring self-healing to distributed systems, and has tackled the issues around building lease consumers. Leasing is a fundamental part of Jini, and you'll certainly be using it when you lease service and event registrations as a lease consumer, and probably at other times as well. In most of these cases, you'll be using the high-level APIs described in this chapter. But at times, you may need to get under the hood to tinker with the lower level APIs, or—as you become more proficient with Jini—even build services that expose resources via leasing.

What's Next?

In the next chapter, you'll look at the other half of the leasing equation—building services that export leased resources. The techniques you'll see there will let you come "full circle," exporting leases that can be managed by clients using the classes described in this chapter!

Exporting Leased Resources

Topics in This Chapter

- Custom lease implementations
- How to use the `Landlord` paradigm
- How to use "cookies" to identify leased resources
- Creating a service that exports leased resources
- A custom object storage service

Chapter 13

In the last chapter, you saw how to use, renew, and manage leases that you hold on resources granted by a service. Knowledge about how to use leases in this way—being a lease consumer—is essential for being able to program in Jini. Since service and event registrations are leased, you have to be able to be an effective lease consumer to write even the simplest Jini services and clients.

But there is another side to the leasing equation, which I'll talk about in this chapter. Here, you'll see how to be an effective lease *grantor*. Many times you'll be writing a service that will export some resource to consumers. In such cases, you may very well find it beneficial to lease these resources. By leasing the resources you export to others, your own programs can take advantage of all the benefits that leasing brings to Jini communities: Resources can be automatically freed when clients forget, or are unable, to release their resources themselves. You've already seen what the consumer of a lease has to do. But what are the steps that the grantor must follow?

In this chapter, you'll learn about the idioms and strategies for lease granting, and see the responsibilities that lease grantors have. You'll also see a set of "helper" classes that Sun provides that can make certain types of lease grantors easier to write. You can use these classes if you wish—they may make your life easier—but by the end of this chapter, you should be able to write your own service-side, lease-granting code "from scratch" if you need to. In any case, you should have a greater understanding of the "under the hood" details of how leasing is implemented in Jini.

Finally, you'll see an example of a simple Jini storage service that leases object storage to its clients. This example will illustrate how to write an effective lease grantor and use the Sun-provided "helper" classes.

Leasing Interfaces and Implementations

As you shall see, while Jini provides and standardizes a basic infrastructure for leasing—including the actual Lease interface and a few lease-related exception types—the core Jini interfaces actually say *nothing* about how leasing must be implemented by applications. In fact, when lease holders work with Lease objects, they are actually manipulating an *implementation-specific* lease type that has been provided to them by the lease grantor.

Let's look a bit more closely at how this works. Every lease grantor, whether a lookup service, an event generator, or any other service that uses leasing as a way to control access to its resources, can decide for itself how it should best implement leasing. When it returns a lease to a resource consumer, all the grantor must do is return some object—any object—that implements the Lease interface. When the holders of this Lease object call methods on it to renew the lease, cancel the lease, and so on, the object they hold that implements the Lease interface actually sends a message back to the lease grantor, telling it that the holder wishes to change the state of the lease. The details of how this communication is done are private to the *particular* lease implementation returned by the grantor, and so the actual lease-implementing object returned is also specific to the grantor. In a nutshell, Jini only specifies the client-side interfaces for dealing with leases; lease grantors can implement these interfaces in any way they see fit.

This strategy makes Jini tremendously flexible, and able to work over any number of communication substrates. Particular lease implementations can communicate with lease grantors via RMI, CORBA, or "raw" sockets. They could potentially even communicate over non-TCP networks, or via infrared links, as long as the chosen communications medium is supported by both the lease grantor and the lease holder.

But while this approach is flexible, it also means that providers of leases have a bit more work to do than they might otherwise. They have to decide how to implement leasing internally, and construct implementations of their own proprietary lease protocols as well as the lease implementations that will hide these protocols behind the standard leasing APIs. They also must take care of the internal tasks of cleaning up after expired leases.

Fortunately, Jini provides a set of classes in the `com.sun.jini.lease` and `com.sun.jini.lease.landlord` packages that serve as great starting points for constructing lease providers. Be sure to note, however, that since these classes are not part of the `net.jini` package hierarchy, they are subject to change. But since these classes aren't standardized, there is also no requirement that you use them. If they save you time, great. If not, you may be better off building a completely custom leasing implementation for your service. Of the services provided by Sun's sample implementation of Jini, the "`outrigger`" JavaSpaces service, the "`mercury`" event mailbox service, the "`norm`" lease renewal service, and the "`mahalo`" transaction manager service use these classes; Sun's "`reggie`" implementation of the lookup service and its "`fiddler`" implementation of the lookup discovery service do not.

The Landlord Paradigm

Let's look at what these leasing packages provide in the way of support for building lease grantors. The most important interface is `com.sun.jini.lease.Landlord`. This interface defines an API that can be used with a particular lease implementation to construct most of the implementation of a lease grantor. You will create a new object that implements the `Landlord` interface and is responsible for managing the resources that you are granting under lease to consumers.

Once you've provided an implementation of `Landlord`, you can simply "plug in" a particular lease implementation that Sun gives you that understands how to communicate with `Landlord` implementations. This lease type is called `LandlordLease`, and it is a class that implements the `Lease` interface, and can be shipped as-is to clients when they ask for a lease.

Let's look first at the `Landlord` interface, since this is the first bit of code you'll have to write if you're creating a lease provider.

```
package com.sun.jini.lease.landlord;

import java.rmi.Remote;
import net.jini.core.lease.LeaseMapException;
import net.jini.core.lease.UnknownLeaseException;

import java.util.Map;

public interface Landlord extends Remote {
    public void cancel(Object cookie)
        throws UnknownLeaseException, RemoteException;
    public Map cancelAll(Object[] cookies)
        throws RemoteException;
```

```
        public long renew(Object cookie, long extension)
            throws LeaseDeniedException,
                    UnknownLeaseException,
                    RemoteException;
        public Landlord.RenewResults renewAll(Object[]
                                              cookies,
                                              long[] extensions)
            throws RemoteException;
}
```

This is a relatively simple interface to implement, since it has only four methods. The `cancel()` and `cancelAll()` methods cancel leases, and the `renew()` and `renewAll()` methods renew leases for a specified duration. These methods are invoked when a client holding a `LandlordLease` invokes `cancel()`, `renew()`, and so on.

The `cancelAll()` and `renewAll()` versions are invoked when a set of leases batched together into a `LeaseMap` is canceled or renewed as a group. The `cancelAll()` method returns a `java.util.Map`, which will be null if all the specified leases were cancelled successfully. If some leases could not be cancelled, the map identifies which cancellations failed by storing a mapping from each affected lease's cookie to an exception describing the nature of the failure.

But what are these "cookie" arguments in all of these methods? A cookie is a unique token that you use internally to identify leased resources; you decide on the cookies you will use when you build your `Landlord` implementation. When you ship out a lease to a client, you embed in it a cookie for the resource it represents. When a caller invokes `cancel()` or `renew()` on this lease, the lease performs an RMI method invocation back to your `Landlord` implementation, passing the cookie that uniquely identifies the leased resource. It's up to you to decide on an intelligent mapping between cookies and resources.

Even though `Landlord` is only an interface, it does dictate certain implementation details for you. In particular, your `Landlord` implementation must be a `RemoteObject`, since the `LandlordLeases` that you will send to clients use RMI to communicate back to the `Landlord`.

One other detail to mention here is the return values of the `renew()` and `renewAll()` methods. The return value from `renew()` is simply the new actual duration of the lease. The object that is returned from `renewAll()` is an instance of `RenewResults`, which is a nested class defined inside the `Landlord` interface. This class simply contains an array of new durations for the leases that were successfully renewed, and an array of exceptions for the leases that were denied.

I've talked about how `Landlords` and `LandlordLeases` communicate with each other, and how they use cookies to convey information that uniquely identifies leased resources. But so far, I haven't said anything about *how* LandlordLe-ases get created and how they get returned.

For the latter part—how leases get returned—you're on your own. Jini, and the Landlord interface, define no particular interfaces for getting leases from resource providers. The way leases are asked for and returned is up to the particular service that grants leases. You've even seen a couple of different ways to ask for and receive leases so far in the standard Jini services: You ask for lookup registrations by calling register() on a lookup service, and the lease is returned in a ServiceRegistration; you ask for event solicitations by calling notify() on a lookup service, and the lease is returned in an EventRegistration. The particular APIs you decide on to allow clients to ask for resources and get leases are completely up to you, and should be chosen based on what makes sense for your particular service and the resources you are exporting.

As for how leases get created, the Landlord classes do have something to say. The com.sun.jini.lease.LandlordLeaseFactory interface defines an API for "factory" objects that can be used to create LandlordLeases. The Factory class, which is defined as a static nested class within the LandlordLease class, provides a LandlordLeaseFactory implementation that creates these leases.

The way you use this factory is simple. Once you've decided on the API that clients will use to ask for leases, you implement this API by calling into the factory for LandlordLeases to have it create leases that you will return to clients.

The LandlordLeaseFactory API has only one method:

```
package com.sun.jini.lease.landlord;

import net.jini.core.lease.Lease;
import net.jini.core.lease.LeaseDeniedException;

public interface LandlordLeaseFactory {
    public Lease newLease(Object cookie,
                          Landlord landlord,
                          long expiration)
                throws LeaseDeniedException;
}
```

The Factory class inside LandlordLease implements newLease() to return new LandlordLeases. You pass it the cookie that uniquely identifies the resource associated with the new lease, a reference to the Landlord object that the lease will call back to, and the duration to assign to the lease. The expiration here is the *actual* expiration that you are granting the lease for—the client may have asked for a longer value, but here you pass the expiration time that you've decided to grant the lease.

Core Tip: Don't grant leases for *more* time than asked

When a caller asks for a lease and supplies a requested expiration time, you are free to grant a lease that expires at the same time, or sooner than, the requested expiration. But you should never grant a lease for longer than the requested expiration time.

Granting extended leases is simply asking clients to do more work than they would normally do—such as canceling their leases explicitly when they no longer need them.

Identifying Leased Resources

So far, you've seen how `LandlordLeases` communicate with `Landlords`, and how these leases get created by `LandlordLeaseFactories`. Let's now revisit how to associate leases with leased resources, and how to identify resources with the cookies received from client leases.

When you create your `Landlord` implementation, you must decide on a type of object to use as the "cookie" values that you bind into leases, and that uniquely identify leased resources.

When you write your service that exports leased resources, only you understand the internals of how these resources will be stored and arranged. If the resources are kept internally in a hash table, then the hash code of the individual objects may suffice to uniquely identify them. Such an arrangement would also permit the resource that is associated with a given lease to be quickly found given the hash code. So, in this set up, using the hash code as the cookie value that you stuff into leases is a good approach to maintaining this association between the leases you dole out and the resources you keep track of internally.

Other services may have different arrangements for how their leased resources are stored. In almost every case, an effective cookie type will be one that allows quick access to the underlying resource whenever it comes in to the `Landlord`. Second, cookies should be relatively secure so that if a client manages to get hold of a cookie by some means, it cannot forge a lease to a resource that it doesn't hold. Finally, a good cookie type will always *uniquely* identify the *association* between the lease and the resource. That is, for any given pair of resource and lease, there should only be one cookie that identifies this pair.

Let's look at this last requirement in a bit more detail. Suppose the resource to which you are leasing access is an item in a fixed-length array (I'll come back to this hypothetical situation in the example for this chapter). Clients might ask for a lease on a slot in the array. Clearly, the index of the item in the array is one choice for a cookie that uniquely identifies the resource—such a value always identifies only one array item and, when it is returned to the `Landlord`, it can be used to find the associated resource very quickly.

Unfortunately, this cookie only identifies the resource, not the lease; effective cookies must identify *both* parts of the association. Let's look at what can happen if you don't include some identifier for the lease in the cookie. Suppose you grant a lease to a particular item in the array, say item 12, and ship out a lease containing this cookie to a client. Now suppose that this client holds on to the lease for a long period of time, past the lease's expiration time, without renewing it. Now, if the holder of the now-expired lease object contacts the grantor to renew the lease, the cookie—the number 12—will be sent to the landlord without any way of knowing that the lease containing this cookie has already expired. This situation is particularly problematic if the grantor has already issued *new* leases to clients on this same slot 12 in the array—it now has no way to identify or distinguish the expired leases from the newly granted ones.

Because of situations like this, it is necessary to design cookie types in such a way that they not only allow unique and quick access to the underlying resource, but that they also distinguish leases from one another.

Implementing the Landlord Interface

Let's now look at how to build implementations of the `Landlord` interface. These implementations will vary depending on what type of resource you are granting access to, but the basic structure of most `Landlord` implementations will have at least some similarities.

First, as previously mentioned, `Landlords` need to be able to track the resources that they expose via leasing, and map from cookies that they receive into leases. They should design these cookies so that they can tell if a client is using a lease that has already expired, or is otherwise no longer valid, so that they can report `UnknownLeaseException` back to the caller.

Second, `Landlords` need to decide on their policies for granting leases. This means that they should decide what the maximum lease duration they will grant is, and when they should deny leases. Some `Landlords` may always grant a requested lease for any resource, as long as it is within certain bounds. Other `Landlords` may grant different lease times depending on the resource that is being asked for.

Finally, `Landlords` also need to do their own cleanup and management of resource deallocation whenever leases expire. That is, Jini doesn't provide any classes that developers can use that will automatically deallocate resources whenever leases expire. So, when you build your `Landlord` implementation, you'll need to figure out how best to implement deallocation.

A common implementation approach would be to have a thread that wakes up periodically and scans all the resources to see which are held by expired leases. Those resources could then be deallocated and any necessary bookkeeping could be done to flag that the resources are available for re-leasing. Another strategy would be to only do the work to determine if a resource should be deallocated "on demand." That is, whenever the `Landlord` gets another request to cancel or renew a lease, it could then scan over the resources it holds to assess which can be deallocated.

Strategies like the first are more appropriate when there is a possibly large set of resources that the service grants access to, and freeing unused resources as soon as possible will be a win. Strategies like the second are simpler to implement and may be beneficial if the number (or total size) of leased resources is small, and the time required to do any deallocation is small enough to not unduly slow down the implementation of `cancel()` or `renew()`.

`Landlords` must take care of how they allocate memory. In particular, they probably will want to create "surrogate" data structures that hold the information needed for lease implementations (expiration times, cookies, and so forth), and not use actual lease objects internally in the `Landlord` themselves.

This is particularly true in the case of the `LandlordLease` implementation that comes with Jini. You might be tempted to just use these `LandlordLease` objects internally to do your lease bookkeeping—after all, they have expiration times and cookies, and all the other tidbits of information that you need to implement leasing. But recall that these objects are meant to be serialized and returned to clients, and that they contain within them remote references to the `Landlord` itself. So, if your `Landlord` uses these objects internally for bookkeeping, changing the values of their expiration times merely has the effect of calling back to the `Landlord` itself! So you will need to create your own bookkeeping data structures that maintain information about expiration times and cookies and keep these associated with leased resources. Other implementations of the `Lease` interface may afford other strategies. For example, if your lease is a remote object, you can keep the one "true" copy of the lease yourself, and return RMI stubs for it to clients. In this case, it may make sense to use the actual remote lease server object as the bookkeeping object for your lease implementation.

Jini provides a handful of interfaces that you can use to assist in the implementation of your `Landlord`, although there is no requirement to use these and, in the case of very simple `Landlords`, the work required to use them may outweigh the benefit you might get.

The `com.sun.jini.lease.LeasedResource` interface provides a way for you to associate with your resources any extra information that's required to do leasing. This interface provides methods for fetching the cookie associated with a resource, and getting and setting the current expiration time for the lease on the resource. If the resources you lease implement this interface, you can easily scan over them, determine which have expired, and map resources into cookies. The example later in this chapter uses this interface, so I present it here:

```
package com.sun.jini.lease.landlord;

public interface LeasedResource {
    public Object getCookie();
    public long getExpiration();
    public void setExpiration(long newExpiration);
}
```

The `com.sun.jini.lease.LeasePolicy` interface works in cooperation with `LeasedResources` to implement a particular leasing policy. This interface has methods that allow you to determine if a `LeasedResource` has already expired, and that will compute an actual granted lease time based on a requested lease time. Particular implementations of this interface, such as `LeaseDurationPolicy` in the same package, fulfill these requests based on initialized parameters that control maximum and default leasing times.

Finally, the `com.sun.jini.lease.LeaseManager` interface provides a way to track lease status. Some implementations of `LeasePolicy`, including `LeaseDurationPolicy` which comes with Jini, allow the use of a `LeaseManager` to monitor leasing. Think of a `LeaseManager` as a listener interface that objects can implement to get callbacks whenever leases are initially granted or renewed.

Again, some of these interfaces may help; others may not be worth the work. In the example you'll see shortly, I'll use the `LeasedResource` interface as a handy tool to associate bookkeeping information with resources, but ignore the other lease helper interfaces.

An Example

Let's look now at an example of how you might implement a lease grantor using the `Landlord` tools that come with Jini (see Listing 13–1). The program shown is a provider of storage "slots"—this means that the program keeps a fixed number of items that it is willing to grant to callers for storage of their objects. Once the slots run out, new clients cannot acquire storage. Slots are leased so that if clients die or do not renew their interest, the slot provider can clean house and deallocate slots.

This example is a (very!) scaled down example of how a more general Jini storage engine might work—such an engine could provide storage of arbitrary Java objects, under lease to consumers.

Let's work through some of the design decisions in this example. First, the slot resources are implemented as a fixed-length array. Thus, there is a natural way to refer to the individual resources—the index of a slot within the array uniquely identifies it. So this index can serve as *part* of the cookie that will be stuffed into leases so that they can be mapped back to resources later. But the program also needs a way to uniquely identify the leases that it has granted. For this task, I've taken a simple approach—the slot provider keeps a counter. Whenever a new lease is issued, it is assigned the current value of the counter and the counter is incremented. So, the cookies for this example are a tuple consisting of both the index of the resource and the unique identifier for the lease.

Since the program will never need to map from the lease counter number *back* into a lease, it doesn't need to keep a hash table or other data structure that maintains all of its leases. It only needs to know when a request comes in if the resource specified by the cookie is still held by the lease specified in the cookie.

Each slot in the table is a class that implements the `LeasedResource` interface, and contains an arbitrary object as a value (this is the object that clients can use to store data in). Each slot knows its expiration time, and the cookie that is associated with the lease that holds that resource. Since slots know their expiration time, the `Landlord` can easily iterate over them and identify ones that have expired. Since slots remember the cookies of the leases that are associated with them, the `Landlord` can easily walk the slots and see if any given cookie matches the cookie for a particular slot.

So we've now decided on how resources will be stored, and how the bookkeeping information needed for leasing will be bound into the resources. The last things to do are to decide on a policy for granting leases, and a strategy for cleaning up unused resources.

The policy used in this example is quite simple—it grants any requested lease up to a maximum time of 10 minutes. Requests for leases longer than 10 minutes are truncated down to this maximum value.

Since this `Landlord` implementation only allows access to a fixed (and small) number of resources, I won't use a thread to wake up and deallocate stored objects. Instead, I'll use the "on demand" approach. Whenever the `Landlord` needs to make a decision to cancel or renew a lease, it scans over the `Leased-Resources` it has and, at that time, deallocates any unused data.

First, let's look at the interface that consumers of slots will use to communicate with slot providers.

Listing 13–1 `SlotProvider.java`

```java
// An interface for our leased slot provider application

package corejini.chapter13;

import java.rmi.Remote;
import java.rmi.RemoteException;
import net.jini.core.lease.UnknownLeaseException;

public interface SlotProvider extends Remote {
    public SlotResult leaseFreeSlot(Object value,
                                    long duration)
        throws RemoteException;
    public Object getValue(Object key)
        throws RemoteException, UnknownLeaseException;
}
```

The interface here, which is a remote interface—it uses RMI for communication between the slot consumer and slot provider—has only two methods. The first, `leaseFreeSlot()`, passes in an object that the slot consumer wishes to be stored in a free slot, along with a requested duration. The method returns a `SlotResult` object (Listing 13–2) if a slot is available, or null if no slots are free.

If a consumer successfully acquires a slot, it can then access the data stored in its slot by passing in a special "key" that identifies the data held there. (In this particular application, only the owner of a slot can access the data held there—the key is a way to ensure that applications can't read each others' slots. You could easily think of modifications to this program to allow sharing of objects among clients.)

The `SlotResult` return value contains the index of the slot, the lease on the slot, and a key to be used to fetch the value back out of the slot again. This key is effectively "opaque," meaning that the client cannot tell what's in it, and shouldn't care; it's merely a token to gain access to the stored data.

Listing 13–2 `SlotResult.java`

```java
// SlotResult encapsulates the return values from a
// leaseFreeSlot() operation.

package corejini.chapter13;

import net.jini.core.lease.Lease;
import java.io.Serializable;


public class SlotResult implements Serializable {
    protected int index;
    protected Lease lease;
    protected Object key;

    SlotResult(int index, Lease lease, Object key) {
        this.index = index;
        this.lease = lease;
        this.key = key;
    }

    public int getIndex() {
        return index;
    }
    public Lease getLease() {
        return lease;
    }
    public Object getKey() {
        return key;
    }
    public String toString() {
        return "slot " + index +
            " leased until " +
            lease.getExpiration();
    }
}
```

Now look at the provider of slots, Listing 13–3. This is code that will implement the remote `SlotProvider` interface, and will grant access to slots on a leased basis. Note that the code shown here, for simplicity, is not a Jini service. Instead, it is a "stand-alone" RMI program that grants access to slots. The goal here is to show how leasing works internally, not how to build yet another Jini program that interacts with lookup and discovery.

> ## Listing 13–3 `SlotProviderImpl.java`

```java
// This is an application that leases storage "slots"
// to consumers.

package corejini.chapter13;

import com.sun.jini.lease.landlord.Landlord;
import com.sun.jini.lease.landlord.LandlordLease;
import com.sun.jini.lease.landlord.LeasedResource;
import net.jini.core.lease.Lease;
import net.jini.core.lease.LeaseMapException;
import net.jini.core.lease.UnknownLeaseException;
import java.rmi.RemoteException;
import java.rmi.RMISecurityManager;
import java.rmi.Naming;
import java.rmi.server.UnicastRemoteObject;
import java.net.InetAddress;
import java.util.Map;
import java.util.HashMap;
import java.io.Serializable;

class CookieType implements Serializable {
    int index;
    int count;

    CookieType(int index, int count) {
        this.index = index;
        this.count = count;
    }

    public boolean equals(Object o) {
        if (!(o instanceof CookieType))
            return false;

        CookieType other = (CookieType) o;

        return other.index == index && other.count == count;
    }

    public String toString() {
        return "idx=" + index + ", count=" + count;
    }
}
```

Listing 13–3 `SlotProviderImpl.java` (continued)

```java
public class SlotProviderImpl extends UnicastRemoteObject
    implements SlotProvider {
    protected LeasedSlot[] slotMap = new LeasedSlot[8];
    protected MyLandlord landlord = null;
    protected LandlordLease.Factory factory =
        new LandlordLease.Factory();
    protected static int nextCount = 0;

    static class LeasedSlot implements LeasedResource {
        protected CookieType cookie;
        protected long expiration;
        protected Object value;

        public LeasedSlot(int index) {
            this(index, -1);
        }
        public LeasedSlot(int index, int count) {
            this.cookie = new CookieType(index, count);
            this.expiration = 0;
        }
        public Object getCookie() {
            return cookie;
        }
        public long getExpiration() {
            return expiration;
        }
        public void setExpiration(long expiration) {
            this.expiration = expiration;
        }
        Object getValue() {
            return value;
        }
        void setValue(Object value) {
            this.value = value;
        }
        void setCookieCount(int count) {
            cookie.count = count;
        }
        int getCookieCount() {
            return cookie.count;
        }
    }
}
```

Listing 13–3 `SlotProviderImpl.java` (continued)

```java
class MyLandlord extends UnicastRemoteObject
        implements Landlord {
    protected static final int MAX_LEASE =
        1000 * 60 * 10;

    public MyLandlord() throws RemoteException {
        super();
    }

    public long getRealDuration(long duration) {
        if (duration > MAX_LEASE ||
            duration == Lease.ANY) {
            return MAX_LEASE;
        } else {
            return duration;
        }
    }

    public void cancel(Object cookie)
        throws UnknownLeaseException {
        long currentTime = System.currentTimeMillis();

        System.out.println(
            "+++ landlord cancel: " + cookie);

        LeasedSlot slot = validateSlot(cookie);

        slot.setCookieCount(-1);
        slot.setValue(null);
    }
```

Listing 13–3 `SlotProviderImpl.java` (continued)

```java
public Map cancelAll(Object[] cookies) {
    System.out.println("landlord cancel all: ");
    Map exceptionMap = null;

    for (int i=0 ; i<cookies.length ; i++) {
        try {
            cancel(cookies[i]);
        } catch (UnknownLeaseException ex) {
            if (exceptionMap == null) {
                exceptionMap = new HashMap();
                exceptionMap.put(cookies[i], ex);
            }

        }
    }

    return exceptionMap;
}

public long renew(Object cookie, long extension)
        throws UnknownLeaseException {
    System.out.println(
            "+++ landlord renew " + cookie +
            " for " + extension);

    LeasedSlot slot = validateSlot(cookie);

    extension = getRealDuration(extension);
    slot.setExpiration(extension +
                    System.currentTimeMillis());
    return extension;
}
```

Listing 13–3 `SlotProviderImpl.java` (continued)

```java
    public Landlord.RenewResults renewAll(
                                Object[] cookies,
                            long[] extensions) {
        long[] granted = new long[cookies.length];
        Exception[] denied = null;

        for (int i=0 ; i<cookies.length ; i++) {
            try {
                long result = renew(cookies[i],
                                    extensions[i]);
                granted[i] = result;
            } catch (Exception ex) {
                if (denied == null) {
                    denied =
                     new Exception[cookies.length + 1];
                }
                denied[i+1] = ex;
                granted[i] = -1;
            }
        }

        Landlord.RenewResults results =
            new Landlord.RenewResults(granted, denied);
        return results;
    }
}

public SlotProviderImpl() throws RemoteException {
    for (int i=0 ; i<slotMap.length ; i++) {
        slotMap[i] = new LeasedSlot(i);
    }

    landlord = new MyLandlord();
}
```

Listing 13–3 `SlotProviderImpl.java` (continued)

```java
public synchronized SlotResult leaseFreeSlot(
                                   Object value,
                                   long duration)
        throws RemoteException {
    long currentTime = System.currentTimeMillis();
    duration = landlord.getRealDuration(duration);

    // return the first unused free slot
    for (int i=0 ; i<slotMap.length ; i++) {
        LeasedSlot slot = slotMap[i];

        if (slot.getCookieCount() == -1 ||
            slot.getExpiration() < currentTime) {
            slot.setExpiration(duration + currentTime);
            slot.setValue(value);
            slot.setCookieCount(nextCount++);

            System.out.println("+++ setting slot " +
                               i + " to " + value);
            System.out.println("    cookie is " +
                               slot.getCookie());

            Lease lease =
                factory.newLease(slot.getCookie(),
                                 landlord,
                                 duration + currentTime);
            return new SlotResult(i, lease,
                                  slot.getCookie());
        }
    }

    // no available slots
    return null;
}

public synchronized Object getValue(Object key)
        throws RemoteException, UnknownLeaseException {
    LeasedSlot slot = validateSlot(key);

    return slot.getValue();
}
```

Listing 13–3 `SlotProviderImpl.java` (continued)

```java
LeasedSlot validateSlot(Object cookie)
        throws UnknownLeaseException {
    long currentTime = System.currentTimeMillis();

    if (!(cookie instanceof CookieType)) {
        throw new UnknownLeaseException(
                        "Bad cookie type");
    }

    int index = ((CookieType) cookie).index;
    int count = ((CookieType) cookie).count;

    if (index < 0 || index >= slotMap.length) {
        throw new UnknownLeaseException(
                        "Bad cookie data");
    }

    LeasedSlot slot = slotMap[index];

    if (slot.getCookieCount() == -1) {
        throw new UnknownLeaseException(
                        "Slot not under lease");
    }

    if (slot.getExpiration() < currentTime) {
        slot.setCookieCount(-1);
        slot.setValue(null);
        throw new UnknownLeaseException(
                        "Already expired");
    }

    if (!slot.getCookie().equals(cookie)) {
        throw new UnknownLeaseException(
                        "Wrong cookie for slot; " +
                        "slot has been released.");
    }

    return slot;
}
```

Listing 13–3 `SlotProviderImpl.java` (continued)

```java
public static void main(String[] args) {
    if (args.length != 1) {
        System.err.println(
            "Usage:  SlotProvider <binding_string>");
        System.exit(1);
    }

    if (System.getSecurityManager() == null) {
        System.setSecurityManager(
            new RMISecurityManager());
    }

    try {
        String host =
            InetAddress.getLocalHost().getHostName();
        String url = "rmi://" + host + "/" + args[0];
        SlotProviderImpl spi = new SlotProviderImpl();
        Naming.rebind(url, spi);
        System.out.println(
            "SlotProvider bound to " + url);
    } catch (Exception ex) {
        System.err.println(
                "Couldn't create SlotProvider: " +
                ex.getMessage());
        System.exit(1);
    }
}
```

The first class here, `CookieType`, defines the cookies that the slot provider will use to associate leases and resources. The `CookieType` class holds two separate values: an index, which is used to identify a particular resource, and a unique counter, which is used to identify a lease. Whenever a cookie of this type comes in, the slot provider can quickly identify the resource it refers to by looking up the index. And, if the resource stores the counter value of the lease that owns it, the provider can easily see if an incoming cookie was sent by the lease that holds the resource, or another, out-of-date lease.

The `CookieType` class is `Serializable` since it will be transmitted along with leases to clients.

The `SlotProviderImpl` class is what actually implements the slot-providing interfaces. The class extends `UnicastRemoteObject` and implements `Slot-Provider`. When a client contacts the slot provider, it will use the methods in the `SlotProvider` interface; this is also the same interface that a proxy would use to communicate with a back-end slot provider, if the code here were implemented as a Jini service. The resources it doles out to clients are elements from an array of `LeasedSlots`. The class also maintains an implementation of `Landlord`, which you'll see shortly, and a counter value that will be incremented whenever new leases are created.

First look at the `LeasedSlot` class that makes up the elements of the resource array. `LeasedSlot` implements `LeasedResource`, so it has methods on it to get the cookie associated with a slot, get the expiration time, and so on. Each slot maintains three pieces of information: the cookie for the slot, the expiration time of the lease that currently owns the slot, and any object that a client may have stored here. If a slot is unowned, its cookie will be set to a special value indicating that the slot is available for leasing. Unowned or expired slots may have zero (uninitialized) expiration times, or may still have the expiration time of the lease that last owned them.

The next nested class that you see here is the `Landlord` that will be used to interact with leases and manage slots. The class `MyLandlord` implements the `Landlord` interface, and extends `UnicastRemoteObject`, so it can work "out of the box" with the Sun-provided `LandlordLease` class. Even though the `Landlord` is a remote object, its methods will never be seen directly by clients—they only access the methods on this class indirectly, through the lease objects that they hold.

The method `getRealDuration()` implements the "policy" for the `Land-lord`—the maximum lease duration and the default lease duration are the same, 10 minutes, and any requested lease is granted as long as it is under this value. Requests for leases longer than 10 minutes are shortened to this value.

The next few methods implement the `Landlord` interface. The `cancel()` method takes a cookie that may identify a lease/resource pairing. The method calls `validateSlot()` to make sure that the cookie does indeed represent a valid slot, and that the slot is indeed held by the lease represented by the cookie. The validation check, defined in the outer `SlotProviderImpl`, makes sure that the cookie is of the needed type (`CookieType`), that its index is within range, that the item referred to by the index is in fact leased, that it's not already expired, and that the slot is owned by the lease represented by the cookie. If any of these conditions are not true, `validateSlot()` raises an `UnknownLeaseException`. Otherwise, it returns the slot identified by the cookie.

Once `cancel()` has a valid slot, it frees the resources associated with the slot by setting the `value` member of the `LeasedSlot` to null, and setting the cookie `count` data to -1, which indicates that the slot is no longer under lease.

The implementation of `cancelAll()` iteratively calls `cancel()` for all the cookies passed to it. If at least one cancellation fails, a new `Map` is created and populated with a mapping for each failed exception. That is, for each lease that could not be canceled, the `Map` that is created and returned by `cancelAll()` associates the lease's cookie with an exception that indicates why the cancellation failed. You may be wondering about the wisdom of returning cookies— which are meant to be internal data structures—as a result of this call. Remember that `Landlord` implementations are never seen directly by clients. Clients only indirectly access `Landlord`s through `Lease`s and `LeaseMap`s. In particular, the `cancelAll()` method is only called from implementations of `LeaseMap`. The `LandLordLeaseMap`, which is the flavor of `LeaseMap` that works with Sun's `Landlord` classes, will "translate" from cookies into client-visible leases when the `map` is returned from the `Landlord` implementation.

The `renew()` and `renewAll()` methods work much the same as `cancel()` and `cancelAll()`; `renew()` first validates an incoming cookie as referring to a legitimate slot, and then computes the actual new duration to use for the lease by calling `getRealDuration()`. The new duration is stored in the `LeasedSlot`. The `renewAll()` method iterates through incoming cookies and calls `renew()` for each one. The results of the complete operation are returned in a `RenewResults` object, which contains an array of new lease times, and an array of exceptions. If the renewal succeeds, then the corresponding item in the `granted` array is set to the new lease duration. If the renewal fails, then the *next* item in the `denied` array is set—that is, failure of item *i* to renew causes the *i+1* element in the exceptions array to be set. And, element *i* of the granted array is set to -1.

The `MyLandlord` class takes care of all the mechanics of lease management for the slot provider. When new leases are created, they are initialized to contain a reference to this `Landlord`, and everything in the cancellation and renewal process happens automatically.

Core Note: Landlord utility classes

For most `Landlords`, *the implementation of* `cancelAll()` *and* `renewAll()` *will be exactly the same—they will iterate through the input cookie arrays, calling* `cancel()` *or* `renew()`, *and will build the appropriate return result.*

Because these implementations are common, Sun has—as of Jini 1.1—provided the `com.sun.jini.lease.landlord.LandlordUtil` *class. This class has two static methods,* `cancelAll()` *and* `renewAll()`, *that provide this functionality. The underlying* `cancel()` *and* `renew()` *methods that these static methods will call out to are defined in a new interface,* `com.sun.jini.lease.landlord.LocalLandlord`.

The end result of these two utility classes is that most custom `Landlord` *implementations will implement* `LocalLandlord` *and then use* `LandlordUtil` *to get the* `cancelAll()` *and* `renewAll()` *functionality "for free."*

I've implemented these methods "by hand" here so that you can see what's involved in producing the correct return results. Most applications will simply use the `LandlordUtil` *class, though.*

We still need to look at the remainder of the `SlotProviderImpl` class to see how it works; in particular, we need to see how it issues leases for new slots. When the `SlotProviderImpl` is first created, it initializes its array of `Leased-Slots` and creates an instance of `MyLandlord` to handle lease cancellations and renewals.

Clients, when they need a slot, will go through the `leaseFreeSlot()` method. This method takes a value that the client wishes to store, and a requested lease duration. It will return a `SlotResult` if a slot was granted, or null if no more slots are available. The implementation of this method is where new leases get created. The code converts the requested duration into an actual duration based on the policy implemented by `MyLandlord`. It then iterates through the array of slots, looking for any slot that is unleased or already expired. The first time it finds such a slot, it sets its expiration to the computed expiration time, stores the client-supplied value, and initializes a new cookie by incrementing the lease counter to get a unique number. The factory is called to produce a new lease with that cookie and expiration time, and a `SlotResult` is returned to the client. The `key` value that is returned in the `SlotResult` to identify the client's data is simply the cookie value.

Note that it is the `leaseFreeSlot()` method that is responsible for freeing data associated with an expired lease. If a client explicitly cancels a lease, then the MyLandlord class will free its data. But data held by expired leases are only cleaned up when a new slot is needed. This is an example of the "on-demand" style of resource deallocation mentioned earlier; an alternative would be to have a thread that periodically wakes up and scans the slot array for expired data that can be freed.

The getValue() method is used by a client to retrieve the data stored in its slot, given a key to that data returned in the SlotResult. The validateSlot() method is called to make sure that the key is legitimate, and that the data stored in the corresponding slot is owned by the holder of the key. If it is, then the value is returned.

Finally, the main() for the slot provider implementation creates a new Slot-ProviderImpl and binds it into the RMI registry, at a name supplied on the command line. Since the code here isn't a Jini service, it cannot rely on discovery and lookup for a slot consumer to rendezvous with the provider. So, the code allows the person running the provider to supply a name that the client can use to find it; more on this when I talk about compiling and running the example.

Let's look now at a simple client (Listing 13–4) that will use the slot provider to store data.

Listing 13–4 `SlotClient.java`

```java
// Exercise the SlotProvider.

package corejini.chapter13;

import net.jini.core.lease.Lease;
import net.jini.lease.LeaseRenewalManager;
import java.rmi.RemoteException;
import java.rmi.RMISecurityManager;
import java.rmi.Naming;

public class SlotClient implements Runnable {
    protected SlotProvider provider = null;
    protected LeaseRenewalManager mgr = null;

    public SlotClient() {
        mgr = new LeaseRenewalManager();
    }

    public void setSlotProvider(SlotProvider sp) {
        provider = sp;
    }

    public void run() {
        SlotResult res1, res2, res3;

        while (true) {
            try {
                res1 = provider.leaseFreeSlot("Hello",
                                              10000);
                if (res1 != null) {
                    mgr.renewUntil(res1.getLease(),
                                   Lease.ANY, null);
                } else {
                    System.out.println("No more slots!");
                }
```

Listing 13–4 `SlotClient.java` (continued)

```java
        res2 = provider.leaseFreeSlot("there",
                                      10000);
        if (res2 != null) {
            mgr.renewUntil(res2.getLease(),
                    System.currentTimeMillis() +
                    (1000 * 20), null);
        } else {
            System.out.println("No more slots!");
        }

        res3 = provider.leaseFreeSlot("World!",
                                      10000);
        if (res3 != null) {
            mgr.renewUntil(res3.getLease(),
                           Lease.ANY, null);
        } else {
            System.out.println("No more slots!");
        }

        try {
            System.err.println("Sleeping...");
            Thread.sleep(1000 * 30);
        } catch (InterruptedException ex) {
        }

        try {
            if (res3 != null) {
                System.out.println(
                  "Value of slot: " +
                provider.getValue(res3.getKey()));
                System.out.println(
                  "Cancelling lease");
                mgr.cancel(res3.getLease());
                System.out.println(
                  "After cancellation.");
                System.out.println(
                  "Value of slot: " +
                provider.getValue(res3.getKey()));
            }
        } catch (Exception ex) {
            System.err.println("Error: " +
                            ex.getMessage());
        }
```

Listing 13–4 `SlotClient.java` (continued)

```
                try {
                    System.err.println("Sleeping...");
                    Thread.sleep(1000 * 30);
                } catch (InterruptedException ex) {
                }
            } catch (RemoteException ex) {
                System.err.println("Bogus: " +
                                    ex.getMessage());
                ex.printStackTrace();
            }
        }
    }

    public static void main(String[] args) {
        if (args.length != 1) {
            System.err.println("Usage: SlotClient <url>");
            System.exit(1);
        }

        if (System.getSecurityManager() == null) {
            System.setSecurityManager(
                    new RMISecurityManager());
        }

        try {
            SlotProvider sp = (SlotProvider)
                Naming.lookup(args[0]);
            SlotClient slotClient = new SlotClient();
            slotClient.setSlotProvider(sp);
            new Thread(slotClient).start();
        } catch (Exception ex) {
            System.err.println(
                    "Couldn't start SlotClient: " +
                    ex.getMessage());
            System.exit(1);
        }
    }
}
```

The `SlotClient` class is an application which iteratively acquires and releases slots from a `SlotProvider`. When the `SlotClient` is started, it creates a LeaseRenewalManager to take care of the leases returned by the SlotPro-viderImpl. We've now come full circle! We're actually supplying the leases that will be managed by the LeaseRenewalManager class.

The bulk of the code here is in the run() method for the class, which continually acquires resources. During each iteration of the loop, the method tries to get three slots. Each is initially leased for 10 seconds and, if a slot can be successfully grabbed, it will be renewed. At each iteration, the first is renewed indefinitely, using the Lease.ANY flag, the second is set to expire 20 seconds from the current time, and the third is also renewed indefinitely. After the three slots are acquired, the code sleeps for a few seconds, and then fetches the value of the third resource to show that it can be successfully retrieved. The lease on this resource is then canceled, and so further attempts to fetch its value result in an UnknownLeaseException. After another sleep, the entire process repeats itself.

The program will continue acquiring one new, indefinitely leased resource each time through the loop. After a while, it will exhaust the resources available in our SlotProviderImpl, and no new slots can be acquired.

Compiling and Running the Examples

Since the SlotProvider program isn't a "real" Jini service (meaning it doesn't use lookup or discovery), it needs a different mechanism to allow its clients to find it. The code here uses the RMI registry as a way to rendezvous with clients. You will specify a "name" on the command line that will be associated with the provider; clients will then find the provider by looking up the name in the RMI registry on the host on which the provider is running.

For any of this to work, you must make sure you're running the RMI registry program, which will act as a simple name server. The program, called rmiregistry, lives in the standard Java bin directory. You should run it on the same host on which the provider will run.

Next, let's move on to building the programs.

On Windows: First, compile the main program files for both the "service" implementation and the client. The Java compiler should build all the class files needed by each, so you can compile the SlotProviderImpl into the service directory and the SlotProviderClient into the client directory.

```
javac -classpath C:\files;
               C:\jini1_1\lib\jini-core.jar;
               C:\jini1_1\lib\jini-ext.jar;
               C:\jini1_1\lib\sun-util.jar;
               C:\service
          -d C:\service
```

```
          C:\corejini\chapter13\SlotProviderImpl.java

javac -classpath C:\files;
                C:\jini1_1\lib\jini-core.jar;
                C:\jini1_1\lib\jini-ext.jar;
                C:\jini1_1\lib\sun-util.jar;
                C:\client
            -d C:\client
        C:\corejini\chapter13\SlotProviderClient.java
```

Next, you need to build the RMI stubs for the two remote classes in this example: the `SlotProviderImpl` and the nested `MyLandlord` class. Make sure that the stubs wind up in the `service-dl` directory since they'll need to be downloadable by clients.

```
rmic -classpath C:\jini1_1\lib\jini-core.jar;
                C:\jini1_1\lib\jini-ext.jar;
                C:\jini1_1\lib\sun-util.jar;
                C:\service
        -d C:\service
corejini.chapter13.SlotProviderImpl
corejini.chapter13.SlotProviderImpl.MyLandlord

mkdir C:\service-dl\corejini\chapter13
cd C:\service\corejini\chapter13
copy SlotProviderImpl_Stub.class
    C:\service-dl\corejini\chapter13
copy SlotProviderImpl$MyLandlord_Stub.class
    C:\service-dl\corejini\chapter13
```

Finally, you're set to run! Make sure you pass in a security policy file and a correct codebase. Start the service first. You'll have to give a name to the slot provider so that the client can rendezvous with it later. This can be any arbitrary string; here I've used "`foo`."

```
java -cp C:\jini1_1\lib\jini-core.jar;
        C:\jini1_1\lib\jini-ext.jar;
        C:\jini1_1\lib\sun-util.jar;
        C:\service
    -Djava.security.policy=C:\files\policy
    -Djava.rmi.server.codebase=http://myhost:8085/
    corejini.chapter13.SlotProviderImpl foo
```

Now start the client. The client needs no codebase since it exports no downloadable code. To allow the client to connect with the provider, you must pass
in an RMI URL on the command line. This should have the host on which the
provider is running, followed by the string that you just used when you ran the
provider (the provider will print the URL you should use when it starts). Be
sure you replace the "turbodog.parc.xerox.com" hostname with the host on
which the provider is running.

```
java -cp C:\jini1_1\lib\jini-core.jar;
        C:\jini1_1\lib\jini-ext.jar;
        C:\jini1_1\lib\sun-util.jar;
        C:\service
     -Djava.security.policy=C:\policy
     corejini.chapter13.SlotProviderClient
                 rmi://turbodog.parc.xerox.com/foo
```

On UNIX: First, compile the main program files for both the "service" implementation and the client. The Java compiler should build all the class files
needed by each, so you can compile the SlotProviderImpl into the service
directory and the SlotProviderClient into the client directory.

```
javac -classpath /files:
                /files/jini1_1/lib/jini-core.jar:
                /files/jini1_1/lib/jini-ext.jar:
                /files/jini1_1/lib/sun-util.jar:
                /files/service
          -d /files/service
     /files/corejini/chapter13/SlotProviderImpl.java

javac -classpath /files:
                /files/jini1_1/lib/jini-core.jar:
                /files/jini1_1/lib/jini-ext.jar:
                /files/jini1_1/lib/sun-util.jar:
                /files/client
          -d /files/client
     /files/corejini/chapter13/SlotProviderClient.java
```

Next, you need to build the RMI stubs for the two remote classes in this example: the SlotProviderImpl and the nested MyLandlord class. Make sure that
the stubs wind up in the service-dl directory since they'll need to be downloadable by clients.

```
rmic -classpath /files/jini1_1/lib/jini-core.jar:
                /files/jini1_1/lib/jini-ext.jar:
                /files/jini1_1/lib/sun-util.jar:
                /files/service
        -d /files/service
corejini.chapter13.SlotProviderImpl
corejini.chapter13.SlotProviderImpl.MyLandlord

mkdir /files/service-dl/corejini/chapter13
cd /files/service/corejini/chapter13
cp SlotProviderImpl_Stub.class
    /files/service-dl/corejini/chapter13
cp SlotProviderImpl\$MyLandlord_Stub.class
    /files/service-dl/corejini/chapter13
```

Finally, you're set to run! Make sure you pass in a security policy file and a correct codebase. Start the service first. You'll have to give a name to the slot provider so that the client can rendezvous with it later. This can be any arbitrary string; here I've used "foo."

```
java -cp /files/jini1_1/lib/jini-core.jar:
         /files/jini1_1/lib/jini-ext.jar:
         /files/jini1_1/lib/sun-util.jar:
         /files/service
     -Djava.security.policy=/files/policy
     -Djava.rmi.server.codebase=http://myhost:8085/
     corejini.chapter13.SlotProviderImpl foo
```

Now start the client. The client needs no codebase since it exports no downloadable code. To allow the client to connect with the provider, you must pass in an RMI URL on the command line. This should have the host on which the provider is running, followed by the string that you just used when you ran the provider (the provider will print the URL you should use when it starts). Be sure you replace the "turbodog.parc.xerox.com" hostname with the host on which the provider is running.

```
java -cp /files/jini1_1/lib/jini-core.jar:
         /files/jini1_1/lib/jini-ext.jar:
         /files/jini1_1/lib/sun-util.jar:
         /files/service
     -Djava.security.policy=/files/policy
     corejini.chapter13.SlotProviderClient
                rmi://turbodog.parc.xerox.com/foo
```

Summary

This chapter has looked at the grantor side of leasing in Jini. In the last two chapters, you've seen a complete leasing loop—all the way from clients asking for leased resources, to services that grant leases, and back to the clients that must manage their leases. You've also looked at some common APIs that Sun provides for granting leases, using the `Landlord` paradigm. These utility classes should be useful for a range of applications—Sun even uses them internally in the sample implementations of some of its services—and can be applied to the leasing needs of many of the services you will write. But even if these classes aren't sufficient for you, or don't provide the abstractions you need, you should have a deep enough understanding of lease granting from this chapter to write your own custom leasing infrastructure.

What's Next?

So far in this book, I've talked about a lot of the things that services need to do—participate in discovery, manage their leases, and so on. In the next chapter, I'll pull together all of the things that you as a service writer need to do to ensure that your services are "well-behaved" in the Jini environment.

The Well-Behaved Service

Topics in This Chapter

- Service responsibilities
- Creating administrable services
- Strategies for user interfaces
- Creating service interfaces

Chapter 14

While Jini takes great care to make it unlikely that a single service can—through bad programming or software failure—disrupt an entire community, there are still a number of responsibilities that services have "to play well with others." You've seen most of these responsibilities already. For one, Jini services must follow the join protocol. This ensures that services will try at all costs to persistently maintain any configuration information that users have placed on them. It also provides guidelines for how Jini services connect to their communities—they must wait for a random amount of time before launching into discovery to prevent packet storms, for instance.

For most services, the join protocol represents the required essentials of being a Jini service; you should not deploy services that do not follow the join protocol, as they can disrupt other services in a community and will be difficult to manage.

But beyond these base requirements, there are a number of other jobs that a service can do to ensure that it is useful and useable in a range of contexts. Services should describe themselves through the use of attributes. Services can and should provide administrative interfaces that allow users to configure them. And services that are suitable for direct user interaction should provide user interface components that allow end users to interact with them directly.

In this chapter, you'll learn about these "extra" requirements that can make the difference between a merely useable service and a well-tuned, product-quality service.

The Responsibilities of a Service

I've already spent a fair amount of time talking about the minimum requirements of services in Chapter 8. The join protocol, described there, lists the specifics of what services must do in order to work reliably and manageably in a Jini community. To recap:

- To prevent packet storms on their networks, services should wait a random amount of time before starting.

- Services should perform multicast discovery, joining any groups they have been configured to join, or the unnamed "public" group if they have not yet been configured.

- Services should use unicast discovery to connect to any explicitly configured URLs for lookup services.

- Services must renew their leases with all their lookup services until told to deregister with a lookup service.

- If a service loses contact with a lookup service found through unicast discovery, it must attempt periodically to reestablish contact with it.

- When a service is asked to change the set of attributes associated with it, it must make this change at all lookup services with which it is registered.

- Services must save configuration information persistently, so that it will be used even after restarts or crashes. This persistent information includes the service's unique ID, any lookup groups it should join, its attributes, and its explicitly configured lookup services.

Fortunately for all of us, most of this complexity is completely hidden! The `JoinManager` class handles all of these interactions, with the exception of persistence.

In the examples in previous chapters, you've seen how to use the `JoinManager`, and how to create services that persistently store their configuration data. With this knowledge in hand, you can create reliable, fully functioning Jini services.

But, well-behaved services can go even further. I've already mentioned a number of the extra steps services can take, which basically boil down to the following three:

- Services can describe themselves using attributes.
- Service can support administration.
- Services can provide a user interface that allows humans to control them.

I talked about the first of these, how services can describe themselves by using attributes, in Chapter 7. The standard set of attributes mentioned there can be used as a way to communicate information in a well-known format to clients; services can, of course, also provide custom attributes, such as the `Capacity` attribute.

In this chapter, I'll mainly focus on the two other extra steps that well-behaved services can take: providing for administration and user interfaces.

You've already seen the basics of administration earlier in this book, but in this chapter you'll learn about administration in detail. Recall that services can support a number of administrative interfaces that allow clients to control them. At a minimum, services should support the `JoinAdmin` interface, which controls their interaction with the join protocol. But there are other standard administrative interfaces available, and many services will also provide custom administrative interfaces. In this chapter, you'll see an example of a version of the `LeaseService` that supports administration.

Finally, services can provide complete user interfaces that allow end users to control them. Even though a service's proxy may implement Java interfaces that might not be known to a given client—which effectively means that the client cannot interact *programmatically* with the service—a service's user interface (UI) may still allow *people* to interact with it directly. There are a number of strategies that you can take to attach a user interface to a Jini service. I'll talk about the pros and cons of each in this chapter, and pay special attention to a solution that the Jini community has agreed upon as a "standard" approach.

If you're deploying services for "real-world" use, either internally in your company or as a commercial product, these extra steps—description, administration, and user interface—can add greatly to the utility of your service.

Core Note: Know and Use the Jini Technology Compatibility Kit

Sun makes available a set of tools called the Jini Technology Compatibility Kit (TCK) that can be used to test a service's compliance with the join protocol and other aspects of being a "well-behaved" Jini service. In fact, passing the requirements of the TCK is necessary for services that wish to use the Jini-compatible logo from Sun.

The TCK is freely available from Sun, and you don't have to be a commercial licensee to use it. You can download it, free of charge, to test your own services, to verify whether third-party services that don't bear the Jini-compatible logo are well-behaved, and to ensure that even logo-bearing services do what they claim.

The Jini TCK is available at:

```
http://developer.java.sun.com/developer/products/jini/
product.offerings.html
```

Again, nothing requires you to pass the compatibility kit's tests, and nothing requires you to take the extra steps mentioned in this chapter to ensure that your service is well-behaved. It's just that if you want to "legally" call yourself a Jini service and use the Jini trademarks, you must pass the compatibility tests.

At the time of this writing, the TCK is at version 1.1, and will certainly grow over time.

Service Administration

Chapter 9 briefly introduced the notion of service administration, and showed some of the common administrative interfaces for services. In this section, you'll look a bit more deeply at administration, and see an example of how to create an administrable service.

Administration through Delegation

Service administration follows a *delegation* model. This means that, rather than having a service's proxy object implement all of the required administrative interfaces, the proxy can return a "surrogate" object that understands how to do administration.

There are a number of reasons for this. First, it allows developers to create the administrative interfaces for a service independently from the service's core functionality. You can build what your service *does* first, and then worry about how to control it.

Second, administrative code may be quite large. By keeping this functionality out of the proxy, you can speed up download times, and reduce the storage requirement in Jini lookup services. Administrative delegate objects are only fetched when needed.

Finally, by providing the ability for administration to be mediated by an object separate from the proxy, developers can choose the best implementation strategy for each. For example, the administrative object for a service may be simply an

RMI stub that communicates directly with the back-end portion of a service. Other service proxies may create the administrative object locally when asked. Still others may ask the back-end part of the service for an administrative object when needed. If Jini required the proxy to implement the administrative interfaces directly, this flexibility would be lost.

These benefits of delegation don't, however, *require* you to create a separate administrative object. A developer can choose to implement the administrative interfaces directly in the service proxy itself. When asked for its administrative object, such a service proxy would simply return a reference to itself.

Administrative Interfaces

You've already seen the basic Jini administrative interfaces in Chapter 9. A service proxy that provides an administration delegate object should implement the `net.jini.admin.Administrable` interface. The object returned by the `getAdmin()` call may implement several common administrative interfaces. Table 14–1 lists the standard interfaces.

Table 14–1 Standard Administrative Interfaces		
Package	*Interface*	*Description*
`com.sun.jini.admin`	`DestroyAdmin`	Controls the termination of a service.
`net.jini.lookup`	`DiscoveryAdmin`	Controls how a lookup service interacts with groups and other lookup services.
`net.jini.admin`	`JoinAdmin`	Controls a service's participation in the join protocol. Should be implemented by all services.
`com.sun.jini.admin`	`StorageLocation Admin`	Controls the location of a service's persistent storage.

In addition to these standard interfaces, certain services may implement their own custom administrative interfaces. For example, a storage engine may support controls that allow users to configure the maximum amount of storage it will grant. Sun's own implementation of the Jini lookup service, `reggie`, supports the `com.sun.jini.reggie.RegistrarAdmin` interface, which allows administrators to change things such as the default maximum lease duration that will be granted.

Implementation of Administrative Delegates

Creators of services have great freedom in how they choose to implement their administrative delegate objects. Some administration objects will be simply RMI stub objects that communicate directly with the back-end service. Others will be more complex objects that "wrap" some protocol that they use to communicate with the service.

There is, however, one restriction that the writers of administrative objects should follow: In general, it's a good idea to not use GUI classes directly in your administrative delegates.

Why is this? Clearly, programmatic administration of services isn't the only thing you'll want to do; you'll also want to be able to directly control services through front-end graphical interfaces. If a service provides a custom administration API, it would certainly be useful if it could supply a user interface that allowed users to work with it!

The reason for this guideline is that not all platforms will have all Java packages available to them. The services you write should be not only *useable* but also *controllable* from as many platforms as possible. Suppose that a service proxy is sent to a machine that has only a limited set of the Java class libraries (such as a PDA or cell phone); most likely, devices like this will be lacking many of the full-blown user interface libraries. Now, if the administrative object for this service relies on such libraries—perhaps because it is a subclass of JFrame or Component, then these machines will be completely unable to even instantiate the administrative object! Even though clients may be perfectly capable of interacting with the object programmatically, they are prevented from doing so because of the constraints placed on the object by its developer. The moral of the story is that you should make your administrative objects as minimal as possible, so that they can be run as widely as possible.

Of course, services can still provide custom GUIs for their administration objects, as well as for themselves; they should, however, take care to not *require* their users to have a full set of class libraries to work. A bit later in this chapter, you'll see how to attach user interfaces to services and administration objects.

An Example: Administering the LeaseService

It's time to explore an example of how to create an administrable service using the LeaseService from Chapter 12 as a starting point. The LeaseService is well-behaved in every way—it follows the join protocol, and takes great care to make any configuration information persistent—with one exception: it is not administrable.

As mentioned before, every service should support the JoinAdmin interface at a minimum. This interface allows users (and programs) to control how the service interacts with the join protocol. Without this interface, you cannot control which groups the service joins, or which lookup services it registers with. So, services should consider this interface to be a requirement.

Additionally, services may want to implement several of the other standard interfaces, or even custom interfaces. In the example of administration for the LeaseService, I'll implement the "big three:" JoinAdmin, DestroyAdmin, and StorageLocationAdmin. You could easily imagine a custom administrative interface for this service—perhaps one that allows users to tune leasing policy variables, such as maximum and default lease times. But, I'll focus only on the standard interfaces here.

The original LeaseService of Chapter 12 was carefully set up to allow it to be extended with administration—its proxy object implemented Administrable and did a remote method invocation back to the service process to fetch an administration object when it was called. The only thing that was lacking from that example was that the back-end service always returned null when asked for its administration object.

To improve the LeaseService, I'll subclass it and override getAdmin() to return a "real" administrative object. I'll also add some extra remote methods that this administrative object will use to communicate with the back-end service to actually change service parameters.

The organization of this example illustrates a very common approach to implementing administration: the service's proxy contacts the back end when it is asked for an administrative object. The back end then returns a serialized administrative object that is initialized with a remote reference that it can use to speak a "private" administrative protocol with the back end.

The code for the example begins with the administrative object (Listing 14–1). Let's start off by examining the administrative object that is returned by the proxy's `getAdmin()` call. This is the actual object that clients will operate on to perform administration.

Listing 14–1 `LeaseAdminProxy.java`

```
// this is the admin object that gets returned to clients.
package corejini.chapter14;

import net.jini.core.entry.Entry;
import net.jini.core.discovery.LookupLocator;
import net.jini.admin.JoinAdmin;
import com.sun.jini.admin.DestroyAdmin;
import com.sun.jini.admin.StorageLocationAdmin;
import java.io.IOException;
import java.io.Serializable;
import java.rmi.RemoteException;
```

Listing 14–1 `LeaseAdminProxy.java` (continued)

```java
public class LeaseAdminProxy implements JoinAdmin,
    DestroyAdmin, StorageLocationAdmin, Serializable {
    protected AdminLeaseService.RemoteLeaseAdmin remote;

    LeaseAdminProxy(
            AdminLeaseService.RemoteLeaseAdmin remote) {
        this.backend = backend;
    }

    // implement destroyadmin
    public void destroy() throws RemoteException {
        backend.destroy();
    }

    // implement storagelocationadmin
    public void setStorageLocation(String loc)
        throws IOException, RemoteException {
        backend.setStorageLocation(loc);
    }

    public String getStorageLocation()
        throws RemoteException {
        return backend.getStorageLocation();
    }

    // implement JoinAdmin
    public Entry[] getLookupAttributes()
        throws RemoteException {
        return backend.getLookupAttributes();
    }
    public void addLookupAttributes(Entry[] attrs)
        throws RemoteException {
        backend.addLookupAttributes(attrs);
    }
    public void modifyLookupAttributes(Entry[] tmpls,
                                       Entry[] attrs)
        throws RemoteException {
        backend.modifyLookupAttributes(tmpls, attrs);
    }
```

Listing 14–1 `LeaseAdminProxy.java` (continued)

```java
public String[] getLookupGroups()
    throws RemoteException {
    return backend.getLookupGroups();
}
public void addLookupGroups(String[] groups)
    throws RemoteException {
    backend.addLookupGroups(groups);
}
public void removeLookupGroups(String[] groups)
    throws RemoteException {
    backend.removeLookupGroups(groups);
}
public void setLookupGroups(String[] groups)
    throws RemoteException {
    backend.setLookupGroups(groups);
}
public LookupLocator[] getLookupLocators()
    throws RemoteException {
    return backend.getLookupLocators();
}
public void addLookupLocators(LookupLocator[] locs)
    throws RemoteException {
    backend.addLookupLocators(locs);
}
public void removeLookupLocators(LookupLocator[] locs)
    throws RemoteException {
    backend.removeLookupLocators(locs);
}
public void setLookupLocators(LookupLocator[] locs)
    throws RemoteException {
    backend.setLookupLocators(locs);
}
public boolean equals(Object o) {
    if (o instanceof LeaseAdminProxy) {
        return backend.equals(
            ((LeaseAdminProxy) o).backend);
    } else {
        return false;
    }
}
```

Listing 14–1 `LeaseAdminProxy.java` (continued)

```
    public int hashCode() {
        return backend.hashCode();
    }
}
```

The administrable object, called `LeaseAdminProxy`, implements the three administrative interfaces and is also `Serializable` since it will be sent from the back end to the client via the proxy's `getAdmin()` method. When the administration object is created, it is initialized with a reference to a remote object that implements the interface the proxy uses to communicate with the back-end service. This interface is nested in the new `LeaseService` subclass that supports administration, and is called `RemoteLeaseAdmin`.

All of the methods on the administrative proxy are simply forwarded to the `RemoteLeaseAdmin` in the service back end. As you'll see, the local administrative APIs are essentially the same as the remote ones in this case. So one possible implementation strategy would be to simply use the stub for the remote interface *as* the administration object. Here, I've taken the approach of creating a separate proxy that calls through to a remote interface, because this is the more general approach, and reflects the way most administrative objects are likely to be built. By separating the implementation of the proxy from the remote protocol, you could imagine more complicated administration objects that cache results locally, or use a more complex protocol to communicate with the back end. Each could evolve independently of the other.

Let's now look at the subclass of `LeaseService`.

Listing 14–2 `AdminLeaseService.java`

```java
// Administrable subclass of LeaseService

package corejini.chapter14;

import net.jini.core.discovery.LookupLocator;
import net.jini.core.entry.Entry;
import net.jini.lookup.JoinManager;
import net.jini.discovery.LookupDiscoveryManager;
import net.jini.lease.LeaseRenewalManager;
import net.jini.admin.JoinAdmin;
import com.sun.jini.admin.DestroyAdmin;
import com.sun.jini.admin.StorageLocationAdmin;
import java.io.File;
import java.io.BufferedReader;
import java.io.BufferedWriter;
import java.io.FileReader;
import java.io.FileWriter;
import java.io.IOException;
import java.rmi.Remote;
import java.rmi.RemoteException;
import java.rmi.server.UnicastRemoteObject;
import corejini.chapter12.LeaseService;
```

Listing 14–2 `AdminLeaseService.java` (continued)

```java
public class AdminLeaseService extends LeaseService {
    protected RemoteLeaseAdmin remoteAdmin = null;
    protected LeaseAdminProxy admin = null;
    protected static boolean done = false;
    protected static Thread thread = null;

    // work around bugs in javac's handling of inner
    // classes and inheritance
    JoinManager getJoinManager() {
        return joinMgr;
    }
    LeaseRenewalManager getLeaseManager() {
        return leaseMgr;
    }
    LookupDiscoveryManager getDiscoveryManager() {
        return (LookupDiscoveryManager)
            joinMgr.getDiscoveryManager();
    }

    void setStorageLoc(String loc) {
        storageLoc = loc;
    }
    String getStorageLoc() {
        return storageLoc;
    }

    // All of our administrative interfaces
    public interface RemoteLeaseAdmin extends Remote,
        JoinAdmin, StorageLocationAdmin, DestroyAdmin {
    }

    public class RemoteLeaseAdminImpl
        extends UnicastRemoteObject
        implements RemoteLeaseAdmin {
        RemoteLeaseAdminImpl() throws RemoteException {
            super();
        }
```

Listing 14–2 `AdminLeaseService.java` (continued)

```
public void destroy() {
    File locFile = new File(getStorageLoc());
    synchronized (AdminLeaseService.this) {
        // stop doing lookup/discovery
        getJoinManager().terminate();
        // empty out the lease manager.
        getLeaseManager().clear();
        // zap persistent storage
        locFile.delete();
        // shut down thread
        done = true;
        thread.interrupt();
    }
}
public void setStorageLocation(String loc)
    throws RemoteException {
    synchronized (AdminLeaseService.this) {
        try {
            // try to pick up the current file
            // and move it.
            File newLocFile = new File(loc);
            File oldLocFile =
                new File(getStorageLoc());

            BufferedReader reader =
                new BufferedReader(
                    new FileReader(oldLocFile));
            BufferedWriter writer =
                new BufferedWriter(
                    new FileWriter(newLocFile));

            char[] buffer = new char[1024];
            int n;
            while ((n = reader.read(buffer)) > 0) {
                writer.write(buffer, 0, n);
            }
            reader.close();
            writer.close();
```

Listing 14–2 `AdminLeaseService.java` (continued)

```java
            setStorageLoc(loc);

            oldLocFile.delete();
        } catch (IOException ex) {
            throw new RemoteException(
                            ex.toString());
        }
    }
}
public String getStorageLocation() {
    return getStorageLoc();
}
public Entry[] getLookupAttributes() {
    return getJoinManager().getAttributes();
}
public void addLookupAttributes(Entry[] attrs)
    throws RemoteException {
    getJoinManager().addAttributes(attrs, true);
    try {
        AdminLeaseService.this.checkpoint();
    } catch (IOException ex) {
        throw new RemoteException(ex.toString());
    }
}
public void modifyLookupAttributes(Entry[] tmpls,
                                    Entry[] attrs)
    throws RemoteException {
    getJoinManager().modifyAttributes(tmpls, attrs,
                                        true);
    try {
        AdminLeaseService.this.checkpoint();
    } catch (IOException ex) {
        throw new RemoteException(ex.toString());
    }
}
public String[] getLookupGroups() {
    return getDiscoveryManager().getGroups();
}
```

Listing 14–2 `AdminLeaseService.java`   (continued)

```java
public void addLookupGroups(String[] groups)
    throws RemoteException {
    try {
        getDiscoveryManager().addGroups(groups);
        AdminLeaseService.this.checkpoint();
    } catch (IOException ex) {
        throw new RemoteException(ex.toString());
    }
}

public void removeLookupGroups(String[] groups)
    throws RemoteException {
    // Note no IOException here.  Adding and setting
    // groups may re-initiate discovery (hence they
    // may raise IOException), but removing cannot.
    getDiscoveryManager().removeGroups(groups);
    try {
        AdminLeaseService.this.checkpoint();
    } catch (IOException ex) {
        throw new RemoteException(ex.toString());
    }
}

public void setLookupGroups(String[] groups)
    throws RemoteException {
    try {
        getDiscoveryManager().setGroups(groups);
    } catch (IOException ex) {
    }
    try {
        AdminLeaseService.this.checkpoint();
    } catch (IOException ex) {
        throw new RemoteException(ex.toString());
    }
}

public LookupLocator[] getLookupLocators() {
    return getDiscoveryManager().getLocators();
}
```

Listing 14–2 `AdminLeaseService.java` (continued)

```java
    public void addLookupLocators(LookupLocator[] locs)
        throws RemoteException {
        getDiscoveryManager().addLocators(locs);
        try {
            AdminLeaseService.this.checkpoint();
        } catch (IOException ex) {
            throw new RemoteException(ex.toString());
        }
    }

    public void removeLookupLocators(
                        LookupLocator[] locs)
        throws RemoteException {
        getDiscoveryManager().removeLocators(locs);
        try {
            AdminLeaseService.this.checkpoint();
        } catch (IOException ex) {
            throw new RemoteException(ex.toString());
        }
    }

    public void setLookupLocators(LookupLocator[] locs)
        throws RemoteException {
        getDiscoveryManager().setLocators(locs);
        try {
            AdminLeaseService.this.checkpoint();
        } catch (IOException ex) {
            throw new RemoteException(ex.toString());
        }
    }
}

public AdminLeaseService(String storageLoc)
    throws RemoteException,
    IOException, ClassNotFoundException {
    super(storageLoc);
}
```

Listing 14–2 `AdminLeaseService.java` (continued)

```java
    // override getAdmin()
    public Object getAdmin() {
        try {
            if (remoteAdmin == null) {
                remoteAdmin = new RemoteLeaseAdminImpl();
            }
            if (admin == null) {
                admin = new LeaseAdminProxy(remoteAdmin);
            }

            return admin;
        } catch (RemoteException ex) {
            System.err.println(
                "Error creating remote admin: " + ex);
            ex.printStackTrace();
            return null;
        }
    }

    public static void main(String[] args) {
        if (args.length != 1) {
            System.err.println(
                "Usage: LeaseService <storage_loc>");
            System.exit(1);
        }

        try {
            AdminLeaseService src =
                new AdminLeaseService(args[0]);
            while (!done) {
                try {
                    thread = Thread.currentThread();
                    Thread.sleep(Long.MAX_VALUE);
                } catch (InterruptedException ex) {
                }
            }
        } catch (Exception ex) {
            System.err.println("Trouble starting: " + ex);
            ex.printStackTrace();
        }
        System.exit(1);
    }
}
```

The code in Listing 14–2 is a subclass of `LeaseService`, and inherits all of its old methods. Only the `getAdmin()` method is overridden, because it must return the administrative object for the service instead of the null value that the original service returned. I've also added a few extra methods here that allow the proxy to communicate with the back end to perform administrative tasks.

The `AdminLeaseService` class defines a nested interface called `Remote-LeaseAdmin`, which defines the way the administrative proxy will communicate with the back end. As mentioned, the local and remote interfaces are—in the case of this example—the same. So the remote interface merely extends the necessary administrative APIs, as well as `Remote`. The nested class `RemoteLeaseAdmin-Impl` provides an implementation of the interface that the administrative objects sent out to clients will communicate with.

The first methods in the `AdminLeaseService` are, unfortunately, necessary to work around bugs that appear in some versions of Sun's `javac` compiler. The bugs prevent inner classes from accessing members contained in their nesting class's superclass. The `getJoinManager()` method and friends simply return members defined in the `LeaseService` class so that they can be accessed by the inner `RemoteLeaseAdminImpl`.

`RemoteLeaseAdminImpl` is a `UnicastRemoteObject`, since the administration object will communicate with it remotely using RMI. This class implements all the various methods that the administration object uses to control the service.

The `destroy()` method is used to shut down the service. It terminates the join process, clears out the lease manager, and deletes the persistent storage associated with the service. It also causes the thread that keeps the "wrapper" process to stop by setting the `done` flag to true. See the implementation of `main()` to see how the flag is used.

The implementation of `setStorageLocation()` tries to "pick up and move" the persistent storage file to the new specified location. The old file is copied to the new and, if no exceptions are raised, the old file is deleted.

The `getStorageLocation()` method is typical of the "get" methods implemented here. It simply returns the current storage location string stored in the superclass. The other "get" methods fetch data out of the `JoinManager` maintained in the superclass.

With the exception of the `destroy()` method, and the various storage location-related methods, everything else controls aspects of the `JoinManager`. The `addLookupGroups()` method is typical of these—it updates the list of lookup groups in the `JoinManager`, and then calls `checkpoint()` to flush the change out to persistent storage. If you're unfamiliar with inner class syntax, you may be confused by the line `AdminLeaseService.this.checkpoint()`. This code merely specifies that the `checkpoint()` method lives in the outer `AdminLeaseService` class, and not in the `RemoteLeaseAdminImpl` inner class.

The only other two distinguished methods in the class are `getAdmin()`, which overrides the null-returning version in the superclass, and `main()`. This version creates the `RemoteLeaseAdminImpl` the first time it is used, and then creates and returns a `LeaseAdminProxy` initialized with the remote object.

The `main()` routine creates a new `AdminLeaseService` object and then loops forever—or until the `destroy()` method shuts the service down. The main thread is recorded so that it can be stopped by `destroy()`.

Providing User Interfaces for Services

In all of the service examples so far, services have been accessed programmatically—through the Java interfaces that they support. This arrangement works fine when both a client and a service can agree ahead of time on what interfaces they will use to work with one another. In fact, because this agreement on interfaces is so important, Sun and its partners are working to define a standard set of interfaces for common network services and devices.

To put it simply, if a client and a service cannot agree on what interfaces they will use, there is essentially no way for them to work together programmatically. If a client finds a service that implements an unknown interface, with methods it does not recognize, the client will have no way of understanding the semantics of the interface—what the service and all of its methods actually *do* and how to use them.

This situation is not as dire as it might seem. Even though a *program* might be unable to use a service that implements unknown interfaces, an actual human *user* may have no problem with such a service. Even if the user doesn't know a remote method call from a bowling ball, he or she is very likely to be able to work with a service that presents an intuitive user interface that hides the programmatic interface.

So, providing intelligent user interfaces for services is important for most services, and virtually essential for those that do not implement standard interfaces. By providing a UI for your service, you make it *directly* accessible to users from programs like browsers that can display the UIs for particular services. So if you have a digital camera and a service that creates thumbnails of images, and the camera has never heard of the thumbnail interface, you may still be able to use these services together if they provide flexible user interfaces, perhaps by directly dragging snapped photos out of the camera's UI and onto the thumbnail service's UI.

In this section, I'll talk about how to build and deliver user interfaces for Jini services.

Several Approaches to Providing UIs

There are several ways one might deliver a user interface for a service. One way would be to make the service's proxy, in addition to implementing the programmatic interfaces that allow clients to drive the service, also implement the needed UI functionality itself. So, your service proxy might be a subclass of JFrame that, when made visible, could display a complete user interface that would allow people to interact with the service.

The downsides of such an approach are exactly the same as the downsides of having administrative objects implement UI functionality directly—if a given client platform doesn't have the necessary UI classes, it will be unable to use the service *at all*, even in a programmatic way. If your service proxy extends a class that is not available in a particular client, that client will not be able to instantiate it and the proxy will be unuseable there. So, this isn't really a viable strategy.

Another approach, and a better one, would be to mirror the style of the Administrable interface—provide a new interface that proxies could implement, perhaps called "Interfaceable," that returns the GUI for a client. While this approach is far better than having the proxy implement the user interface functionality directly, it does have problems. Most importantly, it provides only *one* way to get an interface for a service. Since Jini services may be accessed from any number of devices and machines, each with its own UI capabilities, we'd like a more flexible approach that would allow services to provide multiple UIs— including UIs optimized for desktop computers, voice or telephony interfaces, and perhaps graphical UIs optimized for small devices like cell phones and PDAs. So, any methods on "Interfaceable" should provide some way for clients to specify what sort of interface they are interested in.

This strategy also has the problem that the service itself returns its interface. This prohibits the possibility of adding an interface to a service "after the fact," perhaps by attaching a user interface as an attribute of the service.

A third approach provides user interfaces for services as attributes attached to service proxies. This design provides flexibility, since you can have multiple attributes attached to services, each containing a particular UI implementation. Clients can quickly find the particular UI implementation they need, or can even search for services that implement desired UI functionality. And, if a client doesn't have the class libraries needed for a *particular* UI, the failure to load the desired attribute will be reflected in a very convenient way—by an UnuseableEntryException being raised—without affecting the loading of other attributes or the service proxy itself. This approach is not without its problems, though. Specifically, you must take great care when using serialization to transmit a complex object—like a user interface component—as an `Entry`. I'll talk about this more in the next short example; in practice, this limitation makes it difficult to use this approach for all but the simplest interfaces.

Finally, a fourth approach—and the one that the Jini community is standardizing on—involves a somewhat more complicated use of attributes as a way to associate user interfaces with services. In this approach, a service can have any number of UI "descriptor" attributes attached to it. These attributes can be added by the service, or—solving an issue I mentioned earlier—added after the fact by clients. This approach also allows any number of user interfaces to coexist: you can have graphical, voice, or Web interfaces for the same service. This approach also introduces the concept of different UI "roles" for a service. So a given service might carry a main interface, as well as an administrative interface. I'll discuss this approach in more detail a bit later in the chapter.

Table 14-2 presents a table summarizing some of the choices I've outlined above.

Table 14–2 Service UI Strategies

Strategy	*Pros*	*Cons*
Proxy extends UI class	•Easy to use.	•Supports only one type of UI. •May prevent *any* use of proxy. •Requires proxy (and hence UI classes) to be initialized on service side.
Proxy has method to return UI	•Easy to use. •Same idiom as `getAdmin()`	•Service must build in support for all possible UIs.

Table 14–2 Service UI Strategies (continued)

UI attached as attribute	• Flexible. • Supports easy addition of new UI types. • Supports multiple UIs. • Allows clients to search for services with particular UI types. • Nice failure modes.	• Attributes are created in a different VM than the one in which they'll be used. • Must be careful with serialization.
UI "indirectly" attached as attribute	• Flexible, powerful. • Supports new UI types, multiple UIs. • Service UIs can be added "after the fact." • "Standard" approach adopted by the Jini community.	• Requires a bit of work to set up.

A Simple Example: User Interfaces as Attributes

In the next example of this chapter, you'll see a simple service user interface that's constructed as an attribute that subclasses the Swing UI class JFrame; this user interface provides a basic "splash screen" that identifies the LeaseService from an earlier chapter in a graphically interesting way. The UI also provides a way to access the service's administrative functions. More complicated services could, obviously, support more complicated user interfaces. A storage service might provide graphs and charts showing storage utilization over time. But here, rather than focus on the ins and outs of building large-scale Java user interfaces, I'll focus on one approach to creating service UIs that are useable in the context of Jini.

This approach uses the third strategy I outlined above—attaching a UI as an attribute of the service—and it does have a number of drawbacks, which I'll talk about in the discussion. In the future, after the Jini Community has standardized on the Service UI framework I mentioned briefly, that work will serve as the basis for all Jini user interfaces. While the approach taken here is a suitable stopgap measure for very simple interfaces, I do not recommend it generally.

Figure 14–1 shows the UI for the LeaseService. This "splash screen"-style interface identifies the service, and provides a button that allows users to administer it. Even though the browser code you saw earlier provides a way to access a service's administrative functions, other browsers might not support this ability. So the user interface here has it "built in."

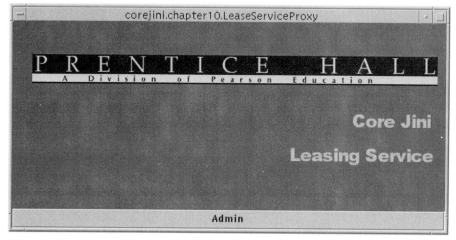

Figure 14–1   *A splash screen for the LeaseService.*

The SplashScreen class (Listing 14–3) is an extension of JFrame, and implements the Entry interface, since it will be sent to clients as an attribute.

Listing 14–3 SplashScreen.java

```java
// A simple frame to display a splash screen

package corejini.chapter14;

import net.jini.admin.Administrable;
import net.jini.core.entry.Entry;
import javax.swing.JFrame;
import javax.swing.JLabel;
import javax.swing.JButton;
import javax.swing.ImageIcon;
import java.awt.event.WindowEvent;
import java.awt.event.WindowAdapter;
import java.awt.event.ActionEvent;
import java.awt.event.ActionListener;
import java.io.InputStream;
import java.io.IOException;
import java.io.BufferedInputStream;
import java.io.BufferedOutputStream;
import java.io.ByteArrayOutputStream;
import java.rmi.RemoteException;
import corejini.chapter11.AdminPanel;
```

Listing 14–3 `SplashScreen.java` (continued)

```java
public class SplashScreen extends JFrame implements Entry {
    protected final static String ICON =
                                "SplashScreen.gif";
    protected final static String DEFAULT =
                                "Core Jini / Leasing Service";

    public SplashScreen() {
        super("Uninitialized splash screen");
    }
    public SplashScreen(Object proxy) {
        super(proxy.getClass().getName());
        setProxy(proxy);
    }

    // Set the proxy object that the splash screen is for
    public void setProxy(Object proxy) {
        Object admin;

        if (proxy == null) {
            admin = null;
            return;
        }

        setTitle(proxy.getClass().getName());

        try {
            if (proxy instanceof Administrable) {
                admin = ((Administrable) proxy).getAdmin();
            } else {
                admin = null;
            }
        } catch (RemoteException ex) {
            admin = null;
        }

        addWindowListener(new WindowAdapter() {
            public void windowClosing(WindowEvent ev) {
                setVisible(false);
                dispose();
            }
        });
```

Listing 14–3 `SplashScreen.java` (continued)

```java
JLabel label;
byte[] buffer = null;

// Fetch the splash screen as a resource.  This gets
// it using the same classloader that loaded this
// object.
try {
    InputStream resource =
        getClass().getResourceAsStream(ICON);
    if (resource == null) {
        label = new JLabel(DEFAULT);
    } else {
        BufferedInputStream in =
            new BufferedInputStream(resource);
        ByteArrayOutputStream out =
            new ByteArrayOutputStream(1024);

        buffer = new byte[1024];
        int n;

        while ((n = in.read(buffer)) > 0) {
            out.write(buffer, 0, n);
        }
        in.close();
        out.flush();

        buffer = out.toByteArray();

        if (buffer.length == 0) {
            label = new JLabel(DEFAULT);
        } else {
            label =
                new JLabel(new ImageIcon(buffer));
        }
    }
} catch (IOException ex) {
    label = new JLabel(DEFAULT);
}

getContentPane().add(label, "Center");
```

Listing 14–3 `SplashScreen.java` (continued)

```java
        if (admin != null) {
            final Object fadmin = admin;
            JButton button = new JButton("Admin");
            button.addActionListener(new ActionListener() {
                public void actionPerformed(ActionEvent ev){
                    JFrame frame = new JFrame(
                                    "Lease Service Admin");
                    frame.getContentPane().add(
                                    new AdminPanel(fadmin),
                                     "Center");
                    frame.pack();
                    frame.addWindowListener(
                            new WindowAdapter() {
                        public void windowClosing(
                            WindowEvent ev) {
                        setVisible(true);
                        dispose();
                    }
                });
                    frame.setVisible(true);
                }
            });
            getContentPane().add(button, "South");
        }

        pack();
        setVisible(true);
    }
}
```

When instances of the `SplashScreen` attribute are sent to clients, they will be transmitted as serialized objects, and reconstituted upon arrival at the client. When a `SplashScreen` attribute is reconstituted, it will create an as-yet invisible frame with a title bar that says "Uninitialized splash screen." When a client application wishes to initialize the splash screen and make it visible, it calls the `set-Proxy()` method on it, passing in the proxy object for the `LeaseService`. This method is one API that both the consumer of these attributes and the attribute writer must agree on. Just like in the service UI case, Jini will certainly standardize on interfaces that will be used to initialize user interface attributes as it evolves; in this example, though, both parties agree on the `setProxy()` call.

Core Alert: Take care when sending serialized UI components

In this example, I'm sending a very simple graphical component to a client as a serialized object. But in general, you should be very careful when returning UI components from services to clients. For one thing, if a service creates a UI component (say, a `JTextArea`*) and attaches it as an attribute, the UI component is initially constructed inside the service. Just naively sending it to the client may not work, as listeners inside the component may point to objects inside the server. So you may need to supply an "initialize" method that clients will invoke on returned objects that correctly set up their state for execution inside the client.*

Other approaches outlined earlier, particularly the fourth one, do not have this problem since UI components are created in the client's JVM.

When the proxy is set in the attribute, it loads a resource that contains the image to be displayed in the splash screen, and creates a button that can be used to bring up the administrative GUI panel we created earlier.

There are a couple of points to make about this code. First, when you create GUI attributes—or any attributes for that matter—you need to ensure that they are properly serializable. The code shown here implements `Entry`, which is a claim to the system that we know what we're doing. But this class has to take special care to make sure that it will behave properly when transmitted to clients.

In particular, note that the code here doesn't hold on to any references to the proxy object. You might think that, rather than forcing the client to call `set-Proxy()` to tell the GUI about its proxy object, the service that created the proxy could "pre-initialize" it with the proxy. But if the code retains a reference to the proxy object, it will be sent along with the rest of the attribute to the client when it is serialized. Since the client presumably *already* has the service's proxy—retrieved via a call to `lookup()`, or through an event—this is almost certainly not what you want!

Also note the call to `getResourceAsStream()`. This method loads a "resource" (in this case an image file) by using the class loader that loaded the attribute itself. Since the attribute was originally published by some service, that service must take care to set the codebase when it runs so that the URL that points to the attribute's code, as well as this image file, can be found by clients. The codebase set by the publishing service will be used to fetch the attribute's code and resources whenever the serialized `SplashScreen` object is reconstituted at the client.

This is an important point and deserves restating—when you set a codebase URL in your service, any downloadable classes your clients need will be loaded from this URL, as will any supporting classes or files. So, for example, in this program, you would put both the splash screen GUI code and the image itself on a directory exported by an HTTP server, and set the codebase to point to this server.

When a client needs the GUI class, it will be retrieved via a class loader initialized to load from the codebase URL. The RMI semantics used by Jini essentially take care of this for you, since the serialized GUI class will be stored at the lookup service with its codebase associated with it. And when the client then needs to load the image resource, it will be fetched using the same class loader that loaded the GUI code. Here you see that the image resource is loaded using the *same* class loader that loaded the `SplashScreen` class (`getResourceAsStream()` is called on the `SpashScreen` class object, which means that the resource is loaded from the same class loader that loaded `SplashScreen`—in other words, the class loader that uses the codebase URL). If the client had used one of its own "local" classes to try to load the image resource, most likely a `ClassNotFoundException` would result—since the class loaders of these local classes would not know to read classes from the codebase URL.

Setting a codebase is a way to ensure that, no matter who needs to use your classes or any of their supporting files, they can be properly fetched from the correct location at run time. You just have to remember to use a class loader that is properly initialized to load from the codebase URL. The easiest way to do this—as shown here—is simply to "reuse" the class loader from a class already loaded remotely.

Finally, note the use of member data here. The `SplashScreen` implementation is not readily searchable by the data contained in it. Clients *can* find it by looking for the classes and interfaces it implements. But because there is no public, nonstatic, nontransient data here, the contents of the `SplashScreen` attribute are not searchable. This is fine for the example here, but in more complicated attributes, you may want to make sure that they expose searchable data to clients.

Now that you've seen how the `SplashScreen` attribute works, let's look at another extension of the `LeaseService` that publishes these attributes.

Listing 14–4 `AttrLeaseService.java`

```java
// Extend the administrable lease service to attach a UI
// attribute to it.

package corejini.chapter14;

import net.jini.core.entry.Entry;
import net.jini.lookup.entry.ServiceInfo;
import java.io.IOException;
import java.rmi.RemoteException;

public class AttrLeaseService extends AdminLeaseService {
    public AttrLeaseService(String storageLoc)
        throws RemoteException, IOException,
                ClassNotFoundException {
        super(storageLoc);

        Entry[] entries = new Entry[2];

        entries[0] = new ServiceInfo("Prentice-Hall",
                                     "LeaseService",
                                     "LeaseService",
                                     null,
                                     "Prentice-Hall",
                                     "v1.0");
        entries[1] = new SplashScreen();

        joinMgr.addAttributes(entries);
        checkpoint();
    }

    public static void main(String[] args) {
        if (args.length != 1) {
            System.err.println(
                "Usage: LeaseService <storage_loc>");
            System.exit(1);
        }
```

Listing 14–4 `AttrLeaseService.java` (continued)

```
        try {
            AttrLeaseService src =
                new AttrLeaseService(args[0]);
            while (!done) {
                try {
                    thread = Thread.currentThread();
                    Thread.sleep(Long.MAX_VALUE);
                } catch (InterruptedException ex) {
                }
            }
        } catch (Exception ex) {
            System.err.println("Trouble starting: " +
                                ex.getMessage());
            ex.printStackTrace();
        }
        System.exit(1);
    }
}
```

This class (Listing 14–4) is an extension of `AdminLeaseService` that simply attaches a couple of attributes to the published proxy object. Here, you see how to attach a `ServiceInfo` object, and the new `SplashScreen` user interface shown earlier. The attributes are added by simply calling out to the `JoinManager`, stored in the original `LeaseService` class, and then checkpointing to make sure the change is saved.

The ServiceUI Approach

In the beginning of the discussion on how to create user interfaces for services, I mentioned four separate strategies. The last one I mentioned involved using attributes "indirectly" as a way to obtain interfaces. In this approach, attributes contain a "factory" object that is capable of producing user interfaces, rather than "raw" user interfaces themselves.

This approach has a number of advantages. First off, it has all of the same advantages of the "direct" attribute approach—it allows services to have multiple user interfaces at the same time, it allows clients to attach new user interfaces that the service writer may not have thought of, it lets clients search for services that have particular interfaces, and it lets clients continue to use the service's proxy directly without forcing them to have any user interface classes installed.

Additionally, this approach brings with it two other important benefits. First, and most importantly, it allows the user interface to be instantiated in the client's JVM. The other attribute-based strategy I mentioned—where UIs are serialized and attached directly as attributes—requires that the interface be first created in the service, serialized, attached as an attribute, and then deserialized in the client. In most cases, serializing Java objects for transport to a new JVM is no big deal. But serializing UI classes for transport requires special care. Many UI components will retain references to data structures that reside in the JVM in which they were instantiated. Swing components, for example, may hold references to enclosing frames, event queues, and various native components. Unless you exercise extreme caution when sending these components to a different machine, you are very likely to wind up with a serialized user interface that doesn't work when it is deserialized in the client.

A second benefit of the factory-based approach is that it keeps the size of attributes down. Even if a client fetches an entire `ServiceItem` for a desired service, it is likely that only one of the user interfaces attached to the service will actually be used. If `ServiceItems` contained multiple full-blown interfaces (most of which would never be used anyway), then the download of `Service-Items` would be incredibly expensive, and incredibly wasteful. Typically, the factories that can make UIs will be far smaller than the UIs themselves, and—since the UIs aren't created until needed—this arrangement will put fewer resource requirements on clients.

The Jini Community at Work

When Jini 1.0 was released, there was no consensus on how user interfaces would be associated with services. The Jini designers had their hands full putting together the basic building blocks of the system. It was clear to everyone involved, though, that for Jini to be useful, the community would have to standardize on a common way of attaching user interfaces to services.

The attribute-as-factory approach described above is the result of an effort by members of the Jini community to define a common means for clients and services to associate user interfaces with services. Bill Venners has led this effort and, at the time of the writing of the second edition of *Core Jini*, the *ServiceUI* specification was making its way through the Jini community process.

While other community efforts—such as the definition of common printing and storage interfaces—have been led by industry groups, this is an example of largely a single individual leading Jini into new territory.

At the time of this writing, the ServiceUI specification and code is in flux, so I haven't presented any examples of its use here. As the ServiceUI APIs solidify, I will add examples to `http://www.kedwards.com/jini/` that show how to use them. In the meantime, the sections below illustrate the high-level details of the ServiceUI approach as it exists now.

ServiceUI Essentials

To associate a user interface with a service using the ServiceUI approach, you must provide three separate objects:

- A `UIDescriptor`, which is attached as an attribute and contains details about a particular UI associated with the service.
- The UI "factory" that will be instantiated on the client's VM and used to create the user interface.
- The actual user interface to associate with the service.

The first, and most important, of these is the `UIDescriptor`. The `UIDescriptor` is simply an attribute of type `net.jini.lookup.entry.UIDescriptor`, which—in the proposed specifications—contains the following items:

- A *role*, which indicates how the UI represented by this descriptor will be used. Roles are expressed as strings that name fully-qualified interfaces. For example, the string `net.jini.lookup.ui.MainUI` would be the role for a service's "main" interface. The `net.jini.lookup.ui.AdminUI` role would be the UI for administering the service.
- A *toolkit*, which indicates a distinguishing package name for the classes that the UI will require. For example, the string `javax.swing` would be used as the toolkit for any UI that required the Swing classes. A speech-oriented interface might use `javax.media.speech` as its toolkit.
- A set of attributes that describes the UI represented by the `UIDescriptor`. Most UI providers will attach attributes to describe the types implemented by the factory contained in the `UIDescriptor` (see below), the locales supported by the UI, the packages required on the client to instantiate the UI, and so on.
- A *factory*, represented as a `MarshalledObject`, which can be used to instantiate the UI.

A client that wishes to find services that have, say, a graphical interface for administration, might search for all services that have `UIDescriptor`s with the toolkit field set to `javax.swing` and the role field set to `net.jini.lookukp.ui.AdminUI`. Clients can download the attributes of such services to do more fine-grained examination of the required packages needed to use the UI.

Once a client is ready to instantiate the UI, it first fetches the factory contained in the `UIDescriptor`. This factory is stored as a `MarshalledObject`. This means that the `UIDescriptor` contains the serialized members of a `factory` object, along with a codebase URL that will be used to retrieve the code for the factory, if needed. The client instantiates the factory by calling the `get()` method on the `MarshalledObject`, which deserializes (reconstitutes) the `factory` object. This results in an instance of the factory that the client can then use to create the desired user interface.

After the factory has been instantiated in the client, the client can interact with it to create actual user interfaces.

Core Note: Advantages of storing factories as MarshalledObjects

Note that storing the factory as a `MarshalledObject`, *rather than simply as a "direct" member of the descriptor, has a couple of advantages. First, it means that the factory won't be instantiated when the descriptor is deserialized; rather, it will only be instantiated when the client explicitly calls* `get()` *on the* `MarshalledObject` *containing the factory. Second, since* `MarshalledObjects` *contain codebase URLs, this leaves open the possibility that the code for the factory could be stored at a different location—and loaded using a different class loader—than the code for the rest of the service.*

UI Factories

Clearly, different sorts of UIs will have different requirements—both in terms of the class libraries that they require on the client, and in the amount of "client-side knowledge" that they require to be used.

If a factory returned a voice interface, for example, a client would still have to know how to use this voice interface. By this I mean that the client would have to know how to interact with the object returned by the factory, how to instantiate and dismiss it, and how to "plug it in" to the rest of the client's behaviors.

Because of these differences, the ServiceUI specification supports different types of UI factories. Most clients will be written to "know" how to interact with certain types of factories. A graphical client, for example, would come pre-programmed with knowledge about how to use graphical UIs associated with services—how to place them in `JFrames`, how to call `show()` on them to display them, and so on. Other sorts of clients might know how to interact with other user interfaces, such as voice, HTML, or some other sort of interface.

Note that just because a client has to know how to instantiate and use a certain *type* of UI, it doesn't need to know anything special about any *particular* UI. Most clients will be happy to know that the UI returned from a factory is a `JPanel`, for instance. This allows them to know that they can slap it in a frame, resize it as needed, and show it to the user. They don't have to know exactly what service-specific UI this panel contains to be able to use it.

Because of the requirement that clients be able to make some minimal assumptions about the types of objects that will be returned by factories, the ServiceUI specification defines a number of different factory classes. Each of these factory classes returns a different type of UI object. For example, `JFrameFactory` returns a `javax.swing.JFrame` instance (or a subclass); and `DialogFactory` returns a `java.awt.Dialog` instance (or a subclass). If a client knows the type of the factory it is using, it will know what sorts of objects the factory will return, and how to use them.

The ServiceUI specification provides for a number of common graphical UI factory types, compatible with either AWT or Swing. Other factory types may appear in the future; in general, you should try to use the "standard" types defined by the ServiceUI specification, since uncommon factory types are unlikely to be understood by clients.

UI Roles

I mentioned in the discussion of `UIDescriptors` that each descriptor comes with a role that defines how the UI is meant to be used. A role might be used to distinguish a service's "main" interface from its administrative interface, for example.

Just as clients and services must agree on some common types for UI factories, they must also agree on a set of symbols that denotes UI roles. For example, if all clients and services agree that the string "admin" indicates an administrative UI, then these programs will have a common language for describing how certain UIs should be used. If a client encounters a service with some strange, unknown role name, it will likely have no idea how the UI for that role is intended to be used.

The ServiceUI specification defines a number of role names, specified as fully-qualified names of Java interfaces. Using interface names means that chunks of the role namespace (like `net.jini` or `com.sun`) can be reserved for use by the Jini community, or by certain companies or individuals. Currently, the ServiceUI specification defines three roles:

- `net.jini.lookup.ui.MainUI`, for providing the "primary" end-user interface for a service.
- `net.jini.lookup.ui.AdminUI`, for providing an administrative interface for a service.
- `net.jini.lookup.ui.AboutUI`, for providing some simple descriptive information for a service.

While you can define new roles, you should try to use the standard ones wherever possible. Remember that agreed-upon roles are the common denominator between services and clients; if a client doesn't understand your role, it is unlikely to know how you intend your interface to be used.

Where to Go Next

The ServiceUI approach provides a solid foundation for building user interfaces for Jini services. It allows services to have multiple interfaces, and even supports multiple *types* of interfaces at the same time. Interfaces can be added by the original writers of a service, or they can be added after-the-fact by other clients. And, perhaps most importantly, the ServiceUI framework is designed with extensibility in mind: The basic APIs here can be extended to support graphical, voice, or other styles of user interfaces.

As I said at the start of this section, the ServiceUI specification is still evolving. The discussion I've presented here should be treated as a very tentative overview of what's coming, and not the final word on using the ServiceUI approach. As the Jini community process adopts and enhances ServiceUI, I will post information—and example programs—that you are welcome to download on my Web site. See the "Related Reading" section at the end of this chapter for pointers to Bill Venners' excellent Web site on the ServiceUI project.

Summary

In this chapter, you've looked at not only what the basic requirements of Jini services are, but also how to make services more well-behaved. Custom Jini services should always support join administration, and may support other standard or custom administrative interfaces as appropriate. And, if your service exposes some concept that would "make sense" to end users—and particularly if your service doesn't implement a well-known programmatic interface—you should seriously consider adding a custom user interface to your service via an attribute.

Related Reading

If you're interested in reading up on the full details of the ServiceUI approach, or the thinking behind particular design decisions, Bill Venners' Web site is the authoritative resource:

```
http://www.artima.com/jini/serviceui/index.html
```

What's Next

In the next chapter, you'll pull together everything you've learned so far about services. Chapter 15 presents a complete service, designed to allow access to a host-connected printer. This service uses persistence, follows the join protocol, and is administrable. You'll also see a sample toolkit that can be used to build new services.

A Complete Example: The Print Service

Topics in This Chapter

- A complex, full-featured service
- The Service Writer's Toolkit
- Service persistence
- Custom administration interfaces
- Custom attributes
- Generating events to clients

Chapter 15

I n this chapter, you'll look in detail at a long example—a full-featured Jini service that can provide printing support to clients. The patterns you'll see here are common across many types of Jini services, so you may be able to reuse whole chunks of code from this example in your applications. In fact, certain pieces of the code are "pulled out" into a toolkit to make the job of writing services easier.

In particular, you'll see how services can checkpoint themselves to persistent storage to ensure reliability and crash recovery, how to support service administration and custom user interfaces for services, and—a new topic here—how custom services can generate events to clients to inform them of changes in the state of the service. Perhaps more important than simply focusing on the individual requirements for a Jini service, you'll learn how the various parts of the service mesh together.

The printing service that you'll examine here is meant to be a "gateway" between the Jini world and a host-attached printer. The printing service offers clients an API for printing data and controlling certain print parameters (number of copies and paper orientation). The service itself uses the standard Java printing APIs to cause data sent to it to be rendered onto the default printer on whatever host the service is running. The architecture here follows a very common Jini model, namely that of a software service that controls and mediates access to attached hardware, making it accessible through the Jini interfaces.

Requirements for a Printing Service

Let's begin by looking at what exactly a printing service needs to do. Obviously, at the most basic level, a printing service must support some interface that allows clients to send data to it to be printed. The printing service should be as general purpose as possible; that is, it should be able to accept any type of data for printing. And, even if the print service does not "know" how to print a particular type of data (JPEG files, or some other complex format, for example), the APIs for printing should not limit the types of data that are sent. One way to make arbitrary data printable is to require that the client send to the service a way for the service to render the data onto a printer.

In addition to simply sending data to the print service, a client needs to have some way of communicating various print parameters to the service, such as paper orientation (portrait versus landscape) and the number of copies to print. For its part, the print service must have some way to inform the client when a print job has completed successfully, or when it has failed. Since printing may take a long time, messages about print completion should be delivered asynchronously as *events* so that clients can continue processing while printing happens in the background.

Print administration is also important. A client may wish to determine how many items are in a service's print queue, and select the service with the shortest queue. So the service will need a way to provide information like this. And, since the client should be able to display the print queue to the user, the service needs a user interface that can present this information in a useful way.

Finally, in addition to all of the *specific* requirements of printing, the service must be a well-behaved, full-featured Jini service. This means that it must be able to recover after crashes by saving its state to persistent storage. Even if a service crashes or is shut down in the middle of printing, any pending print jobs—including the current one—should be resumed when the print service restarts. Ensuring this behavior takes a bit of careful coding. Being a well-behaved service also means that the printing service must be fully administrable—not only for controlling and viewing the print queue, but also for controlling the service's participation in the join protocol and other common aspects of participating in Jini communities.

A Service Writer's Toolkit

Many Jini services follow similiar patterns: They consist of a proxy as well as a "wrapper" application that implements the back-end portion of the service. This wrapper not only provides some portion of the service's processing, but also takes care of publishing the service's proxy, and the lease management that's needed to maintain the proxy. Services such as these typically need to checkpoint themselves to persistent storage so that they can recover after crashes. And most of the administrative tasks of these services are also the same: They allow users to configure their join protocol parameters and the location of their persistent storage. They may also allow users to shut them down.

Rather than having to rebuild all of this infrastructure every time you write a new service, you can define a set of Java classes that serve as a *toolkit* for creating common types of services. This chapter presents just such a set of classes, which I'll use to build the print service. These classes will also show up in later chapters in different types of services. You can use these classes as well, if you find yourself designing services that follow the patterns supported by these classes.

The Service Writer's Toolkit defined here provides a number of functions to service writers. In particular:

- The toolkit takes care of persistent data by checkpointing the state of the service to stable storage. If you use these classes, you can extend the checkpoint and restore behavior to read from and write to persistent storage the data that is particular to your new service.

*   The toolkit handles creation of a `JoinManager`, as well as initializing the `JoinManager` with whatever persistent state may be saved from the last run.

*   The tookit takes care of providing administrative interfaces for the `JoinAdmin`, `StorageLocationAdmin`, and `DestroyAdmin` interfaces. By using the toolkit classes, your service will "automatically" use these interfaces, and you can extend the code to support your own custom administrative interfaces.

The code here is useful for a particular set of services: namely, those that fit into the classic mold where the proxy communicates with a back end to do some processing. In the Service Writer's Toolkit, communication happens via RMI: The class from which new services will be derived is an extension of `UnicastRemoteObject`. Likewise, the administrative object is itself an RMI stub which communicates using RMI to a back-end object that implements administration.

There are two classes and one interface that you should understand in order to use this package. The most important is `BasicUnicastService`. This class should be the superclass of any service that uses this framework. You can subclass `BasicUnicastService` to add your own functionality, and a `main()` routine specific to the needs of your service.

`BasicUnicastService` defines a method called `restored()` that subclasses can override. This method will be called when the service is restarted after a crash or a reboot, to give subclasses of `BasicUnicastService` an opportunity to initialize themselves from the persistent data.

Finally, administration is performed by a class called `BasicUnicastAdmin`. This is an object that actually implements all of the administrative functions for a service, and exposes an RMI interface to clients. Clients access instances of `BasicUnicastAdmin` by calling methods on its RMI stub object, which is returned from proxies when `getAdmin()` is invoked. If your service needs specialized administrative behavior, you can easily subclass `BasicUnicastAdmin` to add the behavior you need.

A Superclass for Services

Let's start off by looking at `BasicUnicastService`, as shown in Listing 15–1.

Listing 15–1 `BasicUnicastService.java`

```java
// A class to use as a superclass for RMI-based services.

package corejini.chapter15;

import net.jini.core.lookup.ServiceID;
import net.jini.core.entry.Entry;
import net.jini.core.discovery.LookupLocator;
import net.jini.lookup.JoinManager;
import net.jini.lookup.ServiceIDListener;
import net.jini.lease.LeaseRenewalManager;
import net.jini.discovery.LookupDiscoveryManager;
import java.rmi.Remote;
import java.rmi.RemoteException;
import java.rmi.MarshalledObject;
import java.rmi.server.UnicastRemoteObject;
import java.io.File;
import java.io.Serializable;
import java.io.IOException;
import java.io.ObjectOutputStream;
import java.io.ObjectInputStream;
import java.io.FileOutputStream;
import java.io.FileInputStream;
```

Listing 15–1 `BasicUnicastService.java` (continued)

```java
public abstract class BasicUnicastService
        extends UnicastRemoteObject
        implements ServiceIDListener {
    protected JoinManager joinMgr;
    protected LeaseRenewalManager leaseMgr;
    protected LookupDiscoveryManager luMgr;
    protected String storageLoc;
    protected File file = null;
    protected ServiceID serviceID = null;
    protected Object proxy = null;

    // Store data for crash recovery
    static class PersistentData implements Serializable {
        ServiceID serviceID;
        Entry[] attrs;
        String[] groups;
        LookupLocator[] locs;
        MarshalledObject subclassData;

        PersistentData(ServiceID serviceID, Entry[] attrs,
                    String[] groups, LookupLocator[] locs,
                        MarshalledObject subclassData) {
            this.serviceID = serviceID;
            this.attrs = attrs;
            this.groups = groups;
            this.locs = locs;
            this.subclassData = subclassData;
        }
    }

    public BasicUnicastService(String storageLoc)
            throws RemoteException {
        super();

        this.storageLoc = storageLoc;
        file = new File(storageLoc);
    }

    // subclasses that want to be informed after a
    // restore should override this.
    public void restored(Object subclassData) {
    }
```

Listing 15–1 `BasicUnicastService.java` (continued)

```java
public JoinManager getJoinManager() {
    return joinMgr;
}

public LookupDiscoveryManager getDiscoveryManager() {
    return luMgr;
}

public LeaseRenewalManager getLeaseManager() {
    return leaseMgr;
}

// administration will call this to shutdown.
// clients can override.
protected void shutdown() {
    System.exit(1);
}

protected abstract Object getProxy();

// subclasses override to return initial attributes
protected Entry[] getAttributes() {
    return new Entry[0];
}

public void serviceIDNotify(ServiceID id) {
    serviceID = id;
    try {
        checkpoint();
    } catch (IOException ex) {
        System.err.println("Trouble checkpointing: " +
                        ex.getMessage());
    }
}

protected void checkpoint() throws IOException {
    checkpoint(null);
}
```

Listing 15–1 `BasicUnicastService.java` (continued)

```java
    protected void checkpoint(Object rawSubclassData)
            throws IOException {
        MarshalledObject subclassData =
                new MarshalledObject(rawSubclassData);

        PersistentData data = new PersistentData(serviceID,
                                    joinMgr.getAttributes(),
                                    luMgr.getGroups(),
                                    luMgr.getLocators(),
                                    subclassData);

        ObjectOutputStream out = new
            ObjectOutputStream(new FileOutputStream(file));

        out.writeObject(data);
        out.flush();
        out.close();
    }

    // restore should *only* be called once, at startup.
    protected void restore()
            throws IOException, ClassNotFoundException {
        ObjectInputStream in = new
            ObjectInputStream(new FileInputStream(file));
        PersistentData data =
            (PersistentData) in.readObject();

        if (data == null) {
            System.err.println("No data in storage file.");
        } else {
            System.out.println("Restoring!");
            serviceID = data.serviceID;
            leaseMgr = new LeaseRenewalManager();
            luMgr = new LookupDiscoveryManager(data.groups,
                                    data.locs,
                                    null);
            joinMgr = new JoinManager(proxy, data.attrs,
                                    data.serviceID, luMgr,
                                    leaseMgr);
            // Subclasses override restored() to do subclass
            // specific restore behavior.
            this.restored(data.subclassData.get());
        }
    }
}
```

Listing 15–1 `BasicUnicastService.java` (continued)

```java
// subclasses override this to do their own
// initialization behavior.
protected void initialize() throws IOException,
    ClassNotFoundException {
    proxy = getProxy();

    if (file.exists()) {
        restore();
    }

    if (joinMgr == null) {
        leaseMgr = new LeaseRenewalManager();
        luMgr = new LookupDiscoveryManager(
                                new String[] {""},
                                null, null);
        joinMgr = new JoinManager(proxy,
                            getAttributes(),
                            this, luMgr, leaseMgr);
    }
}

// subclasses write a main that creates a subclass of
// BasicUnicastService and calls initialize() on it.
}
```

The `BasicUnicastService` class is a remote object which extends `UnicastRemoteObject`. This means that it will use RMI for communication with its proxy objects. Instances of `BasicUnicastService` are meant to be constructed with a string that indicates the location of the service's persistent storage.

Creation of a `BasicUnicastService` is a two-stage process. First, a new instance of the class is created by calling the constructor and passing to it a string identifying its storage location for persistent data. Second, the `initialize()` method is called, which "begins" the service proper. Separating the stages of creation gives subclasses more freedom in deciding where and how to add their own custom behaviors. In general, most subclasses will call the `BasicUnicast-Service` constructor in *their* constructors; the `main()` routine for the service will then call `initialize()` on the newly constructed object.

Several of the methods on this class are meant to be overridden by subclasses. In particular, `getProxy()`, `getAttributes()`, `initialize()`, `restored()`, and `shutdown()` can profitably be overridden by subclasses. Of these, `get-`

`Proxy()` is abstract, because `BasicUnicastService` cannot provide a reasonable default implementation of it—only a particular subclass knows what proxy object it will use. The others provide what are hopefully sensible default behaviors that many subclasses will be able to use unchanged.

The `getProxy()` and `getAttributes()` methods simply return the service's proxy object and any initial attributes that should be set on it, respectively.

The `initialize()` method, by default, tries to restore the service from its checkpointed state if the file containing its persistent data exists. It does this by calling out to `restore()`, which will create an initialized `JoinManager` from this data. If the storage file does not exist, or if `restore()` cannot recover the state of the service, then `initialize()` will create a "fresh" `JoinManager`. Subclasses of `BasicUnicastService` that have to do some particular initialization will often override `initialize()`. But they should be sure to call out to their superclass' implementation so that the restoration behavior is preserved.

The `shutdown()` method is invoked from a service's termination administrative APIs just before the service is destroyed. Services can do any special cleanup jobs that they may require here; by default, `shutdown()` simply exits the JVM. The final method that subclasses may wish to override is `restored()`, which is called when a service is recovered from a checkpointed log.

So, let's look at how checkpointing and restoration work. The nested class `PersistentData` is used to contain all of the information written to stable storage. It contains all of the information needed for the join protocol (the service's ID, attributes, groups, and explicit lookup locators), as well as an untyped object called `subclassData`. This object can be used by subclasses to store any information particular to their code. When `checkpoint()` is called, it builds a new `PersistentData` record by fetching the information out of the `JoinManager`, as well as any subclass-specific information passed to it. Subclasses can use this mechanism to pass their own data, specific to their service, to `checkpoint()` so that it will be saved and recovered.

Restoration of persistent information after a restart is accomplished by `restore()`. This method is only called once—when the service is first started. It reads the saved data off stable storage, constructs a `JoinManager` initialized with the recovered information, and calls out to the `restored()` method, passing it the subclass-specific data it recovered. This allows subclasses an opportunity to set up any subclass-specific state that may have been saved to persistent storage.

When you look at the printing service, you'll see how subclasses can use this code. Basically, the steps they must follow are simple: They should override at least `getProxy()`, along with any other methods they may need to change, and provide a `main()` routine that creates a subclass of `BasicUnicastService` and calls `initialize()` on it.

Core Tip: Ensuring that saved data will be loadable in the future

There is one subtlety to note in the checkpoint and restore code. You may have noticed that the subclass-specific data is "wrapped" in a MarshalledObject before it is put into the PersistentData object; likewise, when a PersistentData instance is read, the get() method is invoked to "unwrap" the MarshalledObject and return the original subclass data. Why is this? Think for a moment about the way the PersistentData class works. In the future, when we load saved instances of this class off of the disk, the Java class loader will need to have access to the class files for every class referred to by the PersistentData instance. If you look at the definition of PersistentData, you'll see that the data members in it are references to things like ServiceID and String and LookupLocator—all of which are "standard" classes that come with either Java or Jini, and which we can expect to always be accessible to any class loader trying to recreate a saved PersistentData object.

Of course, subclasses of BasicUnicastService may need to checkpoint arbitrary data to the disk. Some of this data may be in the form of "nonstandard" classes that don't come with Java or Jini. Such classes may not have even originated with the subclass of BasicUnicastService—they may be custom lease implementations provided by clients of the service, for example, which the service wishes to save. How can we ensure that the classfiles for such arbitrary objects can be found at the time the data is recovered from disk?

This is why the subclass-specific data is wrapped in a MarshalledObject. Presumably, nonstandard data will arrive at the service by way of a remote method invocation, in which case they will be "annotated" with a codebase that specifies where the bytecodes for any unknown classes may be found. By wrapping instances of these data in a MarshalledObject before saving to disk, we ensure that the codebase annotation is saved as well. When the PersistentData instance is loaded off the disk, the standard classes will be loaded from the default Java classloader, while the classes required by any object wrapped in the MarshalledObject will be loaded from its specific codebase URL.

This is a general guideline to follow anytime you need to serialize data that may use nonstandard classes. By using a MarshalledObject you can save the data along with the codebase URL needed to access any required classes; this allows these classes to be reloaded from that

URL in the future. Classes that will typically be found in the normal classpath of an application do not need this special treatment, because their classes will be loaded from default locations

A Tool for Administration

Let's now look at how to support administrable `BasicUnicastServices`. When you create a subclass of `BasicUnicastService`, you will need to create a proxy object for your subclass. If your service is to be administrable, then this proxy should implement the `Administrable` interface and return an object which can be used to manage the service as it runs.

Since many of these administrative tasks are common across services—shutting down the service, changing its join parameters, and so forth—many services can share a common implementation of administration.

In this section, I will present a class called `BasicUnicastAdmin` that cooperates with a `BasicUnicastService` to administer it. Instances of `BasicUnicastAdmin` are created with a reference to the service that they will manage. These objects implement all the methods in `JoinAdmin`, `StorageLocationAdmin`, and `DestroyAdmin`. `BasicUnicastAdmin` is itself an RMI server object, and the RMI-generated stub for it is a perfectly acceptable object to return from the service proxy when `getAdmin()` is called.

As a remote object, `BasicUnicastAdmin` must implement an interface that defines the methods that are callable on it remotely. I've created such an interface, shown in Listing 15-2, that extends the administrative interfaces and `java.rmi.Remote`.

Listing 15–2 RemoteUnicastAdmin.java

```java
// A remote interface that groups together all of
// the administrative interfaces supported by
// BasicUnicastAdmin.

package corejini.chapter15;

import com.sun.jini.admin.DestroyAdmin;
import com.sun.jini.admin.StorageLocationAdmin;
import net.jini.admin.JoinAdmin;
import java.rmi.Remote;

public interface RemoteUnicastAdmin
    extends JoinAdmin, DestroyAdmin,
            StorageLocationAdmin, Remote {
}
```

This interface, called `RemoteUnicastAdmin`, defines the over-the-wire proto-col that the administrative objects used in clients will use to speak to the remote `BasicUnicastAdmin` object that resides in the service. Since `BasicUnicas-tAdmin` is an RMI object, its automatically generated stub class can be used as the client-side administrative object.

Next, take a look at the code for the `BasicUnicastAdmin` object itself, as shown in Listing 15–3.

Listing 15–3 BasicUnicastAdmin.java

```java
// A class for handling common administrative chores.

package corejini.chapter15;

import net.jini.lookup.JoinManager;
import net.jini.discovery.LookupDiscoveryManager;
import net.jini.core.entry.Entry;
import net.jini.core.discovery.LookupLocator;
import java.rmi.RemoteException;
import java.rmi.server.UnicastRemoteObject;
import java.io.File;
import java.io.IOException;
import java.io.FileReader;
import java.io.FileWriter;
import java.io.BufferedReader;
import java.io.BufferedWriter;

public class BasicUnicastAdmin extends UnicastRemoteObject
    implements RemoteUnicastAdmin {
    protected BasicUnicastService service;

    protected BasicUnicastAdmin(
            BasicUnicastService service)
        throws RemoteException {
        this.service = service;
    }

    public synchronized void destroy() {
        File locFile = new File(service.storageLoc);
        service.getJoinManager().terminate();
        locFile.delete();
        service.shutdown();
    }
```

Listing 15–3 `BasicUnicastAdmin.java` (continued)

```java
public synchronized void setStorageLocation(String loc)
    throws RemoteException {
    try {
        File newLocFile = new File(loc);
        File oldLocFile = new File(service.storageLoc);

        BufferedReader reader =
            new BufferedReader(
                new FileReader(oldLocFile));
        BufferedWriter writer =
            new BufferedWriter(
                new FileWriter(newLocFile));

        char[] buffer = new char[1024];
        int n;
        while ((n = reader.read(buffer)) > 0) {
            writer.write(buffer, 0, n);
        }
        reader.close();
        writer.close();

        service.storageLoc = loc;
        oldLocFile.delete();
    } catch (IOException ex) {
        throw new RemoteException(ex.toString());
    }
}
public String getStorageLocation() {
    return service.storageLoc;
}
public Entry[] getLookupAttributes() {
    return service.getJoinManager().getAttributes();
}
```

Listing 15–3 `BasicUnicastAdmin.java` (continued)

```java
    public void addLookupAttributes(Entry[] attrs)
        throws RemoteException {
        service.getJoinManager().addAttributes(attrs,
                                               true);
        try {
            service.checkpoint();
        } catch (IOException ex) {
            throw new RemoteException(ex.toString());
        }
    }

    public void modifyLookupAttributes(Entry[] tmpls,
                                       Entry[] attrs)
        throws RemoteException {
        service.getJoinManager().modifyAttributes(tmpls,
                                                   attrs,
                                                   true);
        try {
            service.checkpoint();
        } catch (IOException ex) {
            throw new RemoteException(ex.toString());
        }
    }

    public String[] getLookupGroups() {
        return service.getDiscoveryManager().getGroups();
    }

    public void addLookupGroups(String[] groups)
        throws RemoteException {
        try {
            service.getDiscoveryManager().addGroups(
                                              groups);
        } catch (IOException ex) {
        }
        try {
            service.checkpoint();
        } catch (IOException ex) {
            throw new RemoteException(ex.toString());
        }
    }
```

Listing 15–3 `BasicUnicastAdmin.java` **(continued)**

```java
public void removeLookupGroups(String[] groups)
    throws RemoteException {
    service.getDiscoveryManager().removeGroups(groups);
    try {
        service.checkpoint();
    } catch (IOException ex) {
        throw new RemoteException(ex.toString());
    }
}
public void setLookupGroups(String[] groups)
    throws RemoteException {
    try {
        service.getDiscoveryManager().setGroups(
                                        groups);
    } catch (IOException ex) {
    }
    try {
        service.checkpoint();
    } catch (IOException ex) {
        throw new RemoteException(ex.toString());
    }
}
public LookupLocator[] getLookupLocators() {
    return service.getDiscoveryManager().getLocators();
}
public void addLookupLocators(LookupLocator[] locs)
    throws RemoteException {
    service.getDiscoveryManager().addLocators(locs);
    try {
        service.checkpoint();
    } catch (IOException ex) {
        throw new RemoteException(ex.toString());
    }
}
public void removeLookupLocators(LookupLocator[] locs)
    throws RemoteException {
    service.getDiscoveryManager().removeLocators(locs);
    try {
        service.checkpoint();
    } catch (IOException ex) {
        throw new RemoteException(ex.toString());
    }
}
```

Listing 15–3 `BasicUnicastAdmin.java` (continued)

```java
    public void setLookupLocators(LookupLocator[] locs)
            throws RemoteException {
        service.getDiscoveryManager().setLocators(locs);
        try {
            service.checkpoint();
        } catch (IOException ex) {
            throw new RemoteException(ex.toString());
        }
    }
}
```

`BasicUnicastAdmin` extends `UnicastRemoteObject` since it uses RMI to communicate with its stub object located in the client. The class implements the remote interface `RemoteUnicastAdmin`, which defines the set of methods on the class that are callable remotely; these are the methods of the various Jini administrative interfaces. Although `BasicUnicastAdmin` could have been designed to implement the various individual administrative interfaces directly, using a separate interface—`RemoteUnicastAdmin`—leads to a cleaner design by encapsulating *all* the common administrative interfaces. That is, this separate interface is a design choice, not a requirement.

New instances of `BasicUnicastAdmin` are initialized with a reference to the `BasicUnicastService` that they will manage. All the various methods on the administrative implementation change or retrieve information from the service object, and cause the service object to checkpoint itself after a change. The actual implementations of these methods are similar to the ones you saw in Chapter 14.

To use `BasicUnicastAdmin` in your own services, you would simply instantiate a new instance of the class in your service's wrapper the first time one of your proxies is asked for an administrative object. By returning the RMI-generated stub for `BasicUnicastAdmin` to the client, you can expose the administrative methods to it.

If your service needs to define custom administrative interfaces in addition to the standard interfaces supported here, you can easily subclass `Basic-UnicastAdmin` to provide the extra functionality needed.

In the rest of this chapter, I'll show a print service that leverages the service toolkit code you've just looked at. You'll see how to subclass `Basic-UnicastService` to create new RMI-based services, and how to extend the functionality of `BasicUnicastAdmin` to support custom administrative interfaces.

Defining the Print Service API

Now that you've seen some tools that you can use to create Jini services, it's time to begin building atop these tools to create the printing service.

The first thing you need to do when defining any Jini service is to create the API that clients will use to communicate with it. This is the API that the service's proxy object will implement; clients may look for objects that implement this interface when they search lookup services.

The example shown in Listing 15–4 presents a very simple interface, called Printer, with a single method for controlling printing. This method will take as parameters the data to be printed, a token indicating the paper orientation, the number of copies to print, and a reference to a remote listener object that will be called back when printing completes, either successfully or unsuccessfully.

Listing 15–4 `Printer.java`

```
// This is the interface that the proxy implements.

package corejini.chapter15;

import net.jini.core.event.RemoteEventListener;
import java.rmi.RemoteException;

public interface Printer {
    public void print(int format, int copies, Object data,
                      RemoteEventListener listener)
        throws RemoteException;
}
```

The `format` integer here should be one of the special formatting tokens defined in the `java.awt.print.PageFormat` class: PORTRAIT, LANDSCAPE, or REVERSE_LANDSCAPE. The `copies` argument is simply the desired number of copies; `data` is the data to be printed; and `listener` is an object that will be called back when the status of printing changes. The `listener` can be null if the client doesn't care about being informed of the status of its print jobs.

The Java printing model in Java 2 uses a "callback" printing model, where a method on an object will be invoked whenever the printing subsystem needs to render a page onto a printer. The objects that are called to control printing must implement either the `java.awt.print.Printable` or the `java.awt.print.Pageable` interface. The object that you pass as the `data` parameter here should implement either one of these interfaces to be printable. The object will be sent to the service, which will use it to control the rendering of the object onto a printer.

At the end of this chapter, I provide a list of some simple extensions you can make to this code. One possible modification is an *extensible* printing model, where clients can preregister renderers for particular types. Then, if an object is sent which is not `Printable` or `Pageable`, but has an installed renderer, the print service can still print it. For now, though, you should make sure that all objects you send implement one of the two Java printing interfaces.

Communicating with Clients: Events and Listeners

You saw in the previous section how clients can install a listener that will be called whenever the status of a print request changes. As you'll see, the printing service queues up print requests from clients, and dispatches them one at a time. Since the time between when a client submits a print request and the time it is actually printed (or fails to print) may be quite long, you need to use an asynchronous notification scheme for telling clients about what's happening to their print jobs.

The standard Java event and listener paradigm will do the job here. Clients can, when they issue a print request, pass in a listener that will be sent an event whenever the status of the print request changes. Since the events will be passed between separate JVMs, and will be delivered using a remote method implemented by the client, you'll have to use Jini's remote event facilities. You'll get a chance to look more closely at remote events in the next chapter; you only need to understand some pretty simple details to figure out how events are being used here.

If you recall the discussion on event delivery from way back in Chapter 5, you'll remember that `RemoteEventListener` is the interface that recipients of remote events should implement. This interface has one method, called `notify()`, that is called whenever an event generator delivers an event to a recipient. The `notify()` method of `RemoteEventListener` is defined to take a `RemoteEvent` as a parameter. The printing service that you'll see in a bit will deliver instances of `PrintServiceEvent`, which is a subclass of `RemoteEvent`.

This new event type contains extra information that clients can use to determine if a print request has succeeded or, if it has failed, why it has failed.

Listing 15–5 `PrintServiceEvent.java`

```
// A remote event that signals printer completion/failure

package corejini.chapter15;

import net.jini.core.event.RemoteEvent;
import java.io.Serializable;

public class PrintServiceEvent extends RemoteEvent
    implements Serializable  {
    protected Exception ex;

    PrintServiceEvent(PrintProxy proxy, long seq,
                      Exception ex) {
        super(proxy, 0 /* type */, seq, null);
        this.ex = ex;
    }

    public Exception getException() {
        return ex;
    }
    public boolean printJobFinished() {
        return ex == null;
    }
}
```

The `PrintServiceEvent` class (Listing 15–6) is a subclass of `RemoteEvent`. It contains within it an `Exception` that indicates why the client's print request failed, or will be set to null if the print request completed successfully. The `getException()` method returns the nested exception, and the `printJobFinished()` method can be used to determine whether or not the print request completed.

Note that the constructor for this class is package protected, because only the printing service will ever generate new events. When a new `PrintServiceEvent` is created, it is initialized with a proxy object that indicates the source of the event (this proxy can be used to communicate back with the printing service), an event type ID and a sequence number that together uniquely identify the event, and the exception. I'll talk about type IDs and sequence numbers in more detail in the next chapter, but basically these are ways for clients to uniquely identify and distinguish particular events. In the printing example, sequence numbers are monotonically increasing, and are saved to persistent storage so that they will never be reused. The service could be better behaved by not using zero as the value of all its event type IDs, but this is good enough for now. See Chapter 16 for more details.

The Remote Printing Interface

Now that you've looked at the APIs for printing and for notification, it's time to look at the remote printing interface (Listing 15–7). This is the set of methods and conventions that the proxy object will use to communicate back with the printing service running on some remote machine on the network.

Listing 15–6 `RemotePrinter.java`

```
// This is the interface that the proxy uses to communicate
with the
// service's back end.

package corejini.chapter15;

import net.jini.admin.Administrable;
import net.jini.core.event.RemoteEventListener;
import java.rmi.Remote;
import java.rmi.RemoteException;

public interface RemotePrinter
    extends Remote, Administrable {
    public void print(int format, int copies,
                    Object data,
                    RemoteEventListener listener)
        throws RemoteException;
}
```

As might be expected, the remote printing API defined here looks similar to the "local" printing API that the proxy implements. The `RemotePrinter` interface extends `Remote`, so you know that the service proxy will use RMI for communication with the printing service. The `print()` method has the same parameters as the local version, and the interface extends `Administrable`, so it also supports a `getAdmin()` method that will fetch an administrative proxy object from the remote printing service.

The Print Service Proxy

All the pieces are now in place to develop the proxy object (Listing 15–8) that will be sent to clients of the printing service. You can think of this proxy as a bit of code that mediates between the local printing APIs provided by the `Printer` interface and the remote printing APIs provided by the `RemotePrinter` interface.

The methods of the proxy object do a bit of type checking on their arguments so that some types of failures can be detected locally, without having to do a complete round-trip to the service.

Listing 15–7 `PrintProxy.java`

```
// This is the proxy object that will be sent to
// clients.

package corejini.chapter15;

import net.jini.admin.Administrable;
import net.jini.core.event.RemoteEventListener;
import java.io.Serializable;
import java.rmi.RemoteException;
import java.awt.print.PageFormat;

public class PrintProxy implements Serializable,
    Administrable, Printer {
    protected RemotePrinter remote;

    PrintProxy(RemotePrinter remote) {
        this.remote = remote;
    }
```

Listing 15–7 `PrintProxy.java` (continued)

```java
public void print(int format, int copies, Object data,
                  RemoteEventListener listener)
    throws RemoteException {
    switch (format) {
    case PageFormat.LANDSCAPE:
    case PageFormat.PORTRAIT:
    case PageFormat.REVERSE_LANDSCAPE:
        break;
    default:
        throw new IllegalArgumentException(
                            "Bogus page format");
    }

    if (data == null) {
        throw new NullPointerException("data");
    }

    remote.print(format, copies, data, listener);
}


public Object getAdmin() throws RemoteException {
    return remote.getAdmin();
}


public boolean equals(Object o) {
    if (o instanceof PrintProxy) {
        return ((PrintProxy) o).remote.equals(remote);
    } else {
        return false;
    }
}

// Two objects that are equals() must have the same
// hashCode() value.  So here I override hashCode() to
// return the hash code of the remote object.
public int hashCode() {
    return remote.hashCode();
}
}
```

The `PrintProxy` class implements a handful of useful interfaces: it is `Serializable` since it will be sent over the wire; it is `Administrable` since it can provide an administrative proxy for controlling the service; and it is a `Printer` since it exposes the local printing API to clients.

Whenever the proxy is created, it is initialized with a reference to an object implementing the `RemotePrinter` interface; this reference will be used to communicate with the back-end remote printing service.

The two main methods here, `print()` and `getAdmin()`, forward these invocations to the remote printing service. But, `print()` also embeds a bit of intelligence to check the values of the `format` and `data` arguments; bogus values here will cause exceptions to be raised locally, without the need to go to the printing service to determine that a failure has occurred.

Finally, the `equals()` method reports that two `PrintProxies` are equal if they refer to the same printing service. This implementation of `equals()` is a convenience to clients because the proxy objects returned as the sources of `PrintServiceEvents` can be easily compared against the proxies that clients already hold. Likewise, here I've reimplemented `hashCode()` to have correct semantics. The value returned from this method must be the same for any two objects that are `equals()`; since `equals()` is based on whether two proxies refer to the same remote object, I've changed `hashCode()` to simply return the hash value of the remote object.

Printer Administration APIs and UIs

You've seen that the `PrintProxy` provides an administrative object for the printing service by going through the `RemotePrinter` interface to fetch the object from the back-end service. This administrative object, as you will see, is a subclass of `BasicUnicastAdmin` which implements the "big three" administrative interfaces (`JoinAdmin`, `DestroyAdmin`, and `StorageLocationAdmin`), and also implements a *custom* administrative interface that clients can use to view particular aspects of the print service.

The custom administrative API defined here is quite simple—it provides a way to view the jobs currently queued by the printing service—but it serves as an example of a custom administrative interface. And, since this custom interface is likely to be known to only a handful of specially written clients that have advance knowledge of how to use it, the service needs to provide a user interface that can allow *anyone* to directly interact with it without having to understand the programmatic interface.

First, look at the API for the custom print administration interface as shown in Listing 15–8.

Listing 15–8 `PrintAdmin.java`

```
// A simple interface for printer administration.

package corejini.chapter15;

import java.util.List;
import java.rmi.RemoteException;

public interface PrintAdmin {
    public List getJobs() throws RemoteException;
}
```

This interface has one method, `getJobs()`, that returns the currently queued jobs. You can easily extend the APIs here to provide a richer set of administrative functions, perhaps to reorder or delete print jobs. The `getJobs()` method returns a list of `JobRecords`, each of which contains information about a queued job. You'll see the definition of `JobRecord` a bit later in the discussion of the implementation of the printing service.

Next, take a look at a custom user interface for viewing objects that implement `PrintAdmin`. This interface can be attached as an attribute and sent along with the printing service's proxy object. Clients can then instantiate the attribute and initialize it by passing the service's administrative object to it.

Figure 15–1 shows a screenshot of the user interface. The UI consists of a simple list box containing the queued jobs, in order of first to last. The "Refresh" button contacts the service to retrieve a fresh list of jobs.

Figure 15–1   *The PrintAdminPanel GUI*

The code that implements this user interface and can be used as an attribute is shown in Listing 15–9.

Listing 15–9 `PrintAdminPanel.java`

```
// A user interface for PrintAdmin objects.

package corejini.chapter15;

import net.jini.core.entry.Entry;
import java.awt.BorderLayout;
import java.awt.event.ActionEvent;
import java.awt.event.ActionListener;
import javax.swing.JPanel;
import javax.swing.JButton;
import javax.swing.JList;
import javax.swing.JLabel;
import java.util.List;
import java.rmi.RemoteException;
```

Listing 15–9 `PrintAdminPanel.java` (continued)

```java
public class PrintAdminPanel implements Entry {
    private JPanel panel = null;

    public PrintAdminPanel() {
    }

    public JPanel getPanel() {
        return panel;
    }

    public void setAdmin(final PrintAdmin admin) {
        panel = new JPanel();
        panel.setLayout(new BorderLayout());
        panel.add(new JLabel("Current Print Jobs"),
                            "North");
        final JList list = new JList();
        panel.add(list, "Center");

        JButton refreshButton = new JButton("Refresh");
        refreshButton.addActionListener(
            new ActionListener() {
                public void actionPerformed(ActionEvent ev){
                    List jobs = null;
                    try {
                        jobs = admin.getJobs();
                        System.out.println("Got back " +
                                            jobs.size() + "
                                            jobs");
                    } catch (RemoteException ex) {
                        System.err.println(
                                "Error getting jobs: " +
                                ex.getMessage());
                    }
                    list.setListData(jobs.toArray(
                                    new Object[0]));
                }
            }
        );

        panel.add(refreshButton, "South");

        refreshButton.doClick();
    }
}
```

The `PrintAdminPanel` implements `Entry`, contains within it a `JPanel` which can be embedded in other Swing components, and can be attached to a service's proxy object as an attribute.

`PrintAdminPanel` instances will be created in the service's JVM, serialized and attached as an attribute to the service's registration, and eventually downloaded and reconstituted by a client. When the `PrintAdminPanel` is created, it contains no initialized member data. Clients that wish to display the `PrintAdminPanel` initialize it by calling `setAdmin()` and passing in the administrative object for the printing service. This method creates the panel and the rest of the user interface within it. Clients can then extract the `JPanel` in this object and install it in a `JFrame` or other component to make it visible.

Note that I've taken special care here to ensure that no Swing-related calls are made in the constructor. All of the Swing components are set up in the call to `setAdmin()`, which occurs in the client. This ensures that no Swing components are initialized on the server side, when the object is created, and are thus not serialized. Remember that serialization of Swing components can be problematic.

Internals of the Print Service

With the details of the local and remote printing APIs, as well as the administrative interfaces, out of the way, we can now begin to look at the implementation of the internals of the printing service. The printing service follows many of the same patterns you've seen earlier in this book (a "wrapper" application implements the back-end portion of the service and manages the Jini obligations of the service), and so can be built atop the infrastructure classes from earlier in this chapter.

The service's back end subclasses `BasicUnicastService`, and so communicates with its proxies via RMI. It creates a class to perform administration, which is a subclass of `BasicUnicastAdmin`, with additional methods to support the `PrintAdmin` interface.

Listing 15-10 is the heart of this code.

> ## Listing 15–10 `PrintService.java`

```java
// This is the print service back end.

package corejini.chapter15;

import net.jini.core.entry.Entry;
import net.jini.core.event.RemoteEventListener;
import net.jini.admin.JoinAdmin;
import com.sun.jini.admin.DestroyAdmin;
import com.sun.jini.admin.StorageLocationAdmin;
import net.jini.lookup.entry.ServiceInfo;
import java.awt.print.Printable;
import java.awt.print.Pageable;
import java.awt.print.PageFormat;
import java.awt.print.PrinterJob;
import java.io.Serializable;
import java.io.IOException;
import java.util.HashMap;
import java.util.List;
import java.util.ArrayList;
import java.rmi.server.UnicastRemoteObject;
import java.rmi.Remote;
import java.rmi.RemoteException;
import java.rmi.RMISecurityManager;


public class PrintService extends BasicUnicastService
    implements RemotePrinter {
    protected List queue = new ArrayList();
    protected HashMap agents = new HashMap();
    protected PrintThread printThread;
    protected boolean done = false;
    protected PrintRecord currentRecord = null;
    protected PrintAdmin remoteAdmin = null;
    protected long lastEventSeqNo = 0;
```

Listing 15–10 `PrintService.java` (continued)

```java
public PrintService(String storageLoc)
        throws RemoteException {
    super(storageLoc);
}

// overrides base implementation to get
// correct shutdown behavior
protected void shutdown() {
    done = true;
    notify();
    super.shutdown();
}

// overrides base implementation to also
// save PrintServiceData
protected void checkpoint() throws IOException {
    checkpoint(new PrintServiceData(currentRecord,
                                    queue,
                                    lastEventSeqNo));
}

// overrides base implementation to start
// print thread
protected void initialize() throws IOException,
                               ClassNotFoundException{
    super.initialize();

    printThread = new PrintThread();
    printThread.start();
}
```

Listing 15–10 `PrintService.java` (continued)

```
// overrides base implementation to set some
// attributes.
protected Entry[] getAttributes() {
    Entry[] entries = new Entry[2];
    entries[0] = new ServiceInfo("Prentice-Hall",
                                  "PrintService",
                                  "PrintService",
                                  null,
                                  "Prentice-Hall",
                                  "v1.0");
    entries[1] = new PrintAdminPanel();
    return entries;
}

// overrides base implementation to return
// print proxy.
protected Object getProxy() {
    return new PrintProxy(this);
}

// overrides base implementation to restore
// print service-specific data.
public void restored(Object subclassData) {
    PrintServiceData data =
        (PrintServiceData) subclassData;
    currentRecord = data.currentRecord;
    queue = data.queue;
    lastEventSeqNo = data.lastEventSeqNo;
    System.out.println("Restored!");
}

public void print(int format, int copies, Object data,
                   RemoteEventListener listener) {
    Object agent = getPrintAgent(data);
    PrintRecord record = new PrintRecord(format,
                                          copies, data,
                                          agent, listener);
    queuePrinting(record);
}
```

Listing 15–10 `PrintService.java` (continued)

```java
public Object getAdmin() throws RemoteException {
    if (remoteAdmin == null) {
        remoteAdmin = new PrintAdminImpl(this);
    }

    return remoteAdmin;
}

Object getPrintAgent(Object data) {
    if (data instanceof Printable) {
        System.out.println("Data is printable");
        return data;
    }
    if (data instanceof Pageable) {
        System.out.println("Data is pageable");
        return data;
    }

    // build a list of data's classes and search for
    // them, most specific to least.
    List classes = getClasses(data);

    for (int i=0, size=classes.size() ; i<size ; i++) {
        Object o = agents.get(classes.get(i));
        if (o != null) {
            System.out.println(
                "Found printer for " +
                ((Class) classes.get(i)).getName());
            return o;
        }
    }

    System.out.println("No printer found");
    return null;
}
```

Listing 15–10 `PrintService.java` (continued)

```java
List getClasses(Object data) {
    List classes = new ArrayList();
    Class nextClass = data.getClass();

    while (nextClass != null) {
        classes.add(nextClass);
        Class[] interfaces = nextClass.getInterfaces();
        for (int i=0, size=interfaces.length; i<size;
                                              i++) {
            classes.add(interfaces[i]);
        }

        nextClass = nextClass.getSuperclass();
    }

    return classes;
}

void queuePrinting(PrintRecord record) {
    queue.add(record);
    try {
        checkpoint();
    } catch (IOException ex) {
        System.err.println("Trouble checkpointing; " +
                           "couldn't save job: " +
                           ex.getMessage());
    }
    System.out.println(
        "Printing queueued, waking thread");

    synchronized(this) {
        notify();
    }
}
```

Listing 15–10 `PrintService.java` (continued)

```java
// PrintThread handles the actual mechanics of
// job management and printing
class PrintThread extends Thread {
    public void run() {
        System.out.println("PrintThread cranking...");
        while (!done) {
            PrintRecord record = null;

            System.out.println(
                "Waiting for lock to dequeue");
            //
            // Grab the next item off the queue.  Check
            // currentRecord, since we may be
            // initialized with a print job in progress
            // after a restore.
            //
            if (currentRecord == null) {
                synchronized (PrintService.this) {
                    System.out.println("Dequeueing...");
                    if (queue.size() != 0) {
                        record = (PrintRecord)
                                        queue.get(0);
                        currentRecord = record;
                        queue.remove(0);
                        try {
                            checkpoint();
                        } catch (IOException ex) {
                            System.out.println(
                                "Couldn't checkpoint; " +
                                "job not saved: " +
                                ex.getMessage());
                        }
                    }
                }
            } else {
                record = currentRecord;
            }
```

Listing 15–10 `PrintService.java` (continued)

```
//
// Print it, if we have something to print.
//
if (record != null) {
    Exception ex = printRecord(record);
    if (record.listener != null) {
        PrintServiceEvent ev =
            new PrintServiceEvent(
                (PrintProxy) proxy,
                lastEventSeqNo++,
                ex);
        System.out.println(
            "Sending event from proxy " +
            proxy);
        try {
            record.listener.notify(ev);
        } catch (Exception ex2) {
            System.err.println(
                "Trouble sending event: " +
                ex2.getMessage());
        }
    }
    currentRecord = null;
    try {
        checkpoint();
    } catch (IOException ex2) {
        System.out.println(
            "Couldn't checkpoint; " +
            "job not saved: " +
            ex2.getMessage());
    }
}
```

Listing 15–10 `PrintService.java` (continued)

```java
        //
        // Wait for more stuff on the queue...
        //
        if (queue.size() > 0)
            continue;

        System.out.println("Waiting for lock");

        synchronized(PrintService.this) {
            try {
                System.out.println("waiting...");
                PrintService.this.wait();
            } catch (InterruptedException ex) {
              System.out.println("interrupted...");
            }
        }

        System.out.println(
                "Waking up!  Something to print!");
    }
    System.out.println(
            "Shutting down print thread...");
  }
```

Listing 15–10 `PrintService.java` (continued)

```java
Exception printRecord(PrintRecord record) {
    Exception ex = null;
    System.out.println("Printing data " +
                        record.data);

    PageFormat format = new PageFormat();
    format.setOrientation(record.format);

    PrinterJob job = PrinterJob.getPrinterJob();
    job.setCopies(record.copies);
    job.defaultPage(format);

    if (record.agent instanceof Pageable) {
        job.setPageable((Pageable) record.agent);
        try {
            job.print();
        } catch (Exception ex2) {
            ex = ex2;
        }
    } else if (record.agent instanceof Printable) {
        job.setPrintable((Printable) record.agent,
                        format);
        try {
            job.print();
        } catch (Exception ex2) {
            ex = ex2;
        }
    } else {
        ex = new IllegalArgumentException(
                                "Bad agent");
    }

    return ex;
}
}
```

Listing 15–10 `PrintService.java` (continued)

```java
    public static void main(String[] args) {
        try {
            if (args.length != 1) {
                System.err.println(
                    "Usage: PrintService <datafile>");
                System.exit(1);
            }

            if (System.getSecurityManager() == null) {
                System.setSecurityManager(
                    new RMISecurityManager());
            }

            PrintService service =
                new PrintService(args[0]);
            service.initialize();
            System.out.println("Print Service Started");
        } catch (Exception ex) {
            System.err.println(
                    "Error starting print service: " +
                    ex.getMessage());
            System.exit(1);
        }
    }
}
```

In addition to extending `BasicUnicastService`, the `PrintService` class also implements the `RemotePrinter` interface, with which its proxies will communicate.

When the service is run, its `main()` routine instantiates a new `PrintService` object with a command-line argument that indicates the location of the service's persistent storage. In the constructor for `PrintService`, this argument is passed to the constructor for `BasicUnicastService`, which handles the actual restoration of old data, or creation of the service for the first time.

After creating a `PrintService` object, `main()` calls `initialize()`, which is overridden from the base `BasicUnicastService` superclass. The `initialize()` method calls `BasicUnicastService.initialize()`, which, as you have seen, will try to restore the service, or create a "fresh" `JoinManager` if this is the first time the service has been run. The rest of `PrintService`'s version of `initialize()` creates and starts a `PrintThread`, which is a thread that monitors and dispatches the print queue.

The `PrintService` class overrides a few key methods that are used to determine the behavior of `BasicUnicastService`. The `getProxy()` method is implemented to return a new `PrintProxy`; `getAttributes()` creates and returns two attributes that will be attached to the service's entry wherever it is registered. The first of these is a `ServiceInfo` attribute that describes the printing service; the second is the `PrintAdminPanel` that can provide a user interface to print administration.

The `PrintService` class also initializes some "working" storage that it will use as it runs. The `queue` list contains the current queue of submitted print requests; `agents` is a list of mappings from `Class` objects to print "agents" or "handlers" that know how to render objects of those classes onto a printer; `proxy`—declared in the `BasicUnicastService` superclass—is the print proxy that will be sent to clients.

As you'll see in this example, the notion of print agents is used to separate the data that's being printed from the code that knows how to print it. In this example's current form, all objects sent to the print service should implement `Printable` or `Pageable` so that they can effectively "be their own agents." But the mechanisms here provide a way for you to extend this example to create new printing code that can be used to render objects of *arbitrary* types. I'll talk about how to do this at the end of the chapter.

After initialization, a new `PrintThread` object is created and started. This thread monitors the print request queue and handles printing the requests stored there. It will sleep if the print queue becomes empty, and will be awakened if new items are added. This separate thread allows printing to happen in the background, separate from any other threads in the system that might be servicing administrative calls, performing join duties, and so on.

The facilities in `PrintService` for handling persistent data build on those provided by `BasicUnicastService`. Here, the `checkpoint()` call is overridden to call the superclass' version, passing it an instance of `PrintServiceData` to be saved in addition to the information already saved by `BasicUnicastService`. The `PrintServiceData` object contains the print job currently being serviced (if there is one), the contents of the print queue, and the last sequence number used in an outgoing event.

The `PrintService`'s `restored()` method will be called after the service is resumed, with the subclass-specific data passed as an argument. In the case of `PrintService`, this data will be an instance of `PrintServiceData` (since this is the type of the "extra" data passed to `checkpoint()`). The `restored()`

method initializes the currently printing job, the print queue, and the last event sequence number from this data.

The `checkpoint()` method will be called "automatically" by `Basic-UnicastService` any time that data under its control changes. So, for example, the state of the service is checkpointed whenever a service ID is assigned to it, or the state is modified through the invocation of one of the various administrative methods. But `checkpoint()` is also called directly from `PrintService` whenever any data specific to this subclass of `BasicUnicastService` changes. So, checkpointing is done from the `PrintThread` as print jobs are dispatched. It is important to make sure that your services save their state any time they make a change that will need to be reflected across restarts; they need to make sure that changed data is reliably saved to disk.

Printing

Let's look at the actual mechanics of printing now. The main entry point for printing is the `print()` method. This method takes the data to be printed, some parameters to control printing, and—optionally—a listener that will be called when printing completes, either successfully or unsuccessfully.

The `print()` method first calls `getPrintAgent()` to get an "agent" that knows how to print the data that has just been received. An agent in this context is simply an object that implements either `Printable` or `Pageable`, so that it can be used with Java's printing subsystem, and "understands" how to render a particular type of data. If the object that is passed to `getPrintAgent()` is itself `Printable` or `Pageable`, then it is simply returned—the object is "self-printing," as it already knows how to print itself. Otherwise, the object to be printed is introspected and all the classes and interfaces that it extends or implements are found. These are, in turn, looked up in a hash table to see if any printing agents have been installed for any of these particular types. This is an avenue for future expansion—you can "preregister" agents for common types, such as strings of text and images, and make these printable by the service. Clients could even transmit new print agents to the service to extend its abilities at run time.

Once a print agent has been found for the data, the `print()` method creates a new `PrintRecord` (described below) to hold the information about the request, and queues the record by calling `queuePrinting()`.

The `queuePrinting()` method adds the new record to the end of the print queue, and checkpoints the state of the service. This checkpoint is necessary so that if the service crashes after receiving the print request, but before it can be completed, the service can resume printing without losing data. After checkpointing, `queuePrinting()` calls `notify()` (defined in `java.lang.Object`) to wake up the `PrintThread` if it is waiting for new data to appear in the queue.

The `PrintThread` class is where the heart of printing and queue management lives. One `PrintThread` instance will be created and started whenever the service is run. The `run()` method on this thread essentially sits in a big loop, processing items in the job queue. At the start of a pass, it looks to see if there is currently a job in progress. This will be the case if, for instance, the service crashed while printing and then resumed—the `PrintThread` should dispatch any current print job before moving on to the rest of the queue. If no job was in progress, then it dequeues the item at the head of the print queue, makes this the currently processed job, and checkpoints itself to remember that it is processing this item.

After grabbing an item to print, the thread actually prints it by calling `print-Record()`. This method handles the interaction with the Java printing subsystem by creating a new `PrinterJob`, initializing it with the parameters specified in the client's print request, and then beginning printing. This method causes the `PrintThread` to block until finished, at which point it returns any exception that may have occurred, or null if printing completed successfully.

Back in the `PrintThread`, after `printRecord()` finishes, the client's listener is notified, if one has been provided, by delivering a new `PrintServiceEvent` to it. This event has a fresh sequence number, generated by incrementing the count of used sequence numbers. If event delivery fails—most likely because the client that issued the request has crashed or terminated before the job completed—an exception will be raised and caught, and the service will continue processing normally. The current print job is cleared to indicate that no work is in progress—the job has been completely dispatched—and the state of the service is checkpointed again. Checkpointing also saves the last used sequence number, to ensure that sequence numbers are never reused, and that clients can readily distinguish multiple events from this service.

Finally, if more print jobs are waiting to be printed, the thread continues processing jobs. Otherwise, it blocks by calling `wait()`, which causes it to sleep until new jobs are added and `notify()` is called.

Persistent Data Formats

The `checkpoint()` and `restored()` methods rely on two classes to store data. The first is `PrintServiceData` (Listing 15–11), which contains all the persistent state of the `PrintService` which is not already held by its superclass, `BasicUnicastService`. Instances of `PrintServiceData` will be read from and written to the persistent storage file as the service runs. This class contains the currently executing job, the contents of the entire print queue, and the last used sequence number.

Listing 15-11 PrintServiceData.java

```
// Print service-specific persistent data.

package corejini.chapter15;

import java.util.List;
import java.io.Serializable;

class PrintServiceData implements Serializable {
    PrintRecord currentRecord;
    List queue;
    long lastEventSeqNo;

    PrintServiceData(PrintRecord currentRecord,
                     List queue, long lastEventSeqNo) {
        this.currentRecord = currentRecord;
        this.queue = queue;
        this.lastEventSeqNo = lastEventSeqNo;
    }
}
```

The current record, as well as the items in the queue, are instances of `Print-Record` (Listing 15–12). Each `PrintRecord` contains the information needed to dispatch one print request: the format of the request (portrait, landscape, etc.), the number of desired copies, the data to print, the "agent" that knows how to print it, and the listener that will be called when the job finishes.

```
Listing 15-12 PrintRecord.java
```

```java
// internal bookkeeping for recording print jobs

package corejini.chapter15;

import net.jini.core.event.RemoteEventListener;
import java.io.Serializable;

class PrintRecord implements Serializable {
    int format;
    int copies;
    Object data;
    Object agent;
    RemoteEventListener listener;

    PrintRecord(int format, int copies, Object data,
                Object agent,
                RemoteEventListener listener) {
        this.format = format;
        this.copies = copies;
        this.data = data;
        this.agent = agent;
        this.listener = listener;
    }
}
```

Implementing Print Service Administration

The final big piece of the puzzle is the implementation of administration for the printing service. In this particular case, administration is implemented by a separate nested object that is a subclass of BasicUnicastAdmin. The administrative object that the print service returns to callers is actually the *stub* for this implementation. This arrangement is different than the approach from Chapter 14. In that chapter, the administrative object was a separate proxy that forwarded its methods on to a remote object that lived in the back-end portion of the service. Here, I've simply used the remote object's stub as the administrative object, as there is no difference in the API that is presented to clients and the API that's implemented "natively" by the remote administration object. (Using an RMI-generated stub is actually just the "degenerate" case of the sort of proxy that I've used all along in this book—that is, it's a serializable object that gets sent over the wire so that clients can use the back end. But in the case of the RMI stub, the proxy is automatically generated by `rmic`, and consists of only remote methods, no local ones.)

By basing the implementation of the administrative object on `Basic-UnicastAdmin`, the service gets an implementation of `JoinAdmin`, `StorageLocationAdmin`, and `DestroyAdmin` "for free." The subclass need only implement the methods particular to `PrintAdmin`.

Let's look at how this works. Listing 15-13 shows the interface that the administration implementation will use, called `RemotePrintAdmin`. The administration implementation itself, `PrintAdminImpl`, is shown a bit later. The service's `getAdmin()` method creates an instance of `PrintAdminImpl` the first time it is called, and returns this to its caller. The caller, in this case, will be the `PrintProxy` object, which will simply return this object to callers. Since the stubs for remote objects are returned in place of the actual remote implementations in RMI calls, clients will, after calling `getAdmin()` on their `PrintProxies`, have an RMI stub that refers directly to the underlying `PrintAdminImpl` object.

Listing 15–13 `RemotePrintAdmin.java`

```
// This is the union of the administrative interfaces
// that the print service implements.

package corejini.chapter15;

import java.rmi.Remote;

interface RemotePrintAdmin
    extends RemoteUnicastAdmin,
            PrintAdmin,
            Remote {
}
```

Here you see the `RemotePrintAdmin` interface, which is a "remote" version of the `PrintAdmin` interface. This interface must be declared so that the RMI stubs compiler will know which methods on `PrintAdminImpl` are meant to be callable remotely. The `PrintAdminImpl` class, shown in Listing 15-14, is actu-

ally a nested class within `PrintService`. I've broken it out separately here for
clarity.

Listing 15-14 PrintAdminImpl

```
// An implementation of RemotePrintAdmin, using the
// administration toolkit.

class PrintAdminImpl extends BasicUnicastAdmin
    implements RemotePrintAdmin {

    PrintAdminImpl(PrintService s)
            throws RemoteException {
        super(s);
    }

    public List getJobs() {
        List jobs = new ArrayList();
        synchronized (PrintService.this) {
            if (currentRecord != null) {
                jobs.add(new JobRecord(currentRecord,
                                            true));
            }

            for (int i=0, size=queue.size(); i<size;
                                            i++) {
                jobs.add(new JobRecord((PrintRecord)
                                        queue.get(i),
                                        false));
            }
        }
        return jobs;
    }
}
```

`PrintAdminImpl` implements all the particular administrative interfaces; the
implementations of `JoinAdmin`, `DestroyAdmin`, and `StorageLocationAdmin`
are gained by subclassing `BasicUnicastAdmin`, and the object also implements
the `RemotePrintAdmin` interface by returning details about the currently queued
print jobs when asked. Rather than returning "private," implementation-specific
details about the listeners registered with print jobs and so on, the implementation of `getJobs()` returns a list of `JobRecords` (Listing 15–15). These
`JobRecords` contain some of the same information as `PrintRecords`, but with-

out some of the internal details used by `PrintRecords`. `JobRecords` contain a string describing the printed data, without containing the data itself.

Listing 15–15 `JobRecord.java`

```
// client-visible representation of a job

package corejini.chapter15;

import java.io.Serializable;
import java.awt.print.PageFormat;

public class JobRecord implements Serializable {
    boolean current;
    int format;
    int copies;
    String dataName;
    int jobid;

    JobRecord(PrintRecord rec, boolean current) {
        this.current = current;
        this.format = rec.format;
        this.copies = rec.copies;
        this.dataName = rec.data.toString();
        this.jobid = rec.hashCode();
    }

    public boolean getCurrent() {
        return current;
    }

    public int getFormat() {
        return format;
    }

    public int getCopies() {
        return copies;
    }
```

Listing 15–15 JobRecord.java (continued)

```java
    public String getDataName() {
        return dataName;
    }

    public int getJobID() {
        return jobid;
    }

    public String toString() {
        StringBuffer buf = new StringBuffer();

        if (current) {
            buf.append("[CURRENT] ");
        }
        switch (format) {
        case PageFormat.PORTRAIT:
            buf.append("portrait, ");
            break;
        case PageFormat.LANDSCAPE:
            buf.append("landscape, ");
            break;
        case PageFormat.REVERSE_LANDSCAPE:
            buf.append("reverse, ");
            break;
        }
        buf.append(copies + " copies, ");
        buf.append(dataName);

        return buf.toString();
    }
}
```

A Print Client

Now it's time to build a simple client (Listing 15–16) to test out the service. This client will use discovery to find lookup services, and then search for `PrintServices` there. Once such a service is found, the client will issue a couple of print requests, and register itself as the listener for these jobs so that it can determine whether they succeed or fail. The client will also download the `PrintAdminPanel` attribute for the service and use this to create a UI for the printing service.

Listing 15–16 `Client.java`

```
// A client of the print service

package corejini.chapter15;

import net.jini.discovery.DiscoveryListener;
import net.jini.discovery.DiscoveryEvent;
import net.jini.discovery.LookupDiscovery;
import net.jini.core.lookup.ServiceRegistrar;
import net.jini.core.lookup.ServiceTemplate;
import net.jini.core.lookup.ServiceMatches;
import net.jini.core.event.RemoteEvent;
import net.jini.core.event.RemoteEventListener;
import net.jini.core.entry.Entry;
import net.jini.admin.Administrable;
import java.io.IOException;
import java.io.Serializable;
import java.awt.Graphics;
import java.awt.event.WindowAdapter;
import java.awt.event.WindowEvent;
import java.awt.print.Printable;
import java.awt.print.PrinterException;
import java.awt.print.PageFormat;
import java.rmi.RemoteException;
import java.rmi.RMISecurityManager;
import java.rmi.server.UnicastRemoteObject;
import javax.swing.JFrame;
```

Listing 15–16 `Client.java` (continued)

```java
public class Client implements Runnable {
    ServiceTemplate template;

    // An inner class for discovery
    class Discoverer implements DiscoveryListener {
        public void discovered(DiscoveryEvent ev) {
            ServiceRegistrar[] regs = ev.getRegistrars();
            for (int i=0 ; i<regs.length ; i++) {
                doit(regs[i]);
            }
        }

        public void discarded(DiscoveryEvent ev) {
        }
    }

    public Client() throws IOException {
        Class[] types = { Printer.class };
        template = new ServiceTemplate(null, types, null);

        LookupDiscovery disco =
            new LookupDiscovery(
                LookupDiscovery.ALL_GROUPS);
        disco.addDiscoveryListener(new Discoverer());
    }
```

Listing 15–16 `Client.java` (continued)

```
void doit(ServiceRegistrar reg) {
    Printer printer = null;
    Entry[] attributes = null;

    try {
        ServiceMatches matches =
            reg.lookup(template,
                    Integer.MAX_VALUE);

        if (matches.totalMatches > 0) {
            printer = (Printer)
                matches.items[0].service;
            attributes = matches.items[0].attributeSets;
        } else {
            printer = null;
        }
    } catch (Exception ex) {
        System.err.println(
            "Doing lookup: " + ex.getMessage());
        ex.printStackTrace();
    }
```

Listing 15–16 `Client.java` (continued)

```
if (printer == null)
    return;

System.out.println("Got a printer!");

// issue a couple of print requests.
try {
    printer.print(PageFormat.PORTRAIT, 1,
            new PrintableString("Hello World"),
                new Listener());
    printer.print(PageFormat.LANDSCAPE, 1,
            new PrintableString("Hello Again"),
                new Listener());
} catch (Exception ex) {
    System.out.println("Trouble printing: " +
                        ex.getMessage());
    ex.printStackTrace();
}

PrintAdminPanel panel = null;

for (int i=0, size=attributes.length; i<size; i++)
{
    if (attributes[i] instanceof PrintAdminPanel)
        panel = (PrintAdminPanel) attributes[i];
        break;
}
```

Listing 15–16 `Client.java` (continued)

```java
    if (panel != null) {
        try {
            panel.setAdmin((PrintAdmin)
                            ((Administrable)
                                printer).getAdmin());
        } catch (RemoteException ex) {
            System.err.println(
                "Error getting admin: " +
                ex.getMessage());
            ex.printStackTrace();
        }

        final JFrame frame =
            new JFrame("Print Admin Panel");

        frame.getContentPane().add(panel.getPanel());
        frame.pack();
        frame.setVisible(true);
        frame.addWindowListener(new WindowAdapter() {
            public void windowClosing(WindowEvent ev) {
                frame.setVisible(false);
                frame.dispose();
            }
        });
    }
}
```

Listing 15–16 `Client.java` (continued)

```java
// An inner class for handling events
class Listener extends UnicastRemoteObject
        implements RemoteEventListener {

    Listener() throws RemoteException {
    }

    public void notify(RemoteEvent e) {
        if (!(e instanceof PrintServiceEvent)) {
            return;
        }
        PrintServiceEvent ev = (PrintServiceEvent) e;
        if (ev.printJobFinished()) {
            System.out.println(
                "Job finished successfully!");
        } else {
            System.out.println(
                "Job failed:  " +
                ev.getException().getMessage());
            ev.getException().printStackTrace();
        }
    }
}

public void run() {
    while (true) {
        try {
            Thread.sleep(Integer.MAX_VALUE);
        } catch (InterruptedException ex) {
        }
    }
}
```

Listing 15–16 `Client.java` (continued)

```java
// A string that implements Printable
static class PrintableString
        implements Printable, Serializable {
    String s;

    PrintableString(String s) {
        this.s = s;
    }

    public int print(Graphics g, PageFormat pf,
                     int page)
            throws PrinterException {
        if (page >= 1) {
            return Printable.NO_SUCH_PAGE;
        }

        int xo = (int) pf.getImageableX();
        int yo = (int) pf.getImageableY();
        g.setColor(java.awt.Color.black);
        g.drawString(s, xo+20, yo+60);
        return Printable.PAGE_EXISTS;
    }

    public String toString() {
        return s;
    }
}
```

Listing 15-16 `Client.java` (continued)

```
public static void main(String[] args) {
    try {
        if (System.getSecurityManager() == null) {
            System.setSecurityManager(
                new RMISecurityManager());
        }

        Client client = new Client();
        new Thread(client).start();
    } catch (Exception ex) {
        System.err.println("Bogus: " + ex.getMessage());
        System.exit(1);
    }
}
}
```

When a `PrintAdminPanel` attribute is found, it is initialized by calling the `setAdmin()` method on it. As mentioned in the last chapter, the Jini community is currently working toward a standard set of well-known interfaces for creating UIs. But without this ability in Jini at the time of writing, I had to explicitly "know" that this `setAdmin()` method existed on `PrintAdminPanel` here.

Print jobs are issued to the service by passing it instances of a class called `PrintableString`. This is a simple class, implemented by the client, that wraps a Java string and provides an implementation of the `Printable` interface needed to tell the service how to render a particular data type. `PrintableString` has a `print()` method that renders its string in the default font on the page.

The client also provides a class called `Listener`, which implements `Print-Listener` to receive `PrintServiceEvents`. Whenever events are received, the `Listener` class prints out details about the success or failure of the print job.

Compiling and Running the Examples

To run the sample code here, first compile the service and the client to their respective directories. Next, run `rmic` on the classes that implement remote interfaces: `Client.Listener`, `PrintService`, `BasicUnicastAdmin`, and `PrintService.PrintAdminImpl`. In addition to any RMI-generated stubs, the proxy for the printing service must be downloadable by the client. So, be sure to copy these, and the classes used by them, to the correct download directories.

On Windows:
Compile the top-level class for the service. This will compile any needed classes as well.

```
javac -classpath C:\files;
                C:\jini1_1\lib\jini-core.jar;
                C:\jini1_1\lib\jini-ext.jar;
                C:\jini1_1\lib\sun-util.jar;
                C:\service
        -d C:\service
          C:\files\corejini\chapter15\PrintService.java
```

Next, compile the top-level client class, which will compile all the classes referred to by it.

```
javac -classpath C:\files;
                C:\jini1_1\lib\jini-core.jar;
                C:\jini1_1\lib\jini-ext.jar;
                C:\jini1_1\lib\sun-util.jar;
                C:\client
        -d C:\client
          C:\files\corejini\chapter15\Client.java
```

The client has one class that implements a remote interface, so you must run `rmic` on it to generate the stubs for it.

```
rmic -classpath C:\jini1_1\lib\jini-core.jar;
                C:\jini1_1\lib\jini-ext.jar;
                C:\jini1_1\lib\sun-util.jar;
                C:\client
        -d C:\client
          corejini.chapter15.Client.Listener
```

The server is a bit more complicated. On the server side, there are three classes that implement remote interfaces, including the administration object. You must run `rmic` on these as well.

```
rmic -classpath C:\jini1_1\lib\jini-core.jar;
                C:\jini1_1\lib\jini-ext.jar;
                C:\jini1_1\lib\sun-util.jar;
```

```
        C:\service
    -d C:\service
      corejini.chapter15.PrintService
      corejini.chapter15.PrintService.PrintAdminImpl
      corejini.chapter15.BasicUnicastAdmin
```

Almost done! The stub for the client's event listener will be downloaded by services, so you must copy it to the client's download directory. Also, the client sends an instance of `PrintableString` to the service. Because this isn't a "standard" class that the service would know about, the client must ensure that it is in the download directory also.

```
mkdir C:\client-dl\corejini\chapter15
cd C:\client\corejini\chapter15
copy Client$Listener_Stub.class
        C:\client-dl\corejini\chapter15
copy Client$PrintableString.class
        C:\client-dl\corejini\chapter15
```

Finally, make sure that all of the classfiles that the service exports are in the service's download directory. This includes the stubs for the service's remote objects, as well as any interfaces or other classes referred to by the service's proxy or administrative object.

```
mkdir C:\service-dl\corejini\chapter15
cd C:\service\corejini\chapter15
copy PrintService_Stub.class
        C:\service-dl\corejini\chapter15
copy PrintService$PrintAdminImpl_Stub.class
        C:\service-dl\corejini\chapter15
copy BasicUnicastAdmin_Stub.class
        C:\service-dl\corejini\chapter15
copy PrintProxy.class
        C:\service-dl\corejini\chapter15
copy PrintService$PrintAdminImpl.class
        C:\service-dl\corejini\chapter15
copy PrintAdmin.class
        C:\service-dl\corejini\chapter15
copy RemotePrintAdmin.class
        C:\service-dl\corejini\chapter15
copy RemotePrinter.class
        C:\service-dl\corejini\chapter15
```

On UNIX:

Compile the top-level class for the service. This will compile any needed classes as well.

```
javac -classpath /files:
                /files/jini1_1/lib/jini-core.jar:
                /files/jini1_1/lib/jini-ext.jar:
                /files/jini1_1/lib/sun-util.jar:
                /files/service
       -d /files/service
          /files/corejini/chapter15/PrintService.java
```

Next, compile the top-level client class, which will compile all the classes referred to by it.

```
javac -classpath /files:
                /files/jini1_1/lib/jini-core.jar:
                /files/jini1_1/lib/jini-ext.jar:
                /files/jini1_1/lib/sun-util.jar:
                /files/client
       -d /files/client
          /files/files/corejini/chapter15/Client.java
```

The client has one class that implements a remote interface, so you must run rmic on it to generate the stubs for it.

```
rmic -classpath /files/jini1_1/lib/jini-core.jar:
               /files/jini1_1/lib/jini-ext.jar:
               /files/jini1_1/lib/sun-util.jar:
               /files/client
      -d /files/client
         corejini.chapter15.Client.Listener
```

The server is a bit more complicated. On the server side, there are three classes that implement remote interfaces, including the administration object. You must run rmic on these as well.

```
rmic -classpath /files/jini1_1/lib/jini-core.jar:
               /files/jini1_1/lib/jini-ext.jar:
               /files/jini1_1/lib/sun-util.jar:
               /files/service
      -d /files/service
         corejini.chapter15.PrintService
```

```
corejini.chapter15.PrintService.PrintAdminImpl
corejini.chapter15.BasicUnicastAdmin
```

Almost done! The stub for the client's event listener will be downloaded by services, so you must copy it to the client's download directory. Also, the client sends an instance of `PrintableString` to the service. Because this isn't a "standard" class that the service would know about, the client must ensure that it is in the download directory also.

```
mkdir /files/client-dl/corejini/chapter15
cd /files/client/corejini/chapter15
cp Client\$Listener_Stub.class
          /files/client-dl/corejini/chapter15
cp Client\$PrintableString.class
          /files/client-dl/corejini/chapter15
```

Finally, make sure that all of the classfiles that the service exports are in the service's download directory. This includes the stubs for the service's remote objects, as well as any interfaces or other classes referred to by the service's proxy or administrative object.

```
mkdir /files/service-dl/corejini/chapter15
cd /files/service/corejini/chapter15
cp PrintService_Stub.class
          /files/service-dl/corejini/chapter15
cp PrintService\$PrintAdminImpl_Stub.class
          /files/service-dl/corejini/chapter15
cp PrintProxy.class
          /files/service-dl/corejini/chapter15
copy PrintService\$PrintAdminImpl.class
          /files/service-dl/corejini/chapter15
copy RemotePrintAdmin.class
          /files/service-dl/corejini/chapter15
copy PrintAdmin.class
          /files/service-dl/corejini/chapter15
copy RemotePrinter.class
          /files/service-dl/corejini/chapter15
```

Invoke the service by providing it with a location for its persistent storage, along with the service's codebase and a policy file. The client will download and use stubs and proxies, so it also needs a security policy file. And, since it exports its event listener stub as well as its `PrintableString` class, it needs a codebase. Be sure to use the appropriate separate codebases for the client and the service.

On Windows:
```
java -cp C:\jini1_1\lib\jini-core.jar;
        C:\jini1_1\lib\jini-ext.jar;
        C:\jini1_1\lib\sun-util.jar;
        C:\service
     -Djava.rmi.server.codebase=http://myhost:8085/
     -Djava.security.policy=C:\policy
     corejini.chapter15.PrintService C:\storage

java -cp C:\jini1_1\lib\jini-core.jar;
        C:\jini1_1\lib\jini-ext.jar;
        C:\jini1_1\lib\sun-util.jar;
        C:\client
     -Djava.rmi.server.codebase=http://myhost:8086/
     -Djava.security.policy=C:\policy
     corejini.chapter15.Client
```

On UNIX:
```
java -cp /files/jini1_1/lib/jini-core.jar:
        /files/jini1_1/lib/jini-ext.jar:
        /files/jini1_1/lib/sun-util.jar:
        /files/service
     -Djava.rmi.server.codebase=http://myhost:8085/
     -Djava.security.policy=/files/policy
     corejini.chapter15.PrintService /var/storage

java -cp /files/jini1_1/lib/jini-core.jar:
        /files/jini1_1/lib/jini-ext.jar:
        /files/jini1_1/lib/sun-util.jar:
        /files/client
     -Djava.rmi.server.codebase=http://myhost:8086/
     -Djava.security.policy=/files/policy
     corejini.chapter15.Client
```

Ideas for Future Work

I've already hinted at one of the big possible improvements you could make to this code: You could allow the printing of objects that do not directly implement `Pageable` or `Printable` by using the "agents" framework already present here. You could even consider "widening" the administrative interface to allow clients to transmit new print agents for particular data types to the print service; the print service could store these persistently so that downloaded agents could be available across restarts.

In general, the administrative interface shown here could be improved in several ways. Obvious extensions include the ability to reorder and delete print jobs. The administrative interfaces could also generate events—unlike the events you've already seen that indicate the disposition of *particular* print jobs, these events might tell a system administrator whether a printer is out of paper or needs service.

Finally, the print service shown here lacks a nonadministrative GUI. That is, while there is a special user interface for interacting with the custom `PrintAdmin` API, there is no special user interface for common printing tasks. Such an interface might take the form of a printer icon that is responsive to drag-and-drop operations—dropping an item on the printer could cause it to be added to the print queue. With this ability, the Jini print service could appear on a "desktop" browser application as a printer, and allow any sort of data to be dropped onto it.

Summary

This chapter has presented a set of toolkit classes for building services, as well as a complete example of a Jini service for printing. From this code, you've seen how to create services with persistent state and custom administrative interfaces. You've also seen how to generate events when the status of a print job changes.

The overall form of the printing service and the toolkit class that it is based on is typical of many Jini services: the system is architected as a front-end proxy that communicates using RMI with a back end. This back end brings some resource—in this case, a printer attached to a host computer—into the "Jini world."

When you create your own Jini services, you should find that you're dealing with many of the same tasks and problems that we've looked at here.

Related Reading

At the time of this book's writing, the Jini Printing Working Group was defining a set of standard APIs for print service, using the Jini community process. The working group's drafts and notes are at:

```
http://developer.jini.org/exchange/users/jpgwg/
```

You'll need to become a member of the Jini community Web site (`http://www.jini.org`) to visit these pages.

There is also a more extensive version of the Service Writer's Toolkit, available from my Web site, at:

```
http://www.kedwards.com/jini/swt.html
```

What's Next?

In this chapter, you saw a few simple uses of Jini remote events. The next chapter covers this topic in depth. You'll see how to receive remote events, and how to be a proper and well-behaved generator of remote events. You'll also understand how to create "pluggable" pipelines of events that can interconnect Jini services, and extend the basic event delivery machinery already present in Jini.

In Depth: Remote Events

Chapter 16

You've already seen in this book some examples of how Jini uses remote events, primarily in the context of lookup service events. You've seen how lookup services will generate events to inform interested parties about changes in the services that are members of a community.

But Jini's mechanisms for notification can be used in many other situations. In some cases, you will write clients that interact with services that generate events to inform consumers when there is a change in their state. In this chapter, you'll look in more detail at how to be a proper consumer of remote events.

In other situations, you will be writing your own custom services and applications that will *generate* events. You'll need to understand the patterns that you can use to track your listeners and lease their registrations. You'll also need to understand the idioms of remote communication facilitated by Jini. This chapter also covers these aspects of the Jini event programming model.

But in either circumstance—whether you are consuming or producing Jini events—you should understand why the Jini event architecture was designed as it was. Events in Jini have a superficial similarity with the "classic" Java event paradigm used in local applications. But remote events have some important differences, which you'll learn about in this chapter. Foremost among these differences is the ability to create "generic" chunks of code that can be composed together to form a distributed event "pipeline" of processing.

In this chapter, you'll look at the design rationale behind Jini events, see how to build real applications that use and produce events, and explore Jini's ability to create generic event handlers.

The Need for Notifications

If you're used to programming in Java—or any other modern programming language or environment for that matter—you understand the importance of an *asynchronous notification* mechanism for allowing you to deal with occurrences outside your own program. Asynchronous notification simply means that your program is told, or "notified," whenever something "interesting" happens externally. The "asynchronous" part comes from the fact that notification happens at or about the time that the interesting thing happens, not just when your program happens to ask whether something interesting has happened.

Asynchronous notifications can be contrasted to *polling*, which is another way for programs to learn about changes in some state external to themselves. In polling, a program explicitly checks regularly to see if an interesting change has taken place. Polling has its advantages. For one, the external change can be dealt with when the program is ready to deal with it. But polling has many downsides as well. Most importantly, the polling program must be structured to periodically check the changing entity. Often, the requirements that polling imposes on a program can radically alter the "natural" structure of the program. For instance, if you're polling, you'd better make sure that no single operation you perform will last longer than the minimum sampling interval between polls. Otherwise, there's a chance you could fail to notice an important change.

The alternative is the approach that asynchronous notifications take—rather than having the program check for the change, the program is told that it has changed. The change is dealt with by code in the program, but—here is the key— in a separate flow of control from the main execution of the program. Essentially you provide a "handler" (often called a *callback*) that specifies what will happen whenever an interesting change is detected. Because you are relieved of the burden of constantly checking for that change—since you are explicitly told when the change happens—you don't have to structure your code around polling. And because the code that responds to changes is separated logically from the code that does the other work of the application, your program can be more cleanly structured than otherwise.

Core Note: How asynchronous notification *really* works

I've glossed over many of the details of how asynchronous notification actually works, in the interest of showing the benefits of using asynchronous callbacks. The truth is that there has to be some bit of code in your application that detects the delivery of the notification from the external entity and knows how to invoke your callback.

The code that does this actually uses polling to do its work. This code, often called a dispatcher, hangs out waiting on notifications and then maps particular types of notifications into invocations of particular callbacks. How this works varies from system to system. In many windowing toolkits, including the X Window System's Xt toolkit, the dispatcher is simply a procedure that you turn control of your program over to. Once the dispatcher is running, it grabs notifications and fires callbacks, and everything happens in the same thread of control—the program's main thread. Such systems impose restrictions on how long any single callback can take—since as long as a callback is running, the dispatcher is blocked and no notifications can be received.

Other systems, including Java, use separate threads of control to dispatch notifications and invoke callbacks (Java actually has its own terminology for this, as you'll see shortly). The main benefit of a threaded dispatcher is that the dispatcher need not be blocked while a callback is executing. The downside is that callbacks run in separate threads from the application's main thread, and so you must take care to properly synchronize access to data shared between your callback and your main application code.

If there's a moral here, it's that there's no such thing as a free lunch.

So I've talked about asynchronous notifications in the abstract, but the title of this chapter has the word "events" in it, and I have yet to talk about what asynchronous notifications have to do with events. Events are simply objects that encapsulate some change—a window has appeared on the screen, a button has been pressed, a Web page has finished loading. In virtually every system that uses events, events are categorized into types to provide *specific* information about the change that has taken place. In Java's AWT for example, there are `MouseEvents`, `WindowEvents`, `KeyEvents`, and so on. Each of these event classes has information that describes a *particular* change in the state of the windowing system.

To continue bringing these abstract ideas about notification into concrete Java terms, Java also uses *listeners* to associate handler code with particular event types. Listeners are analogous to callbacks as described earlier—you can install a listener for a particular event and, when that event is received, the dispatcher will invoke your listener to do its job. In Java's AWT, there are about as many listener types as there are event types—`MouseListener`, `WindowListener`, `KeyListener`, and so on. Each of these listeners is an interface with methods that the dispatcher will call when certain events are received. So the methods of `MouseListener` are called when particular mouse-related situations arise; these methods are different than the methods on the other listener classes, because each is tailored specifically for its individual task.

This discussion of notifications, events, and listeners may seem pretty academic. Certainly if you've been doing any Java programming at all—and most readers of this book will be already rather handy with Java—then you already know all of this. But my goal here is to bring out some of the key assumptions that are implicit and very often not even thought about in the Java model—namely that there are specific types of events that are dispatched to specific listeners. This assumption is one of the subtle differences between the "normal" Java event model and the Jini model. Understanding the rationale behind why Java does things the way it does will help highlight the differences in Jini when we get to them.

And, of course, a second reason for going into all this detail is that events are quite simply a fundamental part of any programming model, not to be taken lightly.

Jini Event Design Center

Now that I've talked a bit about what events are and why they're useful, it's time to look at how Jini uses events, and what features of an event system the Jini designers felt were the most important to focus on.

First and foremost, the events that Jini propagates between services and service consumers are *remote events*. This means that the event objects that capture some change in state are sent across VM boundaries: the entity that is sending the event resides in a different VM, and usually even on a different host, than the entity that receives it.[1] The "remoteness" of these events entails all of the difficulties covered in Chapter 2 in the discussion about distributed systems—a sender or a receiver can fail, the time required to send the event can be quite large, and so on. I'll talk specifically about the implications of using events remotely in the next section.

Second, in Jini, event listeners are designed to be *composable*. This means that you can take a set of event listeners and "stack" them together—the output of one listener becomes the input of the next one in the stack.

You could imagine doing something like this in AWT. For example, you could write a class that not only implements `MouseListener`, but also supports the `addMouseListener()` method so that "downstream" listeners could receive events from it. But unlike in the AWT event model, where you would have to create a separate type of listener for each of the dozen or so events that AWT generates (`MouseEvents`, `WindowEvents`, `KeyEvents`, `ActionEvents`, and so on), Jini supports the ability for you to write *one* type of listener that can be "plugged in" for *any* type of remote event.

In practice, this means that if you write a class that generates events, you can send those events to any type of Jini event listener without knowing the details of the listener or requiring it to implement any special interfaces, beyond the basic Jini event listener interface. And the flip-side of this is that any Jini event listener can receive any type of event from any event generator.

Why is this useful, and why have the Jini creators considered this design point to be so crucial to the architecture of a remote event system? You'll find out in the next section, which looks more closely at how remoteness affects an event system.

How Remote Events Differ from Local Events

Chapter 3 touched quickly on some of the differences between remote and local events, but I want to visit these again quickly because these differences manifest themselves throughout the Jini event architecture. Here is another situation where simply making one component of a system remote has great consequences on the architecture of the system.

Because a system running across VMs on disparate hosts is such a different creature than a system running entirely in a single VM, there are a number of implications for an event system designed to work in such a setting. The most important of these are:

- Out of order delivery
- Partial failures
- Latency versus computation trade-offs

---

1. Of course, most Jini applications will also generate and consume local events as well—any application with a graphical interface will certainly use events, for example. So Jini adds only the mechanisms for sending events between entities on different VMs.

I'll quickly revisit each of these to show how they affect remote events.

Out of Order Delivery

In general, it's much more difficult to ensure that messages sent across a network are received in the same order they were sent, especially when messages are sent to multiple consumers. While a remote event delivery system *could* make such guarantees at the expense of performance (using reliable protocols or custom sequencing techniques), the performance hit may be unwieldy for some applications. Further, guaranteeing *global* in-order delivery is extremely hard—if one recipient crashes, do you hold up delivery of events to the other parties to maintain order? These types of guarantees require delivery policies that understand the semantics of the applications involved—whether they require in-order delivery, and how much they're willing to pay for it.[2]

Partial Failures

If you're sending a local event to a component in the same VM, you generally are assured that if you send the event it will be delivered. Any crash or failure that brings down the recipient is almost certain to bring down the sender as well, resulting in a total failure of the application.

Contrast this to the remote setting, where partial failures can occur. In such a setting, the sender may generate an event that goes undelivered because the recipient has failed. The addition of the possibility of partial failure brings a separate parameter of control not present in the local case—if an event cannot be delivered, what should the sender do? Should it try to resend? Should it discard the event? Should it queue the event and hold on to it until the receiver asks for it? If so, how long should it be held?

Local-only event delivery mechanisms simply have no way to express such constraints, because they aren't present in the local-only setting.

Latency Versus Computation

In the local case, events can be generated, sent, and delivered very quickly. Look at AWT for examples of this—you can get an event every time the mouse pointer moves across the screen. In most cases, the work that an application

---

2. I should note that even in Java's local AWT event dispatch system, there are no guarantees of in-order delivery. But in general, such a guarantee could be made far more easily than in a remote setting.

will do when an event is received (update the display, write some data to disk) completely dominates the time required for the event machinery to generate and dispatch the event.

Such is not the case in the remote setting. There, delivery of an event involves serializing the information in the event, sending it across a network, and deserializing it on the other end. The time required to do this can be several orders of magnitude larger than local delivery, and will almost certainly dominate the time spent by an application to respond to or handle the event.

This disparity in delivery times has architectural implications for applications in the remote setting: In general, events will be sent far less frequently than in the local case, and will contain as much information as necessary to allow the application to process the event without the need for another network round-trip. Because the cost of remote events is so high relative to local events, applications may take steps to batch remote events together or make other provisions to try to offset the cost. Again, here you see the semantics of the particular applications involved imposing constraints on the event subsystem.

In all these cases, applications need the ability to express their desires about event *policies*: meaning how and even whether events are delivered. Put simply, there is a much wider variance in what applications may expect from an event delivery system in the remote case than in the local case. There are no single answers for all applications. Some applications may require in-order delivery at all costs; others may not care about order at all. Some applications may insist that events never be dropped, possibly requiring that they be logged for later delivery; others may be perfectly capable of tolerating lost messages. Since there is such latitude in the space of what applications may reasonably require, any useful remote event system must make provisions for applications to specify their own constraints and behaviors.

Addressing Application Semantics

Jini's event model addresses the need to accommodate different application semantics by providing a way for applications to extend, at run time, the event model itself. It does this by supporting the composable event handlers described earlier. That is, if an application needs some special behavior, such as in-order events, or storage of events, or guaranteed delivery, it can simply write a handler that provides this behavior and "plug it in."

Paradoxically, the sorts of behaviors that can be added are open-ended, even though the Jini event programming model says *nothing* about such behaviors in its APIs. That is, there is no call to enableInOrderDelivery() or `storeEventsUntilDeliverable()`. Instead, Jini provides only the bare minimum set of APIs for event delivery, but defines these APIs in such a way that developers can write new behaviors without having to understand the semantics of the events themselves. So you can write code that provides in-order delivery behavior and use it with *any* type of Jini remote event, without having to understand what those events *mean*.

Further, such behaviors can be added either by the generators of events or by the consumers of events. So if you're writing a new service that sends events periodically, and it's important to you that clients receive your events if at all possible, you can create a "reliable delivery" event handler and forward your events to it. This handler could then try to ensure that events are delivered on to their final destinations. Alternatively, the decision to use such an event handler could be made by the consumer of the events. So if you are writing an application that will only periodically wake up to receive events, you can create a "store and forward" event handler and arrange for events destined for you to be sent there. When your application is active, it can contact the event handler to have its events forwarded.

The ability to extend the event model to accommodate such new, application-specified behaviors was an important goal for the Jini designers. And the solution they came up with—composable, application-provided event handlers that can work with any type of event—is elegant and minimal. An alternative like providing "control knobs" in the API for setting and tuning any number of delivery parameters would have only increased the work for event generators—since they would now have to implement *all* these potential delivery policies—but would still likely fall short of the requirements of many applications. The Jini approach is extremely flexible while being minimal and easy to understand.

The Jini Event Programming Model

With this introduction and rationale behind us, let's look at the programming model Jini uses for remote events. As you've seen already, Jini provides an *extremely* minimal set of APIs for dealing with events. But the size of the API set belies the range of tasks it can be applied to.

There are really only two important classes and interfaces: `RemoteEvent` defines a common superclass for all Jini remote events, and `Remote-EventListener` defines a single method that event consumers must implement to receive events. Jini does not define any standard interface for event generators. Instead, the particulars of how clients will ask to receive events will vary from generator to generator. You've already seen how the `notify()` call on Jini `Ser-`

`viceRegistrars` works, which is an example of a service-specific way to ask to receive events.

The RemoteEvent Class

First, take a look at the relevant details of `RemoteEvent`:

```
public class RemoteEvent extends java.util.EventObject {
        protected Object source;
        protected long eventID;
        protected long seqNum;
        protected MarshalledObject handback;

        public RemoteEvent(Object source, long eventID,
                           long seqNum,
                           MarshalledObject handback);
        public long getID();
        public long getSequenceNumber();
        public MarshalledObject
                           getRegistrationObject();
}
```

The `RemoteEvent` class extends `java.util.EventObject`, as all Java events do. `EventObject` implements `Serializable`, so `RemoteEvents` can be transmitted over the wire to other Java VMs and reconstituted as needed. The "source" of a `RemoteEvent` is the object that generated the event. Obviously, this will vary from event generator to event generator.

Event Types

`RemoteEvents` have a few details that are designed to support the uses to which they will be applied in Jini. First, every `RemoteEvent` has an identifier that uniquely describes the "type" of the event relative to the entity that generated it.

Each unique identifier should represent some distinct type of occurrence in the event generator, *not* each and every instance of an event object. So a printer service might use one event type to indicate that the printer is out of paper, and another event type to indicate that the printer has jammed. In such a use, multiple instances of "out of paper" events would have the same event identifier that indicates the type of the event.

In Sun's sample implementation of the Jini lookup service, a new event identifier is assigned to each distinct event registration. That is, the implementation defines the "distinct occurrence" that warrants an event to be a match of the particular service template provided by a client. You could imagine other services that define the space of their identifiers in different ways. As you'll see in the discussion about customizing the event pipeline, using a separate type identifier for each client registration can be a big help when using event delegates.

The set of identifiers that a service may generate is unique only to it. Put another way, there is no global namespace of event identifiers. A printer service may use the integers 1 and 2 to indicate special printer conditions, while a Jini lookup service might use these same numbers to indicate different occurrences specific to it.

In addition to using these type identifiers, Jini services are also free to use subclasses of `RemoteEvent` to describe state changes. You've already seen one example of this in the Jini lookup service. The lookup service sends `Service-Events` to describe changes in the registrations with a particular lookup service. These `ServiceEvents` contain information specific to the change at hand, but are still `RemoteEvents` that can be used, operated on, and forwarded by any code that understands basic `RemoteEvents`.

Sequence Numbers, Idempotency, and Ordering

Each event also contains a *sequence number* that can be used by consumers to determine whether they may have received events out of order. Jini is fairly flexible about how event generators set and use sequence numbers, but there are two basic requirements. First, the Jini specifications dictate that any object that generates events use a different sequence number for those events if and only if the events refer to two distinct occurrences within the event generator. Second, Jini dictates that for any two events A and B from the same generator and with the same event identifier, then A occurred before B if and only if the sequence number of A is lower than the sequence number of B.

I'll walk through an example of how such sequence numbering would work in the familiar printer service. A printer service might define an event type to indicate that the printer is out of paper, and generate events to interested parties whenever this happens. The first requirement imposed by Jini *mandates* that the service *cannot* use the same sequence number in events that result from two occurrences of the printer running out of paper. Also, the service has to use the *same* sequence numbers for events generated from the same "out of paper" occurrence.

This requirement is imposed so that clients that process events can be *idempotent*. That is, that they can, if they choose, be written in such a way that they only deal with the underlying occurrence once, regardless of how many events they may receive notifying them of the underlying occurrence. So if a flaky event generator or a third-party event handler somehow sends multiple events for the same out of paper occurrence, clients can do the right thing by handling these events only once.

The second requirement—that sequence numbers be increasing in value—mandates that if the printer runs out of paper twice, then the sequence number for the events that result from the second occurrence will be higher than the sequence numbers that resulted from the first. This requirement is so that event consumers can tell if they have received events out-of-order. Some consumers, for instance, may simply discard events that arrive after a "logically-later" event that they have already dealt with.

This requirement produces what is known as a *strict ordering* of events. Given any two events that resulted from different occurrences, you can tell which happened later. Note that this strict ordering requirement doesn't say that generators cannot skip sequence numbers—a generator could increment sequence numbers by ten or by a hundred for every occurrence that produces events. Because this is true, clients are limited in the information they can infer from sequence numbers. Clearly, they can infer ordering information, since sequence numbers increase. But if the sequence numbers of two events differ by, say, a hundred, then the client cannot determine if no events, one event, or even a hundred events transpired between the two.[3]

For the most part, implementing these requirements is trivial—event generators can keep a counter for sequence numbers, and make sure that for any event-worthy occurrence they use the same sequence number for any and all events that result from that occurrence. After each round of events is sent off, they simply increment the sequence counter. Event consumers can choose to pay attention to sequence numbers if they wish, or simply deal with the consequences of potentially receiving multiple events that correspond to the same occurrence, or out-of-order events. In most cases, this won't be a big deal.

But event generators can optionally make an even stronger guarantee over and above these "baseline" guarantees designed to support idempotency and ordering. Services can, if they choose, guarantee that not only do their sequence numbers increase, but that sequence numbers are not skipped. This allows consumers to take two sequence numbers from the same generator and with the same type

---

3. Although if the sequence numbers differ by exactly 1, that is if the sequence number of event A is n and the sequence number of event B is n+1, then a client can be assured that *no* events came between A and B, because there is no "gap" for other events to hide in. ·

identifier and determine *exactly* how many intervening events (from the same generator and of the same type) have been generated. A client that received such events would then be able to precisely determine whether it has missed any events and, if so, how many. This guarantee provides what is known as a *full ordering* of events.

The implementation of a service that provides full ordering of events is not much more difficult than a service that provides only the baseline guarantees. Recall that the baseline guarantees can be satisfied by having a global counter within the generator, and incrementing that counter whenever there is an event-worthy occurrence, no matter what the event type. To provide full ordering, a service only needs to make sure that there are *separate* counters for each event type (so that each increases separately from the others), and that counters are incremented by exactly one each time an event-worthy occurrence takes place.

Be sure to remember that *all* these guarantees about sequence numbers are only made for events from a single event generator and with the same event ID. So the sequence numbers of two events from different generators, or two events from the same generator but with different IDs, cannot be compared.

Table 16–1 summarizes the guarantees that services may be able to make about event sequencing:

Table 16–1 Event Sequencing Guarantees

Idempotency	Events have different sequence numbers if and only if they correspond to different occurrences in the event generator	Required by the Jini spec
Strict Ordering	Sequence numbers are increasing, but the event generator may "skip" sequence numbers	Required by the Jini spec
Full Ordering	Sequence numbers are increasing, and are not skipped	Optionally implemented by services

Currently, there is no easy way for services to "advertise" what level of strictness in event sequencing they provide. Clearly, the logical way to do this would be as an attribute on the service's registration with a lookup service, but as of this writing, there is no standard attribute that describes the guarantees a service is willing to make.

Application-Specified Return Data

The final component of `RemoteEvent` is the `MarshalledObject` that is returned by the `getRegistrationObject()` method. This object is a way for an event consumer to have data particular to it "handed back" when a `RemoteEvent` is received. Recall that a `MarshalledObject` is simply the serialized version of whatever object you provide, along with codebase information to allow the implementation of the object to be retrieved later if needed.

Although Jini defines no "standard" interface for event generators, most generators will provide a registration method that allows clients to ask to receive events. Whatever the particulars of these registration methods, they should allow a way for the client to pass in a `MarshalledObject` to be associated with the registration. The event generator should then return this `MarshalledObject` whenever an event is sent to the consumer.

By using this ability to associate arbitrary data with event registrations, clients can simplify some of their bookkeeping chores. Clients can use this "handed back" object to associate client-specific context with event registrations.

The RemoteEventListener Interface

After `RemoteEvent`, the most important interface you must understand is `RemoteEventListener`. This is the interface that any consumer of `RemoteEvents` must implement; fortunately, implementing it is very easy, as the interface has only one method:

```
public interface RemoteEventListener
        extends java.rmi.Remote, java.util.EventListener. {
    public void notify(RemoteEvent ev)
        throws UnknownEventException, RemoteException;
}
```

Whenever an event generator sends an event to you, the `notify()` method on an object that you have designated as a listener for remote events will be called. The actual event that is delivered may be a subclass of `RemoteEvent`, as you've already seen in our look at notifications from lookup services—lookup services actually send a subclass of `RemoteEvent` called `ServiceEvent`, which contains more detailed information about state changes than a generic `RemoteEvent`.

The basic paradigm here is quite simple—you just register for events, using whatever mechanisms are provided by the service you want events from, and then those events get delivered via the `notify()` method.

There are a few points about event delivery that you should be aware of, though. First, the `RemoteEventListener` interface extends `java.rmi.Remote`. This means that the interface itself defines an RMI communication protocol between the event consumer and the event generator. This also means that your implementation of `RemoteEventListener` must be an RMI server object, typically a `java.rmi.server.UnicastRemoteObject`.

Another point to make is that event consumers must take care when implementing the `notify()` method. RMI uses *synchronous* calls, which means that when a service invokes the `notify()` method on your event listener remotely, the service blocks until your code returns. If your code takes a long time before it completes, you will prevent the service from delivering events to others. So it's important that you try to limit the amount of work done in `notify()`. Most times, you will simply place the received event on a queue and then return; the work of dealing with the particular queued events is delegated to a separate thread.[4]

Dealing with Errors

Event delivery errors can happen in the consumer or in the generator. You'll notice that `RemoteEventListener`, the interface implemented by the consumer, declares `notify()` as raising an `UnknownEventException`. Consumers are allowed to raise this exception from `notify()` if they ever receive an event with an unexpected type identifier, or from an unexpected source. This situation indicates that, somehow, either the service or the client has gotten confused, and that unanticipated and unwanted events are being exchanged between them. By raising `UnknownEventException`, the client is claiming that it doesn't want to receive that particular type of event from that event generator again.

As for the generator, if it calls the `notify()` method on a client and receives an `UnknownEventException`, it is free to cancel the client's event registration for that particular type of event. This would ensure that the client never receives that type of event from the generator again.

---

4. Just as clients can take special care not to stay in `notify()` for too long, services can protect themselves from clients which are not so well-behaved. Services that are concerned with performance and robustness may insulate themselves from ill-behaved clients by handing off the *invocation* of `notify()` to a separate, short-lived thread. This allows the service to continue doing other work—including notifying other clients—without having to completely block until `notify()` returns.

Other Event Interfaces

The RemoteEvent and RemoteEventListener interfaces are the most central APIs defined by the Jini remote event model. There is, however, one more common class that, although not required, will be used frequently by Jini applications. This class is EventRegistration, which encapsulates the information associated with a particular client's solicitation of events.

The reason that this class is not "required" by all Jini event generators is that the interfaces to event generators are not standardized—event generators may or may not return an EventRegistration as their needs dictate. The class is commonly used, however, and is defined as a return value from ServiceRegistrar's event solicitation method.

You've already seen this class before, so I won't dwell too long on it. But you should make sure that you understand how the members of EventRegistration will be set and used. Let's look at the particulars of this class.

```
public class EventRegistration
                implements java.io.Serializable {
    protected long eventID;
    protected Object source;
    protected Lease lease;
    protected long seqNum;

    public EventRegistration(long eventID,
                            Object source,
                            Lease lease,
                            long seqNum);
    public long getID();
    public Object getSource();
    public Lease getLease();
    public long getSequenceNumber();
}
```

EventRegistrations are serializable since, obviously, they will need to be sent to clients who are registering for events.

The Lease object referenced here is a representation of the client's lease on its event registration. While event generators don't strictly *have* to lease their event registrations, they are strongly advised to—leasing ensures that any event generator you write will be able to clean up after ill-behaved or crashed clients. You've already seen lots of details on leasing, and explanations for why leasing is important, so I won't go into more detail here. Review Chapter 12 if you want a refresher on leasing.

The other members of `EventRegistration` require a bit more explanation. If you're writing an event generator that returns these `EventRegistration` objects to clients, you need to make sure you properly set up all these fields.

The source object indicates the generator that will deliver remote events. This should be set to the same source that will be used in all `RemoteEvents` generated for this event registration; clients must be able to take the source from a `RemoteEvent` they receive and compare it to the source in the registration.

Likewise, the event ID should be the identifer that will be used in all `RemoteEvents` for this registration. A client should be able to take a `RemoteEvent` and identify the registration that caused that event given the combination of source and event ID in the event.

Finally, the sequence number in the registration should identify the *last* sequence number used by the generator for events of the specified type at the time the registration was granted. Clients can store this number and then compare it to subsequently received events; this will allow them to determine whether they may have missed events that occurred between the time the registration was actually granted and the time the client received its first event from the generator.

As you'll see, correctly setting the source and event ID is necessary so that third-party event handlers can correctly route events to a desired destination. The sequence number must be returned so that clients can determine if they may have missed any events between when the registration occurred and when they actually received their first event.

At this point, you've seen the entire set of APIs used by Jini to deal with remote events! Let's jump into some example programs next.

An Example: Heartbeat Events

In this example, you'll see a Jini service that generates "heartbeat events." These are events that are sent periodically to clients. Clients can ask to receive heartbeat events at certain intervals, such as every minute, every hour, every day, or every week.

The semantics of these events are very simple. In fact, for most clients, simply having an internal thread periodically awaken to generate a notification would be sufficient, and far more lightweight than relying on some external service to generate timer events.[5] But by keeping the amount of application-specific code to a minimum here, I can focus in on the mechanics of event registration, leasing, and delivery—which are, after all, the main goals of this chapter.

This is the first example in the book that implements a real event generator with proper leasing behavior (the example in Chapter 15 sent `Print-`

`ServiceEvents` when a job completed, but the registration process was implicitly "hidden" behind print job submission, and registrations were never actually leased). So here you'll see a more complete event generator as well as a more prototypical event consumer.

To keep the example interesting, I'll be creating some "helper" classes that can be used to support leased event registrations. These classes can easily work in conjunction with the `BasicUnicastService` and other classes from the Service Writer's Toolkit that you saw in Chapter 15. You should be able to reuse these classes in many of your own applications.

I'll talk about the classes to help with event registrations before diving into the service itself.

A Toolkit for Event Registrations

You've already seen in Chapter 15 how it's possible to build a simple "toolkit" for managing tasks common to many services. In this section, you'll learn how to abstract away some of the common functionality needed to handle the leasing and managing of event registrations. Much of this work is simple book-keeping—keeping lists of registrations, expiring leases as necessary, handling the chores of being a lease landlord. As such, much of this work can be handled comfortably by a library of code that can be applied to different applications.

The main class here is called `BasicRegistrationLandlord`. This class follows the standard `Landlord` paradigm you've already seen in Chapter 13, and in fact, works much the same way as the `Landlord` in the `SlotProvider` example. It implements a simple, default leasing policy, it uses RMI for communication with the `LandlordLeases` that are sent to clients, and registrations are kept in a simple data structure that can be easily scanned.

Each event registration is represented internally by an instance of a class called `Registration`. Each `Registration` maintains the cookie that uniquely identifies the lease on the registration, the `RemoteEventListener` that will be notified when an event is delivered, the `MarshalledObject` that will be returned to the listener, and the current expiration time of the registration.

Whenever the `BasicRegistrationLandlord` needs to cancel or renew leases, it scans an `ArrayList` of `Registration` objects, looking for the `Regis`-

---

5. This heartbeat service isn't as daft as it might first appear, however. Services that are inactive for long periods of time, such as a weekly backup service, might use the RMI activation framework to "deactivate" themselves. Having an external service send a message once per week could be the trigger that causes such a service to reactivate itself.

tration that contains a particular cookie. Once it finds it, it updates the Registration's expiration time if it is renewing it, or removes it from the list if it is
canceling it.

Let's look at the code for Registration, as shown in Listing 16–1.

Listing 16–1 Registration.java

```
// This class represents one event registration
// with a BasicRegistrationLandlord.
package corejini.chapter16;

import net.jini.core.event.RemoteEventListener;
import java.io.Serializable;
import java.rmi.MarshalledObject;
```

Listing 16–1 `Registration.java` (continued)

```
class Registration implements Serializable {
    protected Object cookie;
    protected RemoteEventListener listener;
    protected MarshalledObject data;
    protected long expiration;

    // To maintain a registration, we need to remember
    // the cookie for the registration, who the listener
    // is, the client-provided data, and its expiration
    // time.
    Registration(Object cookie,
                 RemoteEventListener listener,
                 MarshalledObject data,
                 long expiration) {
        this.cookie = cookie;
        this.listener = listener;
        this.data = data;
        this.expiration = expiration;
    }

    Object getCookie() {
        return cookie;
    }

    RemoteEventListener getListener() {
        return listener;
    }

    MarshalledObject getData() {
        return data;
    }

    long getExpiration() {
        return expiration;
    }

    void setExpiration(long expiration) {
        this.expiration = expiration;
    }
```

Listing 16–1 `Registration.java` (continued)

```
    // Subclasses can override this if they need to do
    // special things at cancellation/expiration time.  The
    // default implementation does nothing.
    protected void cancelled() {
    }
}
```

This simple class maintains the items necessary for keeping and using a registration, namely the cookie that represents the lease on the registration, the listener that will be called when an event needs to be delivered, the `MarshalledObject` data that should be returned to the consumer, and the expiration time for the registration.

This class is only used internally by the `BasicRegistrationLandlord` and its callers—it is never exposed to lease holders or other event consumers.

Let's now look at the `BasicRegistrationLandlord` class (Listing 16–2), which manages sets of event registrations.

Listing 16–2 `BasicRegistrationLandlord.java`

```
// This class implements some basic functionality to
// lease event registrations.  It can work in
// conjunction with the BasicUnicastService from
// Chapter 14.

package corejini.chapter16;

import net.jini.core.lease.Lease;
import net.jini.core.lease.UnknownLeaseException;
import net.jini.core.lease.LeaseDeniedException;
import com.sun.jini.lease.landlord.Landlord;
import com.sun.jini.lease.landlord.LandlordLease;
import java.rmi.server.UnicastRemoteObject;
import java.rmi.RemoteException;
import java.util.List;
import java.util.ArrayList;
import java.util.Map;
import java.util.HashMap;
```

Listing 16–2 `BasicRegistrationLandlord.java` (continued)

```java
public class BasicRegistrationLandlord
    extends UnicastRemoteObject
    implements Landlord {
    // A simple leasing policy...10-minute leases.
    protected static final int DEFAULT_MAX_LEASE
    = 1000 * 60 * 10;
    protected int maxLease = DEFAULT_MAX_LEASE;
    // Assume that registrations are kept in
    // a list maintained by our clients.
    protected List regs;
    // A factory for making landlord leases
    protected LandlordLease.Factory factory;

    public BasicRegistrationLandlord(List regs,
                            LandlordLease.Factory factory)
        throws RemoteException {
        this.regs = regs;
        this.factory = factory;
    }
```

Listing 16–2 `BasicRegistrationLandlord.java` (continued)

```java
// Change the maximum lease time from the default
public void setMaxLease(int maxLease) {
    this.maxLease = maxLease;
}

// Apply the policy to a requested duration
// to get an actual expiration time.
public long getExpiration(long request) {
    if (request > maxLease || request == Lease.ANY)
        return System.currentTimeMillis() + maxLease;
    else
        return System.currentTimeMillis() + request;
}

// Cancel the lease represented by 'cookie'
public void cancel(Object cookie)
    throws UnknownLeaseException, RemoteException {
    for (int i=0, size=regs.size() ; i<size ; i++) {
        Registration reg =
            (Registration) regs.get(i);
        if (reg.cookie.equals(cookie)) {
            reg.cancelled();
            regs.remove(i);
            return;
        }
    }
    throw new UnknownLeaseException(cookie.toString());
}
```

Listing 16–2 `BasicRegistrationLandlord.java` (continued)

```java
    // Cancel a set of leases
    public Map cancelAll(Object[] cookies)
        throws RemoteException
        Map exceptionMap = null;

        for (int i=0 ; i<cookies.length ; i++) {
            try {
                cancel(cookies[i]);
            } catch (UnknownLeaseException ex) {
                if (exceptionMap == null) {
                    exceptionMap = new HashMap();
                    exceptionMap.put(cookies[i], ex);
                }
            }
        }

        return exceptionMap;
    }

    // Renew the lease specified by 'cookie'
    public long renew(Object cookie, long extension)
        throws UnknownLeaseException,
               LeaseDeniedException,
               RemoteException {
        for (int i=0, size=regs.size() ; i<size ; i++) {
            Registration reg =
             (Registration) regs.get(i);
            if (reg.getCookie().equals(cookie)) {
                long expiration =
             getExpiration(extension);
                reg.setExpiration(expiration);
                return expiration -
             System.currentTimeMillis();
            }
        }
        throw new UnknownLeaseException(cookie.toString());
    }
```

Listing 16–2 `BasicRegistrationLandlord.java` (continued)

```
    // Renew a set of leases.
    public Landlord.RenewResults renewAll(Object[] cookies,
                                          long[] extensions)
            throws RemoteException {
        long[] granted = new long[cookies.length];
        Exception[] denied = null;

        for (int i=0 ; i<cookies.length ; i++) {
            try {
                granted[i] = renew(cookies[i],
                    extensions[i]);
            } catch (Exception ex) {
                if (denied == null) {
                    denied =
                        new Exception[cookies.length+1];
                }
                denied[i+1] = ex;
            }
        }

        Landlord.RenewResults results =
            new Landlord.RenewResults(granted, denied);
        return results;
    }
}
```

Let's look at how this code works. The `BasicRegistrationLandlord` class is a `Landlord` that works with Sun's `LandlordLease` implementation of leasing. So, `BasicRegistrationLandlord` extends `UnicastRemoteObject` since, as you will recall, `LandlordLeases` communicate back to their Landlords via RMI. The class also implements the `Landlord` interface, which defines the contract that `LandlordLeases` expect.

This new `Landlord` manages a single `ArrayList` of `Registration` objects. Each `Registration` is a `Landlord`-internal representation of an event registration made by a client. When a `BasicRegistrationLandlord` is created, it is initialized with a list of `Registrations` and a factory for making new leases (you can refer back to Chapter 13 on exporting resources via leasing if you need to review the details of factories and how the `Landlord` paradigm works).

Many of the methods here are similar to those in the examples of Chapter 13: The `setMaxLease()` method controls the leasing policy by setting the maximum lease duration which will be issued; `getExpiration()` takes a requested duration and returns an actual lease expiration time, given whatever policy is in effect.

But the "meat" of the work here is done by the methods to cancel and renew event registration leases. The `cancel()` method scans the list of `Registration` objects, looking for one with a cookie that matches the input parameter. If it is found, it is removed from the set of managed registrations and its `cancelled()` method is called. While in the implementation of `Registration` shown here, `cancelled()` does nothing; subclasses of `Registration` could override this method to allow some special type of behavior to happen upon cancellation. If the input cookie is not found, then an `UnknownLeaseException` method is raised—presumably a client has held on to a lease longer than its expiration time.

The `renew()` method works in much the same way—it scans the list, looking for a matching cookie. If it is found, the expiration date of the corresponding `Registration` object is updated. If it is not found, an `UnknownLeaseException` is raised.

The two methods that deal with multiple leases at once—`cancelAll()` and `renewAll()`—simply iterate through the cookies passed to them and call the underlying `cancel()` and `renew()` methods. Note that `cancelAll()` returns null if all cancellations succeed, or a `Map` mapping from cookies to exceptions if failures occur.

Note that there is nothing in the `BasicRegistrationLandlord` class that is specific to event registrations—all the particular details about events are hidden away in the `Registration` class. So by substituting a different `Registration` class, you can use this code for managing many sorts of `LandlordLeases`.

A Simple Event Generator

Now that you've got some tools for handling registrations of events, we can look at an event generator. This event generator, called `HeartbeatGenerator`, allows clients to register for "heartbeat" events at various intervals. Clients can ask that they receive events every minute, hourly, daily, or weekly. These registrations are leased to clients using the `Landlord` techniques seen earlier.

The generator itself makes only a "best effort" attempt at sending events. If the generator crashes and then restarts, it does not send "make up" events for the time that it was down. Again, the goal here is to focus on the strategies for building event generators and clients, not on all the application details that might be necessary in a more robust generator of heartbeat events.

Look at the code, as shown in Listing 16–3.

Listing 16–3 `HeartbeatGenerator.java`

```java
// A simple service that sends periodic events.

package corejini.chapter16;

import corejini.chapter15.BasicUnicastService;
import corejini.chapter15.BasicUnicastAdmin;
import net.jini.core.lease.Lease;
import net.jini.core.lease.UnknownLeaseException;
import net.jini.core.event.RemoteEvent;
import net.jini.core.event.RemoteEventListener;
import net.jini.core.event.EventRegistration;
import net.jini.core.event.UnknownEventException;
import com.sun.jini.lease.landlord.LandlordLease;
import java.rmi.Remote;
import java.rmi.RemoteException;
import java.rmi.MarshalledObject;
import java.rmi.RMISecurityManager;
import java.rmi.server.UnicastRemoteObject;
import java.io.Serializable;
import java.io.IOException;
import java.util.List;
import java.util.ArrayList;
```

Listing 16–3 `HeartbeatGenerator.java` (continued)

```java
// The cookie class for our leases.  This class
// identifies leases by their unique event type
// identifiers and the period they're registering
// for.
class HeartbeatCookie implements Serializable {
    int period;
    long eventType;

    HeartbeatCookie(int period, long eventType) {
        this.period = period;
        this.eventType = eventType;
    }
    public boolean equals(Object other) {
        if (!(other instanceof HeartbeatCookie))
            return false;

        HeartbeatCookie cookie = (HeartbeatCookie) other;

        return cookie.period == period &&
               cookie.eventType == eventType;
    }
}
```

Listing 16–3 `HeartbeatGenerator.java` (continued)

```java
// The heartbeat service is a BasicUnicastService
// (see Chapter 15).
public class HeartbeatGenerator
        extends BasicUnicastService
        implements Runnable,
                    HeartbeatGenerator.HeartbeatRequest {
    // 10 minutes
    protected static final int MAX_LEASE = 1000 * 60 * 10;
    protected boolean done = false;
    protected long tickCount = 0;
    // Lists of registrants
    protected List minute = new ArrayList();
    protected List hour = new ArrayList();
    protected List day = new ArrayList();
    protected List week = new ArrayList();
    // Separate landlords for each list
    protected BasicRegistrationLandlord minuteLandlord;
    protected BasicRegistrationLandlord hourLandlord;
    protected BasicRegistrationLandlord dayLandlord;
    protected BasicRegistrationLandlord weekLandlord;
    protected long lastEventSeqNo = 0;
    protected LandlordLease.Factory factory =
        new LandlordLease.Factory();

    protected long nextEventType = 1;

    public static final int MINUTE=1,
                            HOUR=2,
                            DAY=3,
                            WEEK=4;
```

Listing 16–3 `HeartbeatGenerator.java` (continued)

```java
// Saves our class-specific data when we persist
static class Registrations implements Serializable {
    List minute;
    List hour;
    List day;
    List week;
    long nextEventType;
    long lastEventSeqNo;

    Registrations(List minute, List hour,
                  List day, List week,
                  long nextEventType,
                  long lastEventSeqNo) {
        this.minute = minute;
        this.hour = hour;
        this.day = day;
        this.week = week;
        this.nextEventType = nextEventType;
        this.lastEventSeqNo = lastEventSeqNo;
    }
}


// We send particular subclasses of RemoteEvent
public static class HeartbeatEvent extends RemoteEvent
    implements Serializable {
    int period;

    HeartbeatEvent(Object proxy,
                   long eventType,
                   long seq,
                   MarshalledObject data,
                   int period) {
        super(proxy, eventType, seq, data);
        this.period = period;
    }

    public int getPeriod() {
        return period;
    }
}
```

Listing 16–3 `HeartbeatGenerator.java` (continued)

```java
// Callers speak this interface to ask us to send
// heartbeats
public interface HeartbeatRequest extends Remote {
    public EventRegistration register(int period,
                                 MarshalledObject data,
                                 RemoteEventListener listener,
                                 long duration)
        throws RemoteException;
}


public HeartbeatGenerator(String storageLoc)
        throws RemoteException {
    super(storageLoc);

    minuteLandlord =
        new BasicRegistrationLandlord(minute, factory);
    hourLandlord =
        new BasicRegistrationLandlord(hour, factory);
    dayLandlord =
        new BasicRegistrationLandlord(day, factory);
    weekLandlord =
        new BasicRegistrationLandlord(week, factory);
}

// Initialize the superclass and start the
// leasing thread
protected void initialize()
        throws IOException, ClassNotFoundException {
    super.initialize();
    new Thread(this).start();
}
```

Listing 16–3 `HeartbeatGenerator.java` (continued)

```java
// Save the specific registration data
protected void checkpoint() throws IOException {
    checkpoint(new Registrations(minute,
                                 hour,
                                 day,
                                 week,
                                 nextEventType,
                                 lastEventSeqNo));
}

// Use the RMI-generated stub as the proxy
protected Object getProxy() {
    return this;
}

// Restore class-specific data
public void restored(Object subclassData) {
    Registrations regs = (Registrations) subclassData;
    minute = regs.minute;
    hour = regs.hour;
    day = regs.day;
    week = regs.week;
    nextEventType = regs.nextEventType;
    lastEventSeqNo = regs.lastEventSeqNo;
}
```

Listing 16–3 `HeartbeatGenerator.java` (continued)

```java
public synchronized EventRegistration register(
                            int period,
                            MarshalledObject data,
                            RemoteEventListener listener,
                            long duration) {
    // Build a cookie based on the table and token
    long eventType = nextEventType++;
    HeartbeatCookie cookie =
        new HeartbeatCookie(period, eventType);

    // The landlord we'll use for the lease
    BasicRegistrationLandlord landlord;

    // The registration list we'll add it to
    List regs;

    switch (period) {
    case MINUTE:
        landlord = minuteLandlord;
        regs = minute;
        break;
    case HOUR:
        landlord = hourLandlord;
        regs = hour;
        break;
    case DAY:
        landlord = dayLandlord;
        regs = day;
        break;
    case WEEK:
        landlord = weekLandlord;
        regs = week;
        break;
    default:
        throw new IllegalArgumentException(
                                    "Bad period");
    }
```

Listing 16–3 `HeartbeatGenerator.java` (continued)

```java
            // Create the lease and registration, and add the
            // registration to the appropriate list
            long expiration = landlord.getExpiration(duration);
            Registration reg = new Registration(cookie,
                                                listener,
                                                data,
                                                expiration);
            Lease lease = factory.newLease(cookie,
                                           landlord,
                                           expiration);
            regs.add(reg);

            // Return an event registration to the client
            EventRegistration evtreg =
                new EventRegistration(eventType,
                                      proxy,
                                      lease,
                                      0);

        try {
            checkpoint();
        } catch(IOException ex) {
            System.err.println("Error checkpointing: " +
                               ex.getMessage());
        }

        return evtreg;
    }
```

Listing 16–3 `HeartbeatGenerator.java` (continued)

```
protected void sendHeartbeat() {
    tickCount++;

    // Minute listeners
    sendHeartbeats(minute, MINUTE);

    // Hour listeners
    if (tickCount % 60 == 0) {
        sendHeartbeats(hour, HOUR);
    }

    // Day listeners
    if (tickCount % (60 * 24) == 0) {
        sendHeartbeats(day, DAY);
    }

    // Week listeners
    if (tickCount % (60 * 24 * 7) == 0) {
        sendHeartbeats(week, WEEK);
    }
}
```

Listing 16–3 `HeartbeatGenerator.java` (continued)

```java
protected void sendHeartbeats(List regs, int period) {
    // First, scavenge the list for dead registrations,
    // in reverse order (to make us immune from
    // compaction)
    long now = System.currentTimeMillis();
    for (int i=regs.size()-1 ; i >= 0 ; i--) {
        Registration reg = (Registration) regs.get(i);
        if (reg.expiration < now) {
            reg.cancelled();
            regs.remove(i);
        }
    }

    // Now, message the remaining listeners
    for (int i=0, size=regs.size() ; i<size ; i++) {
        Registration reg = (Registration) regs.get(i);
        HeartbeatCookie cookie =
            (HeartbeatCookie) reg.getCookie();
        long eventType = cookie.eventType;

        try {
            HeartbeatEvent ev =
                new HeartbeatEvent(proxy,
                                   eventType,
                                   lastEventSeqNo++,
                                   reg.data,
                                   period);
            reg.listener.notify(ev);
        } catch (RemoteException ex) {
            // Just complain...
            System.err.println(
                "Error notifying remote listener: " +
                ex.getMessage());
        } catch (UnknownEventException ex) {
```

Listing 16–3 `HeartbeatGenerator.java` (continued)

```java
                // Cancel the registration... Here I'll
                // do this by setting its expiration so
                // that it'll be dropped the next time
                // through.
                System.err.println(
                    "Unknown event, dropping: " +
                    ex.getMessage());
                reg.expiration = 0;
            }
        }
    }

    public void run() {
        long timeToSleep = 60 * 1000;
        while (true) {
            long nextWakeup =
                System.currentTimeMillis() + timeToSleep;

            try {
                Thread.sleep(timeToSleep);
            } catch (InterruptedException ex) {
            }

            long currentTime = System.currentTimeMillis();

            // See if we're at the next wakeup time
            if (currentTime >= nextWakeup) {
                nextWakeup = currentTime + (60 * 1000);
                // notify
                sendHeartbeat();
            }
            timeToSleep = nextWakeup -
                        System.currentTimeMillis();
        }
    }
}
```

Listing 16–3 `HeartbeatGenerator.java` (continued)

```
public static void main(String[] args) {
    if (System.getSecurityManager() == null) {
        System.setSecurityManager(
            new RMISecurityManager());
    }

    try {
        if (args.length != 1) {
            System.err.println(
             "Usage: HeartbeatGenerator <storageloc>");
            System.exit(1);
        }

        HeartbeatGenerator gen =
            new HeartbeatGenerator(args[0]);
        gen.initialize();
        System.out.println(
            "Heartbeat generator started.");
    } catch (Exception ex) {
        System.err.println(
            "Error starting heartbeat generator: " +
            ex.getMessage());
        System.exit(1);
    }
}
}
```

This code is based on the `BasicUnicastService` you saw in the last chapter, so many of the concepts here will be familiar to you. The service is structured around separate lists of `Registration` objects, one list per "period" that clients can register for (per-minute events, per-hour events, and so on). For each of these, there is a separate `BasicRegistrationLandlord` that handles the management tasks for that period.

Event Types and Sequence Numbers

Two of the main decisions that any event generator has to make are how to use event type identifiers, and how to use sequence numbers.

Let's look first at how this service uses event type identifiers. Earlier in this chapter, I talked about how events are delivered with particular event type identifiers in them. And remember that the `EventRegistration` objects that are returned to clients contain in them the event type identifier that the client has just registered to receive. The event type identifier is meant to uniquely distinguish some type of occurrence in the generator that causes events to be fired. For this service, I grant a separate event type identifier for each and every client registration; when a client registers to receive, say, hourly heartbeat events, a new event type number is generated and returned to the client.

This strategy is similar to that employed by Sun's implementation of the lookup service, where each registration for notifications by a client is given a separate event type identifier. Other strategies might be possible. For example, rather than granting a separate event type identifier for each and every client registration, one could create a separate type ID for each period that can be requested (`minuteEventID`, `hourEventID`, and so on). But, as you'll see in the discussion on third-party event delegates, using separate event type identifiers for each registration can be useful when using delegates.

For sequence numbers, the `HeartbeatGenerator` keeps a global sequence number counter (called `lastEventSeqNo`). This counter is incremented by one every time a new event is sent. This service only tries to send an event once, when the "due date" comes up for a client. Since there are no retries, the code here doesn't have to do anything special to ensure that multiple events from the same "due date" have the same sequence numbers. Thus, satisfying the requirements for idempotency and strict ordering is easy here.

Note that since each client registration has a different event ID, any single client may see skips in the sequence numbers of events delivered to it. For example, if a client has asked to receive weekly events, it will see gaps in sequence numbers caused by the fact that other clients, who are receiving events at smaller intervals, have been sent the events with the intervening sequence numbers.

So the service here only implements the two required sequence number guarantees. It ensures that distinct sequence numbers are generated if and only if there are two distinct occurrences—in this case, the passing of the "due date" for sending an event. The code does this by only sending one event for each occurrence, and ensuring that sequence numbers are never reused. Likewise, the service also guarantees that sequence numbers are uniformly increasing. The service does this by keeping a global counter and incrementing it each time a new sequence number is needed.

The service *does not* provide the optional "full ordering" guarantee. To provide this guarantee is a relatively simple task, though: In the `Registration` object for each client registration, the service would store the last used sequence number for that *particular* client—or, more accurately, that particular event type identifier, since full ordering imposes restrictions on sequence numbers relative to a particular type identifier.

Defining a Cookie Type

The class `HeartbeatCookie` defines the "cookie type" for the application's leases. You'll recall from Chapter 13 that the definition of a cookie type for a lease is dependent on the particular application that will grant the lease—cookies are meant to be used by the grantor of a lease to uniquely identify the leased resource and the holder of the lease. For this application, the cookie type is defined to hold an integer that represents the period—this is used to identify which registration list the lease is stored in—and the event type identifier that was returned to the client when it registered for events.

Given this cookie definition—period and event ID—the service can uniquely find each and every active registration. First, it can identify which `Registration` list to search and then, since each `Registration` is graced with a separate event ID, it can search for that ID in the list. Essentially, the event ID becomes a unique token for identifying client registrations.

Persistent Data

You'll remember from the last chapter that much of the work of being a `BasicUnicastService` has to do with dealing with persistent data—checkpointing data periodically, and recovering after a crash.

The service here has several key pieces of data that must be reliably saved and recovered. These data are grouped together by the `Registrations` class. Instances of this class maintain references to the four `ArrayLists` of client `Registration` objects, the last-used event type, and the last-used sequence number.

Whenever `checkpoint()` is called, this information is saved to disk, along with whatever other data was saved by the `BasicUnicastService` superclass (mainly data used by the `JoinManager`). And when the service is restored from persistent storage, an instance of `Registrations` is loaded off disk and used to reset the various registration lists and counters.

Registering for and Sending Events

The event-centric portions of this code have to do with how the service handles clients' requests for event registrations, and how events are sent to clients. Let's look at the registration process first.

The `HeartbeatGenerator` service exports a single method to allow clients to register to receive heartbeat events. Remember that Jini provides no "standard" interfaces for event generators—each generator can decide for itself how it will allow clients to solicit events. Here, the `register()` method takes the period that specifies how often the client wishes to receive events, a `MarshalledObject` containing arbitrary data to be returned to the client when the event occurs, a `RemoteEventListener` to send the events to, and a requested lease duration.

When a new request comes in, the service generates a new event type identifier to serve as the ID for events for this registration. This type identifier will also uniquely identify the registration and be used in cookie values. A new `HeartbeatCookie` is created based on the period and the type identifier; this cookie will be used in the leasing process as described in Chapter 13.

After this, a new `Registration` is created that holds the data specific to this particular client's registration—the cookie, the listener to send events to, the client-provided hand-back data, and the current expiration time. A new lease is created, the registration is added to the appropriate list of `Registration` objects, and a new `EventRegistration` is created and returned to the client.

If a client calls `register()` multiple times with the same parameters, the service will dutifully install multiple registrations for it. So the client will receive separate events for each period it has registered for, and each will have a different event type ID.

Note that `Registration` is the service-internal information needed to handle registrations; `EventRegistration` is the information returned to the client, which contains the event type identifier, the "source" of the events (in this case, the proxy object for the service), the lease, and the last-known sequence number for this event type. Here, the last-known sequence number for the client's event type is zero, since the service has never before sent any events to it.

After updating these state variables, the service is checkpointed to disk.

The actual delivery of events is handled by a separate thread. The service's `run()` method wakes up every minute to deliver any events that need to be sent. After each batch of events is delivered, `run()` figures in the time required to actually process all of the events, so that its timer doesn't "drift" off. (I want to ensure that the service sends events roughly every minute, rather than every minute plus whatever time is required to do the delivery. The code here subtracts out delivery time when deciding how long to sleep for the next interval.)

Whenever the thread wakes up, `sendHeartbeat()` is called to process the appropriate registration lists: Minute registrations are sent each time the thread wakes, hourly registrations are sent every 60th wake-up, and so on. The `sendHeartbeats()` method takes care of the actual delivery.

This method first scans the registration list, expiring any out-of-date event registrations. This "lazy" clean-up method—where registrations are only discarded just before the service tries to use them—keeps the code from having to have a separate lease expiration thread and simplifies the design.

After expiring any out-of-date registrations, the code processes all the remaining `Registration` objects in the list. For each, it generates a new `Heartbeat-Event` with a unique sequence number, and initializes it with the source for the event (the service's proxy object), the client's particular event type identifier, the `MarshalledObject` data the client has asked to be returned to it, and the period for which this event is being sent. Note that the proxy and event type are *exactly* what was returned to the client in the `EventRegistration` object—this is required so that clients can compare these values in events that they receive with the values originally returned to them in their `EventRegistrations`.

Once the actual event object has been constructed, it is delivered to the client by calling the `notify()` method on the `RemoteEventListener` provided by the client. This call uses RMI to transport the event to the client's VM, possibly on a different machine somewhere on the network.

There are two ways that `notify()` can fail. The first is with a `Remote-Exception`. This exception will be raised if the client crashes or is unreachable because of network problems. The service here complains when this happens—by printing a message—but otherwise takes no action. It will continue trying to resend events to the client in the future, until its registration expires. So if the client recovers or the network is repaired, the client will receive events normally.

The other way `notify()` can fail is with an `UnknownEventException`. Recall that this exception is raised by clients when they receive an event with an unexpected type or source. Most probably this is caused by either a bug in the service (it delivers an event with a type different than the one returned in the client's `EventRegistration`), or a bug in the client (the client has simply failed to track its event registrations reliably). In either case, when the client raises this exception, it is claiming that it no longer wishes to receive events of this type. So the `HeartbeatGenerator` service drops the client's registration. In this code, it does this by setting its expiration time to zero, so that it will be lazily cleaned up the next time events are delivered.

A Client to Test the HeartbeatGenerator

Now that you've seen how the `HeartbeatGenerator` service works, we can look at a simple client to exercise the service. This application, called `HeartbeatClient`, simply contacts all the Jini lookup services until it finds a `HeartbeatGenerator`. Once the service has been located, it solicits events for each of the four supported periods (minute, hour, day, and week), and renews its leases eternally.

Listing 16–4 provides the code for the client.

Listing 16–4 `HeartbeatClient.java`

```
// A simple client to test the HeartbeatGenerator
// service.

package corejini.chapter16;

import net.jini.discovery.DiscoveryListener;
import net.jini.discovery.DiscoveryEvent;
import net.jini.discovery.DiscoveryGroupManagement;
import net.jini.discovery.LookupDiscoveryManager;
import net.jini.core.lookup.ServiceRegistrar;
import net.jini.core.lookup.ServiceEvent;
import net.jini.core.lookup.ServiceTemplate;
import net.jini.core.event.RemoteEvent;
import net.jini.core.event.EventRegistration;
import net.jini.core.event.RemoteEventListener;
import net.jini.lease.LeaseRenewalManager;
import net.jini.lease.LeaseRenewalEvent;
import net.jini.lease.LeaseListener;
import net.jini.core.lease.Lease;
import java.io.IOException;
import java.rmi.RemoteException;
import java.rmi.RMISecurityManager;
import java.rmi.server.UnicastRemoteObject;
```

Listing 16–4 `HeartbeatClient.java` (continued)

```
public class HeartbeatClient implements Runnable {
    ServiceTemplate template;
    HeartbeatGenerator.HeartbeatRequest
        gen = null;
    LeaseRenewalManager leaseManager =
        new LeaseRenewalManager();
    EvtListener listener;

    // An inner class for discovery listening
    public class DiscListener
            implements DiscoveryListener {
        public void discovered(DiscoveryEvent ev) {
            ServiceRegistrar[] regs = ev.getRegistrars();
            for (int i=0 ; i<regs.length ; i++) {
                doit(regs[i]);
            }
        }

        public void discarded(DiscoveryEvent ev) {
        }
    }


    // An inner class for event listening
    class EvtListener extends UnicastRemoteObject
        implements RemoteEventListener {
        EvtListener() throws RemoteException {
        }
```

Listing 16–4 `HeartbeatClient.java` (continued)

```java
public void notify(RemoteEvent e) {
    if (!(e instanceof
        HeartbeatGenerator.HeartbeatEvent)) {
        return;
    }

    HeartbeatGenerator.HeartbeatEvent ev =
        (HeartbeatGenerator.HeartbeatEvent) e;

    switch (ev.getPeriod()) {
    case HeartbeatGenerator.MINUTE:
        System.out.println("Came from MINUTE");
        break;
    case HeartbeatGenerator.HOUR:
        System.out.println("Came from HOUR");
        break;
    case HeartbeatGenerator.DAY:
        System.out.println("Came from DAY");
        break;
    case HeartbeatGenerator.WEEK:
        System.out.println("Came from WEEK");
        break;
    default:
        System.out.println("Unknown!");
        break;
    }
}

public HeartbeatClient() throws IOException,
        RemoteException {
    Class[] types =
        { HeartbeatGenerator.HeartbeatRequest.class };

    template = new ServiceTemplate(null, types, null);
    listener = new EvtListener();

    LookupDiscoveryManager luMgr =
        new LookupDiscoveryManager(
                DiscoveryGroupManagement.ALL_GROUPS,
                null, null);
    luMgr.addDiscoveryListener(new DiscListener());
}
```

Listing 16–4 `HeartbeatClient.java` (continued)

```java
void doit(ServiceRegistrar reg) {
    if (gen != null)  // bail once we've found it.
        return;

    try {
        gen = (HeartbeatGenerator.HeartbeatRequest)
            reg.lookup(template);
    } catch (Exception ex) {
        System.err.println("Doing lookup: " +
            ex.getMessage());
    }

    if (gen == null)
        return;

    // Sign us up for events!
    EventRegistration evt;
    try {
        evt = gen.register(HeartbeatGenerator.MINUTE,
                null, listener, Lease.ANY);
        leaseManager.renewUntil(evt.getLease(),
                Lease.ANY, null);

        evt = gen.register(HeartbeatGenerator.HOUR,
                null, listener, Lease.ANY);
        leaseManager.renewUntil(evt.getLease(),
                Lease.ANY, null);

        evt = gen.register(HeartbeatGenerator.DAY,
                null, listener, Lease.ANY);
        leaseManager.renewUntil(evt.getLease(),
                Lease.ANY, null);

        evt = gen.register(HeartbeatGenerator.WEEK,
                null, listener, Lease.ANY);
        leaseManager.renewUntil(evt.getLease(),
                Lease.ANY, null);

    } catch (RemoteException ex) {
        System.err.println("Bogus: " + ex.getMessage());
    }
}
```

```java
    public void run() {
        while (true) {
            try {
                Thread.sleep(Integer.MAX_VALUE);
            } catch (InterruptedException ex) {
            }
        }
    }

    public static void main(String[] args) {
        if (System.getSecurityManager() == null) {
            System.setSecurityManager(
                new RMISecurityManager());
        }

        try {
            HeartbeatClient client = new HeartbeatClient();
            new Thread(client).start();
        } catch (Exception ex) {
            System.err.println("Bogus: " + ex.getMessage());
            System.exit(1);
        }
    }
}
```

This is an extremely simple client to exercise the `HeartbeatGenerator` service. The client defines a separate inner class to participate in the Jini discovery process. The client only continues searching until it has found a single `HeartbeatGenerator`. At that point, it registers for events to be delivered every minute, hour, day, and week. The leases for these event registrations are handed off to a `LeaseRenewalManager` so that they will be renewed indefinitely.

The client also defines a separate inner class to receive events. When heartbeat events are delivered, they come through this class's `notify()` method. The client simply ensures that they are indeed `HeartbeatEvents`, and then displays whether the event was sent because of the minute timer, the hour timer, and so on.

Compiling and Running the Heartbeat Examples

To test them out, build and run the HeartbeatGenerator and HeartbeatClient programs. First, compile the code needed for the service, and then build the necessary RMI stubs. Both BasicRegistrationLandlord and HeartbeatGenerator extend java.rmi.server.UnicastRemoteObject, so you have to build stubs for them.

On Windows:

```
javac -classpath C:\files;
                  C:\jini1_1\lib\jini-core.jar;
                  C:\jini1_1\lib\jini-ext.jar;
                  C:\jini1_1\lib\sun-util.jar;
                  C:\service
      -d C:\service
      C:\files\corejini\chapter16\HeartbeatGenerator.java

rmic -classpath C:\jini1_1\lib\jini-core.jar;
                 C:\jini1_1\lib\jini-ext.jar;
                 C:\jini1_1\lib\sun-util.jar;
                 C:\service
      -d C:\service
          corejini.chapter16.BasicRegistrationLandlord
corejini.chapter16.HeartbeatGenerator

mkdir C:\service-dl\corejini\chapter16

cd C:\service\corejini\chapter16
copy BasicRegistrationLandlord_Stub.class
     C:\service-dl\corejini\chapter16
copy HeartbeatGenerator_Stub.class
     C:\service-dl\corejini\chapter16
```

On UNIX:

```
javac -classpath /files:
                  /files/jini1_1/lib/jini-core.jar:
                  /files/jini1_1/lib/jini-ext.jar:
                  /files/jini1_1/lib/sun-util.jar:
                  /files/service
       -d /files/service
          /files/corejini/chapter16/HeartbeatGenerator.java

rmic -classpath /files/jini1_1/lib/jini-core.jar:
                 /files/jini1_1/lib/jini-ext.jar:
                 /files/jini1_1/lib/sun-util.jar:
```

```
            /files/service
      -d /files/service
            corejini.chapter16.BasicRegistrationLandlord
corejini.chapter16.HeartbeatGenerator

mkdir /files/service-dl/corejini/chapter16
cd /files/service/corejini/chapter16
cp BasicRegistrationLandlord_Stub.class
      /files/service-dl/corejini/chapter16
cp HeartbeatGenerator_Stub.class
      /files/service-dl/corejini/chapter16
```

After this, you need to build the files necessary for the client program. Note that the client also needs the `HeartbeatRequest` interface, which is the interface that the service's proxy implements. This interface is contained within the service's code, but is actually used by both the service and the client. So you'll have to copy it out to the client's directory. Since `HeartbeatClient`'s `EvtListener` class extends `UnicastRemoteObject`, you'll have to run `rmic` to generate its stubs.

On Windows:

```
javac -classpath C:\files;
                  C:\jini1_1\lib\jini-core.jar;
                  C:\jini1_1\lib\jini-ext.jar;
                  C:\jini1_1\lib\sun-util.jar;
                  C:\client
      -d C:\client
            C:\files\corejini\chapter16\HeartbeatClient.java

rmic -classpath C:\jini1_1\lib\jini-core.jar;
                  C:\jini1_1\lib\jini-ext.jar;
                  C:\jini1_1\lib\sun-util.jar;
                  C:\client
      -d C:\client
            corejini.chapter16.HeartbeatClient.EvtListener

mkdir C:\client-dl\corejini\chapter16
cd C:\client\corejini\chapter16
copy HeartbeatClient$EvtListener_Stub.class
      C:\client-dl\corejini\chapter16

cd C:\service\corejini\chapter16
copy HeartbeatGenerator$HeartbeatRequest.class
      C:\client\corejini\chapter16
```

On UNIX:

```
javac -classpath /files:
                 /files/jini1_1/lib/jini-core.jar:
                 /files/jini1_1/lib/jini-ext.jar:
                 /files/jini1_1/lib/sun-util.jar:
                 /files/client
      -d /files/client
         /files/corejini/chapter16/HeartbeatClient.java

rmic -classpath /files/jini1_1/lib/jini-core.jar:
                /files/jini1_1/lib/jini-ext.jar:
                /files/jini1_1/lib/sun-util.jar:
                /files/client
     -d /files/client
        corejini.chapter16.HeartbeatClient.EvtListener

mkdir /files/client-dl/corejini/chapter16
cd /files/client/corejini/chapter16
cp HeartbeatClient\$EvtListener_Stub.class
     /files/client-dl/corejini/chapter16

cd /files/service/corejini/chapter16
cp HeartbeatGenerator\$HeartbeatRequest.class
     /files/client/corejini/chapter16
```

Finally, you're set to run the applications! Start the service first, then the client. Be sure to give the service a pathname to use for its stable storage. As usual, replace "myhost" with the hostname on which the client's and the service's HTTP servers are running, and set the appropriate port number.

On Windows:

```
java -cp C:\files\jini1_1\lib\jini-core.jar;
         C:\files\jini1_1\lib\jini-ext.jar;
         C:\files\jini1_1\lib\sun-util.jar;
         C:\service
     -Djava.rmi.server.codebase=http://myhost:8085/
     -Djava.security.policy=C:\policy
         corejini.chapter16.HeartbeatGenerator C:\tmp\hb

java -cp C:\files\jini1_1\lib\jini-core.jar;
         C:\files\jini1_1\lib\jini-ext.jar;
         C:\files\jini1_1\lib\sun-util.jar;
         C:\client
     -Djava.rmi.server.codebase=http://myhost:8086/
     -Djava.security.policy=C:\policy
```

```
corejini.chapter16.HeartbeatClient
```

On UNIX:

```
java -cp /files/jini1_1/lib/jini-core.jar:
        /files/jini1_1/lib/jini-ext.jar:
        /files/jini1_1/lib/sun-util.jar:
        /files/service
    -Djava.rmi.server.codebase=http://myhost:8085/
    -Djava.security.policy=/files/policy
        corejini.chapter16.HeartbeatGenerator /tmp/hb


java -cp /files/jini1_1/lib/jini-core.jar:
        /files/jini1_1/lib/jini-ext.jar:
        /files/jini1_1/lib/sun-util.jar:
        /files/client
    -Djava.rmi.server.codebase=http://myhost:8086/
    -Djava.security.policy=/files/policy
        corejini.chapter16.HeartbeatClient
```

As the service starts up, you should see it report:

Heartbeat generator started.

And then—for as long as you leave the client and the server running—you should see the client output messages to the effect of:

Came from MINUTE

Came from MINUTE

Came from MINUTE

If either you're very bored or very tenacious, you can leave this up long enough to get the hourly, daily, and weekly messages.

This example has shown how to create a simple event client—much like you've seen before—and also a rather robust event generator. This generator takes care of event registration leases, manages sequence numbers correctly, and assigns event type identifiers to allow client registrations to be clearly distinguished from one another.

In the remainder of this chapter, I'll show how to build an event handling delegate service, and use this service "in between" the HeartbeatGenerator and a client.

Third-Party Event Delegates

This chapter has already talked a lot about how Jini was designed to support "third-party" event delegates—these are chunks of code that can add new application-provided functionality to an event system. Further, these delegates are "generic" in the sense that they can operate on any type of event, from any source.

In Jini, these delegates are typically implemented as Jini services that run in separate VMs from the original "upstream" generator, or the final "downstream" receiver. Delegates can be added by either the receiving client or by the sending service, and multiple delegates can be composed together.

I'll briefly review why event delegates are important, and how event delegates can be used in a Jini community. As you've seen in this chapter, the Jini event programming model says nothing about quality of service guarantees, such as what policies a service should follow when an event cannot be delivered to a client, what ordering should be imposed on events, and so forth. These sorts of policies don't just affect performance, they can also drive the entire architecture of a client application.

For example, imagine a client application that is inactive for large periods of time. If this client needed to receive events, then each delivery would cause the client to be reactivated. If the frequency of events is high, then the client may spend nearly all of its time simply reactivating itself so that it can receive an event!

This is a very real example of how the standard event delivery mechanisms in Jini may need to be augmented by applications to support their particular semantics and constraints. In the case of the activatable client, you'd like to have a way for events to be queued up and retrieved periodically. Essentially what you would need is a "mailbox" for events for one that receives events until the client goes to "pick up its mail." Such an event mailbox service could be used not only by Jini clients, but by other services as well.

In the last example of this chapter, you'll learn about building just such an event mailbox service.

Core Note: The "mercury" event mailbox service

When I wrote the first edition of Core Jini, there was no standard event mailbox available anywhere. Since this service seemed like a useful tool—as well as a good way to explain how to build event delegates—I decided to create one as an example for the book.

*With the release of Jini 1.1, however, Sun has provided its own event mailbox service, called "*mercury,*" which I talk about in Chapter 19.* Mercury *provides a somewhat different look-and-feel from the event mailbox I present here. Since it's a more "industrial-strength" service, and since it implements what should become a common API in Jini communities, I encourage you to use that service if you have need of an event mailbox.*

Still, the value of walking through the code for an event delegate holds, however, and so I've decided to leave this example intact for the second edition of Core Jini. If you understand this code, you'll have a better sense for how you can implement your own event delegate services, and what the mercury service is doing "under the hood."

Designing for Composition

Jini supports composable event delegates by relying on a very *standard* and very *narrow* set of APIs for event delivery. By *standard* I mean that every single remote event, no matter what its type, is delivered to a Remote-EventListener. Because there is no other way for Jini remote events to be delivered, you know that if you are a RemoteEventListener you can receive any type of event.

This situation is in stark contrast to, say, AWT's event model. In AWT, there are maybe a dozen separate types of events, each with its own listener classes. Because of the many ways to receive events, it's very difficult to create a "generic" listener—you'd have to implement all dozen or so listener interfaces with all their methods. And if a new event type showed up in the future, you'd be out of luck since you can only implement the event listener interfaces that you know about at compile time.

By relying on only one listener interface, Jini allows your code to listen for any type of remote event, including remote events that may not even be defined at the time your code is written.

The *narrowness* of the Jini APIs means simply that there are very few methods you need to worry about to receive events. In fact, there's only *one*—the `notify()` method. This makes the job of writing a new event listener almost trivial; there are no exotic or rarely used methods that you have to understand in order to "plug in" to the Jini event system.

These properties are present in Jini by design, not by accident. And they mean that any entity, whether it's an event generator or an event receiver, can add event delegates to the delivery path between the two. Multiple delegates can even be composed together on the delivery path—sometimes called the *event pipeline*—to enable rich, new behaviors.

Composition in Practice

Let's move away from the abstract and talk about what composable event delegates mean in practice. I've said that both generators and receivers can add delegates to the event pipeline.

Services that need to enforce some particular event delivery behaviors may choose to provide these behaviors through delegation for reasons of *modularity* and *reuse*. On the modularity front, a service writer may find that separating out a chunk of event processing behavior into a separate service makes sense from a design perspective. And of course, once separated into a separate service, such behavior becomes available for others to reuse—if a set of useful delegates are available to you, why not take advantage of them rather than reinventing the wheel?

Delegates can potentially add all sorts of interesting functionality to the Jini event mechanisms. For example, a service that is rarely active may not wish to be awakened every time an event is delivered. Such a service could use an event mailbox as described earlier. Some clients may find that an event generator does not provide fine-grained facilities for describing the events to be sent. For example, some clients may find the search facilities provided through `ServiceTemplates` and the Jini lookup service to be too limiting, and may use an "event filtering service" to further restrict the set of events they will receive. This delegate would receive all events specified by the initial `ServiceTemplate` parameter, but would only forward those that match some further query specifier.

How Events Are Delivered through the Pipeline

Let's ignore, for the moment, the process of setting up a series of delegates, and focus on what happens when an event is actually delivered from an original generator, through a series of delegates, and down to the intended receiver.

Every delegate, as well as the final receiver, implements the `Remote-EventListener` interface, so `RemoteEvents` can be delivered through the `notify()` method on each of these entities. In most cases, each delegate will be implemented as a service that may be used by any number of clients. So this raises a question: If a delegate is processing and forwarding events from several upstream generators, and these are possibly intended for several downstream receivers, how does the generator know how to route the events?

The answer is that each downstream entity must tell the delegate "before" it in the pipeline that the downstream entity should receive all events from a certain source and with a certain event type that are delivered to the delegate. The delegate must maintain some way to map which events go to which downstream receiver. This information could take the form of a mapping table that specifies, for any given event source and type, which downstream listener to forward them to. Or, as in the case of Sun's "`mercury`" event mailbox service, the mapping may be implicit. `Mercury` will produce a new listener each time a client asks it for a mailbox registration; any events received at that listener will be held until the receiver at the final destination provides the ultimate listener to which the events should be sent.

Figure 16–1 shows an example of a delegate processing events to and from a number of entities. Here you see three event generators sending events to a single delegate. The delegate shown here keeps a mapping table internally so that it can remember how to route events from each of these generators on to the down-stream receivers.

This mapping is established through a registration process that is analogous to the process when an event listener asks a generator to send it events; in fact, you could say that this *is* exactly the same process, since delegates are not only listeners, but generators as well!

Setting up the Pipeline

Each type of delegate will define its own interfaces for allowing it to be hooked into a pipeline. The situation here is the same as for all other event genera-tors—there are no "standard" interfaces for generators (or delegates), because each entity that generates events supports its own way to ask for events that make sense for its particular application domain. You ask lookup services for

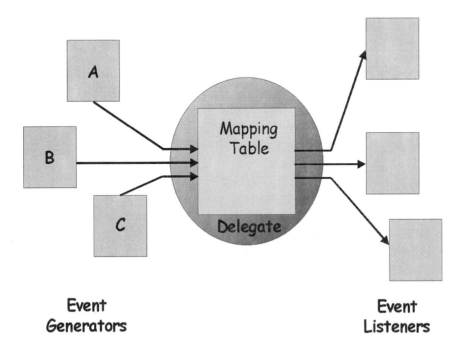

**Event
Generators**

**Event
Listeners**

Figure 16–1   *An event delegate routes events from multiple generators.*

events by invoking the `notify()` method and passing in a `ServiceTemplate`; when registering with the event mechanism of the `HeartbeatGeneratorSer-vice`, you invoke `register()` and pass in the period at which you wish to receive events. Other services may have completely different notions of when events should be sent, and therefore support completely different mechanisms for asking that events be sent.

In general, either the original generator or the original listener will set up the event pipeline; the code idioms they follow are quite different, however. Let's look at each.

Pipelines from the Generator Perspective

Event generators have a somewhat easier task than listeners when they create an event pipeline. Typically, an event generator that wishes to use a delegate to enhance its event processing will obtain a reference to the delegate before it allows clients to solicit events from it. The service will typically register the delegate as its *only* event listener—so all events sent by the service will go straight to the delegate.

When a client contacts the service to receive events, the client passes in a listener to which events should be sent. The service then registers with the delegate—using whatever delegate-specific registration interfaces it supports—and tells the delegate to route events from the service, and of a certain type known to the service, to the `RemoteEventListener` supplied by the client.

In this case, the service already knows everything it needs to construct the pipeline. The service can assign every client registration a unique event identifier, and make sure it never sends any events with that identifier until the registration process is complete, and the client-supplied listener has been registered with the delegate.

Let's talk through an example. Suppose you want to create a reimplementation of the Jini lookup service that routes all its outgoing events through a delegate. The first thing you would do is acquire a reference to the delegate service you intend to use. This delegate would implement `RemoteEventListener` (since it needs to receive your outgoing events), and would presumably have some registration method that would take as parameters an event source, an event type, and a `RemoteEventListener`. Any events received by the delegate that had the specified source and type would be forwarded on to that listener. The reimplemented lookup service would send *all* its events to the delegate, regardless of final source.

The only other significant change would come in the `notify()` method on the service which, you will remember, is how clients ask to receive events from lookup services (the method name `notify()` is unfortunately overloaded in Java and Jini). When the service processes the client's request for registration, it generates a unique event ID for the client and tells the delegate to route events of that type that it receives to the client-supplied listener.

From this point, whenever the service generates any events, they will go directly to the delegate, which will then route them to the client-supplied listener based on the source and type information in the event.

Pipelines from the Listener Perspective

The steps that an event consumer will take to create an event pipeline vary in the specifics because each delegate has its own interfaces for registration. But in general, there are a number of steps that will be largely common, no matter what the particulars of the delegates or other generators.

Most event delegates will use an approach like the Sun event mailbox, in which routes between generators and receivers would be "implicitly" set up by having the client request a *separate* listener from each delegate *before* connecting the pieces together into a pipeline. If a delegate is capable of providing multiple listeners each time a client asks it for service, it can know that *any* events received by that listener are destined for the downstream client. This makes the job of routing events easier, and does away with the race conditions of the previous strategy. This is exactly the approach taken by Sun's `mercury` event mailbox. Chapter 18 goes into more detail on how this works.

Leasing across Delegates

One other important question that must be addressed in chaining delegates is: How does leasing work? Presumably, a delegate won't continue to forward and process events in perpetuity just because you ask it to. This is definitely un-Jini-like! Clearly the answer is to lease event registrations with delegates, just as "normal" event registrations are leased from event generators.

There are a couple of approaches that one could follow here. One strategy would be to have the entity that creates the pipeline do the leasing for *all* the delegates. In such a situation, the client that is consuming the events would get leases back from its registrations with each stage in the pipeline, and renew them using a `LeaseRenewalManager` or some other strategy. If the client crashes, the delegates gradually expire the leased registrations and the pipeline dissolves.

Another approach would be to have each entity in the pipeline handle the lease for the registration for the next upstream member of the pipe that it receives events from. Using this strategy, each delegate might manage the lease for the event registration with the generator that supplies events to it. The client—the actual final consumer of the events—would only manually handle the final event registration lease from its direct generator. Such an arrangement would require each stage in the pipeline to provide a way to pass it a lease to be managed.

This approach may be marginally less work for the client, and has a certain elegance to it—much like in the single-generator, single-listener model, the listener is responsible for telling the generator to continue sending it events. This approach also works well if the eventual recipient will not be active often enough to perform leasing. Presumably the event processing delegates will be implemented as long-lived services, so handing off lease management to them would allow the ultimate recipient to become inactive as needed.

One downside of this approach is that when a problem occurs, leases expire serially, rather than in parallel, as would happen in the first approach. So the total time required for the pipeline to dissolve would be longer.

In the example in this chapter, I'll use the first approach—the client, which is the final receiver of events, handles all the leases for all the delegates.

An Example: An Event Mailbox

Let's move on to the final example of this chapter—an event mailbox service that can store events until they are requested by their final recipient. Receivers can use this mailbox much as just described—they simply interpose it between the original generator of events and themselves. They must "reserve space" in the mailbox service by telling it about the events they expect to receive. Then, once the mailbox has accumulated events for them, they can fetch these events as a "batch" (causing all stored events to be returned in a list), or they can ask that the mailbox deliver them individually using the recipient's normal `notify()` method. This allows the "normal" event processing code to be reused for receiving stored events.

This code builds on the `BasicRegistrationLandlord` code shown earlier in this chapter for managing event registration leases. The mailbox service defines its own particular subclass of `Registration`. Recall that this is the class that stores the service-internal information needed to process event registrations. This subclass (Listing 16–5) is called `EventMailboxRegistration`.

Listing 16–5 `EventMailboxRegistration.java`

```java
// A subclass of registration that holds a
// list of to-be-delivered events.

package corejini.chapter16;

import net.jini.core.event.RemoteEvent;
import net.jini.core.event.RemoteEventListener;
import java.io.Serializable;
import java.rmi.MarshalledObject;
import java.util.List;
import java.util.ArrayList;

class EventMailboxRegistration
    extends Registration implements Serializable {
    protected List mailbox = new ArrayList();

    EventMailboxRegistration(Object cookie,
                            RemoteEventListener listener,
                            MarshalledObject data,
                            long expiration) {
        super(cookie, listener, data, expiration);
    }
```

Listing 16–5 `EventMailboxRegistration.java` (continued)

```
    // Override cancelled to null the mailbox
    protected void cancelled() {
        mailbox = null;
    }

    List getMailbox() {
        return mailbox;
    }

    void appendEvent(RemoteEvent ev) {
        mailbox.add(ev);
    }

    List getAndFlushMailbox() {
        List rv = getMailbox();
        mailbox = new ArrayList();
        return rv;
    }
}
```

The `Registration` superclass holds the lease cookie, the `Remote-EventListener` specified by the client, the `MarshalledObject` that should be returned to the client, and the current expiration time for the registration. The `EventMailboxRegistration` subclass adds only storage for the set of events that are being kept for the client. This class will be used internally by `Event-Mailbox` to store client-by-client information to process events.

The EventMailbox Service

Let's look now at the EventMailbox class (Listing 16–6), which implements the store-and-forward event delegate service.

Listing 16–6 EventMailbox.java

```java
// A "mailbox" for events--a service that stores
// events until asked.

package corejini.chapter16;

import corejini.chapter15.BasicUnicastService;
import corejini.chapter15.BasicUnicastAdmin;
import net.jini.core.lease.Lease;
import net.jini.core.lease.UnknownLeaseException;
import net.jini.core.event.RemoteEvent;
import net.jini.core.event.RemoteEventListener;
import net.jini.core.event.EventRegistration;
import net.jini.core.event.UnknownEventException;
import com.sun.jini.lease.landlord.Landlord;
import com.sun.jini.lease.landlord.LandlordLease;
import java.rmi.Remote;
import java.rmi.RemoteException;
import java.rmi.RMISecurityManager;
import java.rmi.server.UnicastRemoteObject;
import java.io.IOException;
import java.io.Serializable;
import java.util.List;
import java.util.ArrayList;
import java.util.HashMap;
```

Listing 16–6 `EventMailbox.java` (continued)

```java
// Define a new type of cookie to use for our
// leases.
class MailboxCookie implements Serializable {
    protected Object source;
    protected long eventType;

    MailboxCookie(Object source, long eventType) {
        this.source = source;
        this.eventType = eventType;
    }

    public boolean equals(Object o) {
        if (!(o instanceof MailboxCookie))
            return false;

        MailboxCookie cookie = (MailboxCookie) o;

        return cookie.eventType == eventType &&
            cookie.source.equals(source);
    }
}
```

Listing 16–6 `EventMailbox.java` (continued)

```java
// EventMailbox is a BasicUnicastService (see Ch. 13)
public class EventMailbox extends BasicUnicastService
    implements Runnable, EventMailbox.EventMailboxRequest {
    protected LandlordLease.Factory factory =
        new LandlordLease.Factory();

    // This is a hash map keyed by 'source'.  Each
    // value is a list of Registrations.
    protected HashMap mailboxes = new HashMap();

    // This is a hash map of all of the Landlords
    // for the individual registration lists; it
    // is keyed by 'source'.
    protected HashMap landlords = new HashMap();

    // Defines the remote interface that clients will
    // use to communicate with the service.
    public interface EventMailboxRequest
        extends RemoteEventListener, Remote {
        // Get a mailbox.
        public EventRegistration acquireMailbox(
                                        Object source,
                                        long eventType,
                                        long duration)
            throws RemoteException;
        // Get events in a batch.
        public List getEvents(Object source,
                            long eventType)
            throws RemoteException,
                    UnknownLeaseException;
        // Have events re-delivered to the original
        // listener.
        public void deliverEvents(Object source,
                                long eventType,
                                RemoteEventListener listener)
            throws RemoteException, UnknownLeaseException;
    }
```

Listing 16–6 `EventMailbox.java` (continued)

```java
// Serialized data object
static class MailboxData implements Serializable {
    HashMap mailboxes;

    MailboxData(HashMap mailboxes) {
        this.mailboxes = mailboxes;
    }
}

protected EventMailbox(String storageLoc)
        throws RemoteException {
    super(storageLoc);
}

public void initialize()
        throws IOException, ClassNotFoundException {
    super.initialize();
    new Thread(this).start();
}

protected void checkpoint() throws IOException {
    super.checkpoint(new MailboxData(mailboxes));
}

protected Object getProxy() {
    return this;
}

public void restored(Object subclassData) {
    MailboxData data = (MailboxData) subclassData;
    mailboxes = data.mailboxes;
}
```

Listing 16–6 `EventMailbox.java` (continued)

```java
// Clients, when they come in, must have the correct
// key token in their cookies, or we assume that
// they're holding on to an expired cookie.  The
// mailboxcookie.equals() method checks for token
// equality,  but when events come in from generators,
// we still have to find where to stash them--which
// mailbox--but we don't have a token.  So we
// "manually" scan the list looking for any
// registration with matching source and type, but
// ignoring the key.

// Events from generators come in through this method.
public synchronized void notify(RemoteEvent ev) {
    Object source = ev.getSource();
    List regs = (List) mailboxes.get(source);

    // If we don't have an entry for this source, we
    // don't complain with an UnknownEventException--
    // that would prevent us from getting any future
    // events from that source.  Instead we just
    // silently ignore it.
    if (regs == null) {
        System.err.println("Unknown source.");
        return;
    }

    // Iterate through the list looking for the
    // matching cookie.
    for (int i=0, size=regs.size() ; i<size ; i++) {
        EventMailboxRegistration reg =
            (EventMailboxRegistration) regs.get(i);

        MailboxCookie cookie = (MailboxCookie)
                                reg.getCookie();
```

Listing 16–6 `EventMailbox.java` (continued)

```
                    // File the event into the matching mailbox.
                    if (cookie.source.equals(source)) {
                        System.out.println(
                            "Saved event in mailbox");
                        reg.appendEvent(ev);
                        return;
                    }
                }

                // If we don't find a matching mailbox, just
                // ignore it.
                System.out.println("No registration.");
        }

        // Consumers or generators can install a request for
        // mailboxing through this call.
        public EventRegistration acquireMailbox(Object source,
                                           long eventType,
                                           long duration)
            throws RemoteException {
            // Create a cookie for the mailbox and its lease.
            MailboxCookie cookie =
                new MailboxCookie(source, eventType);

            // Create a new list for this source, if we
            // need to.  Also get the Landlord for this
            // source.
            List regs;
            BasicRegistrationLandlord landlord;
            if ((regs = (List) mailboxes.get(source)) == null)
{
                regs = new ArrayList();
                landlord = new BasicRegistrationLandlord(regs,
                                                factory);
                mailboxes.put(source, regs);
                landlords.put(source, landlord);
            } else {
                landlord = (BasicRegistrationLandlord)
                    landlords.get(source);
            }
```

Listing 16–6 `EventMailbox.java` (continued)

```java
    // Compute the expiration time.
    long expiration = landlord.getExpiration(duration);
    EventMailboxRegistration emr = new
        EventMailboxRegistration(cookie, null, null,
                                 expiration);
    Lease lease = factory.newLease(cookie, landlord,
                                   expiration);

    // Add the registration to the list of mailboxes.
    regs.add(emr);

    // Return an event registration to the client.
    EventRegistration mbr =
        new EventRegistration(eventType, source,
                              lease, 0);

    try {
        checkpoint();
    } catch (IOException ex) {
        System.err.println("Error checkpoint: " +
                           ex.getMessage());
    }

    System.out.println("Acquired new mailbox for " +
                       source + ", " + eventType);

    return mbr;
}
```

Listing 16–6 `EventMailbox.java` (continued)

```java
public synchronized List getEvents(Object source,
                                   long eventType)
        throws UnknownLeaseException {
    System.out.println("Getting events.");
    List regs = (List) mailboxes.get(source);

    if (regs == null) {
        throw new UnknownLeaseException();
    }

    MailboxCookie cookie = new MailboxCookie(source,
                                             eventType);

    for (int i=0, size=regs.size() ; i<size ; i++) {
        EventMailboxRegistration reg =
            (EventMailboxRegistration) regs.get(i);
        if (reg.getCookie().equals(cookie))
            return reg.getAndFlushMailbox();
    }

    throw new UnknownLeaseException();
}
```

Listing 16–6 `EventMailbox.java` (continued)

```java
public synchronized void deliverEvents(Object source,
                              long eventType,
                   RemoteEventListener listener)
     throws UnknownLeaseException, RemoteException {
    System.out.println("Redelivering events.");
    List regs = (List) mailboxes.get(source);

    if (regs == null) {
        throw new UnknownLeaseException();
    }

    MailboxCookie cookie = new MailboxCookie(source,
                                        eventType);

    for (int i=0, size=regs.size() ; i<size ; i++) {
        EventMailboxRegistration reg =
            (EventMailboxRegistration) regs.get(i);

        if (reg.getCookie().equals(cookie)) {
            List events = reg.getMailbox();
            // Try to send them.  If we get any
            // exceptions, don't flush the mailbox.
            boolean succeeded = true;
            for (int j=0, evsize=events.size();
                                j<evsize; j++) {
                try {
                    listener.notify((RemoteEvent)
                                events.get(j));
                } catch (RemoteException ex) {
                    System.err.println(
                        "Error sending: " +
                        ex.getMessage());
                    succeeded = false;
                } catch (UnknownEventException ex) {
                    System.err.println(
                      "Client claims they don't want " +
                       "this event type...");
```

Listing 16–6 `EventMailbox.java` (continued)

```
                        Landlord ll = (Landlord)
                            landlords.get(source);

                        if (ll != null) {
                            ll.cancel(reg.getCookie());
                        }

                        return;
                    }
                }

                if (succeeded) {
                    reg.getAndFlushMailbox();
                }

                return;
            }
        }

        throw new UnknownLeaseException();
    }

    public void run() {
        while (true) {
            try {
                Thread.sleep(Integer.MAX_VALUE);
            } catch (InterruptedException ex) {
            }
        }
    }
}
```

Listing 16–6 `EventMailbox.java` (continued)

```java
public static void main(String[] args) {
    if (System.getSecurityManager() == null) {
        System.setSecurityManager(
            new RMISecurityManager());
    }

    if (args.length != 1) {
        System.err.println(
            "Usage: EventMailbox <storage>");
        System.exit(1);
    }

    try {
        EventMailbox mailbox =
            new EventMailbox(args[0]);
        mailbox.initialize();
        System.out.println("running!");
    } catch (Exception ex) {
        System.err.println(
            "Error starting event mailbox: " +
            ex.getMessage());
        System.exit(1);
    }
}
}
```

The `EventMailbox` service extends the `BasicUnicastService` from Chapter 15, and uses many of the conventions of that class. It first defines a new cookie type for maintaining the associations between leases held by clients and internally leased resources. The `MailboxCookie` class maintains the source and event type of an object registration; these will uniquely identify an event registration.

The `EventMailbox` class itself maintains its internal data in the form of two hash maps. The first maintains all the `EventMailboxRegistrations` in effect. It is organized as a `HashMap` of `ArrayLists` keyed by event source. Each `ArrayList` contains the `EventMailboxRegistrations` for that source. Whenever an event arrives, the service can quickly find the particular set of registrations for that source, and then scan the registrations looking for the one that matches the event type at hand.

The second hash map keeps a mapping from event sources to `Basic-RegistrationLandlords`. Recall that the `BasicRegistrationLandlord` class understands how to manage a single `ArrayList` of `Registration` objects. Since the service here stores registrations in a hash map that contains `ArrayLists` as values, there is a separate `Landlord` for each source. This hash map maintains this association.

The remote interface `EventMailboxRequest` defines the protocol that clients will use to communicate with the service. The service's proxy is actually just the automatically generated stub for the `EventMailbox` service. There are three methods defined by this interface. The first, `acquireMailbox()`, is used by clients to reserve a mailbox for events of a particular type from a particular source. "Reserving a mailbox" means that the service will begin storing events that it sees that match the parameters, and not simply dispose of them. This method also takes a requested lease duration.

The second method, `getEvents()`, returns a "batch" of all the events received since the client last checked in. The events are returned as a `List`, and the client's mailbox is cleared.

Note that the `notify()`, `getEvents()`, and `deliverEvents()` methods are synchronized. So `getEvents()` and `deliverEvents()` will have sole access to the mailbox when they run—new events cannot be stored in the mailbox while they are in the process of delivering or returning events.

The final method, `deliverEvents()`, causes any stored events to be sent one at a time to the specified `RemoteEventListener`. After the events have been delivered, the client's mailbox is cleared.

The `EventMailbox` service follows the usual conventions for storing persistent data. The class `MailboxData` contains the hash map of registrations, and is saved to disk every time `checkpoint()` is called; this same information is restored whenever the service is restarted.

The bulk of the work in this service is in its implementation of `notify()` and the three methods defined by the `EventMailboxRequest` remote interface. Let's look at these in detail.

The `notify()` method is called whenever an upstream event generator needs to deliver an event to the mailbox delegate. When an event arrives, its source is looked up in the hash map of registrations to see if any client has registered interest in the source. If there is no `ArrayList` of `EventMailboxRegistrations` for the source, then the service has received a spurious event or—more likely—a client has added it as a listener for an upstream generator, but has not had a chance to acquire a mailbox. Remember that the information needed to acquire a mailbox (the event's source and type) is typically only available from generators (including the Jini lookup service) once the delegate has already been installed as a listener for the generator.

The policy taken by the mailbox service is that it simply drops all events from unknown sources or of unknown types until clients have established a valid mailbox for them.

If there is an `ArrayList` containing registrations from the event's source, then the registrations are scanned in turn to try to find the particular `EventMailbox-Registration` for the event's source and type. If it is found, then the event is appended to the client's mailbox for later retrieval. Otherwise, it is simply dropped.

Whenever a client wants to have the mailbox service begin storing events for it, it calls `acquireMailbox()`. The parameters to this call are the source and type of the events that are to be saved—presumably this is enough information to uniquely identify the destination of the event—and a requested lease duration. Note that the approach here differs from that of `mercury`. The code here uses event source and type as "routing" information, rather than creating a separate listener for each client.

The call creates a new `ArrayList` to hold registrations from this source, if there is none. If this is the first time that this source has been encountered, a new `BasicRegistrationLandlord` is also created to manage leasing for registrations for events from the source.

The normal leasing mechanics are done here—computing an actual expiration time, creating a cookie and a lease, and so on—the registration is added to the appropriate list, and an `EventRegistration` is returned to the client. From this point, whenever an event is received that has a source and type that have been specified in a call to `acquireMailbox()`, the event will be saved in a client-specific mailbox until the client retrieves its events, or its lease on the mailbox expires.

The `getEvents()` method simply finds the mailbox for the client given the specified event source and type, and returns the whole `ArrayList` of events to the client; the mailbox is cleared after this operation. If there is no such mailbox, the service assumes that the client's lease on the mailbox expired, and throws `UnknownLeaseException` to tell the client that its lease is no longer valid.

The `deliverEvents()` method works similarly. The only difference here is that the method takes a `RemoteEventListener` parameter that the service should deliver the events to. The service will call `notify()` in turn for each of the events to deliver them using the "normal" event handling code in the listener. If `notify()` raises an `UnknownEventException`, the service cancels the client's registration. Otherwise, a `RemoteException` while delivering is noted to the standard error output.

Note that here, if a `RemoteException` is raised, the client's event mailbox is not emptied. The service tries to ensure that events are actually delivered to the client before discarding any stored events. If a client crashes in the middle of having its events delivered, it can reconnect later and still retrieve all of its stored events.

A Mailbox Client

Let's now look at the final piece of the puzzle: a client to exercise the `Event-Mailbox`. This is actually the first client in this book that uses *two* services at once. In this case, it will build an event pipeline containing both the `Heart-beatGenerator` as the ultimate event generator, and the `EventMailbox` as an intermediary between the client and the generator. The `MailboxClient` class is a subclass of `HeartbeatClient`—it can reuse all the behavior in the earlier client for finding `HeartbeatGenerators`, and only extend the code to use the event mailbox, as shown in Listing 16–7.

Listing 16–7 `MailboxClient.java`

```
// A subclass of HeartbeatClient that uses a mailbox
// for deferred event delivery.

package corejini.chapter16;

import net.jini.core.lookup.ServiceTemplate;
import net.jini.core.lookup.ServiceRegistrar;
import net.jini.core.event.RemoteEvent;
import net.jini.core.event.EventRegistration;
import net.jini.lease.LeaseRenewalManager;
import net.jini.core.lease.Lease;
import java.io.IOException;
import java.rmi.RemoteException;
import java.rmi.RMISecurityManager;
import java.util.List;
```

Listing 16–7 `MailboxClient.java` (continued)

```java
public class MailboxClient extends HeartbeatClient {
    ServiceTemplate mailboxTemplate;
    EventMailbox.EventMailboxRequest mailbox = null;

    public MailboxClient() throws IOException,
                                  RemoteException {
        Class[] mbtypes =
            { EventMailbox.EventMailboxRequest.class };
        mailboxTemplate =
            new ServiceTemplate(null, mbtypes, null);
    }

    void doit(ServiceRegistrar reg) {
        // Bail once we've found a generator and a mailbox.
        if (gen != null && mailbox != null)
            return;

        // Find a generator.
        if (gen == null) {
            try {
                gen = (HeartbeatGenerator.HeartbeatRequest)
                    reg.lookup(template);
            } catch (Exception ex) {
                System.err.println("Doing lookup: " +
                                    ex.getMessage());
                ex.printStackTrace();
            }
        }

        // Find a mailbox.
        if (mailbox == null) {
            try {
                mailbox = (EventMailbox.EventMailboxRequest)
                    reg.lookup(mailboxTemplate);
            } catch (Exception ex) {
                System.err.println("Doing lookup: " +
                                    ex.getMessage());
                ex.printStackTrace();
            }
        }
```

Listing 16–7 `MailboxClient.java` (continued)

```java
if (gen == null || mailbox == null)
    return;

System.out.println(
    "Got a generator and a mailbox!");

// Remember our registrations...
EventRegistration evtreg = null;
EventRegistration mbreg = null;

// Sign us up for events!
try {
    // Tell the generator to send to the mailbox.
    // Here, we do our own leasing even though the
    // events are sent to the mailbox.
    evtreg =
        gen.register(HeartbeatGenerator.MINUTE,
                     null, mailbox, Lease.ANY);
    leaseManager.renewUntil(evtreg.getLease(),
                            Lease.ANY, null);

    // We need to tell the mailbox to hold on to
    // events with this <source, type>.  We do this
    // by acquiring a mailbox.  We again do our own
    // leasing of this mailbox.
    mbreg =
        mailbox.acquireMailbox(evtreg.getSource(),
                               evtreg.getID(),
                               Lease.ANY);
    leaseManager.renewUntil(mbreg.getLease(),
                            Lease.ANY, null);
} catch (RemoteException ex) {
    System.err.println("Bogus: " + ex.getMessage());
    ex.printStackTrace();
}

System.out.println("Sleeping a while...");

// Wait a while, then ask the mailbox for events.
try {
    Thread.sleep(1000 * 60 * 5);
} catch (InterruptedException ex) {
}
```

Listing 16–7 `MailboxClient.java` (continued)

```java
        System.out.println("Getting events in a batch");

        try {
            List events =
                mailbox.getEvents(mbreg.getSource(),
                                mbreg.getID());
            System.out.println("events:" );
            for (int i=0, size=events.size(); i<size; i++) {
                System.out.println(i + " = " +
                                events.get(i));
            }
        } catch (Exception ex) {
            ex.getMessage();
            ex.printStackTrace();
        }

        System.out.println("Sleeping again...");

        // Now wait a while, then ask the mailbox for our
        // events.
        try {
            Thread.sleep(1000 * 60 * 5);
        } catch (InterruptedException ex) {
        }

        System.out.println("Asking for delivery");

        try {
            mailbox.deliverEvents(mbreg.getSource(),
                                mbreg.getID(),
                                listener);
        } catch (Exception ex) {
            ex.getMessage();
            ex.printStackTrace();
        }
    }
```

Listing 16–7 `MailboxClient.java` (continued)

```java
    public static void main(String[] args) {
        if (System.getSecurityManager() == null) {
            System.setSecurityManager(
                new RMISecurityManager());
        }

        try {
            MailboxClient client = new MailboxClient();
            new Thread(client).start();
        } catch (Exception ex) {
            System.err.println("Bogus: " + ex.getMessage());
            System.exit(1);
        }
    }
}
```

The core of this code is in the `doit()` method. This code is invoked every time a new lookup service is discovered; it searches lookup services until it finds both a `HeartbeatGenerator` and an `EventMailbox`. Once it has these, it goes to work.

The first thing it must do is build the event pipeline. It contacts the `HeartbeatGenerator`, solicits to receive events every minute, and has these events delivered to the mailbox service (the proxy for this service implements `RemoteEventListener`, so that it can receive these events). It then has a `Lease-RenewalManager` renew the lease for this event registration indefinitely.

Next, the client calls `acquireMailbox()` on the `EventMailbox` to tell it to store events from the `HeartbeatGenerator`. The `EventRegistration` returned from the `register()` call on the `HeartbeatGenerator` contains the source and type of the events it will send to its listener; by passing these to `acquireMailbox()`, the client is telling the mailbox that matching events should be held for it.

Finally, the code tests out whether this event pipeline really works! It sleeps for five minutes—to allow some time for events to accumulate in the mailbox—and then calls `getEvents()` on the mailbox to fetch all the queued events. These are printed out, and then the client sleeps for another five minutes, and then it calls `deliverEvents()` to have the events delivered to it via the "normal" `Remote-EventListener` interface defined in the superclass.

Compiling and Running the Examples

Let's now build and run a little distributed system that consists of the new
EventMailbox, the HeartbeatGenerator from the last example, and the
MailboxClient. First, compile the code needed for the service, and build the
necessary RMI stubs. Make sure that you previously compiled Basic-
RegistrationLandlord, HeartbeatClient, and HeartbeatGenerator
from the last examples, as you'll be needing them again. Since EventMailbox
extends java.rmi.server.UnicastRemoteObject, you'll have to build stubs
for it.

On Windows:

```
javac -classpath C:\files;
                  C:\jini1_1\lib\jini-core.jar;
                  C:\jini1_1\lib\jini-ext.jar;
                  C:\jini1_1\lib\sun-util.jar;
                  C:\service
      -d C:\service
        C:\files\corejini\chapter16\EventMailbox.java


rmic -classpath C:\jini1_1\lib\jini-core.jar;
                C:\jini1_1\lib\jini-ext.jar;
                C:\jini1_1\lib\sun-util.jar;
                C:\service
     -d C:\service
        corejini.chapter16.EventMailbox


mkdir C:\service-dl\corejini\chapter16
cd C:\service\corejini\chapter16
copy EventMailbox_Stub.class
    C:\service-dl\corejini\chapter16
```

On UNIX:

```
javac -classpath /files:
                  /files/jini1_1/lib/jini-core.jar:
                  /files/jini1_1/lib/jini-ext.jar:
                  /files/jini1_1/lib/sun-util.jar:
                  /files/service
      -d /files/service
        /files/corejini/chapter16/EventMailbox.java


rmic -classpath /files/jini1_1/lib/jini-core.jar:
                /files/jini1_1/lib/jini-ext.jar:
                /files/jini1_1/lib/sun-util.jar:
                /files/service
```

```
    -d /files/service
        corejini.chapter16.EventMailbox

mkdir /files/service-dl/corejini/chapter16
cd /service/corejini/chapter16
cp EventMailbox_Stub.class
    /files/service-dl/corejini/chapter16
```

After this, you need to build the files necessary for the client program. Note that the client also needs the `EventMailboxRequest` interface, which is the interface that the service's proxy implements. This interface is contained within the service's code, but is actually used by both the service and the client. So you'll have to copy it out to the client's directory.

On Windows:
```
javac -classpath C:\files;
                  C:\jini1_1\lib\jini-core.jar;
                  C:\jini1_1\lib\jini-ext.jar;
                  C:\jini1_1\lib\sun-util.jar;
                  C:\client
      -d C:\client
          C:\files\corejini\chapter16\MailboxClient.java

cd C:\service\corejini\chapter16
copy EventMailbox$EventMailboxRequest.class
    C:\client\corejini\chapter16
```

On UNIX:
```
javac -classpath /files:
                  /files/jini1_1/lib/jini-core.jar:
                  /files/jini1_1/lib/jini-ext.jar:
                  /files/jini1_1/lib/sun-util.jar:
                  /files/client
      -d /files/client
          /files/corejini/chapter16/MailboxClient.java

cd /files/service/corejini/chapter16
cp EventMailbox\$EventMailboxRequest.class
    /files/client/corejini/chapter16
```

Finally, you're set to run the applications! Start the `HeartbeatGenerator` service first, then the `EventMailbox` service, then the client. Be sure to give both the services pathnames to use for their stable storage, and set the hostnames in the codebases appropriately.

On Windows:

```
java -cp C:\files\jini1_1\lib\jini-core.jar;
         C:\files\jini1_1\lib\jini-ext.jar;
         C:\files\jini1_1\lib\sun-util.jar;
         C:\service
    -Djava.rmi.server.codebase=http://myhost:8085/
    -Djava.security.policy=C:\policy
    corejini.chapter16.HeartbeatGenerator C:\tmp\hb


java -cp C:\files\jini1_1\lib\jini-core.jar;
         C:\files\jini1_1\lib\jini-ext.jar;
         C:\files\jini1_1\lib\sun-util.jar;
         C:\service
    -Djava.rmi.server.codebase=http://myhost:8085/
    -Djava.security.policy=C:\policy
    corejini.chapter16.EventMailbox C:\tmp\mb


java -cp C:\files\jini1_1\lib\jini-core.jar;
         C:\files\jini1_1\lib\jini-ext.jar;
         C:\files\jini1_1\lib\sun-util.jar;
         C:\client
    -Djava.rmi.server.codebase=http://myhost:8086/
    -Djava.security.policy=C:\policy
    corejini.chapter16.MailboxClient
```

On UNIX:
```
java -cp /files/jini1_1/lib/jini-core.jar:
         /files/jini1_1/lib/jini-ext.jar:
         /files/jini1_1/lib/sun-util.jar:
         /files/service
    -Djava.rmi.server.codebase=http://myhost:8085/
    -Djava.security.policy=/files/policy
    corejini.chapter16.HeartbeatGenerator /tmp/hb


java -cp /files/jini1_1/lib/jini-core.jar:
         /files/jini1_1/lib/jini-ext.jar:
         /files/jini1_1/lib/sun-util.jar:
         /files/service
    -Djava.rmi.server.codebase=http://myhost:8085/
    -Djava.security.policy=/files/policy
    corejini.chapter16.EventMailbox /tmp/mb


java -cp /files/jini1_1/lib/jini-core.jar:
         /files/jini1_1/lib/jini-ext.jar:
         /files/jini1_1/lib/sun-util.jar:
         /files/client
```

```
-Djava.rmi.server.codebase=http://myhost:8086/
-Djava.security.policy=/files/policy
corejini.chapter16.MailboxClient
```

When you start the `HeartbeatGenerator` service, you should see:

Heartbeat generator started.

After starting the `EventMailbox`, you'll see it report:

Running!

Finally, start the `MailboxClient`. It will contact the mailbox server to get a mailbox assigned to it after it solicits events from the `HeartbeatGenerator`. The `EventMailbox` will print some output when a mailbox is acquired, resulting in something like the following:

Acquired new mailbox for corejini.chapter16.HeartbeatGenerator_Stub
[RemoteStub [ref: [endpoint:
[13.2.116.134:44273](remote),objID:[b3b823:d6dd277b8b:-8000, 0]]]], 2

This apparent mumbo-jumbo is the string representation of the source that the `EventMailbox` expects to receive events from. In this case, the client has specified the `HeartbeatGenerator` as the source, and here you see the `toString()` representation of the RMI stub for the `HeartbeatGenerator`.

As the `HeartbeatGenerator` delivers events to the `EventMailbox`, the `EventMailbox` will record when events are received. It will also display a message when the client application asks for the events to be delivered to it in a batch, or for the events to be "redelivered" to it via its `RemoteEventListener` interface.

Saved event in mailbox
Saved event in mailbox
Saved event in mailbox
Saved event in mailbox
Saved event in mailbox
Getting events.
Saved event in mailbox
Saved event in mailbox
Saved event in mailbox
Saved event in mailbox
Saved event in mailbox
Redelivering events.

The client will start up and indicate when it has acquired the service proxies for both the `HeartbeatGenerator` and the `EventMailbox`:

Got a generator and a mailbox!

The client will next sleep for a few minutes, and then get the events in a "batch" from the mailbox. As the events are returned, they are printed. The output below shows the default `toString()` representation of the `HeartbeatEvents`:

Sleeping a while...
Getting events in a batch
events:
0 = corejini.chapter16.HeartbeatGenerator$HeartbeatEvent
[source=corejini.chapter16.HeartbeatGenerator_Stub[RemoteStub
[ref: [endpoint:[13.2.116.134:44273](remote),objID:
[b3b823:d6dd277b8b:-8000, 0]]]]]
1 = corejini.chapter16.HeartbeatGenerator$HeartbeatEvent
[source=corejini.chapter16.HeartbeatGenerator_Stub[RemoteStub
[ref: [endpoint:[13.2.116.134:44273](remote),objID:
[b3b823:d6dd277b8b:-8000, 0]]]]]
2 = corejini.chapter16.HeartbeatGenerator$HeartbeatEvent
[source=corejini.chapter16.HeartbeatGenerator_Stub[RemoteStub
[ref: [endpoint:[13.2.116.134:44273](remote),objID:
[b3b823:d6dd277b8b:-8000, 0]]]]]
3 = corejini.chapter16.HeartbeatGenerator$HeartbeatEvent
[source=corejini.chapter16.HeartbeatGenerator_Stub[RemoteStub
[ref: [endpoint:[13.2.116.134:44273](remote),objID:
[b3b823:d6dd277b8b:-8000, 0]]]]]
4 = corejini.chapter16.HeartbeatGenerator$HeartbeatEvent
[source=corejini.chapter16.HeartbeatGenerator_Stub[RemoteStub
[ref: [endpoint:[13.2.116.134:44273](remote),objID:
[b3b823:d6dd277b8b:-8000, 0]]]]]

The client will sleep again, and then ask for redelivery of any events stored at the mailbox. This time, when the events are received, they come in via the `notify()` method implemented in the `HeartbeatClient` example earlier in the chapter.

Sleeping again...
Asking for delivery
Came from MINUTE
Came from MINUTE
Came from MINUTE
Came from MINUTE
Came from MINUTE

This example has shown how a client can interpose a third-party event delegate between itself and an existing event generator. The important thing to realize here is that the generator, the `HeartbeatGenerator`, is completely unchanged from the first example of this chapter. The client has added new functionality to the event delivery pipeline, without having to know anything about the `Heart-beatGenerator` other than how to ask it for events, and without needing to make any modifications to the `HeartbeatGenerator`! This functionality has been added solely by the client, with no involvement or knowledge required by the event generator.

Using code like the `EventMailbox` shown here, you can have your clients augment the functionality provided by the event generators they find in a Jini community. And once you've got a "toolbox" of event-handling delegates, you can use them freely with any event generator.

Summary

This chapter looked at Jini's philosophy for remote events, and the actual programmatic interfaces for building event generators and event consumers. The first example in this chapter showed how to construct a generator/consumer pair for simple "heartbeat" events. The generator in this case performed leasing of its event registrations.

The second example of the chapter looked at how to build an event delegate that could be interposed between an event generator and an event recipient. The fact that the generator knew nothing about the delegate meant that you could extend whatever functionality is provided by other delegates in similar ways. And even though this example showed how to use delegation with `Heartbeat-Events`, you could easily use this exact same event mailbox with *any* Jini event source, including Jini lookup services.

What's Next?

The final three chapters of this book will address slightly different topics than what you've seen before: They talk about common Jini services that are built atop the basic Jini infrastructure. Chapter 17 talks about JavaSpaces, a storage service for objects. JavaSpaces is a service defined and provided by Sun, and will be common enough on most Jini networks that you should know how to leverage and use it.

JavaSpaces

Chapter 17

The chapters so far in this book have focused solely on the infrastructure that forms the underpinnings of Jini communities—the plumbing, if you will, that all collections of services have to agree upon in order to form dynamic federations at run time.

This chapter shifts focus to look at one particular service that is built atop the basic Jini substrate. This service—called JavaSpaces—provides a storage facility for Java objects. Using JavaSpaces, Jini services and clients can create and manipulate "spaces"—persistent collections—of Java objects. They can acquire leased storage for Java objects, search for stored objects, and remove stored objects from a space.

And, just as the topics you've already seen or will shortly see—discovery, lookup, leasing, remote events, transactions—constitute the Jini programming model, JavaSpaces is also meant to play a role in that model. JavaSpaces provides a facility for *distributed shared memory* that can be used by any other entity in a Jini community.

In addition to simply providing storage for entities in a Jini community, Java-Spaces can be applied to other uses. The JavaSpaces programming model is quite simple, and yet is powerful and flexible enough that it can be used as the basis for entirely new ways to build distributed applications. Collections of applications can use a JavaSpace as a "shared blackboard" for depositing and retrieving objects. The objects that are stored in a space can represent work to be done (and thus can be used to build producer/consumer-style distributed applications), or simple parcels of data (perhaps used to build distributed voting or bidding applications).

In this chapter, you'll explore this service, look at its basic programming model, and see how it can be applied to a number of distributed systems programming problems.

What Is JavaSpaces?

Many applications in a distributed setting, just as in a local setting, have a need to store data persistently. The JavaSpaces service provides this capability in the form of a full-fledged Jini service that can be found via lookup and used through its proxy, just like any other Jini service.

But what does it mean to be a "storage service?" If someone tells you simply that they have a storage service, there are a number of questions you might ask them about it. For example, what kinds of things can it store? You could imagine a storage service that holds on to sequences of raw bytes for clients. Such a service would be capable of storing anything, as long as it was first serialized to a byte array. Other services might hold actual objects, like the simple "slot provider" example of Chapter 13, which doles out a fixed number of "slots" for object storage to clients.

You could also ask how you retrieve data from the service. The slot provider in Chapter 13 returned a unique "key" value to the client that could be used to retrieve data stored there. Others services might refer to data by a name provided by the client, or some other mechanism.

JavaSpaces takes a very Java-centric approach. Like the slot provider example in this book, it is not a *data* storage service, but an *object* storage service. That is, it holds complete, live Java objects. In fact, it can *only* hold Java objects. But unlike the slot provider, which never actually made any use of the "objectness" of the items it stored, JavaSpaces fully understands the Java type system, and can leverage type semantics to make it a natural fit for applications that need to store, find, and retrieve Java objects.

A Filesystem for Objects

The goal of JavaSpaces is to provide what might be thought of as a "filesystem for objects." That is, JavaSpaces can provide a ubiquitous, natural way to store and use objects, designed to work naturally with object-oriented applications written in Java. And, much like a filesystem, JavaSpaces can provide a way to *share* objects between applications. So just like an application (or a user) can drop a file into a well-known location on a filesystem for retrieval by another application (or user), JavaSpaces can act as a shared communications medium between Jini-aware clients and services—it represents the distributed shared memory component of the Jini programming model, and provides a mechanism for cooperating Jini entities to share and exchange information.

But, typical filesystems only store simple "bags of bits." In the case of systems like UNIX and Windows, these files don't even really have types associated with them. For the most part, it's up to the applications that use them, and established conventions, to associate some meaning and interpretation to these bags of bits known as files that exist in a filesystem.

JavaSpaces, on the other hand, is a very object-centered storage system. Rather than storing simple untyped data, JavaSpaces leverages Java to store whole objects, with all the benefits that come from being a Java object: strong typing, mobile code, secure execution, and so forth. So in a JavaSpace, the stored entities have actual types and may contain code in them.

Another difference lies in how stored entities are found. In a filesystem, access to previously stored data is done through naming. Every file in a filesystem has a name that's unique within that filesystem. If the name is well-known and agreed upon by all parties that will use it (such as `C:\autoexec.bat` or `/dev/tty`), then it can, by convention, have special properties and be used by any number of parties. Searching in a filesystem is typically done by searching for some portion of the name of the file or—in some cases, such as text files—by searching through the actual contents of the file.

In JavaSpaces, names aren't so important. In fact, the "name" of an object is just one of the many attributes of an object that you could use to find it. You can search for objects based on their class, or their superclass, or the interfaces they implement. And you can search for objects based on their attributes, including any attribute that—by convention—is treated as a name.

Attribute-Based Search

So if objects don't necessarily have names that identify them, how do clients use a JavaSpace to store and find objects? The answer is that JavaSpaces uses exactly the same technology as the Jini lookup service for attribute-based searches. Every object stored in a JavaSpace must implement the `net.jini.core.entry.Entry` interface, which means that it can be interpreted as a strongly typed *collection* of the member objects within it. In fact, the only difference between how the JavaSpace and Jini lookup service use attribute searching is that lookup services define how a *set* of templates can match a *set* of entries; JavaSpaces only has tools for matching single entries.

Recall from Chapter 7 that `Entry` is a no-method "tagging" interface that objects can implement to tell the system that the creator of that object is aware of the special ways such objects will be used in lookup services (members of the object are serialized independently and so forth). `Entry` objects in JavaSpaces have exactly the same semantics: They are treated as collections of the public, nonstatic, nonfinal, nontransient objects that are referred to by them.

Each `Entry` can be searched for via a "template" that is matched against its member objects; templates can be used to search based on either the types or the values of objects, and support "wildcards," exactly as shown in Chapter 7. (So now might be a good time to review the matching rules for attributes in Chapter 7, if they've slipped your mind.)

Since these same concepts are used so extensively in the Jini lookup service, you're already used to them. JavaSpaces uses exactly the same attribute-based search rules as the lookup service, although it uses a different set of APIs for storing, searching for, and retrieving objects. These APIs are more closely aligned with the needs of a storage service.

Predecessors to JavaSpaces

Much of the work that went into building JavaSpaces is based on earlier research by David Gelernter, a computer scientist at Yale University. Gelernter designed a system called Linda, which is in many ways a predecessor of JavaSpaces. The central notions in Linda are *tuples*, which are collections of data grouped together, and the *tuple space*, which is a "shared blackboard" into which applications can deposit and retrieve tuples.

These notions are clear analogs of *entries* and *spaces* in the JavaSpace world. But while JavaSpaces owes much to Linda, there are some important differences between the two. First, Linda tuples do not have the strong typing that the Java language provides. That is, while the individual *elements* of a tuple are typed, the tuple as a whole is not. JavaSpaces provides strong typing for not only `Entry` objects, but also the objects referred to by those `Entries`. This strong typing is important to enable JavaSpaces to mesh nicely with applications that expect the strong typing they find in the Java platform. Furthermore, not only are JavaSpace `Entry` objects strongly typed, but they leverage and use the Java type system, meaning that clients can search based on superclass relationships. Linda allows only value matching.

Second, `Entry` objects in JavaSpaces *are* objects—that is, they not only have data associated with them, but actual methods too. Since complete objects can be stored in JavaSpaces, clients can retrieve not only lifeless data, but also the code necessary to operate on this data.

Finally, JavaSpaces meshes well with the Jini conventions and paradigms. Whereas Linda systems typically envision a single, large Linda tuple space, a Jini community will typically have several active JavaSpaces services. Each can support its own, separate storage area for objects. JavaSpaces `Entry` objects are leased by the clients that store them, so the Jini self-healing mandate applies here as well.

The rise in popularity of Java has brought a renewed interest in Linda-descended systems. One of these is the `T Spaces` system from IBM Research. T Spaces is in many ways similar to JavaSpaces, although it is not as minimal. T Spaces provides the ability to modify the behavior of the tuple space through downloaded code, supports database-style indexing and queries, and allows users to set access control security policies on tuples.

Configuring and Running JavaSpaces

Way back in Chapter 1, when you downloaded and installed the basic Jini distribution, I ignored a couple of key services that weren't used in the first part of the book. It's time to go back and take care of the missing pieces now.

If you installed the Jini Starter Kit on your system using the instructions provided in Chapter 1, then everything you need to run JavaSpaces is already installed and in place. You should note that in earlier (pre-1.1) releases of the Jini Starter Kit, JavaSpaces was available as an extra download. If you are still running an older version of Jini, you will need to visit the Sun Web page to download JavaSpaces, or—a better strategy—simply upgrade to 1.1 and get the latest and greatest versions of everything all at once.

Start the Run-Time Services

JavaSpaces provides a new service for the Jini environment, but it also relies on the existing Jini infrastructure to function correctly. As a "normal" Jini service, JavaSpaces requires the "normal" infrastructure, such as lookup services and HTTP servers, to support its downloadable code. But JavaSpaces also requires one service that ships with Jini which you haven't seen yet: the Jini *transaction manager*. Sun's implementation of this service is called `mahalo`.

Just as in Chapter 1, these necessary services can be started via the GUI provided by Sun, or "by hand." I'll walk through the GUI installation first, because it's the easiest and will give you a feel for the steps that are required to start up JavaSpaces. But you should definitely pay attention to the command-line instructions for starting JavaSpaces: having an understanding of the service at this level will be important if you need to move a JavaSpaces installation to a different machine, or need to start JavaSpaces at boot time.

Starting Required Services via the GUI

As you saw in Chapter 1, Jini ships with an easy-to-use graphical interface for starting the services that Jini uses. This interface can only start services on the local machine, so if you have a need to run services on a set of machines, you'll either have to run the GUI on each or, perhaps better, just use the command-line instructions.

Go back, now, and review the instructions in that chapter for how to launch the StartService GUI application. You'll need to start the application and load the same platform-specific property file that you used before. This property file will install the templates for starting the JavaSpace and transaction manager services.

Once the property file is loaded, you'll see the same GUI containing tabbed panes for starting the various services that you saw in Chapter 1. In the following instructions, I'll assume that you've already started a Jini lookup service, as well as an RMI activation daemon on each of the machines on which you will be running the JavaSpaces service or the transaction manager service. For most settings, this can be the same machine that is hosting a lookup service, and so the required activation daemon will already be running. (You do not need a separate activation daemon for each activatable service you run on a given machine; one activation daemon can support all services on one machine.)

You do, however, need to make sure that the HTTP services on your network are correctly configured. Just as with any Jini service, JavaSpaces and the transaction manager need to be able to export downloadable code to clients. The downloadable code for these services is installed into the lib directory under jini1_1. There are two separate JAR files that contain the downloadable code for these services, outrigger-dl.jar and mahalo-dl.jar.

If there is already an HTTP server running with its root directory set to the Jini lib directory, then you can simply "reuse" this HTTP server to serve up the downloadable code for these two new services. Because the Jini installation places all downloadable code for the "core" services, as well as JavaSpaces, together in one directory, it's easy to use one HTTP server to export the downloadable code for the lookup service, JavaSpaces, and the transaction manager.

If you are not already running an HTTP server to export downloadable code for the core Jini services, you will need to start one. See the instructions in Chapter 1 for how to do this.

The common case, though, is the easy one—all the files are installed together and there is one machine that is used for running the Sun-provided Jini services, and on which an HTTP server and activation daemon are both already running. In this case, all you have to do is start the transaction manager and then start the JavaSpaces service.

Click on the *Mahalo_TxnManager* tabbed pane on the GUI to bring up the panel shown in Figure 17–1. Mahalo is the name of Sun's implementation of the Transaction Manager service.

```
┌─────────────────────────────────────────────────────────────────┐
│ StartService                                              _ □ ×   │
├─────────────────────────────────────────────────────────────────┤
│ File                                                              │
├─────────────────────────────────────────────────────────────────┤
│ Mercury │ Norm │ TransientSpace │ FrontEndSpace                   │
│   Transient_Fiddler    │    Activatable_Fiddler   │  Mahalo_TxnManager │
│  Template  │  Run  │  RMID  │  WebServer  │  Reggie  │  LookupBrowser │
│                                                                   │
│        Java Command : java                                        │
│        Java Options : -jar                                        │
│   Setup JVM Options :                                             │
│  Executable Jar File : C:\files\jini1_1\lib\mahalo.jar            │
│            Codebase : http://hostname:8080/mahalo-dl.jar          │
│  Security Policy File : C:\files\jini1_1\policy\policy.all         │
│       Log Directory : C:\tmp\mahalo_log                           │
│  Groups and Locators : public                                     │
│          Server JVM :                                             │
│  Server JVM Arguments :                                           │
└─────────────────────────────────────────────────────────────────┘
```

Figure 17–1   *Starting the transaction manager*

Configuring the transaction manager is easy. Just make sure that the paths to the appropriate security policy files and JAR files are correct, and specify a log directory to use. This is the file that the service will use for persistent storage. On Windows, something like `C:\temp\txn_log` is fine; on UNIX, `/var/tmp/txn_log` works great for development work. The *Manager Name* parameter simply sets a `Name` attribute on the service's registrations with lookup services, for your convenience.

Be sure to set a correct URL for the codebase parameter. The hostname here should be the name of the machine on which you're running the HTTP server that's serving up the JAR files that come with Jini; be sure to change the port number to 8080, if you've been following my recommendations and are running your web server on that port.

Like the lookup service, the transaction manager is an activatable service. That means that once you start the service once, it will be registered with the RMI activation daemon, and will be restarted as necessary whenever `rmid` restarts.

Jini comes with two separate implementations of the JavaSpaces service. One of these is a transient service—meaning that the service does not save information between crashes or restarts—and one is persistent.

For development and debugging work, you may wish to run the transient space. For deployment, I'd definitely recommend the persistent space. For the examples shown here, either will work. The start-up procedures for either should be well familiar to you at this point, since most of the options are the same as for the other Jini services. In the interest of variety, I'll show how to start the transient service.

Click on the *TransientSpace* tab. "Outrigger" is the name of the JavaSpaces implementation provided by Sun. Take a look at the panel here (shown in Figure 17-2), and simply check to make sure that the paths to security policy files and JAR files are correct, and edit the URL to point to the web server on which you're hosting the Jini JAR files. Remember to set the port number to 8080.

Figure 17–2 Starting a JavaSpaces service.

Once you've got these two services configured, the only thing left is to actually start them up. Go to the *Run* panel (Figure 17–3). Assuming that the rest of the needed services are running in appropriate places, all you have to do is start the transaction manager service and then start the JavaSpaces service by clicking on the buttons. You can also use this panel to shut down a service, if you need to .

Starting the Required Services via the Command Line

In this section, you'll see the nitty-gritty details of how to manually start the services required by JavaSpaces. Understanding how this works will give you some insight into how these services work, and will let you do things like write scripts that can automatically start a service when a machine boots.

As mentioned in the last section, the services required to use JavaSpaces are—first and foremost—normal Jini services that require lookup services, HTTP servers, and activation daemons. So you need to make sure that you are running a properly configured lookup service somewhere on your network.

StartService	
Start RMID	**Stop RMID**
Start WebServer	**Stop WebServer**
Start Reggie	**Stop Reggie**
Start LookupBrowser	**Stop LookupBrowser**
Start Transient_Fiddler	**Stop Transient_Fiddler**
Start Activatable_Fiddler	**Stop Activatable_Fiddler**
Start Mahalo_TxnManager	**Stop Mahalo_TxnManager**
Start Mercury	**Stop Mercury**
Start Norm	**Stop Norm**
Start TransientSpace	**Stop TransientSpace**
Start FrontEndSpace	**Stop FrontEndSpace**

Tabs: File | Mercury | Norm | TransientSpace | FrontEndSpace | Transient_Fiddler | Activatable_Fiddler | Mahalo_TxnManager | Template | Run | RMID | WebServer | Reggie | LookupBrowser

Figure 17–3   *Running the services*

To do JavaSpaces development or use JavaSpaces-aware clients, you must run both the JavaSpaces service as well as the Jini transaction manager service. The latter comes with the standard Jini Starter Kit distribution. Both of these services make use of the RMI activation framework, so each should be run on a machine with an instance of `rmid` running on it. If you're running these services on the same machine, or even (as is likely) on the same machine as a Jini lookup service, you can "share" one instance of `rmid` among all of these services.

Also, like any other Jini service, JavaSpaces and the transaction manager need to be able to export downloadable code to their clients. The downloadable code for both services lives in the Jini `lib` directory; `outrigger-dl.jar` contains the downloadable code for JavaSpaces, and `mahalo-dl.jar` contains the downloadable code for the transaction manager.

If you're already running a Jini lookup service on your network, then out of necessity, you're already running an HTTP server that exports the lookup service's downloadable code. Since the downloadable code for JavaSpaces and the transaction manager live in the same directory (by default) as the downloadable code for the lookup service, you can use this same HTTP server to export *all* the code for these three services. Just make sure that there is an HTTP server running somewhere on your network with its root directory set to point to the location of these JAR files. You'll need to remember the machine name and port number of this HTTP service for use in codebase properties, so that JavaSpaces and the transaction manager can tell their clients where to access downloadable code from.

Now, start the transaction manager. The startup arguments for the transaction manager look much like the other Jini services you saw in Chapter 1. The basic form of the transaction manager command line is:

```
java -jar <txn-mgr-jar-file>
    [-Dcom.sun.jini.mahalo.managerName=<name>]
    <txn-mgr-codebase>
    <security-policy-file>
    <log-directory>
    [<lookup-service-groups>] [<lookup-locators>]
```

This format is similar to the other Jini services. The `-jar` option says that the classes to run reside entirely within a JAR file. You can optionally specify a "name" for the transaction manager service (usually "`TransactionManager`" is just fine). After this come the required arguments for the transaction manager. These are the codebase to provide to clients, a security policy file, and a log directory. The codebase should be set to the hostname and port number of the HTTP server that's exporting the `mahalo-dl.jar` file. The security policy file here is used to set the security permissions on any JVMs that are started by the activation daemon to run reactivated code; review Chapter 1 for details on how this works. The log directory is an absolute path to a directory in which the trans-action manager will write its persistent state. You should make sure that this directory doesn't exist when you run the transaction manager; it will be created automatically when it is used.

Finally, you can optionally specify the names of Jini communities to join, and lookup locators to discover. Passing "`public`" as a group name is a special flag that indicates that the transaction manager should become part of the unnamed, public group.

Here are the specific command lines for starting the transaction manager on different platforms.

On Windows:

```
java -jar C:\jini1_1\lib\mahalo.jar
    -Dcom.sun.jini.mahalo.managerName=TransactionManager
    http://myhost:8080/mahalo-dl.jar
    C:\jini1_1\example\txn\policy.all
    C:\temp\txn_log
    public
```

On UNIX:

```
java -jar /files/jini1_1/lib/mahalo.jar
    -Dcom.sun.jini.mahalo.managerName=TransactionManager
    http://myhost:8080/mahalo-dl.jar
    /files/jini1_1/example/txn/policy.all
    /tmp/txn_log
    public
```

Listings 17–1 and 17–2 provide some simple scripts to automate the startup process for Windows and UNIX (the UNIX script should work well on Solaris, Linux, and most other UNIX variants). These scripts are available in the down-loadable code package from the FTP server, as described in the introduction. Be sure you edit the scripts to set the location of your Jini installation, your host-name, and so on.

Listing 17–1 `txnmgr.bat` **Script for Windows**

```
REM Set this to wherever Jini is installed
set JINI_HOME=C:\jini1_1
REM Set this to the host where the webserver runs
set HOSTNAME=hostname

REM Everything below should work with few
REM changes
set POLICYFILE=%JINI_HOME%\example\txn\policy.all
set JARFILE=%JINI_HOME%\lib\mahalo.jar
set CODEBASE=http://%HOSTNAME%:8080/mahalo-dl.jar
set TXN_POLICYFILE=%POLICYFILE%
set LOG_DIR=C:\temp\txn_log
set GROUP=public

java -jar %JARFILE%
    -Dcom.sun.jini.mahalo.managerName=
    TransactionManager
    %CODEBASE% %TXN_POLICYFILE%
    %LOG_DIR% %GROUP%
```

Next, start up the JavaSpaces service. For the examples in this book, start a

---

Listing 17–2 `txnmgr.sh` Script for UNIX

```
#!/bin/sh

# Set this to wherever Jini is installed
JINI_HOME=/files/jini1_1

# Set this to wherever the webserver is running
HOSTNAME=hostname

# Everything below should work with few changes
POLICYFILE=$JINI_HOME/example/txn/policy.all
JARFILE=$JINI_HOME/lib/mahalo.jar
CODEBASE=http://$HOSTNAME:8080/mahalo-dl.jar
TXN_POLICYFILE=$POLICYFILE
LOG_DIR=/tmp/txn_log
GROUP=public

java -jar $JARFILE\
     -Dcom.sun.jini.mahalo.managerName=\
     TransactionManager \
     $CODEBASE $TXN_POLICYFILE \
     $LOG_DIR $GROUP
```

"transient" JavaSpace. I'll talk about what this means a bit later in the chapter.
The prototypical command line for starting a transient JavaSpace looks like this:

```
java -Djava.security.policy=<policy-file>
     -Djava.rmi.server.codebase=<codebase>
     -Dcom.sun.jini.outrigger.spaceName=<name>
     -jar <jar-file>
     [<groups>] [<locators>]
```

You'll have to pass a security policy file here to permit access to system
resources and, once again, the codebase is set so that clients of the JavaSpaces
service will know where to download code needed to use the service. Like the
transaction manager, you can optionally specify a name for the service (usually
"JavaSpaces" is fine), and can provide the names of Jini communities to join, as
well a specific lookup locator URLs. Passing "public" as a group name indicates that the service should join the unnamed, public group.

Here are the command lines for starting a transient JavaSpace for Windows
and UNIX:

On Windows:

```
java -Djava.security.policy=
            C:\jini1_1\example\books\policy.all
        -Djava.rmi.server.codebase=
            http://myhost:8080/outrigger-dl.jar
        -Dcom.sun.jini.outrigger.spaceName=JavaSpaces
        -jar C:\jini1_1\lib\transient-outrigger.jar
         public
```

On UNIX:

```
java -Djava.security.policy=
            /files/jini1_1/example/books/policy.all
        -Djava.rmi.server.codebase=
            http://myhost:8080/outrigger-dl.jar
        -Dcom.sun.jini.outrigger.spaceName=JavaSpaces
        -jar /files/jini1_1/lib/transient-outrigger.jar
         public
```

Here are two scripts, Listings 17–3 and 17–4, for starting the JavaSpaces service on Windows and UNIX.

Listing 17–3 `javaspaces.bat` Script for Windows

```
REM Set this to wherever Jini is installed
set JINI_HOME=C:\jini1_1
REM Set this to the host where the webserver runs
set HOSTNAME=hostname

REM Everything below should work with few
REM changes
set POLICYFILE=%JINI_HOME%\example\books\policy.all
set JARFILE=%JINI_HOME%\lib\transient-outrigger.jar
set CODEBASE=http://%HOSTNAME%:8080/outrigger-dl.jar
set GROUP=public

java -Djava.security.policy=%POLICYFILE%
        -Djava.rmi.server.codebase=%CODEBASE%
        -Dcom.sun.jini.outrigger.spaceName=JavaSpaces
        -jar %JARFILE%
        %GROUP%
```

> **Listing 17–4** `javaspaces.sh` Script for UNIX

```
#!/bin/sh

# Set this to wherever Jini is installed
JINI_HOME=/files/jini1_1

# Set this to wherever the webserver is running
HOSTNAME=hostname

# Everything below should work with few changes
POLICYFILE=$JINI_HOME/example/books/policy.all
JARFILE=$JINI_HOME/lib/transient-outrigger.jar
CODEBASE=http://$HOSTNAME:8080/outrigger-dl.jar
GROUP=public

java -Djava.security.policy=$POLICYFILE \
    -Djava.rmi.server.codebase=$CODEBASE \
    -Dcom.sun.jini.outrigger.spaceName=JavaSpaces \
    -jar $JARFILE \
    $GROUP
```

Now that you've got the transaction manager and JavaSpaces services up, it's time to look more closely at how to build on top of these services!

Transient and Persistent JavaSpaces

I've talked a few times already about the fact that the Sun release of JavaSpaces ships with two different implementations of the service: a *transient* implementation and a *persistent* implementation. In the installation instructions, I've focused solely on the transient JavaSpaces implementation.

The difference between the two is that a transient JavaSpaces service only holds on to the data it stores as long as it is running. Any stored objects will be lost if the service crashes or is otherwise brought down. A persistent JavaSpaces service, on the other hand, logs its stored objects to the disk, so they can recover their state after they are restarted. These are two different *implementations* of JavaSpaces, but they share exactly the same *interfaces*.

In this book, I've recommended going with the transient space for development and testing. The transient space is a bit faster than the persistent space, and—the primary reason for its use here—is easier to set up. In a production environment, though, ensuring that there is no data loss is typically of primary importance, and so the persistent space would be more appropriate.

In case you run into the terminology in your own explorations, the class that implements the transient JavaSpaces service is called `com.sun.jini.outrigger.TransientSpace`. The class that implements the persistent service is called `com.sun.jini.outrigger.FrontEndSpace` (there used to be a persistent space implementation called `PersistentSpace`, but it's no longer available from Sun). The transient implementation lives in the JAR file `transient-outrigger.jar`, which you used earlier when starting the service, while the persistent implementation is in `outrigger.jar`.

Read the JavaSpaces documentation that comes with the Jini Starter Kit for more details on the persistent space.

The JavaSpaces Programming Model

JavaSpaces espouses the philosophy that less is more. The programming model for using JavaSpaces is very minimal—there are only four types of operations that you can do on a JavaSpace.

- You can write a new object into a JavaSpace.
- You can read an object that's in a JavaSpace.
- You can take an object out of a JavaSpace (this is like a read that removes the just-read item).
- You can ask that the JavaSpace notify you when objects that match a certain template are written into the space.

That's it! You cannot get much simpler than that. These four conceptual operations are actually used via a slightly larger set of methods in the `net.jini.space.JavaSpace` interface; these methods provide overloaded versions of some of the operations, and some ways to speed processing in a space.

All these operations support the common Jini notions of leasing—stored objects are leased. A client must renew the leases for a stored object, or the JavaSpace will remove the object. Similarly, the JavaSpaces service leases event registrations, just like a lookup service.

All these operations take `Entry` parameters that specify either the object to be stored (in the case of the write operation), or the template to be matched (in the case of the read, take, and notify operations).

Transactions, in Brief

In addition to lease duration and `Entry` parameters, the write, read, take, and notify operations also allow you to optionally pass a `Transaction` object to them. Transactions are a topic I'll reserve for the next to last chapter of the book—mainly because they're not used very often, especially in beginning Jini programming—but I'll say just a bit about them here.

Transactions, as you may remember from Chapter 3, are a way to group a related set of operations together. So if you're building a banking application and you need to do a transfer between two accounts, you would typically implement this as two separate operations grouped together by a transaction. The first operation decrements an account by a desired amount, and the second increments a different account by the same amount. By "grouping these into a transaction," you're telling the system that it should ensure that both of the operations complete successfully, or that neither of them complete at all.

Transactions provide a way to guard against partial failures. In the banking example, the *last* thing you want is for only one of the two operations to succeed. If this happens, you've either just robbed one client of money, or given another client free money, depending on which operation succeeds. The system is in an inconsistent state because of a partial failure. With transactions, either the whole thing works or it doesn't. If it works, you're happy, and if it doesn't, at least the system is in a known state and you can try to do the transfer later.

One of the reasons that I've saved transactions until near the end of the book is that, of all the current Sun-provided Jini services, JavaSpaces is the only one that uses or supports transactions. And even in the case of JavaSpaces, transactions are optional! Even though all the operations listed above will take a transaction parameter to indicate that they should be run in the context of a transaction, you can simply pass null here. Operations that do not run in the context of a transaction are logically "independent" of one another.

So for the rest of this chapter, I'll mention transactions where appropriate, but won't get into any of the "meat" of transactions until Chapter 18.

JavaSpaces APIs

Let's look at the interface for using JavaSpaces services. This interface, `net.jini.space.JavaSpace`, is implemented by the service proxies for Java-Spaces services. Like all Jini proxies, you don't know (and generally don't care) how the service proxy *implements* this interface. A particular proxy may communicate with a back-end JavaSpace using RMI, or CORBA, or raw sockets. And that service may be implemented using simple in-memory hash tables or with a full-blown database. The one thing that all have in common, though, is that their proxies will implement this one simple interface that allows clients and other Jini services to use them in the same way.

```
package net.jini.space;

public interface JavaSpace {
    public final long NO_WAIT = 0;// don't wait

    Lease write(Entry e, Transaction txn,
            long lease)
        throws RemoteException,
                TransactionException;
    Entry read(Entry tmpl, Transaction txn,
            long timeout)
        throws RemoteException,
                TransactionException,
                UnusableEntryException,
                InterruptedException;
    Entry readIfExists(Entry tmpl, Transaction txn,
                long timeout)
        throws RemoteException,
                TransactionException,
                UnusableEntryException,
                InterruptedException;
    Entry take(Entry tmpl, Transaction txn,
            long timeout)
        throws RemoteException,
                TransactionException,
                UnusableEntryException,
                InterruptedException;
    Entry takeIfExists(Entry tmpl, Transaction txn,
            long timeout)
        throws RemoteException,
                TransactionException,
                UnusableEntryException,
                InterruptedException;
    EventRegistration notify(Entry tmpl,
                    Transaction txn,
                    RemoteEventListener l,
                    long lease,
                    MarshalledObject obj)
        throws RemoteException,
                TransactionException;
    Entry snapshot(Entry e) throws RemoteException;
}
```

I'll discuss the individual methods in more detail below.

Write()

The `write()` method is used to deposit a new `Entry` into a JavaSpace. The arguments are the `Entry` object to be written, the `Transaction` that the write operation should be a part of, and an initial requested lease duration expressed in milliseconds. The `Entry` that is passed to the method is unchanged; it is serialized and a copy of it is stored in the JavaSpace. The method returns a `Lease` object, which can be renewed "manually" by the client, or can be handed off to a `LeaseRenewalManager` or other code for renewal.

If you pass in a `Transaction` to this method, or to any of the other methods in this class, then the operation will not happen until you tell the `Transaction` to "go."[1] This causes the `Transaction` to attempt to perform all of the operations, which will either succeed if all the operations succeed, or fail if one or more of them fails. If any constituent operation fails, then all operations are "undone," and it appears as if the transaction never happened.

If you don't want to worry about this sort of thing just yet, you're in luck, because you can always pass null as the transaction parameter, and calling `write()` will simply cause an object to be written, independent of any other operations.

If you call `write()` and the call returns without raising an exception, you can be assured that the object has been written into the JavaSpace. If a `RemoteException` is raised, then you cannot tell if the write was successful or not.

Read() and ReadIfExists()

The `read()` and `readIfExists()` methods use the provided template to search the JavaSpace. The template is compared against the `Entry` objects stored in the space according to the attribute matching rules in Chapter 7. If a match exists, an `Entry` will be returned, otherwise null will be returned.

Note that the JavaSpaces API provides no way to return multiple values from a search. You should specify your template so that any object that matches the template will satisfy the use to which you intend to put it. If there are multiple matching objects in the space, there is no guarantee that the same object will be returned each time. (Even if there is only one object that matches, a particular JavaSpaces implementation may return *equivalent* yet *distinct* objects each time; that is, JavaSpaces may return two objects that have identical values as reported

---

1. More accurately, the operation *will* happen, but all of the effects of it will be invisible "outside" the transaction. Again, see Chapter 18 for details.

by `equals()`, but they may be separate objects as reported by the `==` operator. So you should be sure that you are aware of this possibility if you plan on comparing objects retrieved from multiple calls to a space.)

Passing in a null template means that *any* `Entry` in the space may be returned.

The difference between these two methods is in how they use their timeout parameters. The `read()` call will return a matching `Entry` if it exists, or wait for the timeout period until a matching `Entry` appears; the `readIfExists()` call will try to return a matching `Entry` immediately if it exists, or null otherwise. It does not wait for a matching `Entry` to appear.

But if `readIfExists()` doesn't wait to see if a matching `Entry` appears, why does it have a timeout parameter? The answer has to do with the way transactions work. When `readIfExists()` is called, the matching `Entry` may be currently involved in a transaction—more accurately, it may be currently affected by some operation that is running as part of a transaction.

For example, the `write()` which placed the matching `Entry` in the JavaSpace in the first place may be one operation in a transaction that has not fully committed yet. Until the transaction commits, the `write()` hasn't "really" happened yet, and the `readIfExists()` call cannot safely return it (if the transaction were to abort, the `Entry` would be removed from the JavaSpace, since an unsuccessful transaction returns the system to the state that it would be in if the transaction had never happened).

This is where the timeout parameter comes in. The `readIfExists()` call may block for the duration specified by the timeout parameter if the only possible match is involved in a transaction. If the transaction "quiesces" before the timeout period, then the `Entry` will be returned. If the timeout elapses and there is no matching `Entry` available that is not involved in a transaction, then null will be returned.

The `read()` call also considers transactions. It will block waiting until a matching `Entry` appears, or until a matching `Entry` that is involved in a transaction stabilizes. If the timeout elapses before either of these occur, then null will be returned.

The `JavaSpace` interface defines a constant, `NO_WAIT`, which can be used as a timeout value to mean that these calls should return immediately.

Take() and TakeIfExists()

The `take()` and `takeIfExists()` calls work just like `read()` and `readIfExists()`—they match a template, possibly block until some timeout elapses, and then return a matching `Entry` or null. The difference is that the `read()` methods leave the matched `Entry` in the JavaSpace; the `take()` methods remove it from the space.

Both the `read()` and the `take()` methods can raise two kinds of exceptions. If a `RemoteException` is raised, then there was some network communication problem, and—in the case of `take()`—the removal of the matching `Entry` may or may not have taken place. If this is unacceptable, you can execute the `take()` operation in a transaction and only commit the transaction once you've already got the return value from the `take()`. This lets you separate the acquisition of the return value of the `take()` from the process of making the removal of the item "visible" to other operations.

With both the `read()` and the `take()` methods, an `UnusableEntry-Exception` occurs when the `Entry` that would have been returned cannot be deserialized—typically this is because of version errors or because the class of the `Entry` is not known to the client. When such a case happens during a `take()`, the `Entry` is still removed, even though no value will be returned to the client.

Notify()

The `notify()` method works much the same way as the method of the same name on Jini lookup services. The method takes an `Entry` as a template that will be matched against future writes to the JavaSpace. If a new `Entry` is written that matches the template, an event will be sent to the listener specified in the `notify()` call.

In addition to the template, the method takes an optional transaction parameter, the `RemoteEventListener` to send events to, a requested lease duration in milliseconds, and a `MarshalledObject` that contains a serialized object that will be returned in any events generated as a result of this registration. The call returns an `EventRegistration` object containing all the usual details—the source and type of the events that will come as a result of the registration, the `Lease` for the registration, and the last sequence number sent for the event type.

Sun's specification for JavaSpaces dictates that the service use *full ordering* for sequence numbers of events from the service. So if you see an event with sequence number 5 and then see an event with sequence number 10, you know that there have been 4 intervening matches of written `Entry` objects that resulted in events not seen by you, possibly because of network problems or out-of-order delivery.

The JavaSpaces service does not guarantee that events will be delivered to registered clients; instead it makes a "best effort" attempt. If it catches a `RemoteException` while trying to send an event to the client (through the invocation of the `notify()` method of the listener), it will periodically try to resend events until the client's lease expires.

Core Note: Documenting service behavior is important!

The sort of details just listed—how the JavaSpaces service generates sequence numbers, what its event delivery policies are—are important to most writers of clients! Since clients care about such details, there's a lesson here for service writers: While advertising such information at run time via attributes is important, good, solid documentation that's available when developers sit down to understand your service is crucial. If you write a new service, documenting such little details can go a long way toward making your service truly useful and useable by other developers.

Snapshot()

The methods just presented represent the core operations in JavaSpaces— they're all you need to know to effectively use JavaSpaces services. But with a little help, you can make your interactions with JavaSpaces much more efficient. This is where the snapshot() method comes in.

The process of serializing an object in Java can be very time-consuming, especially if the object is large or has a complicated series of references within it (hash tables of vectors, for instance). And yet every time you pass an Entry (or any other parameter for that matter) to one of the methods in the JavaSpace interface, the parameters must be serialized for transmission to the service. Some clients will have very regular access patterns: They will write the same object many times, or they may use an Entry as a template to search over and over again for matching objects.

In such cases, it may be a big win to avoid the cost of having to serialize the same object over and over again. The read(), write(), etc., methods cannot really do this for you—for them to check to see if an object you pass in is the same as an object you passed in earlier, they would have to go ahead and serialize the passed object anyway to see if it's identical to the first. So there's no win to be gained by having read() and friends do this check for you. It's something that you, as the caller of these methods, have to plan on.

This is where snapshot() comes in. When you call snapshot(), you pass in an Entry and get an Entry out. The returned Entry can be used in any future calls to the same JavaSpace that you called snapshot() on, and will avoid the repeated serialization process. Essentially, the Entry that you get back from snapshot() is a "token" that identifies the original object and can be sent without repeated serializations of the original object. By using the snapshot()'ed

`Entry` in lieu of the original, you can save a lot of cycles that would have otherwise been spent on serializing the same object over and over again.

There are a few restrictions on how you can use the `Entry` that's returned from `snapshot()`. First, the object is essentially "opaque" to you. It's not the original object you passed in, it's a specialized representation of it that's particular to the JavaSpaces implementation you're talking to. You should be sure not to make any changes to it, or treat it like the original for anything except sending to a Java-Space.

Since the returned object is a specialized representation of the original `Entry`, it is only valid as a parameter to methods on the JavaSpace that generated it. So you cannot produce a snapshot of an `Entry` on one JavaSpace service and expect it to work on another.

Likewise, you cannot transfer the snapshot version of an `Entry` to another JVM (say, via an RMI call) and expect it to work. Particular implementations of the JavaSpaces service proxy may be "smart," using a caching scheme to map snapshots of `Entry` objects to whatever they send over the wire to the back-end service. To permit implementations like this, JavaSpaces makes no guarantees that a snapshot of an `Entry` can be used from a VM other than the one in which it was generated.

You also cannot compare a snapshot to `Entry` objects that are *returned* from a JavaSpaces server. That is, all of the methods that return `Entry` objects return "non-snapshot" objects, or "real entries" in other words. Snapshots are only used as input parameters, not return values.

Finally, even though you can call `snapshot()` on a null `Entry`, the Java-Spaces specification makes no guarantees about what value is returned. The particular JavaSpaces implementation you're talking to may return null as the value of the snapshot `Entry`, so you should be aware of this.

Creating snapshots of the `Entry` objects you pass to JavaSpaces can be a big win if you're writing the same data over and over again, or searching using the same templates over and over again.

An Example: Persistent Event Logging with JavaSpaces

In this example you'll put your newly found knowledge of JavaSpaces to work in a pair of programs. The first contacts the lookup services for a Jini community, receives all the events that describe the changes in membership in the community, produces `Entry` objects that represent these changes, and logs them to a JavaSpaces service. The second program can connect up to a Java-Spaces service and copy out the logged history of a Jini community.

This is a rather simple application of JavaSpaces, but it illustrates the basics of reading and writing data, and shows an example of how to design your classes for easy searchability.

Design for Searchability

What do I mean by "design for searchability?" Recall that `Entry` objects have certain very particular semantics that apply to searching. Every `Entry` that you store in a service is searchable by its type, or by the types or values of the public, nonstatic, nontransient, nonfinal object members within it. This means that if you want to search by a member of an `Entry` that you create, you need to make sure that it meets the criteria for searchability (public, nonstatic, and so on). You also need to make sure that it's an object, rather than a primitive data type, because only objects can be used in a search.

Finally, in addition to the basic rules about the types of objects that can be searched, there's also an element of design here. Namely, because only exact matches count when you're searching by the value of an object, you may need to "pull out" certain aspects of your `Entry` types as members so that they can be searched. For example, if your `Entry` has a hash map as a member, chances are that it will be hard for a client to produce a hash map which will be an exact match for the stored one. This means that searching by value for hash maps is quite difficult. If, on the other hand, you can extract certain key elements from the hash map, and represent them as separate members in the `Entry`, they become more easily searchable.

The lesson here is that even though an `Entry` may contain a bunch of useful data, you may want to represent it differently to make it more easily searchable.

Let's look at the `Entry` classes that will be used for the community logging example. The logging program will record not only information about discovery—what new lookup services have appeared or seem to have gone away—but also information about what services are available. These types of occurrences are different, but share some common information that should be recorded—namely, the group name that the change happened in, and the time of the change.

The approach I've taken here is to define a superclass, called `WatcherEntry`, that's used by all `Entry` classes used by the community watching-and-logging program. Two specific subclasses of it, `DiscoveryEventEntry` and `ServiceEventEntry`, record information specific to discovery and service membership changes.

Take a look at `WatcherEntry` first, as shown in Listing 17–5.

Listing 17–5 `WatcherEntry.java`

```
// This is a superclass for the Entry types that
// we'll use. This stores the time that the
// event arrived, and the group name that was
// being watched.

package corejini.chapter17;

import net.jini.core.entry.Entry;

public class WatcherEntry implements Entry {
    public Long timestamp = null;
    public String group = null;

    public WatcherEntry() {
    }

    public WatcherEntry(String group, long time) {
        this.group = group;
        timestamp = new Long(time);
    }
}
```

This class is the superclass of the other two `Entry` classes you'll see shortly. It implements the `Entry` interface, and has two members which, you will note, satisfy the requirements for searchability. These two members store the group in which the `Entry` records a change, and the timestamp of the change. The timestamp here could be represented as the fundamental type `long`, but I've used the object representation `Long` so that it will be searchable.

Next, look at the two subclasses that record specific events, starting with `Dis-coveryEventEntry` (see Listing 17–6).

Listing 17–6 `DiscoveryEventEntry.java`

```java
// An Entry class that represents a DiscoveryEvent.

package corejini.chapter17;

import net.jini.core.lookup.ServiceRegistrar;
import net.jini.core.discovery.LookupLocator;
import java.rmi.RemoteException;

public class DiscoveryEventEntry extends WatcherEntry {
    public ServiceRegistrar reg;
    public LookupLocator locator = null;
    public Boolean discovered = null;

    public DiscoveryEventEntry() {
    }

    public DiscoveryEventEntry(String group,
                               ServiceRegistrar reg,
                               boolean discovered) {
        super(group, System.currentTimeMillis());

        this.reg = reg;
        try {
            this.locator = reg.getLocator();
        } catch (RemoteException ex) {
        }
        this.discovered = new Boolean(discovered);
    }
}
```

This class extends `WatcherEntry`, so it is still an `Entry` that can be used with JavaSpaces. A new `DiscoveryEventEntry` will be written to the space whenever a new lookup service is discovered, or when the watcher program discards a lookup service because it seems to be down or otherwise misbehaving. Even though a `DiscoveryEvent` may contain information about a whole set of lookup services, a separate `DiscoveryEventEntry` will be written for each lookup service in the set.

The class maintains three pieces of data—the service registrar that was discovered or discarded, the registrar's lookup locator (recall that this is a URL-like class that represents a lookup service), and a flag indicating whether this `DiscoveryEventEntry` is due to a discovery or a discard event.

Here you can see the same patterns as before—all of the data is in the form of public objects. And here I've "broken out" some data that's not strictly necessary, but makes searching easier. A lookup service's `LookupLocator` can be easily retrieved from its `ServiceRegistrar`. So any client that retrieves a `DiscoveryEventEntry` could already determine its URL given the `ServiceRegistrar` stored here. But `ServiceRegistrars` are not easily searchable—to search based on a `ServiceRegistrar`, a client would have to go through discovery itself to fetch a proxy for a lookup service, and then use this in a template to search the space. (It should be noted that there is no requirement for the proxies returned by a lookup service to be exactly the same each time. A proxy may cache state, so even if a client does fetch a proxy and try to search by it, there is no guarantee that it'll match a proxy from an earlier discovery).

But `LookupLocators` are easy to construct. If a client wishes to see the entire discovery and discard history of one particular Jini lookup service, it only needs the host and port of the lookup service to construct a `LookupLocator` that it can use for searching. This is an example of "designing for searchability"—even though keeping redundant information in the `Entry` (a locator that could be derived from the other data) may seem wasteful, it's actually a big help in searching. And there are clearly other useful bits of information you could keep in these entries, such as the service ID of the lookup service that's been discovered or discarded.

Now take a look at the `ServiceEventEntry` class (Listing 17–7).

Listing 17–7 `ServiceEventEntry.java`

```java
// An Entry that represents a ServiceEvent.

package corejini.chapter17;

import net.jini.core.lookup.ServiceID;
import net.jini.core.lookup.ServiceRegistrar;
import net.jini.core.lookup.ServiceItem;
import net.jini.core.lookup.ServiceEvent;
import net.jini.core.entry.Entry;
import net.jini.lookup.entry.Name;

public class ServiceEventEntry extends WatcherEntry {
    public ServiceRegistrar registrar = null;
    public ServiceID serviceID = null;
    // even though these details can be fetched
    // from the service item, breaking them out
    // allows independent searching.
    public ServiceItem serviceItem = null;
    public Object service = null;
    public Integer transition = null;
    public String name = null;

    public ServiceEventEntry() {
    }
```

Listing 17–7 `ServiceEventEntry.java` (continued)

```
public ServiceEventEntry(String group,
                            ServiceEvent ev){
    super(group, System.currentTimeMillis());

    registrar = (ServiceRegistrar) ev.getSource();
    serviceID = ev.getServiceID();
    serviceItem = ev.getServiceItem();
    transition = new Integer(ev.getTransition());
    if (serviceItem != null) {
        service = serviceItem.service;

        // Attach the Name as a separate member, if
        // there is one.
        Entry[] attrs = serviceItem.attributeSets;

        for (int i=0 ; i<attrs.length ; i++) {
            if (attrs[i] instanceof Name) {
                name = ((Name) attrs[i]).name;
            }
        }
    }
}
}
```

This example shows more of the same. `ServiceEventEntry` objects are written into the JavaSpaces service whenever a `ServiceEvent` is received by the watcher. It records information about the type of transition that occurred (whether a new service appeared, an existing service disappeared, or an existing service changed), as well as a set of other data that can aid in searching, or can be used by clients that retrieve these objects. For example, the `ServiceRegistrar` and `ServiceItem` objects are likely to be useful to a client that retrieves this `Entry`, but are not very useful for searching. On the other hand, the `ServiceID` and `Name` members are very useful for searching, even though they could be retrieved from the other data in the class, once downloaded. Note, here, how the `Name` attribute is retrieved from the set of attributes attached to the service's proxy, and stored separately to make it more searchable.

A Community Watcher

Now that you've seen the `Entry` types that will be stored and retrieved from the space, it's time to look at the two programs that will demonstrate how to use JavaSpaces. The first is called `DjinnWatcher`. Once started, this program tries to discover all the lookup services for the group specified on the command line. Whenever a `DiscoveryEvent` arrives, it writes a new `DiscoveryEventEntry` into a JavaSpace.

As the program finds lookup services, it registers with each to receive all types of events from it. This way, the program will be notified when any type of transition occurs in the lookup service, and can store these as `ServiceEventEntry` objects.

Let's look at the program as shown in Listing 17–8.

Listing 17–8 `DjinnWatcher.java`

```java
// Watch for DiscoveryEvents and ServiceEvents for
// a given community.  Create Entry objects for these
// and write them into a space.

package corejini.chapter17;

import net.jini.space.JavaSpace;
import net.jini.core.lookup.ServiceRegistrar;
import net.jini.core.lookup.ServiceEvent;
import net.jini.core.lookup.ServiceTemplate;
import net.jini.core.lease.Lease;
import net.jini.core.entry.Entry;
import net.jini.core.event.RemoteEvent;
import net.jini.core.event.RemoteEventListener;
import net.jini.core.event.EventRegistration;
import net.jini.discovery.DiscoveryEvent;
import net.jini.discovery.LookupDiscovery;
import net.jini.discovery.DiscoveryListener;
import net.jini.lease.LeaseRenewalManager;
import java.util.ArrayList;
import java.rmi.RemoteException;
import java.rmi.RMISecurityManager;
import java.rmi.server.UnicastRemoteObject;
import java.io.IOException;
```

Listing 17–8 `DjinnWatcher.java` (continued)

```java
public class DjinnWatcher implements Runnable {
    protected Class[] types = { JavaSpace.class };
    protected String group;
    protected ServiceTemplate tmpl =
        new ServiceTemplate(null, types, null);
    protected ArrayList regs = new ArrayList();
    protected JavaSpace javaSpace = null;
    protected LeaseRenewalManager leaseManager = null;
    protected static final int ALL_FLAGS =
        ServiceRegistrar.TRANSITION_MATCH_NOMATCH |
        ServiceRegistrar.TRANSITION_NOMATCH_MATCH |
        ServiceRegistrar.TRANSITION_MATCH_MATCH;
    protected EvtListener evtListener;
    protected LookupDiscovery disco;

    // An inner class for listening for remote events.
    class EvtListener extends UnicastRemoteObject
        implements RemoteEventListener {
        public EvtListener() throws RemoteException {
        }

        public void notify(RemoteEvent ev) {
            if (!(ev instanceof ServiceEvent))
                return;

            ServiceEvent sev = (ServiceEvent) ev;

            // Write the data into the space.
            writeEventData(javaSpace, sev);
        }
    }
```

Listing 17–8 `DjinnWatcher.java` (continued)

```
// An inner class for listening for discovery events.
class DiscListener implements DiscoveryListener {
    public void discovered(DiscoveryEvent ev) {
        boolean spaceNotYetFound = (javaSpace == null);
        ServiceRegistrar[] newregs = ev.getRegistrars();
        for (int i=0, size=newregs.length; i<size; i++){
            if (!regs.contains(newregs[i])) {
                // If we don't have a space yet, search
                // for it.  Otherwise, start getting
                // events from the new registrar!
                regs.add(newregs[i]);

                if (javaSpace == null) {
                    // This will register for events
                    // in all known registrars.
                    findJavaSpace(newregs[i]);
                } else {
                    registerForEvents(newregs[i]);
                }
            }
        }

        // We only log discovery events received
        // *after* we find a space.  So if we're still
        // processing the event that found the space for
        // us, we just bail.  spaceNotYetFound records
        // whether the space was found at the time this
        // method started.
        if (spaceNotYetFound)
            return;

        // After adding each to the list, and
        // looking for JavaSpaces, we can log new
        // discovery events if we've found a space
        // already.
        if (javaSpace != null) {
            writeEventData(javaSpace, ev, true);
        }
    }
```

> **Listing 17–8** `DjinnWatcher.java` (continued)

```
public void discarded(DiscoveryEvent ev) {
        ServiceRegistrar[] deadregs =
                            ev.getRegistrars();
        for (int i=0,size=deadregs.length; i<size;
i++){

            regs.remove(deadregs[i]);
        }

        // Log the event, if we've found a space.
        if (javaSpace != null) {
            writeEventData(javaSpace, ev, false);
        }
    }
}

public DjinnWatcher(String group)
    throws IOException, RemoteException {
    leaseManager = new LeaseRenewalManager();
    evtListener = new EvtListener();
    this.group = group;

    if (group == null) {
        System.out.println("Watching public group");
        disco = new
            LookupDiscovery(new String[] { "" });
    } else {
        System.out.println("Watching group " + group);
        disco = new
            LookupDiscovery(new String[] { group });
    }

    disco.addDiscoveryListener(new DiscListener());
}
```

Listing 17–8 `DjinnWatcher.java` (continued)

```
protected void findJavaSpace(ServiceRegistrar reg) {
    if (javaSpace != null)
        return;

    try {
        javaSpace = (JavaSpace) reg.lookup(tmpl);
        if (javaSpace == null) {
            return;
        }
        System.out.println("Found a space!");
    } catch (RemoteException ex) {
        System.err.println("Error doing lookup: " +
                        ex.getMessage());
        disco.discard(reg);
        return;
    }

    for (int i=0, size=regs.size() ; i<size ; i++) {
        System.out.println("Registering for events at "
                + "previously-found registrar: "
                + regs.get(i));
        registerForEvents((ServiceRegistrar)
                        regs.get(i));
    }
}
```

Listing 17–8 `DjinnWatcher.java` (continued)

```java
    // Log discovery events.
    protected void writeEventData(JavaSpace space,
                                  DiscoveryEvent ev,
                                  boolean discovered) {
        System.out.println("Writing DiscoveryEvent " + ev);

        try {
            ServiceRegistrar[] evtregs =
                ev.getRegistrars();
            for (int i=0 ; i<evtregs.length ; i++) {
                DiscoveryEventEntry entry =
                    new DiscoveryEventEntry(group,
                                            evtregs[i],
                                            discovered);
                Lease lease = space.write(entry, null,
                                    60 * 60 * 1000);
                leaseManager.renewUntil(lease,
                                    Lease.ANY, null);
            }
        } catch (Exception ex) {
            System.err.println("Error writing event: " +
                            ex.getMessage());
        }
    }

    // Log service events.
    protected void writeEventData(JavaSpace space,
                                  ServiceEvent ev) {
        System.out.println("Writing ServiceEvent " + ev);

        try {
            Lease lease;
            ServiceEventEntry entry =
                new ServiceEventEntry(group, ev);

            lease = space.write(entry, null,
                            60 * 60 * 1000);
            leaseManager.renewUntil(lease, Lease.ANY, null);
        } catch (Exception ex) {
            System.err.println("Error writing event: " +
                            ex.getMessage());
        }
    }
```

Listing 17–8 DjinnWatcher.java (continued)

```
protected void registerForEvents(ServiceRegistrar reg){
    try {
        ServiceTemplate search =
            new ServiceTemplate(null, null, null);
        EventRegistration evtreg;
        evtreg = reg.notify(search, ALL_FLAGS,
                            evtListener, null,
                            60 * 60 * 1000);
        leaseManager.renewUntil(evtreg.getLease(),
                            Lease.ANY, null);
    } catch (RemoteException ex) {
        System.err.println("Error soliciting events: " +
                            ex.getMessage());
        disco.discard(reg);
    }
}

public void run() {
    while (true) {
        try {
            Thread.sleep(Integer.MAX_VALUE);
        } catch (InterruptedException ex) {
        }
    }
}

public static void main(String[] args) {
    String group = null;

    if (System.getSecurityManager() == null) {
        System.setSecurityManager(
            new RMISecurityManager());
    }

    if (args.length == 1) {
        group = args[0];
    } else if (args.length > 1) {
        System.err.println(
                "Usage: DjinnWatcher [<group>]");
    }
```

Listing 17–8 `DjinnWatcher.java` (continued)

```
        try {
            DjinnWatcher dw = new DjinnWatcher(group);
            new Thread(dw).start();
            System.out.println("Cruising!");
        } catch (Exception ex) {
            System.err.println("Error!   " + ex);
        }
    }
}
```

The `DjinnWatcher` program takes a group name on the command line. You can pass "`public`" here if you want the program to watch the public group. When the program starts, it creates a `LeaseRenewalManager` to handle its leases on the objects it will store in the JavaSpaces service, and—following the usual pattern—creates an inner class for listening for discovery events and an inner class (which is a remote object) for receiving remote events from lookup services.

Before the `DjinnWatcher` can begin logging events, it must find a JavaSpace through the usual lookup mechanisms. So whenever a new lookup service is discovered, the program looks to see if a JavaSpace is registered there if it has not already found one. When a JavaSpaces service is found for the first time, the program contacts all the previously found lookup services to register to receive events from them; the program will also register to receive events from all lookup services that it finds in the future.

Note that there is a limitation with this program and its peer (which you'll see in a bit) that you should be aware of. The program only discovers lookup services in the community it's been asked to watch, and only looks for JavaSpaces services in those communities. So you need to make sure that—for the version of the program shown here—you run a JavaSpaces service that's a member of the community you're planning on watching. This is simply a limitation of this program, not a limitation of JavaSpaces. You can easily change the code to find a lookup service in a different community, but this approach is the simplest for illustrating the techniques that are covered in this chapter.

Likewise, the program stores all the `Entry` objects it writes into the *first* Java-Spaces service it encounters. So you should probably only run one JavaSpace for this example.

The `findJavaSpace()` call works just as you would expect—it uses the `lookup()` method on the lookup services it finds to search for a JavaSpaces service. The `registerForEvents()` call also uses methods you've seen before. It calls `notify()` on the lookup service to ask to receive events in the future, and passes the inner `EvtListener` instance as the listener for events. The management of the renewal of the leases granted on each event registration is performed by the `LeaseRenewalManager` created earlier.

The program shown here is doing quite a bit of work in the thread that does discovery—it is doing a remote call to search the lookup service for JavaSpaces services, and registering with lookup services to receive events. In a "real" application, you would want to do these slow operations in a separate, short-lived thread so that the discovery process isn't blocked while you're doing other things. But the situation isn't too dire for the example here.

Also note that the code here calls `discard()` on the `LookupDiscovery` object whenever a `RemoteException` is caught in `findJavaSpace()` or `registerForEvents()`. Remember that a call to `discard()` tells the discovery machiney that a lookup service is not responding; this allows it to be discovered again, if it returns to the community. Calling `discard()` on a `LookupDiscovery` object causes that object to invoke the `discarded()` method on the discovery listener, so that it can clean up its state as needed.

The main work done by the program is to write `Entry` objects into the JavaSpaces service when it receives a `DiscoveryEvent` or a `ServiceEvent`. These tasks are handled by the two versions of the `writeEventData()` call. One takes a `DiscoveryEvent` and the other takes a `ServiceEvent`. Each `DiscoveryEvent` can contain discovery information for multiple lookup services. So the code here breaks these up into multiple, discrete `DiscoveryEventEntry` objects so that each is represented separately in the log of the history. The `Entry` objects are created and then written into the space (with no transaction), and the lease for the stored object is passed to the `LeaseRenewalManager` for renewal.

The version of `writeEventData()` that takes a `ServiceEvent` is similar. A new `ServiceEventEntry` is constructed from the event and written to the space.

Note here the use of a thread that does nothing but keep the VM from exiting. Since this application uses no other libraries—such as AWT—that would start their own threads, this step is necessary so that the VM doesn't terminate after `main()` completes.

A Consumer of Logged Event Data

Next, you'll see a program that can retrieve stored information about a community and display it. The model that `DjinnConsumer` (Listing 17–9) follows is that, after a `DjinnWatcher` has been running for a while, you can start the consumer, give it a group name, and it will fetch all the accumulated `Entry` objects for the group.

The same limitations that applied to the `DjinnWatcher` implementation apply here—the program will only contact a JavaSpace service that's a member of the group for which the user wants history information, and the program contacts the first JavaSpaces service it finds. So you should make sure that you run a single JavaSpaces service in the group you're logging, unless you decide to modify this program to make it more robust.

Take a look at the code.

Listing 17–9 `DjinnConsumer.java`

```java
// Contact a JavaSpaces service and retrieve the
// logged history for a single group.

package corejini.chapter17;

import net.jini.space.JavaSpace;
import net.jini.core.lookup.ServiceTemplate;
import net.jini.core.lookup.ServiceRegistrar;
import net.jini.core.entry.*;
import net.jini.discovery.DiscoveryEvent;
import net.jini.discovery.DiscoveryListener;
import net.jini.discovery.LookupDiscovery;
import java.rmi.RemoteException;
import java.rmi.RMISecurityManager;
import java.io.IOException;

public class DjinnConsumer implements Runnable {
    protected Class[] types = { JavaSpace.class };
    protected String group;
    protected ServiceTemplate tmpl =
        new ServiceTemplate(null, types, null);
    protected JavaSpace javaSpace = null;


    // An inner class for discovery.
    class DiscListener implements DiscoveryListener {
        public synchronized void discovered(DiscoveryEvent
                                                         ev) {
            if (javaSpace != null)
                return;
```

Listing 17–9 `DjinnConsumer.java` (continued)

```java
            ServiceRegistrar[] regs = ev.getRegistrars();
            for (int i=0, size=regs.length ; i<size ; i++)
{
                JavaSpace js = findJavaSpace(regs[i]);
                if (js != null) {
                    javaSpace = js;
                    doit();
                }
            }
        }

        public void discarded(DiscoveryEvent ev) {
        }
    }

    public DjinnConsumer(String group) throws IOException
{
        LookupDiscovery disco;
        this.group = group;

        if (group == null) {
            System.out.println("Fetching public history");
            disco = new
                LookupDiscovery(new String[] { "" });
        } else {
            System.out.println("Fetching history for " +
                                            group);
            disco = new
                LookupDiscovery(new String[] { group });
        }

        disco.addDiscoveryListener(new DiscListener());
    }

    // Find and return a JavaSpace, if it exists at the
    // registrar.
    protected JavaSpace findJavaSpace(ServiceRegistrar
                                            reg) {
        if (javaSpace != null)
            return null;
```

Listing 17–9 `DjinnConsumer.java` (continued)

```java
    try {
        JavaSpace javaSpace = (JavaSpace)
                                    reg.lookup(tmpl);
        if (javaSpace != null) {
            System.out.println("Found a space!");
            return javaSpace;
        }
    } catch (RemoteException ex) {
        System.err.println("Error doing lookup: " +
                            ex.getMessage());
        return null;
    }

    return null;
}

  protected void doit() {
    System.out.println("Searching for history for " +
                                        group);

    // Make a template to search for the group
    // passed on the command line, any timestamp.
    WatcherEntry tmpl = new WatcherEntry();
    tmpl.group = group;
    tmpl.timestamp = null;

    try {
        // Snapshot it, since we'll be using it
        // over and over.
        Entry snapshot = javaSpace.snapshot(tmpl);
        boolean done = false;
        int i = 0;

        while (!done) {
            Entry result =
                    javaSpace.takeIfExists(snapshot,
                            null,
                            JavaSpace.NO_WAIT);

            if (result != null) {
                printResult(i++, result);
            }
```

Listing 17–9 DjinnConsumer.java (continued)

```
                done = (result == null);
            }

            // Quit once we've got everything.
            System.out.println("Done!");
            System.exit(1);
        } catch (Exception ex) {
            System.err.println("bogus:   " +
                                    ex.getMessage());
            ex.printStackTrace();
        }
    }

    protected void printResult(int i, Entry result) {
        if (result instanceof DiscoveryEventEntry) {
            DiscoveryEventEntry disc =
                (DiscoveryEventEntry) result;
            System.out.println("[" + i + "] " +
                        (disc.discovered.booleanValue() ?
                        "discovered" : "discarded") +
                        " " + disc.locator.toString());
        } else if (result instanceof ServiceEventEntry) {
            ServiceEventEntry serv =
                (ServiceEventEntry) result;
            System.out.println("[" + i + "] " + serv.name +
                        " " +  serv.transition + " " +
                        (serv.service == null ? "" :
                    serv.service.getClass().getName()) +
                        " " + serv.serviceID);
        } else {
            // Someone else added an entry type?
            System.out.println(result);
        }
    }

    public void run() {
        while (true) {
            try {
                Thread.sleep(Integer.MAX_VALUE);
            } catch (InterruptedException ex) {
            }
        }
    }
}
```

Listing 17–9 `DjinnConsumer.java` (continued)

```
public static void main(String[] args) {
    String group = null;

    if (System.getSecurityManager() == null) {
        System.setSecurityManager(
                        new RMISecurityManager());
    }

    if (args.length == 1) {
        group = args[0];
    } else if (args.length > 1) {
        System.err.println("Usage: DjinnConsumer " +
                                        "[<group>]");
    }

    try {
        DjinnConsumer dc = new DjinnConsumer(group);
        new Thread(dc).start();
        System.out.println("Cruising!");
    } catch (Exception ex) {
        System.err.println("Error!  " + ex);
    }
}
}
```

This program is a bit shorter than `DjinnWatcher`, as it doesn't have to solicit events from any lookup services, or maintain a list of discovered lookup services, or log any event data.

The code defines an inner class, `DiscListener`, to perform discovery. Whenever a new lookup service is found for the specified group, `findJavaSpace()` is called to search for a JavaSpaces service and, if one is found, the `doit()` method is called to retrieve the `Entry` objects that describe the community's history.

As in the last example, this code is doing a lot of work in the discovery thread—too much for a "real-world" application, but not too bad for an example designed to show off how to use JavaSpaces. Be sure that if you have to do a lot of computation or invoke any remote calls as a result of discovery in your programs, you create a short-lived thread to do the work without blocking the discovery thread.

The most interesting part of the program is in the `doit()` method, so take a look at that. The `DjinnConsumer` is interested in all `Entry` objects that describe the history of the community—whether they're of type `DiscoveryEventEntry` or `ServiceEventEntry`. The easiest way to search for both is to search for their superclass, `WatcherEntry`. Here, the fact that JavaSpaces understands the Java type system is a big win: The program can search using a `WatcherEntry` as a template and find all the specific `Entry` objects that are instances of classes derived from it.

In this example, the code needs to find all the objects that describe a particular group, so it creates a `WatcherEntry`, sets its `group` member to the group being searched for, and sets the `timestamp` to null. This says that the code wants to match any `Entry` that is of class `WatcherEntry` (or a subclass), and that has an *exact* match in the `group` field for the group. The `timestamp` value is treated as a "don't care" since it's null; it's effectively a wildcard value that will match any value of `timestamp`.

The JavaSpace APIs only allow a client to fetch one item at a time. Since this application will be using the same template over and over again, I've created a "snapshot" of it here. Recall that a snapshot is a way to save yourself the time of serializing an `Entry` over and over again.

After this, `DjinnConsumer` sits in a loop, taking matching items out of the JavaSpace until there are no more. A version of the `take()` call is used so that the code will remove each item as it is matched; `takeIfExists()` is specifically used because the code should try to remove only items that exist at the time the method is called—you don't want to sit around waiting for new items to appear in the future. To prevent the call from blocking because of objects that may be involved in an "unsettled" transaction, the `JavaSpaces.NO_WAIT` flag is used. This indicates that even though a potentially matching `Entry` may be involved in a transaction, the call shouldn't wait for the transaction to complete. In such an event, the method will simply return null to indicate that there are no more matching `Entry` objects in the space.

When each `Entry` is retrieved, it is tested for null and then passed to `print-Result()` for display. Remember that the `take()` and `read()` methods can return null if they don't match any items, or if the matched items are involved in transactions that don't complete before a timeout period elapses. So you need to make sure that you don't just blindly use a returned result without checking it. The loop continues until `takeIfExists()` returns null, which the program interprets as exhaustion of the event data, at which point `DjinnConsumer` exits.

The program as shown here uses the retrieved objects in a very simple way—they are simply printed to standard output in the order they are fetched. You could imagine some more sophisticated visualizations or presentations of the data, or even some less sophisticated ones, such as simply ordering the data based on timestamp, or removing duplicate services by looking at the service IDs in `ServiceEventEntries`.

Compiling and Running the Programs

Okay, it's time to get these things running! Unlike most of the previous examples we've looked at, these two programs aren't clients or servers to each other—they're both clients of JavaSpaces, but don't need to share any downloadable code with each other. In fact, it would be completely acceptable to bundle both of these programs and their associated files into the same JAR file, and allow users to run either from the same JAR.

So I'm going to compile them both to the client directory, and forego the enforced separation that I've usually followed when building a client and a server program. Note that even though you're now building a program to use the JavaSpaces APIs, you don't need to include any JavaSpaces JAR files in the CLASSPATH! Only the net.jini.space.JavaSpace interface is needed at compile time, and that exists in the jini-ext.jar file; the implementation will be delivered at run time by the Jini infrastructure.

On Windows:

```
javac -classpath C:\files;
                 C:\jini1_1\lib\jini-core.jar;
                 C:\jini1_1\lib\jini-ext.jar;
                 C:\jini1_1\lib\sun-util.jar;
                 C:\client
      -d C:\client
        C:\files\corejini.chapter17.DjinnWatcher.java
        C:\files\corejini.chapter17.DjinnConsumer.java
```

On UNIX:

```
javac -classpath /files:
                 /files/jini1_1/lib/jini-core.jar:
                 /files/jini1_1/lib/jini-ext.jar:
                 /files/jini1_1/lib/sun-util.jar:
                 /files/client
        -  d /files/client
        /files/corejini/chapter17/DjinnWatcher.java
        /files/corejini/chapter17/DjinnConsumer.java
```

The only remote object in this example is the nested EvtListener class in DjinnWatcher. You'll need to generate stubs for it via rmic, and copy the stubs to the client-dl directory.

On Windows:

```
rmic -classpath C:\jini1_1\lib\jini-core.jar;
```

```
                C:\jini1_1\lib\jini-ext.jar;
                C:\jini1_1\lib\sun-util.jar;
                C:\client
      -d C:\client
      corejini.chapter17.DjinnWatcher.EvtListener

mkdir C:\client-dl\corejini\chapter17
cd C:\client\corejini\chapter17
copy DjinnWatcher$EvtListener_Stub.class
    C:\client-dl\corejini\chapter17
```

On UNIX:

```
rmic -classpath /files/jini1_1/lib/jini-core.jar:
                /files/jini1_1/lib/jini-ext.jar:
                /files/jini1_1/lib/sun-util.jar:
                /files/client
      -d /files/client
        corejini.chapter17.DjinnWatcher.EvtListener

mkdir /files/client-dl/corejini/chapter17
cd /files/client/corejini/chapter17
cp DjinnWatcher\$EvtListener_Stub.class
    /files/client-dl/corejini/chapter17
```

Now you're set to run! Start up the DjinnWatcher program first, and let it run for a while. While it's running, you may want to start or stop some of the services you've seen earlier in the book, just to give the watcher something to record. Be sure to give the watcher a group to watch; here I've used "public."

On Windows:

```
java -cp C:\jini1_1\lib\jini-core.jar;
        C:\jini1_1\lib\jini-ext.jar;
        C:\jini1_1\lib\sun-util.jar;
        C:\client;
     -Djava.rmi.server.codebase=http://myhost:8086
     -Djava.security.policy=C:\policy
        corejini.chapter17.DjinnWatcher public
```

On UNIX:

```
java -cp /files/jini1_1/lib/jini-core.jar:
        /files/jini1_1/lib/jini-ext.jar:
        /files/jini1_1/lib/sun-util.jar:
```

```
     /files/client:
   -Djava.rmi.server.codebase=http://myhost:8086
   -Djava.security.policy=/files/policy
      corejini.chapter17.DjinnWatcher public
```

As the watcher runs, you should see output as it finds a JavaSpaces service, and logs events to it. Obviously, the more things going on in your community, the more event traces you'll see.

Watching public group

Found a space!

Registering for events at previously-found registrar: com.sun.jini.reggie.Regis-trarProxy@ac2984f

Cruising!

Writing ServiceEvent

com.sun.jini.reggie.RegistrarEvent[source=com.sun.jini.reggie.Registrar-Proxy@ac2984f]

Writing ServiceEvent

com.sun.jini.reggie.RegistrarEvent[source=com.sun.jini.reggie.Registrar-Proxy@ac2984f]

Writing ServiceEvent

com.sun.jini.reggie.RegistrarEvent[source=com.sun.jini.reggie.Registrar-Proxy@ac2984f]

Writing ServiceEvent

com.sun.jini.reggie.RegistrarEvent[source=com.sun.jini.reggie.Registrar-Proxy@ac2984f]

Writing ServiceEvent

com.sun.jini.reggie.RegistrarEvent[source=com.sun.jini.reggie.Registrar-Proxy@ac2984f]

Writing ServiceEvent

com.sun.jini.reggie.RegistrarEvent[source=com.sun.jini.reggie.Registrar-Proxy@ac2984f]

Next, run the consumer program. Note that the consumer, since it exports no downloadable code, doesn't need to have a codebase property set. (It *will*, however, be using downloaded code—namely the proxy for the JavaSpaces service—so it needs a security policy file.) Be sure to use the same group name for the consumer as you did for the watcher.

On Windows:

```
java -cp C:\jini1_1\lib\jini-core.jar;
        C:\jini1_1\lib\jini-ext.jar;
```

```
        C:\jini1_1\lib\sun-util.jar;
        C:\client
    -Djava.security.policy=C:\policy
        corejini.chapter17.DjinnConsumer public
```

On UNIX:

```
java -cp /files/jini1_1/lib/jini-core.jar:
        /files/jini1_1/lib/jini-ext.jar:
        /files/jini1_1/lib/sun-util.jar:
        /files/client
    -Djava.security.policy=/files/policy
        corejini.chapter17.DjinnConsumer public
```

When the client runs, it'll fetch all the history for the group you've specified, and dump it to standard out.

Fetching public history
Found a space!
Searching for history for public
[0] null 2 corejini.chapter5.HelloWorldServiceProxy
b227e764-0e84-4bcf-adca-82f9a98445f1
[1] null 2 corejini.chapter12.LeaseServiceProxy
ce95e89f-a06f-419c-b167-87cdbac61caa
[2] null 1 b227e764-0e84-4bcf-adca-82f9a98445f1
[3] null 2 corejini.chapter5.HelloWorldServiceProxy
b227e764-0e84-4bcf-adca-82f9a98445f1
[4] null 2 corejini.chapter12.LeaseServiceProxy
f2a50050-952e-4c49-9379-e2db24ec4dab
Cruising!
Done!

The output here shows five events that were logged for the public group. In this case, there were two separate instances of two services, HelloWorldService and LeaseService, started after the watcher began its logging. (You know that these services started because of the transition number—"2" is the numerical form of the TRANSITION_NOMATCH_MATCH flag.) The "*null*" here is where the names of the services would be, if they had names. And the long string of numbers and letters at the end is the service ID for each.

This example has shown a simple pair of applications—a writer and a reader—that can cooperate together to produce and display histories of the activity in a given Jini community. The minimalist JavaSpaces API makes applications like this easy. And JavaSpaces follows the basic paradigms of interaction in

Jini—attribute-based search, leased resources, notification using the Jini remote events model—making it a good and useful citizen in many Jini communities.

Applying JavaSpaces to Distributed Computing Problems

This chapter has focused on one particular and obvious use of the JavaSpaces programming model: as a persistent shared repository for objects. Such a use is easy to understand, and has immediate utility for many applications that need to store objects or make them available to others.

But JavaSpaces can also be used in a different way: It can be used as the complete basis for a new distributed systems programming paradigm. This was the original intent of the Linda work on which JavaSpaces was based. While Linda certainly could be used as a simple storage engine, the real goal was to provide a new model for building distributed applications. In this new model, distributed systems would be built around "flows" of objects from application to application, coordinated through the central Linda tuple space.

The idea here is that rather than building custom, remote communication interfaces or protocols for each new distributed application, applications can be defined in terms of the set of objects they write into the tuple space and the set of objects they retrieve from the tuple space. To move the analogy into Java terms, rather than defining and refining new RMI remote interfaces for each new task, the JavaSpaces interfaces would be the common APIs for interaction between applications. Applications would define their own set of `Entry` objects, and associate their own semantics with these objects.

Look at a distributed compute server as an example. Say you want to build a program to speed up builds of a large software project—sort of a distributed `make` application. In the traditional approach, you'd define a set of interfaces that the various components of the system would use to talk to each other. A `Controller` object might do the dependency analysis of the source code and farm out each chunk to one of a set of `Builder` processes. The `Controller` might have methods to `createJob()` to start a new build, and `checkJobStatus()` to see how a build is going. Each `Builder` might support methods to `startBuild()`, `stopBuild()`, and `checkStatus()` to return the status of a compilation local to that one builder. These interfaces would also likely support event passing, so that the central `Controller` could know when an individual build has finished.

In the JavaSpaces model, each of the tasks that needed to be done for a distributed `make` program would be mapped into the concepts of `Entry` objects in a JavaSpace. For example, a centralized coordinating `Controller` process could write `BuildTask Entry` objects into a JavaSpace, while the separate `Builders` would retrieve these objects whenever they were ready to compile a new chunk of the code. When each `Builder` finished a chunk, it would write a `BuildStatus` object into the space, where it would be retrieved by the `Controller`.

In this model, the JavaSpaces service takes care of the mechanics of event propagation and searching for new tasks. New `Builders` can be added dynamically without having to tell the `Controller`—if you run a new one, it simply begins doing `take()` operations on a space when it finds a new `BuildTask`. So it's easy to dynamically expand the capacity of the system.

And rather than defining separate interfaces for each component of the system, the `JavaSpaces` interface is the only API that components of the system need to understand. Rather than providing a host of new methods that need to be implemented and understood by all parties, the handful of JavaSpaces methods are sufficient to build the entire distributed application. All of the semantics of the task at hand get encoded into the objects stored to and retrieved from the space. And many applications can share this same infrastructure to build their systems.

This distributed `make` case is only one example of the sort of applications that could be built on top of JavaSpaces. Addressing this use of the JavaSpaces paradigm is really beyond the scope of this book. The focus here is on enabling you to build and use Jini services, and understanding the mechanics of distributed computing using the tools that Jini provides. JavaSpaces provides another programming model that is logically separate from Jini, but can be used by Jini applications, which can benefit from it.

Further Reading

If you're interested in the research that the JavaSpaces work was based on, you can check out the Linda project home page at Yale:

```
http://www.cs.yale.edu/HTML/YALE/CS/Linda/linda.html
```

The T Spaces work at IBM's Almaden Research Center represents a tuple space-based approach to building distributed systems. `T Spaces` is more functional, and also more complex, than JavaSpaces, which has an extremely minimalistic programming model. The home page for this project is at:

```
http://www.almaden.ibm.com/cs/TSpaces/index.html
```

Finally, the Java Distributed Computing page has information on JavaSpaces, including details of a nifty demo show at the 1998 JavaOne conference in San

Francisco. There, JavaSpaces was used to build a massively parallel compute server out of the thousands of "JavaRing" devices given to attendees—these devices were literally rings that you wore on your finger, and had an embedded Java VM inside them. Using JavaSpaces, parts of a large fractal image were parceled out to individual rings for computation, and then reassembled into a whole.

This page is also a good starting point if you're interested in leveraging the JavaSpaces programming model as a way to build distributed applications as flows of objects.

```
http://www.java.sun.com/products/javaspaces/
```

What's Next?

The next chapter in the book addresses the main issue that I punted on in this chapter—transactions! In the next chapter, you'll look at what sorts of safety guarantees transactions can provide, what the Jini model for distributed transactions is, and see how to use transactions to coordinate operations across multiple services.

Distributed Transactions

Chapter 18

This chapter is dedicated to one of the more seldom used aspects of Jini—distributed transactions. Transactions, as mentioned in Chapter 3, are an important tool for building reliable systems in which computation must span a number of components.

But of the core concepts in Jini—discovery, lookup, leasing, remote events, and transactions—transactions are likely to be the one that you use the least. Of the standard services that ship with Jini, only JavaSpaces uses transactions and even there, transactions are optional.

Still, an understanding of transactions is important for understanding Jini. If you're building Jini-aware programs that need to interact with multiple services, and ensure that results that involve more than one service are carried out accurately, then transactions are the tool that you need.

In this chapter, I'll briefly revisit what transactions can do for you: How transactions can mitigate some of the problems in distributed systems that arise from partial failures, and how transactions can be used to keep a computation in a known state at all times. I'll talk about the classical transaction model that you may be familiar with from database programming, and you'll see how the Jini model differs from that. You'll also see how the Jini transaction APIs are used, particularly from the standpoint of a client application using transactions to coordinate a number of services. Finally, you'll explore an example that uses transactions to coordinate multiple JavaSpaces services.

Consistency and the Evils of Partial Failure

Chapter 2 talked about the differences between building stand-alone applications and true distributed systems. As you recall from that chapter, the key distinction between a stand-alone system and a distributed one is the fact that distributed systems can suffer *partial failures*.

A partial failure is when one component of the system fails, leaving other components functioning. Stand-alone systems, in contrast, typically suffer from *total failures* where the entire application (or the machine on which the application is running) simply dies. Paradoxically, while a total failure might on the surface seem to be a much more dire event, partial failures are the source of many of the problems in distributed computing. There are a couple of reasons for this.

First, detecting whether a partial failure exists can sometimes be difficult. You may not even be able to tell reliably that a component has failed in a distributed system. In a stand-alone system, typically either the system is up and running, or it's crashed; there are no "fuzzy" circumstances.

Second, you may not know if the component that is not responding actually did the work you asked it to do. Say you ask a remote database to withdraw $100 from an account and you never get a response back from it. Should you ask it to do the work again, when it comes back up? Should you assume that it completed?

Total failures in a stand-alone system cause work to stop: The system isn't functioning, and nothing will happen until the system is brought back up. But partial failures in a distributed system can cause *inconsistencies* in the state of the system. These inconsistencies may go unnoticed and can even spread through the system unless you're careful.

A Classical Transaction Model

Stand-alone applications can still encounter consistency problems. Think of a stand-alone database, running on a single machine. This database may dutifully process transfers between bank accounts, until one day it crashes unexpectedly. The database cannot predict when it is going to crash, clearly—if it could, then it would take steps not to crash! And so there is the chance that a crash will occur right in the middle of a transfer, say when money has been removed from one account but not yet added to another. If a crash occurs at just the wrong time, the database could come back up in an inconsistent state—money has been subtracted from the first account but not yet added to the second; this cash is essentially lost to the bit bucket.

To address these problems, the database community adopted the notion of *transactions*. A transaction is a group of computations—such as subtracting an amount from one account and adding it to another—which must be completely executed as a group for the result to be considered valid. Transactions provide a way to "cluster" operations together and make the execution of all of them appear to be like the execution of a single operation: either the operation happens or it doesn't.

Transactions provide what are often called the "ACID" properties to data manipulations, so called because of the initials of the four individual properties:

- Atomicity. Either all of the operations grouped under a transaction succeed, or they all fail: They execute as if they were a single atomic operation.
- Consistency. After the transaction completes, the system should be in a consistent, understandable state. The notion of "consistency" is something that may only be discernible by the human users of the system—therefore, transactions are merely a way to help ensure consistency, not guarantees of consistency itself.
- Isolation. Transactions don't affect one another until they complete. That is, the effects of a transaction that is in the middle of executing will appear "invisible" to other computations outside of that transaction. This property ensures that computations won't be based on bogus data that may change if a transaction fails.
- Durability. Once a transaction completes successfully—meaning that all of its changes have been made permanent—then these changes must not be lost due to any subsequent failure or crash. The results of the transaction must be at least as persistent as the entities that use them.

You should be sure that you understand that transactions don't guarantee that a set of grouped operations will always succeed. Transactions merely guarantee that the operations will either all succeed or all fail, and that—most importantly—the system can tell which has happened.

Transactions in stand-alone systems most commonly ensure that the system will return to a known state after a crash. In the classical banking example, if the debit and credit operations are grouped together into a transaction, then—even if the system crashes in the middle of the transaction—the system guarantees that it will come back into a known state. Either the transaction will have fully completed, and the system can detect this and carry on with its business, or the trans-action will have failed in the middle, in which case none of the component operations take effect and the entire transaction can be retried later.

But even in stand-alone systems, transactions can be used to guard against the failure of individual component operations. In a database, one operation in a transaction may fail because it would cause deadlock or because a disk is full, for instance. Here again, transactions ensure that *none* of the related operations in the transaction take place if any one of them fail.[1]

Core Note: Filesystems have these same problems

I've focused on databases as an example of a system in which crash recovery can be aided by transactions. But you may not know that everyday computer filesystems have many of these same problems!

If you've ever flipped the power switch on a Windows machine without properly shutting it down, you may have been greeted by the dreaded "System not properly shut down. Must run scandisk" message. What has happened here is that the system has been unexpectedly shut down, and must check itself for any inconsistencies. In general, the operating system will not allow itself to fully boot until any inconsistencies have been removed. The scandisk program scans the entire disk looking for information that might be in an inconsistent state.

The same benefits that transactions bring to databases can be applied to filesystems as well. "Journaling" or "log-based" filesystems essentially use a transaction model like the one described here to ensure that filesystems come back up into a known state after a crash. By doing filesystem updates in the context of a transaction, you can guard against data loss, prevent inconsistencies, and save yourself the time and hassle of having to run scandisk after a crash.

Just one more example of the power of transactions!

---

1. This example is actually getting close to the errors that can happen in distributed systems, where only one constituent operation in a transaction fails. Still, in the stand-alone case, it is easy to detect that an operation has failed. This is not always the case in a distributed system.

Two-Phase Commit

Let's look at how transactions actually work. I'll start off by explaining the basic transaction *protocols*—the steps of the transaction process—in the stand-alone case, before moving on to how transactions work in a distributed setting like Jini.

Most transactions in database systems are based on what is known as the *two-phase commit* protocol, sometimes just called 2PC. While transactions have a lot of special terminology surrounding them, the basics are actually surprisingly simple. Two-phase commit says that to get a group of operations to either all succeed or all fail together in a known way, you have to follow a simple two-step process.

In the first step, called the *prepare* step, a coordinating entity (called the *transaction manager*) tells all the parties involved in the transaction to "get ready" to perform their operations. This means that each of the parties, called a *participant*, has to do a few things. First, the participant computes whatever result is being asked for. But rather than writing the result into some permanent storage (onto the disk, or into the database), the result is just saved in a log file. Second, each participant reports back to the central manager whether it was able to successfully move into this state.

If a participant reports that it has successfully prepared itself to move to the next stage, then this is a guarantee to the transaction manager that the participant is willing and able to move to the next step at some point in the future. This stage is shown in Figure 18-1.

In the second step, called the *commit* step, the manager tallies up all these *votes* from the participants about whether they were able to do the first stage. If any of the participants was not able to move into the prepared stage, then the manager calls off the transaction since it cannot be fully completed. But if all the participants report that they are ready, then the manager writes into a log that it is about to complete the transaction, along with a list of all the prepared participants. It then tells each participant to "go." When each participant receives the "go" message, it copies the result from temporary storage into permanent storage, and tells the manager when it has finished. This stage is shown in Figure 18-2.

You may be wondering what happens if a participant fails after the manager has told it to commit, but before the participant actually updates the permanent record. Isn't it possible, in this case, for the update to be lost? If a participant reports that it has successfully moved to the prepare stage, then this is in effect a *guarantee* to the manager that if the manager contacts it in the future, the participant will be able to commit the change. The manager must continue telling par-

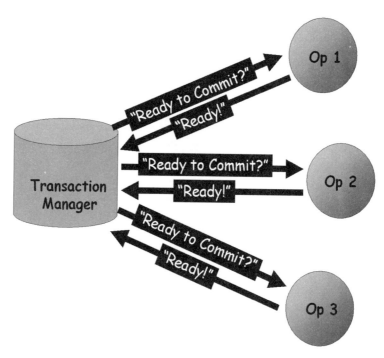

Figure 18–1   *Executing the prepare phase.*

ticipants to commit until it has heard from all of them. As long as even one participant hasn't responded, the manager keeps trying; it is not allowed to clean up after the transaction until all participants have been updated.

All this may seem complicated, but the good news is that most of the time, you don't need to worry about the actual details of how two-phase commit works. If you're writing applications that are doling out operations to services to be executed under transactions, then the Jini transaction APIs hide most of this complexity from you. (Services that expose operations that can happen within transactions have to have a somewhat greater understanding of the protocol, though.)

With this in mind, it's time to move on and look at what the Jini transaction model looks like.

Transactions in Jini

Just like so much else in Jini, the Jini transaction model makes a strong separation between interface and implementation. And while usually in Jini this

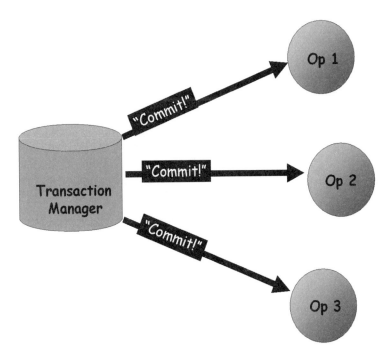

Figure 18–2   Executing the commit phase.

means that objects are described in terms of their Java interfaces, and their implementations are hidden, the Jini transaction model takes this separation one step further.

In Jini, only the two-phase commit protocol itself is standardized. What services do in response to the individual phases of the protocol is up to them. In essence, only the mechanics of the two-phase commit stages are a built-in part of Jini, while the semantics of what transactions "mean" to any given service are not dictated by Jini.

What does this mean in practice? This design decision has several implications.

First, it means that Jini can have one transaction manager that can drive transactions in any number of applications. In more traditional systems, the transaction manager is typically tightly integrated with the rest of the system. In databases, for instance, the transaction manager *is* the database, because transactions are an inseparable part of the database and the transaction manager must have internal knowledge of the database to be able to work.

In contrast, the single Jini transaction manager can drive the two-phase commit protocol for transactions in *any* type of service, even services that the transaction manager has no knowledge of.

Second, it means that Jini as a whole has no way of enforcing *what* any particular service will do when confronted with a transaction. In a database system, transactions are so tightly integrated with the database that operations cannot "escape" from their transaction boundaries, and update data without going through the transaction process.

In Jini, service writers can receive messages from the transaction manager telling them to move to the prepare stage, the commit stage, and so on. But there is no guarantee about what exactly those services will do in response to those messages. Of course, one hopes that if a service writer has gone to the trouble of working with transactions, then the service will preserve sensible transaction semantics.

The approach that Jini takes is very lightweight, and very object-oriented. The two-phase commit protocol itself is the "interface" that transaction participants must understand. The "implementation" of the protocol is up to them. So service writers can choose an implementation that makes sense for them. A database service might keep fully redundant, fully reliable logging information to implement two-phase commit. While an on-line game might use a much faster and looser implementation.

The Players in Jini Transactions

There are three main parties involved in Jini transactions: the transaction manager, the transaction participant, and the transaction client. In Jini, the transaction manager is actually a full-fledged Jini service that simply runs through the two-phase commit protocol when asked. The transaction manager keeps, for each transaction, a list of participants. For each participant, it will send it a message telling it what stage to move to. Essentially the manager is only in charge of the signaling for the two-phase commit protocol. All transaction manager services, including the one in the sample implementation from Sun, implement the `net.jini.core.transaction.server.TransactionManager` interface.

The participant in a transaction is a program that is performing an operation that is grouped with other operations into a transaction. Typically, this will be a Jini service that is allowing some of its operations to be "transactable"—letting them take a transaction parameter so that the operation can be grouped with others. In Jini, transaction participants implement the `net.jini.core.transaction.server.TransactionParticipant` interface.

Finally, the transaction client is the entity that starts the whole process. This may be a Jini application that needs to perform operations on multiple services and ensure that they all happen together. Or in other cases, it may be a Jini service that needs to make use of operations in other services. But whatever the context, there is no required interface that transaction clients must implement. Jini does, however, provide some helper classes that clients can use to make their use of transactions easier. The most important of these is the net.jini.core.transaction.Transaction interface, which provides an object representation of a set of operations grouped into a transaction. The net.jini.core.transaction.TransactionFactory class provides a useful helper for creating new Transaction instances.

The high-level overview of how a transaction is used is pretty simple. First, a client gets a reference to the Jini transaction manager, usually through the standard discovery and lookup process. The client then calls the Transaction-Factory to create a new Transaction object that will be managed by that transaction manager.

After the client has a Transaction object, it can begin grouping together the operations that will make up the transaction. In Jini, this is typically done by sending the Transaction object off to the individual participants as part of a method call to perform some operation. If you think about the JavaSpaces examples from the last chapter, there was no abstract representation of a *write* operation that could be "added" to a Transaction, and the Transaction class has no methods for adding operations to it. Instead, in the JavaSpaces case, certain methods on the service that can operate in the context of transactions simply take a Transaction argument. The JavaSpaces service takes care of creating some bookkeeping information that remembers that the particular operation is associated with a particular transaction, and then *joins* the transaction by telling the transaction manager that it is controlling one of the member operations.

So while the client is *conceptually* adding operations to the transaction, the programming model and APIs simply look like the client is invoking methods on the services just like normal, only with a Transaction object as a parameter.

Once all the member operations have been grouped together—that is, once the client has invoked all of the methods whose operations are to be performed under a particular transaction—the client then tries to commit the operations by calling the commit() method on the Transaction. It is this method that begins the two-phase commit process, or rather, it signals the manager to begin the process and handle the messaging of all the member participants.

Up until this point, none of the participating services have actually executed any of the requested operations. So if you've called write() on a JavaSpace with a Transaction parameter, the write will not actually take effect until you commit the transaction.[2]

At the end of all this, if the commit() call successfully completes, then the client can be sure that all the member operations have successfully completed. The call may raise a `net.jini.core.transaction.CannotCommitException` if any participant cannot move to the prepared stage.

This overview really represents about 90 percent of what you need to know to use Jini transactions. For the most part, transaction clients—which are the part of the puzzle you will most commonly be working with—don't need to understand the mechanics of two-phase commit, logging, or crash recovery. Transaction participants do need to have a deeper understanding of transactions, though. And there are a few subtleties that will even affect clients.

I'll talk about the subtleties a bit later in the chapter, but for now, let's focus on the Jini transaction programming model and how it appears to clients.

Programming with Jini Transactions

In this section, you'll see the Jini transaction interfaces and classes, and see how to build clients that can take advantage of transactions. A bit later, once you've covered the basics, you'll see a simple example of writing a transaction client that can coordinate operations across multiple JavaSpaces services.

The Transaction Manager

The most important part of the Jini transaction paradigm is the transaction manager. As mentioned before, the transaction manager is itself a service which simply handles stepping through the two-phase commit protocol on behalf of clients. Since the transaction manager is a service, it can be shared among other services and clients in a Jini community.

You've already seen how to run Sun's sample implementation of a transaction manager, called `mahalo`, in the last chapter. This implementation, as well as any other alternate implementations that may appear in the future, will implement the `TransactionManager` interface.

I won't present the `TransactionManager` interface here, because it is rarely if ever used directly by clients; but, you should know that it exists, and that if you are writing new services that participate in transactions, you will have to have a greater familiarity with it.

---

2. Actually, the notion of when and how transactions "take effect" is a bit more complicated than this. Even the effects of operations in uncommitted transactions will be visible to other operations operating under that same transaction. More on this a bit later in the chapter, but for now, you can think of the operations as "not happening" until the transaction commits.

Creating Transactions

Once a client has a reference to a `TransactionManager`, obtained via the usual lookup process, it can create transactions as needed. Clients do not create transactions through the `TransactionManager` directly.[3] Instead, they use the `TransactionFactory` class, which is a part of the `net.jini.core.transaction` package.

Take a look at this interface now.

```
package net.jini.core.transaction;

import net.jini.core.lease.LeaseDeniedException;
import java.rmi.RemoteException;

public class TransactionFactory {
    static NestableTransaction.Created
            create(NestableTransactionManager mgr,
                    long leaseTime)
            throws LeaseDeniedException,
                    RemoteException;
    static Transaction.Created
            create(TransactionManager mgr,
                    long leaseTime)
                throws LeaseDeniedException,
                        RemoteException;

}
```

The `TransactionFactory` "fronts" a `TransactionManager`, and provides a more high-level API on top of it. The two static methods here are used to create new transactions, given a Jini `TransactionManager`. You'll notice that transactions are leased to you by the `TransactionManager`. If you are executing a transaction that may take significant time to perform, you will have to handle renewing the leases on the transaction until it is complete.

Leasing governs how long a transaction can be left "open" before an attempt is made to commit it. You need to be sure you renew the lease on a transaction at least until you try to commit it. Once a lease has expired on a transaction, you cannot add more participants to it, and you cannot try to commit it. Once you

---

3. Clients don't create transactions through the `TransactionManager` directly, even though the manager has a `create()` call. Many of the methods used by the various Jini transaction interfaces look very similar, and it can be difficult to tell when you should use what. This is why I'm neglecting the `TransactionManager` API here—to keep the number of superficially similar APIs to a minimum in the interest of cutting down on confusion and focusing on the common tasks that clients will perform.

have begun the commit process, the transaction manager will continue it even if the lease expires, so you don't have to worry about renewing leases through the duration of the two-phase commit process. The lease only governs the time you have in which to add participant operations and begin the commit process.

The first version of the `create()` call is used to create transactions that can be "nested" within other transactions. In the Jini model, transactions can be hierarchical. So if you have a computation that depends on the successful completion of some subgroup of operations, you can execute that subgroup in a nested transaction. I'll talk a bit more about nested transactions later in the chapter, but for now, I'll focus on the second version of the `create()` method.

This method returns an instance of `Created`, a static inner class within the `Transaction` class.

```
public static class Transaction.Created
        implements Serializable {
    public final Lease lease;
    public final Transaction transaction;
    // ... other details elided ...
}
```

This is a simple container class that holds the newly created `Transaction` object, as well as the `Lease` object that can be used to renew or cancel the lease on the transaction.

The Transaction Interface

After a client has successfully found a proxy for a `TransactionManager` and created a new `Transaction`, most of its operations will be performed through this `Transaction` object. Take a look at the `Transaction` interface:

```
package net.jini.core.transaction;

import java.rmi.RemoteException;

public interface Transaction {
    void abort()
        throws UnknownTransactionException,
            CannotAbortException,
            RemoteException;
    void abort(long waitFor)
        throws UnknownTransactionException,
            CannotAbortException,
            TimeoutExpiredException,
            RemoteException;
```

```
    void commit()
        throws UnknownTransactionException,
            CannotCommitException,
            RemoteException;
    void commit(long waitFor)
        throws UnknownTransactionException,
            CannotCommitException,
            TimeoutExpiredException,
            RemoteException;


}
```

The `abort()` method is used to cause a transaction to abort—meaning that the transaction manager essentially cancels the transaction. You can only call `abort()` on a transaction that has not already committed—a committed transaction is considered final and cannot be undone. But if you haven't gone this far, then `abort()` will stop the entire transaction and cause the participants to clean up any state they may have accrued in the process of getting ready to perform the transaction. A call to `abort()` on a transaction that has already committed will raise `CannotAbortException`. This exception will also be raised if a client tries to abort a transaction and the lease on the transaction has already expired.

The call will return as soon as the manager records the fact that the transaction is now in the "aborted" state, but before all the participants have been notified of the change. This prevents the client from having to block until all the messages have gone out to the participants.

The `commit()` method is how clients cause the two-phase commit process to begin. Calling `commit()` signals the transaction manager to begin the protocol. If any participant cannot move to the prepare state, or if the lease on the transaction has expired, or if the transaction has already been aborted, then the `CannotCommitException` is raised. At this point, the client can be guaranteed that *none* of the constituent operations have happened. Otherwise, the method will return as soon as the manager moves into the commit stage. This means that all the participants have moved to the prepare stage, and the manager has recorded the fact that it is *going* to commit, but hasn't necessarily notified all the individual participants. This means that when `commit()` returns, the change is guaranteed to happen, but the effects of it may not have propagated out to all the participants yet. Like the behavior of `abort()`, this behavior keeps clients from having to block as long.

Both `abort()` and `commit()` have versions that take a timeout, expressed as a number of milliseconds. These versions of the calls actually block until all the participants have been notified of the abort or commit operation, or until the timeout elapses. These versions of `abort()` and `commit()` are useful if you want to wait until all the participants in a transaction have a chance to reflect the new data—this method can make stronger guarantees about whether you will see all the results of the abort or commit operation everywhere immediately after you abort or commit. If the timeout elapses before all the participants have been notified, then `TimeoutExpiredException` will be raised. The manager will still continue trying to notify all the participants, but control is returned to you after the timeout.

Core Alert: You can sometimes still see out-of-date data, even with transactions

One of the biggest differences with transactions in a distributed setting, as opposed to transactions in a stand-alone setting, is that in certain circumstances, you can still see out-of-date data. This can happen when a client tells the transaction manager to begin the commit process, but not all participant services have yet been notified to move from the prepare to the commit phase. Once the transaction manager has collected all the votes from participants and knows that all participants are ready in the prepare stage, then it knows that at some point, it will be able to complete the transaction. But the process of notifying all the participants may take an arbitrarily long time.

Stand-alone systems don't have this problem since the individual components can typically be notified of the commit phase virtually instantly. But you should be aware that there may be a time window in which you can see temporarily inconsistent results, even when using transactions.

All these calls can raise `UnknownTransactionException` in addition to whatever other exceptions they may raise. This exception is analogous to the `UnknownLeaseException` you saw in Chapter 12—if you hold on to a `Transaction` object long enough that it becomes unknown to the transaction manager, and then try to use it, you'll get an `UnknownTransactionException`. Common reasons for this exception are when you hold on to a previously aborted or committed transaction for which the transaction manager has already cleaned up its bookkeeping records.

Transaction Participants

Each service that exposes "transactable" methods will play the role of a Jini transaction participant. The `TransactionParticipant` interface is used to coordinate communication between the manager and the participant—the manager will invoke the methods defined by the `TransactionParticipant` interface as it moves all the participants through the two-phase commit process.

Even though you should know that the `TransactionParticipant` interface exists and understand the role it plays, I won't go into the details of it here because it's virtually never used by clients. The `TransactionParticipant` interface is *only* used between managers and participants to regulate the two-phase commit process; it has nothing to say about how clients add new operations to transactions.

Instead, and as you've already seen with JavaSpaces, the particulars about how services allow operations to be added to transactions are up to the individual services. In the case of JavaSpaces, operations are added by simply passing a `Transaction` instance to one of the normal JavaSpaces methods. There are no standardized methods supported by all participants to add operations to a transaction.[4]

Using Transactions with JavaSpaces

In the next program, you'll see a simple example of using transactions with the one standard service that currently supports them: JavaSpaces. By using transactions with JavaSpaces, you can coordinate operations across any number of spaces, transferring objects, updating data sets, and so on, reliably, even in the face of partial failures.

Listing 18–1 shows the basics of working with transactions as a client: It securely moves `Entry` objects between two JavaSpaces. Such a program might be useful for transferring datasets from a JavaSpace running on a slow desktop machine to a large compute server, for example.

Here I'm using transactions for the data movement, because it's important that no data be lost. If I were to simply take an `Entry` out of one space without performing the operation under a transaction, my client (or the destination Java-Space) could crash before the data is written to its destination. Transactions ensure that each move happens completely or not at all.

---

4. In fact, unless you read the documentation for JavaSpaces, you'd never even know that it can participate in transactions. The proxy for JavaSpaces doesn't itself implement `TransactionParticipant`, so you cannot test it to see if you can use transactions with it. Instead, the class that implements the participant functionality for JavaSpaces is hidden within the implementation of the service. This really isn't a problem, since to do pretty much *anything* to a service requires that you know ahead of time what methods it supports and how to use them.

Take a look at the program.

Listing 18–1 `EntryMover.java`

```java
// Safely move a set of Entry objects from one JavaSpace
// to another.

package corejini.chapter18;

import net.jini.space.JavaSpace;
import net.jini.core.lookup.ServiceTemplate;
import net.jini.core.lookup.ServiceMatches;
import net.jini.core.lookup.ServiceRegistrar;
import net.jini.core.lookup.ServiceID;
import net.jini.core.entry.Entry;
import net.jini.core.lease.Lease;
import net.jini.core.transaction.Transaction;
import net.jini.core.transaction.TransactionFactory;
import net.jini.core.transaction.CannotCommitException;
import net.jini.core.transaction.UnknownTransactionExcep-
tion;
import net.jini.core.transaction.server.TransactionManager;
import net.jini.lease.LeaseRenewalManager;
import net.jini.discovery.LookupDiscovery;
import net.jini.discovery.DiscoveryGroupManagement;
import net.jini.discovery.DiscoveryListener;
import net.jini.discovery.DiscoveryEvent;
import net.jini.lookup.entry.Name;
import java.util.ArrayList;
import java.rmi.RemoteException;
import java.rmi.RMISecurityManager;
import java.io.IOException;
```

Listing 18–1 `EntryMover.java` (continued)

```java
public class EntryMover implements Runnable {
    protected Class[] spaceTypes = { JavaSpace.class };
    protected ServiceTemplate spaceTmpl =
        new ServiceTemplate(null, spaceTypes, null);
    protected Class[] txnTypes =
        { TransactionManager.class };
    protected ServiceTemplate txnTmpl =
        new ServiceTemplate(null, txnTypes, null);
    protected ArrayList regs = new ArrayList();
    protected LeaseRenewalManager leaseMgr =
        new LeaseRenewalManager();
    protected JavaSpace js1 = null, js2 = null;
    protected TransactionManager txn = null;
    // This is the ID of any already-found JavaSpace.
    // We need to keep it to weed out duplicates.
    protected ServiceID id = null;

    // An inner class for discovery.
    class Discoverer implements DiscoveryListener {
        public void discovered(DiscoveryEvent ev) {
            System.out.println("Discovered!");
            ServiceRegistrar[] newregs = ev.getRegistrars();
            for (int i=0, size=newregs.length; i<size; i++){
                if (!regs.contains(newregs[i])) {
                    regs.add(newregs[i]);
                    findServices((ServiceRegistrar)
                                        newregs[i]);
                }
            }
        }
        public void discarded(DiscoveryEvent ev) {
        }
    }

    public EntryMover() throws IOException {
        LookupDiscovery disco = new
            LookupDiscovery(
                DiscoveryGroupManagement.ALL_GROUPS);
        disco.addDiscoveryListener(new Discoverer());
    }
```

Listing 18–1 EntryMover.java (continued)

```
// Find all the services we'll need, and then call
// doit()!
protected void findServices(ServiceRegistrar reg) {
    if (js1 != null && js2 != null && txn != null ) {
        return;
    }

    ServiceMatches matches = null;

    if (js1 == null || js2 == null) {
        System.out.println("Searching for JavaSpace");
        try {
            matches = reg.lookup(spaceTmpl,
                                 Integer.MAX_VALUE);
        } catch (RemoteException ex) {
            System.err.println("Error doing lookup: " +
                               ex.getMessage());
            return;
        }

        for (int i=0 ; i<matches.totalMatches ; i++) {
            // If we haven't found a space yet, or if
            // this is a  new space, then use it.
            if (js1 == null) {
                js1 = (JavaSpace)
                    matches.items[i].service;
                System.out.println(
                    "Found first JavaSpace!");
                id = matches.items[i].serviceID;
            } else if (js2 == null &&
                !id.equals(matches.items[i].serviceID)) {
                js2 = (JavaSpace)
                    matches.items[i].service;
                System.out.println(
                    "Found second JavaSpace!");
            }
        }
    }
}
```

Listing 18–1 `EntryMover.java` (continued)

```java
        if (txn == null) {
            System.out.println("Searching for txn mgr");
            try {
                txn = (TransactionManager)
                    reg.lookup(txnTmpl);
                if (txn != null) {
                    System.out.println("Found it!");
                }
            } catch (RemoteException ex) {
                System.err.println("Error: " +
                                ex.getMessage());
                ex.printStackTrace();
            }
        }

        // If we've got two spaces and a transaction
        // manager, then do it!
        if (js1 != null && js2 != null && txn != null)
            doit();
    }

    // Load up the first space with some data, and then
    // move it out under transactions.
    protected void doit() {
        System.out.println(
            "Writing some data to first space");
        for (int i=0 ; i<10 ; i++) {
            Name name = new Name(Integer.toString(i));
            try {
                Lease l = js1.write(name, null, 60 * 1000);
                System.out.println("Wrote: " + name);
                leaseMgr.renewUntil(l, Lease.ANY, null);
            } catch (Exception ex) {
                System.err.println("Trouble writing: " +
                                ex.getMessage());
                ex.printStackTrace();
            }
        }
```

Listing 18–1 `EntryMover.java` (continued)

```
System.out.println("Moving to second space");

Name nameTmpl = new Name(null);

Entry e = null;
boolean done = false;
int idx=0;
ArrayList uncommits = new ArrayList();

while (!done) {
    try {
        System.out.println("Creating transaction");

        Transaction.Created c =
            TransactionFactory.create(txn,
                            10 * 60 * 1000);

        // Manage the lease on the transaction,
        // just in case.
        leaseMgr.renewUntil(c.lease,
                        Lease.ANY, null);

        // Take under a transaction
        e = js1.takeIfExists(nameTmpl,
                        c.transaction,
                        JavaSpace.NO_WAIT);

        if (e == null) {
            done = true;
            continue;
        }

        // Write under the same transaction.
        System.out.println("Moving: " + e);
        Lease l = js2.write(e, c.transaction,
                        60 * 1000);
        leaseMgr.renewUntil(l, Lease.ANY, null);
```

Listing 18–1 `EntryMover.java` (continued)

```
            // Commit!
            if (idx++ % 2 == 0) {
                System.out.println("Committing!");
                c.transaction.commit();
            } else {
                uncommits.add(c.transaction);
            }
        } catch (RemoteException ex) {
            System.err.println("Trouble communicating:"
                                    + ex.getMessage());
        } catch (CannotCommitException ex) {
            System.err.println("Couldn't commit: " +
                                    ex.getMessage());
        } catch (UnknownTransactionException ex) {
            System.err.println("Unknown transaction: " +
                                    ex.getMessage());
        } catch (Exception ex) {
            System.err.println("Other problem: " +
                                    ex.getMessage());
        }
    }

    // Dump out the contents of the spaces, then
    // commit the remaining transactions, then
    // dump again.

    System.out.println("Contents of space 1: ");
    dumpContents(js1);

    System.out.println("Contents of space 2: ");
    dumpContents(js2);
```

Listing 18–1 `EntryMover.java` (continued)

```java
        System.out.println(
            "Committing remaining transactions.");
        for (int i=0, size=uncommits.size(); i<size; i++) {
            Transaction t = (Transaction)
                uncommits.get(i);
            try {
                t.commit();
            } catch (RemoteException ex) {
              System.err.println("Trouble communicating" +
                                  ex.getMessage());
            } catch (CannotCommitException ex) {
                System.err.println("Couldn't commit: " +
                                    ex.getMessage());
            } catch (UnknownTransactionException ex) {
                System.err.println("Unknown transaction: " +
                                    ex.getMessage());
            }
        }

        System.out.println("Contents of space 1: ");
        dumpContents(js1);

        System.out.println("Contents of space 2: ");
        dumpContents(js2);
    }

    protected void dumpContents(JavaSpace js) {
        try {
            Name nameTmpl = new Name(null);

            Entry e = null;
            while ((e = js.takeIfExists(nameTmpl, null,
                        JavaSpace.NO_WAIT)) != null) {
                System.out.println("Removing: " + e);
            }
        } catch (Exception ex) {
            System.err.println(ex.getMessage());
            ex.printStackTrace();
        }
    }
```

Listing 18–1 `EntryMover.java` (continued)

```
public void run() {
    while (true) {
        try {
            Thread.sleep(Integer.MAX_VALUE);
        } catch (InterruptedException ex) {
        }
    }
}

public static void main(String[] args) {
    try {
        if (System.getSecurityManager() == null) {
            System.setSecurityManager(
                new RMISecurityManager());
        }
        EntryMover mover = new EntryMover();
        new Thread(mover).start();
    } catch (Exception ex) {
        System.err.println("Error: " + ex.getMessage());
        ex.printStackTrace();
    }
}
}
```

This program uses discovery to find lookup services, and then searches those lookup services until it finds the other services it needs to do its job. The program requires two separate JavaSpaces and a transaction manager service to work. The findServices() method is called each time a new lookup service is found until the necessary complement of services has been located. Once everything is in order, the program calls doit() to exercise the Jini transaction manager.

The interesting part of this program is in the doit() method, so take a look at it. The method first writes a set of Name entries into the first JavaSpace. This is so that it will have some data to later extract. The program writes ten entries, each of which has a distinct name so that we can see later which have been successfully moved. Note that the writes are *not* done under a transaction, since they do not depend on the success or failure of any other operations.

After this, the program sits in a loop, moving Name objects as it finds them. For each iteration, the program creates a new Transaction by calling out to the TransactionFactory. That is, for each move, a separate transaction is created under which the move will be performed (remember, a single move is the *combination* of a take and a write). Thus, although the client retrieves a single transaction *manager*, it creates many transactions to be processed by that manager on behalf of the client. The program asks for a ten-minute lease, and passes the lease off to a `LeaseRenewalManager` just in case the transaction takes longer to execute than expected.

The heart of the move code is two JavaSpaces operations that happen under the same transaction. First, `takeIfExists()` is called on the first space to remove an entry, and then `write()` is called on the second space to copy it to that space, completing the move. This pair of operations happens under the same transaction to ensure that either they both happen (and the entry is moved) or neither happen (and the entry stays where it is); this way, no entries are lost. Because the move happens under a transaction, the move is not *actually* completed until the transaction under which it operates commits.

Just to make things a little more exciting, only half of the transactions are committed immediately. The uncommitted transactions are kept on a list so that they can be committed later.

After the loop completes—because there are no more entries to be moved—the code prints out the contents of the two spaces, commits the remaining transactions, and then prints the contents of the two spaces again.

Compiling and Running the EntryMover

Getting this example up and running is pretty simple; you simply have to compile the `EntryMover` client and launch it.

On Windows:

```
javac -classpath C:\files;
              C:\jini1_1\lib\jini-core.jar;
              C:\jini1_1\lib\jini-ext.jar;
              C:\jini1_1\lib\sun-util.jar;
              C:\client
    -d C:\client
    C:\files\corejini\chapter18\EntryMover.java
```

On UNIX:

```
javac -classpath /files:
              /files/jini1_1/lib/jini-core.jar:
              /files/jini1_1/lib/jini-ext.jar:
              /files/jini1_1/lib/sun-util.jar:
              /files/client
```

```
-d /files/client
/files/corejini/chapter18/EntryMover.java
```

Now you're set to run it. Before you start, make sure that you've got a transaction manager and *two* separate JavaSpaces running! If you have a lookup service browser running, you can check to see if these necessary services are available on your network. Be sure that you distinguish between a single JavaSpaces service that might be registered on several lookup services, and two separate instances of the JavaSpaces service—you'll actually need two separate JavaSpaces instances running here. Refer back to the instructions in Chapter 17 for details on running these.

On Windows:

```
java -cp C:\jini1_1\lib\jini-core.jar;
        C:\jini1_1\lib\jini-ext.jar;
        C:\jini1_1\lib\sun-util.jar;
        C:\client
-Djava.security.policy=C:\policy
corejini.chapter18.EntryMover
```

On UNIX:

```
java -cp /files/jini1_1/lib/jini-core.jar:
        /files/jini1_1/lib/jini-ext.jar:
        /files/jini1_1/lib/sun-util.jar:
        /files/client
-Djava.security.policy=/files/policy
corejini.chapter18.EntryMover
```

Take a look at the output of the EntryMover program. First, you should see the program searching for and finding the pair of JavaSpaces and the transaction manager.

Searching for JavaSpace
Found first JavaSpace!
Searching for txn mgr
Found it!
Searching for JavaSpace
Found second JavaSpace!

After this, the EntryMover will set up some data for it to move. It will write ten Name entries into the first space.

Writing to first space
Wrote: net.jini.lookup.entry.Name(name=0)

Wrote: net.jini.lookup.entry.Name(name=1)
Wrote: net.jini.lookup.entry.Name(name=2)
Wrote: net.jini.lookup.entry.Name(name=3)
Wrote: net.jini.lookup.entry.Name(name=4)
Wrote: net.jini.lookup.entry.Name(name=5)
Wrote: net.jini.lookup.entry.Name(name=6)
Wrote: net.jini.lookup.entry.Name(name=7)
Wrote: net.jini.lookup.entry.Name(name=8)
Wrote: net.jini.lookup.entry.Name(name=9)

Now here comes the interesting part! The program will begin moving data from the first space to the second. Each move consists of two operations—a `takeIfExists()` and a `write()`—which are grouped together under a transaction. The even-numbered moves will be committed immediately, while the others will be deferred. You'll see the results of all this in just a bit.

Moving to second space
Moving: net.jini.lookup.entry.Name(name=0)
Committing...
Moving: net.jini.lookup.entry.Name(name=1)
Moving: net.jini.lookup.entry.Name(name=2)
Committing...
Moving: net.jini.lookup.entry.Name(name=3)
Moving: net.jini.lookup.entry.Name(name=4)
Committing...
Moving: net.jini.lookup.entry.Name(name=5)
Moving: net.jini.lookup.entry.Name(name=6)
Committing...
Moving: net.jini.lookup.entry.Name(name=7)
Moving: net.jini.lookup.entry.Name(name=8)
Committing...
Moving: net.jini.lookup.entry.Name(name=9)

Finally, look at the results of these moves. The `dumpContents()` method is a destructive way to print out the contents of a JavaSpace. That is, it works by actually taking items out of the space and displaying them. Remember that only the even-numbered transactions were committed—the odd transactions are still pending, and so you shouldn't see the effects of them here.

Contents of space 1:

Contents of space 2:

Removing: net.jini.lookup.entry.Name(name=0)

Removing: net.jini.lookup.entry.Name(name=2)

Removing: net.jini.lookup.entry.Name(name=4)

Removing: net.jini.lookup.entry.Name(name=6)

Removing: net.jini.lookup.entry.Name(name=8)

Sure enough, the first space is empty and the second space shows all the entries put there from the committed transactions only. Now the program will commit the remaining transactions, and you can see what the results are.

Committing remaining transactions.

Contents of space 1:

Contents of space 2:

Removing: net.jini.lookup.entry.Name(name=1)

Removing: net.jini.lookup.entry.Name(name=3)

Removing: net.jini.lookup.entry.Name(name=5)

Removing: net.jini.lookup.entry.Name(name=7)

Removing: net.jini.lookup.entry.Name(name=9)

Remember that the `dumpContents()` method removes the items it displays. So all the even-numbered entries from the first part of the example have now been removed. But here you see that the data from the newly committed transactions have appeared in the second space!

Here, transactions have given us exactly what we want: They provided a way to ensure consistency in the data by grouping operations together.

So far, you've seen how to build applications that are simple transaction clients. In the next section, I'll talk about some of the more subtle aspects of transactions.

Other Transaction Issues and Idioms

This section highlights some of the subtle points of dealing with transactions, as well as some not-so-subtle, but seldom-used aspects of the programming model.

Transactions and Visibility

Earlier in this chapter when I said that operations grouped into a transaction don't actually take place until the transaction is committed, I told a white lie. The more accurate truth is that the operations *do* happen; they're just not visible "outside" the transaction.

I'll illustrate what this means in terms of the example program you've just seen. In that program, a series of move operations were done under transactions, but only half of the transactions were immediately committed. When the dump-Contents() method was called, it only showed the data that had been moved by committed transactions. This might lead you to believe that the JavaSpaces involved in the transactions simply queued up the takeIfExists() and write() calls until the word came down from the transaction manager to invoke them. But in fact, this is not what happened.

What actually happened is that the takeIfExists() and write() operations *did* take place immediately. But their effects were constrained so that they could only be detected by operations that were members of the same transaction!

So the reason dumpContents() didn't see the uncommitted moves *wasn't* because the spaces hadn't done anything yet. It was because dumpContents() itself made calls to takeIfExists() to fetch entries for display, and *those* calls weren't members of the transaction that did the move. In the EntryMover example, you can go back and change the code so that dumpContents() uses one of the uncommitted transactions for its call to takeIfExists() and it will suddenly be able to see the results of all the operations in this uncommitted transaction.

The very logical reason for this is that the operations grouped together in a transaction are meant to be logically related. So it makes sense for them to all "see" the effects of one another. So in the EntryMover example, the write() clearly needs to be able to use the entry returned by takeIfExists() if it is to work properly.

This is a general fact of life in the transactions world that you should be aware of. What actually happens when you use transactions is more complex than simply queueing up operations until all participants are ready to go. Transactions have implications for the visibility of the effects of operations.

You can even use these terms to describe what happens when you don't pass *any* transaction to one of the JavaSpaces methods. What effectively happens is that you get a "transient" transaction that only contains one member operation and commits immediately. So the effects of any of these operations with a null transaction argument is immediately visible to all parties.

Nesting Transactions

If you have very complex sets of operations that you need to group together into transactions, you may think about decomposing the problem down into constituent parts which are themselves composed of many operations. To support situations like this, Jini allows *nested transactions*. Nested transactions are transactions in which member operations are themselves transactions.

The semantics work just the same as in "normal" transactions—for a transaction to succeed, all of its constituent members must succeed. So if one of the members is itself a transaction, all of *its* member operations must succeed.

Nested transactions follow the usual transaction visibility rules—the effects of members of a transaction are only visible to other members of the transaction. The effects of operations in a parent transaction are visible to operations in its subtransactions. The effects of a subtransaction are only visible in the parent when the subtransaction commits. (This is analogous to what happens with individual operations in a transaction—the effects of an operation are visible, even within the transaction, only when it is performed. The commit of a subtransaction is analogous to performing a primitive operation.)

You've already seen, in the interface for `TransactionFactory`, a method for creating "nestable" transactions—meaning transactions that can be nested within other transactions. This method returns a `NestableTransaction.Created` container that holds a `NestableTransaction` and its lease. And the method takes as an argument a `NestableTransactionManager`, which is a subinterface of the regular `TransactionManager`.

Core Note: Mahalo doesn't support nested transactions

Even though the Jini specifications have quite a bit to say about nested transactions, and the semantics of nested transactions are clearly defined, Sun's implementation of mahalo—*its transaction manager—does not yet support nested transactions. So be careful about creating applications that may require nested transaction functionality. While this functionality is certainly coming, it's not available at the time of this writing.*

Events and Sequence Numbers

If you looked carefully at the interface for the JavaSpaces service, you may have noticed that not only do the expected calls like `read()`, `write()`, and `take()` allow a transaction parameter, but so does `notify()`. You may have been curious about why an event registration was allowed to happen inside a transaction, and even what it means for an event registration to happen inside a transaction!

Basically, you can register to receive events within the context of a transaction. This means that you will be able to see any events that arise from changes caused by other member operations in the transaction. This much is probably what you expected. In a nutshell, you will receive events caused by other operations in your transaction, even though these same operations will be invisible event-wise (just as they are invisible result-wise) to anyone outside the transaction, until the transaction commits. Once the transaction commits, then any listeners outside the transaction will receive events about any changes, just as they normally would.

But being able to ask for events from within a transaction context has implications for how event sequence numbers and types work, and how event registration leases are used.

First, an event generator that allows event registrations to happen under transactions *must* use a different event type ID for events that are delivered inside transactions versus those delivered outside, even if those events are of the same logical "type." So, for instance, if a printer service generates out-of-paper events that generally have the same type ID regardless of their destination, that service would have to use a *different* ID for out-of-paper events sent to recipients that registered for events under a transaction.

This requirement is so that third-party delegates won't blindly forward to recipients events that should only be visible to parties that are members of a certain transaction. Recall that such delegates may rely on the event type ID to know how to route the event to downstream listeners. By using a separate type ID, recipients outside the transaction won't receive the events, and recipients inside the transaction can simply tell the delegate to deliver within-transaction events to them. (Of course, if your service doesn't support event registrations within a transaction, you don't have to worry about any of this.)

A second implication has to do with how sequence numbers are generated for events delivered within a transaction scope. Events sent because of an occurrence visible only inside a transaction will have a different sequence number than events sent because of the *same* occurrence if it happens outside the transaction, or when the transaction commits. This is because operations that occur within a transaction, even event deliveries, must be isolated from operations that occur outside a transaction.

Finally, the duration of an event registration that occurs within a transaction is bounded by the duration of the transaction. So even if you ask for a long event registration lease, if the transaction completes (either by committing or aborting), the lease on the event registration will be terminated, even if it hasn't yet expired.

Using Transactions to Hide Data

An interesting twist on the transaction visibility rules can be applied in situations where you need it. The fact that operations that are within a transaction are only visible to other operations within the transaction is not just useful for ensuring that uncommitted data keeps from "polluting" other operations. It can also be used as a nifty way to hide data. By grouping operations into a transaction, you can prevent any other programs from messing with your data, whether intentionally or unintentionally.

Take a look at the `EntryMover` as an example. This is actually a pretty ill-behaved program. It writes a few `Name` entries into a space, and then copies out *all* of the `Name` entries in that space. If some other applications had a brisk trade in `Name` entries going, we would have just scuttled them!

While using transactions as an impromptu information-hiding strategy isn't an approach based in "real" systems security principles, it can be useful in a number of scenarios. One of the scenarios in which it's most useful is when you want to protect yourself from the inadvertent—rather than the determined and malicious—stray program.

You may be wondering how this works. At some point, if you're working with transactions, you'll either have to commit your changes (making them visible to others), or abort the changes (in which case they simply "won't exist"). How can you get any benefit out of this?

The answer is to use operations within a transaction that can return results to a calling program. Let's look at how to do this in JavaSpaces. Say you wish to use JavaSpaces to privately exchange some data with another program. You create a transaction, and then write new objects into the space. You then send the transaction object to the receiver. Essentially this transaction acts like a "key" which allows the receiver access to the data. The key can be exchanged with another client using some means you devise yourself, and which both you and the other client agree upon. Some ways might include sending it over a socket, through an RMI call, or even putting it in a JavaSpace, wrapped in an `Entry`!

The receiver then performs `take` operations on the space, using the key. Once all the data has been fetched, the receiver can simply abort the transaction, and the space will clean up all the tentative entries, as if they had never existed. Of course, the receiver will already have the objects in its hands, returned from the `take` operations.

Again, using transactions for data hiding shouldn't be thought of as a robust approach to system security. But it can help guard against damage done by clumsy programs.

Summary

This chapter has provided an overview of the fundamentals of Jini's distributed transaction model, with a particular focus on the view of transactions from the client. You've seen how transactions can be used to guard against partial failures, and you've looked at Jini's unique transaction model, which separates the two-phase commit protocol from the semantics of transactions.

The example in this chapter has illustrated how to use transactions as a JavaSpaces client, which for the near future will be the most common use of transactions (at least until other transactable services appear). And you've seen some of the deeper implications of using transactions, such as how transactions affect remote event delivery. Using the techniques described here, you should be ready to interact with any number of transaction-supporting services, as they appear on the market.

The Jini Utility Services

Chapter 19

T his final chapter of the book explores a set of new services introduced with Jini 1.1—a collection of *utility services* that can be used by other Jini clients and services. These aren't "end user" services in the sense that they do not provide direct access to some device or application-oriented software. Instead, they are meant to be used as building blocks by other Jini-aware software. In this sense, they have a target audience similar to the transaction manager you learned about in the last chapter.

These three services can be used by any number of Jini clients or services but, as you will see, they are primarily useful when building services that are intended to run in situations with somewhat impoverished network or communications resources, or in situations where your service may be inactive for long periods of time.

The first of these services is the `LookupDiscoveryService`. It can interact with the Jini discovery protocols to find lookup services on behalf of another service or application. The second service, the `LeaseRenewalService`, is similar to the leasing service presented earlier in this book—clients of the service can pass it their leases for renewal. Finally, the third utility service is the `Event-Mailbox`. Again, this service is similar to the one you saw in the earlier chapter on remote events. Your applications can direct remote events to this service for later "pick up."

In this chapter, I'll walk you through the programming models for these services, as well as the rationale behind them. I'll also show you the details of configuring and running them. Finally, you'll get to see an example application that uses all three of these handy services.

Why the Utility Services?

From the brief description of the three services that I outlined above, you may be wondering how much utility these utility services actually provide. Why, you may be asking, would you need a service that can perform discovery for you, when you'd have to use discovery to find such a service in the first place?

The answer—and there is a good one—has to do with the types of environments into which your services may be deployed. Ideally, you'd like to write services that can be run in a wide range of settings, including ones with limited network connectivity.

Imagine, for instance, that you're writing a service that will reside on a wireless device. This could be a digital cell phone, a PDA, or even a standard notebook computer with a wireless modem card attached. In such a setting, it may be *extremely* impractical for your service to assume that it will always have full network connectivity. Obviously, for your service to be useful to any other party, it will need to connect to the network when it's actually working. But you'd like to be able to minimize the amount of "on air" time for simple housekeeping chores. This might be because using the network drains battery power, or simply because your wireless network provider charges for connect time.

Services designed to be run in such environments can make great use of the utility services. For example, you can off-load your leasing chores to a `LeaseRenewalService`, running somewhere on the *wired* network. This service, since it is running in a location that has constant network connectivity, can handle the tasks of renewing any leases you hold without the exceptional sort of costs that would be incurred if your service did these tasks itself. Likewise, the `EventMailbox` can queue events destined for your service so that they can be delivered later, perhaps when the machine hosting your service is "docked" or when it needs to be connected to the network for some other task.

So these services can be a big win when you're developing for restricted platforms. But there's another, much more common, situation when these services come in handy. This is when you're building a service that will use the RMI activation framework to allow itself to be activated on demand.

I've hinted a few times in this book about the activation framework. You know that the "standard" Jini services use activation as a means to allow them to restart automatically after failures. While activation is largely outside the scope of this book, the basic idea is simple.[1] Activation provides a way for you to create remote (RMI) objects that do not need to be active all the time. You *register* your remote objects with the activation system, which will then *activate* your objects—reconstitute and run them—when a remote method call is made on them. In this way, such objects use system resources only when needed.

Activation provides a number of very nice properties, and can be extremely useful when building Jini services. It allows your services to be inactive until they are needed—so you can potentially host massive numbers of remote objects on a single machine, while using no resources until those objects are required. Activation can also provide a way to cause your remote objects to be automatically "restarted," either after a crash or when a machine boots up.

But a key point—and one that necessitates these utility services when building activatable services—is that the activation framework can only activate an object *in response to a remote method call.* As you know, Jini services often need to respond to occurrences that are not represented by RMI calls. The discovery protocols, for example, involve very low-level multicast UDP and TCP messages. There is no RMI traffic involved in discovery, and hence, no way for the activation system to "know" to activate a service, just because some UDP or TCP packets go by.

So this is the other situation where the utility services prove their worth. Since these services will perform full-fledged remote method invocations back to your code, they can serve as "activation triggers," causing your objects to be reactivated in response to various Jini occurrences. These helper services make it possible to build well-behaved, activatable services, easily and robustly. By off-loading certain chores to these services, you know that your code can be made activatable—with all the benefits that brings—and be safely reactivated only when necessary.

When I talk about the descriptions of the specific utility services, I'll say more about how each can be profitably used in situations where you're using activation, or running in low-resource environments. But first, you'll need to get these services up and running on your system!

---

1. Appendix A, which presents a short primer on RMI, does talk a bit about activation, however. If you're curious, you may want to jump ahead and read up on how activation works in a bit more detail. Appendix A presents one final iteration of the trusty "Hello, World" service from Chapter 5, this time designed to use activation.

Configuring and Running the Utility Services

Just like the other Jini services you've seen so far, you can launch the utility services from the `StartService` GUI that comes with Jini, or from the command line. I won't go into great detail on how to use the GUI to launch these services—the property file that comes with the Jini distribution comes with predefined templates for launching them, and the process is much the same as for the earlier services you've seen.[2]

Briefly, visit the panels for the *Mercury, Norm,* and *Activatable_Fiddler* services in the GUI. Mercury is Sun's implementation of an event mailbox; Norm is the implementation of the lease renewal service; and Fiddler is the implementation of the lookup discovery service. There are two versions of Fiddler, one that uses activation and one that does not. I recommend using the activatable one, and give the instructions for it below.

At each panel, simply double-check the paths, in case you've installed anything in non-standard locations, and edit the codebase option to have the proper hostname and port number for the Jini web server (remember to use port 8080, if you've been following the recommendations consistent with the instructions in the book).

After this, you can just go to the *Run* panel to launch these three services.

In the rest of this section, I'll talk a bit more about how these services use activation, and give the gory details for starting the services by hand.

A Refresher: The Lifecycle of Activatable Services

Much like the other Jini services you've seen so far, the three utility services are themselves activatable.[3] As you probably recall from way back in Chapter 1 when you set up the lookup service, being activatable means that these programs have somewhat different life cycles than those of other Java programs with which you may be familiar.

---

2. If you're interested in service startup issues around Jini, you may want to check out the "OutOfBox" project on `http://www.jini.org`. This is a Jini community project, working to make the initial Jini experience—the "out of the box" experience—better and more painless.
3. As I mentioned above, Sun's implementation of the `LookupDiscoveryService` also supports a "transient" (non-activatable) mode, as do several other Sun-provided services. I won't talk about this mode of operation here, though. See the manual pages and release notes for more information.

First, the programs that you run to "start" these services don't actually start them at all. Instead, they simply register the services with the activation framework. It is the activation framework that will launch the services when they are needed.

Second, once you've run the programs to register the services with the activation framework, you generally will *never* have to run these services again. The activation system will take care of launching them for you, as long as *it* is running. (Which means that you should take care that `rmid`—the RMI activation daemon—is running on the host on which you plan to run these services. Further, `rmid` should have access to its log file after restarts, so that it has available to it the information needed to re-launch these services.)

Third, there are actually *two* JVMs involved in the process of starting these services. The first is the JVM that runs the "wrapper" program that registers the services with `rmid`. This is the JVM that you directly start yourself when you run the services as shown below, and is called the "setup" JVM. The second virtual machine is the JVM that `rmid` launches to run a service when it activates it. This is called the "server" JVM. While you typically don't interact with the server JVM directly—since `rmid` starts it and you never see it—you can pass arguments to these services that will in turn get passed to the server JVM. This level of control is only rarely used, however; most users will never exercise any control over the server JVM.

In the sections below, I'll walk you through the details of getting each of the three utility services up and running. The good news is that these services are bundled with the basic Jini starter kit, so if you've installed this kit, they're already on your system. You will have to do a bit of setup work, however.

Starting the LookupDiscoveryService

Sun's sample implementation of the `LookupDiscoveryService` is called `fiddler`. As I mentioned earlier, this service can be run in either its activatable or its "transient" mode; here, however, I'll only talk about using it in the activatable mode.

The basic command line syntax needed to run `fiddler` is:

```
java -jar <fiddler jar file>
    <codebase>
    <policy file>
    <log directory>
    <groups and locators>
```

The syntax here is very similar to that for the other Jini services you've already seen. The first argument, the `-jar` option, names the path to the `fiddler.jar` file that contains the implementation of `fiddler`.

After this are the arguments to the program itself, rather than the arguments to the `java` bytecode interpreter. The `codebase` argument should be a URL that points to the JAR file containing `fiddler`'s downloadable code. This code is bundled in the file `fiddler-dl.jar`, and is installed along with the rest of the Jini JAR files in the Jini 1.1 `lib` directory. If you're already running an HTTP server that is exporting the downloadable code for the core Jini services—which you almost certainly are if you've gotten this far—you can "reuse" this HTTP server. Otherwise, you'll have to start one with a root directory pointing to the Jini 1.1 `lib` directory. Refer back to Chapter 1 if you need the details on how to do this.

The next argument is the full path to a security policy file. This is the policy that will be in effect for the *server* JVM, which is the JVM that will be launched by the activation framework.

After this comes a log directory. `Fiddler`, like the other services you've seen, will record its state into a persistent log directory so that it can be recovered after a restart. You should make sure that the directory doesn't exist, but that all of the directories leading up to it *do* exist. This directory should be on some stable file-system that will survive machine reboots.

Finally, the last argument is a list of Jini groups and locators that indicate which lookup services to discover and join. If you do not specify any groups or locators, `fiddler` will join only the public group. If you do provide arguments, you must make sure that the groups and locators list does not contain any spaces. Multiple groups or locators should be separated by a comma only. Any string which is a valid Jini-format URL will be interpreted as a locator; otherwise, the string will be interpreted as a group name. The group name `public` indicates that `fiddler` should discover lookup services that are members of the public group; the string `all` indicates that it should use multicast discovery to find lookup services that are members of any group; and the string `none` means that `fiddler` shouldn't use multicast discovery at all.

For example, to tell `fiddler` to find lookup services that are members of the `public` group, the `experimental` group, the `ThirdFloor` group, as well as the lookup service named by the URL `jini://idea.parc.xerox.com`, you'd construct a string as follows:

```
public,experimental,ThirdFloor,jini://idea.parc.xerox.com
```

Note again that there are no spaces in this string.

Here is an example of starting the `fiddler` service on Windows to join the `public` group:

```
java -jar C:\jini1_1\lib\fiddler.jar
    http://your_host:8080/fiddler-dl.jar
    C:\files\policy
    C:\temp\fiddler_log
    public
```

And on UNIX:

```
java -jar /files/jini1_1/lib/fiddler.jar
    http://your_host:8080/fiddler-dl.jar
    /files/policy
    /var/tmp/fiddler_log
    public
```

Listings 19-1 and 19-2 show scripts that you can use to start `fiddler` on Windows and UNIX, respectively. Be sure to modify these scripts to use your actual hostname and paths to the installed JAR and policy files.

Listing 19-1 discsvc.bat

```
REM Set this to wherever Jini is installed
set JINI_HOME=C:\jini1_1

REM Set this to the host where the webserver runs
set HOSTNAME=hostname

REM Everything below should work with few changes
set POLICY=%JINI_HOME%\example\lookup\policy.all
set JARFILE=%JINI_HOME%\lib\fiddler.jar
set CODEBASE=http://%HOSTNAME%:8080/fiddler-dl.jar
set LOG_DIR=C:\temp\fiddler
set GROUP=public

java -jar %JARFILE% %CODEBASE% %POLICY% %LOG_DIR% %GROUP%
```

Listing 19-2 discsvc.sh

```sh
#!/bin/sh

# Set this to wherever Jini is installed
JINI_HOME=$HOME/files/jini1_1

# Set this to wherever the webserver is running
HOSTNAME=hostname

# Everything below should work with few changes
POLICY=$JINI_HOME/example/lookup/policy.all
JARFILE=$JINI_HOME/lib/fiddler.jar
CODEBASE=http://$HOSTNAME:8080/fiddler-dl.jar
LOG_DIR=/var/tmp/fiddler_log
GROUP=public

java -jar $JARFILE $CODEBASE $POLICY $LOG_DIR $GROUP
```

Starting the LeaseRenewalService

Sun's sample implementation of the `LeaseRenewalService` is called `norm` and, like `fiddler`, is activatable. Unlike `fiddler`, `norm` does not provide a non-activatable implementation as well.

The command syntax for starting `norm` is basically the same as that for starting `fiddler`. And remember that since both services are activatable, you should follow the guidelines I mentioned earlier—make sure `rmid` is running, make sure `rmid` has access to its log directory, you should only have to run norm once, and so on.

Here is the basic command syntax:

```
java -jar <norm jar file>
     <codebase>
     <policy file>
     <log directory>
     <groups and locators>
```

Just as in `fiddler`, the `-jar` argument names the path to the executable JAR file containing the `norm` implementation, `norm.dl`.

After this, the `codebase` argument specifies the URL from which download-able code can be retrieved. The downloadable code for `norm` lives in the `norm-`

`dl.jar` file in the Jini 1.1 `lib` directory. The next argument is a path to a policy file; this policy file dictates the security permissions for the server JVM. The log directory argument specifies a path to the directory in which `norm` will persistently save its state information. Just as with `fiddler`, this directory should not exist prior to running `norm`, but all directories leading up to it should exist.

The final argument specifies a set of groups or locators to be joined. The argument here works just as it does with `fiddler`—any strings that can be parsed as Jini `LookupLocator` URLs are treated as locators; the special strings `public`, `all`, and `none` can be used to indicate the public group, all groups, or no groups. Be sure that all the tokens you specify here are separated by commas, not spaces.

Here's a sample command line for starting `norm` on Windows, joining the `public` group. As always, be sure to replace the hostname with the name of the machine running your HTTP server, and set the correct paths.

```
java -jar C:\jini1_1\lib\norm.jar
     http://your_host:8080/norm-dl.jar
     C:\files\policy
     C:\temp\norm_log
     public
```

And here's a sample command line for starting on UNIX:

```
java -jar /files/jini1_1/lib/norm.jar
     http://your_host:8080/norm-dl.jar
     /files/policy
     /var/tmp/norm_log
     public
```

Listings 19-3 and 19-4 provide scripts that you can use to start `norm` on these platforms.

Listing 19-3 lease.bat

```
REM Set this to wherever Jini is installed
set JINI_HOME=C:\jini1_1

REM Set this to the host where the webserver runs
set HOSTNAME=hostname

REM Everything below should work with few changes
set POLICY=%JINI_HOME%\example\lookup\policy.all
set JARFILE=%JINI_HOME%\lib\norm.jar
set CODEBASE=http://%HOSTNAME%:8080/norm-dl.jar
set LOG_DIR=C:\temp\norm
set GROUP=public

java -jar %JARFILE% %CODEBASE% %POLICY% %LOG_DIR% %GROUP%
```

Listing 19-4 lease.sh

```
#!/bin/sh

# Set this to wherever Jini is installed
JINI_HOME=$HOME/files/jini1_1

# Set this to wherever the webserver is running
HOSTNAME=hostname

# everything below should work with few changes
POLICY=$JINI_HOME/example/lookup/policy.all
JARFILE=$JINI_HOME/lib/norm.jar
CODEBASE=http://$HOSTNAME:8080/norm-dl.jar
LOG_DIR=/var/tmp/norm_log
GROUP=public

java -jar $JARFILE $CODEBASE $POLICY $LOG_DIR $GROUP
```

Starting the EventMailbox

The implementation of the `EventMailbox` service that comes with Jini 1.1 is named `mercury` and, you'll be pleased to hear, has exactly the same command-line argument syntax as `fiddler` and `norm`. Likewise, this service is activatable, so the usual cautionary tales about running `rmid` are in effect here as well.

Here is the basic command syntax for `mercury`:

```
java -jar <mercury jar file>
    <codebase>
    <policy file>
    <log directory>
    <groups and locators>
```

Mercury's implementation lives in the `mercury.jar` file, and the downloadable code that needs to be exported to clients lives in `mercury-dl.jar`. Both of these files reside in the Jini 1.1 `lib` directory.

Here is an example of running the service on Windows:

```
java -jar C:\jini1_1\lib\mercury.jar
    http://your_host:8080/mercury-dl.jar
    C:\files\policy
    C:\temp\mercury_log
    public
```

And on UNIX:

```
java -jar /files/jini1_1/lib/mercury.jar
    http://your_host:8080/mercury-dl.jar
    /files/policy
    /var/tmp/mercury_log
    public
```

Listings 19-5 and 19-6 provide scripts that you can use to launch the Event-Mailbox service on Windows and UNIX.

Listing 19-5 mailbox.bat

```
REM Set this to wherever Jini is installed
set JINI_HOME=C:\jini1_1

REM Set this to the host where the webserver runs
set HOSTNAME=hostname

REM Everything below should work with few changes
set POLICY=%JINI_HOME%\example\lookup\policy.all
set JARFILE=%JINI_HOME%\lib\mercury.jar
set CODEBASE=http://%HOSTNAME%:8080/mercury-dl.jar
set LOG_DIR=C:\temp\mercury
set GROUP=public

java -jar %JARFILE% %CODEBASE% %POLICY% %LOG_DIR% %GROUP%
```

Listing 19-6 mailbox.sh

```
#!/bin/sh

# Set this to wherever Jini is installed
JINI_HOME=$HOME/files/jini1_1

# Set this to wherever the webserver is running
HOSTNAME=hostname

# Everything below should work with few changes
POLICY=$JINI_HOME/example/lookup/policy.all
JARFILE=$JINI_HOME/lib/mercury.jar
CODEBASE=http://$HOSTNAME:8080/mercury-dl.jar
LOG_DIR=/var/tmp/mercury_log
GROUP=public

java -jar $JARFILE $CODEBASE $POLICY $LOG_DIR $GROUP
```

Now that you're proficient in starting these services, it's time to move on and look at how they actually work.

The LookupDiscoveryService

As I mentioned at the start of this chapter, there are occasions when a service may wish to delegate even the most basic of its Jini responsibilities—including the act of discovering lookup services. Most commonly, this will be because you are writing an activatable service. Since the Jini discovery protocols involve very low-level network traffic—raw TCP and UDP packets, rather than remote method invocations—there is no way for the activation system to reactivate a service in response to discovery traffic.

If an inactive service were not able to be reactivated in response to discovery traffic, then it is possible that the service might *never* properly discover and join the Jini communities that it should be a part of. Consider a case where a new lookup service is added to a community populated by a number of inactive services. Since these services would not be automatically activated by the new lookup service's multicast announcement traffic, the lookup service might never be populated with the services in its community—they would never wake up to register their proxies with the lookup service.

Even if these inactive services were to be periodically awakened, perhaps by a "heartbeat" generator service (of the type you saw in the chapter on remote events), there is a chance that its window of activity might occur during an interval in which the lookup service sends no announcement messages. Because of these reasons, services that are largely inactive can find it difficult to form a functioning community.

The LookupDiscoveryService works around these problems by performing discovery on behalf of the inactive services. Since it is always active, the LookupDiscoveryService will receive all announcement traffic from lookup services. It can then notify any interested services, whether inactive or not, via a remote method call. This call would serve to reactivate any inactive services, which could then take an appropriate response to the discovery events—most likely by joining a new lookup service that appeared on the network.

Other Situations

In addition to the case of activatable services, there are other situations in which the delegation of discovery duties can be a win. One of these is when there are no lookup services accessible from your service via multicast.

This situation can arise if your service is on a multicast network, but there are simply no lookup services within range of it. It can also arise if your service is on some particular subnetwork that doesn't support multicast, but needs access to some communities on the "normal" network that *does* support multicast.

This later situation is not as uncommon as you might think. It may arise because the router configuration in some part of your company does not support multicast. Or it may arise because you are essentially "bridging" a normal TCP LAN environment to a more restricted networking environment. For instance, you may have services that reside on hardware that does not have Ethernet connectivity, but may have some other form of connectivity—infrared, say—that supports unicast TCP layered atop it, but does not support multicast.

In all of these cases, a LookupDiscoveryService can act as a bridge between a collection of lookup services on one part of the network and your services on another. If your service can be configured with one specific reference either to a LookupDiscoveryService, or (by using a locator URL) to a lookup service that contains such a service, then you can use it to perform discovery for you.

The LookupDiscoveryService Programming Model

The basic idea behind the LookupDiscoveryService is simple—you provide it with a list of groups and locators you're interested in hearing about, and it delivers a RemoteEvent to you when any lookup service that is a member of one of these groups, or that is named by one of these locators, is discovered.

All LookupDiscoveryServices, including Sun's fiddler implementation, should implement a standard, simple interface.

```
package net.jini.discovery;

public interface LookupDiscoveryService {
    public LookupDiscoveryRegistration register(
                        String[] groups,
                        LookupLocator[] locators,
                        RemoteEventListener listener,
                        MarshalledObject handback,
                        long leaseDuration)
                            throws RemoteException;
}
```

Your code—whether a client or a service—that wishes to make use of a LookupDiscoveryService will first find and download a proxy for the service, typically using the normal Jini mechanisms. This proxy will implement the LookupDiscoveryService interface. The one method in this interface, register(), is used to ask the LookupDiscoveryService to discover a set of lookup services and deliver events when they are found.

The first argument to `register()` is an array of groups that names the communities to be found. Next is an array of `LookupLocators` that names the specific lookup services that your code is interested in. The `RemoteEventListener` indicates a listener object that will be called whenever a discovery is made; typically this will be a listener that you define on your service, since you ultimately want to learn about discoveries. But it can also be a listener defined by another service, such as the `EventMailbox` service. You'll see how this works a bit later in this chapter. In either case, the listener argument should not be null.

Next, you see a `MarshalledObject` parameter, which serves as a handback. Whenever the `LookupDiscoveryService` delivers events to your listener, this same object will be returned to it. Finally, the `leaseDuration` parameter is used to request that the `LookupDiscoveryService` keep this new registration available and active for the specified amount of time. Each `LookupDiscoveryRegistration` issued by a `LookupDiscoveryService` requires some storage and computation, so these registrations are leased to you. When the lease expires, the `LookupDiscoveryService` knows it can safely clean up the registration associated with the lease.

RemoteDiscoveryEvents

After you have acquired a registration, the `LookupDiscoveryService` will send you events to indicate that new lookup services have been *discovered*, or that currently discovered lookup services have been *discarded*. The `LookupDiscoveryService` continually monitors the multicast announcements it receives from lookup services, and logs and analyzes those announcements for information about the state of the lookup services.

Because of this information that the `LookupDiscoveryService` collects, you will not only receive discovery events when a new lookup service appears that is a member of one of your groups, but also when a currently discovered lookup service joins one of these groups. You will likewise receive discard events if a currently discovered lookup service drops its membership in a group you are interested in. Finally, the `LookupDiscoveryService` will track the announcements it receives from lookup services, and will generate a discard event to you if a lookup service ceases to generate announcements. The semantics of the events here are somewhat richer than those for the raw discovery management classes.

The actual events that are delivered to you are `RemoteDiscoveryEvents`. These events are similar to the `DiscoveryEvents` you've already seen, which are generated by the discovery management libraries. `RemoteDiscoveryEvents` are, obviously, subclasses of `RemoteEvent`, and carry with them all the semantics of such events—the source indicates the `LookupDiscoveryService`

that generated the event; sequence numbers provide strict, not full, ordering; and
each new registration generates a unique event type ID.

```
package net.jini.discovery;

import java.util.Map;

public class RemoteDiscoveryEvent extends RemoteEvent {
    // ... constructor elided ...
    public boolean isDiscarded();
    public ServiceRegistrar[] getRegistrars()
                        throws LookupUnmarshalException,
                               RemoteException;
    public Map getGroups();
}
```

I haven't shown the constructor for this class, since it's only ever used by the
LookupDiscoveryService itself, when it generates these events. First notice
that the event class extends RemoteEvent, so all the usual methods for checking
type IDs, sequence numbers, and so on are present here.

Of the methods specific to this class, isDiscarded() indicates whether this
event was generated in response to a new discovery, or a lookup service being
discarded.

The getRegistrars() method returns the lookup service proxies associated
with this particular discovery or discard. If this event represents a discovery, then
the method will return the newly discovered lookup services; if it is a discard,
then the method will return the proxies for the lookup services that are no longer
members of named groups, or are not responding.

The getGroups() method returns a map in which each key is a ServiceID
corresponding to each lookup service represented by the event. Each value in the
map is an array of Strings naming the groups in which the lookup service is a
member.

Notice the new exception type that the getRegistrars() method can raise:
LookupUnmarshalException. When you call the getRegistrars() method
on the RemoteDiscoveryEvent, the registrar proxies will be deserialized so
that they can be returned to you. If any proxies cannot be properly deserialized
(most likely because of a codebase error when the lookup service that published
the proxy was run), then a LookupUnmarshallException will be raised.
Potential unmarshalling problems are also why the keys in the map returned by
getGroups() are ServiceIDs rather than proxy objects—ServiceIDs, since
they are a part of the core Jini infrastructure, should avoid any deserialization
problems. You can use the LookupUnmarshallException to fetch the proxies

that *were* properly unmarshalled, as well as information about those that were not.

```
package net.jini.discovery;

public class LookupUnmarshalException extends Exception {
    // ... constructor elided ...
    public ServiceRegistrar[] getRegistrars();
    public MarshalledObject[] getMarshalledRegistrars();
    public Throwable[] getExceptions();
}
```

The `getRegistrarss()` method returns to you the lookup service proxies that were successfully unmarshalled. The `getMarshalledRegistrarss()` method returns those proxies that could not be unmarshalled; note that they are returned to you still in their `MarshalledObject` form.

Core Tip: What good is the proxy as a MarshalledObject?

You may be wondering why the `getMarshalledRegistrars()`
method returns anything to you at all—if you can't use the result as a
`ServiceRegistrar`, *why would you want it? The answer is that*
some applications may want to hold on to the `MarshalledObjects`
that are returned from this call, in case they are able to reconstitute
the proxies that these objects represent later.

Most of the time, if a proxy cannot be deserialized, it will be
because of problems downloading the code for the proxy. If the
owner of the service improperly sets the codebase property, then the
proxy is unlikely to ever be deserializable. But if the problem is
simply that the HTTP server on which the proxy's code resides is
down, you may be able to reconstitute the proxy later, by calling the
`get()` *method on the* `MarshalledObject` *that represents it.*

The `getExceptions()` method returns to you an array of exceptions, one for
each of the `MarshalledObjects` in the array returned by `getStillMar-`
`shalledRegs()`. These exceptions indicate exactly why the corresponding
proxies could not be unmarshalled.

LookupDiscoveryRegistrations

The `LookupDiscoveryRegistration` object that is returned to your application is the means by which you interact with the `LookupDiscoveryService`.
Through this object you can fetch the lease for your registration, change the
sets of desired groups and locators, and discard lookup services that you hold
references to but are not responding.

As I mentioned earlier, `LookupDiscoveryRegistrations` are leased to you
from the `LookupDiscoveryService`. You must actively renew this lease, or the
`LookupDiscoveryService` will free your registration; when this happens, any
invocation of a remote method in the registration object will raise a `NoSuchOb-`
`jectException`. This exception likely indicates an error in your leasing code.

```
package net.jini.discovery;

public interface LookupDiscoveryRegistration {
    public EventRegistration getEventRegistration();
    public Lease getLease();
    public ServiceRegistrar[] getRegistrars()
                        throws LookupUnmarshalException,
                                RemoteException;
```

```
    public String[] getGroups() throws RemoteException;
    public LookupLocator[] getLocators()
                            throws RemoteException;

    public void addGroups(String[] groups)
                            throws RemoteException;
    public void setGroups(String[] groups)
                            throws RemoteException;
    public void removeGroups(String[] groups)
                            throws RemoteException;

    public void addLocators(LookupLocator[] locators)
                            throws RemoteException;
    public void setLocators(LookupLocator[] locators)
                            throws RemoteException;
    public void removeLocators(LookupLocator[] locators)
                            throws RemoteException;

    public void discard(ServiceRegistrar registrar)
                            throws RemoteException;
}
```

Many of these methods are self-explanatory, so I'll deal with the easy ones
first. You see in this interface a number of methods that allow you to control the
set of groups or locators in which you are interested. The get methods simply
return the groups or locators currently being searched for. The set methods overwrite the entire set of groups or locators; the add methods add specific groups or
locators to the set; and the remove methods extract members from these sets.

Note that if you've already discovered a lookup service that is a member of
multiple groups, and then you change the set of groups you're searching for to
include *another* of the groups that the lookup service is a member of, you will not
receive an extra event. The LookupDiscoveryService only sends you a discovery event once for each lookup service, unless that lookup service is discarded
and then discovered again.

The getLease() method fetches the Lease object for this registration with the
LookupDiscoveryService. You are responsible for ensuring that this lease is
renewed for as long as you wish to use the registration; as I mentioned earlier, if
you do not renew the lease, any remote method on the registration object will raise
NoSuchObjectException if invoked after the lease has expired. This exception
is an indication that the service has freed any service-side information associated
with the registration object you hold in your application.

The getEventRegistration() method returns to you an EventRegistration object. This object holds details that you may need to work with events

received from the `LookupDiscoveryService`—it holds the type ID for the events that will be sent to the listener you initially presented to the service, as well as the starting sequence number.

As you remember from the discussion of remote events and `EventRegistrations` earlier, the `EventRegistration` class also holds a lease on the registration. In the case of the `LookupDiscoveryService`, the lease on your discovery registration is also used for the lease on your event registration. Since virtually every client of the `LookupDiscoveryService` will both take out a registration with the service *and* direct events from it to a listener, it makes sense to use the same lease for both. So the `getLease()` method on the `EventRegistration` returns the same lease that `getLease()` on the `LookupDiscoveryRegistration` does.

The `getRegistrars()` method, as you might expect, returns to you the list of all of the lookup service proxies that have been discovered so far for your particular registration. Just like the method of the same name on `RemoteDiscoveryEvent`, this call may raise a `LookupUnmarshalException` if there are problems deserializing any lookup service proxy.

But this call has another use as well. Whereas the `getRegistrars()` method on `RemoteDiscoveryEvent` simply returns all of the proxies contained in that event, the method here contacts the back-end service to fetch *all* of the proxies for your registration discovered to date. This call can be useful in helping you to rebuild your picture of all discovered lookup services when, for instance, you believe you might have missed one or more `RemoteDiscoveryEvents`. This call allows you to effectively "resynchronize" with the service, downloading a complete set of lookup service proxies.

Finally, the `discard()` method allows you to "throw away" a previously-discovered lookup service proxy. This most commonly happens when a proxy you are using raises a `RemoteException`—likely indicating that it has crashed or become unreachable. The `LookupDiscoveryService` maintains no direct communication with the lookup services it discovers (although it does monitor their announcement messages). Therefore, it may be unable to reliably detect that a lookup service has failed. By calling `discard()`, you allow the `LookupDiscoveryService` to rediscover it, once the service returns.

The LeaseRenewalService

In this section, I'll talk about the `LeaseRenewalService` that comes with the Jini 1.1 utility services. As you already know, any Jini service will need to periodically renew its leases on its registrations with lookup services. Likewise, nearly all Jini clients will maintain leases on event registrations (at a minimum), and will need to renew those leases. Of course, Jini applications may have leases on any number of other resources as well, such as JavaSpaces entries, transactions, and so forth.

Just as activation can present problems for services that need to be made aware of discovery, activation can also have implications for the leasing behavior of Jini code. One of the chief advantages of activation is that it allows your code to consume virtually no computational resources, and only a modicum of storage resources when it is inactive. Activation allows you to have potentially huge numbers of remote objects on a single server by keeping unused objects inactive.

But if your inactive services maintain leases on their proxy registrations—which they are certain to do—then they would have to reawaken periodically to renew their leases. And activation is not an inexpensive operation. Clearly the requirement to reactivate to do leasing would preclude having large numbers of activatable services on one machine in practice; there would be constant activity as services were activated to renew their leases and then deactivated again afterwards.

The solution—which the `LeaseRenewalService` provides—is to delegate the leasing chores for inactive services to another entity. By delegating leasing, your services can safely deactivate themselves, assured that the leases on their registrations will be renewed as needed. You do not need to make provisions for your code to be reactivated every few minutes to handle the task yourself.

In addition to its usefulness in creating activatable services, the `LeaseRenewalService` is also an important tool when writing services for platforms that may have sporadic (or expensive) network connectivity. The example of a service running on a cellular telephone that I gave at the beginning of this chapter illustrates this. Your device may not always be able to connect to the network readily, or your network service provider may charge you for access time. In such settings, it may make sense to delegate your leasing to an external service to keep your connection time (and fees) to a minimum.

Like any Jini service that grants access to some resource, the `LeaseRenewalService` leases its efforts to clients. So, when you ask the `LeaseRenewalService` to renew a set of leases for you, you take out a lease on this request. You must renew your lease with the `LeaseRenewalService` for it to continue renewing your "downstream" leases that it is responsible for.

The key to all of this, of course, is that the `LeaseRenewalService` will typically grant leases for a period far longer than most other services. If you had to contact the `LeaseRenewalService` every ten minutes to ask it to renew the ten minute leases it is managing for you, you haven't saved yourself anything. So the `LeaseRenewalService` will typically grant leases for days or weeks. During this time, it will dutifully contact the grantors of the leases you've asked it to manage, renewing these leases for whatever durations it can get.

Since you will still have to manage leases on your registrations with the LeaseRenewalService, it kindly provides an interface that will cause it to send events to you just before your registrations with it are about to expire. If your service is activatable, the delivery of such events will reawaken your service, allowing it to renew its lease with the LeaseRenewalService.

Be sure to remember the warnings from Chapter 12—the use of a third-party leasing service, while generally helpful, can also be harmful if used improperly. The use of such a service effectively increases the "window" during which the failure of your service will go unnoticed by its lease grantors. This can mean that the lookup services for your community may continue to hold proxies for your service for a considerable time after it has failed.

The LeaseRenewalService Programming Model

Although the semantics are different, the LeaseRenewalService looks stylistically very much like the LookupDiscoveryService. When using both services, you obtain a registration object that represents your contract with the service. You then manipulate this registration object to control the parameters of interaction with the service, get a lease for the registration, install event listeners, and so forth.

Here is the interface that the LeaseRenewalService's proxy exposes to its clients:

```
package net.jini.lease;

public interface LeaseRenewalService {
    public LeaseRenewalSet createLeaseRenewalSet(
                            long leaseDuration)
                        throws RemoteException;
}
```

The createLeaseRenewalSet() is used to establish a new registration with a LeaseRenewalService. The call returns an instance of LeaseRenewalSet. It is through this interface that you can add leases to be managed, install event listeners, and so forth. The leaseDuration parameter specifies the initially requested duration for your lease *with the leasing service*, not the duration of any of the particular leases it will manage. Of course, this method can raise Remote-Exception if the proxy cannot communicate properly with the back-end portion of the LeaseRenewalService.

The LeaseRenewalSet Interface

Since most of your interactions with the `LeaseRenewalService` will be through the `LeaseRenewalSet`, let's now take a look at that interface:

```
package net.jini.lease;

public interface LeaseRenewalSet {
    final public static long RENEWAL_FAILURE_EVENT_ID = 0;
    final public static long EXPIRATION_WARNING_EVENT_ID =
1;

    public void renewFor(Lease leaseToRenew,
                    long desiredDuration)
                        throws RemoteException;
    public void renewFor(Lease leaseToRenew,
                    long desiredDuration,
                    long renewDuration)
                        throws RemoteException;

    public EventRegistration setExpirationWarningListener(
                        RemoteEventListener listener,
                        long minWarning,
                        MarshalledObject handback)
                            throws RemoteException;
    public void clearExpirationWarningListener()
                            throws RemoteException;

    public EventRegistration setRenewalFailureListener(
                        RemoteEventListener listener,
                        MarshalledObject handback)
                            throws RemoteException;
    public void clearRenewalFailureListener()
                            throws RemoteException;

    public Lease remove(Lease leaseToRemove)
                            throws RemoteException;
    public Lease getRenewalSetLease();
    public Lease[] getLeases()
                    throws LeaseUnmarshalException,
                        RemoteException;
}
```

The most important, and often used, methods in this interface are the two versions of `renewFor()`. It is these methods that allow you to pass your leases from other services to the `LeaseRenewalService` for management.[4]

Both versions of this method have a `leaseToRenew` parameter, which specifies the lease to be managed, and a `desiredDuration` parameter, which indicates the requested lease duration. Be sure to note how the `desiredDuration` argument works: this is the duration you wish your lease to be managed by the `LeaseRenewalService`. Unlike a normal lease duration, this value is not negotiated—what you specify here is the absolute duration for which the service will manage your lease. Of course, even if you ask for the service to manage your lease until the end of time, you must still actively renew the lease on the `Lease-RenewalSet` that contains it, or the service will cease to renew your lease.

You can, of course, specify a `desiredDuration` longer than you think you might need, since you can always remove the lease from the set and cancel it "by hand," or cancel the lease on the entire `LeaseRenewalSet` if you wish all of the leases in that set to expire at their next, natural expiration time. In other words, don't worry about precisely pre-computing the duration you need. Many applications will simply pass `Long.MAX_VALUE` here and cancel their leases explicitly when they no longer need them. You can also effectively change the `member-shipDuration` associated with a lease by calling `renewFor()` on a lease already in the set—this will change the duration to the new value you specify.

The version of the call that takes the `renewDuration` argument allows you to specify the amount of time for which the `LeaseRenewalService` will attempt to renew your lease, each time it negotiates with the original lease grantor. This should be a positive number, or—if the `desiredDuration` is `Long.MAX_VALUE`—then it may be `Lease.ANY`.

The `remove()` method is how you remove a managed lease from a `LeaseRenewalSet`. This call will not cause your lease to be cancelled; instead, it simply tells the `LeaseRenewalService` that you no longer wish it to manage the particular lease. Most often this is because you need fine-grained control over the lease renewal process or—more likely—that you wish to cancel the lease.

The `getRenewalSetLease()` method returns to you the lease on this renewal set. This lease is the "meta lease"—the lease that you must renew to cause all

---

4. Make sure that the leases you pass are, in fact, from a service other than the `Lease-RenewalService` itself. A call to `renewFor()` will raise an `IllegalArgumentException` if you pass it a lease on a `LeaseRenewalSet` (this prevents you from recursively having the service renew your leases for it, which would free you from the responsibility for providing *any* proof of interest). This call will also raise an `IllegalArgumentException` if you pass it a lease that's being managed by another `LeaseRenewalSet` from the same service.

other managed leases to be renewed. The `getLeases()` method returns all of the leases managed by this set. Note that it may raise a `LeaseUnmarshalException`, which indicates that one or more of the leases it manages cannot be deserialized. I'll show the definition of that exception type a bit later.

The other methods in this class control how events from the `LeaseRenewalService` will be sent to you. There are two types of events that the service will generate. The first, `ExpirationWarningEvent`, can be sent to you when the lease on your `LeaseRenewalSet` is about to expire. This event can be used as a "trigger" to cause reactivation of your service. The second type of event is the `RenewalFailureEvent`. This event is generated if, for some reason, one of the leases being managed by the `LeaseRenewalService` could not be renewed. This allows you to become aware that some resource you are using may have become inaccessible because of a lease expiration. I'll talk about the details of these events below, but first you should understand how you register to receive them.

The first thing to note about these events is that your lease for the `LeaseRenewalSet` itself also covers any event registrations you have with the set. In other words, there is no *separate* lease for these event registrations; the situation is much the same as with the event registrations on the `LookupDiscoveryService`. This design choice greatly simplifies your interactions with the `LeaseRenewalService`. There is one lease you must manage for all of your uses of the service.[5]

The `setExpirationWarningListener()` allows you to provide a `RemoteEventListener` that will be called some time before your lease on the `LeaseRenewalSet` expires. The `minWarning` parameter specifies, in milliseconds, how long *before* the lease on the lease set expires you should be notified. Like in any Jini remote event registration, the `handback` parameter specifies a `MarshalledObject` that will be returned in any events that result from this registration.

This method returns an `EventRegistration` object to the caller. As I mentioned before, the lease contained in this registration will be the same as the lease for the `LeaseRenewalSet`. The service uses the value of the constant `EXPIRATION_WARNING_EVENT_ID` as the event type ID for each registration. You should note that if you call `setExpirationWarningListener()` multiple times, you simply overwrite the installed listener. The `EventRegistration` that

---

5. This design decision is why the `LeaseRenewalSet` only allows *single* listeners to be installed for each event type. If the `LeaseRenewalSet` allowed multiple simultaneous listeners to be installed, it would have to lease each separately. The "bundled lease" design choice is why the listener methods follow the `set`/`clear` pattern, rather than `add`/`remove`.

is returned to you is the "same" in the sense that it will have the same event type ID, lease, etc., as before. The `clearExpirationWarning()` method, obviously, removes the expiration listener.

The `setRenewalFailureListener()` method allows you to install a `RemoteEventListener` that will be called whenever the `LeaseRenewalService` is unable to renew a lease in the set. This typically happens when the service receives an exception while trying to renew the lease, or if the grantor of the lease refuses to renew the lease.

Like the `setExpirationWarningListener()`, this method takes a `MarshalledObject` as a handback parameter, and returns an `EventRegistration`. This registration will have the same lease as the `LeaseRenewalSet`, and will use the value of the constant `RENEWAL_FAILURE_ID` as the event type ID. Calling the method multiple times simply overwrites the listener in the registration; calling `clearRenewalFailureListener()` removes the listener, so that no events of this type will be sent.

Exception Classes

As you saw in the discussion of the `LeaseRenewalSet` interface, the `getLeases()` method may raise `LeaseUnmarshalException` if there are problems deserializaing any of the leases it is managing:

```
package net.jini.lease;

public class LeaseUnmarshalException extends Exception {
    // ... constructors elided ...
    public Lease[] getLeases();
    public MarshalledObject[] getMarshalledLeases();
    public Throwable[] getExceptions();
}
```

This exception is clearly analogous to the `LookupUnmarshalException` type shown with the `LookupDiscoveryService`. The `getLeases()` call returns the leases that *could* be successfully deserialized. The `getMarshalledLeases()` method returns the leases that could not be deserialized, in `MarshalledObject` form. And, for each element of the array returned by `getMarshalledLeases()`, there will be a corresponding `Throwable` object indicating why the lease could not be deserialized.

`LeaseUnmarshalExceptions`, much like `LookupUnmarshalExceptions`, represent what could very well be a transient failure to deserialize an object. A likely cause may be an unresponsive HTTP server, for example. You should not treat these leases as implying any information about the state of the corresponding `LeaseRenewalService` or `LookupDiscoveryService`, as the case may be.

Event Classes

This section details the particular subclasses of `RemoteEvent` that are sent to your listeners upon renewal failure or expiration warning. First, take a look at the `ExpirationWarningEvent` class:

```
package net.jini.lease;

public class ExpirationWarningEvent extends RemoteEvent {
    // ... constructor elided ...
    public Lease getRenewalSetLease();
}
```

This simple class extends `RemoteEvent`, and so inherits all of the basic `RemoteEvent` functionality—`getSource()`, `getSequenceNumber()`, and so on. The one useful method here is `getRenewalSetLease()`, which returns the lease for the `LeaseRenewalSet` (just in case you neglected to hold on to a copy of it yourself). Sequence numbers in `ExpirationWarningEvent`s follow the strict ordering principle: sequence numbers are strictly ascending, but are allowed to skip.

Here is the `RenewalFailureEvent`, which will be generated whenever a managed lease in the `LeaseRenewalSet` could not be renewed:

```
package net.jini.lease;

public class RenewalFailureEvent extends RemoteEvent {
    // ... constructor elided ...
    public Lease getLease()
        throws IOException, ClassNotFoundException;
    public Throwable getThrowable()
        throws IOException, ClassNotFoundException;
}
```

Like `ExpirationWarningEvent`s, `RenewalFailureEvent`s are subclasses of `RemoteEvent` and therefore inherit all their methods. The `getLease()` method here returns the lease which could not be renewed (note that this is a different lease than that returned by `getLease()` on `ExpirationWarningEvent`). The method here is declared to raise several exception types that can occur during unmarshalling; these may be raised if there were problems deserializing the particular lease object. The `getThrowable()` method returns any `Throwable` object (usually an `Exception`) that was raised during the `LeaseRenewalService`'s attempt to renew the lease. Like `ExpirationWarningEvent`s, sequence numbers for `RenewalFailureEvent`s follow strict ordering.

The EventMailbox

Now it's time to look in detail at the last of these three utility services, the
EventMailbox. Like the other services, the proxy for EventMailbox imple-
ments only a very narrow interface which returns to you a registration object.
Most of your interactions with the service are through this registration object.

The proxies of all implementations of EventMailbox services, including
mercury, implement the standard interface.

```
package net.jini.event;

public interface EventMailbox {
    public MailboxRegistration register(long leaseDuration)
        throws RemoteException, LeaseDeniedException;
}
```

The single method here, register(), returns an instance of MailboxRegistration. Like any Jini service, this registration is leased from the service; the
leaesDuration parameter lets you request, in milliseconds, how long the initial
lease on this registration should be.

You can think of the register() method as asking the service to create a
new mailbox for you. That is, the call will set up a space for holding events. But,
as of yet, you have not told anyone else how to send events to this mailbox; you
haven't "given out its address," as it were.

Note that the register() method may raise RemoteException if it cannot
communicate with the mailbox service's backend, or LeaseDeniedException
if the mailbox denies the requested lease duration for some reason.

The MailboxRegistration object that is returned allows you to complete
your interactions with the mailbox.

```
package net.jini.event;

public interface MailboxRegistration {
    public Lease getLease();
    public RemoteEventListener getListener();
    public void enableDelivery(RemoteEventListener target)
        throws RemoteException;
    public void disableDelivery() throws RemoteException;
}
```

Each MailboxRegistration has associated with it a lease and a remote
event listener. The lease is, of course, the lease on the registration. You must
renew this lease for the service to keep your mailbox alive. If the lease on a regis-

tration expires, the `EventMailbox` service will free its internal storage area allocated to holding your events; any events stored there will disappear.

In the "real world," every mailbox has an address. Sending a letter to this address causes it to (eventually) wind up in the mailbox. The space you lease from the `EventMailbox` service also has an address, which is a `RemoteEventListener` particular to your registration. Any remote events sent to this listener will wind up in your space, where you can retrieve them later. You fetch this listener by calling `getListener()`. Be sure you understand that this is the listener for *your mailbox*, not any particular listener in your program. The mailbox itself creates the instance of this listener, and the client only fetches it from the mailbox. You can take this listener and pass it around to any service that generates remote events. Any events sent to this particular listener will be queued by the `EventMailbox` service for later delivery to you.

So now you've seen how to create a new "mailbox" inside the `EventMailbox` service (via `register()`), and how to retrieve the address (via `getListener()`) of your mailbox so that you can give it to any event-generating services you encounter. Now the question is how you get any queued events *out* of your mailbox.

The `enableDelivery()` call allows you to connect yourself to your mailbox. You provide a `RemoteEventListener` that will receive any events that are queued in the mailbox, or may be received by it later. As soon as you install a listener via `enableDelivery()`, the `EventMailbox` service will flush out to you any stored events associated with your registration. Your listener will continue to receive any events that arrive at the mailbox as long as it is connected to it. Essentially your listener is "live" in the event delivery pipeline as long as it is installed. Once any event is delivered to you, it is removed from the mailbox.

If you call `enableDelivery()` a second time, your new listener will replace the listener already in effect. To remove your listener, you call `disableDelivery()`. Typically you will do this if your service wishes to deactivate, or otherwise disconnect from the network.

The `enable/disable` calls provide a very effective way for services to connect to a network for some period, retrieve any stored events as well as any "live" events, and then disconnect again. This structure is again perfect for activatable services, as well as services that wish to minimize their connectivity, or perhaps have intermittent connectivity. Most clients of the `EventMailbox` service will set up a mailbox, arrange to have events delivered to it, and then disconnect from the network. The actual `MailboxRegistration` object that represents their mailbox may be saved to persistent storage, to ensure that it will always be accessible in the future. After reconnection to the network, the user of the mailbox will request any saved events (possibly reconstituting the `MailboxRegistration` from persistent storage, if necessary).

Here also you see the value of Jini's notion of "generic" remote events. The `EventMailbox` service, because it provides a generic `RemoteEventListener`, can be made to receive and store events from *any* Jini event source—including the services you've already seen, such as JavaSpaces, the transaction manager, or any of the utility services.

At this point, you've seen the details of how each of these services work. Next, it's time to look at an example of how to use them!

An Example

In this example, you'll see how to use the three utility services. As I mentioned at the start of the chapter, the most common use of these services is to provide support for code that can go inactive for periods of time. This example "simulates" such a service—it creates an interconnected web of Jini services that will collect information about the comings and goings of lookup services on the network. After setting up this little distributed system, the program writes a `MailboxRegistration` into the filesystem and then terminates. At a later time, you can run a separate program that will reconstitute this mailbox and display the information that was captured; note that, because you're using the utility services, you can cause this information to be collected even while none of your applications are running.

This example shows off not only the programmatic details of using the utility services, it also illustrates a common design pattern—setting up a system of services to do work while your code is not connected to the network.

The example is split into two parts. The first part, `Collector.java`, will locate proxies for the needed services, connect them together, and then persistently write out a `MailboxRegistration` object that will be used later to fetch the information. The second program, called `EmptyMailbox.java`, can be run at any time after the first program terminates. It simply reconstitutes the `MailboxRegistration` and begins receiving any queued events, as well as any new events, that describe the state of the community's lookup services.

First, take a look at `Collector.java` in Listing 19-7.

Listing 19-7 Collector.java

```java
// A client that uses the three utility services to
// track discoveries.

package corejini.chapter19;

import net.jini.lookup.ServiceDiscoveryManager;
import net.jini.event.EventMailbox;
import net.jini.event.MailboxRegistration;
import net.jini.lease.LeaseRenewalService;
import net.jini.lease.LeaseRenewalSet;
import net.jini.discovery.LookupDiscoveryService;
import net.jini.discovery.LookupDiscoveryRegistration;
import net.jini.discovery.DiscoveryGroupManagement;
import net.jini.core.lookup.ServiceItem;
import net.jini.core.lookup.ServiceTemplate;
import net.jini.core.event.RemoteEvent;
import net.jini.core.event.RemoteEventListener;
import net.jini.core.lease.LeaseDeniedException;
import java.rmi.MarshalledObject;
import java.rmi.RMISecurityManager;
import java.rmi.RemoteException;
import java.io.File;
import java.io.FileOutputStream;
import java.io.ObjectOutputStream;
import java.io.IOException;

public class Collector {
    private ServiceDiscoveryManager luMgr;
    private LookupDiscoveryService lds;
    private EventMailbox ems;
    private LeaseRenewalService lrs;
    private LeaseRenewalSet leaseSet;
    private RemoteEventListener mboxListener;
    private MailboxRegistration mboxReg;
    // 2-hour run
    private static final long DURATION = 2 * 60 * 60 * 1000;

    public Collector() throws IOException {
        luMgr = new ServiceDiscoveryManager(null, null);
    }
```

Listing 19-7 Collector.java (continued)

```
// Find all of the three utility services.
public void findUtilityServices()
    throws Exception {
    System.out.println("Finding utility services");

    // Service items for the three services
    ServiceItem ldsItem, emsItem, lrsItem;
    ServiceTemplate tmpl;
    long waitDur = 1 * 60 * 1000;          // 1 minute

    try {
        Class[] types =
            new Class[]{ LookupDiscoveryService.class };
        tmpl = new ServiceTemplate(null, types, null);
        System.out.println(
            "Searching for LookupDiscoveryService...");
        if ((ldsItem = luMgr.lookup(tmpl,
                                    null,
                                    waitDur)) == null) {
            throw new Exception(
            "No LookupDiscovery found before timeout");
        } else {
            System.out.println("...found!");
        }
    } catch (InterruptedException ex) {
        throw new Exception("No LookupDiscovery found");
    }
```

Listing 19-7 Collector.java (continued)

```java
    try {
        Class[] types =
            new Class[]{ EventMailbox.class };
        tmpl = new ServiceTemplate(null, types, null);
        System.out.println(
            "Searching for EventMailboxService...");
        if ((emsItem = luMgr.lookup(tmpl,
                                    null,
                                    waitDur)) == null) {
            throw new Exception(
                "No EventMailbox found before timeout");
        } else {
            System.out.println("...found!");
        }
    } catch (InterruptedException ex) {
        throw new Exception("No EventMailbox found");
    }

    try {
        Class[] types =
            new Class[]{ LeaseRenewalService.class };
        tmpl = new ServiceTemplate(null, types, null);
        System.out.println(
            "Searching for LeaseRenewalService...");
        if ((lrsItem = luMgr.lookup(tmpl,
                                    null,
                                    waitDur)) == null) {
            throw new Exception(
                "No LeaseRenewal found before timeout");
        } else {
            System.out.println("...found!");
        }
    } catch (InterruptedException ex) {
        throw new Exception("No LeaseRenewal found");
    }
```

Listing 19-7 Collector.java (continued)

```
    // At this point, we've got all the service items.
    // Do some checking to make sure there aren't
    // codebase problems.

    if (ldsItem.service == null) {
        throw new Exception(
            "No proxy for LookupDiscovery service. " +
            "Check for codebase problems?");
    } else {
        lds = (LookupDiscoveryService) ldsItem.service;
    }

    if (emsItem.service == null) {
        throw new Exception(
            "No proxy for EventMailbox service. " +
            "Check for codebase problems?");
    } else {
        ems = (EventMailbox) emsItem.service;
    }

    if (lrsItem.service == null) {
        throw new Exception(
            "No proxy for LeaseRenewal service. " +
            "Check for codebase problems?");
    } else {
        lrs = (LeaseRenewalService) lrsItem.service;
    }
}

// Create a mailbox registration and record its
// listener.
public void setupEventMailbox()
    throws LeaseDeniedException, RemoteException {
    mboxReg = ems.register(DURATION);

    // Store the listener.
    mboxListener = mboxReg.getListener();

    System.out.println("Event mailbox established");
}
```

Listing 19-7 Collector.java (continued)

```java
// Create a lease renewal set that we can use to
// stuff leases into.  Also sign up to receive
// informational events.
public void setupLeaseRenewals()
    throws RemoteException {
    leaseSet = lrs.createLeaseRenewalSet(DURATION);

    // Have expiration warnings sent to the mailbox
    // 1 minute before the lease set expires.
    leaseSet.setExpirationWarningListener(mboxListener,
                                  1 * 60 * 1000,
                                  null);

    // Have any renewal failures also sent to
    // the mailbox.
    leaseSet.setRenewalFailureListener(mboxListener,
                            null);

    // Now, use the lease renewal service to
    // renew the lease on the mailbox for
    // double the duration.  This lets the mailbox
    // stick around a little longer than the
    // rest of the system.
    leaseSet.renewFor(mboxReg.getLease(),
                2 * DURATION);

    System.out.println("Lease set established");
}
```

Listing 19-7 Collector.java (continued)

```java
public void setupDiscovery()
    throws RemoteException {
    LookupDiscoveryRegistration luReg =
        lds.register(
            DiscoveryGroupManagement.ALL_GROUPS,
            null,           // no locators
            mboxListener,   // Events forwarded to mbox
            null,           // handback object
            DURATION);

    // Add the lease for the registration to the
    // LeaseSet from the LeaseRenewalService so
    // that it will be renewed.
    leaseSet.renewFor(luReg.getLease(), DURATION);

    System.out.println(
        "Discovery registration established");
}

private MailboxRegistration getMboxRegistration() {
    return mboxReg;
}

public static void main(String[] args) {
    if (args.length != 1) {
        System.out.println("Usage: <file>");
        System.exit(1);
    }

    if (System.getSecurityManager() == null) {
        System.setSecurityManager(
                new RMISecurityManager());
    }
```

Listing 19-7 Collector.java (continued)

```java
    try {
        File file = new File(args[0]);
        ObjectOutputStream out =
            new ObjectOutputStream(
                new FileOutputStream(file));

        Collector collector = new Collector();

        collector.findUtilityServices();

        collector.setupEventMailbox();
        collector.setupLeaseRenewals();
        collector.setupDiscovery();

        System.out.println("Services connected.");
        System.out.println("Saving mailbox...");

        Object mboxReg =
            collector.getMboxRegistration();
        MarshalledObject mobj =
            new MarshalledObject(mboxReg);
        out.writeObject(mobj);
        out.flush();
        out.close();
        System.out.println(
            "...mailbox successfully saved to " +
            args[0]);

        System.exit(1);
    } catch (Exception ex) {
        System.err.println("Error: " + ex.getMessage());
        ex.printStackTrace();
        System.exit(1);
    }
  }
}
```

To run this program, you must pass it a filename on the command line into which it will save its serialized MailboxRegistration. The main() for the program installs a security manager, checks the command-line arguments, and begins setting up the distributed system of services.

The first step in this process is handled by the `findUtilityServices()` method. This method uses the `ServiceDiscoveryManager` to look for an instance of a `LookupDiscoveryService`, an `EventMailbox` service, and a `LeaseRenewalService`. Note that the code here calls `lookup()` directly on the `ServiceDiscoveryManager`, passing it a timeout—the code will wait for at most one minute to find each of these services. If one of the necessary services cannot be found, the code raises an exception, causing the program to exit.

After `findUtilityServices()` completes, `main()` sets up each of these three services. The first, and the simplest, is the `EventMailbox`. The program simply creates a new `MailboxRegistration`, and records the registration and its listener for future use. Note that the code passes an initial duration of two hours to the `register()` call. Chances are the mailbox service won't grant a lease of such a lengthy duration, but that's okay: the lease for the service will be passed off to a `LeaseRenewalService` for management.

You see how that works in the next step. The call to `setupLeaseRenewals()` creates a `LeaseRenewalSet` from the `LeaseRenewalService`. It then requests that the leasing service direct any renewal failure or expiration warning messages to the listener previously retrieved from the `MailboxRegistration`. Thus, the mailbox will queue up any events that detail problems that the leasing service may have when renewing leases, as well as the message that indicates that the lease on the `LeaseSet` which holds the entire web of services together is about to expire. Finally, the lease on the `MailboxRegistration` is added to the managed `LeaseSet`, with a managed duration of two hours. This means that the `LeaseRenewalService` will try to renew the lease on the mailbox for two hours, after which point the lease will be allowed to expire naturally.

Finally, the `LookupDiscoveryService` is set up. A new registration is created with the discovery service. This registration will generate events whenever a lookup service that is a member of any group is discovered or discarded. Note that here, again, the listener for the mailbox is installed as the receiver of these events. Any events generated by the discovery service will be delivered to the mailbox service where they will be stored.

The lease for this registration is again passed off to the `LeaseRenewalService` for a two-hour duration.

Be sure you understand how leasing is done in this example. The program creates a single `LeaseRenewalSet` that will contain all of the leases for the various service registrations, except for the lease on the `LeaseRenewalSet` itself. All of these managed leases will be renewed for two hours. The lease on the `LeaseRenewalSet` is *not* renewed in this particular example. So the entire interconnected set of services will exist only so long as the lease on the `LeaseRenewalSet` is valid. The initially requested duration of this lease was two hours, so the system will likely "dissolve" after this time period passes.

Core Note: Mobile code everywhere!

It might be fruitful to pause for a moment here and realize exactly how much mobile code is in use in this example. Back at the start of this book, in Chapter 2, I discussed mobile code and its many uses in the Java and Jini environments. By this point, you've probably become habituated to setting codebases and security policies, without even thinking about it.

In this code, there are literally dozens of examples of mobile code being sent around the network, all in the service of making the Java object-oriented programming model work in the distributed setting. Not only is the code for the various proxies for the utility services being silently transmitted, loaded, and run, the code for the various lease implementations these services use is also being moved across the network. Likewise, the code for every remote event listener is being copied to exactly where it needs to be.

Not only is this code being moved into the `Collector` *example program, it's also being moved between services. Take a look at the remote event listener that you receive from the* `MailboxRegistration`. *The code for this class has been loaded into the JVM running* `Collector`, *so that the program you see here can manipulate it. This code was loaded from the codebase URL specified back when you started up the* `EventMailbox` *service. But look at what happens next: the Collector passes this object off to other services—this listener gets sent to the* `LeaseRenewalService` *and the* `LookupDiscoveryService`. *Each of these services, when they receive the listener, will deserialize it and load the code for it, directly from the codebase URL you specified when you ran the* `EventMailbox`. *RMI's semantics ensure that the original location from which the code for an object was loaded will be preserved in all RMI calls. This lets you take an object downloaded from one service and send it off to another service, and have everything still work normally.*

Finally, after connecting these services together, the program serializes the `MailboxRegistration` to disk. Remember that the `MailboxRegistration` is simply a Java object that maintains a remote reference to the back-end portion of the `EventMailbox` service. By serializing it, you can save this reference for later use. In this particular example, the later use is the `EmptyMailbox` program, which will deserialize the `MailboxRegistration` and use it to receive any events that may have been received between the time the mailbox was created and the time `EmptyMailbox` is run. Note that the `Collector` program, which set all of this up, needn't be running at all during the actual collection phase!

Notice that the `EventMailbox` is being saved as a `MarshalledObject` here. This is because the `MarshalledObject` class preserves RMI's semantics of code loading, which I discussed in the "Core Note" above. When you encapsulate an object in a `MarshalledObject`, the codebase from which it was loaded will be saved as well. This allows the `EmptyMailbox` program, shown below in Listing 19-8, to load the `MarshalledObject` off of disk and, when the `MailboxRegistration` is fetched out of it, any needed code will be loaded from the class's original codebase.

"Normal" serialization—meaning simply writing an object to a file or an array of bytes—doesn't preserve the codebase information. Only serializing an object to or from an RMI remote method call, or to or from a `MarshalledObject`, will preserve this information.

Next, take a look at `EmptyMailbox.java`.

Listing 19-8 EmptyMailbox.java

```
// This client loads a serialized mailbox off of
// disk and receives events from it.

package corejini.chapter19;

import net.jini.core.event.RemoteEvent;
import net.jini.core.event.RemoteEventListener;
import net.jini.event.MailboxRegistration;
import java.io.File;
import java.io.ObjectInputStream;
import java.io.FileInputStream;
import java.rmi.MarshalledObject;
import java.rmi.RemoteException;
import java.rmi.RMISecurityManager;
import java.rmi.server.UnicastRemoteObject;
```

Listing 19-8 EmptyMailbox.java (continued)

```java
public class EmptyMailbox {
    private MailboxRegistration mbox;

    static class LogListener extends UnicastRemoteObject
        implements RemoteEventListener {
        LogListener() throws RemoteException {
        }

        public void notify(RemoteEvent ev) {
            System.out.println("Received from mailbox: ");
            System.out.println("     " + ev);
            System.out.println("     " +
                ev.getClass().getName());
        }
    }

    public EmptyMailbox(String filename) throws Exception {
        File file = new File(filename);
        ObjectInputStream in =
            new ObjectInputStream(
                new FileInputStream(file));

        MarshalledObject mobj = (MarshalledObject)
            in.readObject();

        mbox = (MailboxRegistration) mobj.get();
    }


    public void receiveEvents() throws RemoteException {
        mbox.enableDelivery(new LogListener());
    }
}
```

Listing 19-8 EmptyMailbox.java (continued)

```java
    public static void main(String[] args) {
        try {
            if (args.length != 1) {
                System.err.println(
                    "Usage: EmptyMailbox <file>");
                System.exit(1);
            }

            if (System.getSecurityManager() == null) {
                System.setSecurityManager(
                    new RMISecurityManager());
            }

            EmptyMailbox empty = new EmptyMailbox(args[0]);
            System.out.println("Receiving events...");
            empty.receiveEvents();
        } catch (Exception ex) {
            System.err.println("Error: " + ex.getMessage());
            ex.printStackTrace();
        }
    }
}
```

This program is very simple in comparison to the `Collector` example. The constructor in the code here simply reconstitutes the saved `MailboxRegistra-tion`. It does this by first loading a `MarshalledObject` off of disk, from a path specified on the command line. Then it calls the `get()` method on `Marshalle-dObject` to return the `MailboxRegistration` enclosed within it. It is when the `get()` method is called that the registration is actually deserialized, and the code for it is loaded from the codebase saved in the `MarshalledObject`. This will be the URL that you passed on the command line way back when you started the `EventMailbox` example.

After re-creating the `MailboxRegistration`, the code simply creates a new listener to receive events, and then calls `enableDelivery()`. The listener, called `LogListener`, will print out any received event to the standard output stream.

Note that this program never terminates, even though the connection of services constructed by the `Collector` program will dissolve after about two hours. One possible extension of this program would be to rewrite the `EmptyMailbox` code to shut down after it has received the `ExpirationWarningEvent` from the mailbox. Remember that this event is sent just before the lease on the `Leas-eSet`—which holds the entire web of services together—is about to expire. The

`Collector` already arranges for these events to be delivered to the mailbox. `EmptyMailbox` would know that, a short amount of time after it has received this event, no future events will be coming.

Compiling and Running the Example

First, get the two example programs compiled. You'll have to generate RMI stubs for the `LogListener` class (the only class in this example that extends `UnicastRemoteObject`), and copy the class file for the stub into the `client-dl` directory.

On Windows:

```
javac -classpath C:\files;
                C:\jini1_1\lib\jini-core.jar;
                C:\jini1_1\lib\jini-ext.jar;
                C:\jini1_1\lib\sun-util.jar
    -d C:\client
   C:\files\corejini\chapter19\Collector.java
   C:\files\corejini\chapter19\EmptyMailbox.java

rmic -classpath C:\jini1_1\lib\jini-core.jar;
                C:\jini1_1\lib\jini-ext.jar;
                C:\jini1_1|lib\sun-util.jar;
                C:\client
    -d C:\client
        corejini.chapter19.EmptyMailbox.LogListener

mkdir C:\client\corejini\chapter19
cd C:\client\corejini\chapter19
copy EmptyMailbox$LogListener_Stub.class
    C:\client-dl\corejini\chapter19
```

On UNIX:

```
javac -classpath  /files:
                files/jini1_1/lib/jini-core.jar:
                files/jini1_1/lib/jini-ext.jar:
                files/jini1_1/lib/sun-util.jar
    -d /files/client
   /files/corejini/chapter19/Collector.java
   /files/corejini/chapter19/EmptyMailbox.java
```

```
mkdir /files/client-dl/corejini/chapter19
cd /files/client/corejini/chapter19
cp EmptyMailbox\$LogListener_Stub.class
    /files/client-dl/corejini/chapter19
```

After this, you're set to run the examples. Note that the `Collector` program uses the `ServiceDiscoveryManager`. As you recall from Chapter 10, the `ServiceDiscoveryManager` uses its own remote event listener to receive updates from lookup services. Even though this code isn't written by you, you *must* make some provision for exporting it for the `ServiceDiscoveryManager` to function properly.

You should review the instructions for the examples in Chapter 10 if you need a refresher. If you've already run the examples from Chapter 10, and have not erased the contents of your `client-dl` directory, then the code for the listener should still be installed. You should check to make sure that there is a directory called `net` under `client-dl` that contains the needed listener class files. If not, the example code here will not work, and you should follow the instructions in Chapter 10 for setting this up.

Once you've made sure the `ServiceDiscoveryManager` listener code is properly installed, you're ready to run the `Collector`. Be sure to pass a pathname on the command line to which the `MailboxRegistration` object will be written.

On Windows:

```
java -cp C:\jini1_1\lib\jini-core.jar;
        C:\jini1_1\lib\jini-ext.jar;
        C:\jini1_1\lib\sun-util.jar;
        C:\client
    -Djava.security.policy=/files/policy
    -Djava.rmi.server.codebase=http://myhost:8086/
        corejini.chapter19.Collector C:\temp\collector
```

On UNIX:

```
java -cp /files/jini1_1/lib/jini-core.jar:
        /files/jini1_1/lib/jini-ext.jar:
        /files/jini1_1/lib/sun-util.jar:
        /files/client
    -Djava.security.policy=/files/policy
    -Djava.rmi.server.codebase=http://myhost:8086/
```

```
corejini.chapter19.Collector /var/tmp/collector
```

When the `collector` program starts up, you should be able to see it discover the required services, connect them together, and then save the `MailboxRegistration` to the file you specified.

Finding utility services
Searching for LookupDiscoveryService...
...found!
Searching for EventMailboxService...
...found!
Searching for LeaseRenewalService...
...found!
Event mailbox established
Lease set established
Discovery registration established
Services connected.
Saving mailbox...
...mailbox successfully saved to /var/tmp/collector

At this point, the `Collector` program will exit. You may want to wait a bit and then run the `EmptyMailbox` program. But remember that since the collection of services established by the `Collector` will dissolve after two hours, you shouldn't wait *too* long to run it. Be sure to pass the same filename that you used in the previous example.

On Windows:

```
java -cp C:\jini1_1\lib\jini-core.jar;
        C:\jini1_1\lib\jini-ext.jar;
        C:\jini1_1\lib\sun-util.jar;
        C:\client
    -Djava.security.policy=/files/policy
    -Djava.rmi.server.codebase=http://myhost:8086/
        corejini.chapter19.EmptyMailbox C:\temp\collector
```

On UNIX:

```
java -cp /files/jini1_1/lib/jini-core.jar:
        /files/jini1_1/lib/jini-ext.jar:
        /files/jini1_1/lib/sun-util.jar:
        /files/client
```

```
-Djava.security.policy=/files/policy
-Djava.rmi.server.codebase=http://myhost:8086/
    corejini.chapter19.EmptyMailbox /var/tmp/collector
```

The program will load the `MailboxRegistration` off the disk and reconstitute it. This object doesn't itself contain the events; instead, it contains a remote reference to the `EventMailbox`'s back end. Even though this remote reference has been serialized, stored, and then deserialized, it is still "live" and can be used to contact the service.

Receiving events...

Received event from mailbox:

net.jini.discovery.RemoteDiscoveryEvent[source=com.sun.jini.fiddler.FiddlerProxy@86f01a85]

net.jini.discovery.RemoteDiscoveryEvent

This program doesn't exit. It simply stays active, and tries to continually receive events from the mailbox. Of course, at some point, the lease originally established on the `LeaseRenewalSet` by the `Collector` will expire. It is this lease that holds the entire constellation of services together. So once this happens, the `EmptyMailbox` program will not receive any more events.

This example has shown how to use all three of the utility services to create functionality that persists even after the program that created it exits. A later program can then come and take advantage of that functionality, or the *same* program could be reactivated to use it.

Summary

This chapter has introduced you to a handful of useful new services first introduced in Jini 1.1. These utility services are primarily designed as a way to create services that can deactivate themselves, or services that can function well in low-connectivity environments.

But beyond that, these services show where Jini is headed: toward networks where "applications" are really composed of sets of cooperating services, located dynamically on the network. As more and more Jini services appear—whether these be "end-user"-oriented services such as printers and storage engines, or "utility" services like the ones you've seen here—your options as a Jini developer will only become richer and richer.

APPENDICES

Appendix A

An RMI Primer

This appendix presents a quick-and-dirty primer to the Java Remote Method Invocation (RMI) technology. RMI has been in Java since the days of JDK1.1, but has been significantly enhanced and expanded for the Java 2 release. Jini takes advantage of classes and features that exist only in the Java 2 version of RMI.

This appendix covers the basics of RMI as it exists in Java 2. I'll talk about how to design, compile, and build RMI programs, how to use serialization, how class loading works in RMI, security implications, and how to use the RMI activation framework. This appendix isn't meant to provide full, in-depth coverage of this technology—that could easily be a book in itself! Rather, it's meant to provide enough information about the basics to get you up and running quickly.

Overview of RMI

RMI provides a way for Java applications running in different Java Virtual Machines (JVMs), possibly even on different host computers, to talk to one another. In this sense, RMI is very much like the Remote Procedure Call (RPC) systems that you may be used to: RMI allows a Java program on one machine to call out to a Java method defined by an object that exists on another machine.

But, as you'll see, RMI has some properties that make it unique, and really distinguish it from RPC systems, or even other distributed object systems.

Remote Interfaces

An object that will expose methods that can be invoked by objects on other machines is called a *remote* object. In client/server terminology, this object is the *server*, and the object that invokes methods on it is the *client*. But while it may help you to think of clients and servers for purposes of understanding how a pair of objects interact, RMI doesn't impose any other restrictions on the communication patterns of clients and servers. A server may itself be a client of another object, and a single Java program can—and often will—contain both client and server objects. So it isn't really fair to call RMI a client/server system; it's much more rich than that. But for purposes of clarity, I'll use the term "client" to refer to an object that is invoking methods on a remote object, and the term "server" to refer to the remote object that is allowing its methods to be called remotely.

Before a client can call a method on an object—remote or not—the client must know the interface that the object implements. For example, if someone hands you a plain `java.lang.Object`, you only know how to do a few things to it: call `equals()`, `toString()`, and the other methods that are defined by this class. And even though the object may be a more specific type, such as a `Vector` or a `JPanel`, unless you know more specific information about the type of the object, you cannot use it.

The same is true in RMI, just as it's true in "plain" Java. For a client to invoke a method on a server, it must know what methods the server makes available to it. This set of APIs is called the server's *remote interface*, and it defines the set of methods that can be invoked from outside the server's JVM. Of course, any given server object may also have any number of "local" methods that can only be called by objects that live in the server's JVM.

In RMI, the remote interface of a server is defined by creating a Java interface that extends the `java.rmi.Remote` interface. By extending `Remote`, you're in effect telling RMI that it should create the necessary machinery to allow any methods in your interface to be called remotely. A particular server object that you write, then, is simply an implementation of this remote interface.

Stubs and Skeletons

The JVM only knows how to perform local method invocations: When you write a program that invokes a method on an object, this machinery gets executed to run the method. So then, how do remote invocations work? The answer is that a bit of extra machinery is needed; in the case of RMI, this machinery is implemented in Java code layered atop the JVM, and is not part of the JVM itself.

The first extra bit of functionality RMI requires is a way for the server that implements the remote interface to be able to accept network connections from clients, take data read from those connections, and "turn them into" Java method invocations locally. Second, when a client makes an invocation on a remote object, it must actually make a local invocation on some local object that will then perform the necessary network communication to talk to the remote object. (The client—or any Java code—can only invoke a local object, because this is all the JVM knows how to do directly.) This local object then essentially serves as a representation for the remote object, and takes care of connecting to the server and sending it data to cause the invocation to happen. Once the invocation has finished, any return data must be sent back to the client and reconstituted.

On the server side, this extra functionality is handled by two different classes. First, to handle the network communication, the server object typically will extend a class that knows how to take care of the networking chores involved in RMI. Most of the time, servers will extend a class called `java.rmi.server.UnicastRemoteObject`. This class has all the necessary "smarts" to take care of the low-level networking details that must be done for the receiver to accept network connections.

But, `UnicastRemoteObject` is just a "generic" class that can be extended to provide networking support for all kinds of remote server objects. How do the *specific* methods on a *particular* server object get called? The answer is that a second object, called a *skeleton*, handles taking the data received from the network, figuring out which operation to invoke on the server, and returning the results. The skeleton is paired with a particular server object, because it has to understand what methods are available on a server, and what arguments and return values they have. You can think of a skeleton as providing an "insulation layer" between the server object, which is written pretty much as a normal "local" Java object, and the network.[1]

When a server object has been set up, is listening for network connections, and is ready to receive remote method invocations from clients, we say that the server object has been *exported*. You'll see this term used throughout the RMI documentation, and throughout this book. An exported remote object is simply one that is available to clients for remote method invocations.

On the client side, the situation is similar, but a little simpler. The object *making* a remote call doesn't have to do anything special to "export" itself, or make itself callable from other JVMs. All the client-side machinery has to do is map from local object invocations on the object that represents the server to actual network communication. In RMI, the local object that lives inside the client and handles the chores of packing and unpacking the data and managing the network connection to a server is called a *stub*. Whenever a client "invokes" a method on a remote object, it is actually invoking a method on a local stub object—because this is all the JVM can do inherently. This stub then sends a message to the remote JVM, where it is received and "translated" by the server-side skeleton into a local method call. Figure shows how this happens.[2]

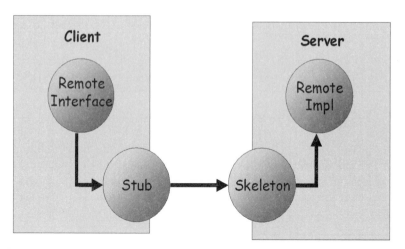

Figure A–1 Clients and servers communicate through stubs and skeletons

1. As of Java 1.2, skeletons are not really needed. The RMI machinery can use reflection to invoke methods on the server object. But unless you pass the -v1.2 option to the RMI stub and skeleton compiler (rmic, which you'll learn about shortly), it will still generate skeletons and use the "old" style of doing things, described here.

2. Java 2 version 1.3 (also known as just "JDK 1.3") adds a new feature called *dynamic proxies* that will eventually pave the way for stubs to disappear also. This feature can, at run time, generate "wrapper" classes that meet some defined interface. Look at the java.lang.reflect.Proxy class for details of this exciting feature.

All this may seem like a lot of work, and in fact, RMI is doing quite a bit "under the covers" to make all this remote communication happen. But the good thing is that, for the most part, *all* this machinery is hidden from both clients and servers.[3] Servers virtually never see their skeletons—even though a skeleton is what actually invokes the remote methods on a server, the server can "believe" that clients are invoking them directly.

Clients actually "see" the stubs for a remote server, but in general, think of the stubs as just being the remote object itself. In RMI, the stub for a server object implements the *exact same* remote interface as the server itself: It has the same methods, raises the same exceptions, and has the same parameters and return types. Stubs even implement the `Remote` interface, so they look like any other remote object. So for all intents and purposes, when you're writing a client, you write your code in terms of the remote interface you're calling out to. You never have to know that it's actually the stub that you're talking to, and not the remote object directly.

Serialization

I said in the preceding section that the stubs and skeletons take care of the networking details, such as packing and unpacking arguments and return values to and from remote calls. So if I have a remote method that takes some input parameters and returns a result, the stubs and skeletons take care of turning these parameters and return values into streams of bytes that can be sent over a network and reconstituted at the other end.

The mechanism for turning an object into streams of bytes and then reconstituting them is called *serialization*, and is a necessary part of RMI, as well as an important part of many other applications.

In the Java language, any object that implements the `java.io.Serializable` interface can be turned into a stream of bytes and then later reconstituted. The `Serializable` interface actually adds no methods that you have to implement; it's merely a "tagging" interface that you use as an indication to Java that you're allowing a given class to be serialized.[4]

---

3. And, as we'll see shortly, you don't even have to write the stubs and skeletons yourself. RMI will create them for you.

4. While you don't have to implement any methods to be serializable, you *can* implement certain methods to override the default serialization behavior. A full discussion of how to do this is outside the scope of this appendix, but look at the documentation for the `Serializable` class for details on how to do this, if you're interested.

Without serialization, RMI would have no way to send complex Java objects across the wire—either as arguments to a method invocation or as return values. Any type that you use as a parameter or return value to or from an RMI *must* be serializable. Primitive types such as `int`, `boolean`, and so on are considered to be serializable, so you can also send or return these in any RMI call.

There are a few other requirements that your classes must meet if they are to be serializable. Even though your class may implement the `Serializable` interface, there are things it can do that prevent it from being serialized. Even worse, these problems cannot be detected at compile time, and so you discover them when you get a `java.io.NotSerializableException` at run time.

The first thing your class must do is ensure that, if it extends a *non*-serializable class, it has a public, no-argument constructor. The presence of this constructor is required for the class to be properly deserialized. Second, you must make sure that your class contains no references to objects that are themselves not serializable. This is why Java cannot fully determine whether your classes are serializable at compile time: You may have an object that would otherwise be serializable, but contains a `Vector` of both serializable and nonserializable objects. If a member of an object cannot be serialized, then the object itself cannot be serialized.

Serialization is deceptively simple. While in most cases, developers can simply tag an object as `Serializable` and then forget about it, there are cases when you may need to take more care with serialization. See the "Further Reading" section at the end of the appendix for some pointers to more information on serialization.

Parameters and Return Values

With the overview of serialization and stubs complete, let's look at exactly how parameter passing works in RMI. First, I'll talk about the simple case—what happens when you pass a reference to a non-remote object as an argument to an RMI method call.

Any parameter or return value that you use in an RMI call must be serializable. RMI will transparently serialize the objects or primitive types you pass or return in remote methods. The fact that RMI serializes the data it sends has some important implications. Unlike local method calls, which pass references to objects, RMI copies the arguments and return values of remote method calls. So the semantics of input and output objects are "pass by value" rather than "pass by reference."

The treatment of remote objects as parameters or return values is a bit different. Let's look next at what happens when you pass a remote object into a remote method as an argument, or return it from a remote method as a result.

RMI works some more "under the covers" magic when it comes to using references to remote objects. Say in the implementation of your server, one of your remote methods returns a reference to `this`. In your server, `this` refers to the actual server implementation object that lives in the server's JVM. But remember that clients always deal with stubs as a way to represent the server; they have no way to *directly* refer to any object in another JVM, so they have to use the stub as a proxy for a remote object. So what you would like to have happen when the server returns a reference to itself is that the client should receive a reference to the server's stub.

To make this happen, remote methods look for input and output parameters that are references to objects that implement `Remote`. Whenever one of these is seen, it is silently replaced with the corresponding stub as appropriate. So if a server returns a reference to itself as the result of a method, RMI "converts" this to a stub so that the client can use it.

This transparent argument swapping ensures the "invisibility" of stubs in both services and clients. Again, both services and clients have the illusion that they're working with local objects, because even things like the `this` reference work and can be exchanged between JVMs. But—when a remote object is being passed or returned—RMI replaces it with its stub so that it can be used from the other JVM.

The effect of this strategy is that remote objects maintain the "pass by reference" semantics of "normal" Java. When you pass a remote object in or out of a method call, what you actually get is a "live" reference to that remote object that can be used by either the client or the server. Passing a remote object doesn't copy the entire object; rather, it just copies the stub, which can be thought of as a reference to a remote object. (And stubs are, in fact, serializable, which means that they are actually passed in remote methods just as non-remote serializable objects are.)

Dynamic Code Loading

Simply saying that all parameter and return types must be serializable glosses over a problem that I haven't addressed yet. Serialization only packages up the member data within an object. That is, serialization takes the contents of a particular instance of a class and puts it in a form that can be written to disk or transmitted over the wire.

But when another program retrieves the packaged (serialized) object, that program cannot reconstitute and use the object unless it has access to the definition of the class that the object implements. That definition is contained in the class file that was produced when the object's source code was compiled. That class file contains the "code" which is required to reconstitute and actually use the object. This code defines how the information contained in the serialized form of the object should be interpreted and translated into the various fields of the actual, live object, as well as the methods that the object implements.

Serialization only packages up the states of all the member variables within the object, not the byte codes for the object iself. Without the necessary code, the serialized data cannot be reconstituted into a "live" object again.

So if you send a serialized object to someone else, how can they use it if they don't get the code along with the data?

This single question—what to do with objects that you may receive that you don't have the code for—leads to one of the biggest differences between RMI and "traditional" RPC or distributed object systems. RMI allows a JVM to dynamically download the *implementation* of a class as needed, not just the data contained in a particular object.

Let's look at what this means in practice. Say you've defined a remote interface that can sort collections of data. This interface might have a method called `sort()` that is defined to take a `java.util.Set` (this interface is a part of the Java 2 "collections framework;" it's essentially an interface that describes the things you can do to a set of data). This method might be defined to return an object that implements the `java.util.SortedSet` interface.

The Java collections framework defines an implementation of `Set` called `HashSet`. As you might expect, this implementation uses a hash map internally, and has certain performance characteristics based on this implementation. Likewise, the collections framework comes with an implementation of `SortedSet` called `TreeSet` that uses a tree data structure internally.

All is fine here, because the server supports a simple method that takes and returns common, known types. But what happens if a client writer decides that he or she needs to use a new, custom implementation of `Set` internally, maybe called `FastSet`? Perhaps this set uses some exotic data structure for performance or space reasons. The `sort()` method is defined to simply take objects that implement `Set`. In the local case, you know you could pass the new `FastSet` and everything would work, because `sort()` only cares that its inputs speak the `Set` interface. This is an example of *polymorphism* in an object-oriented language: As long as you know what interface you want to speak, you don't *care* how that interface is implemented.

But this situation presents a problem in the remote case. In the remote case, the server has never even *heard* of `FastSet`, and it certainly doesn't have the implementation of it available. Whereas in the local case, where the class file is available on the disk at both compile and run time, in the remote case, the server doesn't even know that it *needs* the class file until run time. What you would like to have happen is for the implementation of `FastSet` to be sent to the server, which would allow the server to work on the new `FastSet` and return its results, just like it would in the local case.

It turns out this is exactly what RMI does, and this technique is the source of much of its power. Unlike traditional distributed "object" systems, where a remote object may lose the ability to have unknown subclasses passed into it, RMI allows true "remote polymorphism," where objects work as parameters and results to and from remote methods, just like they would in local methods.

Let's see how this would work in practice. Normally, a Java application finds the implementations of all the classes it needs by looking in its *CLASSPATH*— a set of directories and JAR files that contain necessary class files. RMI extends this basic notion with the concept of a *codebase*. You can think of the codebase as a new location for class files that is provided dynamically to a Java program so that it can access some new class implementations it didn't previously have access to.

In RMI, any program that will *export* classes that may need to be download-able by others must set a codebase that indicates where the implementations of these classes come from. The codebase isn't used to tell the exporting program where to get the classes from. Rather, the codebase is sent to the downloading program, tagged on to the serialization of the object's data. Once the receiver gets the serialized object, it can reconstitute it and, if it doesn't have the class available locally, download it from the location indicated in the codebase. This process of tagging the codebase to the serialized data stream is often called *annotating* the stream with the codebase.

Essentially, the codebase is a way for one program to extend another's CLASSPATH at run time, for particular classes. And whereas the CLASSPATH typically contains only pathnames, the codebase will contain URLs that indicate from where the classes can be downloaded.

A misunderstanding of how codebase works is one of the most common problems faced by beginning RMI programmers. The RMI protocol itself doesn't handle transmitting class implementations around the network. Instead, RMI uses an external facility—the ability of Java programs to copy byte codes from URLs and securely execute them—to provide downloadable code. RMI only supports the mechanisms for "annotating" serialized data streams with the codebase that says where to get the byte codes that implement the serialized class.

In the most common scenario, downloadable code will be placed in a directory served by an HTTP server. Any program that exports downloadable code will then set a codebase that contains an `http` URL that indicates the location of the classes on that server. Codebases are set via properties to the server object's JVM, passed on the command line.

Most new RMI developers commonly think of using downloadable code to support "custom" implementations of types used as parameters or return values in remote method calls. But RMI actually uses dynamic code loading to transmit the stubs for a remote object to a client. This way, the client *only* has to know about the remote interface that the server object implements. The actual stubs that facilitate communication with the server are provided by the server itself. This allows the server to do things such as use custom stubs, or stubs that use custom network protocols, if it chooses. So even the most simple RMI programs will need to support downloadable code, to move stubs around if for no other reason.

Security Implications

Clearly there are security implications to being able to download code from another application on-the-fly. The situation is much like an applet: You're running code that you got from someone else, and you hope that it's not malicious. But just like applets, which provide a restricted environment for downloaded code, RMI can provide a secure environment for running the code that you get from other programs.

In Java, application security is provided by having a `SecurityManager` installed in the run-time environment. To prevent malicious downloaded code from doing harm, RMI will not remotely load *any* code if there is no `Security-Manager` active in the downloading program—instead, the program must be able to find all necessary classes, including stubs, on the local CLASSPATH.

While this situation may be workable for debugging, it's not appropriate for a production environment. To enable downloadable code, you must run with a security manager set. RMI provides a simple security manager, called the `java.rmi.RMISecurityManager`, which can be used. In Java 2, security managers typically are configurable by a *security policy*, which is a file passed on the command line to a Java program. A security policy can define certain "permissions" for the code in an application, based on where the code comes from. So, for instance, you can express notions like, "All code signed by Dave can write to this particular directory, and connect to this particular host on the Internet," or, "Any code downloaded from this site has no filesystem access."

While a full discussion of Java 2 security is outside the scope of this book, you can check the "Further Reading" section at the end of this appendix for some pointers to good material to get you started. But the basics of what you need to know about security and RMI is that if you use a security manager, which you *must* do if you want to use downloadable code, then you *must* set a security policy that tells that security manager what sorts of operations are allowable.

When a security manager is in effect, it controls the behavior of not only downloaded code, but local code as well. By default, almost nothing is allowed, so you'll need a policy file that at least allows your program to access the URLs for remote code.

Chapter 5 of this book presents a "promiscuous" policy file that allows any sort of accesses. This policy is used in all of the examples in the book, because it makes testing and experimentation easier. But for deployment, you should craft a more careful policy file that restricts access more appropriately.

Marshalled Objects

One other handy item in your bag of tricks as an RMI programmer is the `Mar-shalledObject` class. This class, introduced in Java 2, provides a way to represent the serialized form of an object. In general, when you serialize an object, you can write it to a byte array, to a file, or to any other stream of content. The `MarshalledObject` class provides another "container" for the bytes that make up a serialized object.

`MarshalledObjects` are created by passing an object to them in the constructor; this object is serialized and stored within the `MarshalledObject`, and can be later retrieved by using the `get()` method on `MarshalledObject`.

So why would you ever want to use an object to represent a serialized object? Isn't the whole point of serialization to turn the object into something that's not object-like for transmission or storage?

The answer is that, very often, a program will need to hold on to the serialized representation of an object without immediately reconstituting it. The `MarshalledObject` class provides a convenient and standard way to do this.

Suppose, for instance, that you're writing a storage service for objects. Clients may pass in objects that implement `Serializable` for storage by the service. Now, in many cases, the storage service will have no need to reconstitute the objects that are sent to it for safekeeping: The storage service never *looks at* or *uses* the objects, it just holds on to them. If clients pass `Serializable` objects to the storage service through RMI, then those objects will be automatically reconstituted when they arrive at the storage service, which can be an expensive operation, and is simply not useful for this particular application.

In such a case, the storage service could define its interfaces so that it takes `MarshalledObjects` as values to store. `MarshalledObjects` are themselves `Serializable`, so they can be transmitted over the wire to the service. But when they are reconstituted, they become simply `MarshalledObjects`, not whatever arbitrarily complex application-defined class is stored within the `MarshalledObject`.

So using `MarshalledObject` is a good way to transmit and represent objects that shouldn't be automatically reconstituted. But this class provides another handy feature—storing and fetching objects out of a `MarshalledObject` uses RMI-style serialization semantics. So when you store an object in a `MarshalledObject`, it is stored with codebase information that indicates where the implementation of the object can be found. Retrieving an object out of a `MarshalledObject` instance uses this location information to dynamically load the class, if necessary. Also like RMI, when you store a remote object in a `MarshalledObject`, the remote object is silently replaced with its stub.

This feature of `MarshalledObjects` makes them useful as a self-contained representation of everything a client or service might need to know to reconstitute and use an object.

So far I've talked about the basic structure of RMI applications, how parameters are passed and used, how code is downloaded, and how security works. Now it's time to turn these abstract notions into concrete details about how to build RMI applications.

Building with RMI

I'll walk through a quick example of how to write a simple RMI program. While the previous sections focused on the conceptual details of how RMI works, this section looks at the pragmatic details of how to actually go through the steps of writing, building, and running an RMI program.

The first thing you need to do is create the remote interface that will define how a client and server will talk to one another. In Listing A–1, I've defined a simple remote interface, called `NextNumber`, that has a single method. The idea is that a client passes an `int` to this method, which returns the next larger `int` as a result (this is a pretty trivial example, but the goal here is to work out the details of RMI, not focus on a full-fledged application).

Listing A–1 `NextNumber.java`

```
// A remote interface for getting increasing numbers

package corejini.appendixa;

import java.rmi.Remote;
import java.rmi.RemoteException;

public interface NextNumber extends Remote {
    public int getNextNumber(int n) throws RemoteException;
}
```

This interface defines a single method, `getNextNumber()`, which both takes and returns a simple `int`. There are only a couple of things you really must note about this remote interface. The first is that it extends `Remote`. This is the signal to RMI that the interface will be used as a way for a client to speak to a server object that lives in a different JVM. The second is that the `getNextNumber()` method is declared to raise `RemoteException`. In general, *every* method that is callable remotely must be declared to raise this exception in its interface. RMI will cause a client to see this exception if there is trouble communicating with a remote server object.

Now that you've seen the common interface that the server will implement and the client will call, look at the implementation of this interface that the server provides in Listing A–2.

Listing A–2 `NextNumberImpl.java`

```java
// A server object that implements the NextNumber
// remote interface

package corejini.appendixa;

import java.rmi.RemoteException;
import java.rmi.RMISecurityManager;
import java.rmi.Naming;
import java.rmi.server.UnicastRemoteObject;
import java.net.InetAddress;
import java.net.UnknownHostException;
import java.net.MalformedURLException;

public class NextNumberImpl extends UnicastRemoteObject
    implements NextNumber {
    public NextNumberImpl() throws RemoteException {
        if (System.getSecurityManager() == null) {
            System.setSecurityManager(
                new RMISecurityManager());
        }

        try {
            String host =
                InetAddress.getLocalHost().getHostName();
            String url = "rmi://" + host + "/nextNumber";
            Naming.rebind(url, this);
            System.out.println("Server bound to: " + url);
        } catch (UnknownHostException ex) {
            System.err.println("Couldn't get local host");
            System.exit(1);
        } catch (RemoteException ex) {
            System.err.println("Couldn't contact " +
                                "rmiregistry.");
            System.err.println("Are you sure you're running "
                                + rmiregistry?");
            System.exit(1);
        } catch (MalformedURLException ex) {
            // Shouldn't happen
            System.exit(1);
        }
    }

    public int getNextNumber(int n) {
        return n+1;
    }
}
```

> **Listing A–2** `NextNumberImpl.java` (continued)

```
    public static void main(String[] args) {
      try {
        NextNumberImpl server = new NextNumberImpl();
      } catch (RemoteException ex) {
        System.err.println("Trouble creating server: " +
                                        ex.getMessage());
        ex.printStackTrace();
      }
    }
}
```

This class has a `main()` routine, which creates an instance of `NextNumber-Impl`, which implements the remote interface. As you see here, `NextNumber-Impl` extends `UnicastRemoteObject`—which means that it has the "smarts" necessary to be a remote object. That is, by extending `UnicastRemoteObject`, `NextNumberImpl` inherits the machinery that allows it to export itself as a remote object. Further, `NextNumberImpl` implements `NextNumber`—which means that it provides a concrete implementation of the interface that the clients will know how to speak.

Take a look at the constructor for this object. The first thing the code does is to set a security manager. In this case, strictly speaking, there will be no downloaded code: The interfaces are defined to take and return primitive types (`int`s), and the server doesn't need to download any stubs (remember that it's the *client* that downloads the *server's* stub object). But virtually all RMI programs of any complexity *will* need to use downloadable code, so I've gone ahead and set the security manager here, just to reinforce the point.

Next, the code must address an issue that I haven't discussed yet: How does the client find the server after it's running? This is called the *rendezvous problem*. There may be many `NextNumberImpl`s running on the network. How does the client specify which one it wants?

RMI provides a program called the *registry*, which is used to map from string names to remote objects. You can think of the registry as a name server that clients can contact when they need to find a remote object. Clients pass a name in and get a remote object out. The registry actually stores the stubs for the remote objects, so that clients can just download them and go.

The `Naming` class shown here supports interactions with the registry. Here, the code creates a URL-style string that provides a name for it. The string consists of a protocol part ("`rmi`"), followed by the local hostname, and then a unique name for the server ("`nextNumber`"). The protocol, together with the hostname, tells the `Naming` class the location of the particular registry you wish to use. The name "`nextNumber`" is the string—or ID—you wish your remote server to be known by. This complete URL defines a unique name for your remote server object, which clients can use to find it. The URL will be printed out when the server runs; you can pass this string to a client program so that it can find the server at run time.

I won't spend a lot of time talking about the registry here, because it's not used much in the rest of this book—instead, the programs in this book, even the ones that use RMI, use Jini's lookup and discovery protocols to find remote programs.

Core Note: The RMI registry versus Jini Lookup Services

If you've read the sections of this book that discuss the Jini lookup service, and you feel that you understand that concept, then think of the registry as nothing more than a "poor man's" lookup service. That is, just as Jini services register with the Jini lookup service, remote server objects are registered with the RMI registry. And just as clients query Jini lookup services for references to registered services, clients can also query the RMI registry for references to the remote servers that have registered their stubs in the registry (you will see how this is done in the next example). The most important difference between the RMI registry and the Jini lookup service is that only names (String objects) associated with remote servers are registered in the RMI registry, whereas services register their IDs, object types, and attributes with the Jini lookup service. Although the type-based lookup provided by the Jini lookup service results in many more powerful features—features that, because it is string-based rather than type-based, the RMI registry cannot provide—both entities provide conceptually the same service: registration and lookup.

This registry binding process can raise several exceptions if it cannot get the hostname for the local host, if the registry is not running, or if you pass it a bogus URL. The code here just exits if any of these happen.

Next you'll see the actual implementation of the `getNextNumber()` method. Perhaps surprisingly, this method is implemented *exactly* like a purely local version of the same method! The RMI machinery that's in place means that you only have to write the core application logic for remote methods, and RMI takes care of everything else.

Next you'll see the client side of the RMI equation. In Listing A–3, you see a simple client program that can contact the registry to find the server, and invoke its method remotely.

Listing A–3 NextNumberClient.java

```
// A client to test the NextNumber server

package corejini.appendixa;

import java.rmi.Remote;
import java.rmi.RemoteException;
import java.rmi.RMISecurityManager;
import java.rmi.NotBoundException;
import java.rmi.Naming;
import java.net.MalformedURLException;

public class NextNumberClient {
    public static void main(String[] args) {
        if (args.length != 1) {
            System.err.println("Usage: NextNumberClient "
                                  + "<url>");
            System.exit(1);
        }

        if (System.getSecurityManager() == null) {
            System.setSecurityManager(
                new RMISecurityManager());
        }
```

Listing A–3 `NextNumberClient.java` (continued)

```java
        Remote r = null;

        try {
            r = Naming.lookup(args[0]);
        } catch (RemoteException ex) {
            System.err.println("Couldn't contact registry.");
            System.err.println("Are you sure you're running "
                                        + "rmiregistry?");
            System.exit(1);
        } catch (NotBoundException ex) {
            System.err.println("There is no object bound to "

                                        + args[0]);
            System.err.println("Are you sure you ran the " +
                                        "server?");
            System.exit(1);
        } catch (MalformedURLException ex) {
            System.err.println("The string " + args[0] +
                                " is not a valid RMI URL");
            System.err.println("Make sure you use a " +
                        "properly-formatted rmi: // URL");
            System.exit(1);
        }

        try {
            if (r instanceof NextNumber) {
                NextNumber nn = (NextNumber) r;
                System.out.println("Next number after 1 is " +
                                        nn.getNextNumber(1));
                System.out.println("Next number after 2 is " +
                                        nn.getNextNumber(2));
                System.out.println("Next number after 3 is " +
                                        nn.getNextNumber(3));
            } else {
                System.err.println("Uh oh, the name " +
                                        args[0] +
                                        " isn't a NextNumber");
            }
        } catch (RemoteException ex) {
            System.err.println("Couldn't start client: " +
                                        ex.getMessage());
            ex.printStackTrace();
        }
    }
}
```

The client program consists only of a `main()` that contacts the registry to find a `NextNumber` server, and then calls the `getNextNumber()` method on it repeatedly to test it out.

The client program expects to get an RMI-formatted URL on the command line, which should name an instance of the server object. This should be the same URL that the server prints out when it starts. Next, the client installs an RMI security manager. The client application *will* be downloading code from the server—in this case, the stubs for the server. So the code here needs to install a security manager so that the code can be loaded remotely.

You should, however, note one of the common "gotchas" with RMI development: If you neglect to install a security manager, but happen to have the stubs in your CLASSPATH, then the program will continue to work normally because it will simply load the stubs in the "standard" way from the local CLASSPATH. But this same program will break if the classes cannot be found locally. So, even for testing, it's a good idea to go through all the steps that would be required to deploy this program in an actual remote setting where it doesn't have local access to the stubs.

After setting the security manager, the code calls the `lookup()` method on the `Naming` class, passing it the URL from the command line. Remember that the URL that is passed to `lookup()` tells that method both the particular registry to query, as well as the name associated with the remote server object that the client desires. The `lookup()` method contacts the indicated registry and asks the registry to return the stub for the named object. The method may fail in a number of ways—if the registry isn't running, if the URL is bogus, or if there is no remote object bound to that name. In all of these cases, the program simply exits.

Finally, after fetching the object, the program is ready to do some work! The code checks to make sure that the remote object it got back is indeed a `Next-Number`. This remote object should be the stub for the `NextNumberImpl` server, which implements the `NextNumber` interface. If this isn't the case, then someone else has bound another type of remote object to the URL passed on the command line. That is, someone else has registered with the indicated registry, and using the name "nextNumber," a remote object that doesn't implement `NextNumber`. When such a situation occurs, the program exits. If the remote object returned from the registry *is* a `NextNumber`, then the program calls the `getNextNumber()` method on it a few times, printing the results.

Note here how the code must trap any `RemoteExceptions` that are raised by the calls to `getNextNumber()`. The server may crash, the network may become partitioned, or any number of other network-related failures can happen. RMI presents all of these as `RemoteExceptions`.

This is a pretty simple example—no code is being downloaded except for the stubs for the `NextNumberImpl`—but it shows the basics of what you have to do to work with RMI. Next, I'll walk through how to get this code up and running.

Compiling the Example

The first step to getting everything running is to compile the server, the client, and the interface. The warning noted in the last section—that clients and servers must take care that they do not "accidentally" load classes from their CLASSPATHs that should be loaded remotely—applies here. For this example, I'll be compiling everything into the same directory. But in general, this is a bad idea that can mask many problems in coding and configuration that only show up at run time.

Read Chapter 5 for details on the "proper" way to configure your environment. The guidelines there cover details like compiling clients and servers into separate directories, setting up separate HTTP servers to export the downloadable code needed for each, and so on. The rest of this book follows those guidelines to ensure that there is no unwanted "crosstalk" of classes between clients and servers.

The first step, on either Windows or UNIX, is to compile all the files.

```
javac NextNumber.java
      NextNumberImpl.java
      NextNumberClient.java
```

If you look in the directory, you should see `.class` files for each of these. You may be wondering about where the stub and skeleton classes come from. I haven't shown the code for any of these classes, but clearly they get used extensively by RMI.

The answer is that there is a separate step in the compilation process to create stubs and skeletons for remote objects. RMI uses a *stubs compiler* program to generate these classes; the compiler is called `rmic`, and it lives with the rest of the standard Java tools. Unlike `javac`, which takes pathnames, `rmic` takes fully qualified Java class names. The class names you pass it are the classes that *implement* remote interfaces. So, in this case where we have one remote implementation, you would run `rmic` on `NextNumberImpl`:

```
rmic corejini.appendixa.NextNumberImpl
```

If you now look at the contents of the directory, you'll see a couple of new class files there: `NextNumberImpl_Stub.class` and `NextNumber-`

`Impl_Skel.class`. These are the stub and skeleton classes, generated by `rmic` from the `NextNumberImpl` class file. If you're curious about what these classes actually do, you can pass the `-keepgenerated` option to `rmic`, which tells it to leave Java source files for the stubs and skeletons in the directory.

Running the Programs

The first thing you must do before you run these programs is start the RMI registry process! Many developers try to experiment with RMI and run into trouble because they forget this simple first step. The registry lives in the `bin` directory in the standard Java distribution. You can run it by typing `rmi-registry` on the command line. You should *at least* run the registry on the machine on which your server object will live; in general, it's helpful to run a registry on every machine on your network that may potentially support RMI programs.

Now it's time to run the client and server programs. The server in this case needs to export downloadable code (its stub class), and the client needs to be able to access this code. In a production environment, the way you would typically do this is to place the stub class on an HTTP server somewhere on your network. Alternatively, you could even implement a tiny, low-function HTTP server within the RMI server program yourself.

HTTP servers are configured to use one directory on the filesystem of the computer on which they run as their "root" directory. This is the directory from which they serve content. To make a class file accessible from an HTTP server, you'd place it under the server's root directory, creating separate directories for each package name in the fully qualified class name.

So, for example, suppose you have an HTTP server running on Windows with a root directory of `C:\http`. The stub class for this example would live at `C:\http\corejini\appendixa\NextNumberImpl_Stub.class`. On Solaris, with a root directory of `/var/http`, the class would live at `/var/http/corejini/appendixa/NextNumberImpl_Stub.class`. Alternatively, you could bundle any required classes into a JAR file and place the JAR file in the HTTP server's root directory.

In the following examples, I'll assume that you've placed the stub class file appropriately on an HTTP server running on the machine `myhost`. I'll be using this hostname to construct a codebase to tell clients where they can find the downloadable code. If the stub class file is installed as just described, then the codebase URL would be `http://myhost/`. If the class file for the stub is installed in a JAR file in the server's root directory, then you would name the JAR file in the codebase; for example, `http://myhost/stubs.jar`. Be sure to make certain that if your codebase specifies a directory rather than a JAR file, it includes the trailing slash.

After you're all set for downloadable code, you also need to take care of security. Remember that as long as code is running with a security manager, it must have a security policy that allows it access to filesystems and network resources. In Chapter 5 of this book, I use a policy file that grants all permissions to code—essentially allowing them unfettered access to the system. Recall the warnings earlier in this appendix about using this policy file in a production system, but it will serve our purposes fine for now.

Both the codebase and the policy file are passed as properties to the JVM on the command line. Now I'll show how to run the server. Assume for this example that the policy file lives in C:\files\policy on Windows and /files/policy on UNIX.

On Windows:

```
java -Djava.security.policy=C:\files\policy
     -Djava.rmi.server.codebase=http://myhost/
     corejini.appendixa.NextNumberImpl
```

On UNIX:

```
java -Djava.security.policy=/files/policy
     -Djava.rmi.server.codebase=http://myhost/
     corejini.appendixa.NextNumberImpl
```

The server should print the URL that it binds itself to in the registry; for example, on my workstation, it reports:

Server bound to: rmi://turbodog.parc.xerox.com/nextNumber

Be sure to remember this string as you'll have to pass it on the command line to the client. Speaking of which, let's now run the client. The client has a security manager, so it too needs to have a policy file passed to it. But unlike the server, the client exports no downloadable code. So you don't have to set a codebase, because the client doesn't have to tell anyone where to get class files from. Be sure you pass the URL that the server prints out on the command line.

On Windows:

```
java -Djava.security.policy=C:\files\policy
     corejini.appendixa.NextNumberClient
        rmi://turbodog.parc.xerox.com/nextNumber
```

On UNIX:

```
java -Djava.security.policy=/files/policy
     corejini.appendixa.NextNumberClient
```

```
rmi://turbodog.parc.xerox.com/nextNumber
```

After all this work, the output isn't particularly spectacular: The client will simply print out as it invokes messages on the server.

Next number after 1 is 2

Next number after 2 is 3

Next number after 3 is 4

This example does show all the basics that you need to know to work with RMI, though.

In case you didn't try this example because you don't have an HTTP server running on your network, or don't want to take the time to copy class files to it, you should try to run it anyway. The client will "fall back" to using the local CLASSPATH, which means that the example will probably work anyway— since you probably built the client and the server in the same directory.

Again, even though things may work this way, it isn't the recommended way to develop RMI-based software because it hides problems that can show up later when the client and the server *don't* share the same filesystem.

The next section covers one last aspect of RMI that is useful when developing Jini applications: the RMI activation framework.

The Activation Framework

The final topic in this primer on RMI is *activation*. Activation is, simply, a way for Java to start remote server objects "on demand" as they are needed. In the example program in this appendix, you saw how the `NextNumberImpl` server was written—it consisted of a `main()` routine that created and registered a remote object, and then continued running. The server object was only available to clients as long as the program was running. If the program stopped, the remote server object would be garbage collected and would cease to exist, just like any local "normal" Java object.

Activation, introduced in Java 2, provides a way to structure your programs around remote objects that are only "live" when they are necessary, and can basically "go to sleep" when they are not needed. The process of making an object "go to sleep" is called *deactivation*; the reawakening of an object is called *activation*. The facilities provided by the RMI activation framework can be extremely useful when you have remote objects that may need to do work only rarely, or when you have large numbers of remote objects, and the cost of keeping them all "live" at the same time may be prohibitive.

Beyond these two fairly obvious uses of activation, it brings an additional benefit as well: Because activation provides a way for server objects to be started as needed, it can be a powerful tool for creating software that can automatically recover after a crash. If an activatable remote object is shut down or crashes, or the machine on which it is running crashes, activation can be used as a way to bring it back to life when it is needed.

Players in Activation

The high-level description of activation above begs the question: If activatable objects can be reconstituted and made live on demand, who is doing the activation?

The answer is that activation is implemented by a set of cooperating entities. First, there is the activatable object itself. This is the remote server object that may be activated and deactivated as necessary. Second, there is a "wrapper" program that takes care of telling the RMI activation subsystem about this new activatable server object. This wrapper program will typically call out to a few methods to provide details about how the activatable object should be activated, and then exits. The wrapper is analogous to the `main()` program in the `Next-NumberImpl`—it handles the chores of setting up the remote server object. But in the case of the `NextNumberImpl` program, the wrapper must continue running for as long as the server is to be callable. A wrapper for an activatable object, on the other hand, will simply specify details about how the object should be activated, and will then typically exit.

Both of these classes—the activatable object and the program that sets it up—are written by you. The third entity, however, is a standard part of the Java 2 distribution, and is the most important part of the activation picture: the RMI activation daemon, or `rmid`. The activation daemon should be run on any computer on which activatable objects may be started and stopped; there only needs to be one instance of `rmid` on any computer, no matter how many activatable objects will be run there. It is the activation daemon that records the information needed to restart activatable objects.

You may be wondering exactly *where* a newly activated object will be run. Instantiating and running newly activated remote server objects *inside* the activation daemon would be problematic—the JVM running `rmid` would get bogged down doing many things other than simply handling activation and, perhaps even worse, this strategy would mean that remote objects from different applications would be sharing the same JVM. Each of these remote objects may have different security restrictions, and may require different levels of permissions set for them.

So the activation daemon uses the fourth and final entity of the activation framework to take care of actually "hosting" activated objects: *activation groups.* Activation groups are essentially complete, separate instances of the JVM that exist solely to host groups of activated objects. These fresh JVMs are started as needed by `rmid`. In many cases, a whole set of activatable objects created by one wrapper program can share the same JVM. So the activation framework provides a way for wrappers to describe the characteristics of the activation group that will run their activatable objects. Wrappers can use different activation groups to run different activatable objects, and can select security policy files for the JVMs that will run their objects.

This constellation of entities—activatable objects, the wrapper programs that create them, the activation daemon, and JVMs associated with activation groups—cooperate together to support objects which can be activated on demand.

I've decided to cover activation, which many will think of as an "advanced" topic, in this book because it can be so useful for writing Jini services. Activation is helpful for creating long-lived remote server objects that can automatically recover after a crash—which, in a nutshell, is a pretty reasonable description of the functionality that a Jini service must provide.

Using the Activation Framework

In this section, I will give a quick overview of what you have to do to use the activation framework. These details will largely be the same no matter what sort of activatable object you're writing. I'll present the steps below, and then give a bit more detail on each. Afterwards, I'll walk through an example: one final iteration of the "Hello, World" service from Chapter 5, to show how activation is used in practice.

1. Make sure the activation daemon is running on your system!
2. Create the implementation for your activatable object. This will be the remote server object that can be started on demand.
    - Extend the `java.rmi.Activatable` class if you're creating a new activatable object.
    - Declare a two-argument constructor that takes a `java.rmi.activation.ActivationID` and a `java.rmi.MarshalledObject`.
    - Implement the remote methods on your activatable object, as you normally would.
3. Create the implementation for your wrapper program. This program handles the "setup" for the activatable server object.

- Make sure you install a security manager, typically a `java.rmi.RMISecurityManager`.
- Create a `java.rmi.activation.ActivationGroupDesc` that contains the information necessary to start a JVM with the appropriate parameters to run your activatable object.
- Create a `java.rmi.activation.ActivationDesc` that contains the information needed for the activation subsystem to properly activate your object. Register the `ActivationDesc` with the activation daemon so that it has the information to re-create your object. Registering will return the stub for your activatable object.
- You can either bind your activatable object in the RMI registry (if you want callers to find it by name), register it with the Jini lookup serice (if you want callers to find it by service ID, type, or attributes), or simply pass its stub to any interested parties.

I'll walk through these steps in a bit more detail. The first one, running the activation daemon, is easy. You simply type `rmid`; the executable lives in the standard Java `bin` directory.

Creating your activatable object is likewise pretty easy—in fact, creating an activatable remote object is essentially no harder than creating a standard, non-activatable remote object, although the two do follow slightly different patterns. First, an activatable object should extend `java.rmi.activation.Activable`, rather than `java.rmi.server.UnicastRemoteObject`. The `Activatable` class is itself a subclass of `UnicastRemoteObject`, so you still inherit all of this functionality.[5] Also, whereas nonactivatable remote objects must have a no-argument constructor, activatable remote objects must instead have a two-argument constructor. The first argument is the `ActivationID`, which provides a unique identifier for the activatable object, as well as some other information. The second argument is a `MarshalledObject`. As you'll see, the wrapper program can provide an arbitrary `MarshalledObject` instance that will be passed to the activatable object when it is instantiated; this mechanism provides a simple one-shot way for the wrapper to pass data to the activatable object.

The constructor for your activatable object must also call the superclass constructor on `Activatable`. There are a number of variants of the `Activatable`

---

5. The activation framework also provides a way to create activatable objects which are *not* subclasses of `Activatable`. The discussion of how to do this is outside the scope of this primer; see the "Further Reading" section at the end of this appendix for more details.

constructor, and you should check the API documentation for specific details. In most cases, the simplest constructor should be used, which takes an `ActivationID` (which should be the same one passed to your activatable object's constructor), and a port number (which should typically be zero).

These two tasks—extending `Activatable` and providing the special constructor—are the only "special" things you have to do to create an activatable remote object. After doing these, you simply implement the remote methods of your implementation, just as you normally would.

The construction of the wrapper program is a little more complicated, but typically follows a pretty fixed pattern. The wrapper will need to communicate with the activation daemon, and possibly the RMI registry. Both of these are themselves RMI programs, and so the wrapper must be prepared to use the stubs downloaded from these services. The first step in any wrapper is to install a security manager, so that it can execute downloadable code. And, recall, once you've installed a security manager, you'll have to pass a policy file to the wrapper's JVM as well.

Next, the wrapper must prepare information to tell the activation system about how to create activation group JVMs to run its activatable objects. Since activatable objects are run in separate JVMs, the wrapper needs to set up any information that would normally be passed in on the command line to a JVM. At a minimum, this typically includes a security policy file for the JVMs started to hold activated objects.[6] This information is contained within a class called an `ActivationGroupDesc`, which describes how the activation system should create activation groups. This information is "registered" with the activation system, which can then start activation group JVMs as needed.

While the activation group descriptor contains information about how to start JVMs to run activatable objects, you still need to create a description of how to instantiate and run those activatable objects within their activation group. So the next thing the wrapper does is create an activation descriptor (`ActivationDesc`) which contains information such as the codebase URL that indicates where the activatable object's implementation can be retrieved, and

---

6. If you have done development using the first release of Jini, version 1.0, you may have noticed that many of the Jini services required *two* security policy files on the command line. The first was used to establish the security policy for the *setup* JVM, and the second was used to set the security policy for the *server* JVM (the JVM launched by the activation system). A restructuring of the wrappers for the common Jini services in Jini 1.1 obviated the need for the setup security policy. Still, many other activatable programs *will* follow the common pattern of specifying a security policy for both JVMs.

an arbitrary `MarshalledObject` that will be passed to the activatable object's constructor when it is created.

Finally, this activation descriptor is "registered" with the activation subsystem. The registration process tells the activation framework that a new activatable object is available and ready to be called; the server object will be created as necessary. When the object is registered, an RMI stub for it will be returned. Note that at this point, the activatable object need not be "live" for there to be a stub for it. This stub can be passed around, or bound to a name in the RMI registry, all without causing the object to be activated until one of its remote methods is called.

Once the wrapper has set up the necessary information to describe the object and the activation group that should run it, it can simply exit. The activation subsystem will take care of instantiating the object the first time one of its remote methods are called on its stub.

An Example

This example shows an extension of the trusty "Hello, World" series of examples in Chapter 5. This version of the service is similar to `HelloWorldServiceBackend` from Chapter 5—both versions will publish proxies that communicate via RMI to a back-end object. But, unlike the example in Chapter 5 where the back end was a simple remote object, here the back-end server object will be fully activatable.

You should be sure to note the structure of this program—the program is very similar to the Chapter 5 example. The first notable difference is that the service's back-end object, rather than extending `UnicastRemoteObject` as in Chapter 5, extends `Activatable` and follows the usual patterns for activatable objects. Second, the `getProxy()` method in the wrapper program is a bit more complicated than the one in Chapter 5. Here, the method must set up all the needed boilerplate so that the service's back-end object can be activated.

Listing A-4 shows the code for this example:

Listing A-4 HelloWorldServiceActivatable.java

```java
// Create an extension of the service that uses
// RMI to communicate with an activatable back-end
// process.

package corejini.appendixa;

import java.io.IOException;
import java.io.Serializable;
import java.rmi.RemoteException;
import java.rmi.Remote;
import java.rmi.MarshalledObject;
import java.rmi.RMISecurityManager;
import java.rmi.server.UnicastRemoteObject;
import java.rmi.activation.Activatable;
import java.rmi.activation.ActivationID;
import java.rmi.activation.ActivationDesc;
import java.rmi.activation.ActivationGroup;
import java.rmi.activation.ActivationGroupID;
import java.rmi.activation.ActivationGroupDesc;
import java.rmi.activation.ActivationException;
import java.util.Properties;
import corejini.chapter5.BackendProtocol;
import corejini.chapter5.HelloWorldServiceInterface;
import corejini.chapter5.HelloWorldServiceWithLeases;
import corejini.chapter5.HelloWorldServiceProxy2;
```

Listing A-4 HelloWorldServiceActivatable.java (continued)

```java
public class HelloWorldServiceActivatable
    extends HelloWorldServiceWithLeases {
    // Need to pass a policy file to the activation
    // daemon...
    private static String policyFile;
    // ...as well as a codebase.
    private static String codebase;

    // The main difference between this example and
    // HelloWorldServiceRemote (in Chapter 5) is that
    // in this case, the back-end RMI object is activatable.
    // So we need a new back-end object that extends
    // Activatable but still implements BackendProtocol.
    public static class ActivatableBackend
        extends Activatable
        implements BackendProtocol {
        int nextMessage = 0;
        String[] messages = { "Hello, World",
                              "Goodbye, Cruel World",
                              "What's Up, Doc?" };

        public ActivatableBackend(ActivationID id,
                                  MarshalledObject data)
            throws RemoteException {
            super(id, 0);
        }

        public synchronized String fetchString()
            throws RemoteException {
            String str =  messages[nextMessage];
            nextMessage =
                (nextMessage + 1) % messages.length;
            return str;
        }

        // Should put itself back to sleep after a while.
    }
```

Listing A-4 HelloWorldServiceActivatable.java (continued)

```java
    // Constructor for the wrapper simply lets
    // the superclass constructor run.
    public HelloWorldServiceActivatable()
        throws IOException {
    }

    protected HelloWorldServiceInterface createProxy() {
        try {
            // Create a descriptor for a new activation
            // group to run our back-end object in.
            Properties props = new Properties();
            props.put("java.security.policy", policyFile);
            ActivationGroupDesc group =
                new ActivationGroupDesc(props, null);
            // Register the group and get the ID.
            ActivationGroupID gid =
            ActivationGroup.getSystem().registerGroup(group);
            // Now create the group.
            ActivationGroup.createGroup(gid, group, 0);

            // Create an activation descriptor
            // for the object.
            String location = codebase;
            MarshalledObject data = null;
            ActivationDesc desc =
                new ActivationDesc("corejini.appendixa." +
                    "HelloWorldServiceActivatable$" +
                    "ActivatableBackend",
                    location, data);

            // Create the 'back-end' object that will
            // implement the protocol.
            BackendProtocol backend =
                (BackendProtocol)
                    Activatable.register(desc);
            return new HelloWorldServiceProxy2(backend);
```

```
        } catch (RemoteException ex) {
            System.err.println(
                    "Error creating backend object: " +
                    ex.getMessage());
            ex.printStackTrace();
            System.exit(1);
            return null; // not reached
        } catch (ActivationException ex) {
            System.err.println("Problem with activation: " +
                                ex.getMessage());
            ex.printStackTrace();
            System.exit(1);
            return null; // not reached
        }
    }

    // Create the service and start its lease
    // thread.
    public static void main(String args[]) {
        if (args.length != 2) {
            System.err.println(
                    "Usage: HelloWorldServiceActivatable " +
                    " <policy file> <codebase>");
            System.exit(1);
        }

        if (System.getSecurityManager() == null) {
            System.setSecurityManager(
                new RMISecurityManager());
        }
```

Listing A-4 HelloWorldServiceActivatable.java (continued)

```
        try {
            // Pass in the policy file and codebase from
            // the command line.
            HelloWorldServiceActivatable.policyFile =
                args[0];
            HelloWorldServiceActivatable.codebase =
                args[1];

            HelloWorldServiceActivatable hws =
                new HelloWorldServiceActivatable();

            // Start the lease renewal thread.
            hws.leaseThread = new Thread(hws);
            hws.leaseThread.start();
        } catch (IOException ex) {
            System.out.println("Couldn't create service: " +
                                ex.getMessage());
        }
    }
}
```

If you've already looked at the examples from Chapter 5, the first thing you'll notice is how similar this version of the service is to `HelloWorldServiceBackend`. Both versions of the service define "back-end" server objects that return strings when asked; the `getProxy()` methods of each create the particular back-end object and initialize a proxy with a remote reference to that back-end object.

The first thing to notice about this version, though, is that the `ActivatableBackend` object subclasses `Activatable`. Most of the "smarts" in making an object activatable live in this class. `Activatable` itself is a subclass of `java.rmi.UnicastRemoteObject`, so any object that's activatable will automatically inherit all of the code necessary to make its methods callable from remote JVMs. You'll also see that this class implements `BackendProtocol`, which is the same remote interface used by the Chapter 5 `HelloWorldServiceBackend` example for communication between proxies and back-end objects. Note that the constructor for the `ActivatableBackend` class takes two parameters, an `ActivationID` and a `MarshalledObject`. The RMI activation system requires that activatable objects support a constructor with exactly these arguments. Whenever an object is activated, the activation system will use this constructor to re-instantiate the object. The `ActivationID` parameter uniquely identifies this particular activatable object, and should be passed through to the superclass constructor. (The other "0" argument in the call to the superclass constructor is the port number on which the newly activated object will be bound. Specifying "0" here means to use any port number.) The `Mar-shalledObject` parameter is a way to pass "extra" data into the constructor; when you first register your activatable object with the activation system, you can provide a `MarshalledObject` that will be passed back to you whenever you're activated.

The other major difference between this class and the previous class is in the implementation of `getProxy()`. The code here must set up all the details that will allow the activation system to launch a new activation group JVM, and create an instance of the `ActivatableBackend` object in it. Afterwards, it must fetch a reference to the back-end object's stub from the activation system, and initialize and return a proxy that contains a reference to this stub.

The first thing the method must do is create an `ActivationGroupDesc` that describes how the JVM that will contain the activatable back-end object will be started. The `ActivationGroupDesc` is how you pass properties to "child" JVMs that will run activatable objects. Here, you see that the program creates a set of properties and sets up a security policy that will be used by any child JVMs. The next steps are largely boilerplate—they get an ID for the group and create an actual activation group from the descriptor information.

After this, the code must create an activation descriptor for the back-end object. While an `ActivationGroupDesc` describes the properties of the JVM that will execute activatable objects, the `ActivationDesc` is used to describe the objects *within* that group. It provides details on the class name and codebase for any activatable objects in a group. In the code here, you see that the program creates a new `ActivationDesc`, indicating the name of the activatable back-end object, the codebase that will be used to locate its code, and a `MarshalledObject` that will be passed to the object upon activation (here, this object is null).

Finally, after this, `getProxy()` is ready to register the `ActivationDesc`. The process of registering the descriptor for an activatable object returns the stub for the object. At this point, invoking any remote method on the stub will cause the activation system to launch the activatable object, if it is not running already. Here, you see that `getProxy()` registers the descriptor, and then uses the returned stub to initialize the proxy that will be stored in the lookup service. I'm using the Jini lookup service, rather than the RMI registry, here because the code from which this example is derived already uses the lookup service. From this point, any client that fetches and uses the proxy will cause an RMI to be made to an instance of the `ActivatableBackend` class, running inside a JVM created by the activation system. If no instance of the back end is available, the activation system will create one as needed.

The `main()` for this program simply sets up the policy file and codebase as passed on the command line, and installs a security manager.

Compiling and Running the Example

Compiling this example is basically the same as compiling the earlier remote version of the "Hello, World" service from Chapter 5. Note that since the code here extends code from Chapter 5, you *must* follow the instructions in that chapter for building the examples there; all of the service and proxy code from that chapter will need to be compiled and installed into the correct locations before you try to run this example. The steps below give the specific instructions for this one example only.

Compiling

On Windows:

```
javac -classpath C:\files;
               C:\jini1_1\lib\jini-core.jar;
               C:\jini1_1\lib\jini-ext.jar;
               C:\jini1_1\lib\sun-util.jar;
               C:\service
     -d C:\service
C:\files\corejini\appendixa\HelloWorldServiceActivatable.java

rmic -classpath C:\service;
               C:\jini1_1\lib\jini-core.jar;
               C:\jini1_1\lib\jini-ext.jar;
               C:\jini1_1\lib\sun-util.jar
     -d C:\service
corejini.appendixa.HelloWorldServiceActivatable.Activatable-
Backend

mkdir C:\service-dl\corejini\appendix A
cd C:\service\corejini\appendixa
copy
  HelloWorldServiceActivatable$ActivatableBackend_Stub.class
  C:\service-dl\corejini\appendixa
```

On UNIX:

```
javac -classpath /files:
                 /files/jini1_1/lib/jini-core.jar:
                 /files/jini1_1/lib/jini-ext.jar:
                 /files/jini1_1/lib/sun-util.jar:
                 /files/service
  -d /files/service
/files/corejini/appendixa/HelloWorldServiceActivatable.java

rmic -classpath /files/service;
                /files/jini1_1/lib/jini-core.jar;
                /files/jini1_1/lib/jini-ext.jar;
                /files/jini1_1/lib/sun-util.jar
      -d /files/service
corejini.appendixa.HelloWorldServiceActivatable.Activatable-
Backend

mkdir/files/service-dl/corejini/appendix a
cd /files/service/corejini/appendixa
cp
 HelloWorldServiceActivatable\$ActivatableBackend_Stub.class
 /files/service-dl/corejini/appendixa
```

Running

First, since the service is activatable, make sure you're running the activation daemon, rmid, on the system on which the service's back end will run. If you're developing on the same machine on which you're running a Jini lookup service, then there's no need to start a separate rmid—your service and the lookup service can "share" a single instance of rmid.

The instructions below show you how to start the service. For the client, you can "reuse" any of the clients we've used before—since the new service simply provides a re-implementation of *exactly* the same interface as before, the clients are none the wiser. This is the power of Jini: You can swap particular implementations of a service in and out at run time, and clients will simply use whichever one they find that meets their requirements.

On Windows:

```
java -cp C:\jini1_1\lib\jini-core.jar;
         C:\jini1_1\lib\jini-ext.jar;
         C:\jini1_1\lib\sun-util.jar;
         C:\service
     -Djava.rmi.server.codebase=http://myhost:8085/
```

```
   -Djava.security.policy=C:\policy
 corejini.appendixa.HelloWorldServiceActivatable
   C:/policy
   http://myhost:8085/
```

On UNIX:

```
java -cp /files/jini1_1/lib/jini-core.jar:
       /files/jini1_1/lib/jini-ext.jar:
       /files/jini1_1/lib/sun-util.jar:
       /files/service:
    -Djava.rmi.server.codebase=http://myhost:8085/
    -Djava.security.policy=/files/policy
 corejini.appendixa.HelloWorldServiceActivatable
    /files/policy
    http://myhost:8085/
```

Note that to run the example, you must pass the location of a security policy file and the codebase on the command line as arguments to the program. These are used to construct the descriptor information that the activation system will use to launch the activatable back-end object; the policy file and codebase set via properties on the command line are used for the *wrapper* program to function. You should be sure you understand the differences between these two sets of parameters—one set is for the wrapper's JVM, and one set is for the JVMs that are launched by `rmid`.

The behavior of this example from the perspective of clients is exactly the same as that of the remote example in Chapter 5: Each time a client runs, it will contact the back-end object and fetch a different string. But here, the object that clients communicate with can be started on demand by the activation system.

Fully Utilizing Activation in a Jini Service

You may have noticed that the wrapper program in this example does not exit after the activatable object has been registered. Since the wrapper continues running, doesn't this negate the whole benefit of using activation? The answer is that, yes, to a large degree this example is not a very effective user of the facilities offered by activation. The code shown here uses an activatable object *only* for the remote server that returns strings; all of the Jini-related code is still contained in the wrapper. This is why, in this example, the wrapper continues to run—it must run so that it can discover lookup services, publish the proxy, and renew leases. Without these, the back-end object—even though it is activatable and can be started on demand—will "drop out" of the Jini community.

You might be tempted to re-architect this little example so that the activatable object performs not only the back-end duties required of the "Hello, World" service, but also the Jini duties of discovering lookup services, renewing leases, and so on.

You can certainly do this, and achieve many of the benefits of activation. In particular, you can create an activatable service that can be started whenever the activation daemon starts, or whenever any client performs an RMI method invocation on its stub. But making a *well-behaved* activatable Jini service is a bit more work. The reason for this is that the activation system only becomes involved in on-demand activation of objects as a result of an RMI message. Certain aspects of Jini, such as the discovery protocols, involve low-level network traffic over sockets. The activation daemon doesn't listen for such traffic, and doesn't know how to activate remote objects in response to them.

So the trick is to be able to have inactive services become active whenever any "interesting" Jini event occurs, whether or not that event manifests itself as an RMI message. The answer to this quandry is the suite of services discussed in Chapter 19 of this book. While they have many uses, one of the chief motivations for these services was the desire to be able to produce robust, activatable services without the need for continually running wrapper programs. The `LookupDiscoveryService`, for example, will perform the duties of discovering lookup services *on behalf* of another (possibly inactive) service. When the `LookupDiscoveryService` notices that a lookup service has appeared, it can inform the inactive service, which can then reactivate to take whatever action it wishes. The `EventMailboxService` provides a way for inactive services to queue event delivery until they are active. And the `LeaseRenewalService` provides a means for inactive services to delegate their lease renewals to another entity.

Again, these utility services are useful for more than just writing activatable services. But they can be a big win when you want your activatable service to fit cleanly into a Jini environment, without requiring a long-lived wrapper.

Other Activation Topics

This last section of the appendix presents a few additional bits of information about the activation framework and how to use it.

"Lazy" References

One of the benefits of activation is that you can think of references to activatable objects as being "lazy." That is, references to these objects contain the persistent handle information that allows the activation subsystem to know which object should be started, if it is not already running. After an activatable reference is used the first time, a "regular" remote reference is used to contact the server object directly, without having to go through the activation system again.

Because the activation system can convert one of these persistent handles to a "live" remote reference as needed, references to activatable objects are *always* useable, even across restarts of the object. References to a normal remote object, on the other hand, become invalid after the object has crashed and then been restarted. References to activatable objects provide a useful way to have a persistent reference to a server object that is valid even across restarts.

Deactivation

Even though the activation framework will automatically start an activatable object the first time it is needed, it will not automatically deactivate objects when they are no longer required. The reason for this is simple—the decision about when to deactivate an object is best left to the object itself. Some objects may prefer to never deactivate themselves, while others may use complicated heuristics that are based on the number of times a method has been invoked over a period of time.

But regardless of how or whether they decide to do it, activatable objects can deactivate themselves as needed. You can call the `Activatable.inactive()` method, passing an `ActivationID`, to deactivate an object.

Activatable objects can also be *unregistered*. While deactivation is a temporary state—a deactivated object will be reactivated when it is needed—unregistering an object means that it is removed from the activation system. You can call `Activatable.unregister()`, passing in an `ActivationID`, to unregister an object. This allows you to "clean up" activatable objects that you no longer wish to use.

Getting the Most from the Activation Daemon

There are a couple of commonly overlooked ways to exploit the activation daemon that can be helpful when building systems with activatable components. The first is that you can set up your programs to be automatically restarted when the activation daemon restarts. Recall that the activation daemon records persistent information about the activatable objects it knows about. When you create the activation descriptor for your object, you can optionally say that you would like the object to be restarted when the activation daemon starts, as opposed to on-demand restarting.

This feature is useful if you know that your activatable objects are likely to be heavily used, and you want them started as soon as possible. If you've configured `rmid` to start when your computer boots, this feature can be used to launch activatable objects at boot time. Further, this same facility will be used to restart any activatable objects that crash (for example, if, in UNIX, you issue the `kill` command to terminate the lookup service, `rmid` will immediately restart it, even though `rmid` itself never goes down).

The activation daemon stores its persistent state in a log in the filesystem. By default, this log is a directory called `log` under the directory from which `rmid` was started. You can pass the `-log` option to `rmid` to change the location of the log directory. When `rmid` starts, it consults its log directory (if it exists) to recover information about activatable objects it knows about, and to launch any objects that have requested restart service.

The activation daemon also provides a handy way to shut itself down. If you need to stop the `rmid` process for some reason (perhaps because its log is on a filesystem that is full), you can run `rmid -stop`. This command will cause any currently running `rmid` process to shut down.

Further Reading

This appendix has taken a very shallow look at a topic that is actually quite deep. If you're not familiar with RMI or Java 2, there may be a number of topics that you would like to read up on.

The new security architecture is one of the biggest changes that Java 2 has brought, and many developers are confused by it. The book *Just Java 1.2*, by Peter van der Linden, has an entire chapter devoted to Java 2 security, and is worth checking out.

If you just want a high-level overview, the following URL has details on the Java 2 security permissions mechanism:

```
http://www.javasoft.com/products/jdk/1.2/docs/guide/
security/permissions.html
```

This page at the JavaSoft Web site has details about the syntax of policy files. This information will be useful if you want to customize the policy file used by the examples in this book into something more robust.

```
http://www.javasoft.com/products/jdk/1.2/docs/guide/
security/PolicyFiles.html
```

If you want more details about RMI, you should check out Sun's page on the RMI implementation in Java 2. This page includes low-level specifications, examples, release notes, and API documentation. It also has coverage of the RMI activation framework.

```
http://www.javasoft.com/products/jdk/1.2/docs/guide/rmi/
index.html
```

If you want to read up on serialization, this Sun page has specifications, examples, and so on about all the ins and outs of object serialization:

```
http://www.javasoft.com/products/jdk/1.2/docs/guide/
serialization/index.html
```

If you're curious about the new dynamic proxies feature of 1.3, you may want to visit the release notes on reflection for this JDK release:

```
http://www.javasoft.com/products/jdk/1.3/docs/guide/
reflection/proxy.html
```

Finally, the frequently asked questions (FAQs) list for both RMI and serialization is available from Sun at:

```
http://www.javasoft.com/products/jdk/1.2/docs/guide/rmi/
faq.html
```

Appendix B

Common Java and Jini System Properties

T his final appendix provides a reference to the many properties commonly used when developing Jini applications. Properties, as you remember, are special settings that can be used to tune the behavior of the Java run-time and class libraries. Properties are typically passed as arguments on the command line when the JVM is started, using the -D option.

So, for instance, to set the `java.rmi.server.codebase` property to `http://myhost/`, you would type:

```
java -Djava.rmi.server.codebase=http://myhost/
```

Properties can also be set programmatically, as is typically done when setting up an activation group descriptor for configuring the parameters of a JVM launched from the activation framework.

If you wish to pass properties to `rmid`, the RMI activation daemon, you can pass properties to the JVM running `rmid` itself, or to the JVMs launched *by* `rmid` (the "server" JVMs). To set a property in the `rmid` JVM itself, you use the same -D syntax that you see above. To set a property in any server JVMs launched by `rmid` (or to pass any other option to those JVMs, for that matter), you use the -C option of rmid. For example, to set the sun.rmi.server.log-Calls property to true (which will log all remote calls made on code running in that JVM), you'd use the syntax:

```
rmid -C-Djava.rmi.server.logCalls=true
```

Passing properties through to the JVMs launched by rmid can be particularly useful when debugging activatable services, including the core Jini services such as the lookup service.

Tables B–1 through B–11 list the properties used by the RMI and activation packages in Sun's reference implementation of Java 2, as well as properties dictated by the Jini specifications, and properties particular to Sun's sample implementation of Jini.

Table B-1 RMI Server Properties

java.rmi.server.codebase	This property specifies where the implementations of classes that are exported by the VM on which it is set can be found. The property will be passed to VMs that need to download code remotely, effectively augmenting their CLASSPATHS at run time. Sets of URLs can be specified separated by spaces (you may have to enclose the value of the property in quotes on your platform, to keep the spaces from being parsed incorrectly).
java.rmi.server.disableHttp	RMI can "tunnel" through HTTP to allow invocation of remote methods through firewalls. If set to "true," HTTP tunneling is turned off. The default is "false" (tunneling is enabled).
sun.rmi.server.exceptionTrace	If set to true, this property will cause all server-side exceptions to be reported to System.err, in addition to being reflected back to the caller. The default is false.

Table B-1 RMI Server Properties (continued)	
`java.rmi.server.hostname`	By default, RMI uses the IP address of the host on which a remote object is exported to construct references to it. If this property is set, its value is treated as the hostname or IP address of the server and is used instead of the IP address that would be used otherwise. This property can be helpful if an RMI server uses DHCP and references to it should not contain a fixed IP address. By default, this property is not set.
`java.rmi.dgc.leaseValue`	This property sets the lease duration that RMI grants to clients that reference remote objects, specified in minutes. The default is ten minutes.
`java.rmi.server.logCalls`	If set to true, an RMI server will log calls to `System.err`. The property is set to false by default.
`java.rmi.server.useCode-` `baseOnly`	This property, if set to true, disables local loading of classes referenced by remote methods—meaning that classes are only loaded from the codebase URLs, not from the local CLASSPATH. This property can be useful for ensuring that there is no "crosstalk" between clients and services because they share a CLASSPATH.
`java.rmi.server.useLocalHost-` `name`	If this property is set to true, then RMI will embed hostnames—rather than IP addresses—in references to remote objects. This property can be overridden by setting `java.rmi.server.host-` `name`, in which case the value specified there is always used.
`java.rmi.server.randomIDs`	If true, object identifiers for remote objects will be generated using a cryptographically secure random number generator. The default is false.

Table B-2 RMI Activation Properties	
`java.rmi.activation.port`	This property indicates the port number on which the `ActivationSystem` is exported. This property should be set if the `rmid` activation daemon runs on a port other than the default.
`java.rmi.activation.activator.class`	This property specifies the class that implements the `java.rmi.activation.Activator` interface, which is used to control how clients communicate with the activation daemon. This property is used to name the implementation class so that the appropriate stub class can be found.
`sun.rmi.activation.execTimeout`	The value of this property specifies how long `rmid` will wait for an activation group to start up; the default is 30000 milliseconds.
`sun.rmi.activation.snapshotInterval`	The value of this property dictates how many state changes must occur before `rmid` will write its state to the disk. The default is 200.
`sun.rmi.log.debug`	If true, details about `rmid`'s logging will be written to `System.err`.
`sun.rmi.rmid.maxstartgroup`	The value of this property indicates the number of launched-but-not-yet-ready activation group JVMs may be pending. Attempts to create new activation groups will be queued if this number is exceeded, until some pending groups become ready. The default value is 3.

Table B-2 RMI Activation Properties (continued)

`sun.rmi.server.activa-` `tion.debugExec`	If true, `rmid` will print debugging information about its attempts to start new activation groups.

Table B-3 RMI Logging Properties

`sun.rmi.loader.logLevel`	Set this property to `verbose` to have the RMI class loader print out details about all of the classes it loads, or attempts to load. Note: Since services like the lookup service are started via activation, to set this property on a lookup service, you must use the `-C` option on `rmid`, which allows you to set properties on spawned JVMs, as opposed to the JVM running `rmid` itself.
`sun.rmi.server.logLevel`	Set this property to `verbose` to enable useful debugging output from the RMI server object framework (exporting, receiving remote invocations, and so on).
`sun.rmi.dgc.logLevel`	Enables debugging of RMI's internal distributed garbage collection algorithms.
`sun.rmi.transport.logLevel`	Enables debugging output of RMI's low-level transport layer.
`sun.rmi.trans-` `port.proxy.logLevel`	Enables transport-level logging in the default `RMIServerSocketFactory` class; this may be useful for RMI traffic that is passed over HTTP.
`sun.rmi.trans-` `port.tcp.logLevel`	Enables debugging of RMI's use of TCP/IP.

Table B-4 Other RMI Properties	
`sun.rmi.dgc.checkInterval`	This property represents (in milliseconds) how often RMI checks for expired distributed garbage collection leases. The default is 300,000 milliseconds (5 minutes).
`sun.rmi.dgc.cleanInterval`	The value of this property represents, in milliseconds, the maximum that that RMI will wait to retry a failed DGC "clean" call. The default is 180,000 milliseconds.
`sun.rmi.dgc.server.gcInterval`	Specifies the maximum interval in milliseconds between garbage collections of the DGC heap.
`sun.rmi.dgc.client.gcInterval`	Specifies the maximum interval in milliseconds between garbage collections of the client-side DGC heap.
`sun.rmi.transport.tcp.localHostNameTimeOut`	Specifies, in milliseconds, the maximum time RMI will wait to obtain a fully-qualified hostname for the local host. The default is 10,000 milliseconds.
`sun.rmi.transport.tcp.readTimeout`	This value, in milliseconds, specifies how long RMI will wait before it times out a connection. The value here is passed to `Socket.setSoTimeout()`. The default is 2 hours.
`sun.rmi.transport.connectionTimeout`	Specifies the time in milliseconds for which a socket connection attempt may go unconnected. The default is 15,000 milliseconds.
`sun.rmi.transport.proxy.connectTimeout`	Specifies, in milliseconds, the maximum time RMI will wait for a connection to succeed before "rolling over" to try to establish an HTTP connection. The default is 15,000 milliseconds. This property is only used when `http.proxyHost` is set and the value of `java.rmi.disableHttp` is false.

Table B-5 Jini Discovery Properties

`net.jini.discovery.debug`	If this property is set to any value, debugging information about the Jini discovery and join protocols will be printed to `System.err`.
`net.jini.discovery.mtu`	This property indicates the maximum allowable size of multicast packets on your system. It must be a value between 512 and the actual maximum size your network supports. This property can be used to increase the allowed size of multicast request and announcement messages. Its default value is 512.
`net.jini.discovery.ttl`	This property sets the time-to-live (TTL) parameter used by multicast request and announcement. This value controls the "radius" of multicast messages. The value must be set to an integer between 1 and 255; the default is 15.
`net.jini.discovery.timeout`	This property sets the amount of time a client or service will wait for a response from a lookup service when using the unicast discovery protocol. The value should be set to the timeout, in milliseconds. The default is 60,000 (one minute).
`net.jini.discovery.inteface`	When this property is set to a hostname or an IP address, the network interface named by that hostname or address will be used for multicast discovery. If this property is not set, the an arbitrary interface will be used as determined by the operating system defaults.

Table B-6 Join Properties

`com.sun.jini.join.debug`	Setting this property to any value causes Sun's implementation of the `JoinManager` to display debugging information about the join process. This can be useful, for example, to determine if you are using a bogus proxy or attributes.

Table B-7 `Reggie` (Sample Lookup Service) Properties

`net.jini.discovery.announce`	This property controls how often the `reggie` lookup service will announce its presence via multicast announcement. The value is expressed in milliseconds, and the default is 120,000 milliseconds (every two minutes).
`com.sun.jini.reggie.unicast-Timeout`	When `reggie` responds to a discovering entity performing unicast discovery, this property controls the timeout period for which `reggie` will try to send a unicast response. The value is expressed in milliseconds, and the default is 60,000 (one minute).
`com.sun.jini.reggie.proxy.debug`	Setting this property to any value causes the service proxy for `reggie` to print out debugging information to `System.err` as it runs. You should be sure to set this property on a client that has downloaded the service proxy; not the lookup service itself.

Table B-8 `Mahalo` (Sample Transaction Manager) Properties

`com.sun.jini.use.registry`	*NOTE: This property was available in Jini 1.0 only. It is not supported in later releases.* If this property is set to a non-null value, then `mahalo` will bind itself to the RMI registry, in addition to registering itself with the Jini lookup service. This facility is only present to allow debugging and development of `mahalo`, and shouldn't be used in practice.

Table B-8 `Mahalo` (Sample Transaction Manager) Properties

`com.sun.jini.rmiRegistry-Port`	*NOTE: This property was available in Jini 1.0 only. It is not supported in later releases.* This property controls the port on which `mahalo` looks for the RMI registry. This property only works in conjunction with the `com.sun.jini.use.registry` property above.
`com.sun.jini.mahalo.managerName`	This property sets the "name" of the `mahalo` instance. When `mahalo` is bound into the RMI registry, the name sets the name that the service is bound to. When `mahalo` is registered with the Jini lookup service, an attribute of type `net.jini.lookup.entry.Name` is created with this value and attached to the service's registration.
`com.sun.jini.mahalo.debug`	If set, this property enables the output of debugging information. The value should be a comma-separated list of the subsystems to debug. Currently, only `startup` is supported here.

Table B-9 `Outrigger` (Sample JavaSpaces Service) Properties

`com.sun.jini.use.registry`	*NOTE: This property was available in Jini 1.0 only. It is not supported in later releases.* If this property is set to a non-null value, then `outrigger` will bind itself to the RMI registry, in addition to registering itself with the Jini lookup service. This facility is only present to allow debugging and development of `outrigger`, and shouldn't be used in practice.

Table B-9 `Outrigger` (Sample JavaSpaces Service) Properties

`com.sun.jini.rmiRegistryPort`	*NOTE: This property was available in Jini 1.0 only. It is not supported in later releases.* This property controls the port on which `outrigger` looks for the RMI registry. This property only works in conjunction with the `com.sun.jini.use.registry` property above.
`com.sun.jini.outrigger.space-Name`	This property sets the "name" of the `outrigger` instance. When `outrigger` is bound into the RMI registry, the name sets the name that the service is bound to. When `outrigger` is registered with the Jini lookup service, an attribute of type `net.jini.lookup.entry.Name` is created with this value and attached to the service's registration.
`com.sun.jini.outrigger.back-end.vm.options`	This property is used to set command-line arguments to the VM, which will run the `BackEndSpace` part of a persistent JavaSpaces service. You must set the property on the VM running the `FrontEndSpace`, which is the portion of the persistent space directly launched on the command line.
`com.sun.jini.outrigger.java`	This property controls the name of the JVM used to run the `BackEndSpace` portion of a persistent JavaSpace. By default, the executable "`java`" is used.

Table B-9 `Outrigger` (Sample JavaSpaces Service) Properties	
`com.sun.jini.outrigger.back-end.gcInterval`	This property controls how aggressive the `BackEndSpace` portion of a persistent JavaSpace will be in invoking the garbage collector. Persistent JavaSpaces consist of a `FrontEndSpace` that writes log entries to a spool which is consumed by a `BackEndSpace`. The value of the property controls how many log entries must be written before the persistent store is garbage collected. The default is 5. This property must be set on the JVM running the `BackEndSpace`.
`com.sun.jini.outrigger.debug`	Enables output of debugging information. The value should be a comma-separated list of subsystems for which debugging should be enabled. See the manual pages for full details.

Table B-10 `Fiddler` (Sample Lookup Discovery Service) Properties	
`com.sun.jini.fid-dler.server.debug`	This property lets you specify tuples that indicate which `fiddler` subsystem you wish to debug, and where the debugging output for that subsystem should be written. For example, you can pass the string `all` to generate debugging output for all subsystems, `events` to debug event generation, and so on. You should check the manual page for `fiddler` for complete details. Also, note that this property is set by passing it on the command line (not using the `-D` syntax) to the `fiddler` wrapper program.

Table B-11 Mercury (Sample Event Mailbox) Properties

com.sun.jini.mercury.debug	This property lets you select individual mercury subsystems you wish to debug, and direct the debugging output for each subsystem to a log file, or to standard out. For example, you can debug service initialization by passing the string init, or registration expiration by passing expiration. See the mercury manual page for full details. Also, note that this property is set by passing it on the command line (not using the -D syntax) to the mercury wrapper program.
com.sun.jini.mercury.eventsPerLog	Controls the number of events written to each log file. The default is 10.
com.sun.jini.mercury.streamPoolSize	This property controls the maximum number of concurrent event log input and output streams that may exist. The default is 10.

Table B-12 Norm (Sample Lease Renewal Service) Properties

com.sun.jini.norm.debug	Much like the debug properties for fiddler and mercury, this property lets you selectively debug certain norm subsystems. See the manual page for norm for full details. Also, like those other two services, be sure to note that this property is set by passing it on the command line (not using the -D syntax) to the norm wrapper program.

Table B-13 ServiceDiscoveryManager Properties

com.sun.jini.sdm.debug	Set to any non-null value to display stack trace information for exceptions that would normally be silently consumed. This property is useful in diagnosing common problems, such as bad listener codebase or bad definitions of equals() on service proxies.

Table B-13 `ServiceDiscoveryManager` Properties	
`com.sun.jini.sdm.dis-` `cardWait`	When you discard a service through the Service-DiscoveryManager, the reference to that service is temporarily placed in a "limbo" storage area until the ServiceDiscoveryManager ascertains that it has, in fact, disappeared from the lookup service. This allows the ServiceDiscoveryManager to determine when a service should be considered to be "rediscovered." This propertly controls the time (in milliseconds) that the ServiceDiscoveryManager will wait to see if a discarded service disappears from the lookup service. The default is 10 minutes.

Index